COMPARATIVE RELIGIO

Judaism, Christianity, Isla

Comparative Religious Law provides for the first time a study of the regulatory instruments of Jewish, Christian and Muslim religious organisations in Britain in light of their historical religious law. Norman Doe questions assumptions about the pervasiveness, character and scope of religious law, from the view that it is not or should not be recognised by civil law, to the idea that there may be a fundamental incompatibility between religious and civil law. He proposes that religious law pervades society, is recognised by civil law, has both a religious and temporal character, and regulates wide areas of believers' lives. Subjects include sources of law, faith leaders, governance, worship and education, rites of passage, divorce and children, and religion-State relations. A Charter of 'the principles of religious law' common to all three Abrahamic faiths is proposed, to stimulate greater mutual understanding between religion and society and between the three faiths themselves.

NORMAN DOE, DCL (Lambeth), LLD (Cambridge), is Professor of Law and Director of the Centre for Law and Religion, School of Law and Politics, Cardiff University, and Chancellor of the Diocese of Bangor in the Church in Wales.

COMPARATIVE RELIGIOUS LAW

Judaism, Christianity, Islam

NORMAN DOE

Cardiff University

CAMBRIDGE
UNIVERSITY PRESS

CAMBRIDGE
UNIVERSITY PRESS

University Printing House, Cambridge CB2 8BS, United Kingdom

One Liberty Plaza, 20th Floor, New York, NY 10006, USA

477 Williamstown Road, Port Melbourne, VIC 3207, Australia

314–321, 3rd Floor, Plot 3, Splendor Forum, Jasola District Centre, New Delhi – 110025, India

79 Anson Road, #06–04/06, Singapore 079906

Cambridge University Press is part of the University of Cambridge.

It furthers the University's mission by disseminating knowledge in the pursuit of education, learning, and research at the highest international levels of excellence.

www.cambridge.org
Information on this title: www.cambridge.org/9781107167131
DOI: 10.1017/9781316711569

© Norman Doe 2018

First published 2018

Printed and bound in Great Britain by Clays Ltd, Elcograf S.p.A.

A catalogue record for this publication is available from the British Library.

ISBN 978-1-107-16713-1 Hardback
ISBN 978-1-316-61780-9 Paperback

CONTENTS

v

PREFACE

This book has been stimulated by three developments in the past ten years or so. First, in 2007, the Centre for Law and Religion at Cardiff Law School established the Interfaith Legal Advisers Network. The first of its kind in the United Kingdom, the Network was set up in response to a number of high profile civil court cases involving religion, including cases concerning religious dress, sacred animals and faith schools, and the considerable challenges for faith groups posed by State law on religion. The purpose of the Network is to facilitate discussion about such issues, providing the members with a greater understanding of their respective systems of religious law and the common legal issues they face as they interact with the law of the State. The lesson which members have taught each other – not least its Jewish, Christian and Muslim members – is the potential of comparative religious law for fuller mutual respect between the major faith traditions of the world in contemporary society.

Secondly, whilst there have been numerous notable studies which have compared Jewish and Islamic law, it is not until recently that a meaning-ful comparison could be made between these juristic traditions and those of global Christianity. With its first symposium in 2013, a Panel of Experts has met four times each year in Rome (2013–2016) to produce a Statement of Principles of Christian Law (2016), and then, in Geneva (2017), to feed this statement into the work of the World Council of Churches (which has its headquarters in Geneva), particularly its Faith and Order Commission. The statement was developed by a rigorous examination of the legal systems of the Anglican, Baptist, Catholic, Lutheran, Methodist, Orthodox, Presbyterian and Reformed traditions worldwide – commonly styled (at the World Council of Churches) as among the 'historical churches' of global Christianity. The work of the Panel is an innovative project which seeks to re-imagine the ecumenical enterprise – the focus of which hitherto has been on Christian belief and doctrine – through recognition of and working with the laws of churches, and the principles of law which may be induced from them, to underscore that such laws link Christians in common action in the life of the faithful.

Thirdly, since the well-known 2008 lecture of the then Archbishop of Canterbury, Dr Rowan Williams, on the place of civil law and religious law in England, religious leaders, politicians, judges and scholars have made numerous assumptions about the pervasiveness, character and scope of religious law in British society today. These have ranged from the view that religious law is not recognised by the civil law of the State, from the opinion that it should not be recognised by the law of the State, to the view that there may be a fundamental incompatibility between religious law and the law of the State. This book questions these assumptions. It does so by examining a large body of legal evidence, which indicates that religious law plays a vital role in the institutional lives of Jews, Christians and Muslims as they live out their faiths in civic society alongside State law – and that their study might be used imaginatively for these three faiths to respond to the call of the Woolf Commission in 2015 to work together on a 'statement of principles to guide the development and evaluation of policies relating to the common good'. Articulating principles of religious law common to Judaism, Christianity and Islam is an obvious starting-point for this constructive proposal.

I have enjoyed the support of a great many people in the process of writing this book. To my colleagues at the Centre for Law and Religion at Cardiff Law School I owe a particular debt of gratitude: Mark Hill, Frank Cranmer, Paul Goodliff, Stephen Farrell, Siôn Hughes-Carew, Paul Colton, Richard Deadman and Jane Steen particularly. The same applies to all those from the various traditions studied here who have provided help. These include colleagues in the Interfaith Legal Advisers Network, particularly David Frei (Registrar of the London Beth Din), as well as Dr Muhammad Mansur Ali and Dr Abdul-Azim Ahmed of the Centre for the Study of Islam in the UK at Cardiff University, and colleagues on the Christian Law Panel of Experts. A key influence on the method used in this book has been the work of the Anglican Communion Legal Advisers Network. I had the privilege (2002–2007) to work on a draft for the Network of a statement of principles induced from the laws of the 44 churches of the worldwide Anglican Communion. These were refined and adopted by the Network and launched at the Lambeth Conference in 2008: *The Principles of Canon Common to the Churches of the Anglican Communion* (Anglican Communion Office, London, 2008). This also taught me a great deal about the possibilities of comparative study of religious legal systems. To the convenor of that Network, Canon John

Rees (Legal Adviser to the Anglican Consultative Council), I owe an equally large measure of gratitude, as to its other members. At Cardiff Law School, Sharron Alldred, Helen Calvert, Sarah Kennedy and Jenna Poole have as ever provided first-class support, as has, in the research directorate, Rhian Griffiths. At Cambridge University Press, I am especially grateful, as always, to Finola O'Sullivan, Editorial Director, Law, for her continued faith in the project and her infinite patience, as well as that of her colleagues. Finally, I thank my long-suffering family – my wife Heather, our children Rachel, Elizabeth and Edward, my brother Martin and Susan, and, before their sad passing in 2011 and 2016 respectively, my father James and mother Julia – for their constant and unfailing support. Finally, in the event that I have not described the materials accurately, explained them adequately or assessed their value sensibly, I am solely responsible.

Norman Doe
Cardiff Law School
Wales
March 2017

TABLE OF ABBREVIATIONS

AMIC	Aberdeen Mosque and Islamic Centre
AMS	Assembly of Masorti Synagogues
AR	Articles of Religion (The Thirty-Nine Articles), Church of England
BAES	Borehamwood and Elstree Synagogue (US)
BCM	Birmingham Central Mosque
BCOM	Bolton Council of Mosques
BDBJ	Board of Deputies of British Jews
BHRS	Brighton and Hove Reform Synagogue
BUGB	Baptist Union of Great Britain
BUS	Baptist Union of Scotland
c.	Canon (Roman Catholic) in the Code of Canon Law 1983
Can.	Canon (Anglican)
CFM	Council for Mosques (Bradford)
CIC	*Codex Iuris Canonici* (1983), Code of Canon Law (Roman Catholic)
CJM	Central Jamia Masjid (Southall)
Con.	Constitution
CPD	Constitutional Practice and Discipline (Methodist Church in Great Britain)
CTJC	Cambridge Traditional Jewish Congregation
ECFR	European Council for Fatwa and Research
ECHR	European Convention for the Protection of Human Rights and Fundamental Freedoms (Council of Europe)
EHC	Exeter Hebrew Congregation
ELCIRE	Evangelical Lutheran Church in Ireland
ELS	Elstree Liberal Synagogue
EWCA	England and Wales Court of Appeal Civil division
FCUK	Fatwa Committee UK
FMU	Forced Marriage Unit
FOS	Federation of Synagogues (Orthodox)
IFIS	Inter Firm Islamic Societies
ISC	Islamic Sharia Council
JJBS	Jewish Joint Burial Society

LC	Lambeth Conference (Anglican)
LCGB	Lutheran Church in Great Britain
LIS	Lancaster Islamic Society
MAT	Muslim Arbitration Tribunal
MBCOL	Muslim Burial Council of Leicestershire
MCB	Muslim Council of Britain
MCGB	Methodist Church in Great Britain
MCI	Methodist Church in Ireland
MCW	Muslim Council of Wales
MINAB	Mosques and Imams National Advisory Board
MJMRIC	Markazi Jamia Masjid Riza and Islamic Centre (Huddersfield)
MPP	Manual of Practice and Procedure (UFCS)
MRJ	Movement for Reform Judaism
NASFAT	Nasru-Lahi-Il-Fathi Society of Nigeria, United Kingdom and Ireland
NHAYS	North Hendon Adath Yisroel Synagogue
NHC	Norwich Hebrew Congregation
NLRS	North London Reform Synagogue
NUIM	Noor-Ul-Islam Mosque (Bury)
PCI	Presbyterian Church in Ireland
PCLCCAC	*The Principles of Canon Law Common to the Churches of the Anglican Communion* (Anglican Communion Office, London, 2008)
PCW	Presbyterian Church of Wales
PGM	Palmers Green Mosque, Muslim Community and Education Centre for Islamic Studies
PLJC	Peterborough Liberal Jewish Community
RMC	Reading Muslim Council
SO	Standing Orders
SSRS	Sukkat Shalom Reform Synagogue (Wanstead)
UFCS	United Free Church of Scotland
UIDHR	Universal Islamic Declaration of Human Rights (Islamic Council of Europe 1981)
ULPS	Union of Liberal and Progressive Synagogues
UOHC	Union of Orthodox Hebrew Congregations
URC	United Reformed Church
US	United Synagogue (Orthodox)
USCJ	United Synagogue of Conservative Judaism
WCCMJ	World Council of Conservative-Masorti Judaism (Masorti Olami) (or World Council of Conservative Synagogues)
WLJC	Wessex Liberal Jewish Community

Introduction

This book explores various assumptions that have been made in public discourse over recent years about the pervasiveness, character and scope of religious law in British society today. It does so by examining the laws and other regulatory instruments of Jewish, Christian and Muslim organisations in the United Kingdom, with a particular emphasis on England and Wales.[1] First, it has been assumed that the religious law of Islam and some Jewish traditions govern the whole of the life of the faithful, whereas those of other Jewish traditions and Christianity do not. For example, in 2012, in a case (about the schooling of children in Haredi Judaism), Sir James Munby stated:

> Even for the devout Christian attempting to live their life in accordance with Christ's teaching there is likely to be some degree of distinction between the secular and the divine, between matters quotidian and matters religious. But there are other communities, and we are here concerned with such a community, for whom the distinction is, at root, meaningless, for whom every aspect of their lives . . . of their being, of who and what they are, is governed by a body of what the outsider might characterise as purely religious law. That is so of the devout Muslim, every aspect of whose being and existence is governed by the Quran and the Sharia. It is so also of the ultra-orthodox Jew, every aspect of whose being . . . is governed by the Torah and the Talmud. I therefore agree entirely with . . . Hughes LJ . . . The issue is: 'not simply a matter of choice of school but a much more fundamental one of way of life. "Lifestyle" scarcely does [it] justice. It is a matter of the rules for living.'[2]

---

[1] According to the Census of 2011, 59.3 per cent of the population of England and Wales regarded themselves as Christian (c. 33.2 million), 4.8 per cent as Muslim (c. 2.7 million), and 0.50 per cent as Jewish (c. 260,000); and for Scotland: Christians 54 per cent, Muslims 1.4 per cent, and Jews 0.1 per cent. Moreover, the register of the Charity Commission shows over 22,000 religious charities in England and Wales: see M. Hill, R. Sandberg and N. Doe, *Religion and Law in the United Kingdom* (Netherlands: Wolters Kluwer, 2nd edn, 2014) paras. 13 and 178.

[2] *Re G (Education: Religious Upbringing)* [2012] EWCA Civ. 1233.

Secondly, there are assumptions about the accommodation by civil law of religious law – from the view that religious law is not recognised by civil law, through the opinion that they could be recognised by it, to the view that it is not possible to have legal pluralism in society. For instance, in 2008, the then Archbishop of Canterbury, Most Reverend Dr Rowan Williams, proposed that some form of 'transformative accommodation' should be found between English law and *sharia*; but in Parliament in October 2008, Bridget Prentice MP, Parliamentary Under Secretary, Ministry of Justice, stated: 'Shari'a law has no jurisdiction in England and Wales and there is no intention to change this position.'[3] Moreover, the current Archbishop of Canterbury, Most Reverend Justin Welby, said in an interview in 2017 that *sharia* should not be part of English law: 'I don't think that we should have elements of sharia law in the English jurisprudence system'; rather: 'We have a philosophy of law in this country, and you can only really cope with one philosophy of law within a jurisprudential system. The English courts always have to prevail, under all circumstances, always.'[4]

Thirdly, it has been assumed that religious law is fundamentally theocratic and so somewhat incompatible with democracy. In a case in 2010, for example, Sir John Laws stated that to give legal protection to a moral position because it was based on Christianity or any other religion would be 'deeply unprincipled'; he said: 'in the eye of everyone save the believer religious faith is necessarily subjective, being incommunicable by any kind of proof or evidence. It may of course be *true*; but the ascertainment of such a truth lies beyond' the law 'in the heart of the believer'. To do otherwise, he said, would be 'divisive, capricious and arbitrary', especially 'in a society where all the people [do not] share uniform religious beliefs'. Also: 'our constitution would be on the way to a theocracy, which is of necessity autocratic. The law of a theocracy is dictated without option to the people, not made by their judges and governments. The individual conscience is free to accept such dictated law; but the State, if its people are to be free, has the burdensome duty of thinking for itself.'[5]

---

[3] For the lecture, 'Civil and religious law in England' (7 February 2008), and the Written Parliamentary Answer by Bridget Prentice MP (23 October 2008), and other reactions to the lecture and the issues raised in it, see R. Griffith-Jones, ed., *Islam and English Law: Rights, Responsibilities and the Place of Shari'a* (Cambridge: Cambridge University Press, 2013) 20–33 and 35 and the other studies therein.

[4] *Church Times* (9 February 2018) 6.

[5] *McFarlane v. Relate Avon Ltd* [2010] EWCA Civ. 771.

Fourthly, it is sometimes assumed that religious law is not 'law' properly so-called in so far as it lacks the binding and enforceable qualities of law – that many such laws are conventional or social norms, or else obsolescent 'historical relics'.[6] There are also related questions about whether religious law has a dynamic nature responsive for example to claimed processes of secularisation in wider society, as well as how they are created, interpreted and applied in the contemporary daily life of the faithful.[7]

Fifthly, it has been assumed it may be possible for faith leaders in Britain to formulate a statement of principles which articulate shared values for public life. For example, in the context of faith in society today, the Woolf Commission in 2015 proposed that: 'when so much is dominated by the sole value of individual choice, faith leaders and other opinion leaders need to initiate discussions on the values, political and personal, they have in common with each other'. Therefore: '[a] national conversation should be launched . . . by leaders of faith communities and opinion leaders in other ethical traditions to create a shared understanding of fundamental values underlying public life'; moreover, crucially: 'The outcome might well be, within the tradition of Magna Carta and other such declarations of rights over the centuries, a statement of principles to guide the development and evaluation of policies relating to the common good.'[8]

This book tests these and associated assumptions. It explores whether religious law is more pervasive in society than is often presumed in aspiring to touch the day-to-day lives of Jews, Christians and Muslims alike. It includes primary religious law (traditional, historical or classical religious law) and secondary religious law (the modern regulatory instruments of Jewish, Christian and Muslim religious organisations, most typically in the form of their constitutions). This book also examines whether religious law makes provision for the applicability of civil law to the faithful – and the extent to which elements of religious law, and decisions based on them, are recognised expressly or tacitly by the civil law of the State and its institutions (such as by parliamentary statute, the civil Charity Commission or the decisions of the courts). It is suggested

---

[6] A. Huxley, 'Introduction', in A. Huxley, ed., *Religion, Law and Tradition: Comparative Studies in Religious Law* (Abingdon: Routledge, 2002) 1.
[7] R. Sandberg, 'The Reformation of religious law', *Quaderni di Diritto e Politica Ecclesiastica* (Bologna: Il Mulino, 2017) 97–110.
[8] Woolf Commission, *Living with Difference* (2015) 3.14.

that the modern regulatory instruments of the religious organisations studied here are vehicles for mutual accommodation between State and religion – the State would not recognise them unless they were consistent with civil law, and the religious organisation would not make them if they were inconsistent with primary religious law. The book also assesses the degree to which the fundamentals of religious law are theocratic, dictated by God and sourced in conceptions of revealed divine law – but also whether, at the same time, religion is governed by rational laws, humanly created and how it is more temporal, secular or functional than has been presumed. Indeed, much in the laws of Jewish, Christian and Muslim entities today is driven by civil law and civic standards, which are incorporated into secondary religious law as the product of practical reason.

In turn, the book explores how religion and religious belief are juridified through their deployment in the modern regulatory instruments of Jews, Christians and Muslims, and through the translation of elements of classical Jewish, Christian and Islamic law into their modern norms of conduct. It also uncovers the levels of legal pluralism – and juridical diversity – both within and across the three religions. However, and paradoxically, but critically, there are profound similarities between the laws of Jews, Christians and Muslims, which enable articulation of principles of religious law common to the three Abrahamic faiths. The study, therefore, responds to the call of the Woolf Commission in 2015 for faith leaders to work towards a statement of principles to guide the development and evaluation of policies relating to the common good. It does so by offering for debate a statement of 'the principles of religious law' common to Jews, Christians and Muslims. Therefore, the book seeks to make a contribution to the abundant, rich and rapidly growing scholarly literature and public debate on the prevalence of religious law in modern society and its recognition by civil law.[9]

The sources examined include materials and literature on the fundamental elements of what for the sake of exposition are here styled as the classical, traditional or historical sources of Jewish, Christian and Islamic law. These fundamental elements are presented as succinctly as possible

---

[9] The study may be associated with wider scholarship on the creation of norms in the field of religion: see e.g. H. Årsheim and P. Slotte, *The Juridification of Religion?* (Leiden: Brill, 2017): this explores the juridification of religion in State constitutional law, the expansion and differentiation of State laws on religion, the increase in conflict solving (involving religion) by recourse to State law and the increase in the exercise of State judicial power over the law of the State on religion and religious law.

in the form of principles of classical religious law, and note is taken where appropriate of contested areas where fundamentals are the subject of disagreement as between traditions within each of the three faiths. The principal focus of the book, however, is the modern regulatory instruments of Jewish, Christian and Muslim organisations operating at national, regional and local levels, including synagogues, churches and mosques. These documents include the constitutions and other formal regulatory instruments of such organisations, as well as their religious soft-law in the form of guidance, codes of practice, policy documents and other informal normative instruments. The book is the first of its type to compare such instruments in the context of the classical religious law of the Abrahamic faiths. It also sets out, where appropriate and briefly, relevant civil law on the areas studied.

As to structure, the book deals with: jurisprudence – the objects of faith communities and the sources and purposes of religious law (Chapter 1); the faithful – the status and duties of believers and their membership of religious organisations (Chapter 2); and faith leaders – training, appointment and functions (Chapter 3). There then follows: governance – institutions of religious organisations, and their authority and structure (Chapter 4); and the resolution of religious disputes – the interpretation of religious law, informal dispute resolution and religious courts and tribunals (Chapter 5); followed by the topics of belief, worship and education – the profession of religious belief, the administration of worship and religious schools (Chapter 6); the rites of passage – in the early years of life and adolescence, the rites of spiritual development and commemoration and funeral rites (Chapter 7); and then marriage, divorce and children – the formation of marriage, the process and effect of divorce and children at home and in the synagogue, church and mosque (Chapter 8). The book next treats property and finance – the ownership of property, the maintenance of the synagogue, church and mosque, and the regulation of finance, income and expenditure (Chapter 9); and religion, the State and wider society – religious approaches to the State and compliance with its law, human rights and religious freedom, and the extent to which the three religions engage with natural law thinking (Chapter 10). For Jewish and Islamic law, the book uses legal terms from both Hebrew and Arabic,[10] and for Christianity, where appropriate, Latin (mostly for terms used in Roman Catholic law).

---

[10] English spellings of these words will vary, depending on the religious/cultural tradition in question.

Needless to say, there is a growing body of literature on systems of religious law, but few on comparative religious law – and none on the modern regulatory instruments of Jewish, Christian and Muslim religious organisations in Britain in the context of their primary religious laws. First, there is non-comparative literature on the religious law of individual faiths. There is a vast literature on Jewish law,[11] and on Islamic law,[12] but, perhaps remarkably, there is very little on Christian law,[13] as compared for instance with Buddhist law or Hindu law,[14] though there are denomination-specific books on the laws of individual churches within Christianity,[15] and there are also books devoted to Biblical law.[16] However, with their focus on classical religious law, these books do not generally deal with the modern legal instruments of religious organisations. Secondly, whilst recent years have seen a rapid growth in the literature on the law of the State on religion (national and international),[17]

---

[11] E.g. N.S. Hecht, B.S. Jackson, S.M. Passamaneck, D. Piatelli and A.M. Rabello, eds., *An Introduction to the History and Sources of Jewish Law* (Oxford: Oxford University Press, 1996), M. Elon, *Jewish Law: History, Sources, Principles* (Philadelphia and Jerusalem: Jewish Publication Society, 1994), and the seminal I. Herzog (1888–1959, Chief Rabbi of Israel), *The Main Institutions of Jewish Law*, 2 volumes (London and New York: The Soncino Press Limited, 1939, Paperback Edn, 1980).

[12] See e.g. G. Picken, ed., *Islamic Law*, 4 volumes (Abingdon: Routledge, 2010); J. Schacht, *An Introduction to Islamic Law* (Oxford: Clarendon Press, 1991), C.G. Weeramantry, *Islamic Jurisprudence: An International Perspective* (London: Macmillan, 1988), and A.R.I. Doi, *Shariah: The Islamic Law* (London: Ta Ha Publishers, 1984). There are also books on aspects of Islamic law, e.g. M.C. Bassiouni, *The Shari'a and Islamic Criminal Justice in Time of War and Peace* (Cambridge: Cambridge University Press, 2014).

[13] See e.g. N. Doe, *Christian Law: Contemporary Principles* (Cambridge: Cambridge University Press, 2013).

[14] See e.g. R.R. French and M.A. Nathan, eds., *Buddhism and Law: An Introduction* (Cambridge: Cambridge University Press, 2014), D.R. Davis, *The Spirit of Hindu Law* (Cambridge: Cambridge University Press, 2010) and W.F. Menski, *Hindu Law* (Oxford: Oxford University Press, 2003).

[15] E.g. on Roman Catholic canon law: G. Sheehy *et al.*, *The Canon Law: Letter and Spirit* (Dublin, Veritas, 1995); the law of the Church of England: M. Hill, *Ecclesiastical Law* (Oxford: Oxford University Press, 4th edn, 2018); Presbyterian law: J.L. Weatherhead, ed., *The Constitution and Laws of the Church of Scotland* (Board of Practice and Procedure, Edinburgh, 1997); and in the Reformed tradition, e.g. P. Coertzen, *Church and Order: A Reformed Perspective* (Leuven: Peeters, 1998).

[16] See e.g. D. Daube, *Studies in Biblical Law* (Cambridge: Cambridge University Press, 2008), N.J. Ruane, *Sacrifice and Gender in Biblical Law* (Cambridge: Cambridge University Press, 2013), and J. Burnside, *God, Justice and Society: Aspects of Law and Legality in the Bible* (Oxford: Oxford University Press, 2010).

[17] However, books such as L. Zucca, *Law, State and Religion in the New Europe* (Cambridge: Cambridge University Press, 2012) or N. Doe, *Law and Religion in Europe* (Oxford: Oxford University Press, 2011) do not deal directly with religious law as such.

it is increasingly recognised that understanding religious law is required for a fuller appreciation of State law on religion.[18] But there is generally a lack of attention given in these studies to religious law itself so as to enable an understanding of how it interacts with State law and society.[19] At the same time, there is a growing literature on secular law as it applies to Islam.[20] Thirdly, there is little on comparative religious law across the major world faiths. There is no English language equivalent to the book by Silvio Ferrari – this publication examines classical religious law (and the Christian component is Roman Catholic canon law only), not the modern regulatory instruments of Jewish, Muslim or other Christian organisations.[21] The same applies to the book *Religion, Law and Tradition* – this publication explores the category 'religious law', but its editor concludes that it is difficult to define, and the materials on the different systems are presented in parallel not comparatively.[22] Again, the Christian focus is very narrow – only Roman Catholic canon law.[23] Classical Islamic law and Jewish law are compared, for instance, in the book by J. Neusner and T. Sonn.[24] However, the book does not include Christianity based on the (contestable) view that Christianity is not a religion of law. Nor does the

---

[18] See e.g. C. Hamilton, *Family, Law and Religion* (London: Sweet & Maxwell, 1995), P. Edge, *Religion and Law* (Aldershot: Ashgate, 2006), A. Bradney, *Law and Faith in a Sceptical Age* (Abingdon: Routledge, 2008) and P. Cane, C. Evans and Z. Robinson, eds., *Law and Religion in Theoretical and Historical Context* (Cambridge: Cambridge University Press, 2008).

[19] E.g. R. Ahdar and I. Leigh, *Religious Freedom in the Liberal State* (Oxford: Oxford University Press 2nd edn, 2013) or J. Rivers, *The Law of Organized Religions* (Oxford: Oxford University Press, 2011). R. Sandberg, in his *Law and Religion* (Cambridge: Cambridge University Press, 2011) and *Religion, Law and Society* (Cambridge: Cambridge University Press, 2014) calls for greater attention to be paid to religious law in these law and religion studies.

[20] E.g. Y. Sezgin, *Human Rights under State-Enforced Religious Family Laws in Israel, Egypt and India* (Cambridge: Cambridge University Press, 2013), and E. Brems, *The Experiences of Face Veil Wearers in Europe and the Law* (Cambridge: Cambridge University Press, 2014). A. Shachar, *Multicultural Jurisdictions: Cultural Differences and Women's Rights* (Cambridge: Cambridge University Press, 2013), on religious tribunals (especially in Canada), is close to aspects of this book.

[21] Silvio Ferrari, *Lo spirito dei diritti religiosi: Ebraismo, cristianismo e islam a confronto* (Milan: Il Mulino, 2002). There are also the studies on individual faiths in the Italian journal *Daimon: Diritto Comparato delle Religione* (Milan: Il Mulino), under the direction of S. Ferrari and others.

[22] A. Huxley, ed., *Religion, Law and Tradition* (2002).

[23] A.-J. Kwak, ed., *Holy Writ: Interpretation in Law and Religion* (Aldershot: Ashgate, 2009): this compares legal and theological methods of interpretation.

[24] J. Neusner and T. Sonn, *Comparing Religions through Law: Judaism and Islam* (Abingdon: Routledge, 1999).

book explore the implementation of classical Jewish and Islamic law in modern regulatory instruments. Again, in the field of religious studies, sociology of religion and comparative religion, while little attention has to date been given to religious law itself, some notable scholars are increasingly, but briefly, recognising the importance of religious 'self-regulation'.[25]

The present book studies a range of Jewish, Christian and Islamic religious organisations. First, within Judaism,[26] it examines the regulatory instruments of organisations across various Jewish traditions represented in Britain (with about 409 synagogues), including, Orthodox, Conservative, Reformed and Liberal and Progressive Judaism, as well as a selection of their member synagogues and other bodies, including the Board of Deputies of British Jews, 'the representative body of British Jewry'.[27] Organisations studied in the Orthodox tradition are: the United Synagogue (founded 1870) under the religious authority of the Chief Rabbi, with 50 member synagogues, ten affiliate synagogues and one associate synagogue – those studied include the Stanmore and Canons Park Synagogue and the Borehamwood and Elstree Synagogue;[28] and the Federation of Synagogues (founded 1887), which provides centralised services to member Orthodox communities that 'retain their individuality and distinct identity' – 19 constituent and eight affiliated *shuls*.[29] Occasional reference is also made to the Union of Orthodox Hebrew

---

[25] J.A. Beckford and J.T. Richardson, 'Religion and regulation', in J.A. Beckford and N.J. Demerath, eds., *The Sage Handbook of the Sociology of Religion* (London: Sage, 2007) 396.

[26] It is believed the first Jews came from Normandy with William the Conqueror in 1066. However, the Edict of Expulsion issued by King Edward I, 18 July 1290 (on the Jewish Fast of Tisha B'Av) banished the entire Jewish population. Yet, in 1656, Rabbi Menashe Ben Israel successfully petitioned Oliver Cromwell to allow their readmission. Within 50 years, the offices of the Chief Rabbi and the London Beth Din were set up to provide a religious authority for Jewish communities in London and elsewhere: see Jewish Policy Research Report (for the Board of Deputies of British Jews): Synagogue Membership in the United Kingdom in 2016 (2017), compiled by D.C. Mashiah and J. Boyd (2017).

[27] The Board was founded in 1760 when seven deputies were appointed by the elders of the Spanish and Portuguese Congregations (Sephardic) to form a committee to pay homage to George III on his accession; the Ashkenazi Community also appointed a committee and it was agreed that both committees should hold joint meetings. The book does not deal with the Jewish Leadership Council, a charity bringing together the major British Jewish organisations to work for the good of the British Jewish community; it has Constituent Members, a Council and Trustees: www.thejlc.org/.

[28] United Synagogue (Orthodox) (US): www.theus.org.uk/. Members of the United Synagogue are chiefly in the south east, but also in e.g. Sheffield.

[29] Federation of Synagogues (FOS): www.federation.org.uk/.

Congregations (founded 1926), which is an umbrella organisation of Haredi communities in London and Manchester (so-called 'Strictly' or 'Ultra-Orthodox'); it seeks 'to protect traditional Judaism', with nearly 90 affiliated synagogues (and over 6,000 members) under the authority of its own Rabbinate.[30] Secondly, the United Synagogue of Conservative Judaism (based in New York) has communities (*kehillot*) in Britain which offer 'dynamic, pluralistic, accessible, egalitarian and traditional' Judaism;[31] and the World Council of Conservative-Masorti Judaism (Masorti Olami), otherwise known as World Council of Conservative Synagogues (established 1957 in New York).[32] Thirdly, there is the Movement for Reform Judaism, a national umbrella organisation of 41 autonomous synagogues, among which Finchley Reform Synagogue, Brighton and Hove Reform Synagogue, North London Reform Synagogue and Sukkat Shalom Reform Synagogue Wanstead are studied here.[33] Also studied is the Union of Liberal and Progressive Synagogues (founded 1902) – part of global Liberal Judaism, this seeks 'continuity of Jewish faith, tradition, practice and ethics within a contemporary framework', with 30 or so congregations in the United Kingdom;[34] members studied include Elstree Liberal Synagogue, Peterborough Liberal Jewish Community and Wessex Liberal Jewish Community.[35] Other local synagogues are also studied.[36]

---

[30] Board of Deputies of British Jews (BDBJ) (www.bod.org.uk/jewish-facts-info/jews-in-numbers/) classifies the Union of Orthodox Hebrew Congregations (UOHC) as 'Strictly Orthodox'. Its synagogues constitute some 37.4 per cent of all British synagogues. Its spiritual leadership is in the hands of its Rabbinate led by the Av Beis Din.

[31] United Synagogue of Conservative Judaism (USCJ): www.uscj.org/; it succeeds the United Synagogue of America (incorporated 1916).

[32] Masorti Olami is an International Jewish Organization within the World Zionist Organization.

[33] Movement for Reform Judaism (MRJ): www.reformjudaism.org.uk/. The Associated British Synagogues was founded in 1942, later renamed the Associated Synagogues of Great Britain, and in 1958 adopted the name Reform Synagogues of Great Britain, which in 2005 became the Movement for Reform Judaism.

[34] Union of Liberal and Progressive Synagogues (ULPS): *Affirmations of Liberal Judaism* (London: revised edn, 2006) Preamble. The head office is in London. It is linked to the World Union for Progressive Judaism.

[35] Liberal Judaism and the Movement for Reform Judaism have created an alliance, accounting for about one third of synagogue-affiliated Jews in the UK in 82 communities (but these remain within their respective movements), for collaboration in such areas as student chaplaincy and social justice: ULPS: www.liberaljudaism.org/what-we-do/alliance-for-progressive-judaism/.

[36] These include Norwich Hebrew Congregation, North Hendon Adath Yisroel Synagogue, Cambridge Traditional Jewish Congregation and Bristol Hebrew Congregation.

The Christian churches and other organisations studied are similarly from a range of traditions represented in British society – Episcopal, Presbyterian and Congregational. From the Episcopal tradition (in which a church is led by bishops) is, first, the Catholic Church, composed of the Roman or Latin Church and the Oriental Churches, a global communion with the papacy in Rome at its centre.[37] Oriental Catholic Churches are distinct from Orthodox Christianity; that is, they are a family of churches worldwide but with no central system of government; the Oriental Catholic Churches are not included in this study, though occasional mention is made of Orthodox Churches.[38] Secondly, there are those Episcopal churches that belong to the worldwide Anglican Communion (a fellowship of autonomous churches most of which, institutionally, are historical derivatives of the Church of England which was established following separation from Rome in the 1530s during the Reformation).[39] They include the established Church of England, disestablished Church in Wales, Scottish Episcopal Church and, as it straddles Northern Ireland and Ireland, the Church of Ireland – the similarities between their laws and those of others in the global Anglican Communion have been articulated in the Principles of Canon Law Common to the Churches of the Anglican Communion (2008).[40] Moving to the Protestant churches, products of the sixteenth-century Reformation and beyond, are the minority Lutheran Church in Great Britain[41] and, originally an eighteenth-century development, the Methodist Church in Great Britain and the Methodist Church in Ireland (which, again, straddles Northern Ireland and Ireland).[42] As well as the

---

[37] Catholicism embraces Christians in communion with the Pope. The Catholic Church (Latin and Oriental), with the Pope at its head, has a hierarchy of bishops and priests who are regarded as having authority entrusted by Christ to the Apostles and to St Peter in particular whose successor is conceived to be the Pope. Doctrinally, it adheres to tradition and the teaching authority of the church.

[38] For Orthodox canon law, see N. Doe, *Christian Law* (2013).

[39] The Communion has 44 churches worldwide in communion with the See of Canterbury: see N. Doe, *Canon Law in the Anglican Communion: A Worldwide Perspective* (Oxford: Clarendon Press, 1998).

[40] *The Principles of Canon Law Common to the Churches of the Anglican Communion* (London: Anglican Communion Office, 2008).

[41] Central to Lutheranism, which began with Martin Luther (sixteenth century), are justification by faith, preaching the gospel and administration of the sacraments, received in faith without any human merit.

[42] Methodism was inspired by John and Charles Wesley: salvation by God's grace was possible for all.

United Reformed Church in Great Britain,[43] the Presbyterian Churches examined here are the Presbyterian Church of Wales, Church of Scotland, Presbyterian Church in Ireland and United Free Church of Scotland.[44] In the congregational tradition, for the Baptist tradition (which holds that the local church is the primary expression of Christianity), the book studies the Baptist Union of Great Britain and occasional reference is made to the Baptist Union of Scotland.[45] The similarities between the laws of these and other historic churches, across the ecclesial traditions (including those of the Orthodox tradition) have recently been articulated by a Panel of Experts in Christian Law (meeting in Rome 2013–2016, and in Geneva in 2017) in a statement of principles of Christian law (Rome, 2016).[46]

It is estimated that 90 per cent of Muslims worldwide are Sunni, and about 10 per cent are Shi'a.[47] Since the death of the Prophet Muhammad, Sunnis and Shi'a differ, *inter alia*, over the leadership of the Muslim community. Sunnis (guided by the *Sunnah* or exemplary behaviour of the Prophet) accept the legitimacy of the Prophet's first four successors (Abu Bakr, Umar, Uthman and Ali). Shi'a Muslims follow Ali alone, cousin and son-in-law of Muhammad, believing that the Prophet's authority passed only to his descendants. Shi'a rejection of the authority of the first three successors accounts for the substantial differences between the beliefs of the Sunnis and Shi'a. Shi'a rely on decisions of later and more modern leaders – for example, *ayatullahs* who have no direct equivalent in Sunni Islam. There are differences also among Sunnis (e.g. Deobandis, Bareilvis and Maududis) and Shi'a (e.g. Dawoodi Bohras in the Isma'ili branch of Shi'a Islam). In turn, Muslims differ in their personal commitment to Islamic practice (as a matter of conscience) and

---

[43] 'Reformed' refers here to bodies with historical roots in the French and Swiss-led Reformation (Calvin, Zwingli *et al.*). It is part of the World Communion of Reformed Churches, a merger of the World Alliance of Reformed Churches and the Reformed Ecumenical Council in 2010.

[44] The Church of Scotland is the 'national church' under the Church of Scotland Act 1921.

[45] The modern Baptist tradition was founded in the Netherlands in 1609 by John Smyth, a cleric who left the (Anglican) Church of England and taught that the church should receive its members by baptism after they had consciously acknowledged their faith; he opposed infant baptism.

[46] The Panel's statement is published in M. Hill and N. Doe, 'Principles of Christian Law', 19 *Ecclesiastical Law Journal* (2017) 138–155.

[47] Muslims believe the Quran was revealed verbally by God to Muhammad through the angel Gabriel (*Jibril*) over a period of circa 23 years from 609 CE, when Muhammad was 40, to 632 when he died.

Muslim communities are subject to local, ethnic, doctrinal, political, cultural or other differences. Of about 2.7 million Muslims in Britain, and around 1,600 mosques, at least 96 per cent, and about 1,520 (96 per cent) mosques, are Sunni, and about 67 (2 per cent) Shi'a. Most Sunni mosques broadly follow the principles of Deoband, that is about 700–800, and about 350 Bareilvi.[48] Thus, the principal focus of what follows is Sunni Islam.

In turn, it has been estimated that there are about 3,000 Muslim organisations in the United Kingdom: about half are involved in running mosques and community centres, most are local, about half are registered charities and many have a small membership. However, several act as umbrella organisations, mostly around specific issues.[49] A range of Muslim religious entities and their regulatory instruments is studied here.[50]

Nationwide, these include the Muslim Council of Britain (founded 1997), which lists over 400 organisations as affiliates, covering about 179 mosques (e.g. Deobandi, Maududi and Bareilvi). Also studied is the Mosques and Imams National Advisory Board, founded 2006, which recommends ways in which imams and mosque management committees should conduct themselves;[51] it has delegates from mosques under the auspices of, for example, the Muslim Council of Britain, Muslim Association of Britain (founded 1997), British Muslim Forum (founded 2005, with about 270 member organisations) and Al-Khoei Foundation.[52] Then there are, for instance, the Nasru-Lahi-Il-Fathi Society of Nigeria, United Kingdom and Ireland; Muslim Arbitration Tribunal; Inter Firm Islamic Societies; and Fatwa Committee UK (part of the European Council for Fatwa and Research). Regional organisations studied include the Muslim Council Wales (founded 2003), affiliated to the

---

[48] M. Naqshbandi, *Islam and Muslims in Britain: A Guide for Non-Muslims* (London: City of London Police, 2012) 1.2, 3.2 and 3.3.1. The Bareilvi community was founded in India in the 1880s; the Indo-Pakistani Deobandi movement in 1867 and the Maududis follow the teaching etc. of Abul Ala Maududi (1903–1979).

[49] M. Naqshbandi, *Islam and Muslims in Britain* (2012): Guide 4.9.

[50] Other 'umbrella organisations' include the: Union of Muslim Organisations (founded 1970) with approximately 200 affiliated organisations; and the Sufi Muslim Council (founded 2006).

[51] Mosques and Imams National Advisory Board (MINAB) gives specialist advice to the Charity Commission for England and Wales in the field of Muslim charities: see M. Hill *et al.*, *Religion and Law* (2014) paras. 13 and 178.

[52] Al-Khoei Foundation: http://religiouseducationcouncil.org.uk/members/rec-members/al-khoei-foundation.

Muslim Council of Britain; Council for Mosques Bradford (with 80 affiliates, e.g. mosques and Islamic faith schools); Bolton Council of Mosques; Reading Muslim Council; Muslim Burial Council of Leicestershire; and at the more local level: Birmingham Central Mosque; Central Jamia Masjid (Southall); East London Mosque; Palmers Green Mosque, Muslim Community and Centre for Islamic Studies; Markazi Jamia Masjid Riza and Islamic Centre (Huddersfield); and Noor-Ul-Islam Mosque (Bury).[53]

Each chapter that follows surveys a vast amount of material drawn from 80 different regulatory systems. As a result, the chapters include extensive quotations from, and footnotes which refer to, the primary legal materials of the religious organisations studied. These are designed not only to provide evidence for the propositions that appear in the text, but also to allow the regulatory instruments of the faith groups to speak for themselves. Unless the text or context provide otherwise, references to regulatory instruments in the footnotes are merely examples – when legal provisions are unique to a religion or to a tradition within it, this is indicated. Secondary literature is listed in the Bibliography.

Where possible, to declutter the footnotes, the many website references used (for documents containing information on, and guidance and policy of, the religious organisations studied) are gathered together in the Bibliography. An Appendix of the principles of religious law is included towards the end of the book. These, it is argued, are what emerge from a comparative study of the primary and secondary religious law of Jewish, Christian and Muslim religious organisations in Britain today. In all this, the book seeks to contribute to debate and scholarship in a detailed analysis of previously unexplored and evolving legal instruments, to enhance mutual understanding and respect between these faiths, the State and wider society, and to provide a stable comparative methodology for fuller interreligious dialogue through its focus on concrete juridical data. It does so by offering for debate a proposed Charter of Abrahamic Law carrying 'the principles of religious law' common to all three faiths: Jewish, Christian and Islamic.

---

[53] Others include: the Al-Ikhlas Centre (Cardiff) and Darul Isra Muslim Community Centre (Cardiff); Aberdeen Mosque and Islamic Centre; Lancaster Islamic Society; and Islamic Sharia Council.

1

The Laws: Communities, Sources and Functions

Judaism, Christianity and Islam identify a range of sources of law applicable to their faithful. On the one hand, there is what might be styled the classical, traditional or historical sources of law (primary religious law), including sacred texts. On the other hand, there are the modern regulatory instruments of Jewish, Christian and Muslim religious organisations (secondary religious law), such as synagogues, churches and mosques. Each religion has clearly defined ideas about the purposes of these organisations, as well as the character, purposes and scope of their systems of religious law. At the institutional level of synagogues, churches and mosques, regulatory instruments have a number of forms; constitutions predominate. Alongside these formal sources of law (binding legislation), Jews, Christians and Muslims also make religious soft-law (or quasi-legislation): guidelines, codes of practice, policies or other more informal and usually persuasive but nevertheless normative instruments. This chapter treats the objects of the religious organisations, the classical legal sources and the forms and purposes of their regulatory instruments. The legal evidence on each of these matters illustrates the theocratic foundations of religious law, its positivisation in the modern juridical instruments of the faith communities studied, as well as their temporal character and the degree of legal pluralism between and within the faiths. The chapter also proposes the existence of common principles of religious law induced from the similarities between their laws.

The Objects of a Synagogue, Church and Mosque

Each of the religious organisations studied here, across the three faiths, presents in its regulatory instruments an understanding of itself, its component parts and its purposes or institutional objects. Whilst the objects have a religious dimension, they may also have a secular aspect, in terms of wider public benefit, in order for the organisation to obtain charitable status under the civil law of the State, and for its own

14

regulatory instruments to be acceptable to the civil Charity Commission of England and Wales.[1]

Synagogues and Kehillot

In Judaism, a synagogue is traditionally defined as a house of prayer (*beit tefilah*), a house of study (*beit midrash*) and a house of meeting (*beit knesset*).[2] That the purposes of the community, at a synagogue, are to pray, study and meet (for other activities), represents the core objects of Jewish religious organisations today, as appears in their legislation, whether they belong to Orthodox, Conservative, Reform or Liberal and Progressive Judaism – the differences between these traditions are not substantial. Nationwide, in Orthodox Judaism, the United Synagogue, a charity constituted in accordance with the (civil) United Synagogues Act 1870, comprises the 'Member Synagogues' as defined in its Statutes.[3] Its objects are: (1) to found, build, maintain, conduct, promote and develop within the United Kingdom, synagogues which conform to the Form of Worship for persons of the Jewish religion; (2) to advance education and to provide instruction in religious subjects to persons of the Jewish religion, in conformity with the Form of Worship, and to provide means of burial for persons of the Jewish religion; (3) the relief of poor persons of the Jewish religion; (4) to advance the charitable purposes of other Jewish bodies by making grants or loans to them including contributing with other Jewish bodies to the maintenance of a Chief Rabbi and of other 'ecclesiastical persons', and to other communal duties devolving on metropolitan congregations; and (5) any other charitable purposes in connection with the Jewish religion.[4] The synagogue may, subject to any contrary or other direction of its Honorary Officers, do all such lawful things as are necessary to attain these objects.[5] A member synagogue

---

[1] Most of the religious organisations studied here are charities (including charitable companies) under civil law. Whilst the Charities Act 2011 is silent on governing documents for charities (though it is different for a charitable incorporated organisation (CIO)), the Charity Commission has guidance on the matters it regards as mandatory: *Guidance: Changing Your Charity's Governing Document* (CC36), published 5 August 2011: 2. 'When a charity is formed, its purposes and the rules for how it should operate are set down in a governing document.'

[2] Synagogue is from the Greek word συναγωγή, *synagogē*, which means 'assembly'.

[3] United Synagogue (US): US: Statutes 1. See below for its Statutes and other regulatory instruments.

[4] US. Statutes 4.   [5] US. Bye-Laws 3.

must further the objects of the United Synagogue in such manner as the Honorary Officers may from time to time determine that the maintenance and conduct of a synagogue conforms to the Polish or German ritual for persons of the Jewish religion.[6]

Similarly, the Federation of Synagogues provides centralised services to its member Orthodox communities, 'while allowing them to retain their individuality and distinct identity'.[7] Its objects are to: (1) establish and maintain Jewish places of worship and community and educational centres; (2) provide judges (*dayanim*), Rabbis and other religious officiants; (3) establish, maintain and support organisations and other activities for Jewish religious, educational, cultural and social purposes; (4) establish, promote, carry on and assist institutions, organisations, associations and other activities for the promotion, provision and maintenance of *kashrut* (including ritual laws on food); and (5) provide and maintain cemeteries and funeral services for Jews.[8]

Much the same ideas are found in Orthodox instruments adopted at local level. For example, the objects of the North Hendon Adath Yisroel Synagogue (formerly affiliated to the Union of Orthodox Hebrew Congregations) are 'to purchase, lease or hire, maintain and provide a place of worship (synagogue) for Orthodox Jews, to conduct Divine Services and to foster the religious, educational and social development of its members'.[9] The objects of the Cambridge Traditional Jewish Congregation include co-operation with other bodies engaged in the advancement of the Jewish faith 'in making known publicly the view of the Jewish faith on moral and social issues'.[10] The Exeter Hebrew Congregation, which was founded in 1763 and is 'an independent, unaffiliated body', provides for 'the religious, spiritual and cultural needs of Jews in the City of Exeter and County of Devon',[11] and its objects are 'to promote the

---

[6] US: Bye-Laws 2.
[7] Federation of Synagogues (FOS): www.federation.org.uk/; see also Laws 2: 'The name of the Federation shall be, in Hebrew, Chevrat B'nei Yisrael and, in English, "The Federation of Synagogues".'
[8] FOS: Laws 3.
[9] North Hendon Adath Yisroel Synagogue (NHAYS): Constitution, Art. 2; see also Art. 4: affiliation: the synagogue maintains representation on the North West London Communal Mikvah Committee.
[10] Cambridge Traditional Jewish Congregation (CTJC): Declaration of Trust (1981), Preamble.
[11] Exeter Hebrew Congregation (EHC): Con. Preamble and Schedule Regulations. Its Chevra Kadisha was founded in 1757.

religious and other charitable activities' of that Congregation.[12] In turn, the objects of the Exeter Hebrew Congregation Trust (a charity), as set out in its trust deed, are 'the advancement and promotion of the Jewish religion and heritage by the provision and maintenance of a synagogue and burial ground by regular religious worship and educational and social activities and such other activities as may promote the welfare and Jewish identity of its members and other charitable purposes'.[13]

As to Reform Judaism and Liberal Judaism, whilst legal pluralism exists to the extent that each synagogue has its own regulatory instruments, there is little difference as to objects; however, some are spelt out briefly, and others in considerable detail, often with explicit use of religious categories. Within the Movement for Reform Judaism,[14] the objects of the North London Reform Synagogue, by way of example, are the advancement of the Jewish religion through the provision of religious services in a form determined by its Council, the provision and maintenance of a place of worship and the arrangement of marriages, burials and cremations for the members; the advancement of education, in particular through the provision of classes in Hebrew and religion; and such other charitable objects as its Council may consider from time to time advisable.[15] Similarly, within the Union of Liberal and Progressive Synagogues,[16] the objects of the Wessex Liberal Jewish Community, for instance, are to advance the Jewish religion, for the benefit of the public and in accordance with the Affirmation of Liberal Judaism (which sets out its beliefs), particularly by providing places for worship, learning and social activities; to promote and encourage religious activities; to provide Hebrew and religion classes and other religious educational activities; and to advance such charitable activities as the Community itself decides.[17]

---

[12] EHC: Con. Schedule of Regulations, 3.   [13] EHC: Con. Trust Deed (4 May 1994) 1.
[14] MRJ is itself both a registered charity and a company: www.reformjudaism.org.uk/.
[15] North London Reform Synagogue (NLRS): Laws of Sha'arei Tsedek, Art. 1. See also SSRS: Con. Art. 2: 'The Synagogue is a Congregation of Jews as defined by the Beth Din of the Movement for Reform Judaism and its successors formed with the objects of providing and maintaining a Synagogue for the purpose of public worship and advancing religious, education and charitable activities.'
[16] ULPS (with its head office in London) is a charity and a company: www.liberaljudaism.org/.
[17] Wessex Liberal Jewish Community (WLJC): Con. Art. 3; ULPS: *Affirmations* (2006)

In contrast, the objects of Elstree Liberal Synagogue are more detailed, designed around 'the advancement of Liberal Judaism for the public benefit'.[18] To further these objects, its Council may *inter alia*: (1) provide and maintain a place of worship and arrange and conduct religious services; (2) provide, arrange and conduct religious education; (3) solemnise marriages; (4) make provision for burial and cremation; (5) perform such other religious rites and charitable duties as Council determines; (6) co-operate with other charities, voluntary bodies and statutory authorities operating in furtherance of the objects or of a similar charitable purpose; (7) determine and decide all questions relating to: (a) the religious practices and services of the synagogue and the religious education of the children of members, (b) the membership of the synagogue, (c) the administration of the synagogue and its affairs and (d) the furtherance of its declared objects, including the delegation of such of its powers as it sees fit in pursuance of such objects; and (8) all such other lawful acts and things conducive to the achievement of its objects.[19] The objects of Peterborough Liberal Jewish Community also include various religious activities, such as the *barmitvah*, *batmitvah*, conversions, burial and cremation, other religious rites/ceremonies, and implementing nationwide Liberal Judaism 'policies and initiatives at local level'.[20]

In turn, in the Conservative tradition, several communities in the United Kingdom are affiliated to the United Synagogue of Conservative Judaism (based in New York) – an association of 'sacred communities' (*kehillot*) committed to 'a dynamic Judaism that is learned and passionate, authentic and pluralistic, joyful and accessible, egalitarian and traditional'. The function of the *kehillot* is to empower Jews to seek the presence of God, meaning and purpose in Torah and *mitzvot*, to fully engage with Israel and to be inspired by Judaism to improve the world and the Jewish people by connecting all *kehillot* with a common sense of community, shared sacred mission and purpose. The objects of the United Synagogue of Conservative Judaism itself are to: (1) transform and strengthen the *kehillot* in their effort to inspire meaningful prayer, sustain a culture of continuing lifelong Jewish learning, nurture religious

---

[18] Elstree Liberal Synagogue (ELS): Con. Art. 3; the Constitution was approved at the Annual General Meeting 2015: Con. Art. 1.

[19] ELS: Con. Art. 4.

[20] PLJC (affiliated nationally to Liberal Judaism, a constituent member of the World Union of Progressive Judaism): Con. Art. 3.

and spiritual growth and promote excellence in *kehilla* leadership; (2) ensure educational excellence true to the vision of Conservative Judaism for children and adults in the *kehillot*; (3) engage the next generation of *kehilla* leadership; and (4) encourage and build new *kehillot*.[21]

Similarly, several communities are affiliated with the World Council of Conservative-Masorti Judaism;[22] its 'mission' is to renew and strengthen Jewish life 'by building the Masorti movement throughout the world', to advance 'the interests and principles of Masorti Judaism' through working with its affiliates and to be an effective spokesperson for Masorti Judaism. It does so by emphasizing the study of Torah, in the fullest sense, and the transmission of its principles from generation to generation, the unity of the Jewish people and centrality of the synagogue in their lives and the importance of maintaining a centrist, dynamic Jewish practice. The latter is based on *halacha* and *mitzvot*, and is grounded in Jewish knowledge and observance, reflecting a love of tradition but embracing modernity and the positive aspects of change. It must also emphasise the centrality of Israel and knowledge and use of Hebrew; 'the values of egalitarianism, pluralism, tolerance and democracy in the development of ... Jewish tradition'; co-operation among Jews who respect each other within 'the framework of Jewish belief'; and it must support efforts to organize new *kehillot, havurot* [groups] and *minyanim* [persons required for a religious service] committed to Masorti Judaism', and 'train religious and lay leadership needed to realize its objectives'.[23]

Churches and Church Universal

In Christianity, based on traditional understandings of the church (ecclesiology) before, at and since the Reformation,[24] the church as an institution may define itself by its autonomy, polity and objects. A church is a community which may be international, national, regional or local. It has a distinct membership, or other body of persons associated with it, who are organised in territorial or non-territorial units such as provinces,

---

[21] USCJ: Bylaws 1.1–2; it engages exclusively in religious, educational and charitable activities for the purpose of the US (civil) Internal Revenue Code of 1986, s. 501 as amended or similar statute.

[22] World Council of Conservative-Masorti Judaism (Masorti Olami) (WCCMJ) (or World Council of Conservative Synagogues): By-Laws I; moreover: 'All Masorti Olami officers and members of the Board of Directors shall have subscribed to the Jerusalem Program.'

[23] WCCMJ: By-Laws II.

[24] See e.g. A.V. Dulles, *Models of the Church* (Dublin: Gill & Macmillan, 2nd edn, 1988).

districts or congregations. It is autonomous in its system of governance or polity. And a church has among its objects the advancement of the mission of Jesus Christ, which includes proclaiming the Gospel, administering the sacraments and serving the wider community.[25] These principles of Christian law derive from the similarities between the laws of churches.

Within the Episcopal tradition, the Roman Catholic Church – a global or 'universal' church in which 'subsists' the 'church universal' – is 'established and ordered in this world as a society', which exists for 'the salvation of souls', 'to preach the Gospel to all people' and 'proclaim moral principles', to worship and administer the sacraments, and to govern the faithful; in turn, the universal church includes particular churches, such as a diocese which is overseen by a bishop.[26] An autonomous Anglican Church, like the Church of England, Church in Wales, and Scottish Episcopal Church, is a member of the global Anglican Communion, and asserts its place in the 'church universal'; its objects are, typically, to 'minister the doctrine and sacraments and discipline of Christ', respond to human need and establish 'the values of the Kingdom' of God.[27]

Within the Protestant traditions, a Lutheran church is a national or local assembly of the faithful shaped by authoritative Reformation texts and its 'biblical foundations'. As part of the Church of Christ, its objects are, typically, to declare the teachings of the apostles, confess the faith and engage in worship and Christian service; and it may be a member of the Lutheran World Federation.[28] At local level, in the Lutheran Church in Great Britain, a congregation is 'a community of baptised Christians who meet regularly for the proclamation of the Gospel and administration of the Sacraments'. It participates in the mission of God by meeting for worship, teaching and fellowship; witnessing to the Gospel in the world; serving God's creation; providing pastoral care for members; serving and ministering to the community; and reflecting the love of God by proclaiming and living the Good News in the world. Each

---

[25] Christian Law Panel of Experts, *Principles of Christian Law* (2016) I.1.1–5.
[26] *Codex Iuris Canonici* (CIC) (1983), Code of Canon Law (Roman Catholic): Bks. II–IV; *Lumen Gentium*, Vatican II, Dogmatic Constitution (1965) 1, 8, 10–11.
[27] The Principles of Canon Law Common to the Churches of the Anglican Communion (PCLCCAC) (Anglican Communion Office, London, 2008): Principle 10.
[28] The Reformation texts include the Augsburg Confession (1530) and Formula of Concord (1577); see e.g. Lutheran Church in Great Britain (LCGB): Rules and Regulations, Statement of Faith, 7–9.

congregation must: provide services of worship at which the Word of God is preached and the Sacraments are administered; provide pastoral care; and enable all members to carry out their own particular role within the priesthood of all baptised believers. The congregation must also teach both adults and children through Bible studies, Confirmation and Baptism classes and other appropriate media; encourage responsible and appropriate stewardship among members; take part in the mission of the church through diaconal work (service and care for the world) and response to human need (justice and peace issues); and reach out to others, in the local geographical area and members of the wider community.[29]

The Methodist Church in Great Britain is a union of the Wesleyan Methodist Church, Primitive Methodist Church and United Methodist Church, by which it became 'a united church or denomination under the name of the Methodist Church'; its objects are the advancement of 'the Christian faith in accordance with the doctrinal standards and the discipline of the Methodist Church' and any charitable purpose, *inter alia*, of any connexional, district, circuit, local or other organisation of the church. The church also 'cherishes its place' in the church universal as well as its membership of the World Methodist Council.[30] Similarly, the World Communion of Reformed Churches includes Presbyterian, Reformed, Congregational and United Churches; its churches are 'called together in the name of the one God, Father, Son and Holy Spirit. Under the sovereign God, with Christ's followers across the globe, sharing one baptism, the members of the communion belong to the one holy catholic and apostolic church'.[31] For example, the objects of the Presbyterian Church of Wales and its units include sharing in the mission of God to the world, proclaiming the good news of God, establishing fellowships, administering its ritual ordinances, providing pastoral care, religious education, community service, and 'taking a stand for justice and peace'.[32]

---

[29] LCGB: Rules and Regulations: Congregations.

[30] Methodist Church in Great Britain (MCGB): Constitutional Practice and Discipline, Deed of Union, s. 2.3 and 4; Book VI: World Methodist Council; and Methodist Church Act 1976, s. 4.

[31] World Communion of Reformed Churches: Con. Preamble. E.g. United Reformed Church in Great Britain is a union (1972) of the Congregational Church in England and Wales and Presbyterian Church of England; it united in 1981 with the Reformed Churches of Christ and in 2000 with the Congregational Union of Scotland.

[32] Presbyterian Church of Wales (PCW): Handbook of Rules, 1.1; 1: Governance; 2: Members; 3: Courts; 4: Ministry; 5–7: Property; 8: Procedure; 9: Declarations; 10: Services.

For Baptists a church is defined as the local church and congregation. The Baptist World Alliance consists of autonomous member churches and other bodies, such as Baptist Unions and Conventions of local churches: 'extending over every part of the world' as 'an expression of the essential oneness of Baptist people in ... Christ, to impart inspiration to the fellowship, and to provide channels for sharing concerns and skills in witness and ministry'.[33] The Baptist Union of Great Britain is composed of 'the Churches, Associations of Churches, Colleges, and other Baptist organizations and persons who are for the time being in membership with the Union'. The object of the Union is 'the advancement of the Christian religion, especially by the means of and in accordance with the principles of the Baptist Denomination' in order, for example, '[t]o cultivate among its own members respect and love for one another, and to all who love the Lord Jesus Christ', to spread the Gospel (e.g. by ministers and evangelists and by establishing churches), to afford opportunities for 'united action on questions affecting the welfare of the member churches', and to promote good relations between Baptists at home and abroad. A local church shares these objects.[34]

Mosques and Islamic Centres

There are many Muslim organisations in Britain, including associations of mosques and Islamic centres, each with its own objects.[35] For example, at national level, there is the Muslim Council of Britain, which is a registered charity. First, the preamble of its constitution sets out its ethos – it aspires to be a community 'enjoying what is right, forbidding what is wrong, and believing in Allah' (Qur'an 3:110), conscious of the injunctions to 'Hold fast, all together, to the bond with Allah and be not divided' (Qur'an 3:103) and helping one another to God-consciousness and not to sin and transgression (Qur'an 5:2). Secondly, as to

---

[33] Baptist World Alliance: Con. Preamble: 'This Alliance recognizes the traditional autonomy and interdependence of Baptist churches and member bodies'; Art. II: it is e.g. to witness to the Gospel, assist members 'in their divine task of bringing all people to God' through Christ and promote 'Baptist principles'.

[34] Baptist Union of Great Britain (BUGB): Con. Arts. 1–4: its basis is the authority of Christ, baptism by immersion and the duty to evangelise; Art. 5: it acts through its Assembly; Art. 6: admission of a (local) Baptist church.

[35] See above Introduction. See also Universal Islamic Declaration of Human Rights (UIDHR) (Islamic Council of Europe 1981): Art. XIV: this deals with freedom of association.

composition, foundations and character, it is 'an accord of mosques, Muslim associations and institutions' in the UK; and, as to religious law, it 'shall be informed and guided by the Qur'an and the Sunnah in all its aims, policies and procedures'. Moreover, the Council is 'an independent body working for the pleasure of Allah to promote consultation, co-operation and coordination on Muslim affairs'. As 'a non-sectarian body', it seeks 'the common good without interfering in, displacing or isolating any existing Muslim work in the community'. It is also a 'broad-based representative organisation ... accommodating and reflecting the variety of social and cultural backgrounds and outlook of the community'. And it is a body which bases its 'policies and decisions on consensus and the largest practicable measure of common agreement', which, through 'a system of representation and accountability' seeks 'to draw on the ... skills of individuals and the strengths of organised bodies to meet ... challenges ahead in preparing the case for, and advocating, the responsibilities and rights of Muslims living in Britain'.[36]

Thirdly, its aims and objectives are: to promote co-operation, consensus and unity on Muslim affairs in the United Kingdom; to encourage and strengthen existing efforts for the benefit of the Muslim community; to work for a more enlightened appreciation of Islam in wider society; to establish a position for the Muslim community within society that is fair; to work to eradicate disadvantages and discrimination faced by Muslims; and to foster better community relations and work for the good of society as a whole.[37] Any organisation in Britain whose activities are primarily for the benefit of Muslims in Britain, or which operates from Britain with staff drawn from Britain for the benefit of the Muslim *ummah* is eligible for membership if it subscribes to the preamble, aims and objectives and conforms to the following principles: (1) it must profess the Muslim faith, declaring knowingly and voluntarily its belief in 'the Qur'an as the true Word of God revealed to the Prophet Muhammad'; (2) it must have a Constitution, Standing Orders or Bye-laws (which must be provided to the Council);[38] (3) its delegates must be motivated by the desire to serve the community, and abide by the procedures and standing orders that govern the conduct of the Council and its affairs; (4) it must accept the Council Constitution and is able and willing to abide by its provisions and will do its best to uphold and implement agreed policies (collective

---

[36] Muslim Council of Britain (MCB): Con. (2012) Preamble and Declaration of Intent; Art. 8.1: it is an unincorporated association.
[37] MCB: Con. Art. 1: name; and Art 2: aims and objectives.   [38] MCB: Con. Art. 3.1.

responsibility); and (5) it must do its best to promote mutual respect and co-operation with member organisations and use the framework of the Council to resolve difficult issues with other member organisations (pledge of mutual respect and co-operation).[39]

Similarly, the objects of the Nasru-Lahi-Il-Fathi Society of Nigeria, United Kingdom and Ireland, which is also a registered charity, are to: advance the Islamic Faith in accordance with the statement of faith (Quran and Hadith), particularly in providing mosques, libraries, hospitals, educational institutes, and translating the Quran into different languages; promote religious harmony in particular among Muslims of differing traditions; and relieve financial hardship, sickness and distress. It must also advance education especially among women by providing schools and other institutes and disseminating publications; and provide or assist in the provision of facilities for recreation and other leisure time occupations, particularly for young people, in the interests of social welfare with 'the object of seeking to improve conditions of life'.[40]

At regional level, the Muslim Council of Wales is an affiliate of the Muslim Council of Britain and was founded 'to serve the needs of the Muslim community across Wales'. It works with 'Mosques, Charities, Institutions and local partners' for 'the common good'; represents the needs of Welsh Muslims at local government level; 'has strong relationships with all faith communities' in Wales; and seeks 'to enhance the quality of life for Welsh Muslims, build community cohesion and encourage active citizenship'.[41] Its ethos, 'informed and guided by the Sunnah in all its aims, policies and procedures', mirrors that of the Muslim Council of Britain, basing 'its policies and decisions on consensus (*shura*) and the largest practicable measure of common agreement' with 'a system of representation and accountability'.[42] Whilst its objects too generally mirror those of the Muslim Council of Britain, it adapts these to the Welsh context; for example: to promote 'an accurate image of Islam and Muslims' in Wales 'representing the true message of Islam and its teachings'; to broaden integration between Muslims and non-Muslims for the creation of a cohesive Welsh society; to present an

---

[39] MCB: Con. Art. 3.
[40] Nasru-Lahi-Il-Fathi Society of Nigeria, United Kingdom and Ireland (NASFAT): Con. (2006) Clause C; the headquarters of the Society must be located in London.
[41] It was founded in 2003 'to reflect the devolved structure of Welsh government as well as the unique historical, social and religious context of Wales'.
[42] Muslim Council of Wales (MCW): Declaration of Intent.

Islamic perspective on issues of importance to the Welsh public; and to empower Muslims in Wales 'through political and social activism'.[43]

Likewise, the Bolton Council of Mosques (with about 25 mosques for the residents of Bolton and its neighbourhood) seeks advancement of the Islamic religion by, in particular, encouraging the foundation of mosques, promoting racial–religious harmony between Muslims and non-Muslims in order 'to foster mutual understanding and toleration' and promoting other charitable purposes for the benefit of the Muslim Community.[44] The purposes of the Council for Mosques (Bradford) are: to lobby on behalf of the Muslim community on local and national matters such as law and order, health, education and interfaith relations; to offer 'guidance on a wide range of Islamic cultural and religious issues, provide Muslim burial services and work with key partners to provide community support'; and as 'a multi-denominational platform inclusive of all major Islamic schools of thought' to protect 'the religious sanctity of the Islamic code of life'. It is also to encourage understanding between members that will lead to co-operation and mutual support in common areas of concern, thus facilitating consultation, the provision of information and advice on religious matters, 'particularly those affecting policy and practice'; provide advocacy and representation on issues affecting the wellbeing of the Muslim community in Bradford and beyond; and foster links with other faith communities to facilitate under-standing with regard to common concerns.[45]

At local level, a mosque (from the Arabic *masjid*, a place for prostra-tion) will have its own objects.[46] Its own management or leadership committee should be clear about its intentions (*niyyah*) and 'define the mission or aims and agree to a set of objectives'.[47] Mosques engage in a wide range of activities around three principal objects: providing wor-ship, educational programmes and welfare services.[48] The objects of

---

[43] MCW: Con. Objects.   [44] Birmingham Central Mosque (BCM): Con. Art. 3.
[45] Council   for   Mosques   (CFM)   (Bradford):   Con.   Preamble;   and: www.councilformosques.org/about-us/our-aims/.
[46] M. Naqshbandi, *Islam and Muslims in Britain* (2012): Guide 4.1.
[47] Faith Associates: www.faithassociates.co.uk/training-faith-leaders/, Muslim Women's Guide to Mosque Governance, Management and Service Delivery (2016) 49: The Mosque: its structure, management and governance.
[48] Charity Commission: *Survey of Mosques in England and Wales* (2009). See also Central Mosque (affiliated to Jamiatul-Ulama Kwa Zulu Natal South Africa, Council of Muslim Theologians): *Model Constitution of an Islamic Organisation*, Aims and Objectives, e.g. 'To enjoin what is right and forbid what is wrong in all facets of the Muslim community

some Muslim bodies are brief. For instance, the Central Jamia Masjid (Southall) seeks 'to advance the religion of Islam and in particular the Sunni Muslim Faith and in furtherance of that objective the Masjid may be used to teach, propagate and preach Islam according to the Sunni Schools of Thought', that is, the schools of Imam Abu Hanifa, Imam Hanbali, Imam Malik and Imam Shafi'i.[49] Similarly, the objects of the Noor-Ul-Islam Mosque (Bury) are to provide an educational and spiritual centre for young Muslims, including a library and study facilities, and to advance the Islamic religion in the Borough of Bury by providing a mosque, a Muslim burial ground, and education in 'the principles of the Sunni Islamic faith' – but it must not be connected with 'any form of political organization . . . locally, nationally or internationally'.[50]

By way of contrast, the objects of the Lancaster Islamic Society, a charity, are more detailed, namely: to establish, operate and maintain a *masjid* for congregational and other prayers, religious rites and activities;[51] to establish, operate and maintain institutions to disseminate Islamic teaching, training and education; and to strive to create an environment of social and spiritual needs of Muslims and encourage learning and discussion about Islam among its members and the wider community. It also aims to establish, operate and maintain institutions to enhance the religious and social causes of the community, for example, libraries, cemeteries, *da'wah* institutions, social-welfare schemes; enjoin what is right and forbid what is wrong in all facets of the Muslim community, promoting and propagating Islamic teachings and adopting all means to achieve these 'in accordance with Shariah'; and raise funds for such causes to enhance 'the cause of Islam and the Muslim community', promote good race relations; and do such other things as are charitable in law and for the public benefit.[52]

---

and to actively promote and propagate Islamic teachings and to adopt all means for the achievement of this objective in accordance with Shari'ah.'

[49] Central Jamia Masjid (CJM) (Southall): Con. Art. 3.

[50] Noor-Ul-Islam Mosque (NUIM) (Bury): Con. Art. 2.

[51] Moreover: 'In the event of a dispute concerning a matter being of religious purpose, the congregation shall acquire a ruling whether such a matter falls under the definition of "religious activity", from a *bona fide* Ulama body affiliated or aligned to the above institutions or their successors or appointees.'

[52] Lancaster Islamic Society (LIS): Con. Aims and Objectives 1–9; Affiliation: 'In matters of religious guidance and directives, the congregation shall be affiliated to Markazi Masjid, Dewsbury . . . to recognise the religious authority for the purposes of obtaining religious sanction and approval of the congregation's . . . activities.'

The Sources and Forms of Religious Law

All three religions have a strong and rich juristic tradition. In each, the theocratic basis of law comes to the fore – the revealed law of God. Within each faith group, the regulatory instruments of the religious organisations studied represent the formal modern sources of religious law. They exist under a variety of titles and contain binding norms of conduct. Sometimes, they deploy elements of classical religious law in the form of sacred texts, which act as the material sources for these instruments.

Torah and Halakhah

Within Judaism, *halakhah* represents the whole system of Jewish law by which a Jew 'walks' through life (*halakh*, 'to go' or 'to walk'),[53] namely: 'the complex of norms incumbent on Jews', those which are 'commanded by God', and those which reflect the basic values God considers desirable, even if He did not actually command them; the dominant subject matter of *halakhah* is worship of God and all norms are ultimately grounded on revelation.[54] The modern category *mishpat ivri* (literally, Jewish law) is used for the whole legal system or else those elements of the legal system which deal with 'non-religious' or 'civic matters'; it makes three claims: laws belong to a unified system; there are basic authoritative legal sources within the system, and any valid application of the law must be justified by reliance on these fundamental sources; and the system of law itself provides the means by which its rules are recognised as authoritative.[55]

Central to Jewish law is the Torah – classically, 'everything set forth in the Torah . . . is binding', and the 'source of authority of this basic norm itself is the basic tenet . . . that the source of authority of the Torah is divine command'.[56] The Torah, literally 'teaching',[57] is the will of God

---

[53] It is distinct from *Aggadah*, non-legal ideas/topics (e.g. Jewish history, ethics, medicine, literature); *halakhah* in the earliest Rabbinic period was confined to a particular ruling or decision.

[54] A. Sagi, 'Natural Law and Halakha: A Critical Analysis', *Jewish Law Annual* 13 (2000) 149–196.

[55] H. Ben-Menahem, 'The judicial process and the nature of Jewish law' in N. Hecht *et al.*, eds., *Jewish Law* (1996) 421–437 at 421.

[56] M. Elon, *Jewish Law* (1994) I.233.

[57] The word *torah* may be used in the sense of: a law, group of laws or instructions on a specific topic; the way of life revealed by God through a prophet: 'Remember the Torah of Moses my servant' (Malachi 3:22); a general term for 'instruction' (Proverbs 1:8); and a

revealed to the people of Israel. This revealed divine law is found in the Written Torah (the Pentateuch, the first five books of the Hebrew Bible),[58] and the Oral Torah, given verbally by God to Moses and, in the classical Rabbinic tradition, the teachings of the sages of Israel transmitted through the generations (being elucidations of the revealed law). According to tradition, the Torah contains 613 commands (*mitzvot*) divided into two categories: 248 affirmative commandments (*mitzvot aseh*) and 365 negative commandments (*mitzvot lo ta-aseh*).[59] Moreover, the Torah itself is the fullest version of revealed divine law available to humans and is sufficient for all questions – and the Pentateuch has 'supreme sanctity and authority'.[60]

The principal documentary depositories of the Oral Torah are the Mishnah and Talmud. The Mishnah, a digest compiled by Rabbi Judah (d. c. 217 CE), deals with six topics: agricultural laws, appointed times (e.g. Sabbath), women (marriage and divorce), damages (torts, buying and selling and jurisprudence in general), sanctities (laws of sacrifice) and the laws of ritual contamination.[61] The Talmud contains the teachings of the *Amoraim*, the 'expounders' (c. 200–500 CE);[62] it is a commentary on, or exposition of, the Mishnah and other associated works.[63] Various periods in the historical development of Jewish law followed,[64] each generating its own literature, including: (1) the summary codes of

---

parchment scroll (*sefer torah*) on which the instruction is written (Joshua 1:8) or the scroll with the Five Books of Moses.

[58] The Hebrew Bible is divided into: (1) the Pentateuch (*Torah*), i.e. the five books of Moses: Genesis, Exodus, Leviticus, Numbers and Deuteronomy; (2) the Prophets (*Novim*); and (3) the Writings (*Ketuvim*) or the books of the Hagiographa. After the initial letters, the bible is called the *Tanakh*.

[59] Lists of mitzvot were given e.g. by Moses Maimonides (Rambam) in his *Mishneh Torah*.

[60] I. Herzog, *Jewish Law* (1980) I.1.

[61] The Mishnah (lit. teaching) is in the style of the *Tannaim*, 'repeaters' (to 200 CE); H. Danby, *The Mishnah: Translated from the Hebrew with Introduction and Brief Explanatory Notes* (Oxford: Oxford University Press, 1933).

[62] 'Talmud' (root *limmed*, to learn) means 'teaching' or 'study'. There are two Talmuds: Palestinian and Babylonian. In the Middle Ages, the term *Gemara* was used for *Talmud*; see H.L. Strack and G. Stemberger, *Introduction to the Talmud and Midrash*, translated and edited by M. Bockmuehl (Minneapolis: Fortress Press, 2nd edn, 1996).

[63] Tannaitic works (quoted in the Talmud) include the *Tosefta* ('addition' to the Mishnah), *Mekhilta* ('Measure') on Exodus, *Sifra* ('Book') on Leviticus (also called 'Law of the Priests' – *Torat Kohanim*) and *Sif're* ('Books') on Numbers and Deuteronomy. The last three are known as the Midrash.

[64] Those of the: *Savoraim*, 'reasoners' (c. 500–650 CE); *Geonim*, lit. 'geniuses', of the 'Gaonic period' (c. 650–1038); *Rishonim*, lit. 'firsts' (c. 1038–1563); and *Acharonim*, lit. 'lasts' (c. 1500 to the present). See generally, N. Hecht *et al.*, eds., *Jewish Law* (1996).

Talmudic material;[65] (2) the topic codes, such as *Mishneh Torah* (lit: 'Torah Reviewed', c. 1187) by Maimonides (1135–1204), *Sefer ha-turim* (lit: 'Book of Parts') by Jacob ben Asher (d. 1343), and *Shulhan 'arukh* (lit., 'The Prepared Table') by Joseph Karo (1488–1575);[66] and (3) the commentaries.[67] In addition, historically, Jewish law is found in Rabbinic legislation – 'preventative legislation' (*gezeirah*), to prevent breach of the commandments and 'positive legislation' (*takkanah*), designed to stimulate conduct – and custom (*minhag*), universal/local.[68]

Another important classical source is responsa (*teshuvot*): a responsum (*teshuvah*) is an answer given by an authority in Jewish law to a question (*she'elah*) put to it by, for example, a Rabbi or Rabbinic court on what to do in particular situations.[69] Sometimes the respondents write up and publish their replies for circulation to the wider community. The responsa literature does not always confine itself to the letter of the law but uses persuasion to produce the outcome the respondent considers morally correct. This might appeal, beyond that which *halakhah* may demand, to higher moral standards – 'the standards of the pious' (*middat hasidut*) or 'beyond the letter of the law' (*lifnim mishurat hadin*) or to 'heavenly law' (*dine shamayyim*). Thus, halakhic practice links law and morals, suggesting that Jewish law is not simply preceptive and prohibitive but also exhortatory or recommendatory, encouraging and discouraging conduct.[70]

However, Jewish law is 'a site of struggle and diversity between different conceptions of both structure and objective'.[71] Today, for Orthodox

---

[65] E.g. *Halakhot pesuqot*, 'decided laws', ascribed to Yehudai Gaon (eighth century), and *Halakhot gedolot*, 'great laws', by Simeon Kiyyara (ninth century).

[66] This presents Sefardic (Middle Eastern/North African) rather than Ashkenazic (Franco-German and Eastern European) tradition, largely following Maimonides and Asher. When the Ashkenazic, Polish codifier Moses Isserles (d. 1572) added his notes, this became the standard halakhic code for all Jews.

[67] The rise of Jewish academies in Europe led to the production of commentaries or notebooks (*quntresim*) by e.g. Rashi (acronym of Rabbi Shlomo Yitzhaqui (1040–1105). In Spain, such works were known as *hiddushim* or *novellae* (since they aimed at 'new insights').

[68] I. Herzog, *Jewish Law* (1980) I.20–23; see Chapter 5 for precedent.

[69] L. Jacobs, *Concise Companion to the Jewish Religion* (Oxford: Oxford University Press, 1999) 203: Hebrew, *sheelot u-teshuvot*, literally, 'questions and answers'. The responsa literature developed in the Middle Ages.

[70] B. Jackson, 'Judaism as a religious legal system', in A. Huxley, ed., *Religion, Law and Tradition* (2002) 34 at 43: Jackson argues that this is further evidence of an absence of legal positivism (which separates law and morals) in Judaism.

[71] D. Jackson, 'Judaism as a religious legal system' (2002) 34 at 35

Judaism, *halakhah* at its core represents the revealed will of God expressed in the written and oral Torah, which is unalterable and cannot be overridden, and later formulations or interpretations of it (e.g. codes, customs and responsa) are derived from it with the utmost accuracy and care. Reform Judaism embraces the idea that *halakhah* is no longer normative for, or binding on, Jews today, and each Jew is obliged to interpret it for him/herself so as to create separate personal command-ments – traditional *halakhah* is relative to its own period of development and may be changed to meet new circumstances as method (a way of doing) rather than law. And, broadly, Conservative Judaism falls between these two: it seeks fidelity to *halakhah* which is normative and binding, and believes Jews must practically observe its precepts (e.g. Sabbath, dietary ordinances and ritual purity) but, at the same time, using scien-tific and academic enquiry, maintains that the laws are subject to evolu-tion and as such continue to be part of a flexible juridical tradition.[72]

Jewish entities today use a range of formal regulatory instruments (legislation).[73] For example, in the Orthodox tradition, the United Syna-gogue is regulated, under the (civil) United Synagogues Act 1870, by 'Rules' scheduled to the Act, 'Statutes' and 'Regulations'.[74] 'Statutes' are 'the governing Statutes or Constitution of the United Synagogue'; and 'Regulations' are 'any subordinate rules or regulations made by the United Synagogue' (e.g. Bye-Laws).[75] The Statutes may be altered, amended or added to by Special Resolution passed by a majority of no less than two-thirds of the members of the Council at a special meeting for which there should be not less than 14 days' written notice. However,

---

[72] The popular perception is that Conservative Judaism charges Orthodox Judaism with petrifying halakhah and Reform Judaism with abandoning it. See e.g., for a Liberal viewpoint, J. Cohen, 'Halakhah and the modern temper', in W. Jacob, ed., *Beyond the Letter of the Law: Essays on Diversity in the Halakhah*, in the series Studies in Progressive Halakhah (Pittsburgh, PA: Rodef Shalom Press, 2004) 92 at 92: 'its chief feature is education of oneself or training. Accordingly, the Halakhah is a true mirror reflecting the work of the Jew in shaping his character'; 'as its meaning "conduct" indicates, [it] comprises life in all its manifestations – religion, worship, law, economics, politics, ethics, and so forth'; and: 'Laws which govern the daily life of man must be such as suit and express his religious ideals and ethical aspirations': quoted from L. Ginzberg, *Students, Scholars and Saints* (Philadelphia: Jewish Publication Society, 1928) 112, 114, 117.

[73] See e.g. USCJ: Bye-laws adopted by the Board of Directors (2011 and 2012, amended 2013–2016); and WCCMJ: By-Laws adopted 26 April 2010 and effective 2 May 2010: By-Laws 1.

[74] US: Statutes 1; see also 5.24 on property 'regulations'; and Statutes 14 for the power of Honorary Officers to make 'Regulations'.

[75] US: Bye-Laws 1.

any proposal to alter, amend or remove the synagogue objects must not proceed until it has been approved by the Chief Rabbi by a memorandum in writing.[76] Provision is also made for regulations for its member synagogues.[77] Locally, member synagogues must be administered 'in accordance with such model rules or constitution as shall from time to time be specified by the Honorary Officers' of the United Synagogue.[78]

In similar vein, the (Orthodox) Federation of Synagogues has a constitution contained in its 'Laws',[79] and the trustees may make 'bye-laws, rules or standing orders' as they deem necessary or convenient (for the proper conduct and management of the Federation); the Council may by resolution with 14 clear days' written notice, alter or repeal these, and add to them, but not so as to make the Federation cease to be a charity at civil law without the consent of the (civil) Charity Commission and Federation Beth Din.[80] Likewise, synagogues within the Movement for Reform Judaism must have 'clearly documented aims and rules', in the form of a 'Constitution (Laws) of the community' and 'Codes of Practice', which the trustees of the synagogue must keep up-to-date;[81] the North London Reform Synagogue, for instance, has 'Laws' and its Council may make 'regulations'.[82] Communities within Liberal Judaism also have constitutions,[83] such as that of the Wessex Liberal Jewish Community, a registered charity, whose trustees may also make 'rules or bye-laws'.[84]

Custom, as we have seen, is also a normative source in classical Jewish law. For the Jewish philosopher Philo of Alexandria (c. 25 BCE–50 CE): 'customs are unwritten laws, the decisions approved by men of old, not inscribed on monuments nor on leaves of paper which the moth destroys, but on the souls of those who are in the same citizenship'. Moreover: 'Praise cannot be duly given to one who obeys the written law, since he acts under the admonition of restraint and fear of punishment. But he who faithfully observes the unwritten [law] deserves

---

[76] US: Statutes 54: i.e. Arts. 3 and 4.   [77] See e.g. US: Statutes 14.4.   [78] US: Statutes 49.
[79] FOS: Laws: Definitions: 'Laws' means 'this constitution' (adopted in 1948 and amended 2014).
[80] FOS: Laws 29–31: or an equivalent Beth Din if the Federation ceases to exist.
[81] MRJ: Code of Practice, pp. 4, 5, 14.
[82] NLRS: Laws of Sha'arei Tsedek (Amendments Incorporated to 1999); for regulations as to services, see Art. 14. The minister must be consulted in making these; see also SSRF: Con. Art. 1: 'Laws'.
[83] ELS: the Constitution was approved at the Annual General Meeting 2015: Con. Art. 1.
[84] WLJC: Con. (2011) Arts. 1–2; and Art. 32: rules.

commendation, since the virtue which he displays is freely willed.'[85] In turn, custom is recognised in regulatory instruments today. For instance, the Board of Deputies of British Jews must be guided in 'religious matters', which include 'the religious customs and usages of the Jews by the Ecclesiastical Authorities to whom all such matters must be referred' – and it has a Code of Practice on this matter.[86] Indeed, in the Conservative tradition, for the Committee on Jewish Law and Standards of the Rabbinical Assembly: 'If one wants to cancel an ancient custom, one has to prove that it is a bad custom';[87] and in the Reform tradition: 'when a new ordinance was enacted, it was necessary to see whether it would find acceptance by the people' and if 'the people allows certain practices to fall into disuse, then the practices cease to exist'.[88] In the Movement for Reform Judaism, a synagogue may develop its own 'rules and customs' in relation to education and as to the clothing worn by children at its school.[89] In addition, Exeter Hebrew Congregation conducts its affairs 'in accordance with established Jewish traditions'.[90]

Religious soft-law in the form of normative guidance, policy and codes of conduct is also used today across the Jewish traditions. For example, the (Orthodox) United Synagogue provides for the creation of and compliance with 'guidelines and directions', 'policies and practices'[91] and 'protocol', that is 'any code of conduct for a Local Honorary Officer as established from time to time by [them] for ... the management of a Synagogue'.[92] Similarly, in the United Synagogue of Conservative Judaism, the Board of Directors may provide 'Operating Standards and Procedures', including 'guidelines' as to how to select those directors and a 'Code of Conduct' for the directors once selected.[93] Moreover,

---

[85] *De Specialibus Legibus*, 4.149–150: he was perhaps speaking here of the Oral Torah.

[86] BDBJ: Con. Art. 31: Annexe (Code of Practice).

[87] USCJ: Committee on Jewish Law and Standards: Yoreh deah 367:1: Responsum: The Burial of Non-Jews in a Jewish Cemetery.

[88] P. Haas, 'German Romanticism and the Jews: the intellectual basis for halakhic reform', in W. Jacob, ed., *Beyond the Letter of the Law* (2004) 4 at 14, citing Z. Frankel, *On Changes in Judaism* (1845).

[89] MRJ: Code of Practice, p. 22: 'Education Committee Rules and Customs'; p. 25: school 'customs'.

[90] EHC: Con. Schedule of Regulations, 12.

[91] US: Bye-Laws 8: a committee of Local Honorary Officers must act 'in accordance with [any] guidelines or directions' of the Honorary Officers; 17: 'stated policies and practices'.

[92] US: Bye-Laws 1.   [93] USCJ: Bye-Laws 3.2.

Standards for Congregational Practice are issued for affiliated *kehillot* in order for them to fulfil their own objects; these Standards are 'intended to be consistent with the Purpose, Vision and Mission Statement of USCJ and with the Standards of Rabbinic Practice as adopted by the Rabbinical Assembly and approved *teshuvot* of the Rabbinical Assembly Committee on Jewish Law and Standards'.[94] Likewise, the constitution of the Sukkat Shalom Reform Synagogue (London) provides that the 'Laws' in it must be read in conjunction with its 'Codes of Practice' – and the Laws prevail in the case of conflict between them and the Codes of Practice.[95] Principles are another regulatory category; for instance, the constitution of North Hendon Adath Yisroel Synagogue states: 'All activities of the Synagogue shall be carried out in accordance with the principles of Halachic Judaism as set down in the Shulchan Aruch and its commentaries. No activity contrary to these principles shall be permitted and this clause shall not be amended under any circumstances.'[96]

The Bible and Church Law

As with Judaism, Christianity has a long juristic tradition. Norms of conduct and church order are traceable to the New Testament Church community who devoted themselves to the teachings of the apostles. These norms grew under the legislation of the great councils of the post-apostolic church, developed in the medieval *ius commune* of the western church, and diversified in a plurality of legal systems at the time of and beyond the Reformation of the sixteenth century in the creation of new institutional churches. In all this, Christians became prolific legislators – with laws, rooted in their interpretations of divine law, in a host of forms, from canon law, through constitutions, to local church covenants.[97] A dominant feature of Christian teaching, however, is that salvation of the soul through Christ is fundamentally a matter of faith and divine grace – not compliance with law.

---

[94] USCJ: Standards for Congregational Practice (1957, as amended 2017): with explanations by the Committee on Congregational Standards.
[95] Sukkat Shalom Reform Synagogue (SSRS) (Wanstead): Con. Art. 1.
[96] NHAYS: Con. Art. 3.
[97] See e.g. R.H. Helmholz, *The Spirit of Classical Canon Law* (Athens, GA and London: University of Georgia Press, 1996); and J. Witte, *Law and Protestantism: The Legal Teachings of the Protestant Reformation* (Cambridge: Cambridge University Press, 2002).

Today, Christians have no global system of formal law, which is applicable to all their institutional churches – no single body has competence to make such a system of law; rather, each institutional church within the various traditions has its own body of law, order or polity. However, there are principles of church law common to the historic churches of contemporary worldwide Christianity – and their existence can be factually established by empirical observation and comparison. Churches contribute through their own regulatory instruments to this store of principles. These principles are fundamental to the self-understanding of Christianity; have a living force and contain the possibility of further development or articulation; and demonstrate a degree of unity between the churches, stimulate common Christian actions, and may be fed into the ecumenical enterprise to enhance fuller visible unity.[98] Laws are found in a variety of formal sources, including codes of canon law, charters and statutes, constitutions and bye-laws and books of church order. Customs may have juridical force to the extent permitted by the law of a church. Ecclesiastical quasi-legislation (or soft-law), such as guidelines and codes of practice, is designed to complement the formal laws of churches, and consists of rules that may be prescriptive in form and also generate an expectation of compliance; and: 'Church laws should conform to the law of God, as revealed in Holy Scripture and by the Holy Spirit.'[99]

Among the Episcopal churches, for the Roman Catholic Church 'the highest norm of human life is the divine law itself – eternal, objective and universal', and ascertained by the teaching of the church.[100] The principal source of law for the Latin Church is the Code of Canon Law 1983. The Code distinguishes 'universal law' and 'particular law': universal law is applicable to the Latin Church in all parts of the world; it includes the Code itself, papal decrees and authentic interpretations of a legislator – and it recognises the validity of custom provided it is consistent with

---

[98] Christian Law Panel of Experts, *Principles of Christian Law* (2016): a principle of law common to the churches is a foundational proposition or maxim of general applicability which has substance; is induced from the similarities of the regulatory systems of churches; derives from their juridical tradition or the practices of the church universal; expresses a basic theological truth or ethical value; and is implicit in, or underlies, the juridical systems of the churches.

[99] Christian Law Panel of Experts, *Principles of Christian Law* (2016) I.2: the forms of ecclesial regulation; and, for the law of God, I.3.4: the servant law. See also N. Doe, *Christian Law* (2013) Ch. 1.

[100] Second Vatican Council, Decree 1965, *Dignitatis humanae*, I.3.

divine law, reasonable, rooted in the established customs of a community and approved by the canon law.[101] The Church also uses quasi-legislation.[102]

Anglicans too recognise that church 'Law should reflect the revealed will of God';[103] and the laws of their churches (e.g. 'constitutions', 'canons') present Holy Scripture as the ultimate standard and rule in matters of faith.[104] For example, in the established Church of England, legislation in the form of Measures of its General Synod (on parliamentary approval and royal assent) have the same authority as Acts of Parliament under the civil Church of England Assembly (Powers) Act 1919; Canons are created by General Synod and they must receive royal assent to be operative (Synodical Government Measure 1969); and the church often uses soft-law as a form of guidance and in policy documents and codes of practice. Custom also has its place: pre-Reformation Roman canon law continues to operate in the Church of England (under the Submission of the Clergy Act 1533) through its incorporation into the common law on condition that it is not repugnant to royal prerogative, or any statute or common law – and it does so in the form of customary law.[105] The disestablished Church in Wales, which was formed as a result of the Welsh Church Act 1914, likewise, also has a constitution containing canons, regulations and other instruments (the amendment of which is the responsibility of the Governing Body of the church),[106] as has the Church of Ireland; and the Scottish Episcopal Church has a code of canons.[107]

---

[101] CIC: cc. 12, 16, 22, 29; *Lumen Gentium*, Vatican II, Dogmatic Constitution (1965) 27: 'bishops have the sacred right and duty … to make laws for their subjects, to pass judgment on them, and to moderate pertaining to the ordering of worship and the apostolate'. The Oriental Catholic Churches also have a Code of Canons (1990).

[102] F. Morrisey, 'Papal and curial pronouncements: their canonical significance in the light of the 1983 code of canon law', 50 *The Jurist* (1990) 102. For Orthodox canon law, see P. Rodopoulos, *An Overview of Orthodox Canon Law* (Rollinsford, NH: Orthodox Research Institute, 2007).

[103] PCLCCAC: Definitions, 'Law'; and Principle 2.

[104] Thirty-Nine Articles of Religion (1571): Art. 20: 'it is not lawful for the Church to ordain anything which is contrary to God's Word written'. These Articles are still normative in many churches.

[105] N. Doe, *The Legal Framework of the Church of England* (Oxford: Clarendon Press, 1996) 7–32, 86.

[106] N. Doe, *The Law of the Church in Wales* (Cardiff: University of Wales Press, 2002) Chapter 1.

[107] N. Doe, *Canon Law in the Anglican Communion* (Oxford: Clarendon Press, 1998).

Within Protestant traditions, Lutherans recognise 'the Holy Scriptures . . . as the only infallible source and norm for all matters of faith, doctrine and life', and Lutheran churches have constitutions, rules and regulations.[108] Similarly, the Methodist Church in Great Britain recognises that 'the divine revelation recorded in the Holy Scriptures' is 'the supreme rule of faith and practice', and it is governed by 'Methodist Law' contained in its 'Constitutional Practice and Discipline', 'Standing Orders', and 'usage'.[109] On the basis that it is 'the duty of everyone to accept and obey' the will of God as revealed in Scripture,[110] Reformed and Presbyterian churches employ, variously, 'law', a 'code' with 'legislation',[111] a constitution, bye-laws, and normative doctrinal texts.[112] The Manual of the United Reformed Church in Britain, for instance, affirms Scripture as 'the supreme authority for the faith and conduct of all God's people', provides a model constitution for a local church, recognises customs and regulates itself by soft-law.[113] For the Baptist Union of Great Britain too, Christ is 'the sole and absolute authority in all matters pertaining to faith and practice', and the Holy Scriptures have authority as a revelation of God. Thus: 'Each Church has liberty, under the guidance of the Holy Spirit, to interpret and administer His Laws.'[114] The Union itself has a constitution, and a local church in it may have a constitution, trust instrument, a 'covenant' of members' commitments, and normative doctrinal texts.[115]

Quran and Sunna: Sharia

According to modern commentators, most Muslims consider Islamic law to be divine and sacred in so far as it is rooted in principles revealed in

---

[108] See e.g. LCGB: Constitution (2011) and Rules and Regulations (2011).
[109] MCGB: Constitutional Practice and Discipline, Deed of Union, 4, 19, 25(b): Conference Standing Orders, rules and regulations. See also Methodist Church in Ireland (MCI): Con. s. 6: 'Manual of Laws'; s. 5: 'Rules and Regulations'; Regulations, Discipline and Government, 10.06: 'laws of the Church'.
[110] Presbyterian Church in Ireland (PCI): Code, I.I.III.11.
[111] J.L. Weatherhead (ed.), Constitution and Laws of the Church of Scotland (1997) 16; Manual of Practice and Procedure in the United Free Church of Scotland (2011); The Code: The Book of the Constitution and Government of the Presbyterian Church in Ireland (2010).
[112] PCI: Code, Constitution and Pt. III.15: Trustees' Bylaws.
[113] United Reformed Church (URC): Model Constitution for Local Churches (Mission Council, 2010); PCW: Employee Safety Handbook (undated).
[114] Baptist Union of Great Britain (BUGB): Con. 1.3, Model Trusts for Churches 2003, 2.8.1.
[115] BUGB: Model Trusts for Churches 2003, 2.12 (Church Constitution); Baptist Union of Scotland (BUS): Constitution and Bylaws.

the Quran and Sunna (the traditions of the Prophet Muhammad); they distinguish between the 'religion of Islam' (*din*), 'Islamic jurisprudence' (*fiqh*), the principles of Islamic jurisprudence (*usul al-fiqh*), 'Islamic law' and 'Sharia', though Islam itself embraces the entire religion, including beliefs, rituals, morality and law.[116] Moreover, it is commonly understood that Islamic law has a hierarchy of sources: the Quran, Sunna, analogical reasoning (*qiyas*) and consensus of opinion (*ijma*) among Islamic scholars (*ulama*).[117] First, the Quran is the most important source, but not the source of most law in Islam – it is a book about the relation between God and humans; it consists of approximately 6600 verses; deals predominantly with religion; and contains rules (*ahkam*).[118] The Quran is the word of God revealed to the Prophet Muhammad – divine law – its verses preserved by the Companions of the Prophet who wrote them down. Thus, as 'law is the command of God', so the 'function of Muslim jurisprudence' was and is 'simply the discovery of the terms of that command'; or God is 'the ultimate sovereign and ... the first source of law'.[119] There are several understandings of the nature of the revelation of the divine law: the most common is that the Prophet Muhammad recited the exact words of God to the people; another is that the content of the Quran was revealed to the Prophet by God but that the Prophet used his own words to transfer that message of God to the people; or else the Quran is the Prophet's words, but because the Prophet has a divine personality, his words are also God's.[120]

Secondly, the Sunna or the prophetic reports of the words and deeds of the Prophet Muhammad are a source of law. These are commonly referred to as the sayings of the Prophet (*ahadith*), though the singular *hadith* is often used as a singular or collective term in English. They were collected, transmitted, and taught orally for two centuries after the Prophet's death and later put in written form or codified.[121] However,

---

[116] A. Black, H. Esmaeili and N. Hosen, *Modern Perspectives on Islamic Law* (Cheltenham: Edward Elgar, 2013) 2.

[117] See M. Rohe, *Islamic Law in Past and Present*, trans. G. Goldbloom (Leiden: Brill, 2014) 54–93.

[118] It has been estimated that about 10 per cent of Quranic verses are *ayat al ahkam*, verses on legal rules.

[119] N. Coulson, *A History of Islamic Law* (Edinburgh: Edinburgh University Press, 1964) 75; and B. Weiss, *The Spirit of Islamic Law* (Athens, GA: University of Georgia Press, 1998) 24.

[120] A. Black *et al.*, *Islamic Law* (2013) 7–8.

[121] Collections include those of al-Bukhari (d. 870), Muslim (d. 875), and al-Tirmidhi (d. 892).

some modern jurists do not consider these a complete code of law because about 10 per cent of all sayings (*hadith*) of the Prophet relate to law.[122] These are the primary sources of Islamic law and the others are commonly understood as the secondary sources of law.

The third historical source is consensus (*ijma*), where the Quran and Sunna are silent on a matter. There is considerable debate as to whose opinions are relevant for *ijma*: some argue that only opinions of scholars are authoritative, others that those of non-scholar Muslims are relevant; or else the consensus of the Prophet Muhammad's Companions, the people of Medina or the family of the Prophet have authority. Nevertheless, once an *ijma* is established, it serves as a precedent; but according to most jurists, a decision based on *ijma* generally cannot override a statement found in the Quran or Sunna.[123] Fourthly, there is *qiyas*, the deduction of rules from the Quran or Sunna by analogical reasoning. This provided classical Muslim scholars with a method of deducing laws on matters not explicit in primary sources without relying on unsystematic opinion (*ray* or *hawa*). As such, a rule in the Quran or Sunna may be extended to a new problem provided that the precedent (*asl*) and the new problem (*far*) share the same operative/effective cause (*illa*). Other secondary sources include equity (*istihsan*), custom (*urf*) and personal reasoning (*ijtihad*); that is, exertion by *mujtahid* (learned scholars) to infer the rules of Sharia, 'a creative and comprehensive intellectual effort by qualified individuals and groups to derive the juridical ruling on a given issue from Sharia in the context of the prevailing circumstances of society'.[124]

There are several schools of law (*madhhabs*) in Islam.[125] In Sunni Islam, four main schools developed during the first two centuries of Islam. Each school constitutes a particular interpretation of Islamic law. The Hanafi School, whose origin is attributed to Abu Hanifa (700–767), used opinion (*ray*), analogy (*qiyas*) and preference (*istihsan*) in the formulation of law, made collections of *fatwah* (opinions), and, in emphasising the importance of public interests (*masaleh mursalah*),

---

[122] W. Hallaq, *Sharia: Theory, Practice, Transformation* (Cambridge: Cambridge University Press, 2009) 39–51.

[123] The binding force of *ijma* is based on a *hadith* that the Prophet Muhammad is reported to have said: 'My community will never agree on an error.'

[124] M.H. Kamali, *Shariah Law: An Introduction* (Oxford: One World, 2008) 169.

[125] A.R.I. Doi, *Shari'ah* (1984) 85–112.

asserted that the law must change to meet changing circumstances.[126] The Maliki School, of Malik Ibn Anas (710–795), makes extensive use of *hadith*, offers practical rather than speculative or theoretical teaching and is circumspect about the use of *ray* as an independent source: the primary legal sources were the Quran and Sunna.[127]

The Shafi'i School, founded by Muhammad Al-Shafi`i (767–820), systematised the theoretical bases of law, addressed the differences between the schools, rejected the use of opinion (*ray*) in favour of analogy (*qiyas*), argued for the grounding of all legal deductions in the Quran and Sunna as defined by *hadith* reports and authorised the practice of consensus (*ijma*), thereby developing the fourfold classification of legal sources, giving primacy to the *hadith* over custom: 'On points on which there exists an express ruling of Allah or a Sunna of the Prophet or a consensus of all Muslims, no disagreement is allowed. On the other points, scholars must exert their own judgment in search of an indication in one of the three sources.'[128] The Hanbali school, attributed to Ahmad Ibn Hanbal (780–855), recognises as sources of law: the Quran, *hadith*, fatwas of the Prophet Muhammad's Companions, sayings of a single companion, and traditions with weaker lines of transmission (or lacking the name of the transmitter); it also recognises reasoning by analogy (*qiyas*) when absolutely necessary, encourages the practice of independent reasoning (*ijtihad*) through study of the Quran and *hadith* but rejects *taqlid* (imitation) and blind adherence to the opinions of other scholars.[129]

Within Shia Islam, the Jafari School, named after Jafar al-Sadiq (d. 748), recognises four sources of Islamic law: the Quran, Sunna, consensus and human reason, which is capable of inferring categorical judgments drawn from pure and practical reason.[130]

Given the complex plethora of diverse sources of the classical religious law of Islam, it is not surprising that the view has developed in Britain,

---

[126] E.g. the *Hedaya* of Marghanini (d. 1197), a law textbook and the collection of maxims by Nujaim (d. 1563). The school is seen as relatively liberal and is followed by about one third of Muslims.

[127] C.G. Weeramantry, *Islamic Jurisprudence* (1988) 52.

[128] See *Islamic Jurisprudence: Shafi'i's Risala*, trans. by M. Khadduri (Baltimore: Johns Hopkins University Press, 1961).

[129] It is considered the most conservative Sunni school and is the official school in Saudi Arabia.

[130] Since 1959, the Jafari School has been given the status of 'fifth school' along with the four Sunni schools by Azhar University in Cairo. For reason, see Chapter 10 on natural law. The focus of Sufism, Islamic mysticism, is on spiritual development over legalism.

captured in the Independent Review into the Application of Sharia in England and Wales, presented to Parliament in February 2018, that: 'Sharia is an all-encompassing term which includes not only law in the western sense of the word but religious observances such as fasting and prayer, ritual practices such as halal slaughter, and worship in general'; and: 'Sharia is written jurisprudence and law developed on the basis of a diversity of opinions among jurists in the classical period of Islam.' Thus: 'The word sharia is used in diverse ways by Muslims and this leads to varying degrees of understanding and application.'[131]

Muslim religious organisations today use a variety of regulatory instruments, formal and informal – and it is not uncommon for these to refer to categories in the classical Islamic law. At national level, for example, the Muslim Council of Britain has a constitution. Its General Assembly may pass 'ordinary resolutions' (by a simple majority of the delegates present and voting) and 'special resolutions' relating to constitutional amendments (which must be adopted by two-thirds of the delegates present and voting). Notice of any proposed constitutional amendment must be submitted to the Secretary General of the National Council at least six weeks in advance of the General Assembly meeting, who must circulate the proposed amendment to all appointed delegates at least 14 days before the General Assembly meeting.[132] Provision also exists for Standing Orders.[133] Moreover, the General Assembly may make 'policies' and 'policy guidelines' in the best interests of the Muslim community of Britain,[134] and the Executive Committee may also issue 'guidance', and its decision-making must ordinarily be by way of 'consensus'.[135] The constitution also invokes Sharia: 'Any member of the National Council engaged in acts contrary to the Shariah shall be liable to removal from [that] Council.'[136] By way of contrast, the constitution of the Nasru-Lahi-Il-Fathi Society of Nigeria, United Kingdom and Ireland, provides that the members 'submit and agree that this constitution shall be the authority on all issues or matters affecting the

---

[131] *The Independent Review into the Application of Sharia Law in England and Wales*, presented to Parliament by the Secretary of State for the Home Department by Command of Her Majesty (February 2018) Cm 9560: Foreword.

[132] MCB: Con. Art. 4.1: a special resolution is also needed for dissolution of the MCB; Art. 9: process for the amendment of the constitution and standing orders: see below Chapter 4.

[133] MCB: Con. Art. 9.   [134] MCB: Con. Art. 4.2.   [135] MCB: Con. Art. 4.3.

[136] MCB: Con. Art. 5.2: there is a right of appeal in accordance with Art. 5.3: see Chapter 5.

Society in so far as they are not inconsistent with injunctions of the Holy Quran and the Hadith'.[137]

At local level, mosques use a range of legal instruments; the following are typical.[138] The Central Jamia Masjid (Southall) has a constitution (which was registered by the mosque solicitors with the Charity Commission of England);[139] the Board of Trustees, which decides 'matters of policy and shall exercise its own discretion in accordance with the principles in the Holy Quran and Sunnah', must invest funds 'in accordance with the Shari'a and the law of the land', may make 'regulations and by-laws for the guidance and control of the affairs of the Masjid and to define and settle the manner in which compliance with the decisions of the Masjid shall or may be secured or enforced, and to enforce any by-laws and regulations of the Masjid and any directions given by it'; and the *masjid* also has a corpus of 'rules' – the expression '"regulations of the Masjid" means the Constitution and Rules and other Regulations (if any) including by-laws for the management of the Masjid for the time being'.[140] The constitution of Noor-Ul-Islam Mosque (Bury) invokes 'the principles of the Sunni Islamic faith' (education must be in accordance with them), and it contains 'rules of procedure' and 'by-laws', which must not be 'inconsistent' with the constitution;[141] and that of Kingston Muslim Association adopts the Hanafi school of Islamic law.[142]

The model constitution of an Islamic organisation issued by the Central Mosque uses a wide range of categories from classical Islamic law in its treatment of mosque governance. First, it recommends that a constitutional preamble should provide that: 'Sovereignty over the entire universe belongs to Almighty Allah alone ... the path to success is Deen-e-Islam [religion of Islam] alone as enshrined in the Shari'ah ...

---

[137] Con. (2006) Clause X.

[138] Inter Firm Islamic Societies (IFIS) CUBE Network, founded 2011, brings together formal and informal Muslim interest groups within professional organisations; it provides a 'Sample Constitution of an Islamic Society'.

[139] CJM: it was approved and amended on 23 October 2016. See Con. Art. 8.1. for amendment.

[140] CJM: Con. Art. 4; and: '"By-law" means any by-law of the Masjid made under the rules of the Masjid for the time being in force'.

[141] NUIM: Con. Art. 2: principles; Art. 5: rules; Art. 6: by-laws (made by the Committee); Art. 11: constitutional change. See also BCM: Con. Art. 6: constitutional amendment: 'No amendment may be made that would have the effect of making the Charity cease to be a Charity at [civil] law.'

[142] Kingston Muslim Association: Con. Art. 4; see also Art. 24: the Association also makes Rules and Bylaws.

the final and perfect guide unto humanity is the Holy Messenger Muhammad.' Secondly, 'Muslims shall conduct their affairs based upon ... Shura [consultation].' Thirdly, 'permanent and entrenched' articles of a mosque constitution, in the 'basic founding principles', should include the provision that: 'The basis of the functions of the congregation in all its affairs shall be to adhere strictly to the tenets of Shari'ah, the Islamic Law, as expounded by the four Sunni juristic schools of thought ... Hanafi, Shafi, Maliki and Hambali Schools commonly referred to as the Ahlus-Sunnah-wal-Jama'ah.' Fourthly, 'In matters of religious guidance and directives, the congregation shall be affiliated to the Jamiatul-Ulama or ... body appointed by [it] ... [and] recognize the Jamiat's religious authority for the purposes of obtaining religious sanction and approval for [its] ... activities.' Fifthly, the constitution should also provide for the Shura Committee to make, amend and review 'policies of the congregation for the management and control' of it and for a Code of Conduct, 'a document' with 'Islamic requirements and guidelines for Shura Members and Trustees of Islamic Trusts'.[143]

The Purposes of Religious Law

The purposes of Jewish, Christian and Islamic laws are articulated not only in the works of jurists but also in the modern regulatory instruments of the religious bodies studied here. They are shaped fundamentally by the self-understanding of each of the religions and their institutional manifestations. Ideas about the purposes of law also involve understandings about the structure, subject matter and effect of norms, in terms of how they generate the duty of obedience by the faithful – the rule of law.

The Walk through Life

In classical Judaism, the purpose of halakhah is to guide or teach the people (as they 'walk' through life).[144] However, the law is obligatory. Among the commandments (mitzvot) of the Torah, a commandment (mitzvah) may be either a positive precept or negative prohibition. The purpose of a positive commandment is to require an action, in order to bring the actor closer to God; a negative commandment forbids an

---

[143] Model Constitution of an Islamic Organisation: Preamble, Basic Founding Principles, Affiliations, Aims and Objectives, Powers and Duties of the Shura Committee.

[144] 2 Chronicles 19: King Jehoshaphat sends his officers a book of law to 'teach' the people.

action, and its breach distances the actor from God. Moreover, some commandments seek to regulate relations between humans and God and others seek to regulate the relations between human and human. Any violation of the commandments is conceived as a transgression or sin (*aveira*), which may be committed intentionally, in deliberate defiance of God (*pesha*), knowingly, but not intending to defy God (*avon*), or unintentionally (*chet*). Also, a person may be obligated (*chayyav*) to act, an action may be exempt (*patur*) from sanction or else an action may be permitted (*mutar*).[145]

Today, understandings of the purpose and the effect of *halakhah* vary as between the traditions. For Orthodox Judaism, *halakhah* is binding and unalterable; for Reform Judaism, the purpose of *halakhah* is to guide but not to control, and so it is alterable; and for Conservative Judaism, *halakhah* is binding but subject to flexible evolution. More particularly, for some Orthodox jurists, *halakhah* has three qualities: its authorship in God; its claims to perfection in 'the draftsmanship of its biblical foundations, and the social and spiritual values which it embodies'; and its scope – that is religious/ritual matters, and social/civic matters – and its purposes – including 'norms of behaviour', which, as a 'covenant' with God, the faithful cannot unilaterally change in any generation. Indeed, some argue that there is an increasing tendency to view Jewish law in positivist terms, as a system of positive law, in which deciding matters 'not in accordance with the Halakhah' is disapproved,[146] though *halakhah* provides for its own relaxation on the basis of 'equitable settlement or compromise, *pesharah*'.[147] However, some Reform jurists propose that: 'we respect [*halakhah*] and seek its guidance. Some of its provisions have faded from our lives. We do not regret that fact. But as to the laws that we do follow, we wish them to be in harmony with tradition'; 'the law is authoritative enough to influence us, but not so completely as to control us. The Rabbinic law is our guidance but not our governance';[148]

---

[145] For the basic concepts, see I. Herzog, *Jewish Law* (1980) 41–64.

[146] B. Jackson, 'Judaism as a religious legal system' (2002) 34 at 36–37; and M. Silberg, *Talmudic Law and the Modern State*, trans. B.Z. Bokser (New York: Burning Bush Press, 1973) 51, 57. Ultra-conservatives deny the moral authority of the current generation to initiate halakhic change.

[147] I. Herzog, *Jewish Law* (1980) I.56. See also below Chapter 5 for 'equitable' decisions by a Beth Din.

[148] Rabbi S.B. Freehof, *Reform Judaism and the Legal Tradition: The Tintner Memorial Lecture* (New York: Association of Reform Rabbis, 1961) 10: 'I follow the tentative

in short, *halakhah* has 'a voice but not a veto'.[149] Similarly, for the Union of Liberal and Progressive Synagogues, the classical sources of law are 'great literary expressions of the Jewish spirit ... an inexhaustible source of wisdom to which we constantly turn for guidance and inspiration'.[150] The Union also affirms 'the importance of individual autonomy', and, therefore, its communities should 'legislate only in so far as it is necessary to do so' on the basis that 'individuals need guidance, and communal life requires rules'. Therefore, 'in the guidance we offer and in the rules we make, we endeavour to reconcile tradition with modernity' and, thus, the Union affirms 'the need to harmonise Rabbinic Law (*Halachah*) with the social realities and ethical perceptions of the modern world'.[151] Conservative Judaism seeks a middle course; on the one hand, 'Halakhah, or normative Judaism, is the primary expression of the Jew's relation to God, and the one authentic path to Jewish existence', that is Halakhah is 'not in a creed but in a program of conduct ... the performance of religious commandments';[152] on the other hand, an 'ideal Conservative Jew' is one 'trying to grow in commitment and knowledge' – 'Each of us should continually climb the ladder of observance ... to learn and grow.'[153]

The religious organisations today attribute a different purpose, authority and binding effect to their various regulatory instruments. In the Orthodox tradition, the laws of the United Synagogue, for example, are designed for its 'better management and administration'.[154] First, a member synagogue is 'administered' in accordance with the Founding Act (i.e. the United Synagogues Act 1870), 'Statutes, Regulations and Bye-Laws' of the United Synagogue 'to further the objects of the United Synagogue' as well as for the 'maintenance and conduct' of the member synagogue.[155] Secondly, the laws of the United Synagogue generate the obligation of compliance: with regard to the 'regulatory powers of the

---

formula that the halakhah is our guidance not our governance. I do not claim this as an adequate principle', but 'as a rule-of-thumb'.

[149] D. Golinkin, 'The responsa of Rabbi Solomon B. Freehof: a reappraisal', in W. Jacob, ed., *Beyond the Letter of the Law* (2004) 190 at 196: Golinkin suggests, however, that the sources, style and content of Freehof's responsa are based on traditional *halakhah*.

[150] ULPS: *Affirmations* (2006) Arts. 9–13.

[151] ULPS: *Affirmations* (2006) Arts. 40 and 41.

[152] Rabbi Isaac Klein, *A Guide to Jewish Religious Practice* (New York and Jerusalem: The Jewish Theological Seminary of America, 1979, 1992) 2; xxiii: Klein describes his book as 'my code'.

[153] USCJ: The 'Ideal' Conservative Jew: Eight Behavioural Expectations: Jewish Living (1957, as amended 2017).

[154] US: Statutes 1.   [155] US: Bye-Laws 2.

United Synagogue', the Local Honorary Officers, Board of Management, members, officers, agents or servants of a member synagogue 'shall be subject' and 'conform to' the United Synagogue Statutes and Regulations.[156] The same applies to compliance by a member synagogue with the United Synagogue Bye-Laws.[157] Thirdly, however: 'In the event of a conflict between these Synagogue Bye-Laws and the Statutes or Regulations of the United Synagogue, the Statutes or Regulations of the United Synagogue shall prevail.'[158]

Much the same ideas appear in the normative instruments of other Jewish traditions. The United Synagogue of Conservative Judaism adopts Standards for Congregational Practice in order to enable its *kehillot* 'to seek the presence of God, to seek meaning and purpose in Torah and *mitzvot*, to fully engage with Israel, and to be inspired by Judaism to improve the world and the Jewish people'; these Standards are 'intended to be consistent with the Purpose, Vision and Mission Statement of USCJ and with the Standards of Rabbinic Practice as adopted by the Rabbinical Assembly and approved *teshuvot* of the Rabbinical Assembly Committee on Jewish Law and Standards'; and: 'They are promulgated with the intention of increasing the level of engagement and practice to the greatest extent feasible by USCJ affiliated *kehillot*.'[159]

In a similar vein, the Movement for Reform Judaism provides in its soft-law that a synagogue should be 'set up with clearly documented aims and rules by which it will be run, and which should include the legal powers it needs to achieve its aims' vested in 'a clearly identifiable body of people who take responsibility, and are accountable, for controlling the charity so that it is economically and effectively managed'. Members of the synagogue Council are 'to be aware of the Constitution (Laws) of the community, the Codes of Practice and Areas of Responsibility documents and are to obey its rules whilst trying to keep to the spirit of their content'. Norms should also reflect change: 'The custodian trustees … have … the responsibility of maintaining the Laws of the Synagogue and keeping the Areas of Responsibility and Codes of Practice documents up-to-date.'[160] And, for worship, the regulations of North London

---

[156] US: Bye-Laws 26.   [157] US: Bye-Laws 27.1.

[158] US: Bye-Laws 27.2. See e.g. the Orthodox Norwich Hebrew Congregation: Laws and Con. 1.2: 'Every member of the Congregation shall conform to this constitution and any subsequent amendment thereof.'

[159] USCJ: Standards for Congregational Practice (1957, as amended 2017).

[160] MRJ: Code of Practice, pp. 4, 5 and 14.

Reform Synagogue aim 'to ensure the proper and dignified performance of the Services'.[161]

Likewise, in the Union of Liberal and Progressive Synagogues, the trustees of Wessex Liberal Jewish Community may make 'rules or bye-laws' to facilitate and to control: conduct of business; the rights and privileges of members; the conduct of members 'in relation to one another', employees and volunteers; the procedure at meetings; the keeping of records; and 'all such matters as are commonly the subject matter of the rules of an unincorporated association'. Moreover, in terms of their effect: 'The rules or bye-laws shall be binding on all members'; but 'No rule or bye-law shall be inconsistent with, or shall affect or repeal anything contained in [its] Constitution.'[162] The Exeter Hebrew Synagogue too operates under a constitution and trust deed; its former 'Laws, Rules and Regulations ... for the guidance of the Congregation' were replaced with Regulations 'for [congregational] government and conduct'; and: 'Every member shall be given a copy of these Regulations and shall be bound by them.'[163]

Church Order and Mission

Christians have for centuries developed ideas on the purposes, structure, effect and relaxation of law, largely along the lines that church law, as a form of applied theology, exists to enable and regulate the institutional life of the church.[164] First, according to the principles of Christian law of the so-called historic churches, with respect to law as 'servant': church law exists to serve a church in its mission and in its witness to the salvific work of Christ; laws contribute to constituting the institutional organisation of a church and facilitate and order its activities; theology may shape law and law may realise theological propositions in norms of conduct and behaviour; and church laws should conform to the law of God, as revealed in Holy Scripture and by the Holy Spirit.[165] For the Roman Catholic Church, canon law

---

[161] NLRS: Laws, Art. 14.   [162] WLJC: Con. Art. 32.

[163] EHC: Con. Schedule of Regulations, 1.

[164] For historical debate about the purposes of church law, see e.g. R.H. Helmholz, *The Spirit of Classical Canon Law* (1996); and J. Witte, *Law and Protestantism* (2002).

[165] Christian Law Panel of Experts, *Principles of Christian Law* (2016) I.3.

'facilitates ... an orderly development in the life of both the ecclesial society and of the individual persons who belong to it';[166] indeed, canon law itself teaches that the 'salvation of souls [is] the supreme law'.[167] Orthodox canon law is 'at the service of the Church ... to guide her members on the way to salvation'; its main function is 'the spiritual growth of the faithful'.[168] For Anglicans, a church needs laws 'to order, and so facilitate, its public life and to regulate its own affairs for the common good': 'Law is not an end in itself' but exists 'to uphold the integrity of the faith, sacraments and mission, to provide good order, to support communion amongst the faithful, to put into action Christian values, and to prevent and resolve conflict'.[169] Within the Protestant tradition, the rules of the Presbyterian Church of Wales seek 'to safeguard the unity of the Church, and to secure uniformity in the procedures of its courts'; the model constitution of the United Reformed Church is designed 'to signify collective identity', to 'satisfy the outside world', to 'make the Church's working transparent' and to 'obviate later disagreement within the fellowship' of the church;[170] and, likewise, a local Baptist church has a constitution in order to 'govern', 'regulate' and 'enable' the life of that church.[171]

Secondly, as to their scope, structure and binding effect, the principles of Christian law provide that church laws principally deal with ministry, government, doctrine, worship, rites, admonition and discipline and property; consist of various juridical formulae (e.g. precepts, prohibitions and permissions); may be cast as rules, rights and duties and functions and powers; and may be binding or exhortatory. Moreover, all members of a church are subject to its laws, to the extent that the law provides. Later laws may abrogate earlier laws. Laws should be prospective (not retrospective unless this is clearly provided for in them), and they should be clear, stable and coherent. Also, a church

---

[166] *Sacrae disciplinae leges* (1983): Apostolic Constitution by which the Code was promulgated.
[167] CIC: c. 1752.
[168] L. Patsavos, *Manual on Orthodox Canon Law* (New York, Hellenic College, Holy Cross Orthodox School of Theology, 1975), Part II (un-numbered page).
[169] PCLCCAC: Principles 1, 2.5; See e.g. Church in Wales: Con. Prefatory Note: law exists 'to serve the sacramental integrity and good order of the Church and to assist its mission and its witness to the Lord Jesus Christ'.
[170] PCW: Handbook of Rules 1.2; URC: Model Con. for Local Churches, Notes.
[171] BUGB: Model Trusts for Churches 2003, Sch., 4.1–4.6.

may have in place a mechanism for the enforcement and vindication of the rights and duties of the faithful.[172] For example, the Roman Catholic Code of 1983 affects only the Latin Church, but its provisions bind all the faithful directly in the particular churches, bishops, clergy and laity alike;[173] Anglican clergy undertake to obey the lawful and honest directions of their bishops, but in the Church of England the Canons bind clergy but not (of their own force) the laity;[174] and a precondition to admission to the Lutheran Church is acceptance of the constitution and bye-laws.[175]

Thirdly, according to the principles of Christian law, a church law may be relaxed, by competent ecclesial authority, by means of dispensation, economy or other form of equity for the spiritual good of the individual and the common good of the church.[176] In Roman Catholic law, dispensation is 'the relaxation of a merely ecclesiastical law in a particular case'; it may be granted 'within the limits of their competence, by those who have executive power, and by those who either explicitly or implicitly have the power of dispensing, whether by virtue of the law itself or by lawful delegation'. However, laws which define what constitutes juridical institutions or acts cannot be the subject of dispensation. The Pontiff enjoys extensive powers of dispensation and a bishop may dispense with both universal and particular law when this is for the good of the faithful, but cannot dispense from procedural laws, penal laws or in those cases reserved to the Apostolic See. Dispensation must not be granted without 'a just and reasonable cause'; the dispensing authority must consider the circumstances of the case and the gravity of the law from which dispensation is sought; otherwise, the dispensation is illicit and (unless given by the legislator) invalid. The power to dispense must be construed restrictively and a dispensation ends when the reasons for it ceases.[177] Anglicans also recognised dispensation, to the extent this is authorised

---

[172] Christian Law Panel of Experts, *Principles of Christian Law* (2016) I.4.

[173] CIC: cc. 1 and 11–12.

[174] E.g. Church of England: Can. C14: 'I will pay true and canonical obedience to the Lord Bishop of C and his successors in all things lawful and honest'; for the laity, see *Middleton v. Crofts* (1736) 2 Atkins 650.

[175] LCGB: Rules and Regulations, Congregations, 1: a congregation must 'accept and uphold the Governing Documents (Constitutions and Rules and Regulations)'.

[176] Christian Law Panel of Experts, *Principles of Christian Law* (2016) I.4.

[177] CIC: cc. 87–93; pastors may sometimes dispense: see e.g. cc. 1079, 1196, 1245.

by the law of a church,[178] on the basis that laws cannot cover all facets of ecclesial life.[179]

Provision for dispensation is less evident in Protestant legal instruments. However, in Presbyterianism, for example in the United Free Church of Scotland, the General Assembly has a *nobile officium*: 'the power of the General Assembly, as Supreme Court to act in special circumstances beyond or even against its own rules or forms of procedures' as 'shall seem to the General Assembly right and needful for doing justice in the particular case'.[180] This is echoed in Baptist regulatory instruments in relation to the relaxation of procedural rules applicable to ecclesiastical assemblies.[181]

The Pathway of Muslims

In classical Islam, *sharia*, literally 'the path cleared (by God)' or 'the path to the watering place', is a pathway ordained by God for the guidance of mankind, and one that must be followed by Muslims.[182] It is concerned with the whole of Muslim life, the total religious, political, social, domestic and private life of the faithful: God says: 'We have sent down to you the Book explaining all things' (Quran 16:89). It prescribes how Muslims should conduct themselves in accordance with their religion, and includes duties owed towards God (*ibadat*) and towards other humans

---

[178] PCLCCAC: Principle 7: the applicability of law; 1: later laws abrogate earlier laws; 2: laws are prospective and should not be retrospective in effect unless this is clearly provided for in the laws; 3: laws cannot oblige a person to do the impossible; 4: persons cannot give what they do not have; 5: laws should be applied in the service of truth, justice and equity; 6: laws may be dispensed with in particular cases on the basis of legitimate necessity provided authority to dispense is clearly given by the law. For the principle of economy in Orthodox canon law, see N. Doe, *Christian Law* (2013) 40.

[179] PCLCCAC: Principle 3: the limits of law; 1: laws should reflect but cannot change Christian truths; 2: laws cannot encompass all facets of ecclesial life; 3: laws cannot prescribe the fullness of ecclesial life, ministry and mission; 4: laws function predominantly in the public sphere of church life; 5: the principal subjects with which laws deal are ecclesiastical government, ministry, discipline, doctrine, liturgy, rites, property and ecumenical relations; 6: some laws articulate immutable truths and values.

[180] United Free Church of Scotland (UFCS): Manual of Practice and Procedure, Glossary of Latin Terms and V.II.8. Compare J.L. Weatherhead, ed., *Constitution and Laws of the Church of Scotland* (1997) 53: *nobile officium* 'cannot override law, but [can provide] only the want of it when necessary'.

[181] See e.g. BUS: Bye-Laws, Standing Orders 12: 'Standing Orders [of the Assembly] may be suspended in the interests of considering the subject then before the meeting.'

[182] J. Hussain, *Islamic Law and Society* (Leichhardt, NSW: The Federation Press, 1999) 26.

(*mu'amalat*). Profession of faith (*shahadah*), together with ritual practices (*ibadat*), daily prayers (*salat*), almsgiving (*zakat*), fasting (*sawm*) and pilgrimage (*hajj*) constitute the five pillars of Islam.[183] Moreover, *sharia* is concerned as much with ethical standards as with legal rules; it indicates what a person is entitled or bound to do, and what a person ought in conscience to do or refrain from doing. As such, Islamic law classifies human actions into five categories: obligatory action (*wajib*) or duty (*fard*); recommended or desirable but not obligatory action (*sunna* or *mandub*); permitted action (*mubah*); objectionable or disapproved but not prohibited action (*makruh*); and prohibited action (*haram*).[184] Thus: *sharia* 'has a much wider scope and purpose than an ordinary legal system in the western sense of that term'.[185]

The divisions in the subject matter of Islamic law are classically understood to be: (1) penal law – offences against persons are treated by punishment (*qisas*) or giving compensation (*diyah*); (2) the law of transactions – sale (*bay*), hire (*ijarah*), gift (*hibah*) and loan (*ariyah*), and a dominant idea is the prohibition against usury (the doctrine of *riba* prohibits any form of interest on a capital loan or investment) and gambling; (3) family law – a patriarchal outlook dominates the traditional Islamic law of family relationships, which deals with the formation of marriage, the maintenance of the family, and divorce; (4) succession and inheritance – testamentary disposition may be limited to one-third of the net estate (i.e. the assets remaining after payment of funeral expenses and debts) and two-thirds of the estate pass to the heirs of the deceased under the rules of inheritance; (5) procedure and evidence – traditionally, *sharia* was administered by a court of a single *qadi*, who was judge of both facts and law, though the *qadi* may consult a professional jurist, a *mufti*. There is no hierarchy of courts and each *qadi* controls court procedure with the assistance of a clerk (*katib*).[186]

The effect of *sharia* depends on the sources of law in question; classically, the Quran is the most authoritative. The Quran takes priority over the Sunna and jurists should resort to the Sunna for legal guidance only when no clear guidance may be obtained from the Quran – the purposes of the Sunna, therefore, are to confirm the law contained in the Quran; to give an adequate explanation to matters treated in general

---

[183] See below, Chapters 6 and 7.   [184] See M. Rohe, *Islamic Law* (2014) 10–11.
[185] A.R.I. Doi, *Shari'ah* (1984) 85–112.
[186] J. Schacht, *An Introduction to Islamic Law* (Oxford: Clarendon Press, 1964, reprint 1991) 124–198.

terms in the Quran; to clarify verses in the Quran where there may be ambiguity; and to introduce a new rule not appearing in the Quran. In turn, the authority of *hadith* is classified according to the reliability of their transmitters and strength of their *isnad* (chain of narrators); for example, *mutawatir* – a *hadith* reported by a large number of trusted people (its authenticity is virtually guaranteed); *mashhur* – a *hadith* reported from one or more Companions of the Prophet has become well-known and has been transmitted (during the first or secondary generation after the death of the Prophet) by a large number of people; and *ahad* (or solitary) – a *hadith* reported by one person (jurists disagree as to the value depending on the competence of the transmitter). Similarly, the authority and effect of the secondary sources is dependent on the qualities of the person who exercises *ijtihad* or those involved in forming *ijma*; and the concept of *darura* (necessity) enables the relaxation of law when just to do so.[187]

The modern regulatory instruments of Muslim organisations also contain ideas about the purposes, effects and authority of those regulatory instruments. For example, at national level, the constitution of the Muslim Council of Britain may be amended 'for the sole purpose of ensuring the smooth functioning of the [Council] in the attainment of its objectives';[188] and an organisation is eligible for membership of the Council if, *inter alia*: 'Its delegates to the [Council] will abide by the procedures and standing orders that govern the conduct of meetings and the affairs of the [Council]'; and: 'It accepts the Constitution of the [Council] and is able and willing to abide by its provisions'; and, in terms of its religious soft-law, 'it will do its best to uphold and implement agreed policies' and 'promote mutual respect or co-operation with other member organisations and use the [Council] framework ... to resolve difficult issues with other member organisations'.[189]

At local level, mosques may present the purposes of their rules in mundane terms; for example, those of Central Jamia Masjid (Southall) are 'for the management', or to 'regulate and control', the affairs of the masjid.[190] However, the constitution of Lancaster Islamic Society

---

[187] See e.g. J. Hussain, *Islamic Law* (1999) 29–35; see also 36–37: the closing of the gate of *ijtihad* (the doctrine of *taqlid*, which admits no variation from the interpretation of Shariah laid down before the eleventh century) and the (e.g. Shia) rejection of this.

[188] MCB: Con. Arts. 9 and 11.   [189] MCB: Con. Art. 3.

[190] CJM: Rules: Preliminary, iv and 7.4; see also 11 on 'compliance' with civil charity law. See also Central Mosque: MCIO, Powers and Duties of the Shura Committee: policies may be made 'for the control and management of the affairs of the congregation'.

provides that: 'Obedience in line with Allah's guidance [is] to achieve human excellence' – and the purpose of an Islamic organisation is 'to bring about the collective potential of the whole community for the good of mankind with due respect and regard to all forms of life and nature'. In order to achieve these goals, the following are among the essential characters of individuals and organisations: kindness (Quran: 10:26); goodness (Quran: 11:114); patience and perseverance (Quran 3:200); forgiveness (Quran 7:199); tolerance (Quran 2:256: 'Let there be no compulsion in religion'); humility (Quran 25:63); equity and justice (Quran 5:9); and equality of mankind (Quran 59:13).[191] The binding character of religious aspects of the model constitution of an Islamic society issued by Inter Firm Islamic Societies is summed up thus: 'The Society may not undertake any activity which violates the Islamic standards of this constitution.'[192] A mosque constitution might also provide for an undertaking to be made by members to comply with its internal rules; for instance, at Noor-Ul-Islam Mosque, before being admitted, each person must 'undertake to observe and to be bound by the provisions of the constitution and bye-laws of the Mosque'.[193] Also, the model constitution issued by the Central Mosque provides that mosque property 'shall at all times be subject to the Shari'ah law relating to Waqf and Masjids'.[194]

Conclusion

A comparison of Judaism, Christianity and Islam indicates a high degree of similarity as to the objects of the religious organisations in these traditions, their juristic sources, and the purposes, structure and effect of their regulatory instruments. For all three religions, the law revealed by God and represented in the Torah, Bible and Quran, and their original historical interpretations, represent the primary source for religious law. To this extent, the religious law of all three faiths is theocratic in foundation. Beyond this, legal pluralism is the principal feature of these traditions. The modern movements of Judaism each differ in their presumptions about the authority of halakhic sources. Christians differ

---

[191] LIS: Con: Objects.
[192] Central Mosque (Inter Firm Islamic Societies): Model Constitution for Islamic Societies, Art. 11.3.
[193] NUIM: Con. Art. 3; see also 6: bye-laws must not be inconsistent with the constitution.
[194] Central Mosque: Model Con., Status of Masjid and Waqf Properties, 1.

in their precise interpretations of the authority of the Bible. Muslims too differ in the relative weight given to the various secondary sources of *sharia*. However, all three religions agree about juristic consensus, opinion and custom as sources of legal rules. Jews, Christians and Muslims also agree about the objects of their organisations, including synagogues, churches and mosques. These are to worship God, to educate the faithful and to provide service in society. The religious organisations all use regulatory instruments to govern their communal lives; all have constitutions, statutes, rules, or other regulatory forms, including soft-law in the guise of codes of practice, policy documents and guidance. To this extent, secondary religious law is the product of the use of practical reason. Jews, Christians and Muslims also agree that the purpose of their religious law is to guide the faithful in their spiritual lives, and to facilitate and control the faithful in the communal institutional life of the particular religious organisation. However, whereas the religious law of all three faiths aspires to cover the whole of life (religious and civic or social), their regulatory instruments differ in terms of, for instance, the authority of religious tradition in the interpretation of divine law; the prevalence of references to the classical sources of religious law; and the technical mechanisms to relax religious law. To the extent that the regulatory instruments of these religious organisations are created by designated religious authorities and are at the same time acceptable to the civil Charity Commission of England and Wales, they are recognised by civil law.

2

The Faithful: Status, Duties and Rights

The laws of Jews, Christians and Muslims serve not only the wider objects of their religious organisations but also the faithful within them. One traditional and significant element of Jewish, Christian and Islamic laws is the classification of the faithful into two broad categories: the followers and the faith leaders. The juridical instruments of all three religions provide for the admission of people into a religious organisation and they define what it means to belong to it. Definitions of a member or other similar category, and the conditions used for admission, vary between the faiths. Moreover, all three traditions spell out the functions of members. Several provide for the enjoyment and discharge of prescribed rights and duties by all the faithful, regardless of whether they are followers or leaders. At the same time, they articulate the duties and to a lesser extent the rights applicable only to followers. This chapter examines the modern juridification of classical elements of religious law in the contemporary regulatory instruments of the religious communities studied, the extent of the religiosity of these instruments, the incidence of legal pluralism as between the various traditions within each of the religions and the extent of juridical unity which emerges from the legal similarities within and between the three faiths.

The Membership of the Faith Community

Judaism, Christianity and Islam all have norms which define the status of a believer, the conditions which must be satisfied to belong to the religion, and the requirements for the admission of a person to the membership of a synagogue, church or mosque.

The Jewish People and Synagogue Membership

The English word 'Jew' is derived from Latin (*iudaeus*), in turn, based on the Hebrew word *yehudi* meaning 'from the tribe of Judah' – and, for traditional *halakhah*, Jewish status depends on the status of the mother or on conversion to Judaism.[1] However, today there are subtle differences between the various traditions within Judaism as to the definitions of 'Jew' in the context of the admission of persons to synagogue membership, and the process of conversion. Some draw on the classical texts of Jewish law. For instance, the Laws of the (Orthodox) Federation of Synagogues provide that 'Jew' means 'any person who is a Jew according to the rules set out in the Shulchan Aruch [of Joseph Caro (1488–1575)], as interpreted by the Federation Beth Din'. Moreover: 'Jewish' means: 'the adjectival description of practices, culture, places of worship, institutions or organisations of Jews in accordance with the rules set out in the Shulchan Aruch' as similarly interpreted.[2] In turn, membership of a Federation synagogue is open to any individual who agrees to be bound by the rules of that synagogue and the Federation Laws and Bye-Laws, applies for membership in the form required and is approved by the Honorary Officers of that synagogue. Any dispute about membership must be dealt with by the Honorary Officers of the synagogue: if they are unable to resolve it within 28 days, or the individual complains about how the dispute is being handled, it must be referred to the Trustees; if they are unable to resolve it, or the individual similarly complains, it must then be referred to the judges of the Federation Beth Din – and their decision on the matter is final.[3]

In the (Orthodox) United Synagogue: 'The Halachic (Jewish legal) definition of a Jew is one who is born of a Jewish mother or has converted according to the Halacha.'[4] Full members are those persons who are members of a member synagogue; affiliated members those who are members of an Affiliated Synagogue; and associate members those who are members of an Associated Synagogue.[5] Non-Synagogue Membership is open to 'other persons of the Jewish faith' who are, for example, permanently resident in any home or other institution for the care of people.[6]

---

[1] I. Herzog, *Jewish Law* (1980) I.41: '*Bene-Brith*, Sons of the Covenant, is a legal expression comprising both native Jews and proselytes, that is, all the full members of the [Jewish] religio-polity.'

[2] FOS: Laws 1.1: the meanings of 'Jew' and 'Jewish' are to be determined by an 'equivalent rabbinical authority as approved by the Trustees if the Federation Beth Din has ceased to exist'.

[3] FOS: Laws 28.1–2.   [4] US: www.theus.org.uk/article/conversion-2.

[5] US: Statutes 6.1.1–3; see also Statutes 2.

[6] US: Statutes 6.1.4: the United Synagogue has an 'absolute discretion' to admit non-Synagogue Members.

Anyone wishing to become a member of a synagogue must make an application in the form required by the Honorary Officers. No one may be accepted who is indebted to any Member or Affiliated Synagogue without written consent of its own Local Honorary Officers.[7] Membership is annual. The Local Honorary Officers may 'for good and substantial reason, if they consider it in the best interests of the Synagogue', reject an application on written notice; before doing so they must inform the person of this intention and give 'the right to make oral representations and state any case in writing to them'.[8]

The (Orthodox) North Hendon Adath Yisroel Synagogue, for example, provides that: 'Any person of the Jewish Faith shall be acceptable as a member ... provided that the Membership Application is endorsed by the Rabbi.' Moreover, Associate Membership is open to those who are members of other Orthodox Synagogues and Burial Societies and who wish to participate in the services and activities of the synagogue.[9] However, at Cambridge Traditional Jewish Congregation, for membership purposes, '"Jews" are those [who] would normally be accepted as such by the Chief Rabbi of the United Hebrew Congregations of the British Commonwealth of Nations.'[10]

In the Movement for Reform Judaism, synagogue members 'shall be Jews (as defined by the Bet Din of the Movement for Reform Judaism)'; and children (whose mothers are Jewish) of a member, or children who have converted to Judaism, under the age of 21 and unmarried, are regarded as members entitled to attend all synagogue religious services and to such other rights and privileges as are laid down by the Council.[11] The synagogue must: (1) confirm Jewish lineage; (2) obtain a copy of the *ketubah* (marriage contract) of a couple who applies, or of the parents' *ketubah* if the couple is not married, or of the *ketubah* from a previous marriage to cover children; (3) a non-Jewish male partner may become an associate – but the children will be Jewish – or convert if he so wishes; (4) if a partner is female and is not Jewish, the children are not considered Jewish, but she may convert together with the children; however,

---

[7] US: Bye-Laws 5.1–3: see below Chapter 9.   [8] US: Bye-Laws 5.4–5.

[9] NHAYS: Con. Art. 5: Associate Members are not entitled to nominate or vote at Annual or Extraordinary General Meetings nor to permanent seating. The fee is set by the Executive.

[10] CTJC: BL III.

[11] MRJ: Areas of Responsibility and Code of Practice Documents (Constitution): p. 9. Council may also elect Honorary and Associate Members; but no one is admitted whom 'we feel will give the community a problem'. See NLRS: Law Art. 11(a): membership is for 'all persons of the Jewish faith'.

the children of a non-Jewish mother cannot attend its school. There is a membership form for a couple and single member, a separate one for 21–25 year olds, and one for associates.[12] At local level,[13] in North London Reform Synagogue, for example, anyone who desires membership must make written application to the Secretary in the form determined by the Council. Applications must be placed before Council who may accept or reject them, or Council may delegate consideration of an application to a sub-committee, which, by majority vote, accepts or rejects it. Council may elect honorary members entitled to receive notice of and to attend but not vote at General Meetings and to such other rights as the Council may confer upon them.[14]

The definition of 'Jew' in Conservative Judaism lies between these two positions.[15] The United Synagogue of Conservative Judaism supports every affiliated *kehilla* in developing its own criteria for membership – it is committed to assisting and welcoming vibrant and caring Jewish communities 'to fully engage the spiritual gifts of all community members'; celebrates 'the diversity among and within our kehillot'; encourages 'the engagement of all those who seek a spiritual and communal home in an authentic and dynamic Jewish setting'; and calls on all of its kehillot 'to open their doors wide to all who want to enter' in order to strive to make the words of Isaiah a reality: 'My House will be called a house of prayer for all people' (Isaiah 56:7).[16]

Liberal Judaism recognises equilineal descent: individuals born of a Jewish father and non-Jewish mother should be treated in exactly the same way as those born to a Jewish mother and a non-Jewish father 'and considered Jewish if so brought up . . . within the context of a synagogue'. This is confirmed when the child reaches the age of *barmitzvah* or *batmitzvah*: 'There is no certificate, no conversion, no *Beit Din*, no Rabbinic determination of the status of the child, but a quiet acknowledgement that this individual teenager is a full member of the Jewish community, that they have never been anything other than Jewish and that one parent – together with upbringing and education (and not the

---

[12] MRJ: Areas of Responsibility and Code of Practice Documents (Constitution): p. 10.

[13] BHRS: Con. Art. 10: membership is open 'to anyone acting in general conformity with the practice of the Movement for Reform Judaism *Beit Din* '; the trustees determine membership applications.

[14] NLRS: Law, Art. 11(d)–(e); see also SSRS: Con. Art. 4.

[15] Statement of Principles of Conservative Judaism (1988) 45: voluntary practice.

[16] USCJ: Standards for Congregational Practice (1957, as amended 2017): Standard V.

religion of the other parent) – determines Jewish status.'[17] Moreover, Liberal Judaism welcomes 'into our congregations all who have a good claim to be regarded as Jewish, regardless of marital status or sexual orientation'.[18]

In turn, at local level, Elstree Liberal Synagogue is typical: 'the Jewish faith' must be interpreted according to the rules of the Rabbinic Conference of the Union whose decision is final; a full member is a person over 18 years of age 'of the Jewish faith and who subscribes to the principles of Liberal Judaism and of the Synagogue'.[19] Applications are made in a form prescribed by the Council, which determines the matter in private and may hold an interview to do so; however: 'An application for membership . . . may be refused by the Council without any requirement for them to assign any reason' and a register is kept of members and their children.[20] Similarly, at Wessex Liberal Jewish Community, full membership is open to 'all Jewish people, who are aged eighteen or over who want to adhere to Liberal Jewish principles and practices who are approved by the trustees. A Jewish person is one who is accepted as such by Liberal Judaism.' Associate membership is open 'to non-Jewish spouses, civil partners and other partners of full members'; an associate counts as a member for the purposes of the burial society and Charity Commission but has no vote. The trustees may create or amend classes of member and fix their rights/duties; trustees may also elect any person as an honorary member entitled to receive notice of and to attend, but not vote at, General Meetings, and these honorary members are to have such further rights, duties and privileges as may be agreed by the trustees. A person who wishes to become a member must apply in such form as the trustees direct; the trustees 'will consider and decide on applications . . . at the earliest opportunity'; they may only refuse an application if 'asking reasonably and properly, they consider it to be in the best interests of the charity to refuse the application'; they must inform the applicant of the reasons for the refusal within 21 days of the decision, and must consider any written representations the applicant

---

[17] ULPS: www.liberaljudaism.org/lifecycle/jewish-status-conversion/.

[18] ULPS: *Affirmations* (2006) Art. 37.

[19] ELS: Con. Art. 5: an associate is one over 18 and of the Jewish faith who because of a commitment to another synagogue does not wish to be a full member; a 'friend' is one over 18 who is the non-Jewish spouse or long-term partner of a full member or associate or one who has 'an interest in Judaism'.

[20] ELS: Con. Art. 5: the application is made to the Membership Officer; the Honorary Secretary maintains the register.

may make about the decision. The trustees' decision following these representations must be notified to the applicant and 'shall be final'. The community trustees must keep a register of members, which must be made available to any member upon request with the permission of the members whose names and addresses appear in the register.[21]

As to conversion, for the (Orthodox) United Synagogue: 'Judaism is not a proselytising religion [and] does not actively seek to convert non-Jews to the faith'; it 'is accepting of any person who sincerely wishes to belong to the Jewish people'; and 'conversion entails a commitment to a fully observant and practising Jewish life style'.[22] The London Beth Din deals with conversions (*geirut*),[23] applications from non-Jewish people to convert to Judaism, and it administers 'the overwhelming majority of orthodox conversions in the UK'. Applicants include individuals who have become deeply motivated on their own accord to become Jewish, developed an interest through a relationship with a Jewish person, have a Jewish father and non-Jewish mother or have been converted in other countries or under the auspices of another authority and seek to validate/regularise their Jewish status in the UK.[24] As 'a general rule', the Beth Din accepts a *bona fide* conversion administered overseas by 'a reputable, orthodox Beth Din', but it would 'expect' such a person 'to be living a fully observant and practising Jewish life style'. As for a citizen of, or ordinarily resident in, Great Britain, 'it would be expected that [the person] would apply for a conversion in this country'; if they travel overseas for conversion, this 'will not necessarily be recognised by the London Beth Din'. Once converted, a person is 'considered fully Jewish in every respect'. The Beth Din is 'invested by Jewish law with the authority and responsibility to judge objectively, the sincerity and suitability' of applicants, 'not just to maintain standards of Jewish law and to be the guardian of Jewish status but to ensure that it is acting in a way that is best for the applicant'. Conversion 'should not be pursued because of some idealised notion of what it means to be a Jew, as a gesture of personal sacrifice for the sake of love, or in the expectation that it will resolve a mental or emotional anguish' – 'there should be no ulterior motive other than the genuine desire to join the Jewish people and its destiny'. While the Beth Din 'does not condone inter-faith marriages for Jews, it will also consider applications from non-Jews who are in a

[21] WLJC: Con. Art. 8.   [22] US: www.theus.org.uk/article/conversion-2.
[23] US: www.theus.org.uk/article/about-london-beth-din.
[24] US. www.theus.org.uk/article/conversion-2.

relationship with or are civilly married to a Jewish person'. Four criteria should be in place before the Beth Din finalises the conversion: (1) knowledge of Jewish laws and customs as to daily life and festivals; (2) consistent, practical observance of Jewish law and principles in daily life; (3) direct, lived experience of Jewish community; and (4) an inward readiness to take on responsibilities of being a Jew or Jewess. This last is the most difficult for the Beth Din to assess as it is a matter of the heart; while the first three criteria provide some evidence of the fourth, it is nevertheless not possible to know with certainty, so: 'The Beth Din will not finalise a conversion until ... reasonably satisfied that the candidate has in his or her heart of hearts resolved to commit to an orthodox Jewish life.'[25]

Similar norms exist in the Movement for Reform Judaism. Conversion takes about 18 months and must be sponsored by a Rabbi.[26] The candidate must: become involved in the local Jewish community (e.g. regular attendance at the synagogue including attending Shabbat services); acquire basic Jewish knowledge (the *Beit Din* requires formal tuition for at least a year before the candidate comes to a court); acquire basic Hebrew skills (e.g. be able to read Hebrew prayer books); and change how they run their home and daily, weekly and annual routines.[27] Children who are under 13 may convert with their converting parent, and, depending on their circumstances, children between 13 and 16 may convert with a parent. Young people over the age of 16 'should be expected to convert in their own right', but the *Beit Din* expects that all uncircumcised males over the age of 16 should be circumcised as this is the traditional gateway into the covenant (see below Chapter 7). A conversion under the auspices of the Reformed Movement *Beit Din* will be recognised by progressive synagogues worldwide, but not by Orthodox Judaism; and if the convert is male and no *brit milah* is carried out, the conversion may not be recognised by Masorti Judaism in the UK.[28]

By way of contrast, the Union of Liberal and Progressive Synagogues affirms 'the need for an inclusive attitude to Jewish identity', welcomes

---

[25] US: www.theus.org.uk/article/conversion-2: the process is usually completed within two or three years. An administration fee is payable and costs include tuition and accommodation with a family.
[26] MRJ: Areas of Responsibility and Code of Practice Documents (Constitution): p. 10.
[27] A fee is payable to the *Beit Din*.
[28] MRJ: www.reformjudaism.org.uk/resources/life-cycle/. See below Chapter 7 for *brit milah*.

'sincere proselytes' and makes 'the process of conversion no more difficult than it needs to be'; and, short of conversion, its Rabbinic Board may
issue a Certificate of Status to confirm the Jewish identity in cases of
doubt.[29] The process towards conversion requires 'substantial commitment', usually lasts 15 months, is administered and validated centrally by
Liberal Judaism, but it is taught locally. An applicant is first interviewed
by a Rabbi to ascertain that the motives for conversion are for the sake of
embracing the religion. To assist the applicant to make an informed
decision, there must be some preliminary reading and experience of
Jewish life and worship, usually by attending synagogue services for at
least three months before a formal course of instruction. This consists of
lessons in the Jewish religion, history, literature and the Hebrew language. During it, the applicant is supported by the community to gain
personal experience of all the Jewish festivals in the annual cycle so that
they will begin to feel part of a Jewish community. When the sponsoring
Rabbi is satisfied that a sufficient basis of Jewish knowledge and
experience has been acquired, the candidate is asked to submit two essays
and then appears before the Rabbinic Board of Liberal Judaism (with
three Rabbis sitting). If they are satisfied with the sincerity of the candidate, they sign a certificate indicating their approval – the sponsoring
Rabbi also signs the certificate. The candidate then has an Admittance
Ceremony in their new Community at which their status as a Jew is
affirmed. Liberal Judaism strongly recommends circumcision for male
converts; however, if an exemption is sought, candidates must consult a
doctor, preferably a member of the Association of Liberal and Reform
Mohalim. All converts are advised to perform the ritual of *tevilah* (ritual
immersion in a *mikveh* or ritual bath) as a valuable and experiential way
to confirm the change in status.[30]

Similarly, in Conservative Judaism, conversion must be voluntary; and,
for example, if a woman converts when pregnant, the child does not
require conversion; the child of a Jewish mother and gentile father is
considered a Jew without conversion;[31] also, a married gentile may
convert even though the convert intends to remain married to the
unconverted gentile spouse. Such conversion should take place, however,
only after proper counselling and consultation assuring that the convert
will be able to practise the Jewish religion without interference by the

---

[29] ULPS: *Affirmations* (2006) Art. 37.
[30] ULPS: www.liberaljudaism.org/lifecycle/jewish-status-conversion/.
[31] I Klein, *Jewish Religious Practice* (1992) 440–448: this also deals with the process.

non-Jewish members of the family.[32] The Assembly of Masorti Synagogues too has a 'welcoming' and 'practical approach' to prospective
converts; conversions are supervised and approved by its Bet Din.[33]

The People of God and Church Membership

In Christianity: 'Baptism constitutes the incorporation of a person into
the Church of Christ.'[34] Some historic churches expressly use in their
legal instruments the category church 'member', others do not. Nevertheless, each church has an identifiable group of the faithful associated with
it. The Christian faithful constitute the people of God. All the faithful
should be equal in dignity. Baptism generates duties and rights for the
faithful. The faithful includes lay and ordained people.[35] In terms of
'church membership' and other forms of belonging, a church is made
up of those incorporated into it in accordance with its proper laws and
customs. However, a church should serve, in appropriate ways, all who
seek its ministry regardless of membership. Membership in a church, for
the purposes of participation in its government, may be based on any or
all of: baptism; baptism and confirmation or other mature demonstration
of faith; and such other conditions as may be prescribed by law. The
names of persons belonging to a church may be entered on one or more
rolls or other registers of membership subject to such conditions as may
be prescribed by law. Names may be removed from such rolls and
registers in accordance with the law.[36]

First, with regard to all the faithful, according to Roman Catholic
canon law, Christ's faithful (*christifideles*) are 'incorporated into the
Church of Christ through baptism'. The faithful constitute the 'people
of God' and each 'participates in their own way in the priestly, prophetic
and kingly office of Christ'. Moreover, each is called according to his/her
own condition 'to exercise the mission which God entrusted to the
Church to fulfil in the world'.[37] However, by 'divine institution, among
Christ's faithful there are in the Church sacred ministers, who are in law

---

[32] Rabbi Ben Zion Bergman: Responsum (2000).
[33] Assembly of Masorti Synagogues (AMS): www.masorti.org.uk/bet-din/bet-din.html.
[34] Christian Law Panel of Experts, *Principles of Christian Law* (2016) VII.1.3: see below
Chapter 7 for its administration.
[35] Christian Law Panel of Experts, *Principles of Christian Law* (2016) II.1.1–4.
[36] Christian Law Panel of Experts, *Principles of Christian Law* (2016) II.2.1–4.
[37] CIC: c. 204; c. 96: 'By baptism one is incorporated into the Church of Christ and
constituted a person in it.'

also called clerics; the others ... lay people'.[38] Further, by virtue of baptism all Christ's faithful (lay and ordained) enjoy in the church 'a genuine equality of dignity and action' and the right to contribute, 'each according to his or her own condition and office, to the building up of the Body of Christ'.[39] A baptised non-Catholic may be 'received into' the Catholic Church on accepting full communion. Also, after the lapse of a suitable period, 'persons who have manifested a willingness to embrace the faith in Christ are to be admitted to the catechumenate in liturgical ceremonies'; and: 'Through instruction and an apprenticeship in the Christian life catechumens are suitably to be initiated into the mystery of salvation and introduced to the life of faith, liturgy, charity of the people of God and the apostolate' – neophytes must be instructed in the gospel truth and baptismal duties.[40]

The same distinction exists in Anglicanism: 'the *laos* is the whole people of God, but for the purposes of law, a lay person is a person who is not in holy orders'.[41] Yet, all persons are 'equal in dignity before God' and 'as human beings created in the image and likeness of God [are] called to salvation through Jesus Christ'.[42] As Lutherans teach 'the priesthood of all believers',[43] so Methodists recognise the common ministry of Christian service through baptism and the priesthood of all believers,[44] distinguish lay and ordained persons[45] and embrace the equality of the faithful – for instance, for the Methodist Church in Ireland: 'every member of the Church is equal in spiritual privilege, has the same access to God through Christ, and is charged with the duty of establishing His Kingdom upon earth. The acknowledgment of this

---

[38] CIC: c. 207: 'Their state, although it does not belong to the hierarchical structure of the Church, does pertain to its life and holiness'; see also cc. 96–112 for the canonical status of physical persons.

[39] CIC: c. 208; see also *Catechism of the Catholic Church* (London: Continuum International Publishing, 1994), paras. 871–873.

[40] CIC: cc. 11, 788: and their names are registered; c. 789: neophytes are instructed in the faith.

[41] PCLCCAC: Principle 25.1.   [42] PCLCCAC: Principle 26.

[43] LCGB: Rules and Regulations, Statement of Faith, 6: 'as baptized Christians we are all children of God, at once sinners and saints ... incorporated into the priesthood of all believers'.

[44] MCGB: Constitutional Practice and Discipline, Deed of Union 4: the church holds 'the doctrine of the priesthood of all believers and ... believes that no priesthood exists which belongs exclusively to a particular order or class ... but [for] corporate life and worship special qualifications for ... special duties are required' for ordained ministry.

[45] MCGB: Constitutional Practice and Discipline, Deed of Union 1(xiv): 'lay' means 'a person who is neither a minister nor a deacon'

spiritual equality ... has led to the recognition of laypersons as being of an equal status with ministers in all the Courts of the Church.'[46] Much the same applies in the United Reformed Church in Britain: 'The Lord Jesus Christ continues his ministry in and through the Church, the whole people of God called and committed to his service and equipped for it.'[47] By way of contrast, whilst the juridical instruments of a local Baptist church present the congregation as a manifestation of the Body of Christ, for some the congregation is composed of 'members' and 'ministers' and for others it is composed of 'members' and 'ordained ministers', but these instruments do not yield a full juridical treatment of the equality of each category of ecclesiastical person.[48]

Secondly, in Roman Catholic canon law the term 'member' is not generally used to designate a person who belongs to the church; rather, as seen above, the fundamental category is that of 'Christ's faithful' who constitute the people of God.[49] In any event, baptised persons 'are in full communion with the Catholic Church here on earth who are joined with Christ in his visible body, through the bonds of profession of faith, the sacraments and ecclesiastical governance'.[50] At the local level, a parish, for example, is a 'community of Christ's faithful established within a particular church'.[51] The parish priest of the place in which a baptism was conferred must carefully record in the register of baptism the names of baptised persons, the date and place of their birth, and the date and place of the baptism; there are also confirmation registers.[52]

By way of contrast, Anglicans use the concept of church 'member'. Whilst a church 'should serve all who seek its ministry, membership in a church' may be based on any or all of: baptism; baptism and confirmation; baptism, confirmation and communicant status or

---

[46] MCI: Con. s. 1; and Regulations, Discipline and Government, 1.01: 'all believers in Christ may know their sins forgiven, live day by day with the peace of God in their souls and ... may be enriched with all the privileges that belong to the children of God'; 'Christians [may be] made perfect in love through the obedience of faith'.

[47] URC: Manual A.16.

[48] BUGB: Baptists in Local Ecumenical Partnerships, s. 3: 'Most Baptists appoint members to serve as Deacons and/or Elders to work with a minister.'

[49] See however CIC: c. 111: 'Through the reception of baptism a child becomes a member of the Latin Church if the parents belong to that Church.'

[50] CIC: c. 205.   [51] CIC: c. 515.

[52] CIC: c. 877; see also c. 895: those baptised persons who have been confirmed are to be recorded in the confirmation register of the diocesan curia or when prescribed by the Bishops' Conference or the diocesan bishop in the register to be kept in the parish archive.

regular attendance at public worship.[53] Anglican churches also provide for the reception of persons into the institutional church.[54] In turn, there are various classes of member: a communicant is a person who has received Holy Communion at such frequency and on such occasions as may be set by law; and a communicant in good standing is a communicant who for a prescribed period has been faithful in worship and has supported the work and mission of the church.[55] Names may be entered on a parish roll or other register of membership, subject to any conditions as prescribed by law, enabling eligibility for selection to participate in governance and other functions and offices. However, names may be removed from the roll only in accordance with the law, justice and equity.[56] Membership of a church implicitly involves profession of the faith, acceptance of its doctrine, government, law and discipline and enjoyment of fundamental and other rights and duties of the faithful.[57]

The Lutheran Church in Great Britain also has various categories of church member; for example: 'A voting member in a congregation of the [Church] is a baptised person aged 18 years or over who has publicly confessed the Christian faith after a period of instruction in the teachings of the Lutheran Church . . . and who has been duly received into membership of the congregation by its Council'; and: 'A baptised member is a person who has been duly baptised in the name of the Father and of the Son and of the Holy Spirit.' The Council of the congregation must maintain a register of members.[58] In similar vein, the law of the Methodist Church in Great Britain provides that: 'All those who confess Jesus Christ as Lord and Saviour and accept the obligation to serve him in the life of the Church and the world are welcome as members of the Methodist Church.' However, a candidate must be approved by the Church Council and publicly received (and baptised and confirmed if

---

[53] PCLCCAC: Principle 27.1–2; 3: a church may receive as a member any person who qualifies under its law.

[54] N. Doe, *The Legal Framework of the Church of England* (1996) 224–225.

[55] PCLCCAC: Principle 27.4–5.

[56] PCLCCAC: Principle 27.6–7. See e.g. Church in Wales: Con. VI.2: entry on the parish roll confers 'eligibility to exercise voting rights'.

[57] PCLCCAC: Principle 27.8.

[58] LCGB: Rules: the teachings of the Lutheran Church are those based on Luther's Small Catechism.

not already baptised and confirmed) at a service – the Church Council must maintain various registers of the church members.[59]

Presbyterians too define membership of the institutional church, impose conditions for admission to it and provide for membership rolls. The Presbyterian Church of Wales is typical: 'The meaning and standards of membership are based on our doctrine regarding the nature and purpose of the Church of God on earth.' Accordingly, the admission of a new member is 'a responsible act on the part of all members of a local church under the guidance of the Minister and/or the Elders'. In turn: 'Membership is open to any individual interested in promoting the Objects who is accepted as a new member of the [PCW] according to the Rules [or] is a member transferring from another Denomination according to the discretion of the Trustees'; the Trustees 'must keep a register of the names and addresses of members'. To be admitted as member, a person must make 'a profession of faith in God and belief in Christ, and vows to be loyal to them and faithful to all the ordinances of the church'.[60]

Submission to the Will of God

In classical Islamic law, a *Muslim* is one who submits to the will of God (as *Islam* is submission to the will of God) – the plural *muslimun* refers to the collective body of those who adhere to the Islamic faith and so belong to the entire community of believers (*ummah*). A person has the status of a Muslim by birth – if their father is a Muslim – or by conversion. To demonstrate Muslim status, a person must recite the *shahadah*, witnessing there is no God but Allah and Muhammad is the messenger of God. Therefore, conversion entails recitation of the *shahadah*; paying *zakah*, saying five daily prayers, a pilgrimage to Mecca and fasting during Ramadan follow. Male converts are expected to be circumcised and female converts to adopt modest dress. Both sexes often adopt Muslim names and no longer eat pork or drink alcohol. Conversion is to be voluntary: 'There is no compulsion in religion' (Quran 2:256).[61]

---

[59] MCGB: Constitutional Practice and Discipline, Deed of Union 8(a)–(c); Standing Orders 050; Deed of Union 9: Class Book; Standing Orders 054: the Membership Roll is kept by the Pastoral Committee of the Council; the Community Roll lists non-members in pastoral care.

[60] PCW: Handbook of Rules, II: Membership and Model Con. Art. 4.

[61] J.L. Esposito, ed., *The Oxford Dictionary of Islam* (Oxford: Oxford University Press, 2003) 57, 217.

The modern regulatory instruments of Muslim organisations define membership based on a combination of religious and secular criteria, including profession of the Islamic faith, acceptance of a particular school/tradition within Islam, residence in a prescribed area and acceptance of the constitution of the faith community. According to one guidance document, 'all masjids are open to anyone as a matter of principle', but 'the only sense in which most worshippers are "members" of a masjid is by habitual attendance'. Moreover, as most *masjid* management organisations are registered charities, they must have some form of constitutional governance, 'which implies some form of membership criteria' – and these in practice vary widely.[62]

At national level, the Muslim Council of Britain recognises 'the Muslim *ummah*' and its affiliated organisations are 'restricted only to those who profess the Muslim faith, who declare knowingly and voluntarily: "*La ilaha illa Allah Muhammad Rasul Allah*" and believe in the Qur'an as the true Word of God revealed to the Prophet Muhammad (peace be on him) and that there is no prophet after him'.[63] By way of contrast, membership of the Nasru-Lahi-Il-Fathi Society of Nigeria, United Kingdom and Ireland is open to 'All Muslims from all parts of the world whether male or female who are interested in propagating Islam'; but a prospective member must be sponsored by at least two members and must attend at least five meetings with prescribed officers on a regular basis before being considered for membership.[64]

The model constitution issued by the Central Mosque is more specific – for the purposes of the constitution: 'a Muslim shall be any person whose belief systems shall not be at variance with the requisite beliefs of Islam as expounded by the scholars of the Ahlus-Sunnah wal Jama'ah and as interpreted by the *bona fide* Ulama bodies of the Republic of South Africa, such as Qadianis, Ahmedies, Bahias, Zikrees, Ismaili and other Shia groupings, notwithstanding [that person's] claims of being "Muslim"'.[65] In turn, there are two types of 'membership of the congregation'. A full member must be: (1) a Muslim; (2) a Musallee, that is, 'any Muslim male of 18 years or above residing' in the relevant district 'who frequents the congregational prayers at any of the congregational prayer facilities controlled by the organisation'; (3) a resident of the relevant district for more than six months; (4) a person who has not permanently

---

[62] M. Naqshbandi, *Islam and Muslims in Britain* (2012): Guide 4.5.3.
[63] MCB: Con. Art. 3.1.   [64] NASFAT: Con. Arts. E and F.
[65] Model Constitution of an Islamic Organisation: Right of Admission to the Facilities 1–2.

relocated to another vicinity out of the district; and (5) one who has completed a membership application form and submitted it to the membership officer of the congregation and shall have succeeded in such membership application. An application may be accompanied by a token membership fee payable towards the congregation funds determined by the Shura Committee. A member must produce a membership card at general meetings and other instances if so required by a decree of the Shura Committee, renewable biennially, and has the right to vote at prescribed meetings.[66] An associate member must be a Muslim or Musallee and a resident of the relevant district who has not permanently relocated to another district.[67] The Shura Committee must maintain 'a proper register of members' and issue membership cards to all full members to identify them at general meetings and for other purposes.[68]

At the local level, various approaches are used for the definition of membership of a mosque or Islamic centre/society. First, some mosques make explicit but general reference to the observance of Islamic duties. For example, the constitution of Central Jamia Masjid (Southall) provides that: 'Membership of the Masjid shall be confined to persons of the Muslim faith who observe the obligatory duties of Islam and refrains from forbidden things (Munkarats) and who are interested in and willing to contribute actively to further the objectives of the Masjid'; registration is free provided that the Board of Trustees may determine to make eligible any other person who in the opinion of the Board 'shall have rendered or be capable of rendering special service to the Masjid'; nevertheless: 'Only practising Sunni Muslims who attend this Masjid and live within the borough of Ealing, Hillingdon or Hounslow and are members of the [Masjid] shall be eligible to take part in a trustee election.'[69]

Secondly, for other mosques the dominant criterion for admission to membership is belief; at Markazi Jamia Masjid Riza and Islamic Centre (Huddersfield): 'All persons who accept the teaching of the Quran, Hadith and of Khulafa-e-Rashdeen, Hazrat Imam Azam Abu Hanifa, Aima Ahle Bait, Hazrat Shah Abdul Haq Muhaddis Dhelvi, A'La Hazrat Shah Ahmed Raza Khan Brailvi, and who follows the school of thought known as Sunnah and Jamaat Brailvi may be members upon their

---

[66] Model Constitution of an Islamic Organisation: Full Membership 1–8.
[67] Model Constitution of an Islamic Organisation: Associate Membership 1–4.
[68] Model Constitution of an Islamic Organisation: Shura Committee 11.
[69] CJM: Rules 1.

undertaking ... to abide by this constitution and such rules as are ... properly made ... thereunder.'[70]

Thirdly, as well as status, area affiliation and subscription, for some frequency of attendance at prayer is a pre-condition; at Lancaster Islamic Society, a full member of the congregation is a Muslim of 18 years or above residing in Lancaster, or the district of, who frequents the congregational prayers at any of the prayer facilities controlled by the organisation; has been a resident for more than six months; and has not been permanently relocated to another vicinity out of the district of Lancaster.[71]

Fourthly, at Reading Muslim Council, for instance, membership is open *inter alia* to individuals (over 18) who are Muslims or non-Muslims interested in promoting 'the welfare of Muslims' and pay annual subscriptions set by the Executive Committee.[72]

Fifthly, an undertaking to observe the rules of the mosque community may be a prerequisite. At the Noor-Ul-Islam Mosque (Bury): 'Every Muslim residing in the Metropolitan Borough of Bury, aged eighteen years or more, is eligible [for] membership of the Mosque. Every person shall before being admitted ... undertake to observe and be bound by the provisions of the constitution and bye-laws of the Mosque. Members shall pay such entrance fee ... as the Committee may from time to time determine. The Mosque will keep a register of members and enter therein ... the name and current address of each member' and the date of their admission.[73] Provision may also be made to refuse admission and for an appeal; for example, the Markazi Jamia Masjid Riza and Islamic Centre (Huddersfield) has a rule that any person whose application to be entered in the register is refused by the committee may appeal to the Trustees whose decision on the matter will be final and absolute.[74]

Generally, the regulatory instruments of Muslim organisations do not explicitly deal with conversion to Islam. However, guidance of London Central Mosque Trust and Islamic Cultural Centre provides Shahadah (Declaration of Faith in Islam): 'with the pronunciation of this testimony,

---

[70] Markazi Jamia Masjid Riza and Islamic Centre (Huddersfield) (MJMRIC): Con. Art. 3: i.e. AHLE-SUNNAT-WA-JAMAAT (BRAILVI).
[71] LIS: Con: Membership, 1–3.   [72] Reading Muslim Council (RMC): Con. Art. E.
[73] NUIM: Con. Art. 3. See also: IFIS CUBE Network: Sample Constitution of an Islamic Society, Art. 3: a member of the society is one 'who has positively requested to be a member ... and agrees to abide by this constitution'; and Aberdeen Mosque and Islamic Centre: Con. Arts. 3.1–3.3.
[74] MJMRIC: Con. Art. 6.

or Shahadah, with sincere belief and conviction, one enters the fold of Islam'; and: 'for the Pleasure of God, all of one's previous sins are forgiven, and one starts a new life of piety and righteousness'.[75] The declaration is: 'I testify that there is no true god [deity] but God [Allah], and Muhammad is the Messenger and servant of God.'[76] The Trust recommends that the candidate wash the whole of their body with the intention of embracing Islam. On arrival at the mosque, the Imam usually asks appropriate questions to ensure full conviction and to explain the principles of Islam. As there is no compulsion in religion, no one can be forced to change their religion or to convert to Islam; this must be a person's 'own independent decision'.[77] Faith Associates also recommend that mosques should pay greater attention to the needs of converts, refer them for support available locally and nationally by trained Muslim men and women and provide for, *inter alia*, Shahadah certification (if this does not involve a person being coerced into changing their name 'since this is not a requirement for a convert to Islam'); a copy of the Quran; a prayer guide; books on the life (*seerah*) of Prophet Muhammad, the *hadith* and spirituality; a prayer mat; and access to study facilities such as Arabic courses.[78]

The Duties and Rights of the Faithful

The juridical instruments of all three religions contain elaborate provisions on the functions of the faithful. Across the religions, the instruments may present duties and rights applicable to all the faithful (followers and leaders), or alternatively they spell out duties and rights applicable specifically to the followers. Moreover, needless to say, duties imposed on an individual may generate correlative rights for another, and, *mutatis mutandis*, rights vested in one may generate duties for another. This indicates the profound interdependence of religious rights and duties. Failure to fulfil religious responsibilities may in turn result in the suspension or termination of membership, which are considered in the last section of this chapter and in Chapter 5 on discipline. What is

---

[75] The guidance cites Quran 3:19 and 3:85 and Al-Bukhari.

[76] Namely: 'Ashhadu anna Laa ilaaha illaa Allah, wa anna Muhammadan rasulu Allah'.

[77] London Central Mosque Trust and Islamic Cultural Centre: www.iccuk.org/page.php? section=religious&page=conversion.

[78] Faith Associates (FA): www.faithassociates.co.uk/training-faith-leaders/, Mosque Governance (2016) 84: Caring for Converts.

clear is that duties aspire to apply to Jews, Christians and Muslims alike in their daily lives – they are more than fundamental to a way of life, but are rather rules for living.[79]

The Observant Jew

Within Judaism, the classical understanding is that compliance with commandments of the Torah enables the faithful to be close to God – so, today, for Orthodox Judaism, the '*mitzvot* lead us to holiness, sanctify our lives and bring us closer to God';[80] thus: 'the standard of observance required by Jewish law, of every Jewish person', includes 'commitment to observe all Mitzvot', Shabbat (Sabbath), observance, maintaining *kashrut* (Jewish dietary laws) in and outside the home, and laws as to marriage and family purity; the ability to read Hebrew, follow a synagogue service, observe the festivals, be familiar with the halachic and moral principles required to run an observant Jewish home, and belong to a synagogue and participate in community life.[81] However, in Reform Judaism: 'The possibility of attaining holiness (*kedushah*) is one of the criteria for the observance of a commandment. Precepts such as prayer, Torah study, philanthropic deeds and others should lead to sanctification. The litmus test of holiness should determine the value of every religious act in the daily life of Jews in our generation.'[82] In point of fact, for some within Progressive Judaism, holiness may entail 'a departure from, or extension of, halakhic definitions and aims to set a standard, or rationale, for the observance of commandments', or else to inform, guide or regulate it;[83] and: 'We feel obligated to lead a life of *mitzvot*. At the same time we insist . . . that the observance of the *mitzvot* must be in harmony with the freedom of the individual conscience.'[84]

---

[79] See the Introduction for *Re G (Education: Religious Upbringing)* [2012] EWCA Civ. 1233.

[80] D. Golinkin, *Halakhah for Our Time* (New York: United Synagogue Youth, 1991) 11–12. See also I. Herzog, *Jewish Law* (1980) I.46–61: rights and duties.

[81] US: www.theus.org.uk/article/conversion-2.

[82] Rabbi Moshe Zemer (1932–2011), *Evolving Halakhah* (Woodstock, VT: Jewish Lights Publishing, 1998) 50; the book was first published in Hebrew as *The Sane Halakhah* (Tel Aviv: Dvir, 1993).

[83] J. Cohen, 'On the standard of holiness in Jewish law', in W. Jacob, ed., *Beyond the Letter of the Law* (2004) 143–155.

[84] Union of Progressive Jews in Germany, issued in 2001: see J. Rayner, 'Ethics versus ritual', in W. Jacob, ed., *Beyond the Letter of the Law* (2004) 119 at 130–131.

In turn, regulatory instruments across the Jewish traditions display a degree of legal pluralism with respect to the duties and rights of the faithful around the principle that for 'the fully observant Jew, Jewish law or *Halacha* provides a central model for how to lead an affirmed spiritual life'.[85] First, in a member synagogue of the (Orthodox) United Synagogue: 'Where any person shall be accepted as a member of the Synagogue that person shall, subject to these Bye-Laws, be entitled to the rights and privileges of a member of the Synagogue [and] subject to the obligations of membership.'[86] First, as to their rights and privileges, every member is entitled: (1) to attend and worship at the synagogue in accordance with the Form of Worship of the synagogue and to attend educational and social activities organised by the synagogue making any supplementary payment as required by the Local Honorary Officers;[87] (2) to otherwise participate in the religious observances, governance and ceremonies of the synagogue, including in particular the right for male members to be called to the reading of the law, to be married at or under the auspices of the synagogue, provided the synagogue is duly authorised by the Board of British Deputies; (3) to arrange for the celebration of the *barmitzvah* of his/her son at or under the auspices of the synagogue, in accordance with such arrangements from time to time agreed between the member and the synagogue; (4) to arrange for the celebration of the *batmitzvah* of his/her daughter in a manner approved by the Rabbi of the synagogue; (5) to participate in the governance of the synagogue; (6) to be awarded such religious or other honours as the Local Honorary Officers and the Rabbi determine; and (7) to attendance of the Rabbi or a duly qualified officiant appointed by the United Synagogue at the funeral and tombstone setting of any member or unmarried children under 21 of a member, if this takes place at a cemetery of the United Synagogue.[88] However, the availability of the Rabbi at services, observances and celebrations is subject to his contract of employment and must be exercised after consulting with the Local Honorary Officers – such rights are construed and take effect accordingly.[89] Secondly: 'Every

---

[85] BDBJ: *The Employer's Guide to Judaism* (2004: updated 2015) 1.
[86] US: Bye-Laws 6. The rights and privileges are out in Schedule 1 and the obligations in Schedule 2.
[87] US: Bye-Laws, Sch. 1.1: The Rights and Privileges of Membership.
[88] US: Bye-Laws, Sch. 1.2: The Rights and Privileges of Membership; 1.3: Members may exercise their rights in accordance with their seniority as members of the Synagogue: see below Chapter 7.
[89] US: Bye-Laws, Sch. 1.5.

Member of the Synagogue shall . . . be subject to the following obligations and duties': (1) to pay any and all membership subscriptions or other sums due and payable to the synagogue in a prompt and timely manner; and (2) to comply with the statutes, bye-laws and subordinate regulations of the United Synagogue.[90]

Special provision is made for the Association of United Synagogue Women – under the halachic authority of the Chief Rabbi, it represents all female members of the United Synagogue.[91] The Association seeks to educate, empower and engage women within the US community in all areas of Judaism, including lay leadership, religious practice and social action. It liaises closely with the Office of the Chief Rabbi, the Rabbonim and the leadership of the United Synagogue to promote and advocate the views of women within the whole community bearing in mind the diversity of requirements – its objects include to promote activities for the women of the United Synagogue, which may have a social, welfare, charitable, cultural or educational focus, in order to strengthen the values of traditional Judaism and its observance.[92]

Secondly, in the Movement for Reform Judaism, full members of a synagogue are entitled to attend all religious services held by the synagogue and to such other 'rights and privileges' as are laid down by its Council; honorary members are entitled to attend but not to vote at Annual or Special General Meetings and to such other rights as Council may confer but they are not entitled to membership of the Jewish Joint Burial Society (JJBS); and associate members are not entitled to facilities at the Religious School (*cheder*) for their children, voting rights, the right to stand for Council or serve on the management sub-committee or burial rights.[93] Members also have correlative rights which flow from the duties of synagogue officers; for example, the Administrator (assisted by the Membership Secretary) must: advise members who need

---

[90] US: Bye-Laws, Sch. 2: The Obligations and Duties of Membership.
[91] As to women, see e.g. I. Herzog, *Jewish Law* (1980) I.42: 'Woman is equal to man in respect of legal rights, duties and interests, though not altogether in regard to certain capacities coming within the sphere of personal status, in connection with the right of succession and in a few other matters.'
[92] Association of United Synagogue Women: Constitution (2009) Art. 3: objects. The Association has a President (Art. 4), an executive committee (Art. 5), a general meeting (Art. 6), a triennial meeting (Art. 7), and elections of its Honorary Officers and committee (Art. 8); there are also norms on finance (Art. 9), changing the constitution (Art. 10) and dissolution of the association (Art. 11).
[93] MRJ: Areas of Responsibility and Code of Practice Documents (Constitution): p 9

assistance as to fees or wish to leave the synagogue; encourage new members to participate in synagogue life and services; and provide members with information, for example the synagogue newsletter, prayer books and *cheder* details.[94] Moreover, on admission, a member should be given a membership form, bank standing order and gift aid form; JJBS Funeral Fund Guidelines Booklet; calendar of services and events; booklet about Reform Judaism if appropriate; and a copy of the synagogue history.[95]

At local level, North London Reform Synagogue, for instance, provides that members are 'entitled to all rights and privileges' of membership of the synagogue; and: 'The wife of a Member, if living with him, shall herself be a Member of the Synagogue and shall have the same rights as her husband.' Children of a member, under the age of 21 and unmarried, are 'entitled to attend all religious services held by the synagogue and to such other rights and privileges as shall from time to time be laid down by the Council, and they shall be eligible to serve on any committee or sub-committee or special committee'. Furthermore, every member 'regardless of sex' is eligible for all honorary offices, membership of Council, sub-committees and special committees.[96] In turn, a rule at the Brighton and Hove Reform Synagogue states that: 'It is the duty of each member . . . to exercise his or her powers as a member . . . in the way he/she decides in good faith would be most likely to further the purposes' of the synagogue.[97]

Thirdly, according to the Union of Liberal and Progressive Synagogues: to be a Jew is to be the inheritor of a religious and cultural tradition; to be a practising Jew is to accept with love and pride the duty to maintain and transmit that tradition; and to be a practising Liberal Jew is to believe that tradition should be transmitted within the framework of modern thinking and morality – it is to live according to the prophetic ideal of doing justice, loving kindness and walking humbly with God. In turn, the Union affirms 'the Jewish concept of *B'rit* (Covenant): the special relationship that came to exist between God and our Hebrew and Israelite ancestors'; the responsibility which devolves to descendants to be God's witnesses and servants; the 'commitment to the Jewish people, bearer of Jewish religious and cultural heritage'; the 'duty to defend the civil rights, and to seek the material and spiritual welfare, of

---

[94] MRJ: Code of Practice, p. 8; see also p. 12: honorary and associate membership.
[95] MRJ: Code of Practice, pp. 8–9.   [96] NLRS: Law Art. 11(a)–(c).
[97] BHRS: Con. Art. 10.5.

Jews and Jewish communities everywhere'; and 'pride in Jewish history: a unique record of survival and creativity in many lands and diverse circumstances, including times of persecution and suffering', which reinforce the commitment to survival of Judaism.[98] At local level, Elstree Liberal Synagogue, for example, provides, as to 'Rights of the Various Categories of Membership', that a full member may attend and conduct services, be included in the burial schemes, vote at the Annual Extraordinary General Meeting, become a Council member or Honorary Officer, attend committee meetings, and hold executive positions on committees. An associate member may attend and conduct services and attend committee meetings, and a friend may attend services.[99]

Lastly, for the United Synagogue of Conservative Judaism, an 'ideal Conservative Jew' is one who is 'always trying to grow in commitment and knowledge', climbing 'the ladder of observance'. The 'behavioural expectations', to build the foundations of committed Conservative Jewish lifestyle, are to: support a Conservative synagogue by participating in its activities; study a minimum of one hour a week; employ Jewish values to guide behaviour even if it conflicts with personal feelings or inclinations; increase personal Jewish living by adding at least three new *mitzvot* each year; help in the continual repair of the world; make decisions about Jewish behaviour only after considering its effect on the unity of the Jewish people; increase ties with Israel; and increase knowledge of Hebrew.[100] Guidance on the exercise of rights and duties may be the subject of responsa of the Rabbinical Assembly; for example, women and men are equally obligated to observe the *mitzvot*, with the exception of those determined by sexual anatomy;[101] and, while the Torah explicitly prohibits tattooing, those who violate this prohibition may still participate fully in all synagogue ritual.[102]

---

[98] ULPS: *Affirmations* (2006) Preamble and Arts. 5–7.   [99] ELS: Con. Art. 5.

[100] USCJ: The 'Ideal' Conservative Jew: Eight Behavioural Expectations: Jewish Living. Klal Yisrael, the unity of the Jewish people, 'is a central value of the Conservative Movement'; in making decisions about life or religious practices, Conservative Jews must: think about their impact on the entire Jewish community; avoid taking actions which divide them from other Jews; be involved in synagogue life.

[101] USCJ: Rabbinical Assembly, Committee on Jewish Law and Standards: Yoreh deah 246 (2014): Women and Mitzvot.

[102] USCJ: Rabbinical Assembly, Committee on Jewish Law and Standards: Yoreh deah 130 (1997): Tattooing and Body Piercing.

Christian Discipleship

In Christianity, theologically, the life of the faithful is governed by grace and the Holy Spirit. However, it is a principle of law for the historic churches that the law of a church should generally set out the basic rights and duties of all its members. The laity should promote the mission of the church, and bear witness to the Christian faith through their lives in the world. A layperson should engage in the collective ecclesial life, in proclaiming the Word of God, participating in worship and receiving the sacraments. Lay persons should maintain such Christian standards in their private lives as are prescribed by law, and are encouraged to practise daily devotion, private prayer, Bible reading and self-discipline, bringing the teaching and example of Christ into every-day life, upholding Christian values and being of service to both the church and the wider community.[103] Laypersons may also exercise public ministry when allowed by church law.[104] These are derived from laws such as the following.

Roman Catholic canon law distinguishes the duties and rights of all the faithful, lay and ordained, as well as those specifically applicable to the laity. When incorporated by baptism into the Church of Christ, each of the faithful has 'such duties and rights which, in accordance with each one's status, are proper to Christians, in so far as they are in ecclesiastical communion and unless a lawfully issued sanction intervenes'.[105] The duties of all the faithful include: to preserve communion with the church; to lead a holy life; to show Christian obedience to what sacred pastors (who represent Christ) declare as teachers of the faith and rulers of the church; to provide for the needs of the church; and to promote social justice. Their rights include to make known their needs and wishes to the pastors; to be assisted by their pastors; to worship God; to establish and direct associations (e.g. charitable purposes); to have access to a Christian education; and to vindicate and defend their own rights.[106] The laity have specific obligations and rights: to strive so that the divine

---

[103] Christian Law Panel of Experts, *Principles of Christian Law* (2016) II.3: the functions of the laity.

[104] Christian Law Panel of Experts, *Principles of Christian Law* (2016) II.4; see below Chapter 3.

[105] CIC: c. 96; a person has duties and rights: as well as the laity (cc. 224–231), there are those attaching to e.g. clergy (cc. 273–289), religious (cc. 662–672), married couples and parents (cc. 1135–1136).

[106] CIC: cc. 208–223: 'obligations and rights of all the faithful'; sometimes, a duty and a right coincide: e.g. c. 211: 'All the Christian faithful have the obligation (*officium*) and the

message may be known throughout the world; to permeate the temporal order with the spirit of the gospel; to build up the people of God through marriage and the family; and to acquire knowledge of and proclaim Christian teaching; they are also capable of admission to prescribed ecclesiastical offices.[107] These duties and rights derive from the fundamental dignity of the individual as a human being, and as such are inalienable and inviolable.[108] Moreover: '[i]n exercising their rights, [the] faithful, both individually and in association, must take account of the common good of the church, as well as the rights of others and their own duties to others'. The appropriate ecclesiastical authority is entitled 'to regulate, in view of the common good, the exercise of rights which are proper to Christ's faithful'.[109] All the faithful are subject to church discipline.[110]

By way of contrast, in Anglicanism, all the faithful, lay and ordained are responsible for church life and witness, and should: regularly attend public worship, especially at Holy Communion; practise daily devotion, private prayer, Bible reading and self-discipline; bring the teaching and example of Christ into every-day life; uphold Christian values; be of personal service to church and community; and assist the church financially.[111] Two types of right are envisioned: inherent rights and acquired rights: 'all persons, equal in dignity before God, have inherent rights and duties inseparable from their dignity as human beings created in the image and likeness of God and called to salvation through Jesus Christ. However, baptism is the foundation of Christian rights and duties, and a church should respect both sets of rights and duties'.[112] Also, all the faithful enjoy such rights to government, ministry, teaching, worship, sacraments, rites and property as may flow from their human dignity, baptism, the duties of others 'and the law of that church'; indeed, there is

---

right (*ius*) to strive so that the divine message of salvation may ... reach all people of all times and all places.'

[107] CIC: cc. 224–231: the 'obligations and rights of the lay members of Christ's faithful'.

[108] CIC: c. 208.

[109] CIC: c. 223. The exercise of conscience is important here: CCC, paras. 1776–1802.

[110] CIC: c. 11: canon law binds those baptised or received into the church who enjoy the sufficient use of reason and have completed seven years of age; for discipline, see cc. 1311, 1321–1323, 1341.

[111] PCLCCAC: Principle 26.6.

[112] PCLCCAC: Principle 26.1–3; 4: a church should respect rights and duties founded on the dignity of the human person and on baptism and those afforded by church authority; 5: the church is concerned with the welfare of people in all its aspects, physical, mental and spiritual.

to be no unlawful denial of equal rights, status or access to the life, membership, government, ministry, worship, rites and property of a church on grounds of race, colour, ethnic, tribal or national origin, marital status, sex, sexual orientation, disability or age.[113] All the faithful, as appropriate to their state, participate in teaching, governing and sanctifying; lay persons exercise authority in church life and governance according to law, and are subject to discipline to the extent and in the manner prescribed by law.[114]

Whereas Roman Catholic and Anglican laws begin with duties and move to rights, in the Protestant traditions the reverse is often the case. For example, Methodists provide for the 'privileges and obligations of membership' (particularly holy living and participation in the sacraments and worship).[115] The Methodist Church of Ireland is typical: 'Every member shall have their name recorded in the Membership Register and should receive pastoral support and encouragement in their discipleship from the local minister and lay leaders'; but only those whose names are recorded in the Membership Register are entitled to be members of the Church Council, Circuit Executive, District Synod or Conference.[116] As to obligations: 'All members are expected to (a) attend the means of grace, especially the ministry of the Word, united prayer, and the Sacrament of the Lord's Supper, (b) join with others in Christian fellowship, (c) engage in some form of Christian service, [and] (d) financially support the ongoing work and mission of the church through regular giving, so far as can reasonably be expected.'[117] These rules are built on the classical Methodist principle that the faithful are 'helpers one of another', in their covenantal relationships, which clearly expresses the interdependence inherent in the exercise of right and duties.[118]

---

[113] PCLCCAC: Principle 26.7–8; 10: 'All the faithful should recognise the unique status and needs of children and young people . . . and a church should make such provision . . . to ensure their special protection'; their mistreatment, especially sexual abuse, offends their humanity and teaching of Christ.

[114] PCLCCAC: Principle 25.1.

[115] The General Rules of Societies (1743): duties include 'doing no harm' (e.g. profaning the Lord's Day), 'doing good' (e.g. feeding the hungry, visiting and helping the sick), and attending the ordinances, private prayer, searching Scriptures, fasting and abstinence – habitual failure to observe these 'rules' may lead to admonition and exclusion; MCGB: Constitutional Practice and Discipline, Deed of Union 9: privileges and duties.

[116] MCI: Regulations, Discipline and Government, 2.04 and 2.05, 2.07.

[117] MCI: Regulations, Discipline and Government, 2.06.

[118] MCI: Regulations, Discipline and Government, 1.03: The General Rules of Our Societies.

The Reformed churches also speak of the 'rights and privileges' and 'privileges and responsibilities' of church membership. These clearly reflect the interconnectedness of the faithful, their responsibility for mutual assistance and the interplay of both duties and correlative rights, and rights and correlative duties.[119] They may also include a duty on members to respect the ordained ministers.[120] Presbyterians have particularly well-developed compendia of the rights and duties of members[121] on the basis that, for example, '[t]o be a member of the Church of God is a great privilege and involves a corresponding responsibility and duty'.[122] The 'one another passages' of Scripture are a basis for rights and duties of members in a local Baptist church;[123] and, moreover: 'it is the duty of every Disciple to bear personal witness to the Gospel of Jesus Christ, in Family and Public Worship, in the observance of the ordinance of Baptism and the Lord's Supper, in conduct and in the Evangelisation of the world'.[124]

The Five Pillars of Islam

In classical Islamic law, the duties of Muslims are summed up in the so-called five pillars: belief (*imaan*) in God and that Muhammad is the Messenger of God, in the angels, the prophets and the revelation of God in the Quran; prayer (*salat*) – Muslims are required to pray five times a day (at dawn, midday, mid-way through the afternoon, after sunset and

---

[119] URC: Manual A.19: Christian service implies 'mutual and outgoing care and responsibility', worship, prayer, proclamation of the gospel, witness and 'obedient discipleship in the whole of daily life'.

[120] UFCS: Manual of Practice and Procedure, Ch. 3, s. 1: 'It is the duty of members to give faithful attendance on Gospel ordinances; to give their minister all dutiful respect, encouragement and obedience in the Lord; to submit to the Session'; and 'to promote the peace and prosperity of the congregation'.

[121] PCI: Code, I.I, paras. 5–9: 'All who profess [Christ] are called to be members of the visible Church in the fellowship of a congregation, with all the rights and responsibilities attached'; members must e.g. make diligent use of the means of grace, share in worship, 'render whole-hearted service to Christ'; their children are entitled to e.g. baptism, nurture and pastoral care; 'All baptised persons ... are entitled to the pastoral care and instruction of the Church and are subject to its discipline.'

[122] PCW: Handbook of Rules, II: members have 'a responsibility for the worship and whole work of the church, and a duty to take part in that work ... in terms of money, time and talents'; their 'regular use' of the means of grace is 'a duty owed to God and a necessity of the Christian life'; other duties are e.g. showing church unity (by neighbourly love and a forgiving spirit) and living the Gospel in personal and public life.

[123] See N. Doe, *Christian Law* (2013) 61.   [124] BUS: Con III.3

at night); fasting (*sawm*) – this is prescribed in the month of Ramadan (the ninth month in the Islamic lunar calendar) in which adult Muslims in good health may neither eat nor drink during daylight hours; giving *zakat* – each year a Muslim should give a proportion of their accumulated wealth to the poor and needy; and the pilgrimage to Mecca (*hajj*) if they are able to afford it once in a lifetime at one time of the year, at the time of *Eid ul-Adha* – a pilgrimage at other times is called *umra*.[125] The duties are discharged in a balanced way; according to the Universal Islamic Declaration of Human Rights (1981), each Muslim has 'obligations proportionate to his capacity and shall be held responsible *pro rata* for his deeds'.[126]

These duties do not generally appear in the modern regulatory instruments of Muslim communities. However, there are exceptions. For example, the purposes of each of the five pillars of Islam are set out by Birmingham Central Mosque in its soft-law: 'Manifestation of faith in human life in the form of rituals ... serves very important specific purposes': belief provides a focus for worship; prayers five times each day provide spiritual sustenance; *zakat* is 'a socially responsible way of distributing wealth to the poor and needy'; fasting is the best way to teach discipline over desire; and *hajj*, incumbent on all Muslims, seeks to provide an exercise in collectiveness and equality.[127] Under the rules of Central Jamia Masjid (Southall), members must 'observe the obligatory duties of Islam', refrain from 'forbidden things (Munkarats)' and 'contribute actively to further the objectives of the Masjid'.[128] And in Lancaster Islamic Society, a Muslim must exercise 'obedience' to the guidance of Allah in order 'to achieve human excellence', 'adhere strictly to the tenets of Shari'ah' (as expounded by the Sunni schools), and practise, for example, kindness, goodness, patience, forgiveness, tolerance, humility, justice and respect for the equality of mankind.[129]

More often, duties are cast in terms that are more mundane. For example, while not listing the five pillars of Islam, the constitution of the Muslim Council of Britain recognises 'the responsibilities and rights of Muslims living in Britain'.[130] All its delegates must: 'be motivated by

---

[125] J. Hussain, *Islamic Law* (1999) 12.   [126] UIDHR (1981): Preamble.

[127] BCM: Seven Articles of Muslim Faith: https://centralmosque.org.uk/. See also e.g. Ibid.: Five Pillars of Islam.

[128] CJM: Rules 1.

[129] LIS: Con: Basic Founding Principles. Quranic verses are cited to justify each duty.

[130] MCB: Con. Declaration of Intent.

the desire to serve the community'; abide by procedures and standing orders that govern the conduct of its meetings and affairs; accept its constitution and be able and willing to abide by it; do their best to uphold and implement agreed policies; promote mutual respect and co-operation with other member organisations; and use the framework of the Council to resolve difficult issues with other member organisations.[131] Neither does the Nasru-Lahi-Il-Fathi Society of Nigeria, United Kingdom and Ireland list the five pillars, but 'members shall be encouraged to attend Asaalat regularly' (its Sunday spiritual meeting), and observe the Islamic festivals.[132] A common duty, however, is to pay a subscription, as at Noor-Ul-Islam Mosque (Bury) where members pay such subscription as the Committee may determine.[133]

The constitutions of mosques also set out the rights of members. For instance, the model constitution issued by the Central Mosque provides that members: have 'the right' of entry to the *masjid*, the use of the graveyard, 'and so forth'; may stand for election to the Shura Management Committee; and have the right to vote at meetings. An associate member may use the facilities of the congregation such as the cemetery, education, etc., but not vote at meetings.[134] Rights to participate in the mosque governance are common,[135] and these are dealt with in Chapter 4. In recent years, a body of case law has been developed by the civil courts with respect to the exercise of the duties imposed by classical Islamic law and the rights of Muslims to discharge these duties based on civil rights to freedom of religion under the European Convention on Human Rights and equality–religious discrimination law.[136]

The Termination of Membership

All three religions provide norms to terminate the membership of a person belonging to a faith community based on the death or

---

[131] MCB: Con. Arts. 3.3–3.6.   [132] NASFAT: Con. Art. O: Asaalat; V: festivals.

[133] NUIM: Con. Art. 3. See also MJMRIC: Con. Art. 4.

[134] Model Constitution of an Islamic Organisation: Right of admission to the Facilities, Panel of Elected Officials 1, Full Membership 1–8, Associate Membership 1–4.

[135] See e.g. CJM: Rules 1; and MJMRIC: Con. Art. 5.

[136] See e.g. *Ahmad* v. *Inner London Education Authority* [1978] QB 36: a refusal to allow a Muslim teacher to take time off during school hours to attend prayers was upheld as consistent with the European Convention for the Protection of Human Rights and Fundamental Freedoms (ECHR) (Council of Europe).

resignation of the person or their removal as the result of due process administered by the relevant religious authority.

Mumar

In classical Judaism, apostasy involves the rejection of Judaism or defection by a Jew to another religion.[137] The historical approach to the effects of apostasy broadly survives across the Jewish traditions today – individuals cannot divest themselves of their Jewish status: in Orthodox Judaism, 'the apostate (*mumar*), however damnable, has not altogether lost his status as a Jew'; in Conservative Judaism, 'an apostate never ceases to be a Jew' and after repentance before a court may 'be readmitted formally into the Jewish community'; and in Reform Judaism the status of a Jewish apostate is 'the same as' that of 'converts who return to their original religion' – they 'remain Jewish and are to be considered Jewish for all purposes'. Thus, 'an adult proselyte who has become a Jew voluntarily cannot annul this process in any way', and a 'child of an apostate female proselyte, or of a male married to a Jewish woman, would be considered Jewish and would need no formal conversion to Judaism'.[138]

The modern regulatory instruments of Jewish communities do not explicitly deal with apostasy. However, they do contain norms on the termination of membership of the community in question. In the (Orthodox) United Synagogue, membership, which is not transferable between individuals, ceases on the death of the individual concerned, and, in the case of full, affiliated or associate members, if the person ceases to be a member of the synagogue concerned. Further, a member may at any time resign from membership of the synagogue by giving to the synagogue notice in writing.[139] The United Synagogue also provides for the suspension or termination of membership. The Local Honorary

---

[137] Hebrew words used by Rabbinical scholars include *mumar* (literally, 'the one that was changed'), *poshea Yisrael* (literally, 'transgressor of Israel'), and *kofer* ('denier'). Other words are *meshumad* ('destroyed one'), one who has abandoned his faith, and *min* the negation of God and Judaism, implying atheism. Apostasy was forbidden and punishable: Deuteronomy 13:6–11.

[138] Orthodox: I. Herzog, *Jewish Law* (1980) I.60; Conservative: I. Klein, *Jewish Religious Practice* (1992) 446: readmission involves immersion in a *miqweh*; Reform: W. Jacob and M. Zemer, *Conversion to Judaism* (Pittsburgh, PA: Rodef Shalom Press, 1994), Selected Reform Responsa, 213: An Apostate Proselyte.

[139] US: Statutes 6.2; Bye-Laws 5.9–10.

Officers may, 'for good and substantial reason, if they consider it in the best interests of the Synagogue', suspend or restrict the rights of membership of any member of the synagogue, or terminate the membership of any member. They may do so if, before suspending or terminating the membership, they give the person concerned 'the reasons for the suspension or termination and the right to make oral representations and to state any case in writing to them'. Where membership is suspended or terminated, the individual is not 'entitled to exercise any of the rights and privileges of membership' nor 'attend the Synagogue to participate in the Form of Worship or other religious observances ... or to participate in [its] educational, social and other activities'. However, at the discretion of the Honorary Officers, participation in the Funeral Expenses Scheme of the United Synagogue may be maintained. Where membership has been suspended or terminated, the member concerned is, within 14 days of notification of that decision, 'entitled to appeal against the decision to the [nationwide] Honorary Officers' of the United Synagogue. On an appeal, the Honorary Officers must give the individual concerned the right to make oral representations and to state any case in writing to them. An appeal must be dealt with within 30 days. For the purpose of hearing and determining any such appeal, the Honorary Officers may call for such information as they shall determine.[140]

Much the same pertains in other Jewish traditions. For example, in Wessex Liberal Jewish Community, membership is terminated if the member dies, resigns by written notice, fails to pay any sum due within six months of it falling due or is removed by a resolution of the trustees that this is in the best interests of the charity.[141] Thus, 'A member may be deprived of membership and of all rights and privileges of membership, provided that the approved procedure for removing a person from membership is followed.' At least three-quarters of the trustees must agree to the removal, and reasons must be given in writing within seven days of the decision. The removed person may appeal against the decision within seven days of being given the written reason. The appeal

---

[140] US: Bye-Laws 5.6–5.8.

[141] WLJC: Con. Art. 9: a resolution to remove a member may only be passed if the member is given 21 days' written notice of the meeting of the trustees at which the resolution will be proposed and the reasons for this, and if the member has been allowed to make representations to the meeting; and at least three-quarters of the trustees agree to removal of membership; a person removed may not claim refund of any unexpired part of their subscription

must be in writing to a designated trustee. Any person who is so removed has no claim to refund any unexpired part of their subscription.[142]

The norms at North London Reform Synagogue are somewhat more rigorous: 'Any Member may be deprived of membership and of all rights and privileges thereof by a resolution passed at a special meeting of the Council convened for the purpose'; not less than three-quarters of Council must be present at the special meeting and not less than two-thirds of those present must vote in favour of it. Such a resolution requires confirmation by a resolution passed at a Special General Meeting if such meeting is requested by the member within 14 days after notice of the Council resolution has been sent to him by registered post. A member whose membership has been so terminated has no claim for refund in respect of the unexpired part of his subscription, but Council may in their discretion make such a refund.[143] And in the Exeter Hebrew Congregation, a member ceases to be a member if his/her subscription is six months in arrears, whether or not such subscription has been formally demanded, and if the Committee of Management has resolved that he/she cease to be a member; or if the person by written notice to the Secretary has resigned membership; or if by a two-third majority of the Committee of Management that person is requested to resign.[144]

Excommunication

In Christianity, Christian status acquired by baptism (which effects incorporation into the church universal) is generally regarded as indelible. As a result, few churches have norms on apostasy; however, whilst in Roman Catholic canon law there is no provision for formal defection from the Catholic Church,[145] apostasy is 'the total repudiation of the

---

[142] WLJC: Con. Arts. 8.9–8.10. See also ELS: Con. Art. 5: Council may by 75 per cent majority of those present and entitled to vote and for 'good reason' terminate the membership of any individual, provided the individual concerned has: received at least 14 days written notice of a motion proposing the termination of their membership from the synagogue; and the right to be heard by the Council, accompanied by a person of the choosing, before a final decision is made. Prior to the vote by the Council being taken, the individual concerned and their associate are required to leave the meeting.

[143] NLRS: Law, Art. 11(f): Art. 16, on the calling of a Special General Meeting does not apply in this case, but the secretary must convene a Special General Meeting within not less than two or more than eight weeks. See also BHRS: Con. Art. 10(6)–(7): grounds and process.

[144] EHC: Con. Schedule of Regulations, 10.

[145] CIC: c. 11: canon law binds those baptised or who have been received into the church and who enjoy the sufficient use of reason and have completed seven years of age; for discipline (cc. 1311, 1321–1323, 1341), see Chapter 5.

Christian faith', and the penalty is automatic excommunication for laity and for clerics, excommunication, suspension, deprivation or penal transfer.[146]

Nevertheless, church laws may provide for the termination of membership of the institutional church and for the removal of names from church rolls and registers in accordance with the law.[147] Methodist law is typical: whilst death and resignation both terminate membership,[148] 'a member, who in the judgment of the Church Council, has persistently failed to fulfil the Obligations of Membership, despite being reminded of those obligations, shall be regarded as having withdrawn from membership of the church and their name shall be removed from the Membership Register'.[149] Similarly, a Lutheran church council may remove from the register those who have not supported church life or public worship 'over a significant period'.[150]

Churches also provide for the withdrawal of spiritual benefits, short of terminating membership, by means of excommunication. In the Roman Catholic Church, excommunicates and those who obstinately persist in manifest grave sin are not to be admitted to Holy Communion, nor is anyone who is conscious of grave sin without previously having been to sacramental confession.[151] In Anglicanism, no minister shall without lawful cause deny the Holy Communion to a baptised Christian who devoutly and humbly desires it; in the Church of England, this is a prohibition imposed by civil law in the form of a Reformation parliamentary statute still in force – the Sacrament Act 1547. However, a person, in the absence of repentance and amendment of life, may be denied Holy Communion, for living openly in grievous sin or contention, causing scandal to the congregation or bringing the church into disrepute.[152] The churches provide for appeals to the bishop. Restoration to Holy Communion is reserved to the bishop or priest, as the case may be

---

[146] CIC: c. 751: offence; c. 1364: penalty; cc. 1323–1324: baptized persons who fall into apostasy or schism as a matter of conscience do not incur these censures.

[147] Christian Law Panel of Experts, *Principles of Christian Law* (2016) II.2.1–4.

[148] MCGB: Constitutional Practice and Discipline, Standing Orders 057: resigning membership.

[149] MCI: Regulations, Discipline and Government, 2.08.

[150] LCGB: Rules and Regulations, Individual Membership in a Congregation, 2.

[151] CIC: cc. 915–916.

[152] PCLCCAC: Principle 69. See e.g. Church of England: Can. B16: summary exclusion to prevent e.g. scandal; Scottish Episcopal Church: Can. 26: 'it is the inherent right of a Bishop . . . to repel offenders from Communion'.

under church law, or in cases of appeal to the competent authority. The effects of excommunication are such as may be prescribed by law.[153] In the Methodist Church, a person who 'by prolonged absence severs himself or herself from Christian fellowship' is to be removed from the class book of the local church and so ceases membership of it.[154]

Riddah

Historically in Islam, apostasy is the renunciation of Islam (*riddah*, *irtidad*). Some *hadith* speak of apostasy as punishable by death – though some schools of law allowed imprisonment instead of death for apostate women, and some allowed an apostate (*murtad*) to repent – but it was debated as to whether an apostate may be allowed, encouraged or disallowed to do so. Apostasy was therefore included in crimes for which there were believed to be divinely instituted punishments – and there are consequences in the afterlife for those who 'turn from' or 'renounce' God, *yartaddu* and 'those who disbelieve after having believed' (Quran 3:8; 5:6; 9:66).[155] Modern scholars argue against the death penalty for apostasy on the basis of the absence of reference to it in the Quranic verse: 'And if any of you turn back from their faith and die in unbelief, their works will bear no fruit in this life and in the Hereafter; they will be a Companion of the Fire and will abide therein' (Quran 2:217); the verse which states that there is no compulsion in religion (Quran 2:256) is also invoked here.[156]

The modern regulatory instruments of Muslim organisations provide for voluntary withdrawal as well as for compulsory removal from the membership.[157] As to the latter, for instance, the Muslim Council of Britain provides for the suspension and removal of its delegates. For example, any member of the National Council who misses two consecutive meetings of the Committee without reasonable cause may be disqualified from attending further meetings if the Committee passes a motion supported by at least two-thirds of those present and voting and who declare the member as disqualified. Moreover, any member of the

---

[153] PCLCCAC: Principle 69.6–9. See e.g. Scottish Episcopal Church: Can. 26: a right of appeal against the decision of the bishop to the College of Bishops.

[154] MCGB: Constitutional Practice and Discipline, Standing Orders 054.

[155] J.L. Esposito, ed., *Oxford Dictionary of Islam* (2003): 22: the marriage of an apostate is void.

[156] A. Black *et al.*, *Islamic Law* (2013) 225–226.

[157] IFIS CUBE Network: Sample Constitution of an Islamic Society, Art. 3: 'a member is free to withdraw ... at any time'.

National Council engaged in acts contrary to the Shariah shall be liable to removal from the National Council. A member of the National Council may be suspended from membership on any ground provided that the member has been given written notice of charges against him two weeks in advance and he is given the opportunity to make written or oral representations to the National Council before the decision to suspend is made. The decision to suspend requires a two-third majority vote of the total membership of the National Council. The member against whom a decision to suspend has been made has a right to appeal against that decision. The member must inform the Convenor of the Board of Counsellors of the intention to appeal within seven days of the receipt of notice, and the Board must within five working days appoint a panel to consider the appeal. The panel must within two months of the appeal give its decision, confirming, revoking or reducing the suspension. The decision of the Board of Counsellors shall be final.[158]

At the local level too, rules enable the termination of membership of a mosque or other body, as is the case at Markazi Jamia Masjid Riza and Islamic Centre (Huddersfield): names entered in the register may be removed by the committee/trustees if the person acts in a manner likely to bring the organization into disrepute or breaks its rules.[159]

Conclusion

Jews, Christians and Muslims all have laws applicable to the faithful: their status and their membership of institutional faith communities, their duties and rights (which apply for all three faiths to the whole of life), and their loss of status and institutional faith community membership. In terms of status, in classical Jewish law, a person is a Jew by conversion or if their mother is Jewish; in classical Islamic law, a Muslim is a person born of a Muslim father or by conversion; and a person is incorporated into the Church of Christ by baptism. The level of the religiosity of the modern regulatory instruments of the faith communities studied varies as between the religions, the traditions within each religion and the topics

---

[158] MCB: Con. Arts. 5.1–5.3.
[159] MJMRIC: Con. Art. 5. See also e.g. Aberdeen Mosque and Islamic Centre (AMIC): Con. Art. IV.10: the Executive Committee may dismiss an inactive member who refuses to resign if three of the five trustees and five of the seven Executive Committee members agree to it; see also Art. XI: 'judiciary procedure' for *inter alia* violations of the constitution.

regulated. There is a high level of religiosity, in terms of the translation of classical religious legal categories into the modern formal regulatory instruments, in relation to the duties and rights of the faithful, though by no means evenly so; most of the Muslim instruments studied do not refer to the five pillars of Islam, for example. Indeed, whilst regulatory instruments sometimes explicitly incorporate the terms of classical religious law, more often than not the dominant feature of these instruments is their functional or secular character – their norms on these matters are often presented without explicit reference to traditional distinctly religious categories. There is also little use of religious soft-law to regulate status, admission to or the termination of membership of the religious community – these matters are all dealt with by legislation. However, soft-law is used in some Muslim communities with regard to the rights and duties of the faithful. Moreover, as to applications for membership and its termination, the standards of due process are used which broadly mirror those in civil law. Indeed, there is a high level of legal pluralism, not only as between the traditions within each religion but also as between the religions themselves. Whilst Jews provide in their modern regulatory instruments for conversion (generally by means of a declaration by a religious court), Muslim instruments do not (though guidance suggests that more provision should be made for the care of converts to Islam); and Christian instruments are generally silent on the matter of conversion though they do deal with the reception of non-Christian adults by way of baptism. Apostasy is another example: whilst the classical religious law provides for this, the modern regulatory instruments of the three religions do not generally deal with the matter. Nevertheless, there is sufficient legal evidence to indicate a core of principles of religious law, which may be induced from their religious norms, which all three religions share: religious law should provide for the status of the faithful and their admission to the membership of particular faith communities; for admission to the membership of a faith community, each religion may impose such conditions that are consistent with its interpretation of the relevant classical religious law; and each religion may provide for the loss or termination of such membership, provided the process is prescribed by their law with appeal to a designated authority.

3

The Faith Leaders: Appointment and Functions

The juridical instruments of the religious organisations studied here contain elaborate rules applicable to their spiritual or faith leaders: rabbis, ministers and imams. These exercise special functions which are conceived as legally distinct from the followers of the religion whom they serve. The regulatory instruments deal with the status of and the process by which someone becomes a faith leader, and the qualifications required, as well as the procedure for appointing faith leaders to a position within the religious organisation, and the tenure of and the terms on which the position is held. They also treat their duties and rights, the structures for their accountability (including appraisal or review) and termination of tenure and removal from the position held. This chapter examines these matters principally in relation to faith leaders who serve at the local level of a synagogue, church or mosque, though where appropriate their leadership at regional, national and, sometimes, international level is also discussed. It does so against the backdrop of the basic elements of the treatment of faith leaders in classical religious jurisprudence, and it explores the extent to which these elements surface in the modern legislation and soft-law of the religious organisations studied. This field is also fruitful for the articulation of the common principles of religious law. Where appropriate, brief reference is made to civil law, such as on the employment status of faith leaders (as Jewish and Muslim entities often provide in their legislation for the use of contracts of employment – this is far less so in Christian churches).

The Making of a Faith Leader

All three religions have norms on the making of their faith leaders. In some Jewish traditions and in many Christian traditions, the process is known as ordination. The process involves training, selection and authorisation, which may include the laying-on of hands by a competent religious authority. Islam has broad juristic equivalents,

Rabbinical Ordination

In classical Jewish law, a Rabbi is a teacher of Judaism who is also qualified to render decisions under Jewish law.[1] A Rabbi is strictly lay and not 'a Jewish priest'.[2] After emancipation and the emergence of Jewish communities in western society, a need was increasingly felt for a new type of Rabbi, one able to guide the congregation. Orthodox congregations required the Rabbi to be proficient in general learning, to be cultured and to be able to represent the community to non-Jews. Seminaries were founded for the training of Rabbis in, for example, homiletics, philosophy, ethics and history, as well as Rabbinical work (Rabbinics). It is understood that there is little objection in Jewish law to the appointment of a woman as a Rabbi: whilst there are no female Rabbis in Orthodox Judaism, there are in Reform, Liberal and Conservative Judaism.[3] 'Ordination' is often used for the process by which a Jew is appointed as a teacher of the Torah. Ordination (*semikhah*) is based on the verse: 'And he laid his hands [*va-yismokh*] upon him, and gave him a charge, as the Lord spoke by the hand of Moses' (Numbers 27:23) – here Moses lays his hands on his disciple Joshua who was thus able to speak on behalf of Moses as a spiritual leader. In the early Rabbinic period, only scholars who received ordination in the chain reaching back to Joshua were able to act as judges.[4] After the close of the Talmud, full ordination came to an end. While *semikhah* is still used for the ordination of Rabbis, this does not mean full ordination, but is a convention by which a scholar does not render decisions in Jewish law unless authorised to do so by a competent halakhic authority, a person who is ordained. Modern seminaries train students in many disciplines so that ordination in these seminaries is a matter of attesting to the proficiency of the graduates to

---

[1] The term is derived from *rav*, meaning 'great man' or 'teacher'; e.g. Moses is called Moshe Rabbenu, 'Moses our teacher'; the suffix 'i' in the word 'Rabbi' denotes 'my'.

[2] The word *kohen* (priest, plural *kohanim*) means a descendant of Aaron the priest; the priestly caste officiated in the Temple (offering the sacrifices) and, even after its destruction, a *kohen* continues to have a role. The family name Cohen usually signifies that its members were priests. A *kohen* has the privilege of being the first to be called to the reading of the Torah in the synagogue, the right to recite the priestly blessing there and the right to recite the grace after meals. These rules are followed by Orthodox Jews. Reform Jews reject laws as to *kohanim* as they tend to perpetuate a caste system. Conservative Jews are less categorical but for many, laws on *kohanim* are in abeyance today.

[3] However, a significant minority of Conservative Rabbis are opposed to women Rabbis; see below.

[4] N.S. Hecht *et al.*, eds., *Jewish Law* (1996) 124–127; and B. Jackson, 'Judaism as a religious legal system' (2002) 34 at 39.

carry out their Rabbinical functions, and there is often a service or celebration of ordination.[5]

Rabbinical training is provided at various institutions. For example, the Leo Baeck College, London, offers Rabbinical training for Progressive, Reform and Masorti Judaism. The normal route is the five-year Rabbinic Programme, consisting of academic studies, placements and apprenticeships and vocational modules. The first year of the Graduate Diploma in Hebrew and Jewish Studies includes modules in homiletics, services (e.g. weddings and funerals), listening, service-leading skills, education and reflective skills. The second year covers the Jewish life cycle, *chagrim* (the use of festivals) and education (but not bereavement). The third year, a Postgraduate Diploma, is devoted to Jewish care. For a fourth year, the Master of Arts in Applied Rabbinic Theology involves congregational placement and vocational modules on dying, death and bereavement, mental health, spirituality and social action. The fifth year involves transition to the Rabbinate and leadership and management skills.[6] The general criteria for admission to the Rabbinic Programme include: appropriate motivation; academic ability to complete the study; willingness and potential to grow through the programme; religious commitment and personal integrity; loyalty to the Principles of Progressive Judaism; and intellectual maturity. The specific criteria include: proficiency in Hebrew; a Bachelor of Arts degree of a good standard or the academic equivalent; willingness to spend time in an accredited academic programme in Israel; Jewish status (as recognised by a *Beit Din* of the Liberal, Masorti or Reform Rabbinate or an Orthodox *Beit Din*), which must have been held for a minimum of five years prior to entry; a reference, preferably from their community Rabbi; being at least 21 years of age at the time of application; active participation in Jewish community life prior to application;[7] and proficiency in English.[8]

---

[5] L. Jacobs, *Jewish Religion* (1999) 172.

[6] The College also has (for over 50 years) an Interfaith Programme for Jewish–Christian–Muslim dialogue both for its Rabbinic students and the wider community; for over 40 years it has also co-hosted an annual Jewish–Christian–Muslim Student Conference in Wuppertal, Germany and an Annual Jewish-Christian Bible week in Osnabruck, Germany: www.lbc.ac.uk.

[7] E.g. membership of a Liberal, Reform or Masorti Synagogue; regular attendance at Shabbat, Festival and Holy High Day services; regular home observance of major festivals in the Jewish year; and engagement with educational programmes organised in a local synagogue or wider Jewish community.

[8] 'Prospective students for whom English is not a first language must obtain a minimum level B2 on the Common European Framework of Reference for Languages (CERF).'

All candidates are interviewed over a period of three days: this includes an academic interview, and structured and unstructured group interviews. Psychological assessment of the candidate is also required. International students are provided with additional support, such as with respect to personal, welfare, residency and visas.[9]

In Orthodox Judaism, there is no special ceremony for Rabbinic ordination. The usual practice is for a student, after mastering the texts, to present himself to a Rabbi for examination. If the Rabbi believes that the student is competent, he gives him a document stating that he is qualified to render decisions and that he is now given permission to do so. Ordination takes place after a course of Rabbinic studies in a seminary and the certificate of ordination is given by the principal and other teachers of the seminary. There are two levels of ordination: the most basic (*Yoreh Yoreh*) authorizes the recipient to rule on matters of *kashrut* and similar areas of Jewish law on daily life; the more advanced (*Yoddin Yoddin*) authorizes its recipient to rule as a judge (*Dayan*).[10] Among Orthodox synagogues studied, it is rare for explicit mention to be made of *semikhah*; but at North Hendon Adath Yisroel Synagogue, for example: 'Any person having Semicha from a recognized orthodox rabbinical authority shall be eligible for the position of rabbi.'[11] Conservative and Reform Judaism also practise Rabbinical ordination; however, whilst debate still continues among Conservatives,[12] the Reform movement in general admits of the Rabbinical ordination of women.[13] And the Union of Liberal and Progressive Synagogues, which recognises 'no distinction between persons of priestly descent (*kohanim*) and other

---

[9] The College also offers a Bachelor of Arts (Honours) and a Master of Arts in Jewish Education. All the courses at the college are validated by the University of Winchester.

[10] As some consider that Rabbinic ordination today is a remembrance of *semicha*, so it should seek to fulfil as many of the original requirements as possible, e.g. only one qualified to rule in all areas of Jewish law should be ordained: www.myjewishlearning.com/article/ordination-semihah/.

[11] NHAYS: Con. Art. 14.

[12] Statement of Principles of Conservative Judaism (1988) 39: the 'legitimate differences of opinion'; e.g. 'the Jewish Theological Seminary now ordains women as rabbis and certifies them as cantor'.

[13] See generally W. Jacob and M. Zemer, eds., *Gender Issues in Jewish Law: Essays and Responsa* (New York: Berghahn Books, 2001); S. Greenberg, ed., *The Ordination of Women as Rabbis: Studies and Responsa* (New York: The Jewish Theological Seminary of America, 1988); and H. Ner-David, *Life on the Fringes: A Feminist Journey Toward Traditional Rabbinic Ordination* (Needham, MA: JFL Books, 2000).

Jews', affirms: 'Women and men may lead services, become Rabbis and hold any synagogue office.'[14]

Setting Apart for Ordained Ministry

Historically, persons have been assigned to positions of leadership since the earliest days of the church. However, the effect of ordination in terms of the status, character and sacerdotal authority of ordained ministers, and their hierarchical ranking as priests, bishops and the like, were the focus of much disagreement during and beyond the Reformation in the sixteenth century – and disagreements about the recognition of ordinations as between the separate churches of global Christianity continue to challenge ecumenism today.[15] Nevertheless, the historic churches share a number of principles of law applicable to the making of a minister of religion. In Christianity, persons are designated for ministry in a special rite, for most called ordination. Ordained ministry is divine in origin and persons are set apart for it. A church may distinguish between different types of ordained minister. Candidates for ordination must be called by God and by the church to ordained ministry. Vocation to and suitability for ordination are tested by the church through a process of selection, examination and training by a competent authority. Persons are generally admitted to ordained ministry through ordination. Ordination is administered by the competent authority by means of the laying-on of hands and invocation of the Holy Spirit.[16] These principles derive from similarities between the laws of the churches studied.

For the Roman Catholic Church, ordination is a sacrament: 'By divine institution some among Christ's faithful are, through the sacrament of order, marked with an indelible character and are thus constituted sacred ministers; thereby they are consecrated and deputed so that, each according to his own grade, they fulfil, in the person of Christ the Head, the offices of teaching, sanctifying and ruling, and so they nourish the people of God'; the orders are the episcopate, the priesthood and the diaconate.[17] The Church has the duty and right to train persons for sacred ministries and the whole Christian community must foster

---

[14] ULPS: *Affirmations* (2006) Arts. 30 and 32.
[15] See N. Doe, *Christian Law* (2013) Chapter 3.
[16] Christian Law Panel of Experts, *Principles of Christian Law* (2016) III.1.
[17] CIC: cc. 1008–1009; c. 207: clerics; c. 266: by admission to the diaconate, a person becomes a cleric.

vocations. Only men are ordained; a candidate must complete the required probation, possess the requisite qualities and be free of any irregularity or impediment – there is no right to ordination. The minimum interval between diaconate and priesthood is six months, and the right to determine the suitability for ordination rests with the bishop. Baptism and confirmation are required as are sound faith, the right intention, requisite knowledge, a good reputation, moral probity, proven virtue and the physical and psychological qualities appropriate to the order received. The age for ordination is 25 for the priesthood and 23 for the diaconate. Marriage is an impediment to ordination, but there are exceptions. A deacon must make a profession of faith and take the oath of fidelity to the Pontiff. Ordinarily, ordination is celebrated during Mass, on Sunday or holyday of obligation, and in the cathedral. The minister is a consecrated bishop. Orders are conferred by the laying-on of hands and the prayer of consecration, which the liturgical books prescribe for each grade; it is absolutely wrong to compel a man to receive orders.[18]

Similarly, for Anglicanism, the holy orders are bishops, priests and deacons – the 'threefold ordained ministry'.[19] No person is to be a priest or deacon unless called, tried, examined and admitted according to the rite of ordination, and the diocesan bishop has a special responsibility, assisted by the faithful, to provide sufficient priests and deacons and to foster vocations to ordained ministry; the normal age for the diaconate is 23 and that for the priesthood 24.[20] There is no right to ordination: baptism and confirmation are essential, and authority to determine suitability of a candidate rests with the bishop, who must be satisfied the candidate has the necessary spiritual, moral, physical and mental qualities – both men and women may be ordained to the extent permitted by law. A candidate must assent to church doctrine, to use only lawful forms of service, to obey the lawful and honest directions of the bishop and to comply with the law.[21] Progression from diaconate to priesthood is not automatic: normally, a deacon may not be ordained priest for at least one year, unless the bishop has good cause to ordain earlier; laws provide for training, and the production of prescribed documents prior to ordination. The ordination must be in accordance with the ordinal or

---

[18] CIC: cc. 1008–1054.
[19] PCLCCAC: Principle 31. See e.g. Church of England: Can. C1.1; Church in Wales: Book of Common Prayer 1984, v.
[20] PCLCCAC: Principle 32.1–2. See e.g. Scottish Episcopal Church: Can. 11.5.
[21] PCLCCAC: Principle 32.12. See e.g. Church in Wales: Con. VII.66.

other authorised form of service, and it must be administered episcopally under the authority of the diocesan bishop. Valid ordination consists in fulfilment of what the church universal intends with the free consent of the candidate through the imposition of hands by a validly consecrated bishop with the invocation of the Holy Spirit to give grace for the work of a priest/deacon, whichever particular order is bestowed. Ordination cannot be repeated; orders are indelible.[22]

Within the Protestant traditions, for Methodists ordained ministry is also considered divine in origin.[23] Vocation is essential.[24] Candidates must have the necessary qualities: they must be a church member, of the requisite age, and accept the doctrinal standards of the church.[25] There is a rigorous selection process and a period of probation;[26] fundamental to the whole process is the principle that: 'a Minister is constituted by the Call of God, the consent of the members of the Church, the election of the Conference, and the ordination to the office and work of a Minister in the Church of God by prayer and the laying on of hands'.[27] Ordination occurs at the annual Conference: 'Each ordinand shall be ordained by the laying-on of hands with prayer by the [Conference] President or a deputy, assisted by two other ministers ... one of whom may be nominated by the ordinand.'[28] But ordination cannot be repeated.[29]

Likewise, in Reformed and Presbyterian churches, ordained ministry is seen as instituted by Christ.[30] The local church recommends candidates

---

[22] PCLCCAC: Principle 32. See e.g. Church of England: Can. C7. Ordinations usually take place in a cathedral: see N. Doe, *The Legal Architecture of English Cathedrals* (Abingdon: Routledge, 2017) Chapter 1.

[23] MCI: Con. s. 1: 'For ... leadership ... our Lord appointed the Apostles'; 'others were chosen for various offices ... under the guidance of the Holy Spirit and with the concurrence of the local communities' to 'a separated and ordained ministry'.

[24] MCGB: Constitutional Practice and Discipline, Deed of Union 4: 'the call of God who bestows the gifts of the Spirit the grace and the fruit which indicate those whom He has chosen'.

[25] MCI: Regulations, Discipline and Government, 4B: they must normally be under 55.

[26] MCGB: Constitutional Practice and Discipline, Deed of Union 4, Standing Orders 710–729.

[27] MCI: Con. s. 4.

[28] MCGB: Constitutional Practice and Discipline, Standing Orders 321; see also, Deed of Union 4.

[29] MCGB: Constitutional Practice and Discipline, Standing Orders 700: ministers and deacons are ordained to 'a life-long' ministry.

[30] URC: Manual A.20: 'Christ gives particular gifts for particular ministries and calls some ... to exercise them in offices duly recognised within his Church'; the church 'acknowledges their vocation and gives them authority' to exercise it 'setting them apart

who must be eligible, called, trained and examined and ordained.[31] The 'officers of the Church' generally fall into two categories: elders (teaching and ruling) and deacons,[32] and laws provide for the eligibility of candidates,[33] vocation, examination,[34] training and ordination (which is for life) by the Presbytery.[35] In the Baptist tradition, whether a local church subscribes to ordination is a matter for that church – some ordain, but others do not.[36]

The Requisites for Imamship

For Islam, in which the historical division (*fitna*) between Sunni and Shia originated in conflict over leadership (*imamat*) and authority, the title *imam* (leader or the one who stands in front) is applied by Sunnis to the leader of the congregational prayers in the mosque.[37] Historically, Muslim rulers used to appoint the *imam* for the official function of leading the Friday services in the main mosques of capital cities. Sunni Muslims use the title for their prominent jurists, the founders of their legal schools. In Shia Islam, the imam is understood as the divinely

with prayer'; PCI: Code, para. 18.2: 'The authority of any officer . . . is derived from Christ and belongs not to the officer.'

[31] URC: Manual A.23 and K: candidates must be aged 25–55; the local Church Meeting and District Council recommend prior to a National Assessment Conference – Synod decides and training follows; Sch. B and C: affirmations at ordination/induction (e.g. a promise to fulfil the duties of office).

[32] PCW: Handbook of Rules, 2.6: 'An elder . . . is a man or woman called to serve the local church through a ballot held prayerfully and under the guidance of the Holy Spirit'; PCI: Code, I.IV. para. 16: 'permanent officers are the Presbyters (that is, elders) . . . in Apostolic times . . . also called bishops or overseers, and deacons'; there was 'a plurality of Presbyters . . . hence the titles Teaching Elder and Ruling Elder'.

[33] PCW: Handbook of Rules, 4.21–4.25: 'unimpeachable character'; 'a deep experience of the truth of the Gospel'; ability to lead, heal and deliver 'the Gospel . . . with conviction'.

[34] PCI: Code, para. 17: 'Calling to office . . . is an act of God by . . . Christ in the Holy Spirit. This calling is ordinarily made manifest through the inward testimony of a good conscience on the part of the person, the approval of God's people on the part of the Church and the concurring judgment of a court of the Church'; paras. 177–182: the Presbytery commission examines the candidate as to 'his acquaintance with divine truth, his personal faith, and his sense of the responsibilities and duties of the office'.

[35] PCW: Handbook of Rules, 4.1. 4.2: 'A minister at . . . ordination is set apart'; 3.3.9: the Moderator of the Association 'shall lay his hands on the head of each candidate'.

[36] BUGB: Baptists in Local Ecumenical Partnerships, Sect. 3: 'Deacons are not normally ordained, and ordination, commission or recognition of Elders is a matter for each local church and not normally the wider Baptist community.'

[37] The word *imam* is often used interchangeably with the word *khalifah* (the political head of the Sunni Muslim State): see below Chapter 10.

appointed successor of the Prophet Muhammad and is regarded as infallible with authority to make binding decisions in all aspects of human activity.[38] Today, the imam is the person, invariably male, who leads the congregational prayer. However: 'An imam is not a priest, since there are no intermediaries between God and man in Islam'; and, moreover: 'There is no ordination and no sacraments or rites which only a religiously sanctified person may perform.' Therefore: 'In theory, any respectable man with sufficient religious knowledge can act as Imam, and in cases where for some reason, a particular mosque is left without a formally appointed Imam, a member of the congregation will fulfil the function as and when necessary. However, full-time Imams are usually people who have undertaken religious studies, often at Al-Akzar University in Egypt, or in Saudi Arabia. Imams are normally married with families and in western countries where Muslims are a minority, the Imam frequently finds himself called upon to act as community counsellor, Islamic judge or arbitrator, and welfare officer as well as prayer leader.'[39]

The modern regulatory instruments of Muslim organisations do not generally set out the requirements to become an imam.[40] However, the Central Mosque, for example, presents various ways to determine who should function as an imam. First, on the basis of various *hadith*: one who is the most *aqra* (the one who reads the most) has 'the right to be the Imam'; if the candidates are equal on this ground, then the one who has the most knowledge of Sunnah should be the imam; if they are again equal, then the one who made *hijrah* (migration) first should be the imam; and, finally, if they are still equal, then the oldest should be the imam. Secondly, based on opinions of the *fuqaha* (jurists), a person who

---

[38] For the historical qualities required to be an imam, see e.g. *The Pillars of Islam: D'a'im al-Islam of al-Qadi al-Nu'man*, Vol. I, *Ibadat: Acts of Devotion and Religious Observances*, translated by A.A.A. Fyzee, and revised and annotated by I.K.H. Poonawala (Oxford: Oxford University Press, 2002) 190–193.

[39] J. Hussain, *Islamic Law* (1999) 14; see also M. Rohe, *Islamic Law* (2014) 30ff. Traditionally, training involved use of a *mukhtasar*, a handbook of legal material.

[40] M. Naqshbandi, *Islam and Muslims in Britain* (2012): Guide: 4.6.1: in the informal masjids set up in houses, and before the size of the congregation has grown sufficiently to employ an imam, the imam will be chosen from among those present at the time of each *salaah*, based on his knowledge of recitation of sufficient verses of the Qur'an and his reputation for piety. However, for the religious education of children or authoritative sermons on Fridays, when able to afford it, most will seek to employ a full-time imam who meets their financial, ethnic and doctrinal constraints. Usually, this means bringing someone from overseas.

is the most *aqra* is superior to the one who is *afqa* (the most knowledge-able of Sunnah) (Hanafi and Hanbali school); but there is also the opinion that *afqa* is better than *aqra* (Shafa'e and Malik). Thirdly, based on *fatawa* of Hanafi scholars of Deoband, *imamat* (leadership) is the right of the Muslim who is superior in knowledge. In any event: 'Allah does not accept the prayer (*Namaz*) of the person who performs Imamat of people who do not like him; the person who comes for prayer when the time is finishing; and the person who frees a slave and then enslaves him again.' Fourthly, however, the opinion of *Muhaditheen* (experts in the *hadith*) is that whether a candidate is liked or not is immaterial to becoming an imam. Further, it is considered reprehensible (*makruh*) to be led by one who is a sinner (*faasiq*).[41]

As to training *imams*,[42] partnerships between Muslim colleges and public universities have recently been encouraged by secular govern-ment,[43] and a practice has developed of courses at them to be accredited by secular institutions of higher education.[44] For example, the Muslim College, London, is 'a post-graduate Islamic seminary ... geared towards engagement with wider society by providing comprehensive studies of Islam'. The College offers an Imamship Programme to enable

---

[41] Model Constitution of an Islamic Organisation: www.central-mosque.com/fiqh/WhoShouldBeImaam.htm; it is also discussed as to whether it may also be considered obligatory (*wajib*) to be led by one who is a sinner.

[42] M. Naqshbandi, *Islam and Muslims in Britain* (2012): Guide: 4.6.3: the main groups (Sunni Deobandi, Bareilvi, and Mawdudi, and Shia sects) generally have sufficient funds to train imams in Britain, but graduates have only emerged very recently – the smaller ethnic divisions do not.

[43] M. Mukadam and A. Scott-Baumann, commissioned by the Department for Commu-nities and Local Government, *The Training and Development of Muslim Faith Leaders: Current Practice and Future Possibilities* (2010): this recommends the development of greater provision for training in order to improve mutual trust and confidence in wider society.

[44] See R. Jarrar and L. Collard, *A Model for Collaboration in Designing and Delivering Islamic Studies Modules between a HE Institution and a Muslim Community College* (University of Westminster, 2012): this includes a model Memorandum of Understand-ing. In the academic year 2011/12, the following Muslim colleges claimed to be accredited by HEIs: Al-Maktoum College of Higher Education in Dundee (accredited by Aberdeen University), the Islamic College in London (accredited by Middlesex University) and Markfield Institute of Higher Education in Leicester (accredited by the University of Gloucestershire). HEI partners often require the Muslim college to pay large sums for accreditation. Universities may also have centres to study Islam: e.g. Cardiff University's Centre for the Study of Islam in the UK, which promotes scholarly and public under-standing of Islam and the life of Muslim communities in the UK from inter-disciplinary perspectives (e.g. sociological and anthropological).

participants 'to become receptive to the needs of individuals and the congregation they are serving, maintain a high degree of confidence, and develop pastoral skills for the service of the British community'. The scheme delivers 'a comprehensive and holistic training programme that will grant participants all the skills required in Britain's charities, hospitals, prisons, hospices, universities and mosques fully engaging them with all other departments in the organization'. The curriculum includes: British culture and history; introduction to the major issues of Muslim concerns in the light of Fiqh; introduction to the history of Islam and Muslims in Britain; perceptions of Muslims in the West; Islam in the media; major Muslim groups and organisations in Britain; Islam and citizenship; defence forces and imams; Madrassas/school management; mosque management; youth participation; Charity Commission (and its relationship with Muslim organisations); fund-raising; dispute resolution; marriage and divorce: rules and regulations; the national health service and imams (e.g. the importance of hygiene in Islam); education in Britain; sex education; interfaith in the United Kingdom; Dawah work in the United Kingdom; public speaking; British laws affecting Muslims, mosques and Islamic organisations; the prison service and imams; Muslim women in Britain; spirituality, ethics and community building; mental health and bereavement care; immigration laws and imams; Islam and racism; local councils and working with the Muslim community; and counselling and mediation.[45]

Similarly, at the Islamic College, London, the Hawaza Programme provides students with 'a platform for a career as an Islamic lecturer and researcher or as a minister of religion'; it consists of a Bachelor of Arts in Hawaza Studies and Complementary Hawaza Studies. The bachelor's programme 'is consistent with the subjects taught in traditional centres of Hawaza studies such as Qum and Najaf, and incorporates some additional modules that suit the needs of Muslims living in the West'. The first year modules are: Islamic laws; Arabic; logic; research methodology for Hawaza studies; Islamic theology; formative period of the Shi'a; and Qur'anic sciences and approaches to exegesis. These modules are all compulsory. Second-year compulsory modules are: principles of jurisprudence; demonstrative jurisprudence; Islamic ethics; and Hadith studies. Optional modules include: Arabic rhetoric; current issues

---

[45] See: www.muslimcollege.ac.uk. The College also runs an International Programme attended by mature government officers from the Department of Islamic Development, Malaysia.

in Muslim societies; Muslims in the West; and Abrahamic faiths. The compulsory third-year modules are: principles of jurisprudence; demonstrative jurisprudence; Islamic philosophy; Islam and mysticism. Options include: jurisprudential maxims; principles of Qur'anic exegesis; Muslim social and political thought; and Islamic education and teacher training. The Complementary Hawaza Studies programme covers, for example, Islamic law, recitation of the Qur'an, Shi'a Islam, women in Islam, Qur'anic exegesis, and Islamic sects and schools of thought.[46]

The Appointment of Faith Leaders

All the religious organisations studied here have norms on the appointment of faith leaders. Within Judaism and Islam, generally the appointment is made at local level, though the candidate may have to satisfy norms fixed beyond the local setting. In Christianity, since organisational structures are more hierarchical, generally appointment is a partnership of local and wider church units and authorities. The employment status of faith leaders in civil law has been much litigated recently.

The Appointment of a Rabbi

The State courts have recently recognised that: 'It is normal for rabbis to be employed by a particular synagogue',[47] which means that their contracts of employment may be enforced by the civil courts. This arrangement is facilitated by legislation across the various Jewish traditions in Britain. First, in the (Orthodox) United Synagogue, the Chief Rabbi is 'the religious authority of the United Hebrew Congregations of the Commonwealth'.[48] The United Synagogue may support and maintain the Chief Rabbi, in conjunction with other Jewish bodies.[49] At the

---

[46] See: www.islamic-college.ac.uk. Also, the Hijaz College Islamic University (Nuneaton) offers a Diploma in Islamic Law and the London University external LLB: www.hijazcollege.com/.

[47] *President of the Methodist Conference* v. *Preston* [2013] UKSC 29 at para. 36 (*per* Lady Hale).

[48] US: Statutes 2. The office of Chief Rabbi was introduced in 1704; http://chiefrabbi.org/: 'Responsibility for the religious direction and guidance of the United Synagogue is vested in the Chief Rabbi.'

[49] US: Statutes 5.6: it may also support such other communal bodies or organisations as it determines.

local level, 'Rabbi' means 'the Senior Rabbi or Minister of the Synagogue';[50] and: 'So far as necessary and affordable for the proper discharge of the objects of the Synagogue there shall be a Rabbi of the Synagogue who shall be an employee of the United Synagogue', appointed in accordance with the Bye-Laws.[51] The Rabbi of the synagogue must be appointed by the United Synagogue in consultation with its Local Honorary Officers, Board of Management and members of the synagogue; for that purpose, whenever a vacancy occurs in the office of Rabbi of the synagogue, the Local Honorary Officers must notify the United Synagogue, and with the United Synagogue, prepare a list of candidates from among whom a short list is drawn up by the Selection Committee; all short-listed candidates must be interviewed by a Selection Committee appointed by the Local Honorary Officers. The Selection Committee consists of such persons, and wherever possible at least one must be female, as the Local Honorary Officers may determine. However, at least two members of the Selection Committee must be from the Board of Management of the member synagogue. The Selection Committee may co-opt non-voting advisors. It must report to the Board of Management after the interviews and a candidate is selected by a resolution of the Board passed by at least 75 per cent of its members participating in a poll for that purpose. Minutes or a copy of the resolution must be sent to the nationwide Honorary Officers. The voting at the Selection Committee must be conducted by secret ballot, and it must not include any postal or proxy voting. The candidate chosen must be appointed as Rabbi of the synagogue.[52]

At (Orthodox) North Hendon Adath Yisroel Synagogue, for example: 'The conditions of employment, including remuneration and other conditions shall be incorporated in an Agreement ... signed by the Honorary Officers and the Rabbi'; it should be for a limited period, normally five years, but not exceed ten years, and subject to a review at its termination. The Selection Committee advises on the terms of the agreement.[53]

---

[50] US: Bye-Laws 1.   [51] US: Bye-Laws 16.1.   [52] US: Bye-Laws 16.
[53] NHAYS: Con. Art. 14. See also NHC: Con. Arts. 5.3–5.5: 'A candidate for ministerial office or for a vacancy as Reader shall be appointed to that office by the Committee ... The duties of the Minister or Reader shall be outlined by written agreement concluded when the position is formally offered and formally accepted. The engagement, termination of engagement and variation of duties of other staff or provider of services shall be determined by the Committee.'

Secondly, a synagogue constitution in the United Synagogue of Conservative Judaism should provide for the election of 'an ordained rabbi'. Candidates must be solicited in accordance with the rules of the Joint Commission on Rabbinic Placement (of the Jewish Theological Seminary, the Rabbinical Assembly and the United Synagogue of Conservative Judaism). The Rabbi must be elected by the Board or congregation at a meeting called for that purpose, on the recommendation of the Board (of Trustees). In this process, the congregation must use the United Synagogue of Conservative Judaism Guide to Contractual Relations and Standards for Congregational Practice.[54] Moreover: 'Congregations should enter into reasonable written contracts with staff, enforceable under local law, in terms consistent with the highest ethical and moral standards of Jewish practice and tradition.' Congregations should conduct annual evaluations of professional staff, using the best available instruments and techniques. Congregations, clergy and professionals should agree to and seek the resolution of all disputes through the mediation and arbitration processes of the United Synagogue Committee on Congregational Standards. Indeed: 'An arbitration clause providing for binding dispute resolution by the United Synagogue Committee on Congregational Standards should be included in all contracts with clergy and professional staff.'[55] Provision may also exist to appoint to the office of synagogue cantor (or *hazzan*).[56]

In a similar vein, the appointment of a Rabbi within the World Council of Conservative-Masorti Judaism is not simply a matter for a synagogue at local level: 'It is the policy ... that its member congregations and institutions adhere to the (Rabbinic) Placement Policy and Guidelines established by the International Rabbinic Assembly when

---

[54] USCJ: A Guide to Writing and Revising Congregational Constitutions and Bylaws (2010) Art. X; see also USCJ: Standards for Congregational Practice (1957, as amended 2017): Standard I.

[55] USCJ: Standards for Congregational Practice (2017): Standard IX. Congregations should refer to 'Crafting a Contract between the Synagogue and the Professional: Protecting the Partnership while Providing for Separation'; 'Model Rabbinic Engagement Agreement – Synagogue with Rabbi'; and 'Putting the Partnership under the Microscope: The Process of Review and Assessment of a Congregation's Professionals and Leadership'.

[56] USCJ: A Guide to Writing and Revising Congregational Constitutions and Bylaws (2010) Art. XI: candidates for the office are elected by a congregation in accordance with the rules of the Commission on Cantorial Placement (of the Cantors Assembly); the *hazzan* acts as the *ba'al nusach* (religious musical expert) and principal *sheliach tzibbur*, in consultation with the Rabbi and religious committee, and with due deference to the Rabbi's authority as *mara d'atra* of the congregation.

seeking to engage rabbis'; and: 'all rabbinic placements are coordinated through the Director of Placement and such regional commissions as the International Rabbinical Assembly has established'; concerns about the policy should be sent to the Executive Operations Committee for the International Rabbinical Assembly to review.[57]

Thirdly, within the Movement for Reform Judaism (which has a Senior Rabbi),[58] the appointment is made locally. At Sukkat Shalom Reform Synagogue (Wanstead): 'A resolution passed at a General Meeting shall be required authorising the engagement of a Rabbi. The Council shall be empowered to offer a Contract of Employment to any such Rabbi';[59] and at Brighton and Hove Reform Synagogue, there may be as many Rabbis as may be decided by the Members in an Annual General Meeting. A vacancy must be advertised in appropriate journals. Applications should be received by a specially appointed sub-committee whose recommendation should go before the Charity Trustees and then before the membership at a General Meeting. The Rabbi is appointed by a two-third majority of the members at a General Meeting and on appointment must make a written declaration of adherence to the synagogue 'laws'.[60]

Fourthly, within the Union of Liberal and Progressive Synagogues, which likewise has a Senior Rabbi,[61] the Union itself guides and a regional community decides on the appointment of its own faith leader – as at Wessex Liberal Jewish Community: 'Any decision to appoint a Minister as an employee ... must be approved by at least two-thirds of the general membership'; their 'recruitment and terms of employment ... will be decided by [its] Council, with appropriate guidance from Liberal Judaism'.[62]

The constitutions of synagogues also provide for the termination of the appointment of the Rabbi.[63] For example, at North Hendon Adath Yisroel Synagogue (Orthodox): 'The contract of any salaried officials may be suspended or terminated by the Board of Management in the event of gross misconduct, persistent neglect of duties or failure to satisfactorily carry out duties allocated to him subject to contract and

[57] WCCMJ: By-Laws VII: Joint Commissions.
[58] MRJ: www.reformjudaism.org.uk/leadership/.   [59] SSRS: Con. Art. 6.
[60] BHRS: Con. Art. 21(1)–(2).
[61] ULPS: www.liberaljudaism.org/who-we-are/whos-who/.
[62] WLJC: Con. Arts. 16.1–16.2. See also ELS: Con. Art. 8(3): 'The Minister of the Congregation'.
[63] NHIC. Con. Art. 5.

to statute.'[64] Similarly, at Brighton and Hove Reform Synagogue the Rabbi may be dismissed from office by a vote taken by a paper ballot of not less than two-thirds of the members present and voting at a General Meeting convened for the purpose.[65]

The dismissal of an Orthodox Rabbi by the Chief Rabbi was considered by the civil courts in R v. *Chief Rabbi, ex parte Wachmann*. The Rabbi sought judicial review of the declaration of the Chief Rabbi, following an investigation into allegations of adultery with members of his congregation, that he was religiously and morally unfit to occupy his position. It was held that for judicial review to be available against the decision of the Chief Rabbi: 'there must be not merely a public but potentially a governmental interest in the decision-making power in question'; and: 'where non-governmental bodies have ... been held reviewable, they have generally been operating as an integral part of a regulatory system which, although it is itself non-statutory, is nevertheless supported by statutory powers ... clearly indicative of government concern'. Further: 'the court would never be prepared to rule on questions of Jewish law' and it would not 'be easy to separate out procedural complaints from consideration of substantive principles of Jewish law which may underlie them'. Importantly: 'this court is hardly in a position to regulate what is essentially a religious function – the determination whether someone is morally and religiously fit to carry out the spiritual and pastoral duties of his office'. As a matter of general principle: 'The Court must inevitably be wary of entering so self-evidently sensitive an area, straying across the well-recognised divide between church and state'; therefore: 'if judicial review lies here, then one way or another this secular court must inevitably be drawn into adjudicating upon matters intimate to a religious community' – this it was not prepared to do.[66]

---

[64] NHAYS: Art. 17. See also NHC: Con. Arts. 5.3–5.5: 'Termination of an appointment as Minister or Reader shall be by the Committee'.

[65] BHRS: Con. Art. 21(3)–(11): communication with the media may be initiated only by agreement with the Chairman.

[66] [1992] 1 WLR 1036. On the other hand, it is suggested that under civil law, a dismissal which violates the terms of a contract of employment with a Rabbi (including Rabbis within the United Synagogue, whose contracts are recognised in the United Synagogue Bye-Laws, themselves statutory in the sense that they function on the basis of the United Synagogues Act 1870) would be reviewable judicially by a civil court on the basis of private law (as opposed to public law as in *Wachmann*).

Appointment to Ecclesiastical Office

In Christianity, as to the historic churches, ministers are assigned to ecclesiastical offices. An ecclesiastical office: is a position constituted by law; exists independently of the person who occupies it; enables the discharge of functions of the particular ministry attaching to it; may be held by a person(s) with such qualifications as are prescribed by law; and is filled by a variety of means, often by appointment or election. The jurisdiction or authority which attaches to an office is determined by or under law. Authority attaching to an office may be delegated to the extent provided by law. The authority to exercise ecclesiastical office ceases upon lawful dissolution of the office, expiration of the stated term of office, attainment of the prescribed age limit or the death, resignation, transfer, retirement or removal of the office holder.[67]

These principles are derived from the similarities which emerge from a comparison of the regulatory systems of the churches studied. In the Roman Catholic Church, only clerics may obtain offices which require the power of order and governance. Clerics have no right to an ecclesiastical office, but, unless lawfully excused, must accept and faithfully discharge the office committed to them by their bishop.[68] Every cleric must be incardinated in (or tied to) a particular church (generally a diocese).[69] There are extensive provisions on the free conferral of ecclesiastical offices.[70] Appointment to the office of parish priest belongs to the diocesan bishop who may confer it on whomsoever he wishes, unless someone else has a right of presentation or election. To assess the suitability of a priest for office, the bishop must consult the vicar forane (or dean), conduct suitable enquiries and, if appropriate, seek the views of priests and laity.[71] Appointment is for an indeterminate period, but a

---

[67] Christian Law Panel of Experts, *Principles of Christian Law* (2016) III.2. See also *President of the Methodist Conference* v. *Preston* [2013] UKSC 29: the Supreme Court decided that, on the facts, a Methodist Minister was not an employee but was an office holder.

[68] CIC: c. 274; see also cc. 129, 228.

[69] CIC: cc. 265–272; c. 269: the diocesan bishop is not to incardinate a cleric unless e.g. 'the need or advantage of his particular Church requires it'; c. 270: excardination may be granted for a 'just reason'.

[70] CIC: cc. 145–196; c. 147: free conferral; c. 149: the cleric 'must be in communion with the Church, and be suitable, that is, possessed of . . . qualities . . . required for that office by universal or particular law'; simony invalidates tenure; c. 150: only priests have the cure of souls; c. 153: vacancy; c. 156: written appointment.

[71] CIC: cc. 523–524; c. 521: to be a parish priest, the candidate must be outstanding in sound doctrine and uprightness of character, endowed with zeal for souls and other virtues

specified period may be permitted by the Bishops' Conference.[72] The bishop may appoint an assistant priest, if he judges this to be opportune, after consulting the parish priest and vicar forane.[73]

In Anglican churches, in order to exercise public ordained ministry within a diocese, authorisation must be obtained from the diocesan bishop.[74] The bishop may confer authority to the minister publicly by means of appointment to a particular office (such as that of a parish priest), licence, written permission or such other process prescribed by law. The laity, or their representatives, may participate in the appointment of clergy to an office or other public ministry in such a manner, and to such an extent, as may be prescribed by law. Authorisation to exercise public ministry in a diocese may be refused only on grounds provided for in the law. No bishop, priest or deacon coming from another diocese may exercise public ministry in the host diocese without prior permission from the host diocesan bishop. Before permitted by the bishop to minister in the diocese, clergy from another diocese must produce to the host bishop such evidence of ordination and good standing as is lawfully required.[75]

On the Protestant side, there are equally elaborate provisions for the appointment of ordained ministers to office. For example, in the Methodist Church in Great Britain, ministers are stationed by the (national) Conference: 'stations' are 'the comprehensive list adopted annually by the Conference for the ensuing connexional year of ministers, deacons, probationers, arranged according to Circuits, institutions, offices and other spheres of work to which they are appointed or in which they are authorised to serve'.[76] A connexional Stationing Committee is appointed annually by the Conference to recommend to the Conference the stations, for the ensuing year, of ministers, deacons and

---

[72] CIC: cc. 520–522; c. 527: the priest is put in 'canonical possession' of the parish under procedures of particular law or lawful custom but the ordinary may dispense from this.

[73] CIC: c. 547; c. 548: the vicar forane is also known as the dean or archpriest.

[74] PCLCCAC: Principle 42.1; 34.1: charge of a parish; 34.2: assistant clergy.

[75] PCLCCAC: Principle 42.1–6. See e.g. Church of England: Can. C10 and Patronage (Benefices) Measure 1986: appointment is by (1) presentation/nomination by the patron (e.g. bishop) consulting parish representatives (with appeal against refusal to the archbishop); (2) admission/institution by the bishop; and (3) induction.

[76] MCGB: Constitutional Practice and Discipline, Deed of Union 1(xxxi), Standing Orders 770–783; Deed of Union 1xxviii: 'Probationer means a person ... admitted by the Conference ... for the ministry or diaconate and is stationed by [it] but ... not yet ... admitted into full connexion.'

probationers.[77] Ministers in 'active work exercise their ministry ... primarily in the setting in which they are stationed' (i.e. a pastoral charge in a circuit); probationers serve in a circuit under the oversight of a Circuit Superintendent and do not have a pastoral charge in a circuit.[78] Similar rules apply to deacons.[79] The United Reformed Church has equivalent rules,[80] as do Presbyterians: for instance, in the Presbyterian Church of Wales: 'It is the responsibility of the elders to inform Presbytery that a church/pastorate wishes to call a minister'; the Presbytery will 'take the voice of the churches' in a general meeting and if the vote is favourable, the Presbytery will seek the permission of the Association for the Presbytery to visit the pastorate and establish a Pastorate Committee to consider candidates whose names are submitted to the church for election and then the Presbytery confirms the election – all the arrangements regarding the ministry are to be made with the consent of the Presbytery. The minister must retire at 67, and a resignation is to be tendered to the Presbytery.[81] In the Baptist tradition, it is the local church that extends a call to a minister or pastor, and receives their resignation or terminates their ministry.[82]

Christians also provide for the removal of ministers. In the Roman Catholic Church, office is lost on the expiry of a predetermined time,

---

[77] MCGB: Constitutional Practice and Discipline, Standing Orders 322–323: it also advises on stationing policy; Standing Orders 323: the Stationing Advisory Committee advises e.g. on movement of ministers. See also Guidance on the Stationing of Ministers and Deacons: MCGB: Constitutional Practice and Discipline, Bk. VI, Pt. 2, S. 1.

[78] MCGB: Constitutional Practice and Discipline, Standing Orders 700: this is the case whether the minister is full-time or part-time.

[79] MCGB: Constitutional Practice and Discipline, Standing Orders 701: deacons in active work exercise ministry primarily where they are appointed.

[80] URC: Manual L: a minister is called to a pastorate if 'concurred with' by the District Council; A.23: elders who are elected by the church meeting are inducted for such period as the church determines.

[81] PCW: Handbook of Rules, 4.3–4.8; also: 2.6: an elder is called through a ballot held, 'prayerfully and under the guidance of the Holy Spirit', every seven years but a Presbytery may authorise one earlier; an elder wishing to resign informs the minister and elders and the Presbytery decides.

[82] BUGB: Baptists in Local Ecumenical Partnerships, s. 2: 'ministers ... are usually called to a pastorate without a fixed term and move in response to a call to another pastorate' with advice from the Regional Minister; Model Trusts for Churches 2003, 6.1: a church appoints its own ministers 'who have been baptised, who affirm the Declaration of Belief, who hold to the authority of the Holy Scriptures', 'who ... practise ... baptism and whose name appears in the register' of ministers; the minister may be removed by the church.

reaching the age limit defined by law, resignation, transfer, removal and deprivation.[83] The parish priest must offer resignation at 75.[84] Provision is made to relinquish the clerical state for the lay state.[85] In Anglicanism, the withdrawal or termination of authority to exercise public ministry must be carried out in accordance with grounds and process prescribed by law.[86] Clergy may tender a resignation to the bishop but must resign or may be removed if their incapacity or unfitness to discharge ministry is lawfully established. Clergy must retire from office at the age fixed by law but may continue in ministry with the approval of the bishop or other competent authority in the manner and to the extent prescribed by law. A person may voluntarily relinquish the exercise of holy orders. Relinquishment may be reversed in such circumstances as may be allowed under the law. A person may be deposed from holy orders by lawful pronouncement of a competent ecclesiastical authority. Deposition disables the exercise of holy orders, either irreversibly or reversibly, as the case may be, according to the law.[87]

As to Protestant churches – for example, the Methodist Church – a minister or deacon wishing to resign from full connexion must notify the Conference President who refers the notice to an advisory committee for consideration; the minister or deacon is present at the committee. The committee advises the President as to whether the resignation should be accepted and, if so, the date from which it should take effect. The committee also advises the President, Circuit Superintendent and District Chair whether a public announcement should be made and, if so, to whom and in what terms.[88] Reformed churches also provide for resignation, retirement and removal.[89] In the Presbyterian Church of Wales, the minister must retire at 67, and a resignation is tendered to the

---

[83] CIC: cc. 184–189: a person may resign for 'just cause'; resignation from 'grave fear unjustly inflicted' is invalid; c. 189: resignation may be accepted for 'a just and proportionate reason'; cc. 190–191: 'a grave reason' is needed to transfer against the will of the office-holder; cc. 192–195: removal is by a decree for 'grave reason'; c. 194: a person who loses the clerical state is removed from office by law; c. 196: 'Deprivation of office [is] a punishment'; cc. 1740–1752: R. Ombres, 'The removal of parish priests', 1 *Priests & People* (1987) 9–12.

[84] CIC: c. 538.   [85] CIC: c. 293.   [86] PCLCCAC: Principle 42.7.

[87] PCLCCAC: Principle 47. For the laws of the Anglican churches in England, Wales and Scotland, see N. Doe, *Canon Law in the Anglican Communion* (1998) 88–92, 157.

[88] MCGB: Constitutional Practice and Discipline, Standing Orders 760; 761: for reinstatement the person must apply to the President.

[89] URC: Manual A.21 and Sch. C.

Presbytery.[90] Likewise, it is the local Baptist church that receives the resignation of a minister/pastor and terminates their ministry in that church.[91]

The Appointment of an Imam

As to Islam, the norm is for an imam to be appointed at local level by the religious authority competent in the form typically of a committee.[92] The constitutions of some mosques are very brief on the matter, others more detailed. At Markazi Jamia Masjid Riza and Islamic Centre (Huddersfield), for instance, the management committee, with the consent of the trustees, may (if the need arises) appoint an imam based on an 'employment contract' prepared by it and approved by a simple majority of its members. The committee with consent of the trustees may also terminate the contract by a simple majority in accordance with the 'agreed procedures' adopted by it.[93]

The Aberdeen Mosque and Islamic Centre has rather more detailed rules. Together the Board of Trustees and the Executive Committee may appoint an imam for 'a contract-term' of five years, which may be renewed indefinitely by mutual agreement between the imam, Executive Committee and Board of Trustees. Any vacancy in the post of imam should be advertised both nationally and internationally. A panel of four persons conducts a formal interview; it must include the Chair of the Board of Trustees, President and General Secretary of the Executive Committee, and an independent member of the community appointed by the Committee and Board. A candidate for appointment as imam must: be Muslim and over 25; have a formal academic qualification in Islamic Studies; preferably, have memorised the Holy Quran; be highly

---

[90] PCW: Handbook of Rules, 4.3–4.8; also: 2.6: an elder is called through a ballot held, 'prayerfully and under the guidance of the Holy Spirit', every seven years but a Presbytery may authorise one earlier; an elder wishing to resign informs the minister and elders and the Presbytery decides; 4.17: part-time and non-stipendiary ministry.

[91] BUGB: Baptists in Local Ecumenical Partnerships, s. 2: ministers are usually called to a pastorate without a fixed term and move in response to a call to another, with advice from the Regional Minister. ·

[92] M. Naqshbandi, *Islam and Muslims in Britain* (2012): Guide: 4.6.2: in the small number of Arab-run informal *masjids*, the role of imam is honorary, because many of those who attend will be able to act as imam for the prayers, having Arabic as their first language. A dozen or so large Arab-dominated *masjids* (e.g. Regents Park and Aclam Road centres in London) may have Arab mother tongue scholars employed as imams.

[93] MJMRIC: Art. 16.

proficient in the English and Arabic Languages; provide references; have a legal right to be resident in the UK; preferably, has held a similar position in the UK or abroad; and have good communication skills, leadership qualities and good all-around general knowledge.[94] The courts of the State have recognised that an imam may be an employee at civil law and thus may enforce a contract of employment.[95]

The Functions of Faith Leaders

There are key similarities between the three religions as to the functions, duties and rights of faith leaders: preaching, administration of ritual and care of the faithful. Religious organisations in all three religions translate and embellish classical religious concepts into detailed norms of conduct on the roles of Rabbis, ministers and imams. They differ, however, as to arrangements for their accountability in the organisation, the level at which a religious authority (usually regional or local) may exercise their oversight and the provision of schemes for the periodic appraisal of the faith leaders.

The Duties and Rights of Rabbis

In classical Judaism, Rabbis must devote themselves to learning (in the study of the Torah), guiding the community in spiritual affairs and acting as a judge in matters of religious law.[96] There is profound convergence between traditions and movements within Judaism: together with study of the Torah, a Rabbi has to be a teacher, preacher, pastor, counsellor, governor and fund-raiser. First, in the (Orthodox) United Synagogue, the Rabbi of a member synagogue is 'the spiritual head of the Synagogue in connection with the furtherance of its Objects', saving the responsibilities/rights of the nationwide Honorary Officers, Local Honorary Officers or Board of Management 'to duly administer and manage the affairs of the Synagogue in accordance with the Bye-Laws, Statutes and Regulations of

---

[94] AMIC: Con. Art. XIV.1–XIV.4.
[95] *Ur-Rehman* v. *Doncaster Jahia Mosque* [2012] UKEAT 0117–12–1008: it was accepted by both the Employment Tribunal and Employment Appeal Tribunal that the Imam in question was an employee for the purposes of the civil law; see also *Hasan* v. *Redcoat Community Centre* (2013) unreported.
[96] L. Jacobs, *Jewish Religion* (1999) 192.

the United Synagogue'.[97] Moreover: 'The Rabbi of the Synagogue shall carry out and discharge such duties as shall be specified in his Contract of Employment with the United Synagogue'; more particularly, but without prejudice to the contract terms and conditions, the Rabbi has 'the general function and duty to supervise all of the religious services and activities of the Synagogue, including the provision of such educational, social and pastoral and other care to the members ... of the Synagogue and their families'. All such religious and other activities must be conducted in accordance with the objects of the synagogue and the Statutes and Regulations of the United Synagogue. No one other than the Rabbi is entitled to officiate or preach at any religious services held at the synagogue without the consent of the Rabbi under the ultimate authority of the Chief Rabbi.[98] These and other norms, for example, as to termination of office, appear in the constitutions of synagogues.[99]

The Rabbinical Council of the United Synagogue is the professional association of the United Synagogue Rabbinate. Its key objective is to support and promote the well-being and success of Rabbis and their families within their local communities and across the United Synagogue as a whole. As well as representing the interests of Rabbis in conversations with the United Synagogue Trustees and leading head office professional staff, provision exists for the personal and professional development of Rabbis (and support for their families) through a range of activities (e.g. residential conferences). The Council has an organising committee which is elected, meets regularly and consists of an Executive and a Committee; the Executive meets on a regular basis with the Chief Rabbi, Dayanim of the London Beth Din and United Synagogue Chief Executive. The Council is also represented at meetings of the United Synagogue Trustees and offers input to most of its working groups (e.g. Living and Learning, Community Division, and Strategic Review). The Council works with the London School of Jewish Studies (Hendon) to foster 'career-long dynamism, sensitivity, integrity, compassion, effectiveness and professionalism'.[100]

---

[97] US: Bye-Laws 16.1.   [98] US: Bye-Laws 16.2.
[99] NHAYS: Con. Art. 14: 'It shall be the duty of the Rabbi to supervise all religious and ritual activities of the Congregation, including its traditional rites and to deliver discourses, from time to time, in the Synagogue, to take part in ceremonies, celebrations or gatherings which may be held or performed within the Congregation, subject to the terms of the individual Agreement between the Rabbi and the Congregation.'
[100] US, www.theus.org.uk/article/rcus

Secondly, in similar vein, the constitution of a congregation in the United Synagogue of Conservative Judaism should provide that: 'The rabbi shall have the responsibility of teacher and preacher of the congregation ... enjoy the freedom of the pulpit [and] seek the advice and guidance of the board (of Trustees)'; and: 'as *mara d'atra* [decisor of Jewish law] shall be the halakhic authority of the congregation'. In exercising this authority, the Rabbi must give due consideration to the *minhag* (traditions) of the congregation, and the views of its lay leaders and members, as expressed in the communications, meetings, or polls of the membership. If not a member of the Rabbinical Assembly, the Rabbi is expected, nonetheless, to adhere to the standards expected of its members. In addition, the Rabbi is an *ex officio* member, without vote, of all congregation committees. Renewal (or termination) of the contract with the Rabbi must be upon the recommendation of the Board or a committee and voted upon by the congregation at a meeting called for this purpose (and, on termination, the policy agreed by the United Synagogue of Conservative Judaism and the Rabbinical Assembly must be complied with).[101] The Rabbinical Assembly, the international association of Conservative Rabbis, promotes Conservative Judaism, publishes learned texts, prayer books and other Jewish works and administers the Committee on Jewish Law and Standards for the Conservative movement.[102]

Thirdly, and by way of contrast, the Movement for Reform Judaism enumerates a wider range of rabbinical functions within an explicit framework of accountability. On the one hand, in relation to religious practice, the Rabbi of a member synagogue enjoys 'the freedom of being the spiritual leader of the synagogue'; is 'the final authority on all issues of ritual and Halacha'; must in sermons 'have regard to reasonable wishes and requests of the members of the synagogue and its Council'; will, with the Warden, oversee all services and *B'Nei Mitzvot*; will liaise with the parents of the *B'Nei Mitzvot*, *cheder* (or religious school) teachers, tutors of any kind and Warden on a regular basis; is involved in organising *shiva* service cover when required; will liaise with the Chair of House and

---

[101] USCJ: A Guide to Writing and Revising Congregational Constitutions and Bylaws (2010) Art. X. See also Standards for Congregational Practice (2017): with explanations by the Committee on Congregational Standards: Standard I: 'The authority of the rabbi as the spiritual leader and mara d'atra (decisor of Jewish law) of the congregation is a basic tenet of Conservative Judaism.'

[102] The Assembly was established in 1901: www.rabbinicalassembly.org.

Head of Security when wishing, or planning, to use the building for visits etc.; and will help to maintain the *yarhzeit* list in conjunction with the Secretary. On the other hand, in terms of accountability, the Rabbi must undergo a periodic review of his/her performance by a committee appointed by the synagogue Council;[103] meet with the Warden and Chair of Council on a regular basis to discuss all matters relating to his/her position and report to Council on all areas of his/her work on a regular basis; meet with the Religious Activities Committee and the Education Committee regarding his/her religious and educational roles work; consult with the members of Council responsible for care in the community and also discuss membership; and be responsible for developing and maintaining contact with the wider Jewish community and the general community in the area covered by the synagogue. Also, in the wider Jewish world, the Rabbi must be involved with the Assembly of Rabbis of the Movement for Reform Judaism, including the development of liturgy and guidelines for religious practices; if required sit on the Bet Din of the Reform movement; and endeavour to handle correspondence and communications as quickly as possible.[104]

At local level, a particularly full treatment of rabbinical functions is found at Brighton and Hove Reform Synagogue. The duties and terms of remuneration of the Rabbi are prescribed by the Charity Trustees. The religious instruction of children of members is the responsibility of the Rabbi, working with the Charity Trustees and the Cheder Committee. The Rabbi is responsible for the form and content of the services in consultation with the Wardens and Charity Trustees. Religious services must be held on Sabbaths and Holy Days and on such other occasions as the Rabbi may direct, in the synagogue or such other place as the Charity Trustees approve. The Rabbi, with the Wardens and in consultation with the Charity Trustees, is responsible for the ritual used by the synagogue; but if there is no permanent Rabbi, the Wardens and Charity Trustees take responsibility. The Rabbi must not charge any fee for the performance of rabbinical duties for a synagogue member but may accept a donation to synagogue funds for any service he performs for non-

---

[103] The review is based on the contract with the Rabbi and its final form must be presented to and discussed with the Rabbi by the Chair of Council, and a copy is presented to the Council and put on file. The Rabbi must be employed by Council after consultation with the members of the synagogue at a Special General Meeting; see above for the appointment of the Rabbi.

[104] TMRJ: Areas of Responsibility and Codes of Practice Documents: pp. 5–6.

members or which is not part of his prescribed duty. The Rabbi must not officiate in another congregation or accept any appointment which might conflict or interfere with his duties as Rabbi of the synagogue without the prior consent of the Chairman or, if absent, the Vice Chairman.[105]

The Functions of Ordained Ministers

Norms on the functions of Christian leaders of church communities were set out in embryonic form in the New Testament, developed in the early ecumenical councils, systematised in the medieval canon law of the western church and diversified at and beyond the Reformation in the sixteenth century.[106] Today, it is a common principle of Christian law, among the historic churches, that ordained ministers must be duly authorised by their church in order to exercise ministry. Ministers are to preach the Word of God, teach the faith, administer the sacraments and provide pastoral care. They should fashion their ministry after the example of Christ and must lead their private lives in a way that befits their sacred calling. They may engage in such other occupations, including offices held beyond the local church, as are not forbidden by church law or competent authority. Further, ministers are accountable for the exercise of their ministry to the competent church authority in the manner prescribed by law.[107]

Roman Catholic canon law provides a set of duties and rights applicable to all clerics, as well as specific functions applicable to parish clergy. First, since they all work to build up the body of Christ, clerics are united 'in the bond of brotherhood and prayer' and must 'seek to co-operate with one another', promote the mission of the laity, and show reverence and obedience to the Supreme Pontiff and their own Ordinary.[108] All clerics must: seek holiness in their lives; fulfil their pastoral ministry; nourish their own spiritual life with Scripture, Eucharist, prayer and spiritual retreats; observe 'perfect and perpetual continence' and celibacy; refrain from associations inconsistent with the clerical state; hold church doctrine; reside in their diocese unless permitted otherwise by the

---

[105] BHRS: Con. Art. 21(3)–(11): communication with the media may be initiated only by agreement with the Chairman.

[106] See N. Doe, *Christian Law* (2013) Chapter 3.

[107] Christian Law Panel of Experts, *Principles of Christian Law* (2016) III.3.

[108] CIC: cc. 273, 275; c. 274: only clerics exercise governance; c. 384: the bishop is to care for priests, defend their rights, ensure that they fulfil their duties and have an adequate means of livelihood.

Ordinary; wear suitable ecclesiastical dress; and do their utmost to foster peace based on justice – they are forbidden everything 'unbecoming to their state' (e.g. to assume public office involving the exercise of civil power, and practise commerce or trade except with lawful permission).[109] Secondly, deacons are the ordinary ministers of baptism, have various roles at the Eucharist, may celebrate marriages if delegated and may act as minister of the Word.[110] Thirdly, at parish level, the 'care of souls' (cura animarum) is reserved to priests, the co-operators of the bishops; the functions of a parish priest include: administration of baptism, assistance at marriages, conducting funerals, celebrating the Eucharist on Sundays and holydays, instructing and prudently correcting the faithful, preaching and visiting the faithful entrusted to his care.[111] The parish priest also acts on behalf of the parish, must ensure that parish goods are administered in accordance with law, and must reside in the parochial house (or elsewhere if the bishop permits).[112] As well as parish clergy, within the diocese the bishop appoints a Vicar General, Episcopal Vicars and Vicars Forane to assist in the governance of the diocese and oversight of clergy.[113]

Anglicanism is similar: ministry is service, a gift of God, and the public ministry of ordained persons is exercised under Episcopal authority in various forms including parish ministry,[114] to which, like all offices, prescribed functions attach.[115] First, all clergy: (1) should fashion themselves after the example of Christ and should not engage in any occupations, habits or recreations inconsistent with their sacred calling but lead a disciplined way of life appropriate to their clerical state; (2) must be

---

[109] CIC: c. 276: holiness, etc.; c. 277: continence and celibacy; c. 278: the right of association; c. 279: studies; c. 280: common life; c. 281: remuneration; c. 282: a simple way of life; c. 283: residence; c. 284: dress; c. 285: conduct inconsistent with their state; c. 286: commerce; c. 287: justice.

[110] See e.g. CIC: c. 757: ministry of the Word; c. 288: permanent deacons.

[111] CIC: cc. 149–150: cures; c. 757: co-operators; c. 527: possession; cc. 528–530: rights and duties.

[112] CIC: c. 532: temporal goods; c. 533: residence; c. 535: registers; cc. 540–552: cases of absence.

[113] CIC: cc. 475–481: a Vicar General helps to govern the diocese; an Episcopal Vicar assists in a specific area or activity; cc. 553–555: a Vicar Forane oversees clergy, visits parishes and oversees property in a district.

[114] PCLCCAC: Principle 28: the exercise of ministry is structured, authorised, representative and accountable.

[115] PCLCCAC: Principle 29; 29.1: ecclesiastical offices include the offices of primate, archbishop, bishop, dean, archdeacon and parish priest; an ecclesiastical office is 'a stable substantive position constituted by law.'

diligent in liturgical life, particularly the Eucharist, personal prayer, self-examination and study, especially Holy Scripture; (3) must not engage in any secular employment or other occupation without permission from the diocesan bishop; (4) must reside within the territory of the ecclesiastical unit to which they are assigned unless the bishop permits otherwise; (5) are subject to the jurisdiction of their diocesan bishop and must comply with that bishop's lawful and honest directions; and (6) should dress in a manner suitable to the performance of their ministry as may be a sign and mark of their calling both to those within their charge and to society at large.[116] Secondly, a deacon must care for people in need and assist the priest (subject to the priest's direction), but must not exercise functions reserved to the order of priests.[117] Thirdly, working with the bishop, a priest is to: (1) proclaim the Gospel through preaching and teaching, administer the sacraments and provide pastoral care; (2) preside at the Eucharist, pronounce the absolution; (3) visit those within their charge for spiritual consultation and advice, prepare candidates for baptism, confirmation and reception and instruct children within their care in the Christian faith.[118] Fourthly, a parish priest has the primary authority and responsibility for the care of souls exercised under the general authority, oversight and pastoral direction of the diocesan bishop.[119] Fifthly, in the exercise of their ministry, clergy must uphold the professional ethic of public ministry (e.g. honesty, integrity and efficiency) and standards in the delivery of pastoral care, respect for colleagues and confidentiality.[120] Moreover, an Archdeacon assists the bishop in governance within the archdeaconries of a diocese; and an Area Dean must report to the bishop any matter in a parish within the deanery which it may be necessary or useful for the bishop to know about (e.g. illness).[121]

---

[116] PCLCCAC: Principle 41: clerical discipleship. See e.g. Church of England: Can. C26.1: personal prayer, self-examination and study; Can. C14.3: 'I swear by Almighty God that I will pay true and canonical obedience to the Lord Bishop of C and his successors in all things lawful and honest'; Scottish Episcopal Church: Can. 19: secular employment without the permission of the bishop; Church in Wales: Con. VII.48–51: residence.

[117] PCLCCAC: Principle 33.1–3.   [118] PCLCCAC: Principle 33.4–6.

[119] PCLCCAC: Principle 34; see e.g. Scottish Episcopal Church: Cans. 17.3 and 38.4.

[120] PCLCCAC: Principle 43: trust; 44: accessibility; 45: respect for custom; 46: disclosure of confidential information received outside confession may be subject to disciplinary process.

[121] PCLCCAC: Principle 33.6. See e.g. Church of Ireland: Con. II.38–42: Church in Wales: Con. VII.2.

Much the same is found in Methodism: whether as presbyters or deacons, ministers are to preach the Word, administer the sacraments and provide pastoral care.[122] For example, in the Methodist Church in Ireland: 'Christ's Ministers in the Church are Stewards in the Household of God and Shepherds of His Flock.'[123] A minister is ordained to the ministry of Word and Sacrament, in full connexion with the Conference, and answerable to Synod and Conference in matters of discipline and doctrine.[124] As such, a minister is to: (1) win and watch over souls as one who must give account; (2) feed and guide the congregation by regular and faithful preaching, teaching and pastoral visitation; (3) recognise that the quality of her/his life and witness will determine her/his effectiveness under God; (4) exercise self-discipline so that no offence is given to anyone; and (5) act with particular responsibility when her/his actions may be the cause of physical or moral harm. They must also: obey reverently the ministers placed in authority over them; attend to all matters of Methodist discipline; meet and confer with the Church Council; regard colleagues as co-workers in the Gospel and when necessary defend each other's character and reputation; engage in study, training and professional development;[125] and dress publicly in a manner appropriate to their representation of Christ.[126] Also, an appraisal is undertaken of his/her work once every two years.[127]

Likewise, in the United Reformed Church, ordained persons are to preach the Word, administer the Sacraments, provide pastoral care and conduct their lives in a manner compatible with their calling, either as

---

[122] MCGB: Constitutional Practice and Discipline, Standing Orders 701.7–8: deacons share in leadership of pastoral care, worship and mission of the Circuit and its Churches and must account for their ministry in the Convocation of the Methodist Diaconal Order; Standing Orders 740–745: presbyters and deacons must uphold the authority of the Conference, attend synod, and 'confer together, encourage and watch over one another'.

[123] MCI: Con. s. 1.   [124] MCI: Regulations, Discipline and Government, 4A.01.

[125] MCI: Regulations, Discipline and Government, 4A.03; Code of Pastoral Practice (Methodist Church in Ireland) (CPP) (Manual App. 11).

[126] Ibid: 'The Minister has a representative role in the wider community ... It is vital that when in the public eye, Ministers conduct themselves in a manner appropriate to the occasion in terms of behaviour, public speaking and dress code, especially dress for funerals and the conduct of worship.'

[127] MCI: Regulations, Discipline and Government, 4A.05: Accompanied Self-Appraisal Scheme (1999); each District Synod must appoint a District Appraisal Officer and Group to conduct appraisals and report to the District Superintendent.

ministers[128] or as elders and deacons.[129] Presbyterian ministers are similarly charged. The Presbyterian Church of Wales is typical: 'A minister at his/her ordination is set apart by the Church to lead it in this varied ministry by entrusting him/her especially with the preaching of the Word, the administration of the Sacraments, the pastoral care of members and their instruction in the Christian faith and with leading the Church in its work (both missionary and humanitarian) in the local community, the nation and the world.'[130] Elders, along with the minister, have responsibility 'as a team for the life, worship and witness of the local congregation'; they are 'to visit the sick, to teach the young, to guide and support those who are seeking Christ, and to train and encourage believers', and 'to work with their fellow elders and the ministers to build up the body of Christ through all the courts of the Church'.[131] In Baptist polity too, the minister is the 'pastoral overseer' of a local church, and within it a preacher, teacher and administrator.[132]

Moreover, ministry is subject to oversight, an essential of ecclesial order. Oversight is exercised by such authority as is designated by law. A church may have a system of international oversight or leadership. A minister has such international functions of oversight or leadership as are permitted by the law. International church offices include those of pope, patriarch, primate, president, moderator or general secretary. These are appointed or elected to office by competent ecclesial authority. A church may assign to an office of oversight a coercive jurisdiction or a moral authority.[133]

In the Roman Catholic Church, oversight of local ministry is entrusted to the bishop: 'By divine institution, bishops succeed the apostles through the Holy Spirit who is given to them. They are constituted pastors in the

---

[128] URC: Manual A.21; Manual G: the Ministries Committee of the General Assembly is responsible for their pastoral support (including supervision, appraisal, self-evaluation and counselling).

[129] URC: Manual A.23; Sch. B: affirmations made by elders at ordination and induction include acceptance of office and a promise to perform the duties faithfully.

[130] PCW: Handbook of Rules, 4.2–4.21: 'There are three particular aspects to the work of the Ministry, the preaching of the Word, the administration of the Sacraments, pastoral work and mission. A Minister is required ... to be of unimpeachable character; to possess a deep experience of the truth of the Gospel.'

[131] PCW: Handbook of Rules, 2.6; 4.1–4.2: 'those who are ordained are maintained by the whole Church and responsible to it'. See also UFCS: Manual of Practice and Procedure, Ch. 1, s. 1.

[132] BUGB: Model Trusts for Churches 2003, 6.1: 'pastoral overseers'.

[133] Christian Law Panel of Experts, *Principles of Christian Law* (2016) III.4.

church, to be teachers of doctrine, priests of sacred worship, and the ministers of governance' (if in communion with the Pope and the other bishops). Bishops entrusted with a diocese are 'diocesan bishops'.[134] Appointed by the Pope,[135] the diocesan bishop: has all ordinary, proper, and immediate power required for his office, legislative, executive and judicial, and oversees discipline; must protect and explain doctrine, preach frequently, and oversee the ministry of Word and catechesis; and must set a personal example of holiness, promote that of the faithful, celebrate mass regularly, ordain clergy, reside in the diocese, and conduct a visitation of the diocese every five years, and report on this to the Pope.[136] Anglicanism is similar – oversight by bishops is fundamental to church polity.[137] A priest becomes a bishop by consecration administered by three validly consecrated bishops.[138] A diocesan bishop is elected by an electoral body consisting of representatives of the episcopate, clergy and laity.[139] A diocesan bishop is the chief pastor, minister and teacher of the diocese, and a governor and guardian of discipline. For example, the bishop must foster the spiritual welfare and unity of the diocese, minister the Word and Sacraments, ensure the worthiness of public worship, preside at the Eucharist, administer ordination and confirmation and uphold church doctrine; the bishop is also president of the diocesan assembly and resides in the diocese.[140]

The Methodist Church in Great Britain employs the concept of 'super-intendence' for the oversight of a district (which consists of circuits of local churches). Each district has a Chair, a minister in active service, elected by the Conference, and appointed for a renewable term of six years 'to further the work of God in the District'. The District Chair must use 'all the gifts and graces [he] has received' in order 'to be a pastor to the ministers, deacons and probationers and to lead all the people of the district in the work of preaching and worship, evangelism, pastoral care,

---

[134] CIC: cc. 375, 376.

[135] CIC: c. 377: every three years, the Conference draws up a list of potential candidates.

[136] CIC: cc. 273, 375, 380, 381–399: the bishop visits the Pope in the year of the report; cc. 401–402: the diocese is vacated when the bishop dies, resigns or is transferred/deprived; he may resign with papal consent, and at 75 should do so, or if he cannot fulfil his office due to ill health or other reason.

[137] PCLCCAC: Principle 15.10.   [138] PCLCCAC: Principle 35.

[139] PCLCCAC: Principle 36: See e.g. Church in Wales: Con. VIII.9. In England, a person is nominated by the Crown and elected by the College of Canons of the cathedral of the relevant diocese.

[140] PCLCCAC: Principle 37.

teaching and administration'. The Chair presides over the District Synod, and, with its members, is responsible to Conference for 'the observance within the District of Methodist order and discipline'. It is also 'the duty of the Chair to exercise oversight of the character and fidelity of the ministers and ... in the District', and to visit annually the circuits of the district or arrange for a Circuit Superintendent to do so;[141] and the Superintendent shares with other ministers appointed to it the pastoral charge of the circuit and has oversight of ministers, deacons and probationers who minister there.[142] By way of contrast, in Presbyterianism, the regional Presbytery exercises oversight, leadership and encouragement to ministers, office-holders and congregations in the Presbytery; normally, the Presbytery elects a Moderator from amongst the ministers, elders and deacons of the Presbytery to hold office for one year and to call the meetings of the Presbytery.[143] Similar functions are performed by Presidents in the United Reformed Church,[144] and, to a lesser extent, by the Presidents of Baptist Associations.[145]

The Role of the Imam

Turning to Islam, there are various policy documents that address the functions and continuing development of imams. Some deal with general skills. For example, Faith Associates offer 'effective communications

---

[141] MCGB: Constitutional Practice and Discipline, Deed of Union 42(a); Standing Orders 420–426; see also Standing Orders 545(4) (a) and 574: the involvement of the Chair in various appointments; Standing Orders 1110(4): the Chair may act as 'local complaints officer'. See also Standing Orders 754: the Warden of the Methodist Diaconal Order, acting in conjunction with the Convocation, is responsible for the oversight of the character and fidelity of the deacons and diaconal probationers.

[142] MCGB: Constitutional Practice and Discipline, Standing Orders 522–523; Standing Orders 700.9.

[143] Church of Scotland: Act VIII 1996; PCW: Handbook of Rules, 3.3: the Moderator of an Association of churches is elected by the Association (by secret ballot) from the elders every three years and holds office for one year.

[144] URC: Manual B.2 and C.7: the Moderator of a Synod (a minister appointed by General Assembly for a seven-year term) must 'stimulate and encourage the work of the [URC] within the province or nation', preside over Synod meetings, 'exercise a pastoral office towards the ministers', nominate ministers to vacant pastorates, preside at ordinations and/or inductions of ministers and commissioning and/or inductions of church-related community workers, and submit an annual report to General Assembly.

[145] N. Doe, *Christian Law* (2013) 109: Association officers include the Moderator, elected to preside at Association meetings, report on its affairs and supervise its work.

strategies' providing training workshops and seminars to imams, scholars and *aalimahs* in 'non-theological skills' in areas of traditional and new age social media, such as public speaking and press releases, 'in order to promote a positive message of Islam to a wide target audience'.[146] The constitution for an Islamic organisation affiliated to the Central Mosque should make provision for the Shura Committee to pay the salaries or remuneration, and to maintain houses of residence for, the imam or *muadhin* (the mosque official who summons the faithful to prayer five times a day).[147] And East London Mosque has three imams who provide religious teaching (in English, Arabic, Bengali and Somali), *hajj* training and counselling for new Muslims through the Islam Awareness Project, and, for instance, on bereavement, cultural challenges, generational issues and matrimonial problems.[148] However, generally, the constitutions of the Muslim bodies studied do not set out the role of imams. This is in marked contrast to the legislation of Jews and Christians.

The constitution of Aberdeen Mosque and Islamic Centre, therefore, is unusual in its particularly full treatment of the matter. The 'duties of Imam' are: (1) provision of religious services for obligatory prayers, Islamic festivals and celebrations and periods of fasting – however, the Imam may delegate some such duties to other properly qualified and competent persons with the consent of the Executive Committee, but the Imam remains responsible for providing religious services in the proper form and at the proper time; (2) provision of religious services and the traditional duties of the Imam associated with the birth, death, and burial of the members of the Muslim community; (3) the performance of Islamic marriage in accordance with the (civil) marriage regulations in Scotland; (4) propagation of Islam and giving *da'wa* (bringing people to faith) to both Muslims and non-Muslims; (5) the collection of *zakat* and its distribution among those who deserve it, with the agreement of the Executive Committee; (6) limited fund-raising at the request of the Executive Committee; (7) providing religious education for the children of members of the community – the extent and contents of the teaching curriculum must be decided with the Executive Committee;

---

[146] Faith Associates: www.faithassociates.co.uk/training-faith-leaders/.
[147] Model Constitution for an Islamic Organisation: Powers and Duties of the Shura Committee 1–3. See also e.g. Lancaster Islamic Society: Con. Powers and Duties of the Shura Committee, 1–2.
[148] ELM: Religious and Spiritual Services. www.eastlondonmosque.org.uk/

(8) supervision of adult Islamic classes and Quranic studies; (9) counselling members of the Community in religious and ethical matters; (10) the pastoral care of students at educational institutions in Aberdeen and the Aberdeenshire area, including representation to the authorities if necessary; (11) the co-ordination of hospital and prison visits – the Imam may delegate this task to other persons with the consent of the Executive Committee; (12) provision of hospitality to visiting Islamic scholars and religious groups; (13) representing Aberdeen Mosque and Islamic Centre in different activities and events, and liaising with local authorities such as the council, prisons, and police. The Executive Committee may, with the consent of the Imam, add other duties that may be permanent or temporary.[149] A Muslim wishing to talk publicly in any part of the Mosque/Centre at any time must seek the consent of the Imam or Executive Committee; and no announcements are to be made without agreement of the Imam or Committee.[150]

Moreover, at Aberdeen Mosque and Islamic Centre, the Imam is entitled to a holiday fixed at five weeks per calendar year. Holidays must be booked in advance so that the Executive Committee may make arrangements for the period to be covered. The Imam must co-ordinate the arrangements with the Executive Committee. A notice of one month is required for holidays. Unpaid holidays may be granted for valid reasons.[151] The salary of the Imam is paid by the Executive Committee directly to his bank account or by cheque. Tax and Insurance is covered according to the relevant Scottish law. Sick leave on full pay extends to two months; the next two months will be on half pay.[152] Once more, before the appointment begins or the term is renewed, the Mosque and Islamic Centre and the intended Imam must sign a contract of service approved by the Board of Trustees and Executive Committee. The contract may be terminated by either side three months in advance of the date of vacating the post of Imam. Any decision for termination of the contract of service must be taken by three out of the five trustees and five out of the seven Executive Committee members must agree to it.[153]

Some Muslim organisations also regulate the hosting of imams from outside the community. For instance, Palmers Green Mosque Community and Education Centre may invite Imams from the wider community to speak at any mosque event and to deliver Friday sermons, in order to

---

[149] AMIC: Con. Art. XIV.5.   [150] AMIC: Con. Arts. XIII.1–XIII.2.
[151] AMIC: Con. Art. XIV.6a.   [152] AMIC: Con. Art. XIV.6b.
[153] AMIC: Con. Art. XIV.7.

enrich members' knowledge of religion, enhance their education, widen their understanding of 'Islamic rulings' and general knowledge and give motivational inspiration through sharing experience. The mosque has a responsibility to its community 'to ensure that they critically assess the information received as to its value to them' and that the information is 'aligned to the ethos and values of Islam, [the Mosque] and British Values'. To this end, the Mosque 'requires that all individuals and organisations hosted by Palmers Green Mosque adhere to certain guidelines'. The talk should be given in 'a universally understood language, English', and the speaker should not: solicit donations or partake in any fund-raising activities during the event; publicise other organisations or events or partake in any marketing activities or distribution of any sorts of literature; promote any one school of thought or matter of *fiqh* in a manner which could potentially be divisive to the Muslim community; discuss or explore highly sensitive areas of Islam; or promote/propagate any illegal activities, discrimination or hate crime. The mosque provides that respect needs to be shown for scholars and other legitimate opinions.[154]

Finally, the Muslim Council of Britain has issued national guidance to its institutional members to ensure that imams comply with the law of the State and the interests of wider society in the performance of their religious functions. Imams must: (1) provide 'the correct Islamic guidance to the community, especially to our youth, as to our obligation to maintain the peace and security of our country'; (2) observe the utmost vigilance against any mischievous or criminal elements infiltrating the community and provoking any unlawful activity,[155] and liaise with the local Police and give them the fullest co-operation in dealing with any criminal activity including terrorist threats;[156] (3) engage proactively with the media to refute any misconception about Islam and the Muslim community; (4) develop active contacts with other faith communities and civic organisations in order to help maintain social peace and good community relations, and in the event of any tragic incident taking place, give the fullest co-operation to the Police and other

---

[154] Palmers Green Mosque, Muslim Community and Education Centre for Islamic Studies (PGM): Guidelines on Speakers and Imams: www.mcec.org.uk/.

[155] This cites Quran 35:10: 'And those who criminally plot evil deeds, a severe punishment awaits them; and all their plotting is bound to come to nought.'

[156] This cites Quran 5:2: 'Help one another to virtue and God-consciousness and do not help one other to sin and transgression.'

authorities; and (5) 'most importantly', seek 'Allah's help and support and pray for His guidance and protection all the time'.[157] In turn, Bradford Council for Mosques' Advisory Committee of Senior Ulama is to provide 'practical advice and support on religious, cultural and social aspects of living as a Muslim'.[158] For the civil courts, an imam's religious decisions are not subject to judicial review.[159]

Conclusion

There are profound similarities and differences between the regulatory instruments of Jews, Christians and Muslims with regard to the qualifications, appointment, functions and removal of their faith leaders. First, all three make provision for the training of their faith leaders, rabbis, ministers and imams. Both Judaism and Christianity set apart persons as religious leaders: Rabbinical ordination finds a direct parallel in the ordination of Christian ministers – and for Christians ordained ministry is instituted by God. In Islam, to become an imam no religious rite is required, though for example knowledge of the religion is a prerequisite before acceptance by the community, and there exist various imamship programmes provided at Muslim colleges. Unlike the Christian Episcopal churches (as compared with the Protestant churches which speak of the priesthood of all believers), there is today no priestly class in Judaism or Islam in the sense of mediation between God and the faithful. Secondly, the regulatory instruments of all three religions make extensive and elaborate provision for the appointment of religious leaders. However, there is a degree of legal pluralism within the traditions of each religion. Generally, Jewish norms entrust the right to appoint a Rabbi at the local level of the synagogue, though in the Orthodox United Synagogue, the appointment must be acceptable to the Chief Rabbi. In Christianity, for the Episcopal churches parish clergy are appointed by the bishop, though provision exists for lay participation in the process. For Muslims, the appointment of an imam is a democratic matter for a committee of the

---

[157] MCB Community Guidelines to Imams and British Muslim Organisations (2004): these guidelines, issued in the form of a letter by the MCB Secretary General, were to be conveyed in the Friday sermon: www.mcb.org.uk/mcb-community-guidelines-to-imams-and-british-muslim-organisations/.

[158] CFM: www.councilformosques.org/about-us/constitution-and-membership/.

[159] *R v. Imam of Bury Park, ex parte Sulaiman Ali* [1994] COD 142: they lack sufficient public element.

mosque. The removal of faith leaders echoes these arrangements – and the process must be carried out in accordance with the relevant procedural norms. The regulatory instruments of Jewish and Muslim organisations provide for a Rabbi and imam to enter into a contract of employment, so they may be treated as employees for the purposes of civil law and their contracts of employment will be recognised by the State. The courts of the State may regard Christian ministers of religion as office-holders or employees. With regard to their functions, there is a high level of the juridification of religion – service is key – all three religions translate and embellish classical religious concepts into norms which spell out the duties of Rabbis, ministers and imams. The core functions of Rabbis, ordained ministers and imams – and these are shared by all three religions – are to lead the faithful in worship, to assist in administration of religious rites and to provide instruction and pastoral care. Unlike Judaism and Islam, however, Christian laws make extensive provision for the oversight and appraisal of ordained ministry: for instance, in Episcopal churches, this is provided by the bishop, in the Methodist Church by a system of superintendence and in the Presbyterian Church by the regional presbytery. By way of contrast, legislative instruments of only a minority of the Jewish and Muslim bodies studied provide for periodic appraisal of Rabbis and imams.

4

The Governance of Communities: Institutions and Officers

The history of the three faiths is rich in debate about the nature, location and exercise of authority in terms of religious governance. The modern regulatory instruments of Jewish, Christian and Muslim organisations reflect directly different religio-political postures on the governance of the faithful arising from distinctive understandings of the nature of the faith community and the location of institutional authority within it. However, regardless of their particular positions on authority and the implications of these for religious polity, the regulatory instruments also reveal profound similarities and differences between the faiths and traditions within them. Institutional structures may be nationwide, or at regional, and/or local level – and some may be part of a wider international structure; yet, the traditions differ at each level in terms of the authority vested in these institutions – their jurisdiction (and functions), composition and officers. To this extent, there is sometimes a high degree of legal pluralism within the religions. The regulatory instruments of the entities studied also yield shared principles of religious governance – whilst their activities may be religious, in terms of the structure of the institutions themselves, what comes to the fore is their functionality/secularity rather than religiosity: the separation of powers; institutional interdependence; subsidiarity (making strategic and operational decisions at the most appropriate level); representation (the role of democracy/consensus); and due process (the rule of law). The institutional organisation of legislative and administrative powers is studied here – judicial power (in courts or tribunals) is treated in Chapter 5.

The Nationwide Institutions of Governance

Organisations within each religion have nationwide institutions of government. Whilst the principles of representation, division of functions and accountability are shared, there is diversity within and between the religions as to the degree to which such nationwide institutions have competence over the local religious community – in some cases, this is a coercive jurisdiction, in others a moral or persuasive authority.

The Nationwide Institutions of Judaism

Historically, the Sanhedrin was the supreme legislative and judicial body for Judaism; on the destruction of the Temple in Jerusalem (70 CE), it ceased to function in its full form and today there is no central legislature or court with universal authority over all Jews worldwide in their various traditions and movements.[1] Nevertheless, *takkanot* and *gezerot* are still recognised forms of Rabbinic legislation; though the terms often interchange – a *takkanah* may denote Rabbinic legislation which prescribes a new action and a *gezerah* a Rabbinic ruling extending or limiting an existing observance.[2] The traditions differ, however, as to the authority of Rabbinic legislation. While for Orthodox Judaism, such legislation cannot contradict the Torah (and 'anything new is forbidden by the Torah' (Moshe Sofer (1762–1839)), Reform Judaism criticises what it considers the 'novel doctrine of Rabbinic infallibility ... advanced in fundamentalist Jewish circles ... to suppress any movement for change in the halakhah', in the sense that 'it is forbidden to question, let alone disagree with, the views of a given scholar or group of scholars, because they represent da-at Torah'.[3] Indeed, the traditional principle of *va'asu seyag laTorah* (make a fence to protect the Torah) is not meant 'to fossilize Jewish life' but to guarantee 'the right of contemporary Jewish authorities to legislate even radical, innovations to help the Jewish people survive and fulfil the Divine will as they could best determine'.[4]

---

[1] After 70 CE, it was located in various cities.

[2] Both enable Rabbis 'of every generation to legislate and even to contradict a law from the Torah': R.S. Rheins, 'Asu Seyag LaTorah: make a fence around the Torah', in W. Jacob and M. Zemer, eds., *Re-Examining Progressive Halakhah* (New York: Berghahn Books, 2002) 91 at 97: e.g. Rabbennu Gershom's prohibition on polygamy (permitted by the Torah) is a *gezerah*, as it limits an existing observance; Rheins cites M. Lewittes, *Principles and Development of Jewish Law* (New York: Bloch Publishing, 1987) 93ff; and M. Elon, *Jewish Law* (1994) 490ff. Rheins gives as an example of the permissible contradiction of Torah, the *takkanah* permitting self-defence on the Sabbath: I Maccabees 2:39–41.

[3] R. Gordis, *The Dynamics of Judaism* (Bloomington: Indiana University Press, 1990) 82; *da-at Torah* is literally 'Torah knowledge'.

[4] R.S. Rheins, 'Asu Seyag LaTorah: make a fence around the Torah' (2002) 91 at 95. See also S.B. Freehof, *Reform Jewish Practice* (1963) 13: 'Reform Jewish practice is not fixed. It is still changing', and M. Elon, *Jewish Law* (1994) II 495ff, 505–533.

As such: 'Rabbinic legislation which contradicted the Torah may be enacted in order to protect the spiritual and physical well-being of the Jewish people' and 'to safeguard the Torah' – but this does not mean that 'the Rabbis assumed the power to speak with the same eternal authority as the Torah'; also, while 'Rabbis are not empowered to add or abstract from the Torah, they are empowered to declare *takkanot* and *gezerot* that strengthen Judaism'.[5] A Jewish community may also legislate by custom (*minhag*), 'a particular normative behaviour that has been continuous and unquestioned' – 'the people can create law through custom' to determine 'which view is to be accepted when the halakhic authorities disagree as to what the law is [on] a particular matter'.[6] However: 'custom abrogates the law only if it is the custom of respected people'; importantly, 'it is the right of a community to continue to engage in a halakhically sanctioned practice in the face of a new law mandated by another halakhic authority'; and 'existing custom [may be] invoked as the explicitly stated, valid halakhic basis for certain conduct'; but if 'there is no existing custom, one falls back on halakhah and not popular creativity'.[7]

Turning to modern regulatory instruments of Jewish organisations nationwide,[8] first, the institutional pattern which emerges is that each Jewish organisation, across the traditions, has a central governing body (typically a council or other assembly), an administrative or executive body (such as a body of trustees or directors) and officers (including a President). The institutional structure of the Union of Liberal and Progressive Synagogues is typical, with its Council (with representatives from member synagogues), Board of National Officers (its executive), President and Chief Executive; and its Rabbinic Conference which advises on religious issues.[9] Secondly, the governing body is composed

---

[5] R.S. Rheins, 'Asu Seyag LaTorah' (2002) 91 at 104: he cites Maimonides.

[6] M. Elon, *Jewish Law* (1994) II.884–885, 901–903: and 'custom overrides the law'.

[7] J.S. Friedman, 'A critique of Solomon B. Freehof's concept of minhag and Reform Jewish Practice', in W. Jacob and M. Zemer, eds., *Re-Examining Progressive Halakha* (New York/ Oxford: Berghahn Books, 2002) 111 at 117, citing S.B. Freehof, *Reform Jewish Practice* (1963) 8 and 119 – this is also the position taken by M. Elon, *Jewish Law* (1994) II.907–909.

[8] The Board of Deputies of British Jews is dealt with below in Chapter 10.

[9] ULPS: www.liberaljudaism.org/who-we-are/whos-who/. The Movement for Reform Judaism has a Senior Rabbi, President, Board, *Beit Din* and Assembly of Reform Rabbis. The Council of Conservative-Masorti Judaism has its corporate officers (including the President and Chief Financial Officer); an Executive Operations Committee; and a Board of Directors; and congregational affiliate members must also establish 'a national Masorti coordinating body': WCCMJ: By-Laws III-X.

inter alia of persons elected or appointed by the member synagogues, has defined functions (including the creation of law), and its meetings are regulated by detailed procedural rules. For instance, the Council of the (Orthodox) Federation of Synagogues is composed of: the Federation Elders (*ex officio*); from an Affiliated Synagogue, the President (*ex officio*), one elected male and one appointed female Delegate; from a Constituent Synagogue, the President, two Wardens and the Financial Representative (*ex officio*), and one elected male and one appointed female delegate; and members co-opted by the Trustees.[10] Council must meet at least four times each year, the Federation President acting as chair with right to vote, speak and determine all points of procedure 'conclusively',[11] and may rescind, amend or add to the Laws by a resolution, of which at least 14 days' written notice must be given, and which must be passed by two-thirds of the delegates.[12] The Federation 'shall be managed by male Trustees', including the President, two Vice Presidents and two Treasurers, who are appointed by Council on the written nomination of delegates.[13] The Trustees have a range of functions in relation to property (see Chapter 9), and may make bye-laws, rules or standing orders for the Federation and its Burial Society; Council may alter these.[14]

Thirdly, officers have prescribed functions. For example, in the United Synagogue of Conservative Judaism, which has a Board of Directors (to e.g. develop organization-wide policies),[15] the General Assembly of Kehillot (which may amend the United Synagogue Bylaws by two-third majority vote,[16] and adopt/modify the Standards of Kehilla Practice) elects the Board of Directors and the Officers.[17] The Officers include

---

[10] FOS: Laws 4: no paid official of the Federation, the Burial Society or a Federation Synagogue is eligible to act as a Delegate; 5: elections and appointments take place every three years; only women vote for female delegates; 6: Council may exclude delegates; 7: vacancies; 8: Elders.

[11] FOS: Laws 9–12: in his absence, the Vice President chairs the meetings or else other prescribed delegates; 13: votes at meetings; 14: votes on grants and expenditure of money.

[12] FOS: Laws 29.   [13] FOS: Laws 15–19. See below Chapter 5 for the removal of Trustees.

[14] FOS: Laws 30 and 31; 20 and 21: they regulate their own proceedings and may delegate functions.

[15] The Board Operating Standards and Procedures must include, but not be limited to, e.g. a Code of Conduct/Disclosure Statement signed annually by every Board member. The Board of Directors may also create and maintain Operating Standards and Procedures for the District Councils.

[16] USCJ: By-Laws 10: or at any two consecutive regular meetings of the Board.

[17] USCJ: By-Laws 4: it meets annually; 2.3: a *kehilla* must accept the Vision and Mission Statement of the United Synagogue and the Standards of Rabbinic Practice of its Rabbinical Assembly.

the President and Chief Executive Officer. The President is the highest ranking official (not a Rabbi), and chairs the Board of Directors, Executive Committee, and General Assembly; guides and enacts Board policy; and signs all contracts which do not require Board approval.[18] The Chief Executive Officer, the highest rank of the professional staff, is responsible for the day-to-day operation of the organization with authority as defined in the Board of Directors' Operating Standards and Procedures.[19]

What follows is a detailed case study of these themes as they appear in the regulatory instruments of the Orthodox United Synagogue, which exercises jurisdiction over member synagogues. The United Synagogue has a wide range of 'powers', Honorary Officers, an Executive Committee, a Council and Committees. First, its powers are to carry out the objects of the United Synagogue (see above Chapter 1), which include: to found synagogues, a district union of non-member synagogues and places of worship; to provide for burial services, schools, the Court of the Chief Rabbi and the preparation, production and supervision of food and drink for Jewish people 'to better conform to their religious beliefs'; to raise funds, make grants/loans for charitable purposes; to found other charities; to co-operate with other organisations, trusts, individuals or bodies corporate (whether they are charitable or not); to employ and pay such officers and staff as may be thought fit and to make appropriate arrangements for the payment of the pensions, if any, of any such officers and staff.[20]

Secondly, the body of Honorary Officers of the United Synagogue is 'responsible for [its] administration and management'.[21] It consists of no fewer than nine or more than 11 'competent persons' who are elected – nine by the Council, including the President (who must be male) and Treasurer – and four male and four female Honorary Officers.[22] To be eligible for election, the person must be at least 21 years of age and have belonged to a member synagogue for two consecutive years, and served on a Board of Management of a member synagogue for at least

---

[18] USCJ: By-Laws 5: the other officers are the Vice Presidents (three), Treasurer and Secretary.
[19] USCJ: By-Laws 6; 7: Nominations Committee.
[20] US: Statutes 5: employees do not include the Honorary Officers or the Council members.
[21] US: Statutes 7.
[22] US: Statutes 8; see also Statutes 10: provided that where any person is elected, that person must not also serve on any Board of Management of a Member, or of an Affiliated or Associated Synagogue.

two years.[23] Honorary Officers may exercise all the powers of the United Synagogue, on its behalf, that are not according to the Statutes required to be exercised by Council,[24] and: (1) subject to Council approval as to composition, appoint and constitute such Standing Committees, and delegate to them such powers and functions as they determine; (2) form Advisory Committees and other Committees, similarly; and (3) subject to Council approval, 'lay down, make, revoke, alter or amend Regulations generally for the better management and administration of the United Synagogue' (e.g. on the constitution of Member, Affiliated or Associated Synagogues). However, their Regulations must be consistent with the Statutes.[25] The Honorary Officers may act notwithstanding any vacancy in their body.[26] Their office is vacated *inter alia* if the officer: ceases to be a United Synagogue Member; becomes bankrupt or of unsound mind; resigns; is precluded under the (civil) Charities Acts from being a Charity Trustee; or is removed 'for good and substantial reason' by a resolution passed by at least three-quarters of the Council, which, beforehand, must give the officer 'the right to be heard and to state any case in writing' to Council.[27] The President chairs the Honorary Officers.[28]

Thirdly, the Honorary Officers must constitute an Executive Committee to dispatch their business and to regulate its meetings as they think fit; and decisions are made by majority vote but the Chairman has a second/casting vote.[29] The Honorary Officers must invite senior paid staff of the United Synagogue to attend and speak at the Executive Committee in an advisory non-voting capacity.[30] The Executive Committee: must, through Regulations made by the Honorary Officers, provide for the constitution of Divisional Management Committees;[31] may appoint its own members to discharge functions allocated by the Honorary Officers;[32] may hold meetings at any time with the Honorary Officers' agreement or on written request of the President or no fewer than three Honorary Officers; and it may 'exercise all the authorities, powers and

---

[23] US: Statutes 9; see also Statutes 11 and 12: terms of office.   [24] US: Statutes 13.

[25] US: Statutes 14; see also Statutes 41.   [26] US: Statutes 15.   [27] US: Statutes 16.

[28] US: Statutes 20: if the President is not present or is unable or unwilling to serve, the Honorary Officers appoint one of their numbers to be Chairman or, as the case may be, Chairman of that meeting.

[29] US: Statutes 17.   [30] US: Statutes 18.

[31] US: Statutes 19: a member of a Divisional Management Committee who is not an Honorary Officer is an Associate Honorary Officer.

[32] US: Statutes 21: Council must be notified; 22: they must also appoint a Clerk of the Honorary Officers.

discretion ... vested in the United Synagogue generally' under its regulations.[33] The Honorary Officers may delegate any of their powers to committees of themselves and/or others as the Honorary Officers think fit; all *bona fide* acts of any meeting or committee of the Honorary Officers (notwithstanding any defect in their appointment or continuance in office) are 'valid as if every such person had been duly appointed or had duly continued in office and was qualified to be an Honorary Officer'.[34] The Honorary Officers must keep proper records and minutes.[35]

Fourthly, there is the Council of the United Synagogue. It consists of: the Honorary Officers; all who, prior to July 1996, served as an Honorary Officer or were elected a life member or elder of the Council; anyone who served as an Honorary Officer in the previous three years; those elected by secret ballot by, and from, members of the Board of Management of each member synagogue (representation from which is dependent on its membership size); and former Presidents of the United Synagogue.[36] The Council must meet at least four times each year, and may regulate its meetings. The President of the United Synagogue or such other Honorary Officer as is selected by the Honorary Officers is Chairman. Council meets when called or on the written request of the President or not less than 35 Council members. Council may exercise all the authorities, powers and discretions of the United Synagogue vested in it by regulation and delegate its powers to committees of such Council or United Synagogue members as it thinks fit. Council receives the audited annual accounts.[37]

The powers and functions of the Council are to amend the Statutes of the United Synagogue by Special Resolution;[38] to elect or remove Honorary Officers; to consent to Regulations made by the Honorary Officers which require its consent; to determine the admission or discontinuance of member synagogues and consider decisions about the sale/disposal of their sites (with representations to the Honorary Officers); and to act as a forum to discuss the affairs of the United Synagogue and discharge of its objects. In particular, it is: to receive and consider the annual budget of the

---

[33] US: Statutes 23–24.   [34] US: Statutes 25–26.

[35] US: Statutes 27; 28: a written Resolution signed by all the Honorary Officers or of their committee members is as valid and effectual as if it had been passed at a meeting of the Honorary Officers or of such committee.

[36] US: Statutes 29; 30–32: these norms deal with tenure of office and casual vacancies.

[37] US: Statutes 33–38. For accounts, see Chapter 8.

[38] US: Statutes 54: see above Chapter 1.

United Synagogue and any reports from the Honorary Officers or any committee as to the way in which United Synagogue affairs are being administered; to make representations and offer advice and guidance to the Honorary Officers in discharging the United Synagogue's objects; and to carry out such other functions as may be allocated to the Council by the Honorary Officers.[39] Moreover, elaborate provision is made for the establishment, functions, procedure and expenditure of committees.[40]

Church Conferences, Synods and Assemblies

For Christianity, historically, the Reformation in particular stimulated perhaps the most far-reaching doctrinal reappraisal of church polity, largely based on arguments that scripture prescribed patterns of church government different from those rooted in the papacy and bishops of the Church of Rome. This is reflected today in the fact that, with the new institutional churches which emerged from the Reformation, it is commonly understood that there are three principal forms of church polity – Episcopal, Presbyterian and Congregational – and the merits of each, and whether they fuel Christian disunity, continue to arouse debate amongst contemporary theologians.[41] However, regardless of their particular doctrinal positions on authority, all the historic churches have institutions of governance. According to the principles of Christian law, Christ is the ultimate head of the Church universal in all its manifestations. A system of government used by a church reflects its conception of divine law. A church should have institutions to legislate, administer and adjudicate for its own governance. An ecclesial institution has such power, authority or jurisdiction as is assigned to it by law, must comply with the law and may be subject to such substantive and procedural limitations as may be prescribed by law. Ecclesial institutions may be organised at international, national, regional and/or local level.[42]

Whilst an ecclesial tradition may have an international organisation in the form of a church, communion, federation or other global association, with a structure as may be constituted by or assigned to it under its

---

[39] US: Statutes 40.   [40] US: Statutes 41–44.

[41] See e.g. C.O. Brand and R.S. Norman, eds., *Perspectives on Church Government: Five Views of Church Polity* (Nashville, TN: Boardman and Holman, 2004).

[42] Christian Law Panel of Experts, *Principles of Christian Law* (2016) IV.1: Church Governance.

doctrine and law,[43] a tradition may have a national organisation. A church or other ecclesial community organised at national level may have such institutional structure as is prescribed by the legal rules applicable to it. The functions of a national ecclesial entity, and its conference, synod, council or other central assembly, may include the authority to legislate, administer and adjudicate on matters within its competence. The institution is composed of the faithful as are elected or otherwise appointed to it in accordance with the law.[44] These principles are derived from the similarities between the laws of the churches.

First, in the tradition of Episcopal churches, in the Roman Catholic Church,[45] the national Episcopal Conference, 'the assembly of the Bishops of a country or of a certain territory',[46] must draw up its own statutes (to be reviewed by the Apostolic See) which must deal with, *inter alia*, its plenary meetings, a permanent committee of bishops, a general secretary and other offices and commissions; each Conference must elect a President who presides over its plenary meetings and permanent committee. Plenary meetings are to be held at least once each year.[47] The Episcopal Conference may issue decrees only in cases where the universal law so prescribes or by special mandate of the Holy See, on its own initiative or at the request of the Conference; a proposed conference decree must receive two-thirds of the votes at a plenary meeting; and: 'These decrees do not oblige until they have been reviewed by the

---

[43] Christian Law Panel of Experts, *Principles of Christian Law* (2016) IV.2: International Ecclesial Communities: an international ecclesial institution is composed of such persons on such terms of tenure as are assigned to it in accordance with its own juridical instruments. See N. Doe, *Christian Law* (2013) 124–130 for the coercive jurisdiction and authority of the Roman Pontiff and College of Bishops in the Catholic Church, and for the (non-coercive) moral authority, over their autonomous churches, exercised by the institutions of the Anglican Communion, Lutheran World Federation, World Methodist Council, World Communion of Reformed Churches and Baptist World Alliance.

[44] Christian Law Panel of Experts, *Principles of Christian Law* (2016) IV.3: National Church Structures.

[45] CIC: cc. 435–446: neighbouring particular churches may be grouped into provinces to promote inter-diocesan relations; provinces are established, altered or suppressed by the Pope; the provincial council and metropolitan oversee the province; its council may legislate by decrees sent to Rome for approval.

[46] CIC: cc. 447–449; c. 459: relations between Conferences; c. 753: the Conference as teacher.

[47] CIC: cc. 450–454; c. 456: the President must send the minutes of plenary meetings to Rome; c. 457: the permanent committee prepares the agenda and ensures decisions are executed; c. 458: secretary.

Apostolic See and lawfully promulgated'; the competence of a diocesan bishop is also protected.[48]

Also Episcopal, an Anglican Church consists of one or more province(s) (and within them dioceses). The central organ of government is the national assembly, styled variously the General Synod (e.g. England) or Governing Body (Wales) composed of three Houses (or Orders) – bishops, clergy and laity – with representatives elected under elaborate legal rules.[49] The archbishop or primate convenes and presides at meetings held each year – and there are complex procedures for the transaction of business.[50] The principal functions of central assemblies are law-making, policy-making and to a lesser extent administration over a wide range of prescribed subjects of common concern to the whole of the church.[51] The central assembly also has various committees, commissions, boards and other administrative bodies.[52] In the Church of England, for example, the Archbishops' Council, which is a charity, coordinates and promotes the work and mission of the church by supporting it nationally and locally, and by working closely with the House of Bishops of General Synod.[53]

Secondly, across the wide spectrum of Protestant churches, in Methodist polity the Conference is a 'court' with the power to bind: it meets annually under a President.[54] For example, the Conference of the Methodist Church in Great Britain (one of its 'Church Courts and Jurisdictions') meets annually and consists of ministers (in the Ministerial Session) and lay representatives (in the Representative Session). It is responsible for 'the government and discipline of the [church] and the management and administration of its affairs' and has 'all the powers, authorities, rights and duties necessary or desirable in its discretion for

---

[48] CIC: c. 455: Conference decides the manner of promulgation and the time the decrees come into force.

[49] E.g. Church of England: Synodical Government Measure 1969: General Synod has 3 Houses: bishops, clergy and laity.

[50] E.g. Church in Wales: Con. II.20: the archbishop presides; Church of Ireland: Standing Orders of General Synod.

[51] E.g. Church of Ireland: Con. Preamble, Declaration IV: General Synod has 'chief legislative power ... and such administrative power as may be necessary for the Church and consistent with its episcopal constitution'.

[52] See also PCLCCAC: Part III.

[53] Church of England: National Institutions Measure 1998.

[54] MCI: Con. s. 6; Regulations, Discipline and Government, 6: Conference composition, functions, constitutional amendment, procedure, quorum, rules of debate, and President; Regulations, Discipline and Government, 8: General Committee.

such government, discipline, management and administration'. As such, it may: (1) make, amend and repeal Standing Orders or other rules and regulations for the constitution of the Conference consistent with the Deed of Union; (2) found connexional funds for the promulgation of the Gospel and for circuits and local churches and manage connexional property; (3) conduct ordinations; and (4) appoint boards, committees and officers, including its President, and the Methodist Council and Executive can act on its behalf between Conferences and ensure that 'the decisions of the Conference are fully implemented'; the Council also has a Committee on Methodist Law and Polity to advise on Methodist 'legislation and administration', changes to law and their 'coherence with existing usage'; the committee reports annually to the Conference.[55] The President of the Conference must be an ordained minister and is elected by it (designated at the previous Conference by ballot and a majority of the votes cast) to hold office for one year.[56] The President of the Conference: 'plays a significant part in the oversight and leadership of the Church in responding to God's Spirit and developing prophetic vision'; presides at the Conference; stations ministers on vacancies or death;[57] exercises 'a ministry through visits to and encouragement of the constituent parts of the Connexion and beyond';[58] may assist at any Synod, if requested by the Chair or by a majority of the Superintendents in the district; and, if requested to do so, visit any circuit to inquire into its affairs, and to take any steps judged beneficial.[59]

Thirdly, a church of the Reformed tradition has a central assembly composed of ministers and lay representatives with legislative authority. For instance, the General Assembly of the United Reformed Church is 'the central organ [and] final authority, under the Word of God and ... guidance of the Holy Spirit in ... doctrine and order and in all other concerns of its common life', and represents the synods (equal ministerial

---

[55] MCGB: Constitutional Practice and Discipline, Standing Orders 003: Church Courts and Jurisdictions; Deed of Union 18–21: powers; Deed of Union 11, 13–14: membership; Deed of Union 19: Standing Orders; 21: officers and committees; 23: ordination; Deed of Union 26–29 and Standing Orders 110–111: President; Standing Orders 210–216: Methodist Council and Executive (and Audit Committee); Standing Orders 230–232: other committees; Standing Orders 302: General Secretary or 'executive officer'; Standing Orders 338 for the Committee on Methodist Law and Polity.

[56] MCGB: Constitutional Practice and Discipline, Deed of Union 26. The Vice President is a lay member and is elected similarly (ibid., 27).

[57] MCGB: Constitutional Practice and Discipline, Deed of Union 28–29.

[58] MCGB: Constitutional Practice and Discipline, Standing Orders 110.

[59] MCGB: Constitutional Practice and Discipline, Standing Orders 111.

and lay). For example, it oversees the work of the church and can 'alter, add to, modify or supersede the Basis, Structure and any other form . . . of the polity and doctrinal formulations' of the church; constitutional amendment is proposed by a two-third majority of members, referred to the provinces, and effected by majority vote. The General Assembly is assisted in its work by a range of councils and committees.[60] Two Moderators of General Assembly are elected by secret ballot on nomination by a synod: one a minister or church-related community worker and the other an elder.[61]

Similarly, a Presbyterian Church has a General Assembly; its highest court is typically composed of teaching elders from (regional) Presbyteries and ruling elders from the local (Kirk) Sessions. For instance, in the Presbyterian Church of Wales: 'The General Assembly, the Supreme Court of the Church, is a representative body consisting of ministers and elders elected by Presbyteries'; its 'functions . . . are legislative as well as judicial and administrative' as to doctrine, worship, discipline and government; Presbyteries may propose legislative reform to General Assembly and no change may be made to the constitution without approval of the Presbyteries.[62] The Moderator is elected by and appointed to preside over the Assembly and performs such functions as are prescribed by the regulatory instruments of the church; generally, the functions of the Moderator are in the sphere of church governance.[63]

By way of contrast, in the Congregational tradition of church polity, in which the fullness of the Church of Christ is vested in the local church, the national institutions of Baptists have more limited jurisdictions; for instance, in the Baptist Union of Great Britain: 'The general policy of the Union, subject to any directions of the Assembly, shall be decided by a Council', which meets twice a year and consists, for example, of representatives of Associations and the officers and past Presidents; Council may appoint committees and working groups and the

---

[60] URC: Manual B.2.6; 3.1; C: Rules of Procedure; G: Committees: e.g. Mission Council, and Ministries Committee.

[61] URC: Manual C.3; see C. 4 for the General Secretary and C. 5 for the Clerk of Assembly.

[62] PCW: Handbook of Rules, 1.2; 3.4–5.

[63] PCW: Handbook of Rules, 3.4.3.5: the Moderator is elected from the association in three provinces and admitted at a service for installation at which the person is given the Assembly Bible 'as sign of [his] authority'; App. A: the Moderator holds office for one year; chairs meetings of the General Assembly and directs its proceedings; is member of every Board; and visits Presbyteries and Associations by invitation; see also PCI: Code, paras. 99–100; UFCS: Manual of Practice and Procedure, Ch. 5, s. 2.

Assembly may amend the constitution of the Union by resolution passed by a two-third majority vote with notice given at the previous meeting.[64] A Union may also have a President, Directors or Moderators with limited functions due to the autonomy of each member church.[65]

The Principles of Shura and Ijma

The principle of consultation (*shura/mashwara*) is a fundamental in classical Islamic law; it is based on the injunction to Muhammad to consult with his followers (Quran 3:159), and for Muslims to consult with each other in conducting their affairs (Quran 42:38); however, the precise effect of *shura* for democratic governance is debated by Muslim scholars.[66] Nevertheless, the Universal Islamic Declaration of Human Rights (1981) states: 'all public affairs shall be determined and conducted, and the authority to administer them shall be exercised after mutual consultation (*shura*) between the believers qualified to contribute to a decision which would accord well with the Law and the public good'.[67] The concept of *shura* is an important feature of governance in Muslim organisations at national level, consisting as they do, typically, of a national assembly, board of trustees and executive committee (as with Nasru-Lahi-Il-Fathi Society of Nigeria, United Kingdom and Ireland),[68] and other bodies with prescribed administrative and advisory functions (as with the Union of Muslim Organisations).[69]

The focus of this section, by way of a detailed case study, is the Muslim Council of Britain, which has a General Assembly, a National Council and an Executive Committee, a Board of Counsellors and, amongst its

---

[64] BUGB: Con. I.5–9; II.1–10.

[65] BUGB: Con. 2.3: the Vice President is elected annually, becomes President Elect for one year and takes office as President at the annual Assembly; BUS: Con. IX: Core Leaders include the General Director, Ministry Advisor and Mission Advisor; Bylaws VIII: their functions are agreed by Council.

[66] M. Rohe, *Islamic Law* (2014) 314; A. Black *et al.*, *Islamic Law* (2013) 43–44.

[67] Islamic Council of Europe: UIDHR (1981): Preamble.

[68] See e.g. NASFAT: Con. Art. D: Board of Trustees; Art. G: Executive Committee, Management Committee, National Executive Council, National Mission Board, National Council of Elders (open to both males and females); Art. H: Executive Committee; Art. J: Officers (e.g. Chairman); Art. M: Committees (e.g. Education Committee, Finance Committee and Disciplinary Committee).

[69] Union of Muslim Organisations UK: Mosque Council, Advisory Council, Board of Ulema and Youth Council: http://umouk.org/. Also, the Muslim Association of Britain has a National Convention: www.mabonline.net/about/; the Association works closely with the MAB Charitable Trust: www.mabct.org/about-us/.

officers, a Secretary General.[70] It employs the principle of *shura* – alongside this echoes the principle of consensus (*ijma*). First, the General Assembly consists of delegates of Muslim bodies that subscribe to the Principles of Association and pay their annual affiliation fees. National bodies are represented by a maximum of three delegates, regional bodies by a maximum of two, and other bodies by one; the basis of representation must be reviewed from time to time to ensure the number of delegates is appropriate to achieve the objects.[71] The General Assembly is 'the supreme policy-making and ruling body' of the MCB and may adopt resolutions, amend the Constitution and exercise powers necessary to promote the aims and purposes of the MCB.[72] It must elect the Secretary General and Deputy, each for two years but not for more than two consecutive terms, who are responsible to the National Council for implementation of policy and the delivery of any work approved by the National Council or Executive Committee. Every two years, the General Assembly must also elect 30 national representatives (20 per cent must be female) and 12 individuals as zonal representatives to the National Council. No member body and/or its branch/branches may have more than five nationally, or zonally, elected members to the National Council. The number of zones in Scotland, Northern Ireland, Wales and England must be reviewed from time to time by the General Assembly. The General Assembly must be called at least annually by the Secretary General who must call an extraordinary meeting at the request of at least a quarter of the member bodies or half of the elected members of the National Council. Ordinary resolutions are adopted by a simple majority of the delegates present and voting, but for special resolutions – such as constitutional amendments, dissolution or matters 'of special importance' (so decided by a simple majority of General Assembly) – there must be a majority of two-thirds of those present and voting.[73]

Secondly, the National Council has elected, nominated and co-opted members. Its elected members must be at least one half of its members. An approved national or regional body nominates one representative

---

[70] MCB: Con. Art. 4; see also Standing Orders.   [71] MCB: Con. Art. 4.1.

[72] See also MCB: Con. Art. 9: the Preamble and Art. 3.1 of the Principles of Association are not subject to amendment; the Constitution may only be amended by special resolution of the General Assembly; if the Constitution is not affected, National Council may amend the Standing Orders only to ensure the smooth functioning of the MCB in the attainment of its objects. National Council must inform all MCB member bodies of any proposed and agreed amendment; Art. 10: dissolution.

[73] MCB: Con. Art. 4.1.

(who together must not out-number the elected members). The National Council may co-opt persons 'to reflect the diversity of thought, background and gender' in the MCB and 'the variety of social and cultural backgrounds and outlooks of the community'. The National Council is responsible to the General Assembly for 'the efficient and proper functioning' of the MCB, carrying out its own policies and taking initiatives consistent with its own 'policy guidelines in the best interests of the Muslim community'. It must appoint specialist committees on finance and general purpose, research and documentation, media, legal affairs and membership. It meets at least once every three months. Quorum is one third of its members. Wherever possible, National Council decisions must be based on consensus, but if a resolution is voted on, the Secretary General has a casting vote. Matters defined by the National Council as 'of special importance', and those relating to extraordinary items of expenditure beyond a limit agreed by it, require the approval of two-thirds of the members. All other matters are decided by a simple majority.[74]

Thirdly, the Executive Committee consists of the Secretary General (chair), Deputy Secretary General, Treasurer, three Assistant Secretary Generals and duly appointed Advisors. Its role is 'to oversee that the MCB is functioning properly and that the decisions made by the National Council are properly implemented', to which end it: may set up Committees or Task Groups to deliver any task or programme of action; may supervise and guide the Specialist and other Committees as appropriate; and must call for and consider reports from the chairpersons of all Specialist Committees. The Executive Committee meets at least once every month, and its decisions are by consensus, but if the Secretary General so decides by majority vote in a secret ballot.[75]

Fourthly, as its principal administrative officer, the Secretary General is: to convene the General Assembly, prepare the working papers and agenda and maintain a record of proceedings and resolutions in a Minutes Book; to direct the work of the National Council in implementing policies set by the General Assembly; to present a report of activities to the annual meeting of General Assembly; to serve as 'the official

---

[74] MCB: Con. Art. 4.2: there are also rules on notice of meetings, quorum, chairing, voting and vacancies; see also Art. 4.5: the functions of these specialist committees.

[75] MCB: Con. Art. 4.3: the Secretary General must invite the immediate past Secretary General to attend Executive Committee in an *ex-officio* capacity for one year following completion of their term.

spokesperson of the MCB'; to be responsible for maintaining a record of proceedings and resolutions of the National Council in a Minutes Book; and to convene and chair the Executive Committee.[76] Three Assistant Secretaries General assist the Secretary General in roles determined by the Secretary General at the Executive Committee.[77]

Fifthly, the Board of Counsellors is an advisory body – it advises on proposals from and to the General Assembly, National Council, Executive Council and its Specialist Committees; it also acts as the body for grievance and dispute resolution in accordance with the Governance Protocols. The Board members must be notified of meetings of the National Council, which they may attend as observers but do not vote; it must also elect one member as its Convenor and another as its Secretary (both for two years renewable for one more term); and it may set up Committees to carry out its functions and responsibilities. Board members are appointed by the National Council and hold office for six years or less – they must be 'experts in Shariah and Muslims of good repute who have achieved distinction in other fields'. The Board meets at least twice a year and must record its meetings in a minute book kept by its Secretary.[78]

Governance at the Regional Level

Each religion has institutions of government which function at regional level. Whilst the principles of representation, division of functions and accountability are shared, there is diversity within and between the religions as to the degree to which such regional institutions may exercise authority over the local religious community or are subject to the coercive or moral/persuasive authority of their national institutions.

Unions, Districts and Communities

Some provision may be made for regional structures within Judaism. For example, the (Orthodox) nationwide United Synagogue may promote or form or assist in doing so a union of synagogues, in any district, for persons of the Jewish religion who conform to the Polish or German ritual, including synagogues not being member synagogues, in such

---

[76] The Deputy Secretary General deputises for the Secretary General in his/her absence and must assist the Secretary General in the performance of his duties.
[77] MCD. Con. Art. 4.4.   [78] MCB₁ Con. Art. 4.6.

manner as is mutually agreed by the United Synagogue and governing bodies of such non-member synagogues.[79] Similarly, the United Synagogue of Conservative Judaism Board of Directors may create and organize regions geographically aligned, to which all member *kehillot* must be assigned, and regulate their operations; each one of these regions is a 'district', and its President is a 'District Council Chair'.[80]

However, the nationwide statutes of the (Orthodox) United Synagogue and the bye-laws of the United Synagogue of Conservative Judaism do not further regulate such regional unions and districts. By way of contrast, the membership of the Union of Liberal and Progressive Synagogues may include regional bodies with their own system of government and law. For example, Wessex Liberal Jewish Community (which currently has no synagogue) has a Council (composed of the elected Honorary Officers and other members who serve as its Charity Trustees) which manages 'the community' and must meet at least four times each year, decide matters by a majority of votes (the chair having a casting vote), and be quorate.[81] The Honorary Officers – the chair, Treasurer, secretary and membership officer – are elected by the community General Meeting.[82] To be a trustee, a person must be a community member and qualified as a Charity Trustee under civil law.[83] The trustees 'manage the business of the charity' and may, for example, raise funds, acquire, maintain and dispose of property, and pay for goods and services;[84] delegate their powers and functions to a committee of two or more trustees,[85] and make 'rules or bye-laws' with respect to the conduct of their business; admission, rights and privileges of members and their conduct 'in relation to one another' and to employees and volunteers; procedures at meetings; and the keeping of records. The General Meeting may alter, add to or repeal these rules or bye-laws; the trustees must adopt such means as they think sufficient to bring the rules and bye-laws

---

[79] US: Statutes 5.

[80] USCJ: BL 3.2. Also WCCMJ: By-Laws III: congregations may set up regional coordinating bodies.

[81] WLJC: Con. Art. 21; see also Art. 22: conflicts of interests; Art. 23: validity of decisions.

[82] WLJC: Con. Art. 18: the trustees may also appoint trustees to act as officers.

[83] WLJC: Con. Art. 17: Council may also co-opt a further two members; Art. 20: the trustees cease to hold office e.g. on resignation, on ceasing to be a member and on being disqualified under civil law.

[84] WLJC: Con. Art. 18: moreover: 'No alteration of [the] constitution or any special resolution shall have retrospective effect to invalidate any prior act of the trustees.'

[85] WLJC: Con. Art. 24: the trustees may revoke the delegation; committees must report to Council.

to the members' notice; and: 'No rule or bye-law shall be inconsistent with, or shall affect or repeal anything contained in, the Constitution' of the community.[86] However, no amendment may be made to the constitution which would: have the effect of making the charity cease to be a charity under civil law; alter the objects of the community or its provisions on applying its income and property to its trustees, without the consent of the (civil) Charity Commission. Any provision on for instance membership may be amended by resolution passed by a simple majority of members voting at a General Meeting – a copy of it must be sent to the Charity Commission.[87]

Dioceses, Circuits and Presbyteries

Regional structures are more elaborate in Christianity. Within the historic churches, and under the principles of Christian law, the form and authority of any regional assembly depend on the polity of the tradition in question, Episcopal, Presbyterian or Congregational. As such, regional ecclesial organisations may be in the form of a diocese, eparchy, synod, district, classis, presbytery, association or other regional unit. A regional ecclesial unit may have such institutions, in the form of a synod, council, classis, presbytery or other assembly, as are prescribed by the law applicable to it. A regional institution exercises such authority and functions as are conferred on it by the ecclesial community to which it belongs or the constituent churches associated with it. A regional assembly or other institution is composed of the faithful who are elected or otherwise appointed to it by those competent to do so under the law.[88]

First, according to Roman Catholic canon law, a diocese is a portion of the people of God entrusted to a bishop who nurtures it with the co-operation of the *presbyterum*; 'it constitutes a particular church' in which 'the one, holy, catholic and apostolic Church of Christ truly exists and functions'; a diocese has a defined territory and juridical personality, and may only be established by the supreme authority.[89] The diocesan bishop 'governs the particular church ... with legislative, executive and judicial power, in accordance with the law'; the bishop exercises legislative power

---

[86] WLJC: Con. Art. 32. For the Annual and General Meetings, see Arts. 10–15.
[87] WLJC: Con. Art. 7.
[88] Christian Law Panel of Experts, *Principles of Christian Law* (2016) IV.4: Regional Church Structures.
[89] CIC: cc. 368–369; see also cc. 370–371 for e.g. territorial prelatures and vicariates.

himself (it cannot be delegated), executive power personally or through Vicars General or Episcopal Vicars, and judicial power personally or through a Judicial Vicar.[90] The Diocesan Synod assists the bishop and consists of clergy and laity elected by the Diocesan Pastoral Council. The bishop convenes, presides at and dissolves the Synod. He is its sole legislator (members have only a consultative vote), and signs and publishes the decrees which he communicates to the Metropolitan and the Episcopal Conference.[91] The Diocesan Curia consists of institutions and persons who assist the bishop in diocesan governance.[92] The bishop may also be assisted by a Presbyteral Council,[93] Finance Committee[94] and Pastoral Council, which must meet at least once a year.[95]

Secondly, the territory of each Anglican Church is divided into dioceses; a diocese is a territory under the spiritual leadership and oversight of a diocesan bishop and assisted by a representative assembly (typically a Synod or Conference). The creation, division, amalgamation and dissolution of a diocese are usually the responsibility of the central national church assembly.[96] The diocesan assembly consists of houses composed of the bishop, and elected representatives of the clergy and laity; meetings are convened and presided over by the bishop and are usually annual.[97] It may have competence to legislate for the diocese in relation to prescribed matters as well as jurisdiction over its more localised ecclesiastical units (such as parishes); the diocesan assembly must also consider any matter referred by the central assembly and implement the lawful directions of

---

[90] CIC: c. 391; c. 381: a bishop has 'all the ordinary, proper and immediate power required for the exercise of his pastoral office, except in matters which ... the Supreme Pontiff reserves to the supreme or to some other ecclesiastical authority'; c. 134: an 'ordinary' is e.g. a diocesan bishop.

[91] CIC: cc. 460–468: the bishop determines the manner of election and number of lay members.

[92] CIC: cc. 469–494: the officers include the Vicar General, Episcopal Vicar and Chancellor.

[93] CIC: cc. 495–502: he must consult the Council as to matters prescribed under e.g. cc. 461, 515, 1263 and 1742; the College of Consultors has prescribed functions when the diocese is impeded or vacant.

[94] CIC: cc. 492–494: its members (clerical or lay) must be persons of outstanding integrity and skilled in finance and civil law; the bishop must also appoint a financial administrator: see below Chapter 9.

[95] CIC: cc. 511–514: those 'outstanding in firm faith, high moral standards and prudence'.

[96] PCLCCAC: Principle 20: a diocese consists of the faithful in a territory overseen by a bishop.

[97] See e.g. Church of England: Synodical Government Measure 1969, s. 4; Scottish Episcopal Church: Can. 50; Church in Wales: Con. IV.

the latter to which it must make an annual report.[98] The diocesan assembly has an executive organ (its Standing or Executive Committee) which acts with the authority of the assembly between its sessions, advises the bishop and discharges other functions assigned to it by the assembly; the diocesan assembly may also establish a variety of committees, boards, commissions and other bodies, such as on ministry, liturgy and finance, under the control of the diocesan assembly.[99]

Thirdly, Methodist churches have a system of districts, consisting of circuits, which are subject to the jurisdiction of the (national) Conference. For instance, the Conference of the Methodist Church in Great Britain designates a district 'to advance the mission of the Church in a region, by providing opportunities for circuits to work together and support each other, by offering them resources of finance, personnel and expertise, which may not be available locally and by enabling them to engage with the wider society of the region as a whole'.[100] The United Reformed Church too has regions with representative District Councils.[101] In Presbyterian polity, the Presbytery is a court which gives spiritual leadership to the ministers, officers and congregations within its bounds; it appoints a moderator (minister, elder or deacon responsible for order) and a clerk, has a membership of an equal number of ministers and representative elders elected by the Kirk Sessions, and meets to legislate, adjudicate on disputes and administer its affairs.[102] For example, an Irish Presbytery is 'the body primarily responsible for corporate oversight of the congregations and causes assigned to it by the General Assembly'; it may issue 'ordinances' but must observe 'the laws and directions of the Assembly'; and it 'superintends' the 'spiritual and temporal affairs of its congregations'.[103] Baptist Unions may also

---

[98] PCLCCAC: Principle 20: the bishop may give/withhold consent to proposed legislation if allowed, but may not legislate unilaterally; see e.g. Church in Wales: Con. IV.43: Acts of the Diocesan Conference.

[99] For executive committees, see e.g. Church in Wales: Con. IV.16; for boards, etc., see e.g. Church of England: Diocesan Boards of Finance Measure 1925, ss. 1–3: the Board must comply with synod directions.

[100] MCGB: Constitutional Practice and Discipline, Standing Orders 400.

[101] URC: Manual B.2.3: the District Council (moderator and representatives of local churches) meets annually to discharge tasks under the URC Acts 1972, 1981, 2000; see also B.2.4: the Provincial (or National) Synod.

[102] J.L. Weatherhead, ed., Constitution and Laws of the Church of Scotland (1997) 97: Act VIII, 1996: moderator; Act III, 1992: membership.

[103] PCI: Code, paras. 61–79: it consists of ministers and ruling elders appointed by each Kirk Session, has officers (moderator, clerk), meets four times per annum, forms new

have a system of regional associations but these do not enjoy jurisdiction over the autonomous local church.[104]

Muslim Regional Councils

Muslims also have regional organisations.[105] Some are governed by skeletal norms, others by norms that are more detailed. On the one hand, the Bolton Council of Mosques, for instance, has skeletal norms. Its secretary and two members elected either by the mosque committee or the mosque Annual General Meeting represent each of its 25 or so mosques in Bolton and its neighbouring area on the council Management Committee – the mosque secretary must notify the council secretary of its Annual General Meeting.[106] The Management Committee meets at least once each month with the Executive Committee of the Council, and two-thirds of member mosques must be represented on the Management Committee for a quorate meeting.[107] The composition of the council Executive Committee includes persons from the Management Committee representing each mosque; the Executive Committee appoints the Council officers, including the Chairman, the Secretary, and the Treasurer who serve for two years but who may be re-appointed at the council biennial General Meeting. The duties and powers of the council Management Committee include: safeguarding the interests of its members; carrying out its objects and 'general policy'; removing a committee member who is 'irresponsible in his behaviour and duties towards the [Council] or the Muslims in the community or to mankind in general'; and directing the Executive Committee.[108] The council Chairman is to protect the constitution, to preside at the Management and Executive

congregations if authorised by General Assembly, ordains, installs and oversees ministers (e.g. in preaching, doctrine), and enquires into the work of Kirk Sessions and Congregational Meetings; 256: annual report to the General Assembly.

[104] See N. Doe, *Christian Law* (2013) 145–146.

[105] See e.g. IFIS CUBE Network: Sample Constitution of an Islamic Society: Art. 5: Regional Society Representation.

[106] Bolton Council of Mosques (BCOM): Con. Art. 13: any mosque member may be co-opted onto a council sub-committee with approval of the management committee; Art. 9: councillors and MPs are not eligible to hold office.

[107] BCOM: Art. 12: provision is made for extraordinary meetings of the Management Committee and for an Annual General Meeting and Extraordinary General Meeting, which may amend the constitution.

[108] BCOM: Arts. 14–15; see also Art. 16: Executive Committee.

Committee meetings, and, quasi-judicially, 'to reconcile differences and to establish peace and harmony'.[109]

On the other hand, the Council for Mosques (Bradford) is an example of somewhat more detailed governance norms. Importantly, the Council itself must 'respect the independence of all our member organisations' and so performs an advisory (*shoorahi*) role. First, membership of the Council is open 'to all Mosques and other Islamic faith-based establishments in the Bradford district, with the exception of those belonging to any organisation opposed to Muslim interests'; members must 'take an oath of allegiance to abide by the Council ... constitution'. Applications to join are decided by the Executive Committee, and membership is terminated if approved by the full Council, which consists of two representatives nominated by each member organisation – the representatives must not be engaged in 'activities that are against Islam or shariah (Islamic law)'. Secondly, the Council: lobbies on behalf of the Muslim community on local and national matters such as law and order, health, education and interfaith relations; offers 'guidance on a wide range of Islamic cultural and religious issues'; provides Muslim burial services; and works with partners to give community support. Thirdly, the Executive Committee is elected by the Council members, comprises a President, two Vice Presidents, General Secretary (elected at the Annual General Meeting), Joint Secretary and Treasurer (appointed by the Executive Committee) and manages 'all aspects of the organisation's administration'. In turn, the Management Committee is appointed by the Executive Committee consulting the full Council, consists of Council and co-opted members and past Presidents and advises the Executive Committee and provides 'guidance and direction on ... policy matters'. Sub-committees are appointed at the discretion of the Executive Committee, which in doing so must consult with the Management Committee, and provide advice on for example education, law and order, health and bereavement. The Advisory Committee of Senior Ullama of the Council provides, amongst other things, 'practical advice and support on religious, cultural and social aspects of living as a Muslim'.[110]

---

[109] BCOM: Art. 17; see also Art. 18: Secretary; and Art. 19: Treasurer.
[110] CFM: www.councilformosques.org/about-us/constitution-and-membership/; and: www councilformosques.org/our-work/guidance/.

Governance at the Local Level

Each religion has institutions of government at local level. Whilst the principles of representation, division of functions and accountability are shared, there is diversity within and as between religions as to the degree to which local institutions are subject to the coercive or moral/persuasive authority of national and/or regional institutions.

Synagogues: Councils and Officers

Whilst all the Jewish organisations studied here share broadly similar institutional structures, there are subtle differences as between the traditions, not least in terms of the breadth and depth of the coverage of their norms. First, for the (Orthodox) United Synagogue, to be admitted as a member synagogue,[111] the congregation must notify its desire 'by resolution passed in accordance with the laws and regulations ... in force with respect to that Synagogue'.[112] The Council of the United Synagogue may then admit the synagogue which has 'the like rights and obligations with those of the then existing Member Synagogues'.[113] The Council may also found a synagogue.[114] The Council may discontinue a member synagogue as a place of worship if it holds a meeting of all its members to consider their views. If Council so determines, the Honorary Officers may then take steps to discontinue the synagogue as a place of worship, in particular with regard to its property and affairs (subject to any relevant trusts). If the land and buildings of the member synagogue are to be sold or otherwise disposed of, the Honorary Officers must notify Council at its next meeting.[115]

A member synagogue is governed by its body of Local Honorary Officers, Board of Management and Annual General Meeting. The body of Local Honorary Officers consists of no fewer than three positions, or, if the Board of Management so determines, five positions. If three positions, the Local Honorary Officers must include two Wardens and a Financial Representative, and if five positions, there must be a Chairman, Vice Chairman, two Wardens and a Financial Representative. Males and

---

[111] US: Statutes 2: 'Member Synagogues' are listed in Sch. 1. See also Stats. 50–51: the admission of Affiliated (listed in Sch. 2) and Associated Synagogues (listed in Sch. 3).

[112] In the absence of such laws and regulations, it must do so by resolution passed at a meeting of its members of the age of 21 and above, by the majority of persons present at such meeting.

[113] US: Statutes 46.   [114] US: Statutes 47.   [115] US: Statutes 48.

females may be elected as Local Honorary Officers; but when there are three such officers, the two Wardens must be male; if there is a vacancy among the officers, when there are four of these, the Wardens and one of the other Local Honorary Officers must be male; the Chairman and Wardens must always be male. The Financial Representative holds office for two years from their election until the end of the relevant Annual General Meeting. The other Local Honorary Officers hold office for one year.[116] However, no one may hold office for more than six consecutive years, and no Local Honorary Officer assumes office before agreeing to abide by the Protocols issued by the nationwide Honorary Officers.[117]

Subject to a direction of the nationwide Honorary Officers, the Local Honorary Officers are 'responsible for the day to day conduct and management of the Synagogue'. They may: delegate to the Board of Management such of their powers or functions as they decide; form Committees of the Board of Management or other synagogue members and delegate to them such functions as they think fit; and appoint (in accordance with the guidelines or directions of the Honorary Officers) employees (other than the Rabbi) who are then subject to the direction of the Local Honorary Officers or Honorary Officers.[118] The Local Honorary Officers must ensure that the synagogue adheres to the statutes and bye-laws of the United Synagogue, and the policies of its Honorary Officers; and that an Administrator of the synagogue is appointed to discharge such administrative functions as the Local Honorary Officers must determine.[119] They must meet as often as they consider necessary, although seven days written notice must be given, and must attend any meeting which is requested by the nationwide Honorary Officers or by the Chief Executive of the United Synagogue.[120]

Each member synagogue must have a Board of Management consisting of the Local Honorary Officers and no fewer than ten or more than

---

[116] Namely, unless the Board of Management determines prior to an AGM that the Local Honorary Officers are elected for less than a year, that is, until the end of the next but one AGM following their election.

[117] US: Bye-Laws 7. See also 10: no one may be a Local Honorary Officer, or must vacate their office, who e.g. ceases to be a Synagogue member; becomes bankrupt or of unsound mind; resigns; becomes precluded/suspended from acting as a Charity Trustee under civil law; or has been found, in the opinion of the nationwide Honorary Officers, guilty of gross misconduct or default in the discharge of his role.

[118] US: Bye-Laws 8: a committee of Local Honorary Officers must act 'in accordance with [any] guidelines or directions' of the Honorary Officers of the United Synagogue.

[119] US: Bye-Laws 17.

[120] US: Bye-Laws 9: the meeting must be quorate and a record kept.

24 others elected at the Annual General Meeting. Half of the seats are reserved for male members of the synagogue and half for female members. Board members, other than Local Honorary Officers, hold office for one year.[121] The Board, for example: determines the composition of the body of Local Honorary Officers and the Board itself; discusses the synagogue's affairs; assists and advises the Local Honorary Officers on day-to-day administration; receives and considers the annual budget prepared by the Local Honorary Officers (making representations as it thinks fit); determines which candidate for appointment of a Rabbi should be recommended to the Synagogue Members; and discharges such other functions as may be allocated by the Local Honorary Officers.[122] The Board must meet at least four times each year and on requisition of the Honorary Officers or of one-third of Board members. It is chaired by the Chairman of the Local Honorary Officers (or if absent the Vice Chair). Matters are determined by a majority vote but the Chairman has a second/casting vote. The Honorary Officers or their authorised representatives may attend and speak (but not vote) at a Board meeting.[123]

An Annual General Meeting of members must be held at a date decided by the Local Honorary Officers: to receive the Local Honorary Officers' report and synagogue accounts; to elect the Local Honorary Officers and Board of Management; and to consider any advisory motions appearing on the agenda for the meeting. Not less than 28 days written notice of the meeting must be given (with the agenda) by the synagogue administrator to all synagogue members. The national Honorary Officers, after notice to the Local Honorary Officers, may send representatives to any (Annual) General Meeting who may speak but not vote.[124] Provision also exists for Special General Meetings, which may be called by the Local Honorary Officers or national Honorary Officers.[125] Every member present has one vote, but the Chairman has a second/casting vote, and the minutes must be kept.[126] The constitutions of other Orthodox synagogues may have similar rules.[127]

---

[121] US: Bye-Laws 11: normally, they cannot hold six consecutive terms of office; 12: casual vacancies.

[122] US: Bye-Laws 12.

[123] US: Bye-Laws 13: there are also rules on quorum, notice of meetings and minutes; 14: vacation of office; 15: conflicts of financial interest.

[124] US: Bye-Laws 18.   [125] US: Bye-Laws 19.

[126] US: Bye-Laws 20; 21: this contains elaborate rules on all elections and challenges to their validity.

[127] See e.g. NHC: Laws and Con. e.g. Art. 1: Local Honorary Officers. For the Board of Management, Annual General Meeting, and Officers, see also e.g. NHAYS: Con. Arts. 6,

Secondly, the Movement for Reform Judaism has a Code of Practice which provides for synagogue governance. A synagogue must have a Council to: (1) serve the charity without regard to members' personal interests; (2) preserve its independence from the direct control of others; (3) manage and account for its resources; (4) comply with relevant (civil) law and respect the legal and human rights of the individual; (5) serve the synagogue objects, conduct its affairs openly (whilst respecting confidentiality), and carry out its external relations, fund-raising and publicity in a way that enhances its own reputation and that of charities generally. The Council should be: co-operative and creative, not 'an end unto itself [but] an integral part of the community, open and responsive to new ideas and new personnel'; constantly renewing itself and synagogue life; a learning environment to develop skills/expertise; the final arbiter in synagogue affairs; and responsible for managing the synagogue, personnel, staff and committees, and for electing a member to the Board of Deputies of British Jews. Moreover, in making policy, Council is 'to be aware of the Constitution (Laws) of the community, the Codes of Practice and Areas of Responsibility documents and ... obey its rules whilst trying to keep to the spirit of their content'. Its Chair is, *inter alia*, to: oversee its work; arbitrate on disputes in the community or Council; help set policy for the year with the Honorary Secretary or Administrator (its Vice Chair); attend (if possible) the Movement for Reform Judaism Council meetings; represent and speak on behalf of the synagogue; attend as many communal events and religious services as possible; attend all synagogue sub-committee meetings on a regular basis; manage the Rabbi and the Administrator; and write a report for the synagogue newsletter. Provision also exists for annual and special general meetings, appointing a delegate to attend meetings of the Movement of Reform Judaism, reporting to Council thereon.[128]

In turn, member synagogues rehearse or elaborate on these national norms.[129] North London Reform Synagogue is typical: 'The management and affairs of the Synagogue shall be invested in a Council, who may delegate day-to-day matters to an Executive Committee' composed of the

---

12–13: no decisions as 'to religious matters made by any ... Committees shall be valid unless and until sanctioned by the Rabbi'.

[128] MRJ: Code of Practice, pp. 4–6, 14. See also p. 8: the Honorary Secretary.

[129] See also e.g. BHRS: Con. 11: General Meeting of Members; Annual General Meeting; 12–20: Charity Trustees and Council; 23: President, Trustees, Wardens; and SSRS: Con. Art. 8: Honorary Officers; 9: Council; 10. Annual General Meeting; 11: Elections; 13–14: Committees.

Chairman, Honorary Treasurer, Honorary Secretary, Rabbi, and up to four Council Members 'responsible collectively for the co-ordination of all Synagogue affairs'.[130] The Annual General Meeting: elects Council members and officers, including a President (whose rights and duties are fixed by Council);[131] receives the report of the Council, Treasurer, Auditor and Sub-Committees;[132] and approves amendments to the Laws (which are sent to the civil Charity Commission).[133]

Thirdly, the Union of Liberal and Progressive Synagogues is itself committed to the synagogue as a 'democratically governed community' in which 'women and men may ... hold any synagogue office'.[134] For example, Elstree Liberal Synagogue has a Council empowered to: (1) provide and maintain a place of worship and arrange religious services; (2) provide, arrange and conduct religious education; (3) solemnise marriages; (4) provide for burial and cremation; (5) perform such other religious rites and charitable duties as it may determine; (6) raise funds; (7) acquire, maintain and dispose of property and employ staff; (8) co-operate with other charities, voluntary bodies and statutory authorities; (9) determine and decide all questions relating to the religious practices and services of the synagogue and religious education of members' children; (10) decide all questions as to the administration of the synagogue and its affairs, appoint such committees as it may think fit and do all such other lawful acts to achieve the synagogue objects.[135] The synagogue has four Honorary Officers: Chairman, Vice Chairman, Secretary and Treasurer – these must be full synagogue members who have served at least one full year as Ordinary Officers of the Council in the past. They are also the Council Executive Officers.[136] The Council consists of not less than ten or more than 14 Officers: the Honorary Officers and not less than six or more than ten Ordinary Officers elected at a General Meeting. Only full members of the synagogue are eligible to be Officers of the Council.[137] All officers are elected for two years and may

---

[130] NLRS: Laws, Arts. 2 and 3.   [131] NLRS: Laws, Arts. 8–9.

[132] NLRS: Laws, Arts. 15–18.

[133] NLRS: Laws, Art. 20: i.e. Art. 1: objects; and Art. 22: dissolution.

[134] ULPS: *Affirmations* (2006) Arts. 15 and 32.   [135] ELS: Con. Art. 4.

[136] ELS: Con. Art. 7.

[137] ELS: Con. Art. 8: provision also exists to co-opt members. The Minister of the Congregation, representative to the Board of Deputies of British Jews, Honorary President and representative to the ULPS Council may attend but not vote at Council meetings.

be re-elected at the next Annual General Meeting,[138] but cease if, *inter alia*, disqualified under civil charity law or removed by Council 'for good reason' after being heard.[139] Council must hold at least ten ordinary meetings each year.[140] The General Meeting may elect an Honorary Life President in recognition of distinguished service to the synagogue and community.[141] Council must appoint representatives to the Council of the Union of Liberal and Progressive Synagogues.[142]

Lastly, each United Synagogue of Conservative Judaism *kehillah* should have an annual meeting, a board of trustees, and congregational officers – and there are detailed rules on their functions.[143] Moreover, congregations 'should enter into reasonable written contracts with staff, enforceable under local law, in terms consistent with the highest ethical and moral standards of Jewish practice and tradition'.[144] However, unlike the Orthodox United Synagogue, there are general norms on how these institutions are to exercise their functions in terms of relations with other *kehillot*. For example, each congregation must respect the boundaries of other congregations (*Hasagat G'vul*). Boundaries may be physical or, under halachic precedent, demographic, ritual or moral. Thus, a *kehillah* may not solicit members of other congregations, and, if it proposes to expand to another community, it should consult that community, accommodate its concerns and not endanger its survival.[145]

Parish Councils to Kirk Sessions

In the historic churches of Christianity, regional ecclesial units may be divided into or constituted by local churches or congregations existing at the most localised level. A church organised locally may be in the form of a parish, circuit, congregation or other ecclesial unit. Its assembly, styled variously a council, meeting, session or other body, has such authority

---

[138] ELS: Con. Art. 9: there are qualifications: e.g. no one may remain in office for over ten years.
[139] ELS: Con. Art. 10: 75 per cent must vote in favour of removal; Art. 11: conflicts of interest.
[140] ELS: Art. 12: this also deals with committees; as well as chairmanship, quorum, voting and minute keeping.
[141] ELS: Con. Art. 13: the office does not carry voting or administrative rights.
[142] ELS: Con. Art. 14: they may be removed or substituted at any time by Council.
[143] USCJ: A Guide to Congregational Constitutions and Bylaws (2010) Arts. VII–IX.
[144] USCJ: Standards for Congregational Practice (2017): Standard IX.
[145] USCJ: Standards for Congregational Practice (2017): Standard X.

and functions as are lawfully inherent to it or conferred on it by the institutions of the wider ecclesial entity to which it belongs. It, in turn, is composed of those members of the faithful who are lawfully elected or otherwise appointed to it. All ecclesial units at each level are interdependent.[146] Lay people may be elected to these institutions and hold offices associated with them. Indeed, the law should enable the laity to exercise public ministry in those offices or other positions lawfully open to them. They may be admitted to such offices and positions if they are suitable, qualified, selected and admitted by a competent ecclesial authority for such term as is prescribed by law. Lay ministers and officers exercise such public and representative ministry in or on behalf of a church and perform such functions as may be prescribed and permitted by its laws. The authority to discipline, dismiss or reappoint a lay minister or officer depends on, and its exercise must comply with, church law.[147]

First, in Roman Catholic canon law each diocese is divided into parishes.[148] A parish is 'a certain community of Christ's faithful stably established within a particular church, whose pastoral care, under the authority of the diocesan bishop, is entrusted to a parish priest as its proper pastor'. It has juridical personality and the bishop alone is competent to erect, suppress or alter parishes.[149] After the bishop has consulted the Presbyteral Council, and if he judges it expedient, a Pastoral Council is to be established in each parish; the pastor presides, and through the council the faithful assist in fostering pastoral activity; the council has a consultative (not determinative) vote and is governed by norms determined by the bishop. Each parish must also have a Finance Committee to assist the parish priest in the administration of the parish. The pastor is administrator of parish property and keeps its records and archives.[150]

---

[146] Christian Law Panel of Experts, *Principles of Christian Law* (2016) IV.5: The Local Church.

[147] Christian Law Panel of Experts, *Principles of Christian Law* (2016) II.4: Public Ministry Exercised by Lay Persons; public ministry, a gift of God, is the fulfilment of a function assigned in a church to an office or other position exercised under authority on behalf of that church in the service of its mission and witness to the Gospel.

[148] CIC: c. 374: for common action, neighbouring parishes may be grouped (e.g. in vicariates forane).

[149] CIC: c. 515; c. 518: personal parishes may also be set up according to rite, language or nationality.

[150] CIC: cc. 532–537, 1220, 1279, 1281–1288.

Similarly, an Anglican diocese too consists of more localised ecclesial units, such as archdeaconries and deaneries, and within these, parishes, the territorial organisation of which is usually in the keeping of the diocesan assembly.[151] Each parish is governed by an assembly (typically a Parochial Church Council) consisting of clergy and representatives of the laity elected at an annual meeting; the assembly is usually under the chairmanship of the minister in charge of the unit and elaborate rules cover meetings, quorum and decision-making.[152] The council and minister must co-operate in exercising spiritual, governmental and administrative functions; typically, the assembly must: promote the whole mission of the church, pastoral, evangelistic, social and ecumenical; report to the diocesan assembly; elect officers; implement matters referred to it by the diocesan bishop or assembly; administer property; and co-operate at visitations.[153] Similar arrangements exist in Lutheran congregations/parishes.[154]

Secondly, within Methodism, in the Methodist Church in Great Britain, the circuit is a unit of one or more local churches and 'the primary unit in which local churches express and experience their interconnexion in the Body of Christ'. The purposes of the circuit include the deployment of resources for ministry (people, property and finance), and promoting and supporting the work of the Society 'to the end that every member may share actively in world mission'. The Circuit Meeting, composed of the Circuit Superintendent (who presides), ministers and elected representatives from each local church, is 'the principal meeting responsible for the affairs of a Circuit' and 'the development of circuit policy'. It exercises a 'combination of spiritual leadership and administrative efficiency' and is the focal point of 'the working fellowship of the churches in the Circuit, overseeing their pastoral, training and evangelistic work' and the encouragement of leadership.[155] The Church Council is 'the principal meeting responsible for the affairs of a Local Church' or 'Society'.[156] It is composed

---

[151] For archdeacons and deaneries, see e.g. Church of Ireland: Const., II.42; Church of England: Synodical Government Measure 1969, s. 3: a deanery has a synod (an archdeaconry, divided into deaneries, does not).

[152] E.g. Church in Wales: Con. VI.24: meetings etc. of the Parochial Church Council.

[153] E.g. Church in Wales: Con. VI.22: mission. See also PCLCCAC: Principle 21.

[154] LCGB: Rules and Regulations, Congregations, 1–2.

[155] MCGB: Constitutional Practice and Discipline, Deed of Union 1; Standing Orders 500–517; 501: changes to Circuits are in the keeping of the Conference.

[156] MCGB: Constitutional Practice and Discipline, Deed of Union 1; see also Standing Orders 61, 600 and 602.

of ministers and lay representatives elected by the annual General Church Meeting and has 'authority and oversight over the whole area of the ministry of the church'.[157]

Thirdly, within the United Reformed Church, a local church consists of members associated locally for worship, witness and service; the Church Meeting is presided over by the minister and meets quarterly to, for example, further the church's mission, offer ministry in the locality, call ministers with the consent of Synod, elect elders and officers, and admit and transfer members. In turn, the Elders' Meeting (the minister and elders) has 'spiritual oversight'; it is presided over by the minister to, for example, foster witness and service to the community, evangelism, Christian education, ensure that public worship is regularly offered and the sacraments duly administered, provide for the pastoral welfare of the congregation and arrange for pulpit supply in a vacancy.[158]

Fourthly, in Presbyterianism, the Session (Kirk Session or Council) is the court of the local church.[159] For example, in the Presbyterian Church in Ireland, the Kirk Session consists of the ordained minister(s) and ruling elders of the congregation and has a moderator (minister) and a clerk; it meets at least twice a year to provide for 'the oversight and government of the congregation'. The Kirk Session is 'the governing body of a congregation' and must watch over and promote the spiritual interest of the congregation, contribute to Christian witness and service in the local community and authorise co-operation with other churches. It calls meetings of the congregation, provides for administration of the ordinances of sacrament and word, appoints officers, exercises authority over the congregation as to doctrine and conduct (including adjudication in disciplinary cases), keeps a roll of members, promotes stewardship and appoints representatives to the Presbytery and General Assembly.[160] It may also call such Congregational Meetings as the Presbytery may determine to consider, for example, the state of religion and needs of the community, promote mission, foster fellowship, authorise transactions (e.g. as to property), appoint trustees

---

[157] MCGB: Constitutional Practice and Discipline, Standing Orders 603: duties; 604: committees; 605: formation; 610: members; 621: Meeting.

[158] URC: Manual B.1 and B.2.

[159] J.L. Weatherhead, ed., *Constitution and Laws of the Church of Scotland* (1997) 103, Act XVII, 1931: Kirk Session. Ruling elders are ordained by Kirk Session.

[160] PCI: Code, paras. 25–44; 141–147: transaction of business; 148–155: rules of debate; 156–160: voting; see also PCW: Handbook of Rules, 3.1: District Meeting.

and raise funds.[161] In Baptist polity, the local church has its own institutions of governance.[162]

Mosques and Shura Committees

The principles of *shura* and *ijma* in classical Islamic law are used in modern Muslim regulatory instruments as an important feature of governance at local level.[163] Once more, a distinction is made between governing, managing and administering. Three approaches may be offered by way of examples. First, the Mosques and Imams National Advisory Board has issued 'best practice' guidance on the 'self-regulation' of mosques so that they have 'an accountable system of representation'; it contains 'standards'. Members should have: principles of good corporate governance; services that are provided by suitably qualified or experienced personnel who are not impeded from participating in activities (e.g. for young people and women); and schemes to promote the civic responsibility of Muslims in wider society. Mosques should 'self-certify whether they fully meet or partially meet' the standards. The Board randomly selects 50 per cent of mosques that claim to meet all the standards to assess how they do so. If the assessment finds the mosque does not meet the standards, when it has self-certified that it does, the Board supports it through a capacity-building scheme.[164]

Secondly, under the model constitution issued by the Central Mosque, each mosque must have a Shura/Management Committee composed of a Panel of Elected Officials and a Board of Life Trustees. With regard to the Panel of Elected Officials, a person may stand for election at the Biennial General Meeting of the congregation if that person: is a full member of the congregation; frequents congregational prayers; is an upright and

---

[161] PCI: Code, paras. 45–46; 46–52. Church of Scotland: Church Courts Act (Act III 2000) s. 37.

[162] See P. Goodliff, 'Baptist church polity and practice', 168 *Law and Justice* (2012) 3.

[163] See e.g. CJM: Con. Art. 4: Board of Trustees; Art. 5: elections; Art. 28–29: general and extraordinary meetings; NUIM: Con. Art. 4: the Mosque Committee includes a President, Secretary and Treasurer; Art. 5: procedure; Art. 6: meetings and sub-committees; and IFIS CUBE Network: Sample Constitution of an Islamic Society: Art. 4: Executive Committee; Art. 7: Sub-Committees; Art. 8: Meetings; Art. 9: Amendments to the Constitution; Art. 10: Elections.

[164] MINAB: www.minab.org.uk/. The Board awaits the outcome of the 'Better Mosques: A Community Consultation' (2018) on how 'a structured and national approach to developing better mosques in the UK' might be achieved: www.ourmosquesourfuture .org.uk/consultation.

practising Muslim of repute in the community; undertakes to attend all meetings (and submit an apology to the Ameer for non-attendance due to compelling reasons); has lodged a completed nomination form with the electoral officer of the Shura Committee a month before the election indicating an intent to stand for office; and has officially received and studied the code of conduct for Shura members.[165] Other congregation members may be co-opted by the Shura Committee. The elected officials must not exceed 20 or be fewer than ten unless the committee determines otherwise, and they hold office for two years but may stand for 'term after term'; they cease office if proven 'beyond doubt' to have committed a disqualifying act/offence as set out in the constitution until the Board of Life Trustees decides the matter.[166]

To join the Board of Life Trustees, a person must be one: of impeccable standing in the community with a recognized record of 15 years' service to the congregation; nominated by the Shura Committee; and elected by a two-third majority of the Shura Committee. The Board, *inter alia*: protects the congregation's assets; mediates or arbitrates in disputes in the congregation and Shura Committee; and acts as the final authority if dissolution occurs. The Board is presided over by the *Ameer* (President) of the Shura Committee. Life trusteeship does not preclude the holding of executive positions in the Shura Committee. The total number of life trustees must not exceed ten or be fewer than seven. Life Trustees are on the Shura Committee for life and may not transfer their trusteeship; they cease to hold office on death, if they reside for one year outside the relevant district, or if it is proven beyond doubt that they have committed a disqualifying act as set out in the constitution until the Board decides the matter.[167]

The functions of the Shura Management Committee are, *inter alia*: (1) to maintain the *masjid*, madrassa, and other properties, provide for the remuneration of the Imam(s), Muadhin(s), employees and others and to manage congregation finances; (2) to make, amend and review policies of the congregation for the control and management of its affairs; (3) to manage and control any institution which is established or acquired by the congregation; (4) to engage persons to deliver lectures on religious subjects and oversee the general education of *musallees*; (5) to maintain a

---

[165] Model Constitution of an Islamic Organisation: Panel of Elected Officials 1–2.
[166] Model Constitution of an Islamic Organisation: Panel of Elected Officials 3–8.
[167] Model Constitution of an Islamic Organisation: Board of Life Trustees. Provision also exists for Honorary Life Trustees; see also Cessation of Office, 1–5.

register of members, elected members and trustees and an inventory of congregation assets; (6) to establish (and dissolve) committees; (7) to appoint an Ameer, Deputy, Secretary and Treasurer, electoral officer, membership officer and other officers; and (8) generally to further the cause of Islam and the Muslim community under the congregation's objects.[168]

For the Management Committee to carry out business efficiently: 'Mashwara shall be conducted in the correct Islamic spirit and as set out in the Code of Conduct for the Management Committee'. For example: all special resolutions must be in writing and signed by all committee members; the Mashwara must be held fortnightly with no fewer than one Mashwara every month; notice of meetings must be displayed at the *masjid* at least two days in advance; and, echoing the principle of *ijma*, 'Decision-making ... shall as far as possible be ... on the basis of unanimity' – if not possible, the majority view prevails, and in the event of equality of votes, the chairman has the decisive vote.[169]

A general meeting of the congregation must be held in each second consecutive year and a special general meeting may be held at the discretion of the Shura Committee or if requisitioned by no fewer than 50 members. The biennial meeting (which is presided over by the Shura Committee), for example: receives and considers the financial statement of the congregation; elects members to the Shura Committee; and passes resolutions (by closed ballot or show of hands as decided by the Shura Committee).[170] A special general meeting may amend the constitution by a two-third majority vote.[171]

Lancaster Islamic Society, for example, uses Central Mosque's model constitution.[172]

Thirdly, other mosques mirror in different ways these fundamentals of governance. For example, the Markazi Jamia Masjid Riza and Islamic

[168] Model Constitution of an Islamic Organisation: Powers and Duties of the Shura Committee 1–14.
[169] Model Constitution of an Islamic Organisation: Mashwara/Management Committee 1–11.
[170] Model Constitution of an Islamic Organisation: General Meetings 1–8; there are rules on notice, quorum and minutes.
[171] Model Constitution of an Islamic Organisation: Amendments.
[172] LIS: Con: Shura/Management Committee; Panel of Elected Officials; Board of Life Trustees; Powers and Duties of the Shura Committee; Mashweras of the Management Committee; Biennial and Special General Meetings' Cessation of Office of Shura Members.

Centre (Huddersfield) has a Management Committee appointed from its members by the Trustees; it must select a chairperson, secretary, treasurer and joint treasurer from its members who hold office for three years.[173] Decisions are made by majority vote.[174] The Management Committee may make standing orders and rules for the use of the Masjid and Islamic Centre, consistent with the constitution and subject to review at the Annual General Meeting.[175] The constitution may be revoked or altered by a majority at the Annual General Meeting, subject to the approval by the Trustees.[176] Similar norms exist at Reading Muslim Council, which 'shall be administered and managed in accordance with this constitution by the members of the Executive Committee',[177] who are elected by the Annual General Meeting; the Executive Committee must elect from its own members a Chairman, Vice Chairman, Secretary and a Treasurer. They are elected for three years.[178] The Executive Committee must hold at least two ordinary meetings each year.[179] The Council Chairman presides at the Executive Committee (or, if absent, the Vice Chairman). Every matter is determined by a majority vote, the chair has a casting vote and minutes must be kept.[180] The Executive Committee must call an Annual General Meeting of Council members and present to it prescribed reports and accounts,[181] and it may call a special general meeting at any time – the secretary may also call a special general meeting if at least ten members request this in writing stating the business to be considered.[182] The Constitution of the Council may be altered by a resolution passed by not less than two-thirds of the members present and voting at a general meeting, and a copy of the alteration must be sent by the Executive Committee to the (civil) Charity

---

[173] MJMRIC: Con. Art. 7.

[174] MJMRIC: Con. Art. 8; see also Art. 9: quorum; Art. 10: minutes.

[175] MJMRIC: Con. Art. 11.   [176] MJMRIC: Con. Arts. 13 and 17.

[177] RMC: Con. Art. B.

[178] RMC: Con. Art. F; see also Art. G: Executive Committee proceedings are not invalidated by any vacancy in their number, failure to appoint or defect in their appointment or qualification; Art. H: Executive Committee members cease to hold office on e.g. being disqualified under civil charity law.

[179] A special meeting may be called at any time by the chairman or any four members of the Executive Committee on not less than seven days' notice to the other committee members.

[180] RMC: Con. Art. J; Art. O: the committee must make an annual return to the Charity Commissioners.

[181] RMC: Con. Art. P: this also provides for nominations for election to the Executive Committee.

[182] RMC: Con. Art. Q; Art. R: the secretary; Art. S: notices.

Commissioners.[183] Aberdeen Mosque and Islamic Centre too has a Board of Trustees (who must be 'good Muslims'), Executive Committee, President, several Sub-Committees and an Annual General Meeting.[184]

Conclusion

Despite the historical differences within and between the three faiths about the nature, origin and location of religious authority, the legal instruments of the entities studied here all have structures of consensual governance at national, regional, and local levels. At each level, norms deal with the composition, functions and interdependence of institutions. However, institutions at these levels enjoy different degrees of legislative and administrative authority (including strategic and operational decision-making in terms of governing, managing and executing). In this sense, there is a high level of legal pluralism or diversity with and between the faiths. At the national level, Jews and Christians have institutions with either a coercive or a moral authority over regional and more usually local religious communities; this is less the case with Islam. Regional structures are more developed in Christianity than in Judaism or Islam: diocesan assemblies in the Episcopal churches share much in common with the assemblies of Protestant districts and presbyteries – all have authority to govern at that level, but in the Baptist tradition regional associations may guide but not direct the local church, which is autonomous. At the most local level too, the religions all have assemblies, charged with the governance of synagogues, churches and mosques. To this extent, arrangements are also the product of the use of practical reason. Little use is made of religious soft-law in prescribing the institutional structures of their religious organisations – but soft-law is used by Muslim organisations in the form of model constitutions for mosque governance. A principle of the separation of functions is evident across the faith groups; typically, the right to legislate is entrusted to a body representative of all the faithful; management and sometimes strategic decision-making is vested in an executive body; and day-to-

---

[183] RMC: Con. Art. T: no amendment may be made to e.g. the name or objects of the charity.
[184] AMIC: Con: Art. IV: Board of Trustees; Art. V: Executive Committee; Art. VII: sub-committees; Art. VII: ad hoc committees; Art. IX: Annual General Meeting and Extraordinary General Meeting; Art. X: Amendments; Art. XII: Executive Committee Selection; Art. XV: Enforcement; Art. XVI: Dissolution.

day administration is assigned to a variety of officers, including trustees. There is little evidence that such arrangements are sourced directly in divine law. It is a principle of religious law that institutions of governance should be representative of members of the faith community, lawfully elected or otherwise appointed – to that extent, particularly as most of the entities here (or institutions within or associated with them) enjoy charitable status under civil law, their regulatory instruments seek to set democratic standards in religious governance. Whilst performing a range of religious activities within their governmental functions, the structures of these institutions are characterised by their functionality or secularity rather than their religiosity. They are rational. However, concepts and categories from classical religious law do surface from time to time in the modern regulatory instruments of the faith organisations studied, such as: the Jewish concepts of Rabbinic leadership and lay governance; the Christian concepts of collegiality, counsel and consent; and the Islamic concepts of consultation (*shura*) and consensus (*ijma*).

5

The Resolution of Disputes: Courts and Tribunals

The study of religious courts is commonplace in contemporary scholarship. However, to-date, there has been no comparative study of the treatment of tribunals and other dispute-resolution structures under the modern regulatory instruments of the faith communities treated here. The juridical instruments of Jewish, Christian and Muslim organisations provide a very wide range of mechanisms to enforce religious discipline and to resolve internally disputes amongst the faithful, including disagreement about the interpretation of religious law. Whilst the governance of discipline is sometimes within the competence of nationwide governing bodies, or else prescribed officers within them, generally the regulatory instruments reserve the responsibility of resolving disputes, which involve both faith leaders and followers (for example in Christianity by way of visitation), to the regional and/or local religious authorities. In addition, the three religions operate a court or tribunal system to deal with disputes involving faith leaders and, often, the followers. Elaborate provision is made for due process. The idea of a religious offence is a common and fundamental feature of the disciplinary systems of all three religions as is the provision of sanctions. This chapter examines norms on the interpretation of religious law, the informal resolution of disputes and the formal resolution of cases by religious courts, tribunals and other fora. It also explores the degree of religiosity or secularity of these norms, the extent of legal diversity within and between the religions and whether similarities between the legal instruments lead to shared principles in religious law on conflict resolution.[1]

---

[1] For a study of courts of the Abrahamic religions which operate in the USA, see M.J. Broyde, *Sharia Tribunals, Rabbinical Courts and Christian Panels* (Oxford: Oxford University Press, 2017).

The Interpretation of Religious Law

The interpretation of law is not only fundamental to the adjudication of disputes, it is also fundamental to the understanding of the nature and terms of religious practice. As such, the faith communities studied here make provision for the interpretation of religious law in a number of ways, outside the formal processes in courts or tribunals.

The Role of Rabbinical Assemblies

In classical Judaism, if in a responsum a Rabbinical decisor or *posek* (plural *poskim*) proposed an interpretation of the law, this could have been binding on whoever posed the question or for the immediate community; the authority of the interpretation depended on the stature of the *posek*, the quality of the interpretation and/or its reception by other Rabbis and communities – and in cases of disagreement, the majority opinion prevailed.[2] Today, there are various approaches to the interpretation of *halakhah*. Orthodox Judaism advocates strict or traditional interpretation. Conservative Judaism proposes that *halakhah* binds, but interpretation should be flexible so as to accommodate changes in circumstances. Reform, Liberal and Progressive Judaism proposes that *halakhah* may not bind strictly and that interpretations must suit the context.[3] In any event, institutionally, each tradition has its own Rabbinical authorities to interpret *halakhah* – and the modern regulatory instruments of Jewish entities often provide for their own interpretation by prescribed religious authorities.

First, with respect to the interpretation of *halakhah*, the Orthodox 'halakhic method' involves 'a set of rigorous techniques of textual interpretation that, when applied to the literary sources of Jewish law, distinguish objectively "right" understandings from "wrong" ones'; though some argue that: 'The judge or the *posek* must not say ... "bring the book, let us look up the law, let me decide the *halakhah* automatically, in

---

[2] R.S. Rheins, '*Asu Seyag LaTorah*' (2002) 91 at 96, citing Maimonides: Introduction to the *Mishnah*: 'every *mitzvah* ... was given to [Moses] with detailed explanations'; and: 'When a situation arose on which no explanation had been heard from the prophet (Moses), they determined a response by means of deduction, logical argument guided by the thirteen methods of Torah interpretation ... Whenever a disagreement developed, they followed the majority opinion, as the Torah prescribes (Exodus 23:2).'

[3] See above Chapter 1. See also S. Ettinger, 'The prohibition against consulting two authorities and the nature of halakhic truth', 18 *The Jewish Law Annual* (2010) 1–19.

accordance with the written word"'; rather: 'It is their duty ... to study carefully the sources of the law and to subject them to thorough analysis, to test them in the crucible of their training, knowledge, and reason, and to arrive thereby at the correct determination of the law.'[4] But for the Conservative tradition: 'Jewish law must be preserved but ... it is subject to interpretation by those who have mastered it, and ... the interpretation placed upon it by duly authorized masters in every generation must be accepted with as much reverence as those which were given in previous generations.'[5]

In turn, for some in Reform-Liberal Judaism, 'there is no such thing as the one objectively correct answer to a question of *halakhah*' – there is no single 'halakhic method ... to produce the right interpretations of Jewish legal texts'. Rather, halakhic interpretation is 'a flexible and dynamic intellectual activity, capable of meeting new challenges and accommodating changing insights', and prepared 'to slip the stifling bonds of precedent', not a 'mechanical application of black-letter rules'. The *posek*, therefore: 'may not defer to the authority of codes and compilations' but 'must claim ... freedom of judgment that belongs to all knowledgeable students of Jewish law, the freedom to arrive at one's own conclusions based upon one's own reading of the sources, no matter how innovative, even if those conclusions disagree with [those] of other rabbis'. This is so because 'circumstances of life, transformations in culture, scientific and technological developments in each ... generation create halakhic problems that demand resolution'; and so: '"good" liberal halakhic practice is a piece of writing to which we resonate and around which we coalesce as a community'.[6] In short, legal diversity exists in Judaism as to the interpretation of classic religious law.

Secondly, the regulatory instruments of Jewish religious organisations provide for the interpretation of these instruments by prescribed authorities within the organisation. Here, there seems to be less juristic diversity. In the (Orthodox) United Synagogue, the teaching of the Chief

---

[4] M. Washofsky, 'Against method: Liberal halakhah between theory and practice', in W. Jacob, ed., *Beyond the Letter of the Law* (2004) 17 at 27, quoting Ben Zion Meir Hai Uziel (1880–1953).

[5] I. Klein, *Jewish Religious Practice* (1992) xxii.

[6] M. Washofsky, 'Against method' (2004) 17 at 19–20, 27. See also W. Jacob, 'Writing responsa: a personal journey', in W. Jacob, ed., *Beyond the Letter of the Law* (2004) 103 at 100–109.

Rabbi may include interpretations of *halakhah*,[7] and the Rabbinical Council, the association of the United Synagogue Rabbinate, supports Rabbis in their professional development (which may include the development of halakhic method); indeed, its organising committee meets regularly with the Chief Rabbi, Dayanim of the London Beth Din and the United Synagogue Chief Executive.[8] Moreover, as to United Synagogue statutes: 'If any doubt or question shall arise as to the proper construction or application of ... these Statutes ... application may be made by the Honorary Officers to the Charity Commissioners for England and Wales, for their opinion and advice ... which ... when given, shall be binding on [those] Officers.'[9] Instruments commonly include interpretation or definition sections; and, for example, in the (Orthodox) Federation of Synagogues: 'Headings in the Laws are used for convenience only and shall not affect the construction or interpretation of the Laws.'[10]

Within the United Synagogue of Conservative Judaism, the Rabbinical Assembly has a Committee on Jewish Law and Standards which 'sets halakhic policy for Rabbinical Assembly Rabbis and for the Conservative movement as a whole'. It has 25 Rabbis (voting-members), five lay representatives (non-voting) and one cantor to represent the Cantors' Assembly (non-voting). It discusses 'all questions of Jewish law posed by members of the Rabbinical Assembly or arms of the Conservative movement'. When a question is placed on the agenda, each member writes *teshuvot* (responsa), which are discussed by the relevant subcommittees, and then heard by the Committee, usually at two meetings. Papers are approved when a vote is taken with six or more members voting in favour. Each paper is written in response to a specific question posed by a Conservative Rabbi. Committee members may submit concurring or dissenting opinions, which are attached to a decision but these have no 'official' status. Approved *teshuvot* represent 'official halakhic positions' of the Conservative movement; however: 'Rabbis have the authority ... as *marei d'atra*, to consider the Committee's positions but make their own decisions.' Therefore: 'When reviewing *teshuvot*, it is important ... that each of these Questions ... should be brought to [the] local

---

[7] For the Torah Thoughts of the Chief Rabbi, or *Divrei Torah* (singular *Dvar Torah*) literally, 'word(s) of Torah', i.e. Torah thought that is shared with others, see: http://chiefrabbi.org/dvar-torah/.

[8] US: www.theus.org.uk/article/rcus.   [9] US: Statutes 55.

[10] FOS: Laws 1.3: section 1 of the Laws is the interpretation section.

Conservative rabbi [as] *mara d'atra*, or local religious decisor, of a particular community' – the Committee *teshuvot* 'are not meant to, nor can they, substitute for the opinions of a local rabbi'.[11] In short, the Committee 'provides guidance in matters of *halakhah* for the Conservative movement', 'as interpreted by [its] rabbis', but each Rabbi has 'authority for the interpretation and application of all matters of *halakhah*'.[12]

Within the Movement for Reform Judaism (which also has an Assembly of Reform Rabbis), again laws of synagogues provide for their own interpretation; North London Reform Synagogue is typical: 'The Council of the Synagogue shall be the sole authority for the interpretation of these Laws and its decision upon any matter not provided for by these Laws shall be final and binding.'[13] It is also common for the constitutions of synagogues to include a 'definitions and interpretation' section;[14] some may also provide that a constitution should be interpreted in conjunction with specified codes of practice.[15] Likewise in the Union of Liberal and Progressive Judaism (which has a Rabbinic Conference), at Elstree Liberal Synagogue: 'The Council shall be the sole authority for the interpretation of this Constitution and its decisions upon any matter not provided for by this Constitution shall be final and binding.'[16]

Christian Texts and Contexts

Christianity has deep historical traditions as to the interpretation of church law and the role of the opinion of learned jurists in terms both of the legal text and its context.[17] Today, with respect to the historic churches, according to the principles of Christian law, laws should be interpreted by reference to their text, context and precedent; a church has authority to interpret its own law; and for the interpretation of law, recourse may be had to the purposes of the law, the mind of the legislator, and the faith and practice of the church.[18] These principles derive from the laws of churches.

---

[11] USCJ: www.rabbinicalassembly.org/jewish-law/committee-jewish-law-and-standards.
[12] This provision appears in the responsa of the Committee on Jewish Law and Standards: see e.g. Yoreh deah 370:1 (2010).
[13] NLRS: Laws, Art. 21; for an identical rule, see SSRS: Con. Art. 22.
[14] BHRS: Con. Art. 1.   [15] SSRS: Con. Art. 1.   [16] ELS: Con. Art. 24.
[17] J. Brundage, *Medieval Canon Law* (London: Longman, 1995) 168–174, and, for *consilia*, 180–181.
[18] Christian Law Panel of Experts, *Principles of Christian Law* (2016) I.5.

Within the Episcopal tradition, Roman Catholic canon law provides that: laws are 'to be understood in accord with the proper meaning of the words . . . in their text and context'; if the meaning remains doubtful, recourse is to be taken to parallel passages, to the circumstances of the law and to the mind of the legislator.[19] However, there is no system of binding judicial precedent in Roman Catholic canon law: the decision of a church court or tribunal does not have the status or force of law: it binds only the parties to it and it affects only the matter for which it was given. The only authentic and binding interpretation of a law which itself possesses the quality of law is that as promulgated by the legislator, and this is treated merely as a descriptive, declaratory or confirmatory statement of existing law; judicial decisions may be consulted as persuasive authorities and (unless a matter of penal law is involved) 'the case is to be decided in the light of . . . the jurisprudence and praxis of the Roman Curia'.[20]

For Anglicans too: 'Laws should be interpreted by reference to their text and context' and 'according to the proper meaning of their words'; and: 'Authoritative interpretations of law may be issued by church courts or tribunals, or by commissions or other bodies designated to interpret the law, in such cases, in such manner and with such effect as may be prescribed by the law.'[21] However, if 'the meaning of laws remains in doubt recourse may be had to analogous texts, the purposes and circumstances of the law, the mind of the legislator, the jurisprudence of church courts and tribunals, the opinion of jurists, the principles of canon law and theology, the common good, and the practice and tradition of that church and of the church universal'.[22] Moreover: 'The decision of a church court or tribunal has such binding or persuasive authority for other courts or tribunals as may be provided in the law.'[23]

Among the Protestant traditions, Methodists have much the same approach,[24] and the Methodist Church in Great Britain has a Committee

---

[19] CIC: c. 17. See also L. Örsy, *Theology and Canon Law: New Horizons for Legislation and Interpretation* (Collegeville, MN: The Liturgical Press, 1992).

[20] CIC: cc. 16, 17, 19. The Pontifical Council for Legislative Texts gives authentic interpretations with papal authority; the tribunals commonly consult, adopt and follow the decisions of the Roman Rota – and decisions of the Rota and Apostolic Signatura are regularly published for the guidance of the lower courts: see generally, N. Doe, 'Canonical doctrines of judicial precedent: a comparative study', 54 *The Jurist* (1994) 205.

[21] PCLCCAC: Principle 8.1–3.   [22] PCLCCAC: Principle 8.4.

[23] PCLCCAC: Principle 24.14.

[24] MCGB: Constitutional Practice and Discipline, Deed of Union 1; Standing Orders 008: laws should be interpreted according to their text and context.

on Methodist Law and Polity which advises Conference as to 'the interpretation and application of its laws and Standing Orders'.[25] In the
Reformed tradition too, the authority to interpret laws is entrusted to
the church assemblies,[26] though laws may carry definition sections and
provide that terms be interpreted according to their text and context.[27]
Indeed, the Baptist Union of Great Britain settles disputes on 'any issue
as to the meaning, construction, or effect' of provisions of a Baptist trust
instrument and its decision 'shall be binding and conclusive'; but: 'The
Union may not override any validly made determination of a duly
convened Church Meeting or ... Association in regard to the subject
matter at issue, when it shall appear to the Union that such determination was within the powers of the Church Meeting or Association [as] to
the subject matter at issue.'[28]

The Fatwa and Mufti

Classical Islamic law, as we have seen, provides a range of techniques for
the interpretation of *sharia*, based on, for instance, consensus (*ijma*),
deduction by analogical reasoning (*qiyas*), personal reasoning (*ijtihad*)
and precedent (*asl*).[29] Moreover, it is a jurist (*mufti*) who gives, on
request, an authoritative but non-binding opinion or interpretation on
a point of Islamic law.[30] However, it has been argued that it is incorrect
to view the Muslim community in Britain today as one in which religious
authority is both respected and exercised hierarchically. There are two

---

[25] MCGB: Constitutional Practice and Discipline, Standing Orders 338; see also Standing
      Orders 123(3), 126(1)(b) and 131(19), (25): the committee proposes amendments and
      scrutinises all new legislative proposals as to their coherence with existing usage.
[26] URC: Manual B.2.6: General Assembly has 'final authority ... to interpret all forms and
      expressions of the polity practice and doctrinal formulations' of the church.
[27] PCI: Code, X: e.g. para. 137: definitions listed must be employed 'unless the context
      otherwise requires'; PCW: Con. for a Local Church, Art. 1: Interpretation.
[28] BUGB: Model Trusts for Churches 2003, 14.1; 14.3: the rule against overriding a Church
      Meeting 'protects the autonomy of a ... Church Meeting'; parties include the church, its
      members, an Association or the Union; 14.2: 'The Union may, in its discretion, decline to
      entertain any referral ... if it does not consider the subject matter ... to be of a
      sufficiently serious or relevant nature as to call for its intervention.'
[29] See above Chapter 1.
[30] A. Black *et al.*, *Islamic Law* (2013) 83–106: this also deals with the process of issuing a
      fatwa (*ifta*), the phenomenon of on-line *fatawa*, and the distinction between *fatawa* and
      qada (cases) – the scholar (*mufti*, *alim*) is responsible for the development of law, not the
      judge (*qadi*), who is responsible for cases (*qada*) determined in an adjudicative process:
      see below

aspects to this: principles of authority, and practicalities of applying that authority. The principle is that a new requirement for a religious ruling is ultimately referred to the Quran and the practice of the Prophet and his companions. This is achieved by comparing the new requirement with precedents which themselves have satisfied this condition; the task is still performed by a *mufti*, that is someone who is qualified to make a *fatwa*. A *fatwa* is an individual religious judgement applicable to one case. The body of religious instructions that apply to an action, the *masa'il*, is identified through consensus among scholars across the whole of the Muslim community agreeing that particular rulings apply generally, not just as individual *fatwas* in individual cases.[31]

Practical difficulties include: the fact that Muslim communities are scattered around the world militates against common consensus; entrenchment of factions prevents the emergence of consensus; and, with factionalism and dispersal, there is no longer an agreed standard or recognised qualification that demonstrates a required level of scholarship (except within factions). With no formal network of authority at this level, source texts available, sometimes of questionable or unqualified translation, and a plethora of web-sites which encourage readers to submit questions to 'Islamic authorities' that are often unknown, 'there is a strong tendency for Muslims to make arbitrary decisions about right and wrong practice'. In turn, individual Muslims may pick and choose the religious opinion that suits them, with little incentive to respect the opinion of the imam of their local *masjid* or of scholars associated with any umbrella organisation (such as the Muslim Council of Britain). *Fatwas*, religious judgements reached by *muftis* (i.e. Muslim scholars with specific qualifications), may apply to any contentious subject where a general religious ruling/practice does not exist, cannot be applied to the general case (having been given for a specific case) without much wider consultation and cannot be given by unqualified individuals.[32]

Nevertheless, religious bodies today do make express normative provision for the making and issuing of *fatwas*. For example, the Fatwa Committee UK belongs to the European Council for Fatwa and Research.[33] The latter is an Islamic, specialized and independent entity comprising numerous scholars. First, under its constitution, the objects of the Council are to: bring together scholars who live in Europe to unify

[31] M. Naqshbandi, *Islam and Muslims in Britain* (2012): Guide: 4.7.
[32] M. Naqshbandi, *Islam and Muslims in Britain* (2012): Guide: 4.7.
[33] FCUK: http://fatwacommitteeuk.com/about-us.

jurisprudence with regard to *fiqh* issues; issue collective *fatwas* which meet the needs of Muslims in Europe, solve their problems and regulate their interaction with civic communities, within the general regulations and objectives of *shariah*; publish legal studies and research; and guide Muslims generally and those working for Islam particularly, through spreading proper Islamic concepts and decisive legal *fatwas*.[34]

Secondly, the means by which the European Council for Fatwa and Research seeks to achieve these objects include: forming specialized committees of Council members; relying on appropriate *fiqh* resources particularly those based upon sound evidence; taking full advantage of *fatwas* issued from the various *fiqh* establishments and other scientific/academic bodies; making relentless efforts with the civil authorities in European countries to acknowledge and officially recognise the Council and to consult it in reference to Islamic judgements; holding *shariah* courses to qualify scholars for *da'wa* (bringing people to the faith); holding seminars; and publishing and translating *fatwas* and research into European languages. When it issues a *fatwa*, the Council must observe: (1) the sources of Islamic law agreed on by the majority of the *Ummah* (i.e. Quran, *Sunnah*, *ijma* and *qiyas*); and (2) the other sources of law 'not entirely agreed upon' – for instance, juristic preference (*istihsan*), public interest (*maslaha mursala*), blocking the means to evil (*sadd al-dhara'i*), the presumption of continuity (*istishab*), tradition/custom (*urf*), the *fatwa* of a Companion of the Prophet (*madh-hab sahabi*) and the revealed laws preceding *sharia* (*shar'u man qablana*).[35]

Thirdly, the Council should base its *fatwas* on the juristic thought of the four Sunni schools (*madhahib*), but other schools may also have

---

[34] The Council was established in 1997 at a meeting of over 15 scholars responding to an invitation of the Federation of Islamic Organisations in Europe. Its headquarters are in Dublin. Its Constitution provides that the Council may admit scholars, not normally resident in Europe, if their selection is approved by the absolute majority of members. Such members must not constitute more than 25 per cent of the total members of the Council at any one time. In selecting members, the representation of European countries with a significant Islamic presence must be taken into consideration as well as their representation of the jurisprudential schools (*madhahib*). In approving a nomination for new membership, the recommendation of three trusted scholars is to be sought.

[35] See e.g. European Council for Fatwa and Research (ECFR): Final Statement: 25th Ordinary Session (Istanbul, 6–10 October 2015): Fatwa 2/25, Method of Calculating Zakah. The question is what is the method to calculate Zakah? The answer: 'the contemporary majority of the Muslim scholars and most of the specialized sessions in Zakah calculate the Zakah of money and commodities on the basis of the minimum of gold'.

'immense wealth' if their jurisprudence is supported by sound evidence and satisfies the best interests of the community. Sound evidence means that which is from an authorised and accredited source, does not create difficulty or inconvenience and takes into consideration the aims of *sharia*. *Fatwas* and resolutions are issued in the name of the Council through its ordinary and emergency sessions, by virtue of a consensus where possible, or by absolute majority. A member who has objections to, or reservations about, a *fatwa* may record these under the 'customary practice in *fiqh* councils'. The President and Council members may not issue *fatwas* in the name of the Council without its approval. However, each member may issue a *fatwa* with his personal capacity but without mentioning his status within the Council or using its official letterhead. To qualify as a member, a person must: have an appropriate legal (*shar'i*) qualification at university level, or to have been committed to the meetings/circles of the scholars and then be licensed by them; have sound Arabic knowledge and good conduct; be resident in Europe; and approved by the absolute majority of the members of the Council.[36]

Muslim organisations also provide for disputes about the interpretation of their own modern regulatory instruments. Various schemes are used. On the one hand, norms may require internal resolution. For example, in the Muslim Council of Britain, the decision of the National Council on the interpretation of any provision in the Council Constitution is 'final when the General Assembly is not in session'.[37] On the other hand, provision may be made for submission to a religious authority outside but associated with the organisation. This may be to an organisation in Britain, such as in Lancaster Islamic Society: 'The interpretation of the Shari'ah Law ... shall be carried out by competent scholars of bona-fide Ulama bodies of the Markazi Masjid Dewsbury or their appointees or successors.'[38] Or else recourse may be made to a European body: 'On matters related to Islamic Law (Sharia) the Aberdeen Mosque and Islamic Centre shall adopt the decisions of the European Council for Fatwa and Research.'[39] Also, its Fiqh Committee, which consists of three members chaired by the Imam, must: provide advice to the Executive Committee on Islamic law (*shariah*) and in so doing take into full consideration the view of the European Council for Fatwa and Research; seek to answer any religious questions in the light of

---

[36] ECFR and FCUK: http://fatwacommitteeuk.com/about-us.   [37] MCB: Con. Art. 11.
[38] LIS: Con: Shari'ah.   [39] AMIC: Con. Art. 1.4.

the Quran and Sunnah; and consult the European Council for Fatwa and Research when necessary.[40]

In turn, provision may be made for an initial internal resolution on one matter and recourse to a non-European body on another. At the Central Jamia Masjid (Southall), for instance, the Board of Trustees is 'the sole authority for the interpretation of the rules and ... regulations ... made by [it] and the decision of the Board ... shall be final and binding', but 'any dispute concerning the correct interpretation of the Holy Quran or any Hadith between the Trustees and/or Executive Members not being resolved amicably amongst themselves ... shall be referred for Fatwa' to the Majlis-e-Ulama, Bradford (UK) or the Mufti-e-Darul Aloom, Korangi (Karachi). It is for the Board to decide by a majority vote which decision to accept or what further action to take.[41] In a similar vein, the model constitution issued by the Central Mosque for an Islamic organisation provides that: 'The interpretation of the Shari'ah Law ... shall be carried out by competent scholars of bona-fide Ulama bodies of the Republic of South Africa or their appointees or successors'; terms in the text of the constitution are to have such meanings as are assigned in it to them 'unless the context clearly indicates or requires otherwise', and they are to be understood 'in the context of the articles' in the constitution; however: 'In the event of there being a difference of opinion in the interpretation of this constitution or matters not dealt with herein, the Board of Life Trustees' decision in the matter along with written confirmation from the Jamiatul-Ulama [Kwa Zulu Natal] will be final and binding.'[42]

The Quasi-Judicial Resolution of Disputes

The juridical instruments of Jewish, Christian and Muslim organisations often provide for the settlement of disputes by means of an essentially administrative process, short of judicial process in courts and tribunals, which necessitates the making of quasi-judicial decisions. We have already seen how communities provide for the quasi-judicial resolution of, for example, refusals to admit individuals to their membership, the termination of that membership and the removal of faith leaders and officers, as well as for rights of appeal in these matters to designated

---

[40] AMIC: Art. 7.3.   [41] CJM: Rules: 35.
[42] Model Constitution of an Islamic Organisation: Interpretation 1–2, e.g. 'Shari'ah', 'Shura'.

religious authorities.[43] Faith groups differ as to the body/person authorised to settle disputes quasi-judicially whether their decision is binding or
not, and the subjects for which such process may be used.

Shalom Bayit – Peace in the House

From the earliest days, Jews have considered peace (*shalom*) to be one of
the highest virtues. Talmudic Rabbis saw peace as the vessel in which all
blessings are contained – peace is not absence of discord, but a positive
and harmonizing principle in which opposites are reconciled. Today,
some Jews apply the principle of marital peace (*shalom bayit* – peace in
the home) to synagogue life as a basis to resolve discord; for example, for
the United Synagogue of Conservative Judaism, a *kehillah* constitution
should provide that its members are 'to promote *shalom bayit*' in
community life.[44] Common topics treated in the modern norm-
instruments of Jewish entities are complaints, the removal of trustees,
admission to the membership, and arbitration.

First, there are norms on the processing of complaints. For example,
Borehamwood and Elstree Synagogue (a member of the United Synagogue), which is committed to 'working in an open and accountable way
that builds the trust and respect of all its members', has a 'Complaints
Procedure' to ensure that making a complaint is as easy as possible,
prompt, polite and, if appropriate, confidential responses are given with
an explanation/apology as required. The complaints policy is reviewed
annually. If the parties are unable to resolve the matter informally, the
complainant should write to the staff member or volunteer who dealt
with them, or their manager, with details of the complaint. They should
receive a response within 15 working days. A person dissatisfied with the
response may write to the chairman within five days of receiving it
requesting the complaint and the response be reviewed, and the chairman must then respond to the complainant within 15 days. The matter
should be resolved as quickly as possible. However, complex cases may
require longer for them to be investigated. If a case requires detailed
investigation, the complainant is sent an interim response and told when
a reply is expected: 'The Synagogue expects all members who have a
complaint to comply with this procedure' as outlined above, but 'to

---

[43] See above Chapters 1–4.
[44] USCJ: Guide to Congregational Constitutions (2010): Art. XVII.

ensure fairness', reserves its right to ignore a complaint not complying with this procedure.[45]

Secondly, as to trustees, for instance, in the (Orthodox) Federation of Synagogues, the Council may pass a resolution by two-thirds of Delegates to remove a trustee if, *inter alia*, it is in 'the best interests of the Federation to do so'; the Trustee may appeal (with time limits fixed) at an appeal hearing whose decision is final. The appeal hearing is 'independent', with persons from a panel of six (appeal panel) appointed by Council from its members with 'no personal or commercial interest' in the matter.[46] Again, Elstree Liberal Synagogue Council may, by the 75 per cent majority, and 'for good reason, relieve an Officer of the Council of Office', if the officer has received at least 14 days written notice of a motion for removal and is given 'the right to be heard by the Council, accompanied by a person of their choosing, before a final decision is made'.[47]

Thirdly, there are norms for the arbitration of organisational/communal disputes. For example, in the Movement for Reform Judaism, the Chair of a member synagogue must work with the Vice Chair (Administrator) 'to arbitrate on any disputes within the community or Council', and must also act as an 'advisor and mediator' with regard to difficult/divisive issues in the community, not through 'authoritarian leadership'. The Chair must: 'put aside his/her own interests'; do the 'best for the community'; convey 'the wishes of management'; and instruct parties in 'carrying out their duties more effectively'.[48] Synagogue laws may also have rules on mediation; for example, at Brighton and Hove Reform Synagogue: 'If a dispute arises between members ... about the validity or propriety of anything done by the members under this constitution, and the dispute cannot be resolved by agreement, the parties to the dispute must first try in good faith to settle the dispute by mediation before resorting to litigation.'[49]

Fourthly, there are norms on disputes associated with the admission of members. For instance, in the Union of Liberal and Progressive Synagogues,[50] Wessex Liberal Jewish Community provides that if the trustees

---

[45] BAES: Guidelines: Complaints Procedure (undated); see also Guidelines: Zero Tolerance (undated): complaints may relate e.g. to verbal or physical abuse or hostile environment: www.borehamwoodshul.org.

[46] FOS: Laws 17.   [47] ELS: Con. Art. 10.   [48] MRJ: Code of Practice, pp. 4–5, 33–36.

[49] BHRS: Con. Art. 33.

[50] ULPS: *Affirmations* (2006) Art. 4 and 13: these affirm the value of 'justice, love and peace', and 'respect for persons, love of neighbour and practical kindness'.

refuse an application for membership, they must inform the applicant of the reasons within 21 days of the decision, and consider written representations the applicant may make; the trustees' decision following these representations must be notified to the applicant and 'shall be final'.[51]

Finally, the United Synagogue of Conservative Judaism has norms on the amicable resolution of disputes, mediation, arbitration and complaints. The organisation seeks to prevent discord within its *kehillot* by requiring amicable resolution; as such, the constitution of a *kehillah* should provide that: 'As Conservative Jews, ethical and moral behaviour is imperative and values of *derech eretz*, and *kavod*, mutual respect and honour, take precedence in guiding our discussions'; so: 'Members shall be required to speak and act accordingly at all times in order to promote *shalom bayit* (peace in the house)'.[52] Its Standards Committee encourages contracts which require that a dispute between a congregation and the professional be sent to it for mediation, followed by arbitration if mediation is unsuccessful. The committee, a neutral body, assists in an 'equitable' resolution.[53] There are also guidelines on processing complaints of harassment and other unethical behaviour, on the basis that every professional and lay leader serves as a *dugma* (role model) – their behaviour is expected 'to exemplify the highest standards of ethical and moral conduct in relationships with one another and ... members of the congregation'. The procedure to investigate a complaint is designed 'to promote a fair and prompt response'; it is not governed by 'formal rules of legal procedure or evidence' but is informal in order to promote direct communication between the parties to the complaint, without involving counsel. However, as each case is different, every congregation reserves the right to modify these procedures as appropriate. Notice of complaint is made to the President of the synagogue and the executive committee (or delegate). An initial investigation determines whether the complaint is credible (with a right of appeal to the board of directors if it is not viewed as credible), followed by a further

---

[51] WLJC: Con. Art. 8.6–8.

[52] USCJ: Guide to Congregational Constitutions (2010): Art. XVII.

[53] USCJ: Kehilla Affiliations and Standards Committee: Standards (2010). See also USCJ: Standards for Congregational Practice (2017): Standard IX. Congregations should refer to Crafting a Contract between the Synagogue and the Professional: Protecting the Partnership While Providing for Separation; Model Rabbinic Engagement Agreement – Synagogue with Rabbi; Putting the Partnership under the Microscope: The Process of Review and Assessment of a Congregation's Professionals and Leadership; and Model Guidelines for Congregational Policy Against Harassment.

investigation, and a recommendation is made to the board of directors, which may, for example, decide to suspend or dismiss the one complained about.[54]

Hierarchical Recourse and Visitation

All the historic churches have a system of discipline based on the norms of the Christian community as laid down in the New Testament,[55] and the subsequent development of church law.[56] A church as an institution has the right to enforce discipline and to resolve conflicts amongst the faithful. The right to exercise discipline has various foundations, including divine and spiritual authority. A church may exercise discipline in relation to both lay and ordained persons to the extent provided by law. The purpose of discipline is to glorify God, to protect the integrity and mission of the church, to safeguard the vulnerable from harm and to promote the spiritual benefit of its members. Discipline is exercised by competent authority in accordance with law.[57] Moreover, ecclesiastical disputes may be settled by a variety of formal and informal means, including administrative process. The competent authority may settle the matter in a process short of formal judicial process in the manner and to the extent provided by law. Anyone who has a sufficient interest in the matter may challenge a decision by recourse to the relevant and competent authority. The institution of visitation is exercised pastorally by a regional or other authority in relation to the local church, or other such entity, in the manner and to the extent provided by law; the aim of it is to monitor, affirm and improve the life and discipline of the entity visited.[58]

Elements of these principles are summed up, for example, in the law of the Methodist Church in Ireland: 'Discipline in the Church is an exercise of that spiritual authority which the Lord Jesus has appointed in His Church. The ends contemplated by discipline are the maintenance of the purity of the Church, the spiritual benefit of the members and the honour of our Lord'. Moreover: 'All Members and Ministers of the Church are

---

[54] USCJ: Guidelines for Policy against Harassment: these refer to halakhic principles (e.g. Micah 6:8).

[55] See e.g. Matthew 18.15-17. See e.g. J. Brundage, *Medieval Canon Law* (1995) 258.

[56] See N. Doe, *Christian Law* (2013) 154-187.

[57] Christian Law Panel of Experts, *Principles of Christian Law* (2016) V.1.

[58] Christian Law Panel of Experts, *Principles of Christian Law* (2016) V.2.

subject to its government and discipline, and are under the jurisdiction and care of the appropriate Courts of the Church in all matters of Doctrine, Worship, Discipline and Order in accordance with the Rules and Regulations from time to time made by the Conference'.[59] Beyond these shared values, the rules on the informal resolution of disputes vary somewhat as between the Christian traditions, not least in terms of the institution which possesses authority to settle disputes quasi-judicially: in Episcopal churches, the bishop plays a central role; in churches with a Presbyterian polity, it is the regional presbytery and its officers; and in a church which has a congregational polity, the local congregation and its officers. Two common mechanisms are hierarchical recourse and visitation – both have adjudicative aspects.

First, with hierarchical recourse rules allow a complainant to appeal against a decision or conduct of a person or body to the superior of that person or body: this process is predominantly administrative without recourse to a church court or tribunal, though the determination by the superior has a quasi-judicial element in the establishment of facts and the application of norms. For example, in the Roman Catholic Church hierarchical recourse is a process which enables an aggrieved party to challenge an administrative act by way of an appeal to the administrator who performed that act, or to the hierarchical superior of that administrator. It takes three forms: conciliation (mediation between the aggrieved party and the administrator to reach an amicable solution without recourse to the superior); a request for reconsideration (when the aggrieved party petitions the administrator to modify or revoke the act, which may be made during both a conciliation and recourse to the superior); and recourse to the hierarchical superior (this may be made directly to the superior for any just reason without having sought a conciliation or a request for reconsideration, for example, recourse is available against a diocesan bishop to the Congregation for the Clergy). The superior has power to confirm, rescind or modify the original executive act.[60] Analogous norms on the quasi-judicial resolution of disputes exist in Anglicanism.[61]

There are also equivalent mechanisms in Protestant churches. For example, when a Synod in the Lutheran Church in Great Britain is to

---

[59] MCI: Cons. s. 5; and Regulations, Discipline and Government, 5.
[60] CIC: cc. 1732–1739; c. 1400.2; administrative acts cover a spectrum of decisions, orders, policies and decrees issued by those with executive authority.
[61] See N. Doe, *Canon Law in the Anglican Communion* (1998) 72–74.

decide on the termination of the membership of congregations wishing to withdraw;[62] and in the Lutheran Church in Ireland, a congregation settles its own disputes, and provision exists for mediation.[63] Similarly, under Presbyterian polity, an inferior assembly may refer a matter to a superior assembly for advice or determination and complain to a superior assembly about the proceedings of any co-ordinate or lower authority.[64] Some Baptist Unions also use systems of arbitration to resolve disputes among church members.[65]

Secondly, while hierarchical recourse involves an appeal that ascends to a superior ecclesial authority or an arbitrator, visitation is a process by which an institutional authority descends to a lower unit to investigate, maintain and improve its discipline. Under Roman Catholic canon law, the bishop is bound 'to visit his diocese in whole or in part each year, so that at least every five years he will have visited the whole diocese, either personally or, if he is lawfully impeded, through the coadjutor or auxiliary bishop, the vicar general, an Episcopal vicar or some other priest'. Persons, Catholic institutes, pious objects, and places within the diocese are subject to Episcopal visitation (but the bishop may visit the members of religious institutes of pontifical right and their houses only in cases stated in the law); the bishop must carry out his pastoral visitation with due diligence ensuring it is not a burden to anyone on grounds of undue expense; the diocesan bishop must submit to the Pontiff a report every five years on the state of the diocese in a form and at a time determined by the Apostolic See.[66] There are various forms of visitation in Anglican canon law.[67] In the Church of England, the diocesan bishop has a right to visit, and in the Church in Wales, a duty to do so; the pastoral and liturgical side of visitation is stressed as well as an examination of the life and ministry of clergy and laity and the administration of

---

[62] LCGB: Rules and Regulations, Termination of Membership.
[63] Evangelical Lutheran Church in Ireland (ELCIRE): Con. Art. 11–14: cases on Parish Council 'jurisdiction', elections and acts; Art. 12.3: in a disagreement between the parish council and Pastor, both sides may ask a person they trust to mediate.
[64] PCI: Code, para. 21.   [65] See N. Doe, *Christian Law* (2013) 161.
[66] CIC: cc. 396–399; c. 400: in the same year as the report, the bishop must visit the Pontiff in Rome.
[67] PCLCCAC: Principle 23: visitation enables the exercise of a supervisory jurisdiction or a pastoral ministry, including enquiry into and assessment of the condition of an ecclesiastical entity; it may be exercised by the primate, archbishop, bishop or other ecclesiastical person to the extent authorised by the law; only those ecclesiastical entities may be visited which are prescribed by law; visitations may be held at such intervals, in such form and with such consequences as may be prescribed under the law.

the parish or other unit in question.[68] In addition, a visitation may be undertaken by the archdeacon who is required to examine prescribed matters.[69] The Church of England also provides procedures to address the breakdown of pastoral relations in a parish.[70]

By way of contrast, in Protestant churches visitation is normally carried out under the authority of assemblies.[71] For example, in the Presbyterian Church in Ireland, the Presbytery must visit each congregation at least once every ten years or sooner when Presbytery considers it necessary. Its purpose is 'to seek the improvement of Church life and work in the congregation and area concerned, by inquiry into all matters affecting the congregation, by the encouragement of members in their Christian witness and service, and by advice or correction in anything found amiss'. The process requires formal notice and examination of documents (e.g. minute books of the Kirk Session and Congregational Committee, communicants' roll, and inventory of church property). The inquiry involves preparatory meetings held separately and privately by the Presbytery with the minister, Kirk Session, and Congregational Committee. This public visitation should address the challenges and opportunities of the congregation – it also includes an act of worship. The Presbytery findings are read publicly to the congregation, which must report after one year to the Presbytery as to how recommendations made as a result of the visitation have been addressed.[72]

Elaborate rules on visitation are also found in the Methodist Church in Great Britain. The President of Conference has 'the right if requested to do so to visit any Circuit, to inquire into its affairs, and to take any steps open to him or her which he or she judges beneficial'.[73] Moreover, in the Irish Methodist Church, a District Superintendent 'shall visit any Circuit in the District when he/she considers it desirable'; but: 'Every Circuit in a

---

[68] Church of England: Can. C18: discretion; Church in Wales: Con. XI.27: duty; Scottish Episcopal Church: Can. 6.1: congregations.

[69] Church of England: Can. C22.5; Church in Wales: Con. XI.17.

[70] Church of England: Incumbents (Vacation of Benefices) Measure 1977 (as amended 1993).

[71] URC: Manual B.2.4: the Provincial Synod is to arrange for regular visitations to local churches for consultation concerning their life and work.

[72] PCI: Code, para. 70; paras. 246–251: guidelines on visitation are authorised by the General Board.

[73] MCGB: Constitutional Practice and Discipline, Standing Orders 111: the President may delegate this power e.g. to the Chair of the District concerned, and may refer any matter to be dealt with by a connexional complaints team. See also Standing Orders 425: the District Chair must visit each circuit annually.

District shall be officially visited by a District Superintendent at least once in three years.' On all such official visits, a meeting of the members of the Circuit Executive must be held at which the District Superintendent presides. At this meeting, the working of the circuit comes under review and special attention is given to the state of the work of God, including openings for evangelistic effort. The District Superintendents must report to the Conference, through the General Committee, as to the circuits officially visited by them during the year.[74] A special Connexional Visitation Commission may also make visitations (organised by the Visitation Secretary) to enquire into the state of church property and mission in the circuit.[75]

Sulh and Tahkim

Islam has two historical vehicles for the amicable settlement of disputes: mediation or conciliation (*sulh*), and arbitration (*tahkim*),[76] because: 'There is no blame on them if they arrange an amicable settlement between themselves; and such settlement is best.'[77] Today, the regulatory instruments of Muslim organisations contain norms on quasi-judicial power, mediation and arbitration, and the processing of complaints.

With regard to disputes resolved by the exercise of quasi-judicial powers, at national level, for example, any member of the National Council of the Muslim Council of Britain who fails to attend two consecutive meetings without reasonable cause, or who engages in acts which are contrary to *sharia*, may be removed if two-thirds of its Committee passes a motion to this effect. Moreover, any National Council member may be suspended on any ground if given two weeks' prior written notice and the opportunity to make written or oral representations to the National Council prior to the suspension, which itself requires a two-thirds vote. In both cases, the person has a right to appeal. The member must inform the Convenor of the Board of

---

[74] MCI: Regulations, Discipline and Government, 9.17.

[75] MCI: Regulations, Discipline and Government, 29.15: 'All Circuits shall be visited from time to time by a Connexional Visitation Commission which shall inquire into the work of the Circuit and the condition of all trust property.' A Baptist regional officer too may in practice visit a local church to offer missional and pastoral support.

[76] A. Othman, '"And amicable settlement is best": *sulh* and dispute resolution in Islamic law', 21 *Arab Law Quarterly* (2007) 64–77; see also A. Black *et al.*, *Islamic Law* (2013) 154–174.

[77] Surah al-Nisa, Verse 4·128.

Counsellors of the intention to appeal within seven days following the decision, and the Board must appoint a panel to consider the appeal within five working days. The panel must give its decision within two months of the appeal, confirming, revoking or reducing the suspension. The decision reached by the Board is final.[78]

As to mediation and arbitration, the model constitution of an Islamic organisation issued by the Central Mosque, for example, has norms on the matter: 'In the event of unresolved disputes within the members of the Shura Committee or the general members of the congregation, a mediation and conflict-resolution committee shall be established by the Ameer from among the Life Trustees, and if deemed necessary, from elected officials' – 'the issue shall then be handed over to the Jamiatul-Ulama [Kwa-Zulu-Natal] or any of its appointees for the formal process of arbitration which shall be binding upon all members of the congregation, the jurisdiction of any court of law being ousted in such matters'.[79] Similar norms are found on the same subject at Lancaster Islamic Society: the mediation is carried out by the Life Trustees, or, if the matter is unresolved, it is submitted to the Dewsbury Darul Uloom (or its appointee) for arbitration which, then, 'shall be binding upon all members of the congregation'.[80]

As to complaints, Palmers Green Mosque (Muslim Community and Education Centre London) is typical, with its policy 'to welcome all complaints, to investigate them fully and resolve them wherever possible'. A complaint is dissatisfaction, whether justified or not, about the policy or actions of the mosque; it may be received verbally or in writing, from within or from outside the mosque. The complaints process has four stages: three internal and one external. First, the complaint should be resolved by the individual responsible for the area of work being complained about. Second, if the complainant feels that the problem has not been satisfactorily resolved, they can contact a Trustee or the Chair. Third, a complainant who remains dissatisfied with the response may ask for the complaint to be discussed at the next Trustees' meeting. Fourth, the complainant may complain externally to the (civil) Charity Commission at any stage. The recipient of a complaint should: note the facts of the complaint; take the complainant's name, address and telephone number; tell the complainant about the complaints procedure and

---

[78] MCB: Con. Art. 5. See also e.g. MJMRIC: Con. Art. 12.
[79] Model Constitution of an Islamic Organisation: Mediation and Arbitration.
[80] LIS: Con: Mediation and Arbitration.

what will happen next; complete the initial sections of the complaints monitoring form; pass this information within one working week to the Chief Executive Officer who may then escalate it to the Board of Trustees at their discretion; and request that the complaint is followed up with a written account by post or by email so that the complaint is recorded in the complainant's own words.[81]

Courts and Tribunals: Judges and Jurisdiction

All the religions have mechanisms for the formal enforcement of their laws and the judicial resolution of disputes in a system of courts, tribunals or other fora. The juridical instruments of the faith communities deal with courts and tribunals in terms of their establishment, composition and jurisdiction – and sometimes explicit provision is made for their independence and as to whether their decisions are binding or not on the parties involved.

Religious groups may also make use of the civil Arbitration Act 1996, which provides: 'parties should be free to agree how their disputes are resolved, subject only to such safeguards as are necessary in the public interest'; as such: 'parties may make such arrangements by agreeing to the application of institutional rules or providing any other means by which a matter may be decided' – and parties may choose for their disputes to be decided 'in accordance with other considerations'. However: 'A party to arbitral proceedings may (upon notice to the other parties and to the tribunal) apply to the court challenging an award in the proceedings on the ground of serious irregularity affecting the tribunal, the proceedings or the award.'[82] On this basis, parties to a dispute may enter into a contract to be bound by a decision of a religious arbitral tribunal and the secular courts are then competent to enforce that decision.[83]

The Batei Din and Dayanim

Historically, in Jewish law, a Bet/Beth Din (or house of law) is a court (according to the Talmud) of three judges (*dayanim*, singular *dayan*),

---

[81] PGM: Complaints Policy: www.mcec.org.uk. See also e.g. Darul Isra Muslim Community Centre (Cardiff): Complaints Policy (undated).

[82] Arbitration Act 1996: ss. 1, 4, 45 and 66.

[83] See e.g. *Khon* v. *Wagschal and Ors* [2007] EWCA Civ. 1022. See also *AI* v. *MT* [2013] EWHC 100 (Fam) concerning the habitual residence of a child in an arbitration of the New York Beth Din under the supervision of the civil family courts.

ordained Rabbis with jurisdiction over, for example, civil matters, divorce, conversion and dietary law.[84] Traditionally, the administration of justice is not primarily about the application of (divinely revealed) rules to a set of facts 'on behalf of God' but is in itself divine in nature; judges must deliver a 'righteous judgment' (Deuteronomy 16.18) and pursue justice (*tsedek*) because justice 'belongs to God' – later the principle emerged that judges adjudicate on the basis of the 'ordinances and laws' (Exodus 18).[85] When the change occurred is the subject of debate amongst Jewish jurists today.[86] Moreover, a Rabbinic court is not by nature a public forum – its proceedings are not publicly reported, and traditionally there was no hierarchy of courts to sustain an appellate system; rather, a Beth Din is viewed as engaged in 'a private activity of moral-religious persuasion'.[87] Whether or not a judicial decision generates a binding or persuasive precedent[88] is, therefore, also debated across the traditions today: 'While the precise role of precedent in Jewish law is a matter of controversy, there is no question that respect for the interpretations of the past is . . . central . . . in halakhic practice' – but, Reform and Liberal Judaism, for example, proposes that a 'precedent (*takdim*) in Jewish law (*mishpat ivri*) may have a persuasive value (*mancheh*), but it is not binding (*mechayev*) upon the judge'.[89] What follows deals with the modern regulatory instruments of Jewish organisations, across the traditions, as they treat the composition, jurisdiction and processes of their courts.

All the Jewish traditions studied here have their *batei din* (singular Beth Din).[90] The (Orthodox) London Beth Din of the United Synagogue,

---

[84] N. S. Hecht *et al.*, eds., *Jewish Law* (1996) 40, 127–129, 134, 219, 332.

[85] B. Jackson, 'Judaism as a religious legal system' (2002) 34 at 37–38; King Jehoshaphat instructs his judges to avoid partiality and corruption and that 'God is with you in giving judgment' (2 Chronicles 19); see also Deut. 1.17; this also explores how the original judicial function was hereditary.

[86] H. Ben-Menahem, 'The judicial process and the nature of Jewish law', in N. Hecht *et al.*, eds., *Jewish Law* (1996) 421–437.

[87] B. Jackson, 'Judaism as a religious legal system' (2002) 34 at 40.

[88] Terms denoting a judicial decision/judgment include: *pesak din, ma'aseh beit din, ma'a-seh*.

[89] M. Washofsky, 'Taking precedent seriously: on halakhah as a rhetorical practice', in W. Jacob and M. Zemer, eds., *Re-Examining Progressive Halakhah* (2002) 1 at 14–15 and 53–54.

[90] G. Douglas, N. Doe, S. Gilliat-Ray, R. Sandberg and A. Khan, *Social Cohesion and Civil Law: Marriage, Divorce and Religious Courts* (Cardiff University, 2011) 26: this also touches on the Sephardic Beth Din of the Spanish and Portugal Jews' Congregation in London and that of the Union of Orthodox Hebrew Congregations.

with its basis in parliamentary statute, must 'provide an ecclesiastical court of Jewish Law (the Court of the Chief Rabbi)'.[91] However, the Beth Din has no written constitution and its functions are spelt out as a matter of law in the contracts of its judges. Its work includes court cases (*dinei torah*), divorces (*gittin*), conversions (*geirut*), Jewish ritual slaughter (*shechita*), personal status and major matters relating to 'communal life' (such as arbitrations).[92] The Rosh Beth Din is its head; the title Av Beth Din is formally held by the Chief Rabbi, who, due to his workload, is not personally involved in the daily work of the Beth Din but is in contact with the judges or *dayanim*, all of whom are Rabbis.[93] For example, as to communal life: 'In Jewish Law, civil disputes between Jewish parties are required to be adjudicated by a Beth Din adopting Jewish law as the law to be applied to the resolution of the dispute.' The Beth Din sits as an arbitral tribunal as to these disputes (e.g. family, financial, partnership, employment and inheritance) and the parties must sign an Arbitration Agreement prior to a hearing taking place. Then, the award given by the Beth Din has the full force of an Arbitration Award and may be enforced (with prior permission of the Beth Din) by the civil courts.[94] At a hearing, the parties are not required, but are allowed, to have legal representation. To commence a Din Torah (hearing), a party must write to the Beth Din with their name, address and contact details for the defendant(s) and should set out the facts of the case and the relief sought. On receipt of the application, provided the facts as stated give rise to a *prima facie* case, the defendant(s) are summoned to a hearing.[95] The judges may also provide answers to questions put by Rabbis and lay people (typically on matters of daily ritual and practice); the answers are not necessarily classified as *responsa* (only when written down, widely displayed and generally accepted); they regularly consult the historic sources of Jewish law and their decisions are not binding precedents but persuasive: the Beth Din will look to a range of opinions and rulings from other *batei din* in reaching its judgments but, as there is no

---

[91] US: Statutes Art. 5.7: see the United Synagogue Act 1870, Sch. 5.

[92] Like the office of the Chief Rabbi, the London Beth Din pre-dates the United Synagogue.

[93] The Hebrew *rosh* means head or leader. The official title of the London Beth Din is D'Kehila Kedosha London Bet Din Vehamedina – The Beth Din of London and the Country. Its 'central authority' is such that by 'convention' neither the Kedassia at Manchester nor Sephardi Batei Din carry out conversions in the UK and virtually all authority in this area is delegated to the London Beth Din.

[94] See: Chapter 10: www.theus.org.uk/article/about-london-beth-din.

[95] The application should be accompanied by a deposit for the sum of £100

hierarchy of tribunals, it is not bound by any prior ruling. There is no appeal against its decision.[96]

The Movement for Reform Judaism too has a *Beit Din*: it is a 'religious court', 'the Jewish law court for Reform Judaism in Britain'; it acknowledges the importance Reform Judaism places on 'personal life choices based on commitment and Jewish knowledge'; and is 'welcoming, compassionate and inclusive, combining modernity with Jewish tradition'. Its jurisdiction covers advice on conversion, or adoption, divorce or 'any other issue concerning Jewish status or other areas of complex Jewish law'. The office of the *Beit Din* arranges the courts, deals with enquiries, ensures that all documentation is available to the individual courts, works with a special group of Rabbis (its Standing Committee) to discuss individual complex cases and keeps 'a clear record of all decisions that have been taken by the courts over the years'. Each individual *Beit Din* consists of three Reform Rabbis (there are no full-time professional judges), all members of the Assembly of Reform Rabbis, who volunteer their services on a rotating basis – most work as congregational leaders, so they understand the needs and concerns of those who appear before them. The Convenor must attend the court, take notes, inform the Rabbinic panel of the circumstances of the case and ensure 'consistency of judgement' across the courts.[97] Similarly, the Union of Liberal and Progressive Judaism has a Beit Din which deals, for instance, with divorce, conversion and religious practice,[98] and the World Council of Conservative-Masorti Judaism 'supports the work of regional *batei din*'.[99] In Britain, the Assembly of Masorti Synagogues is 'part of the European Bet Din' which provides, for example, for mediation and rulings on Jewish law.[100] Whilst the civil courts may enforce the decision of a Beth Din when it acts as an arbitral tribunal, as judicial review is not available to question the disciplinary decisions of a Rabbinical authority,[101]

---

[96] G. Douglas *et al.*, *Religious Courts* (2011) 34, 43: oaths are rarely taken; witnesses are not required to corroborate evidence; the judges have formal qualifications in Jewish law from required recognised Orthodox institutions and other Batei Din from which it may seek opinions are mainly in Israel.

[97] MRJ: www.reformjudaism.org.uk/resources/life-cycle/.

[98] ULPJ: see e.g. www.liberaljudaism.org/lifecycle/divorce/.

[99] WCCMJ: By-Laws VII. See also Manchester Beth Din: www.mbd.org.uk/site/page/beth-din.

[100] AMS: www.masorti.org.uk/bet-din/bet-din.html.

[101] *R* v. *Chief Rabbi ex parte Wachmann* [1992] 1 WLR 1026: see above Chapter 3.

they may not be able to review the legality of the decisions of a Beth Din on dietary matters.[102]

What follows is a detailed study of the Federation of Synagogues and its Beis Din, a 'Rabbinical Court' which deals likewise with marriage authorisation, divorce, status and conversions, and acts as an arbitral tribunal offering alternative dispute resolution services and legally binding arbitration or mediation. As to arbitration, a Din Torah is a hearing before a recognised Beis Din 'in accordance with Jewish law'. The dispute could be a commercial or personal matter, which would normally be heard in a civil court. Process is relatively quick, cheap and informal and determined by its Dayanim, some of whom may be members of the (secular) Chartered Institute of Arbitrators. It is 'a fundamental rule of Jewish law that a dispute between two Jews should be referred to a Beis Din for decision, and not be taken to the civil courts'; so: 'it is ... the religious and moral duty of any Jew who wishes to pursue a claim against a fellow-Jew, or any Jew who is called by a fellow-Jew to a Beis Din, to have the matter dealt with by [it], and to accept and carry out any decision of the Beis Din'.[103]

The procedural rules of the Beis Din of the Federation of Synagogues are detailed. Any Jew may seek a Din Torah against a fellow-Jew (or even against a non-Jew) if both parties agree to submit to its jurisdiction. If a Jew is summoned by a fellow Jew to a civil court, the respondent may refer the matter to the Beis Din, which will call on the claimant to withdraw the matter from the civil court and refer it to the Beis Din instead. The Beis Din will not hear a case if a civil court process is pending. The respondent has the right in Jewish law to choose which Beis Din to attend; whilst not permitted, in Jewish law, to refuse to submit to the jurisdiction of a Beis Din, he may decline to attend a particular Beis Din if he prefers to have the matter heard in another Beis Din. The matter is usually heard by at least three Dayanim, or, if both parties agree, by a single Dayan. The date of a Din Torah depends entirely on the parties' co-operation and court agenda, but it is usually not more than two and three weeks, or sometimes days, after the initial application, and the time allocated depends on the complexity of the case and demands of the court calendar. Costs are determined on a sliding scale in accordance with the time involved. Process commences when the claimant writes to the Beis Din stating a wish to apply for a Din Torah, or

---

[102] R v. *London Beth Din ex parte Bloom* [1998] COD 131.
[103] FOS: www.federation.org.uk/arbitration/.

by the respondent if civil proceedings have been commenced, or threatened, by the other party, and he wishes it to be adjudicated by the Beis Din instead – but only if the claimant agrees to withdraw the civil suit. Next, the Registrar of the Beis Din will examine the application, and, if satisfied that a *prima facie* case is made out, issue a summons to both parties requesting them to attend for a formal hearing. All parties summoned are expected to confirm in writing whether they will attend. A respondent who chooses to have the case heard by a different Beis Din should inform the Registrar.[104]

Where parties, in the course of a hearing, reach agreement, it may not be necessary for the Beis Din to make a formal ruling. However, it is advisable for the agreement to be referred to the Beis Din, which may record it as an enforceable 'Consent Award'. Although a Beis Din decision, under Jewish law, automatically binds Jewish parties to the dispute, it is not binding in civil law; but, by signing the Deed of Arbitration,[105] the award of the Beis Din binds them in civil law also. Since the parties have bound themselves voluntarily to comply with the Beis Din award, there is usually no right of appeal: the decision is therefore final. If, however, relevant facts were not put before the Dayanim at the hearing, these should be referred to the Registrar, and may result in a re-hearing. For enforcement, if a party fails to comply with the award within the specified time, the other party should inform the Beis Din, which will then call upon the defaulting party to comply with the award within a specified time, failing which permission is given to the other party to have the award enforced in the civil courts.[106]

Where a party summoned fails to attend the hearing without reasonable explanation, a second summons is issued; if this fails, a third; if this fails, the other party is given permission to take such action as he may wish to pursue the claim, and may, in such circumstances, then refer the

---

[104] The claimant will be sent an application form to complete and return to the Registrar of the Beis Din. Where there are relevant documents (e.g. a contract), these too should be submitted.

[105] The Registrar then signs the deed as a witness. This brings the dispute within the Arbitration Acts of 1950, 1979 and 1996, and ensures that all parties comply with the decision of the Beis Din.

[106] The civil courts have enforced Beis Din awards on a number of occasions; see e.g. *Cohen v. Baram* [1994] 2 Lloyd's Rep. 138; and *Kohn v. Wagschal and Ors* [2007] EWCA Civ. 1022. However, in *Soleimany v. Soleimany* [1999] QB 785 the Court of Appeal refused to enforce an award of the Beth Din applying Jewish law where the underlying transaction involved commission of illegal acts in Iran.

matter to the civil courts. However, if after an initial summons it is clear that the party rejects the authority of the Beis Din and will not submit to its jurisdiction, the other party may be permitted to take such action as he wishes to pursue, including referral to a civil court with no further summons.

Each party may bring witnesses, but should notify the Registrar well in advance with full details of their identity and the other party who may bring counter-witnesses. If documents are required for clarification of an issue, they will usually be requested by the Dayanim at the hearing. To ensure their objectivity and impartiality, Jewish law forbids a Dayan to hear one side of a dispute in the absence of the other, or to read any documents relating to the dispute before the case commences. However, the Dayanim may review relevant documents in advance of the first hearing if both parties agree. Normally, the parties present the case in person, but they may bring or be represented by a legal adviser (or *to'en*) provided the Registrar is notified. Having signed the Deed of Arbitration, the hearing commences. The parties may either have the judges determine the case in accordance with strict rules of law and evidence, or empower them to exercise a degree of discretion where this seems 'equitable'. The claimant is called on to present the claim – then the respondent presents the defence or counter-claims. The Dayanim may question either party. The claimant may make further statements, and the respondent may be invited to reply. The Dayanim may reach their decision at the first hearing (or after a short recess) or adjourn to consider it further.[107]

The system of law normally applied by the Beis Din of the Federation of Synagogues is Jewish law, as formulated in the Talmud and codified in Maimonides and the Shulchan Aruch. However, other systems of law may be relevant. In such cases, the Beis Din uses 'the doctrine of incorporation' – 'rules of law derived from other legal systems may be incorporated, or assimilated, into Jewish law'. This occurs, for example, in contractual or commercial cases, if the parties relied upon a contract or commercial deed made in accordance with civil law. The decision as to which law to apply is that of the Dayanim. Finally, the Beis Din makes its decision, which is written up in an 'Award' and formally communicated to all parties. As a matter of 'common practice', the award will state what

---

[107] For instance, until specified documents or witnesses are produced – further hearings may be needed.

the decision is, what remedies, if any, are to be applied and within what timescale, and a summary of the legal reasoning.[108]

The Federation of Synagogues also has a Beis Horo'oh for small claims, and the case is heard by a single Dayan. Claims must meet the prescribed criteria, namely: claims must not exceed £5,000; both parties must consent to the process; each side must pay a nominal fee of £50 (for claims above £2,500, the fee is £100); parties may *not* bring a legal adviser or a professional representative but must represent themselves; before attending, a *shtar borerus* (arbitration agreement) must be signed; a brief written *psak* (giving the ruling but no detailed reasoning) must be presented to the parties within 72 hours; and an appointment to attend must be made in advance.[109] The Beis Din may also adjudicate disputes about the eligibility of any paid officials of the Federation, of the Burial Society or of a Federation Synagogue to act as a Trustee, and 'the decision of the Federation Beis Din (Ecclesiastical Court) shall be final'.[110]

Christian Courts and Tribunals

Christianity has a long tradition of using church courts, with qualified judges, defined jurisdiction and detailed procedural rules.[111] The same applies today in the historic churches. According to the principles of Christian law, a church may have a system of courts, tribunals or other such bodies to provide for the enforcement of discipline and formal and judicial resolution of ecclesiastical disputes. Such bodies may exist at international, national, regional and/or local levels to the extent permitted by the relevant law. Their establishment, composition and jurisdiction are determined by the law applicable to them. They are established by competent authority, administered by qualified personnel and may be tiered with original and appellate jurisdiction. They exercise such authority over the laity and ordained ministers as is conferred upon them by law.[112] With regard to due process, every effort must be made by the faithful to settle their disputes amicably, lawfully, justly and equitably, without recourse in the first instance to church courts and tribunals.

---

[108] FOS: www.federation.org.uk/beis-din/din-torah-jewish-arbitration/.
[109] FOS: limited evening hours are available in addition to normal working hours; appointments are scheduled in one-hour slots: www.federation.org.uk/small-claims-beis-din/.
[110] FOS: Law 18: if a Trustee dies, resigns or becomes ineligible or incapable, or any vacancy arises, a successor must be elected by the Council as soon as is practicable thereafter.
[111] See e.g. R.H. Helmholz, *The Spirit of Classical Canon Law* (1996) 88–145.
[112] Christian Law Panel of Experts, *Principles of Christian Law* (2016) V.3.

Formal process is mandatory if church law or civil law require it. Judicial process may be composed of informal resolution, investigation, a hearing and/or such other elements as prescribed by law, including an appeal. Christians must be judged in the church according to law applied with equity, and disciplinary procedures must secure fair, impartial and due process. The parties, particularly the accused, have the right to notice, to be heard, to question evidence, to an unbiased hearing and, where appropriate, to an appeal.[113] A church may also have a system of ecclesiastical offences. These, and defences to them, are to be clearly defined in writing and a court tribunal must give reasons for its finding of breach of church discipline. A church has a right to impose spiritual and other lawful censures, penalties and sanctions upon the faithful, provided a breach of ecclesiastical discipline has been established. Sanctions should be lawful and just. They may include admonition, rebuke, removal from office and excommunication. They may be applied to the laity, clergy and office-holders to the extent provided by law. Their effect is withdrawal from some of the benefits of ecclesial life. Ecclesial sanctions are remedial or medicinal. Moreover, a church may enable removal of sanctions.[114] There seems to be no tradition for courts to act as arbitral tribunals under civil law.[115]

First, as to the establishment, jurisdiction and personnel of church courts, the tribunals of the Roman Catholic Church are established on the basis of the Code of Canon Law promulgated by the Pontiff. They are ordered hierarchically and exercise jurisdiction over cases concerning spiritual matters, the violation of ecclesiastical laws and all those cases in which there is a question of sin as to the determination of culpability and imposition of ecclesial penalties.[116] In the diocese,[117] the forum of first instance is the diocesan tribunal, presided over by the bishop exercising judicial power personally or through a judicial vicar who may be assisted by adjutant judicial vicars who are priests, but lay judges may be appointed to assist. The tribunal deals in the main with matrimonial cases and cases concerning dismissal from the clerical

---

[113] Christian Law Panel of Experts, *Principles of Christian Law* (2016) V.4.

[114] Christian Law Panel of Experts, *Principles of Christian Law* (2016) V.5.

[115] However, Church of England courts are subject to the supervisory jurisdiction of the High Court.

[116] CIC: cc. 1401–1416: competent forum; cc. 1417–1418: tribunal grades; cc. 1446–1457: judges.

[117] CIC: c. 391: the bishop exercises judicial power (as well as legislative and administrative); see also c. 469: the diocesan curia assists the bishop 'in exercising judicial power'.

state.[118] The tribunal of second instance is the metropolitan tribunal (the archdiocesan tribunal of a province) or a regional tribunal hearing appeals from the diocesan tribunal.[119] The Pontiff is the supreme judge for the universal church, and may judge personally or through tribunals of the Apostolic See.[120] The Roman Rota is 'the ordinary tribunal constituted by the Roman Pontiff to receive appeals' (e.g. third instance) and the Apostolic Signatura is 'the supreme tribunal', which hears, for example, appeals against Rotal judgments – it also functions as the supreme administrative tribunal in disputes about administrative acts and the competence of the inferior tribunals.[121] Importantly, any member of the faithful may refer a case directly to the Pope; and, moreover: 'There is neither appeal nor recourse against a judgment or decree of the Roman Pontiff.'[122]

In Anglicanism, the relationship between courts or tribunals of original and appellate jurisdiction in the judicial hierarchy is to be clearly prescribed by law, as is their subject matter jurisdiction in disciplinary and other causes. The judges are to be duly qualified, selected and appointed by a designated church authority in accordance with a prescribed procedure, and are to exercise their office impartially, without fear or favour. Church courts and tribunals are independent from external interference and uphold the rule of law in the church.[123] The power to establish courts and tribunals is generally a reserve of the central assembly, but that assembly itself will exercise no judicial power (unless the law expressly allows this).[124] The diocesan tribunal, presided over by a judge appointed by the bishop,[125] has original jurisdiction over the discipline of ordained ministers and in some cases over the laity (and

---

[118] CIC: cc. 1419–1427, 1453, 1601–1618: officers include promoter of justice.

[119] CIC: cc. 1438–1441: a metropolitan tribunal may also be a first instance tribunal in prescribed cases.

[120] CIC: cc. 1442; 1405: contentious cases reserved to the Pope e.g. judging cardinals and bishops.

[121] CIC: cc. 1443–1444: the Rota also acts at first instance in e.g. contentious cases involving bishops; c. 1445: the Apostolic Signatura hears e.g. recourses against rotal judgments; see also cc. 1645–1648.

[122] CIC: c. 1417: referral to the Pope; c. 333: no appeal against a papal judgment.

[123] PCLCCAC: Principle 24: church courts/tribunals should be available as needed to resolve disputes.

[124] See e.g. Scottish Episcopal Church: Can. 52.16: 'General Synod shall have no judicial power'.

[125] See e.g. Scottish Episcopal Church: Can. 54: the bishop is assisted by the diocesan chancellor; Church of Ireland: Con. VIII.5–6: the bishop is 'the judge in the Diocesan Court' with the chancellor acting as assessor.

the commission of ecclesiastical offences by them).[126] With respect to appeals, the laws provide for limitation periods, grounds of appeal, leave to appeal and powers of the appellate tribunal. The superior tribunals may also have an original jurisdiction over, typically, the trial of bishops, and constitutional, doctrinal and liturgical matters.[127]

The judicial bodies of Protestant churches are ordered similarly. However, the court of first instance is generally at the local rather than regional level.[128] In Presbyterian churches, there are three tiers of judicial forum: the Kirk Session (which adjudicates on disciplinary charges against members);[129] the Presbytery (with authority over ministers and elders and appeals in cases of lay members);[130] and the General Assembly (which may exercise its judicial functions through a Judicial Commission), the decisions of which are 'final and binding'.[131] In Methodist polity, the Class and Local Society are responsible for members' discipline.[132] For example, in the Methodist Church in Ireland, members are subject to the disciplinary authority of the Church Council. Cases involving local preachers are heard by the Circuit Executive (and the District Superintendent presides), with appeal to the District Disciplinary Committee (with seven members from the district), and further appeal to the Conference, which appoints a committee to hear the appeal – the committee is presided over by the Conference President, and only the Conference Ministerial Session may make the final decision as to 'Discipline and Expulsion of Ministers'.[133]

Secondly, as to process, in the Roman Catholic Church, trial is a last resort. Disputants must settle amicably, promptly and equitably out of court – the Episcopal Conference is encouraged to resolve disputes

[126] Church in Wales: Con. IX.8: the Disciplinary Tribunal.

[127] See e.g. Church of England: Ecclesiastical Jurisdiction Measure 1963, ss. 38, 42 and 45: Court of Ecclesiastical Causes Reserved (doctrine, ritual and ceremonial); Clergy Discipline Measure 2008.

[128] LCGB: Rules and Regulations, Disciplinary Procedure for Pastors of the Church: Episcopal Committee, Council Tribunal, with appeal to Board of Appeal.

[129] PCI: Code, paras. 34–44.   [130] PCW: Handbook of Rules, 2.5.1.

[131] PCI: Code, paras. 104–109: General Assembly is 'the supreme court' with jurisdiction to superintend discipline; its decisions are 'final and binding'; PCW: Handbook of Rules, 3.4–5: General Assembly.

[132] Ultimately, discipline vests in Conference: MCGB: Constitutional Practice and Discipline, Deed of Union 18–21.

[133] MCI: Regulations, Discipline and Government, 5: the three tiers; Con. s. 6.4: Ministerial Session; Regulations, Discipline and Government, 10.0.1: the Church Council is responsible for the 'discipline and exclusion of members as required by the laws of the Church'.

without going to trial and to establish permanent offices in every diocese.[134] The purpose of a trial is to prosecute or vindicate the rights of physical or juridical persons, declare juridical facts and pronounce penalties for offences – judicial power must be exercised lawfully. Anyone (whether baptised or not) may bring an action. The faithful have access to the tribunals to vindicate or defend their rights and there is a legal action to defend every right. Provision is made for oral hearings but proceedings are generally in writing; cases must be concluded within a year.[135] There are special norms on contentious trial,[136] matrimonial cases[137] and penal cases.[138] The Ordinary (e.g. bishop) initiates penal processes when all other pastoral means have failed – the accused must be given the opportunity to be heard and be given canonical counsel; if a violation is established, but the person is truly sorry for the offence and promises to make amends, there can be no penalty.[139] Process is not dissimilar in Anglican courts which are, for example to: act impartially; protect the rights of parties to notice of proceedings, to adequate time for preparation of defence, to a presumption of innocence, to be heard within a reasonable time, to question the evidence, to representation and to appeal in appropriate cases on a matter of either fact or law; and to give their decisions, and the reasons for them, in writing.[140]

Among Protestant churches, for process against clergy, the Lutheran Church in Great Britain, for instance, has three stages. First, informal settlement: the bishop (with others) determines whether a pastor's performance, behaviour, practices or beliefs are of sufficient concern as to merit discussion with the pastor; there follows an informal meeting with the pastor. If concerns remain, an action plan may be instituted to resolve

---

[134] CIC: c. 1446: the judge must exhort parties to an 'equitable solution' by mediation or arbitration and decide whether these (cc. 1717–1720) may resolve the matter; c. 1733: the Episcopal Conference.

[135] CIC: cc. 135, 1400; c. 1476: rights to an action; c. 221: vindicating rights; c. 1453: rule against delays; c. 1455: confidentiality; cc. 1456–1457: judicial impartiality; cc. 1458–1462: hearing; cc. 1465–1467: time limits; cc. 1468–1469: place of trial; cc. 1470–1475: admission to hearings; cc. 1476–1480: plaintiff and respondent; cc. 1481–1490: procurators and advocates; cc. 1491–1500: actions.

[136] CIC: cc. 1501–1655: e.g. summons; proofs; inspection; the judge must have 'moral certainty' and weigh the evidence 'conscientiously'; appeals; expenses and free legal aid; execution of the judgment.

[137] CIC: cc. 1671–1707: the competent forum, proofs, documentary process, judgment and appeal.

[138] CIC: cc. 1717–1719: investigation; cc. 1720–1728: process; cc. 1729–1731: compensation for harm.

[139] CIC: cc. 1341–1349, 1717–1732.   [140] PCLCCAC: Principle 24: due judicial process.

the issue. If unsuccessful, the bishop recommends to the Council withdrawal of the pastor's authority to minister and an interim suspension may be imposed pending investigation by the bishop: reasons must be given. Secondly, there is an investigation. Thirdly, if formal disciplinary action is decided upon, there is a hearing before a panel of Council members chosen by the bishop – the pastor is given notice and a right to a hearing (which may be in private). If the bishop and the Council decide to withdraw the pastor's authority to minister, there is a right of appeal to a Board of Appeal appointed by the Council.[141] Parallel processes exist in Presbyterian churches,[142] as well as in the Methodist Churches in Great Britain and in Ireland.[143]

Thirdly, there are offences and defences. For the Roman Catholic Church, a canonical offence is an external violation, imputable to the person by reason of deliberate intent or culpable negligence of a law/precept to which a penalty is attached; it is committed in the public life (external forum) of the church and not in the forum of conscience (internal forum). Penal laws must be interpreted strictly or narrowly.[144] These include offences: against religion and church unity (e.g. apostasy, heresy, schism, blasphemy and harm to public morals); against church authorities (e.g. the use of physical force against the Pope, teaching doctrine condemned by the Pope and profanation of a sacred object); in violation of special obligations (e.g. unlawful clerical engagement in a trade); and against human life and liberty (e.g. inflicting bodily harm, and procuring an abortion).[145] When an external violation occurs, imputability is presumed but may be rebutted and is not penalised if there is a defence – for example, the person is under 16 years of age, is unaware that the action was a violation, acted accidentally, lacked the use reason, acted under duress or acted in self-defence or the defence of

---

[141] LCGB: Rules and Regulations, Disciplinary Procedure for Pastors of the Church.

[142] PCW: Handbook of Rules, 2.5: complaint; investigation; hearing; and appeals (to Presbytery or Association).

[143] MCI: Regulations, Discipline and Government, 9.18–19 and Manual Ch. 5: if informal resolution (by the District Superintendent) fails, and a complaint is made, the District Pastoral Committee investigates and offers counsel or submits the case to the District Disciplinary Committee on a charge. The Synod or the Conference considers the report of the Committee and issues final judgment. See also MCGB: Constitutional Practice and Discipline, Standing Orders 1100–1155.

[144] CIC: cc. 1311–1312: the punishment of offences in general; cc. 1313–1320: penal laws and precepts; c. 18: the narrow interpretation of penal laws; c. 49: those with executive authority may issue precepts.

[145] CIC: cc. 1364 1399: simony is the receipt of payment for conferral of a spiritual benefit.

another.[146] Anglicans too list ecclesiastical offences[147] – such as neglect of duty, immorality, disobedience to law and conduct unbecoming to the office and work of an ordained minister[148] – as do Lutherans,[149] Methodists[150] and Presbyterians. For instance, in the Presbyterian Church in Ireland, offences include: the teaching or conduct of a person under its jurisdiction which have been declared censurable by the Word of God or by the law of the church and anything among the members which gives rise to 'scandal injurious to the purity or peace of the Church' (such as disobedience to its courts).[151]

Penalties, sanctions or censures are understood to be medicinal. For example, Roman Catholic penal law is designed to repair scandal, to restore justice and to reform the offender; however, if a violation of the law is established, but a person is truly sorry for the offence and seriously promises to make amends, he/she cannot be penalised.[152] Penalties may be imposed by a sentence (*ferendae sententiae*) or they may be incurred automatically (*latae sententiae*).[153] They include: penal remedies (used to prevent future violations, such as admonition and rebuke); penances (such as a retreat, alms or fast); expiatory penalties which may be permanent or for a determinate period (to make satisfaction, such as deprivation of office); and medicinal penalties or censures (such as excommunication). Provision also exists for the cessation of penalties.[154] Different penalties apply to different offences, e.g. apostasy, heresy and schism attract a *latae sententiae* excommunication; participation in prohibited rites attracts a 'just penalty'; simony attracts suspension; and

---

[146] CIC: cc. 1321–1330: those who are liable to penal sanctions.

[147] PCLCCAC: Principle 24.9.

[148] See e.g. Church of England: Clergy Discipline Measure 2013; Church of Ireland: Con. VIII.53: immorality; Church in Wales: Con. XI.18: disobedience to law; Scottish Episcopal Church: Can. 54.2: conduct unbecoming.

[149] LCGB: Rules and Regulations, Disciplinary Procedure for Pastors of the Church: failure to observe the rules 'in a serious and persistent manner'.

[150] MCI: Regulations, Discipline and Government, 5.15: complaints may be made as to e.g. the 'moral and religious character' of a minister, failure to preach church doctrine, and failure to fulfil 'the duties of ministerial office'.

[151] PCI: Code, paras. 131–132: (e.g. I Cor. V.9–11); see also BUGB: Ministerial Recognition Rules.

[152] CIC: cc. 1341–1349, 1717–1732.

[153] CIC: c. 1314; the latter includes e.g. procuring an abortion, and a clerical attempt at marriage.

[154] CIC: cc. 1331–1340: forms of penalty; cc. 1341–1352: application of penalties; cc. 1354–1361: cessation of penalties; cc. 1369–1398: the offences which attract special penalties.

clerics who engage in unlawful trading are 'punished according to the gravity of the offence'.[155] Censures for clergy in Anglican churches include deposition, deprivation, suspension, admonition and rebuke.[156] Equivalent arrangements are found in Methodist[157] and in Presbyterian churches.[158]

Sharia Councils and Tribunals

Historically in Muslim practice, a *sharia* court was presided over by a judge – *qadi* or *hakim* – empowered to adjudicate legal disputes in personal matters (e.g. marriage, divorce and inheritance), civil matters (e.g. contracts and torts), and public matters (e.g. criminal activity) on the basis of Islamic law. Whilst in early Islamic law, the *qadi* judged in accordance with his own personal legal interpretations, from the eleventh century judicial discretion was limited in choosing 'appropriate precedents'. Traditionally, the parties represented themselves and the *qadi* passed judgment on the basis of rules of evidence and testimony set out by the various schools of law.[159] The Universal Islamic Declaration of Human Rights (1981) provides that: everyone, 'in case of an infringement of his rights, [is] assured of appropriate remedial measures in accordance with the Law' (i.e. *sharia*); 'no one shall be deprived of the rights assured to him by the Law except by its authority and to the extent permitted by it'.[160]

---

[155] CIC: c. 1364: apostasy, heresy, schism; c. 1365: prohibited rites; c. 1380: simony; c. 1392: trade.

[156] PCLCCAC: Principle 24.9, 11 and 15.

[157] MCI: Regulations, Discipline and Government, 5.03–05: if a charge is sustained the Meeting has power to admonish, rebuke, suspend or remove a person from office; suspension from office may be for a definite or indefinite period, or subject to any condition as to its duration or removal; 2.08: a member, whom the Church Council judges has persistently failed to fulfil the Obligations of Membership, despite being reminded of them, is regarded as having withdrawn from membership and their name removed from the register.

[158] PCI: Code, para. 133: admonition, rebuke, suspension from rights and privileges of church membership, suspension from office, and deposition from office.

[159] A. Black *et al.*, *Islamic Law* (2013) 91: the judge (*qadi*), who is responsible for cases (*qada*), may be guided by the opinions of a scholar (*mufti, alim*). See also, generally, L. Rosen, *The Justice of Islam* (Oxford: Oxford University Press, 2000).

[160] UIDHR (1981): Preamble; see also Art. V: 'No person shall be adjudged guilty of an offence and made liable to punishment except after proof of his guilt before an independent judicial tribunal', 'after a fair trial' and 'after reasonable opportunity for defence' is given; 'Punishment shall be awarded in accordance with the Law, in proportion to the seriousness of the offence and with due consideration of the circumstances under which it was committed', 'No act shall be considered a crime unless it is stipulated as such in

In Britain, today, Muslims have various adjudicatory bodies with defined functions.[161]

According to the Independent Review into the Application of Sharia Law in England and Wales, presented to Parliament by the Secretary of State for the Home Department (February 2018), there is no clear definition of what constitutes a *sharia* council (councils vary in size and make up), nor are there accurate statistics on their number (estimates in England and Wales vary from 30 to 85). *Sharia* councils may be defined as 'a voluntary local association of scholars who see themselves or are seen by their communities as authorised to offer advice to Muslims principally in the field of religious marriage and divorce'. Moreover, they have no legal status or binding authority under civil law. Whilst *sharia* is 'a source of guidance' for many Muslims, these councils have no legal jurisdiction in England and Wales. Thus, if any decision or recommendation of a council is inconsistent with civil law (e.g. Equality Act 2010), civil law will prevail: 'Sharia councils will be acting illegally should they seek to exclude domestic law.' Although they have no binding legal authority, they have a decision-making capacity when dealing with Islamic divorce.[162]

Importantly, however, the Independent Review states: 'Sharia councils are not courts and ... should not refer to their members as judges. It is this misrepresentation of sharia councils as courts that leads to public misconceptions over the primacy of sharia over domestic law and concerns of a parallel legal system'; also, the recommendations included in the Review (in the main as to Islamic divorces, treated in Chapter 8 below) 'are designed to promote equality between religions in ways that

---

the clear wording of the Law'; 'Everyone is responsible for his actions. Responsibility for a crime cannot be vicariously extended to other members of his family or group, who are not otherwise directly or indirectly involved in the commission of the crime in question'.

[161] See G. Douglas *et al.*, *Religious Courts* (2011) 28: e.g. the Association of Muslim Lawyers; in particular, the study examines the work of the Shariah Council of the Birmingham Central Mosque – it provides rulings, guidance and advice on a range of issues including inheritance, marriage and divorce. See also the three case studies in J.R. Bowen, *On British Islam: Religion, Law and Everyday Practice in Shari'a Councils* (Princeton, NJ: Princeton University Press, 2016).

[162] *The Independent Review into the Application of Sharia Law in England and Wales* (February 2018): councils operate in Sunni communities (and are not prevalent in Shia communities), e.g. Islamic Sharia Council (Leyton); Muslim Law (Shariah) Council (Wembley); Dewsbury Sharee Council; and Nuneaton Muslim Arbitration Tribunal (MAT). There seem to be no *sharia* councils in Scotland.

should challenge misconceptions of a parallel legal system and encourage integration'.[163] It is submitted that this view is questionable in light of the use by the other religious traditions studied here of 'courts and tribunals' with 'judges' who administer religious law. Thus, it is suggested that it is acceptable, on the basis of equality, for such councils to present themselves in the same terms as, for example, the Islamic Sharia Council (a charity), which describes itself as 'a quasi-Islamic Court'. It was established in 1982 'to solve the matrimonial problems of Muslims living in the United Kingdom [in] the light of Islamic family law'. It comprises members from 'all of the major schools of Islamic legal thought (*mad'-hab*) and is widely accepted as an authoritative body with regard to Islamic law'.[164] Its function today is to: guide the Muslims in the UK in matters as to religious issues and in solving their matrimonial problems; foster 'the practice of the Muslim faith according to the Quran and the Sunnah'; provide advice on Muslim family life; establish 'a bench of scholars to operate as the Islamic Shari'a Council and to make decisions on matters of Muslim family law referred to it'; and educate the public regarding Islam 'to dispel negative stereotypes'. The Council deals with Muslim marriages, divorces and inheritance issues, disputes in Muslim groups referred to it for resolution, and requests for Islamic injunctions (*fatawa*) pertaining to daily life. Its Fatwa Department may deal with, for example, organ donation, inheritance and wills, insurance, fasting, the 'general *fiqh* of purification', transactions, *zakah*, *salah*, *halal* food, medicine and abortion. The work of its Counselling Department includes: matrimonial disputes resolved in accordance with the Quran and Sunnah; inter-generational conflicts; anger management; conflict resolution for two/more to find an Islamic solution to a disagreement; and mediation through a neutral third party: 'All settlements are based upon Islamic principles.'[165]

What follows deals in depth with the Muslim Arbitration Tribunal, its composition, functions and procedures. The tribunal was established in 2007 to provide a facility for 'the Muslim community ... to resolve disputes in accordance with Islamic Sacred Law' and its 'principles' in

---

[163] Independent Review (2018): p. 10.
[164] The Council is based in Leyton. Its Founding Organisations included the: London Central Mosque and Islamic Cultural Centre; Muslim World League; UK Islamic Mission; Jamia Mosque and Islamic Centre, Birmingham; Islamic Centre, Glasgow; Islamic Centre, Didsbury, Manchester; and Jamia Masjid Hanafiya, Bradford.
[165] Islamic Sharia Council (ISC) Registered Charity No: 1003855: www.islamic-sharia.org/.

such matters as marriage, divorce, inheritance and wills. Moreover, under the Arbitration Act 1996, it operates as 'an effective, efficient and unique Alternate Dispute Resolution organisation which deals with Islamic Sacred Law within the context of the English Legal System'.[166] The tribunal is subject to several values and principles, namely: the Islamic principle of justice *('Adl)* underpins all of its activities and is integral to decisions it makes in all disputes; it will always endeavour to reach a conclusion which is 'fair and equitable' in the circumstances; all matters are considered by it without any prejudice to race, religion, ethnicity, gender or age; and all matters must be conducted at 'the highest level of professionalism'.[167]

The tribunal hears cases as to: Islamic divorce and family disputes (but not e.g. child custody); family mediation; domestic violence; forced marriages; commercial/civil arbitration; inheritance and wills; and mosque disputes, including those between committee members, and those relating to finance (e.g. misappropriation of funds and contracts for projects such as building projects) and the appointment and dismissal of staff. The tribunal has no criminal jurisdiction. For example, as to 'commercial and civil arbitration', as 'many commercial contracts ... contain an Arbitration agreement', the tribunal acts as 'an impartial, judicial' arbitrator in cases involving, for instance, the quality of goods supplied and the interpretation of a trade clause or point of law. The tribunal uses two arbitrators at every hearing – a lawyer qualified in civil law and an Islamic scholar. Hearings must be 'in accordance with the rules of natural justice', but are informal and may be held in private, with the time and place determined by the parties. The judgment (award) may be delivered instantaneously, is binding on the parties in civil law and is generally considered as final, but recourse lies to the High Court on a question of law, with the approval of the parties, or if that court allows

---

[166] The Muslim Arbitration Tribunal (MAT) is based in Nuneaton. It was established in response to Muslims who had 'to resort to unregulated Shariah Councils and the local Imams to provide resolutions to their problems'; and: 'Any decision reached would ... have no backing of the [civil] law' and may have been 'in conflict' with it: www.matribunal.com/why-MAT.php.

[167] MAT: it cites e.g. Surah al-Hujurat, Verse 9: 'Reconcile between them with justice and act equitably; indeed, Allah loves those who act equitably'; Surah al-Nisa, Verse 58: 'and when you judge between people, judge with justice'; and Verse 35: 'And if you fear disagreement between the two, send an arbitrator from his people and an arbitrator from her people. If they both desire reconciliation, Allah will cause it between them. Indeed, Allah is ever Knowing and Acquainted [with all things].'

judicial review of the case. The High Court may ratify, vary or reverse the award, or refer it to the arbitral tribunal for reconsideration.[168]

The tribunal has established procedural rules, which 'regulate and govern' it, 'to secure that proceedings before [it] are settled in so far as possible' in accordance with 'Qur'anic Injunctions and Prophetic Practice as determined by the recognised Schools of Islamic Sacred Law'; as fairly, quickly and efficiently as possible; and where appropriate, tribunal members must ensure the proceedings are in the parties' interests and those of the wider public.[169] Its arbitral decisions are enforceable under civil law. A request for a hearing must be in writing and include, for example: the name and address of the applicant and respondent, and, if the applicant has a representative, their name and address; the grounds for the case and reasons to support them; and so far as reasonably practicable, a list of documents and the name and address of any witnesses the applicant intends to rely on as evidence.[170] The respondent is served with a copy of a request for a hearing.[171] The applicant may withdraw a case orally, at a hearing or at any time, by filing written notice with the tribunal.[172] The tribunal may hear a case in the absence of a party if satisfied that the party: has a representative present at the hearing; is outside the UK; is suffering from a communicable disease or there is a risk of the party being violent or disorderly; is unable to attend due to illness, accident or other good reason; is unrepresented and it is impracticable to give him notice; or has notified the tribunal that he does not wish to attend the hearing.[173] The tribunal may hear cases together (e.g. with a common question of law or fact) and adjourn a case.[174]

In arriving at its decision, the tribunal: may consider but is 'not bound by any previous decision of the Tribunal'; must 'take into account' the Laws of England and Wales and the recognised Schools of Islamic Sacred Law; and must serve on every party, not later than 14 days after the hearing, a written determination containing its decision and the reasons for it; and may decide the procedure to be followed.[175] The tribunal must consist of (as a minimum) a scholar of Islamic Sacred Law and a solicitor or barrister of England and Wales.[176] The tribunal

---

[168] Those arbitrators who are solicitors or barristers must be qualified in the United Kingdom.
[169] MAT: Procedural Rules, s. 1.   [170] MAT: Procedural Rules, s. 2.
[171] MAT: Procedural Rules, s. 3.   [172] MAT: Procedural Rules, s. 4.
[173] MAT: Procedural Rules, s. 5.   [174] MAT: Procedural Rules, ss. 6 and 7.
[175] MAT: Procedural Rules, ss. 8 and 9.   [176] MAT: Procedural Rules, s. 10

may give oral or written directions to the parties relating to the conduct of any case or application, such as to the preparation for a hearing, case management, the giving of evidence, documents, submissions and the examination and cross-examination of witnesses. An applicant may act in person or be represented by any person, but the tribunal must not direct an unrepresented party unless satisfied the party is able to comply with that direction.[177]

The tribunal may allow oral, documentary or other evidence of any fact which appears to be relevant to a case, but it may not compel a party or witness to give any evidence. All witnesses must testify in the form and manner prescribed by Islamic Sacred Law. Where the tribunal directs time limits for filing and serving written evidence, it must not consider such evidence which is not filed or served in accordance with those directions unless satisfied that the overriding objective will not be achieved. If a party seeks to rely on a copy of a document, the tribunal may require production of the original. The tribunal must not take account of any evidence that has not been made available to all the parties.[178] If any party asserts any fact, it is for that party to prove it. The standard of proof required is that of a balance of probabilities.[179] The tribunal must hold its hearings in private unless the parties agree to a public hearing. If a public hearing is held, it may of its own motion exclude the public to: meet the interests of public order or national security; protect the private life of a party or the interests of a minor; achieve its objective; or ensure that publicity does not prejudice the interests of justice, but only if, and to the extent, it is strictly necessary to do so.[180]

Where there has been an error of procedure, the error does not invalidate any step taken in the proceedings, unless the tribunal so orders; the tribunal may take any step to remedy the error. Any determination made in a case/application under the procedural rules is valid notwithstanding that the determination was not made or served within the time period specified in the Rules. The tribunal may at any time amend an order, notice of decision or determination to correct a clerical error or other accidental slip/omission; if so amended, the tribunal must

---

[177] MAT: Procedural Rules, ss. 11 and 13; see s. 12 for notification of hearings.
[178] MAT: Procedural Rules, s. 14; see s. 15 for the language and s. 18 for the filing of documents.
[179] MAT: Procedural Rules, s. 16.
[180] MAT: Procedural Rules, s. 17; s. 19 deals with addresses service and s. 20 with signatures.

serve an amended version on the party on whom it served the original. No appeal may be made against any decisions of the tribunal; but this rule does not prevent any party applying for judicial review with permission of the High Court.[181]

Conclusion

There is profound juridical unity between Judaism, Christianity and Islam with regard to the resolution of religious conflict. All three accept and justify theologically the need to resolve disputes among the faithful based on the ideas of peace and justice. Communities within each religion make provision for the interpretation of religious law through the opinions of persons (such as Rabbis through *responsa* and muftis through *fatawa*) or bodies with juristic expertise (such as Christian commissions) within or beyond the local faith community. They also exhort the amicable resolution of disputes short of formal process. The juridical instruments of the communities often provide for the settlement of disputes by mediation, arbitration, administrative processes to deal with complaints and the use of quasi-judicial powers vested in religious authorities; however, the Christian institutions of hierarchical recourse and visitation find no obvious parallel in Judaism and Islam. All three religions also have courts or tribunals to provide for the enforcement of discipline and the formal resolution of disputes. Each religious organisation studied here has norms on the establishment, composition and jurisdiction of these judicial bodies. Jewish communities may have a Beth Din composed of *dayanim* (typically Rabbis) with jurisdiction over a wide range of religious matters, such as status, conversion, divorce and the making of arbitration awards enforceable under civil law. *Sharia* fora too, with increasingly professionalised personnel and procedures, have a similarly wide jurisdiction – but there is little by way of rights of appeal within the community. However, Christian courts/tribunals are established by the highest legislative authority in each church, with qualified personnel (usually lay), and tiered in terms of original and appellate bodies, but their jurisdiction is more limited, confined mainly to matters of church discipline among the ordained ministers and/or the laity. In Jewish and Muslim organisations, such matters are usually dealt with in a quasi-judicial fashion on the basis of the authority (vested in, for

---

[181] MAT: Procedural Rules, ss. 21 23.

example, a synagogue or mosque committee) to discipline the officers and members of the congregation. For all three religions, recourse to their courts/tribunals is a last resort. Judicial processes vary: Christian disciplinary processes are elaborate and formal, whereas those of Jews and Muslims are generally less so. The principal body of law to be applied in a case is religious law. Nevertheless, in all three religions, there are detailed norms that seek to secure fair and just process – with rights to notice, to representation, to question evidence and to an unbiased or impartial hearing. In the arbitral Jewish and Muslim tribunals, the award is enforceable under civil law, and in disciplinary cases in Christian tribunals, ecclesial offences – usually expressed with a high degree of generality (such as immoral conduct) – are enforceable within the church by means of a range of remedial or medicinal sanctions, censures or penalties. In all these senses, there is considerable uniformity within and between the faiths.

6

The Faith, Worship and Education

The laws of Jews, Christians and Muslims deal with faith, worship and education in religious schools. The profession of faith and the worship of God are fundamental actions of the faithful. Needless to say, faith and worship, and their expression in teaching and in religious services, are important not only for the individual at the personal level but also for the faith groups as communities in the public sphere of their corporate lives. However, the regulation of belief and its manifestation in public teaching and worship have posed particular problems in the history of religion – not least in terms of which religious authority has competence to regulate these matters. On the one hand, there is an assumption that rules should not intrude in belief and worship in so far as these are intimate to the relationship between the individual and God. On the other hand, there is the desire for order – for maintenance of fidelity to the historic religious message and for decorum in worship as an event which goes to the heart of the corporate identity of the faithful. Nevertheless, the modern regulatory instruments of all three religions studied here deal with faith and worship. This chapter explores the extent to which rules of faith communities define legitimate belief, manage the development of teaching, regulate the profession of the faith (in for example preaching and sermons) and maintain or enforce belief-standards. Next, the chapter examines worship and the Sabbath – the nature and purpose of worship, its provision and administration and the conduct and oversight of worship. It also examines norms on the instruction of followers in the faith and religious schools. In doing so, it touches on the interest of the State and its laws in such matters, particularly the religious schools.[1] It also draws conclusions about the centrality of teaching and worship as a religious activity, explores the extent to which norms are theocratic,

---

[1] For secular government combating radicalisation, see e.g. D. Barrett, 'Tackling radicalisation: the limitations of the anti-radicalisation prevent duty', *European Human Rights Law Review* (2016) 531

delineates legal differences between the religious organisations studied and from the similarities between these instruments elucidates common principles of religious law.

The Definition and Profession of the Faith

All three religions have a body of beliefs, which may include teaching on morals and practice. The juridical instruments of the faith communities studied here deal with its location and normativity; transmission of the faith from generation to generation; and the authorities competent to define, interpret, declare and teach the faith. As seen in Chapter 1, the profession or propagation of the faith is listed in legal instruments among the objects of a religious organisation. The function is also particularised in preaching.

The Shema and Darashah

The Jewish *shema* is a basic confession or declaration of faith in the unity of God; the Torah states: 'Hear [*shema*] O Israel, the Lord our God, the Lord is One'; to this verse are added others and 'these words should be spoken of when lying down and when rising up',[2] that is to say, as understood traditionally by the Rabbis, in the morning and in the evening, at the times described in detail in the Talmud and codes. The *shema* also plays a part in Jewish prayer and in worship.[3] However, it has been said that: 'Judaism is a religion of deed, not creed'; and that: 'Dogmas imposed by an authority able and willing to enforce conformity and punish dissent are non-existent in Judaism.'[4] Nevertheless, there is some emphasis on correct belief; for example, the Mishnah states that those who reject resurrection, revelation and morality have no share in the world to come. There have been attempts to devise a Jewish creed, and, since Maimonides, converts traditionally affirmed *ikrei hadat*, 'the

---

[2] Deuteronomy 6:4–9; 11:13–21; and Numbers 15:37–41. The Hebrew *emunah* denotes 'belief'.

[3] For a Conservative perspective, see I. Klein, *Jewish Religious Practice* (1992) 18–20, 60, 64 and 68.

[4] The first statement has been attributed to Moses Mendelssohn (1729–1786), founder of the so-called 'Jewish Enlightenment'; the second is: Israel Abrahams, *Judaism* (London: Constable, 1917) 26. However, Maimonides proposed 13 principles of faith e.g. that God is one, unique, incorporeal and eternal, that God will reward the good and punish the wicked and that the dead will be resurrected.

fundamentals of the faith', the unity of God and prohibition of idolatry.[5] The (Orthodox) United Synagogue, for instance, uses the category 'religious beliefs' of 'the Jewish people';[6] there is a 'Statement' or 'a description of the state of belief in Conservative Judaism';[7] and, in Liberal Judaism: 'Belief ... is not unimportant ... but it is ... true that the greater emphasis ... has always been on action rather than belief, on deed rather than creed.'[8]

First, normatively, belief should pass from generation to generation. For example, the Union of Liberal and Progressive Synagogues holds that: 'To be a practising Liberal Jew ... is to believe that tradition should be transmitted within the framework of modern thinking and morality', and, thus, to 'live according to the prophetic ideal of doing justice, loving kindness and walking humbly with God' upholds 'common beliefs'.[9] The Union affirms that at Mount Sinai, and subsequently through revelation, inspiration, reflection and discussion, people gained 'an ever growing understanding of God's will'; 'this is a continuing process'.[10] It also holds the 'Jewish conception of God', that is 'One and indivisible, transcendent and immanent, Creator and Sustainer of the universe, Source of the Moral Law [and] God of justice and mercy who demands that human beings ... practise justice and mercy in their dealings with one another.'[11] However, as to 'fundamental questions about Jewish belief and practice', 'respect [is] due to all conscientious options'. Thus, as 'truth must be sought open-mindedly from all sources', it affirms 'the spirit of free inquiry', accepts 'modern Bible scholarship, which has shown that the biblical writers, however divinely inspired, were fallible'.[12]

Secondly, information about Judaism may, or should, be disseminated. For instance, the (Orthodox) United Synagogue may disseminate information on all matters which affect its objects and publish materials 'to educate the public and to promote their awareness' of those objects.[13]

---

[5] Mishnah: San. 10:1; S. Schechter, *Studies in Judaism* (Philadelphia: Jewish Publication Society, 1945) Ch. 6: The Dogmas of Judaism; see also the work of (the ninth-century) Saadia Gaon, *The Book of Beliefs and Opinions*, translated by S. Rosenblatt (New Haven, CT: Yale University Press, 1989).

[6] US: Statutes 5.7.

[7] United Synagogue of America, Rabbinical Assembly and Jewish Theological Seminary of America: *Statement of Principles of Conservative Judaism* (1990) 15.

[8] J. Rayner, 'Ethics versus ritual', in W. Jacob, ed., *Beyond the Letter of the Law* (2004) 119.

[9] ULPS: *Affirmations* (2006) Preamble.   [10] ULPS: *Affirmations* (2006) Art. 10.

[11] ULPS: *Affirmations* (2006) Preamble and Arts. 1–2.

[12] ULPS: *Affirmations* (2006) Arts. 25, 28 and 29   [13] US: Statutes 5.16–20.

The Union of Liberal and Progressive Synagogues too seeks 'to transmit [its own] tradition' and to 'spread their common beliefs' through *inter alia* 'services, public meetings, sermons, writing and inspirational leadership'.[14]

Thirdly, from early times, sermons were delivered in the synagogue, especially on the Sabbath and festivals. The usual preaching method was to take scriptural verses and apply them to contemporary religious/ ethical issues – a method known as *derush*, from a root meaning 'to search/enquire'. A sermon became known as *derashah* (plural *derashot*), and preachers as *darshanim* or *maggidim*, 'speakers/tellers'. Until modern times, preaching did not belong to the Rabbi but to a special class well-versed in *halakhah* – this resulted in publication of collections of sermons. In modern times, formal sermons became a regular feature at synagogue services. The modern sermon is also based on scriptural verses, usually from a portion of the weekly Torah reading, and develops a theme systematically for edification rather than for instruction. In Rabbinical seminaries, Orthodox, Reform and Conservative, homiletics is an important subject in Rabbinical formation – and preaching, in turn, central to a Rabbi's work.[15]

In the (Orthodox) United Synagogue, for example, the teaching of the Chief Rabbi in his 'Torah thoughts' (*Divrei Torah*, singular *Dvar Torah*), thoughts shared with others, are published on-line.[16] At local level, no one other than the Rabbi of the synagogue is entitled to preach at any religious service held at the synagogue without the consent of the Rabbi under the ultimate authority of the Chief Rabbi.[17] In the Movement for Reform Judaism, the Rabbi must in sermons consider the 'reasonable wishes and requests of the members of the synagogue and its Council', and preaching may be subject to periodic review of the work of the Rabbi.[18] Similarly, a congregation of the United Synagogue of Conservative Judaism should provide that the Rabbi 'shall have the

---

[14] ULPS: *Affirmations* (2006) Preamble.

[15] L. Jacobs, *Jewish Religion* (1999) 181–182; see generally L. Jacobs, *Jewish Preaching: Homilies and Sermons* (Elstree, UK: Vallentine Mitchell, 2004); see also M. Saperstein, *Jewish Preaching 1200–1800* (New Haven, CT: Yale University Press, 1992).

[16] US: http://chiefrabbi.org/dvar-torah/.

[17] US: Bye-Laws 16.2. See also the Orthodox NHC: Con. Art. 5.3–5: 'A candidate for ministerial office or for a vacancy as Reader shall be appointed to that office by the Committee'; tenure may also be terminated by the Committee; duties must be outlined by written agreement.

[18] MRJ: Areas of Responsibility and Codes of Practice Documents: pp. 5–6.

responsibility of teacher and preacher of the congregation' and 'enjoy the freedom of the pulpit' but 'seek the advice and guidance of the board (of Trustees)' in this.[19] The Union of Liberal and Progressive Synagogues too has sermons to transmit faith.[20]

Norms exist in classical Jewish law for discipline in matters of belief. Traditionally, heresy is holding a belief contrary to the Jewish religion, but while there are Jewish dogmas, 'there has never been any officially accepted formulation of these, no meeting ... of authoritative Rabbis to decide what it is that Judaism teaches in matters of faith'; however, what emerged in Jewish history is a consensus that 'there are limits in matters of faith, broad to be sure, to step beyond which is heretical'. Blasphemy is cursing the name of God; the penalty to be imposed on a blasphemer (*megaddef*) was death; likewise, insulting the Torah, Moses, the other prophets and sages is an offence but not subject to the death penalty.[21] Apostasy involves the rejection of Judaism or defection to another religion.[22] Nevertheless, apostasy does not result in loss of Jewish status: today, for Orthodox Judaism, 'the apostate (*mumar*), however damnable, has not altogether lost his status as a Jew'; in Conservative Judaism, 'an apostate never ceases to be a Jew' and after repentance before a court may 'be readmitted formally into the Jewish community'; and in Reform Judaism, the status of an apostate is 'the same as' that of 'converts who return to their original religion' – they 'remain Jewish and are to be considered Jewish for all purposes'. Thus, 'an adult proselyte who has become a Jew voluntarily cannot annul this process in any way'; and a child of an apostate female proselyte, or a child of a male married to a Jewish woman, is considered Jewish and no conversion is needed.[23]

---

[19] USCJ: A Guide to Writing and Revising Congregational Constitutions and Bylaws (2010) Art. X.

[20] ULPS: *Affirmations of Liberal Judaism* (1992, revised edn 2006) Preamble.

[21] L. Jacobs, *Jewish Religion* (1999) 87; N.S. Hecht et al., *Jewish Law* (1996) 50.

[22] Hebrew words used by Rabbinical scholars include *mumar* (literally, 'the one that was changed'), *poshea Yisrael* (literally, 'transgressor of Israel'), and *kofer* ('denier'). Other words are *meshumad* ('destroyed one'), one who has abandoned his faith and *min* the negation of God and Judaism, implying atheism. Apostasy was forbidden and punishable: Deuteronomy 13:6–11.

[23] Orthodox: I. Herzog, *Jewish Law* (1980) I.60; Conservative: I. Klein, *Jewish Religious Practice* (1992) 446: readmission involves immersion in a *miqweh*; Reform: W. Jacob and M. Zemer, *Conversion to Judaism* (1994), Selected Reform Responsa, 213: An Apostate Proselyte.

The Proclamation of Faith and the Definition and Development of Doctrine

In the history of Christianity, there have of course been many landmark disputes about doctrine: questions regarding where in the church authority lies to define doctrine, and the extent of permissible dissent. Such disputes are in large measure the cause of the institutional separation of churches.[24] However, today there is juridical unity between historic churches about these matters. According to the principles of Christian law, each church teaches as its doctrine on matters of faith and practice. The doctrine of a church is rooted in the revelation of God as recorded in Holy Scripture, summed up in the historical Creeds, conveyed in tradition and expounded in instruments – texts and pronouncements issued by persons and institutions with lawful authority to teach. The doctrinal instruments of churches may have elements which themselves may generate norms of conduct. The doctrine of a church may be interpreted and developed afresh to the extent and in the way prescribed by law.[25] The proclamation of the Word of God is a fundamental action of the church and a divine imperative incumbent on all the faithful. A church has both the right and the duty to instruct the faithful and to proclaim the Gospel. Preaching is inherent to ordained ministry. Authorised persons may deliver sermons or other forms of preaching for the glory of God, the edification of the people and the exposition of church doctrine. However, Biblical texts must be treated respectfully and coherently, building on tradition and scholarship so that scriptural revelation may continue to illuminate, challenge and transform thinking and doing.[26] Moreover, a church has a right to enforce its own doctrinal standards and discipline. The faithful should be taught and encouraged to believe church doctrine. Ordination candidates and others may be required to subscribe, assent or otherwise affirm their belief in, or loyalty to, the doctrine of their church. The faithful should respect, honour and uphold the doctrine of their church. Any person who offends church doctrine may be subject to disciplinary process. A church has the right to determine the limits of permissible theological opinion, and to interpret

---

[24] See e.g. H. Chadwick, *East and West: The Making of a Rift in the Church* (Oxford: Oxford University Press, 2003).

[25] Christian Law Panel of Experts, *Principles of Christian Law* (2016) VI.1: The Definition of Doctrine.

[26] Christian Law Panel of Experts, *Principles of Christian Law* (2016) VI.2: Proclamation of the Faith.

its own doctrine and doctrinal standards.[27] These principles are derived from the similarities between elaborate norms in the legal systems of the denominations.

For the Roman Catholic Church, the teaching function (*magisterium*) belongs to the ordained ministers: supreme teaching authority is entrusted to the Pontiff and the College of Bishops who may declare infallible doctrine – by which faith or morals on a matter of truth is solemnly defined – and proclaim truth, as contained in the written Word of God or in tradition, and which exists in the deposit of faith entrusted to the church and proposed as divinely revealed.[28] Alternatively, the Pontiff or College of Bishops may proclaim doctrine on faith or morals non-definitively, as might the bishops (while not infallible in their teaching), individually or collectively, in matters of faith.[29] Doctrine is found, for example, in the documents of the Second Vatican Council and the Catechism of the Church (issued by the apostolic constitution *Fidei Depositum*).[30]

For Anglicans, doctrine is the teaching by the church on any matter of faith which a church receives, believes and represents anew from generation to generation by virtue of its belonging to the One, Holy, Catholic and Apostolic Church.[31] Thus: 'The faith of Our Lord Jesus Christ is taught in the Holy Scriptures, summed up in the Creeds, and affirmed by the ancient Fathers and undisputed General Councils'; Holy Scriptures contain 'all things necessary to salvation and are the rule and ultimate standard of faith', the Apostles' Creed represents 'the Baptismal Symbol', and the Nicene Creed is recognised as 'the sufficient statement of the Christian faith'. Moreover, the Thirty-Nine Articles of Religion, the Book of Common Prayer and the Ordinal 1662 of the Church of England, 'grounded in the Holy Scriptures, and in such teachings of the ancient Fathers and Councils ... as are agreeable to the Holy Scriptures',

---

[27] Christian Law Panel of Experts, *Principles of Christian Law* (2016) VI.3: Doctrinal Discipline.

[28] CIC: c. 749.1: Pontiff; c. 749.2: College of Bishops; c. 749.3: 'No doctrine is understood to be infallibly defined unless this is manifestly demonstrated'; c. 750: Word of God and tradition; c. 748: all are bound to seek the truth but none to embrace Catholic faith against their conscience.

[29] CIC: cc. 752, 753, 386; the Sacred Congregation for the Doctrine of the Faith is also active in this field.

[30] Apostolic Constitution *Fidei Depositum*, on the publication of the *Catechism of the Catholic Church*, prepared following the Second Vatican Council, Pope John Paul II (1994).

[31] PCLCCAC: Principle 48.1

represent the historic sources of lawful doctrine for a church in the Anglican Communion.[32] Furthermore, each church must maintain 'the Faith, Doctrine, Sacraments and Discipline of the One, Holy, Catholic and Apostolic Church, and its own doctrinal formularies shall be compatible with the faith revealed in Holy Scripture, summed up in the Creeds, and received, practised and held by the church universal in the light of tradition and reason'. Yet, a church may draw up its own doctrinal formularies in terms suitable to the present day and needs of its people and circumstances, so that the faith may be presented loyally and intelligibly from generation to generation.[33] Competence to develop, reformulate or alter doctrinal formulae is entrusted only to the national/provincial assemblies of a church, subject to such substantive limitations and procedural requirements as may be prescribed by its law to ensure the protection of the faith of the church universal. No new doctrinal formulae may be approved by a central church assembly without the consent of the House of Bishops or equivalent.[34]

Much the same approach is found in the Methodist Church of Great Britain: 'The doctrines of the evangelical faith, which Methodism has held from the beginning, and still holds, are based upon the divine revelation recorded in the Holy Scriptures'; the church 'acknowledges this revelation as the supreme rule of faith and practice'. The doctrines to which preachers are pledged are contained in Wesley's Notes on the New Testament and the first four volumes of his sermons.[35] The Conference is 'the final authority within the Church with regard to all questions concerning the interpretation of its doctrines'.[36] Again, the principal source of Presbyterian doctrine is 'the Word of God as set forth in ... the Old and New Testaments', 'the only infallible rule of faith and practice, and the supreme standard of the Church'. Doctrine is also located in the 'subordinate standards',[37] which 'expound' what is revealed in Scripture,[38] or set out what a church understands 'the Word of God to

---

[32] PCLCCAC: Principle 49.1. See e.g. Church of England: Can. A2–5.
[33] PCLCCAC: Principle 50.1–2.
[34] PCLCCAC: Principle 50.3–6. See e.g. Church in Wales: Con. II.34–43: the Governing Body.
[35] MCGB: Constitutional Practice and Discipline, Deed of Union, 4.
[36] MCGB: Constitutional Practice and Discipline, Deed of Union 4–5 and Bk. V, Historic Texts..
[37] Church of Scotland Act 1921, Sch., Articles Declaratory.
[38] PCW: Handbook of Rules 2.1: 'The Gospel is the standard and inspiration of the life of the Christian'; 9.5: Short Confession; 9.6: Short Declaration of Faith and Practice.

teach on certain important points of doctrine and worship' – these include typically the Westminster Confession of Faith and Larger and Shorter Catechisms. A General Assembly has the right to 'deliberate upon', 'superintend' and declare the church's mind on doctrine.[39] Like the United Reformed Church,[40] for the Baptist Union Christ is 'sole and absolute authority in all matters [of] faith and practice, as revealed in the Holy Scriptures'.[41]

In turn, the proclamation of the Word of God is a fundamental action of the church and a divine imperative for all the faithful for the evangelisation of the world; this is the position in the Roman Catholic and Anglican churches,[42] as well as those of the Protestant tradition.[43] Moreover, in the Roman Catholic Church preaching is of 'great importance' and a homily must set out 'those things which it is necessary to believe and to practise for the glory of God and the salvation of all'; and Anglican clergy have the responsibility to preach sermons, but the laity may also be authorised to do so – the preacher 'must endeavour with care and sincerity to expound the word of truth according to Holy Scripture, to the glory of God and to the edification of the people'.[44] For Methodism, 'the main doctrines of the Christian faith should be more plainly and systematically set forth in public preaching, so that the Methodist people may be established in the faith'.[45] Similarly, in the Presbyterian Church of Wales: 'Our purpose is to ... spread the Gospel of the Lord Jesus Christ as it is revealed in the Holy Scriptures and expounded in our doctrinal standards' by *inter alia*: 'Preaching the Gospel', 'Religious Biblical education' and training, 'Missionary work and evangelising at home and abroad', and 'Providing and publishing literature'.[46] Also, each church may enforce its own doctrinal standards and discipline: the faithful should believe church doctrine; ordination

[39] PCI: Code, III.10–14, 104; PCW: Handbook of Rules 3.4.4: General Assembly has a Doctrine and Worship Panel with 'expertise in worship and doctrinal matters' to 'give guidance on ... Doctrine and Worship'.

[40] URC: Manual A.12; A.17: a 'statement' of its faith.

[41] BUGB: Model Trusts for Churches 2003, 2.8: Declaration of Principle.

[42] Matt. 28.18–20; CIC: cc. 747–748: 'It is the obligation and inherent right of the Church ... to preach the Gospel to all people'; PCLCCAC: Principle 48.

[43] LCGB: Rules and Regulations, Statement of Faith, 7–8; MCGB: Constitutional Practice and Discipline, Deed of Union 4; PCW: Handbook of Rules, 1.1; BUGB: Con. 4.

[44] See, respectively: CIC: cc. 757, 759, 760–772; PCLCCAC: Principles 48 and 51.

[45] MCGB: Constitutional Practice and Discipline, Standing Orders 524; see also PCW: Handbook of Rules, 9: preaching is an ordinance; URC: Manual A.13.

[46] PCW: Handbook of Rules, 1.1. See also PCI: Code, II.9.

candidates and others may be required to subscribe, assent or otherwise affirm their belief in or loyalty to that doctrine; and the faithful should not publicly manifest, in word or deed, a position contrary to church doctrine and those who do so may be subject to correction by disciplinary process.[47]

Iman and Khutbah

Belief or faith (*iman*) is a pillar of Islam common to all Muslims irrespective of their particular tradition, namely belief in God and that Muhammad is the Messenger of God, in the angels, the prophets and the revelation of God in the Quran.[48] Moreover, there is a close connection between faith and action, such that faith manifests itself in conduct: 'no human acts are acceptable to God, for no one can be righteous before God unless he is a believer in the true faith'; and faith consists in 'professing by the tongue, believing with the heart, and acting in accordance with its [Islamic] tenets' – that is an act of faith comprises verbal expression, internal conviction and performance of prescribed acts.[49] However, faith is a matter of free choice and a gift from God: no one is to be compelled to believe – 'There is no compulsion in religion' (Quran 2:256).[50] Nevertheless, believers are commanded by God – 'religion to a Muslim is essentially the Divine Law';[51] and *dawah* (call/invitation) is the means by which God brings people to faith and authorities invite individuals/communities back to God.[52] Modern regulatory instruments represent some of these fundamentals.

First, some have statements of the faith, which may be appended to the constitution of the organisation in question.[53] For example, Birmingham Central Mosque has its Articles of Muslim Faith, namely, seven 'basic beliefs [which] shape the Islamic way of life': (1) Belief in the Oneness of

---

[47] CIC: c. 752: *obsequium* is owed to non-definitive doctrine; for doctrinal offences, see cc. 751, 1323–1324, 1369, and 1364; PCLCCAC: Principle 53: doctrinal offences and subscription; MCGB: Constitutional Practice and Discipline, Standing Orders 010(1): 'No person shall be appointed to office in the Church who teaches doctrines contrary to those of the Church'; PCI: Code, 205: statements at ordination.

[48] J. Hussain, *Islamic Law* (1999) 12.

[49] Al-qadi al-Nu'man, *The Pillars of Islam*, translated by A.A.A. Fyzee and revised by I.K.H. Poonawala (Oxford: Oxford University Press, 2002) 3, 5.

[50] J.L. Esposito, ed., *Oxford Dictionary of Islam* (2003) 57, 217.

[51] S.H. Nasr, *Ideals and Realities of Islam* (Westport, CT: Praeger, 1966) 95.

[52] Quran 16:125: 'Call to the way of your Lord with wisdom and good preaching.'

[53] See e.g. NASFAT: Con. Art, C: 'the statement of faith'.

God: there is One God, Supreme and Eternal, Creator and Provider, Merciful and Compassionate; moreover: 'He is God of all humankind, not of a special tribe, race, or group of people [but] God of all races and colours, of believers and unbelievers alike'; and 'God asks us to know Him, to love Him, and to follow His Law, for our own benefit and salvation'; (2) Belief in the Angels of God, 'pure and spiritually obedient beings, created by God to fulfil His commands and worship Him tirelessly'; (3) Belief in the Revelation of God, sent to His Prophets and Messengers (including the Quran);[54] (4) Belief in the Prophets and Messengers of God (such as Noah, Moses, Solomon, Jesus and Muhammad, who 'were beings endowed with Divine Revelations and appointed by God to teach humankind how to submit to His will and obey His Laws'); (5) Belief in the Day of Judgment (*Yawm al-Din*), Heaven and Hell; (6) Belief in Pre-Measurement (*Qadar*), that Almighty God has knowledge of, and control over, everything that exists in all time and space; and (7) Belief in Resurrection after Death – all who have died will be brought back to life (resurrected) to face the judgment rendered to each by God.[55]

Second, Muslims must profess their faith. For example, a convert must recite the *shahadah*, witnessing there is no God but Allah and Muhammad is the messenger of God. Membership of an organisation in the Muslim Council of Britain is 'restricted only to those who profess the Muslim faith, who declare knowingly and voluntarily: "*La ilaha illa Allah Muhammad Rasul Allah*" and believe in the Qur'an as the true Word of God revealed to the Prophet Muhammad ... and that there is no prophet after him'.[56] Under the model constitution issued by the Central Mosque, 'a Muslim shall be any person whose belief systems shall not be at variance with the requisite beliefs of Islam as expounded by the scholars of the Ahlus-Sunnah wal Jama'ah';[57] and its *masjids* must disseminate 'Islamic teaching' and 'propagate Islamic teachings'.[58] The Markazi Jamia

---

[54] These also include the Torah, the Gospel, the Scrolls of Abraham and the Psalms of David.

[55] BCM: Seven Articles of Muslim Faith: www.centralmosque.org.uk. See also the Islamic Council of Europe, Universal Islamic Declaration of Human Rights (1981) Preamble: a statement of Muslim beliefs.

[56] MCB: Con. Art. 3.1.

[57] Model Constitution of an Islamic Organisation: Right of admission to the facilities of the congregation 1–2; that is, 'as interpreted' by prescribed Ulama bodies in South Africa.

[58] Model Constitution of an Islamic Organisation: Aims and Objectives 1, 2, 4; Powers and Duties of the Shura Committee 1: madrassa.

Masjid Riza and Islamic Centre (Huddersfield) must advance 'the Islamic faith for the public's benefit'; and membership is open to all who accept 'the teaching of the Quran, Hadith and of Khulafa-e-Rashdeen, Hazrat Imam Azam Abu Hanifa, Aima Ahle Bait, Hazrat Shah Abdul Haq Muhaddis Dhelvi, A'La Hazrat Shah Ahmed Raza Khan Brailvi', and follow the school of thought known as Sunnah and Jamaat Brailvi.[59] Propagation of the faith occurs primarily in the mosque, as at the Central Jamia Masjid (Southall) – this may be used to 'teach, propagate and preach Islam according to the Sunni schools of thought' and to 'popularise Islam' through cultural and social activities 'consistent with the tenets and doctrines of Islam'.[60]

Third, Muslim organisations may have committees devoted to propagation of the faith; for instance, the Nasru-Lahi-Il-Fathi Society of Nigeria, United Kingdom and Ireland has an Education Committee to: make recommendations on educational matters to the Executive Committee; monitor 'the quality and relevance of lectures delivered by the preacher(s)'; liaise with the Mission Board on the quality of lectures and arrange seminars for 'pilgrims to the holy land (Mecca)'; assume responsibility 'for the contents and quality of the educational programmes used for the children'; arrange for visiting Islamic Scholars to deliver special prayers and lectures; and organise training and workshops so as 'to keep [the committee members] abreast of [the] latest developments in [the] Islamic world and advise the society accordingly'.[61]

Fourth, in classical Islamic law, a *khutbah* is a sermon or speech given by an imam during the Friday midday service at the mosque and on the occasion of the two major festivals (*Id al-Adha* and *Id al-Fitr*); it consists of expressions praising God, blessings on Muhammad and his family and Companions, and exhortation to the community about their responsibility in this world and in preparation for the hereafter.[62] The Friday sermon is usually quite short, must be recited in Arabic and must contain some text of the Quran; it is also customary for the imam to provide a speech (*bayaan* or *wyaz*), in English, before the sermon.[63] Thus, preaching sermons are included among the duties of imams. For example, at Aberdeen Mosque and Islamic Centre, the imam is responsible for

---

[59] MJMRIC: Con. Art. 2 and 3: i.e. Ahle-Sunnat-Wa-Jamaat (Braivli).
[60] CJM: Con. Art. 3.   [61] NASFAT: Con. Art. N.2.
[62] J.L. Esposito, ed., *Oxford Dictionary of Islam* (2003) 174.
[63] M. Naqshbandi, *Islam and Muslims in Britain* (2012): Guide 9.3.

'propagation of Islam and giving *da'wa*' (bringing people to faith).[64] Also, a Muslim wishing to talk publicly to the congregation in any part of the Mosque/Centre must seek the consent of the Imam or Executive Committee; and no announcements are to be made in it without the prior agreement of either.[65] One model constitution provides that it is for the mosque executive committee to approve 'candidates to perform the Friday sermon'; and an officer is assigned to produce the Friday sermon rota, assist in selection of titles and circulate the Friday sermon.[66]

Indeed, some organisations also regulate hosting imams from outside the community. For instance, Palmers Green Mosque Community and Education Centre may invite imams from the wider community to speak at any mosque event and to deliver Friday sermons, in order to enrich members' knowledge of religion, enhance their education, widen their understanding of 'Islamic rulings' and motivate the people through the sharing of experience. However, the mosque has a responsibility to its community 'to ensure that they critically assess the information received' as to its value to them and that the information is 'aligned to the ethos and values of Islam, [the Mosque itself] and British Values'. To this end, the Mosque 'requires that all individuals and organisations hosted by Palmers Green Mosque adhere to certain guidelines'. The talk is to be in 'a universally understood language, English', and the speaker should not: - solicit donations or fund-raise at the event; publicise other organisations or events or partake in any marketing activities or distribution of any sorts of literature; promote any one school of thought or matter of *fiqh* in a manner which could potentially be divisive to the Muslim community; discuss highly sensitive areas of Islam; or promote/propagate any illegal activities, discrimination or hate crime. The mosque provides that respect needs to be shown for scholars and other legitimate opinions.[67]

As was seen in Chapter 3, historically, apostasy is the renunciation of Islam (*riddah, irtidad*) and a crime which attracts the death penalty. However, unlike the modern laws of Christians, the modern regulatory instruments of the Muslim organisations studied here do not contain provisions on apostasy or the penalties which attach to it.

---

[64] AMIC: Con. Art. XIV.5.
[65] AMIC: Con. Art. XIII.1–2. See also M. Naqshbandi, *Islam and Muslims in Britain* (2012): Guide 4.8.4: it is a religious requirement that no trace should remain of Quranic text on material being disposed of.
[66] IFIS CUBE Network: Sample Constitution of an Islamic Society, 4.8 and 4.9.
[67] PGM: Guidelines on Speakers and Imams www.mcec.org.uk

The Administration of Worship

The worship of God is one of the central functions of a faith community. The laws of Jews, Christians and Muslims on communal worship seek to strike a balance between fidelity to historic patterns of worship and freedom of expression in worship including the need to adapt to changing times, uses and needs. What follows deals with legal understandings of worship, its administration and the exercise of authority over it.

Jewish Worship and Shabbat

Communal worship is the subject of much regulation in Judaism, traceable to the Torah and custom, and marked by both historical continuity and change to reflect 'the nearness and holiness of the divine' – at its core are the benedictions, the *shema* and its special blessings, the reading of the Torah and the *haftarah* (a reading from the prophets after the reading of the Torah).[68] The prayer book for daily and Sabbath prayers is known as a *siddur* (plural *siddurim*) and the book for the prayers for festivals as a *mahzor* (plural *mahzorim*). They have the same basic features but each service or rite has its own distinct elements.[69] In the early nineteenth century, the Reform Movement sought 'to regenerate public worship by enhancing its beauty and relevance, deleting material ... thought to be obsolete, and introducing vernacular prayers, a weekly vernacular sermon, choral and organ music, and new ceremonies', for example confirmation.[70]

Guidance issued by the Board of Deputies of British Jews summarises the holy days. The Sabbath (*Shabbat*) is the Jewish day of rest. It starts on Friday afternoon, about one hour before dusk, and lasts for approximately 25 hours, until after dark the following day; and: 'Jewish law requires Jews to refrain from various acts of "work" on the Sabbath, in commemoration of God's cessation of work on the seventh day of

---

[68] K. Kohler, 'The origin and function of ceremonies in Judaism', Central Conference of American Rabbis, Yearbook, vol. 17 (Cincinnati: Bloch Publishing, 1907) 208, 210, 221.

[69] In Talmudic times, the prayers were recited by heart and not written in orders of service. It is commonly understood that the first prayer book was compiled in the ninth century by Amram Gaon and is known as the Seder Rav Amram Gaon and was followed by the Siddur of Saadiah Gaon in the tenth century.

[70] N. Solomon, 'Public law and traditional faith', in F. Cranmer, M. Hill, C. Kenny and R. Sandberg: *The Confluence of Law and Religion* (Cambridge: Cambridge University Press, 2016) 161 at 168.

creation, as described in the Book of Genesis'; 'prohibited acts of "work"' include travelling (other than by foot), writing, carrying, switching on and off electricity, using a telephone, and any commercial transactions, including buying or selling. Jewish festivals also begin before dusk on the previous day. As the Jewish calendar is lunar, festival dates vary from year to year, and may fall on any week day: 'The laws governing "work" on festivals are for these purposes almost indistinguishable from those concerning the Sabbath, and the same prohibitions and restrictions apply.' Orthodox communities observe 13 festival days, and Progressive communities observe seven: Passover (March/April), comprises for Orthodox two sets of two days or two sets of one-day for Progressive communities; Pentecost (May/June), consists of two days for Orthodox and one for Progressive Judaism; New Year or *Shavuot* (in May/June), is two days for Orthodox and one for Progressive communities; the Day of Atonement or *Yom Kippur* (September/October) is on one day; and Tabernacles or *Succot* (September/October) comprises two sets of days separated by five semi-festive days for Orthodox and two of one day for Progressive Judaism. Moreover, observant Jews pray three times a day, in the morning, afternoon and evening (after nightfall). Some, especially observant men, may attend prayers with a quorum (the *minyan*, ten adult men according to Orthodox tradition), particularly in a period of mourning. In practice, this may mean that they attend a synagogue in the morning and evening.[71]

Modern Jewish regulatory instruments across the traditions deal with the conduct of worship. The (Orthodox) United Synagogue requires worship at a member synagogue to conform to 'forms of worship' approved by the Chief Rabbi, and responsibility for it rests with its Rabbi.[72] Therefore: (1) all religious services or observances must be conducted in accordance with the Polish or German Ritual 'as found in the Authorised Daily Prayer Book of the United Hebrew Congregations of the Commonwealth', but the synagogue may permit a service held 'in accordance with other Orthodox Jewish Ritual' if a service in the Polish or German Ritual is unavailable there, and such services or observances 'are conducted under the supervision and control of [its] Rabbi ... in consultation with [its] Wardens ... under the ultimate authority of the

---

[71] BDBJ: *The Employer's Guide to Judaism* (2004: updated 2015) Section 2: this deals with the duties under civil law of and best practice by employers to accommodate the needs of Jewish employees.
[72] US: Statutes 2, 3, 5.4.

Chief Rabbi'; (2) religious services must be conducted by the Rabbi or may be conducted by any other person employed for that purpose or by any other on an *ad hoc* basis with the consent of the Wardens if the Rabbi is satisfied as to the competence and suitability of the person concerned, under the ultimate authority of the Chief Rabbi; and (3) all members must in exercising members' rights, when attending religious services or observances, 'adhere to the practices of the Jewish Religion as so defined by the Chief Rabbi'.[73] There is an order of precedence in the reading of the Torah in the synagogue, and members exercise rights to do so on the basis of seniority;[74] however, the calling of any person(s) to the reading of the law is a matter within the absolute discretion of the Wardens.[75] Such norms may be embellished at local level on the basis of 'custom'.[76]

Conducting worship in the Movement for Reform Judaism is a partnership between the Rabbi and Wardens. The Rabbi must liaise with the Warden of the synagogue 'on a regular basis to discuss religious activities, services, High Holydays, and Festivals' and 'liturgies, practices and procedures . . . to be used in services'. The Warden must, *inter alia*: chair the Religious Activities Committee; organise the frequency, times and dates of services; oversee 'lay readers' for Friday and Saturday services; attend to the Torah scrolls; liaise with those responsible for singing at the High Holydays, Festivals and Weddings; oversee music; arrange the reading of the Torah; and purchase prayer books.[77] The Movement has prayer books for use on the Sabbath and festival prayer books,[78] and provides norms on 'lay readers', 'scroll readers' and others in worship.[79]

For example, at Brighton and Hove Reform Synagogue: 'The Rabbi is responsible for the form and content of the Services in consultation with the Wardens and the Charity Trustees'; if there is no Rabbi, the Wardens and Charity Trustees have responsibility; and: 'Ritual shall be in conformity with the practice of the Movement for Reform Judaism.' Religious services must be held on Sabbaths and Holy Days, and on such

---

[73] US: Bye-Laws 4.   [74] US: Bye-Laws, Sch. 1.3.   [75] US: Bye-Laws, Sch. 1.4.

[76] See e.g. NHC: Con. Art. 5–6: 'forms of prayer' must conform to 'the form and customs' of the community.

[77] MRJ: Areas of Responsibility and Codes of Practice Documents: pp. 7–8.

[78] MRJ: a prayer book for a festival is a *machzor* and one for Shabbat a *siddur*. The Seder Ha-T'fillot, Forms of Prayer, and the daily and Sabbath Siddur (2008), with services for Shabbat, weekdays, festivals and special occasions, are in a 'flexible format' for 'traditional and creative' worship.

[79] MRJ: *Codes of Practice*, p. 21.

other occasions as the Rabbi directs, in the synagogue or in such other place as the Charity Trustees approve.[80] At North London Reform Synagogue: 'The Council, in consultation with the Minister, shall determine all matters appertaining to the Services and the ritual to be used, and ... make such regulations as may be required to ensure the proper and dignified performance of the Services; and shall assign to members or visitors, irrespective of sex, the duties and privileges to be exercised at the Services.'[81]

In Progressive Judaism, some scholars consider that today rituals are 'less important than other aspects of halakhah', but nevertheless 'remind us of our ethical duties'.[82] As a result, rituals may be modified 'to make them more relevant to the contemporary Jewish community';[83] they are acts required by or conducive to the relationship of the individual or community with God; and private prayer is 'a spiritual exercise for the individual, but public worship has, additionally, a social function', namely: 'It binds the individuals together into a community, and is at the same time a corporate act of self-dedication on the part of the community, to its collective task.' Moreover, rituals in their totality promote 'holiness' and 'moral fitness', but are matters of 'custom'.[84]

The Union of Liberal and Progressive Synagogues affirms the importance of 'prayer and worship, through which the individual and the community seek ever new ways to experience God's presence, to draw spiritual sustenance from their religious heritage, and to dedicate themselves to their responsibilities', and 'the Jewish liturgy', including the recitation of *shema*, public reading of Torah and other writings and 'an abundance of blessings, prayers and hymns composed by Jewish sages, poets and mystics in many lands and ages'.[85] Secondly, it affirms 'the paramount need for sincerity in worship: we may not say with our lips what we do not believe in our hearts'; so: 'though we retain much of the

---

[80] BHRS: Con. Art. 21; see also Art. 25: a person is proposed as Warden by the Rabbi and Charity Trustees and appointed at the Annual General Meeting. See also SSRS: Con. Art. 3: Public Worship.

[81] NLRS: Law, Art. 14.

[82] W. Jacob, 'Writing responsa: a personal journey', in W. Jacob, ed., *Beyond the Letter of the Law* (2004) 103 at 108.

[83] R.S. Rheins, '*Asu Seyag LaTorah*: make a fence to protect the Torah', in W. Jacob and M. Zemer, eds., *Re-Examining Progressive Halakhah* (2002) 91 at 92–93.

[84] J. Rayner, 'Ethics versus ritual', in W. Jacob, ed., *Beyond the Letter of the Law* (2004) 119 at 121, 131–132.

[85] ULPS: *Affirmations* (2006) Arts. 16–17.

traditional Jewish liturgy, we have revised it, with some omissions and modifications, and many amplifications ... [and] use English as well as Hebrew in our services'.[86] Therefore: 'observances must be in accord with our beliefs and individual Jews must be free ... to exercise informed, conscientious choice', which includes 'the details of Sabbath observance and the Dietary Laws'.[87] Thirdly, the Union affirms the importance of *Shabbat* (Sabbath), namely: 'the sanctification of the seventh day as a day of rest and joy, study and worship',[88] and the festivals which it enumerates.[89] Moreover, the Union affirms 'the equal status of men and women in ... ritual',[90] and encourages 'the use of instrumental music in synagogue worship'.[91]

Regional or local communities regulate worship, for example the Wessex Liberal Jewish Community: 'Religious services will be held on those Sabbaths, Holy Days, and on such other occasions as the Council may direct or approve. Every service shall be performed partly in Hebrew and partly ... English and follow the Liberal Judaism prayer books'.[92] And at Elstree Liberal Synagogue, the Council is to 'arrange and conduct religious services', decide what 'religious rites' may be performed, and 'determine and decide all questions relating to the religious practices and services'.[93]

In the United Synagogue of Conservative Judaism: 'The laws, rules and customs of Shabbat, all holy days, and of kashrut, as determined by the Rabbi, are to be observed at all rites, ceremonies and other functions.'[94] A Conservative Jew 'should attend services on *Shabbat* and Festivals', participate 'regularly in a daily *minyan*',[95] and recite the 'statutory prayers' – morning prayer (*shaharit*), afternoon prayer (*minhah*), and evening prayer (*ma'ariv*).[96] Moreover, Shabbat and festivals are 'to be observed in a manner that is essentially spiritual in quality and purpose, and that reflects the sanctity of the day, with ... activities on these days

---

[86] ULPS: *Affirmations* (2006) Art. 31.   [87] ULPS: *Affirmations* (2006) Art. 39.
[88] ULPS: *Affirmations* (2006) Art. 18.   [89] ULPS: *Affirmations* (2006) Arts. 20–21.
[90] ULPS: *Affirmations* (2006) Art. 34.
[91] ULPS: *Affirmations* (2006) Art. 30. Moreover: 'Music is a key part of ... Liberal Judaism' as it has always been in Judaism 'to enhance prayer, spirituality and community': www.liberaljudaism.org/what-we-do/music.
[92] WLJC: Con. Art. 16.3. ULPS has lectionaries for e.g. Torah readings on the Sabbath.
[93] ELS: Con. Art. 4.
[94] USCJ: Standards for Congregational Practice (2017): Standard IV.
[95] USCJ: The 'Ideal' Conservative Jew: Eight Behavioural Expectations: Jewish Living.
[96] I. Klein, *Jewish Religious Practice* (1992) 12. See also the Statement of Principles of Conservative Judaism (1988) 38 for the 'Conservative Prayerbook'.

conducted accordingly'. Halakhic issues such as these 'should be resolved by the Rabbi in consultation with lay leadership' in compliance with the Laws and Customs of the Torah Service.[97] Each *kehillah*, in its constitution, should therefore ensure it is a centre of 'a Jew's liturgical attention', has a Vice President for 'religious observance/services' to 'work with the clergy and religious committee on the schedule and content of religious services [and] holiday observances'[98] and has a qualified *hazzan*, or cantor, elected by a congregation. The *hazzan* is the *ba'al nusach* (religious musical expert) and principal *sheliach tzibbur* (leader of prayers), and acts in consultation with the Rabbi and religious committee, and with due deference to the Rabbi's authority, in all 'activities of the congregation involving liturgical and Jewish music'.[99] The Religious Committee (chaired by the Vice President for Religious Observance): oversees 'all religious services'; may make rules for these subject to the approval of the cantor as to musical issues, the Rabbi as to halakhic issues and the Board of Trustees as to all other issues; offers to the Rabbi and cantor 'advice and guidance regarding the character and mode of . . . services'; and is responsible for appointing *gabbaim* (Wardens) and ushers for religious services. The Vice President is a voting member and the Rabbi and cantor may attend and vote.[100]

The Worship of God and Liturgical Administration

For Christianity, the worship of God is a fundamental duty of the church. With regard to the historic churches, according to the principles of Christian law, worship enables an intimate encounter between a church corporately and the faithful individually with the presence of God. Each church and those bodies within it competent to do so may develop liturgical texts or other forms of service for public worship provided these are consistent with the Word of God and church doctrine. The use of a form of service must be authorised. Forms of service may be found in a book of rites or liturgy, a book of common prayer, a directory of worship or other instrument, and these may include rubrics or other

---

[97] USCJ: Standards for Congregational Practice (2017): Standard II. Congregations should refer to Resources on Shabbat Observance as well as Yad LaTorah – Laws and Customs of the Torah Service: A Guide for Gabba'im and Torah Readers.
[98] USCJ: Guide to Constitutions (2010) Arts. II and VI.
[99] USCJ: Guide to Constitutions (2010) Art. XI.
[100] USCJ: Guide to Constitutions (2010) Art. XV: a *gabbai* (a Talmudic office) is also styled *shamash*.

directions to facilitate worship.[101] A church must provide for public worship. Ordained ministers are particularly responsible for its conduct in accordance with forms of service. Regular attendance at worship, particularly on the Lord's Day, is an expectation on the faithful. The administration of worship in the local church is subject to supervision by those authorities designated by law to provide this.[102] These principles are derived from laws of the churches themselves.

First, as to the nature and forms of worship, in the Roman Catholic Church, worship is 'the first act of the virtue of religion', with adoration, prayer and the participation of the faithful.[103] Liturgy is 'an action of the church' – an expression by the people of their relationship to Christ and the church – a response to God's initiative, a dialogue between the Word and actions of God and his people.[104] The purpose of liturgy is to enable the sanctification of the faithful through worship: the whole church, clergy and laity, shares in the exercise of the office of sanctifying and liturgical actions themselves are not private actions but corporate celebrations of the church with the presence and active participation of the faithful; and the faithful have the right to worship God according to rites approved by the legitimate pastors of the church.[105] Detailed liturgical law exists in ritual books (ordines), their preambles and rubrics.[106] Anglicanism is similar.[107] Norms in service books provide for order and decorum in liturgy, enable the community to participate fully in worship, and ensure adaptability to meet local circumstances, practices and needs.[108] All the faithful should keep the Lord's Day, commonly called Sunday, by regular participation in corporate public worship, hearing the Word of God read and taught, acts of devotion and charity, godly and sober conversation and abstention from all unnecessary labour and business.[109]

---

[101] Christian Law Panel of Experts, *Principles of Christian Law* (2016) VI.4: The Nature and Forms of Worship.

[102] Christian Law Panel of Experts, *Principles of Christian Law* (2016) VI.5: The Administration of Public Worship.

[103] CCC, paras. 2096–2098; 1069: liturgy is a 'public work' in 'the name of/on behalf of the people'.

[104] SC: 1; CCC, paras. 1076–1109.

[105] CIC: cc. 834–837; SC 26; for e.g. prayers, see c. 839; c. 217: the right to worship.

[106] CIC: c. 2.   [107] PCLCCAC: Principle 54.1: the nature of worship.

[108] PCLCCAC: Principle 54.2-5. See e.g. Church of Ireland: Alternative Prayer Book, 1984: 'liturgy becomes worship when the people . . . make the prayers their own prayers, and turn in faith to God'.

[109] PCLCCAC: Principle 54.6: attendance; 7: Sunday.

Much the same is found across the Protestant traditions. In Methodism, 'worship is essential to the life of the Church', 'necessary to Christian fellowship and spiritual growth' and 'the duty and privilege of man who, in the presence of God, bows in adoration, humility and dedication'; however: 'the order of public worship need not be the same in all places but may be modified ... according to circumstances and the needs of men. It should be in a language and form understood by the people, consistent with the Holy Scriptures to the edification of all, and in accordance with the order and Discipline of the Church.'[110] Likewise, the Presbyterian Church of Wales holds: 'Our purpose is to worship God and spread the Gospel of the Lord Jesus Christ';[111] the 'means of grace in a worshipping community are the reading of the Scriptures, prayer, the singing of hymns, the preaching and hearing of the Word and the administration and receiving of the sacraments'; their regular use is 'a duty to God and a necessity of the Christian life'.[112] The United Reformed Church follows suit.[113]

Secondly, there are norms on the development and administration of forms of service. Roman Catholic canon law provides for the formation of liturgical texts and authority over these is entrusted to the Pontiff. It is for the Apostolic See to order the sacred liturgy of the universal church and 'publish the liturgical books [and] review their translations into vernacular languages'. The Conference of Bishops may prepare both the translations and particular ritual texts, adopted to local needs, and arrange for their publication after prior review (*recognitio*) of the Holy See. The Church has a range of texts for different occasions, such as celebration of the sacraments; the principal liturgies are in the Roman Missal (1969), the Roman Ritual (1969–1984) and Roman Pontifical (1968–1984).[114]

In Anglicanism, whilst the Book of Common Prayer 1662 is the normative standard for liturgy, a church may make such revisions, adaptations and innovations in its forms of service as are desirable to meet particular needs and circumstances. It belongs to the central church assembly to approve, amend, continue or discontinue forms of service,[115]

---

[110] MCGB: Constitutional Practice and Discipline, Standing Orders 569: 'creative and culturally appropriate ways ... to meet with God in worship'.
[111] PCW: Handbook of Rules, 1.1.   [112] PCW: Handbook of Rules, 2.1.
[113] URC: Manual A.25.
[114] CIC: c. 826: local ordinary; c. 838.2: Apostolic See; c. 838.3: Conference of Bishops; c. 455.2.
[115] PCLCCAC: Principle 55.1–4.

but these must be neither contrary to, nor indicative of a departure from, the doctrine of the church in any essential matter, nor inconsistent with the Word of God and the spirit and teaching of the Book of Common Prayer 1662.[116] The bishop may authorise for a diocese variations, adjustments or substitutes for, or additions to, any part of a liturgical text under trial use to the extent permitted by law. If permitted by law, a bishop or other ecclesiastical body may also authorise a diocese to use a form of service for which no provision exists in authorised service books. However, no minister in a parish may formulate or use a different form of service without lawful authority.[117] Forms of service must be in a language understood by the people. Local customs may exist in the matter of posture, standing, kneeling or sitting at the time of worship. All persons present should pay reverent attention at the time of worship, give due reverence to the name of the Lord Jesus and stand at the Creed and reading of the Gospel at the Holy Communion.[118]

Methodists also have designated books of worship and hymnals.[119] In the Methodist Church of Great Britain, for example, these are approved by the Conference, though the Faith and Order Committee may make proposals to Conference for the revision of forms of service authorised by it.[120] The law of the Church of Scotland is similar: 'There is no prescribed liturgy in the Church of Scotland, and ministers enjoy considerable freedom in matters of worship'; rather, the principles of worship are in accordance with the Directory for the Public Worship of God 1645 as that 'has been or may hereafter be modified by Acts of the General Assembly or by consuetude'. It is the General Assembly, therefore, that may commend forms of service, but these are not 'regulative' as such. The church has a modern Directory of Worship.[121]

Thirdly, as to the administration of worship, in the Roman Catholic Church, in order to be considered as liturgy, worship takes place when it is carried out in the name of the church by persons lawfully deputed and

---

[116] PCLCCAC: Principle 55.5–6. E.g. Church of England: Church of England (Worship and Doctrine) Measure 1974: General Synod; Scottish Episcopal Church: Can. 22.4: the College of Bishops may allow experimental services.

[117] PCLCCAC: Principle 55.7–9. See e.g. Church of England: Can. B1–5.

[118] PCLCCAC: Principle 54.8–10. See e.g. Church of England: Can. B9: reverence.

[119] MCI: Regulations, Discipline and Government, 3.02: e.g. the Methodist Worship Book (1999).

[120] MCGB: Constitutional Practice and Discipline, Standing Orders 330.

[121] J.L. Weatherhead, ed., *Constitution and Laws of the Church of Scotland* (1997) 28–30. See also Church of Scotland Act 1921, Sch., Articles Declaratory, Art. II.

through acts approved by the authority of the church; and liturgy is conducted under the presidency of the ordained ministers.[122] The supervision of liturgy depends solely on the authority of the church: liturgical supervision resides in the Pontiff and, under the law, the diocesan bishop, who may issue liturgical norms.[123] The liturgical books approved by competent authority must be faithfully observed in the celebration of sacraments: no one on personal authority may add, remove or change anything in them.[124] However, as liturgical law exists to facilitate worship, it should be applied flexibly, with choices and options. The bishop must supervise liturgical discipline and may dispense with the requirements of universal and particular liturgical law in this regard; but a minister cannot unilaterally dispense from liturgical laws, though some writers stress that a governing principle is the *de minimis* rule and the directory rather than mandatory nature of liturgical law.[125]

Liturgical administration is also regulated in Anglicanism. A minister must use in public worship only the lawful forms of service. However, liturgical life should be characterised by flexibility (as authorised by law). Appropriate patterns of worship may vary from place to place, and time to time, and ministers may use their own sensitivity and discretion to conduct worship so that the faithful can participate with sincerity and understanding. A minister may make changes to the authorised form of service; these changes must be lawful, reverent and seemly and not contrary to church doctrine. Rubrics or other directions are to be applied flexibly. Questions of liturgical variation may be referred to the bishop to advise or direct as appropriate.[126] The right to supervise public worship in a parish is invested in its cleric. No minister, lay or ordained, from another parish or diocese may conduct divine services publicly within a parish without the prior consent of its clergy. However, the bishop has authority to order liturgy and public worship within the diocese and to prohibit any unlawful practice.[127] Any minister who fails to provide

---

[122] CIC: c. 834.2; *Lumen Gentium*, Vatican II, Dogmatic Constitution (1965) 11. See also CCEO c. 656: only approved books may be used in liturgy.

[123] CIC: c. 838; SC 22.　　[124] CIC: c. 846.

[125] CIC: cc. 87–88: dispensation (see also c. 392.2); c. 89: ministerial compliance.

[126] PCLCCAC: Principle 56; 57: worship may be dispensed with for reasonable cause; 58: alternatives. See e.g. Church of England: Can B1, C15: '[e]very minister shall use only the forms of service authorised'.

[127] PCLCCAC: Principles 59–60.1–2. See e.g. Church of Ireland: Con. IX.2: '[it] shall be competent for the ordinary to restrain and prohibit in the conduct of public worship any

public worship, to administer the sacraments or to use lawful liturgical ritual or ceremonial, may be subjected to disciplinary process.[128]

The laws of the Methodist Church in Great Britain are similar. Ordained ministers conduct public worship but lay speakers may be appointed to assist.[129] Also: 'No pastor shall hold a religious service within the bounds of a pastoral charge other than the one to which appointed without the consent of the pastor of the charge, or the district superintendent', who ensures that public worship is conducted properly.[130] The Lord's Day is divinely ordained for both private and public worship, rest from unnecessary work, spiritual improvement, Christian fellowship and service.[131] Whilst a Presbyterian Directory of Worship sets out the forms of service, the Kirk Session fixes the time and place and the minister is responsible for the conduct of worship,[132] 'the supervision of worship being a function of Presbyteries, they are to enjoin the discontinuance, or prohibit the introduction of any novel practice in worship which is inconsistent with [church] laws and usages, a cause of division in a congregation, or unfit from any cause to be used in the worship of God'.[133] The United Reformed Church and Baptist Union also have norms regulating the supervision of worship.[134]

Ibadat

There are four obligatory acts of worship (*ibadat*) incumbent on all Muslims when they come of age and are of sound mind and body: the five daily prayers (*salat*), fasting in *Ramadan*, pilgrimage (*hajj*) and the poor-tax (*zakah*). *Salat* is an act of praise, as distinct from supplicatory

---

practice not enjoined in the Book of Common Prayer, or in any rubric or canon enacted by lawful authority of the Church of Ireland.'

[128] PCLCCAC: Principle 60.3–6.

[129] MCGB: Constitutional Practice and Discipline, Standing Orders 700–701.

[130] MCGB: Constitutional Practice and Discipline, Standing Orders 631(1): class leaders and worship.

[131] MCGB: Constitutional Practice and Discipline, Standing Orders 609: this also deals with 'acts of worship' in residential and nursing homes.

[132] PCI: Code, 37.

[133] J.L. Weatherhead, ed., *Constitution and Laws of the Church of Scotland* (1997) 30 and Act VII, 1866; PCI: Code, 19.2: 'Each congregation and each member . . . in all matters of . . . worship . . . is under the immediate jurisdiction of the Kirk Session.'

[134] URC: Manual B.2.2: the Elders' Meeting ensures 'public worship is regularly offered'; BUGB: Model Trusts for Churches 2003, 5.1.1: property may be used as 'a place for public worship'.

prayer, and comprises a combination of standing, reciting verses of the Quran, bowing, prostrating and sitting, all facing the Kaabah in Mecca. It is obligatory for all Muslim men and women (except when menstruating) but may be relaxed for a valid reason (e.g. to save a life). The five daily prayers must be performed each during its allotted period: dawn, noon, mid-afternoon, after sunset, and night. Men are expected to perform *salat* in the mosque. *Salat* occurs: after ritual washing (*wudhu*) of the face, arms and feet; prostrating (*rakah*), kneeling and leaning forward to touch the forehead to the ground; in a clean place (as religiously defined), usually achieved by using a prayer mat (*mursalah*); and behind an arbitrary object that forms a symbolic barrier between the one praying (*sutra*) and those walking around (as it is considered reprehensible to pass in front of a *sutra*).[135] Friday congregational prayers (*salat al-jumah*) are performed at the mosque, the believers in straight lines with men in front and women and children behind or in a separate area; the sermon (*khutbah*) is also part of the service.[136] It is mandatory for each of the five obligatory *salat* to be preceded by the call to prayer (*adhan*). This has to be recited in a loud voice from a raised place outside the *masjid* area, traditionally from the top of a tower (*minar*), which may be satisfied by a single step off the ground just outside the prayer room itself and without amplification. There is no requirement to proclaim the *adhan* from loudspeakers. Most *masjids* are open for the five daily prayers, for each of which a congregation (*jamat*) will form at a fixed time, being led by the imam.[137]

Whilst there is no Sabbath, the day of religious significance is *Yawm-al-Juma'a* (the day of gathering), from Thursday evening to Friday evening. On the Friday morning, men preparing for *juma'a* should clip their nails, shorten a moustache, shave the armpits and pubic hair, take a ritual bath (*ghusl*) and wear clean clothes.[138] The Muslim lunar calendar (*Muharram*) is marked by various festivals and holy days. The first month is one in which the direction of prayer (*qiblah*) was moved from Jerusalem to Mecca and Hussain the grandson of Muhammad was murdered – Sunnis mark this with fasting and Shias by lamentation. The third month (*Rabi' al-awwal*) celebrates *Mawlid*, the birthday of

---

[135] *Salat* consists of units (*rakah*): each complete *salat* comprises two, three or four *rakah* and may last from two to five minutes.

[136] M. Naqshbandi, *Islam and Muslims in Britain* (2012): Guide 2.

[137] M. Naqshbandi, *Islam and Muslims in Britain* (2012): Guide 4.2.

[138] M. Naqshbandi, *Islam and Muslims in Britain* (2012): Guide 9.3

Muhammad – Bareilvis have major events in the *masjid*, and Deobandi, Wahabi and Salafi communities have lectures on the life of Muhammad. For the ninth month (*Ramadan*), obligatory fasting commences the day following the sighting of the new moon and continues for 29 or 30 days until the next new moon – worship in Ramadan is said to be 70 times superior to that at any other time and attendance at *masjids* is much higher; one or more men stay permanently at the *masjids* for the last ten days in a state of seclusion (*ihtikhaf*) for *Lailat-ul-Qadr*, the 'Night of Power'. The tenth month (*Shawwal*) comprises *Eid-ul-Fitr*, the feast of fast-breaking, and *Eid salat* for family gatherings. The twelfth month (*Dhul-Hijjah*) is for pilgrimage to Mecca (in its second week), and *Eid-ul-Adha*, the feast of sacrifice, which includes making gifts.[139]

The purposes of worship and ritual are summed up by Birmingham Central Mosque: 'Manifestation of faith ... in rituals is not a futile exercise ... but it serves very important specific purposes'; for instance: *shahadah* is a focus for worship; prayers five times each day provide 'spiritual sustenance, collectiveness and moral ethics' and a 'strong sense of discipline in our daily affairs'; fasting is the best form of 'teaching oneself discipline over one's desires'; and *hajj* is an exercise in collectiveness and equality.[140]

Modern regulatory instruments often repeat and embellish these elements of Islamic law/practice. For example, Nasru-Lahi-Il-Fathi Society of Nigeria, United Kingdom and Ireland requires: five daily prayers at the prescribed times and congregational Friday prayers (*jumat*); a prayer gathering (*asalatu*) every Sunday morning, which members are 'encouraged' to attend; night vigil prayers (*tahajud*) on the first and third Friday of the month; special prayers (*taraweeh*) and the vigil (*itikaf*) during *Ramadan*.[141] The model constitution issued by the Central Mosque requires a *masjid* to maintain the 'performance of congregational and other prayers and religious rites and activities'.[142] The Central Jamia Masjid (Southall) Board of Trustees may organise 'regular prayers, religious functions and social and cultural festivals for the Muslim community'.[143] East London Mosque is open for all of the five daily prayers; in the daytime, the prayer hall may be used for reading the

---

[139] M. Naqshbandi, *Islam and Muslims in Britain* (2012): Guide 5: such is a Sunnah; and they should apply *ittar*, oil-based perfume.
[140] BCM: Seven Articles of Muslim Faith.   [141] NASFAT: Con. Art. O.
[142] Model Constitution of an Islamic Organisation: Aims and Objectives 1–2.
[143] CJM: Con. Art. 3.

Quran and contemplation. There is a space solely for women. Regular programmes include: *tafsir* (explanation) of the Quran in English, Bangla and Somali; on Saturday a weekly programme open to all the family with a range of speakers and topics; and annual training for *hajj*.[144] Model constitutions may also provide that a mosque should have an officer to manage the cleanliness of prayer spaces and ablution facilities, report any issues as to prayer space or ablution facilities to the management and issue a timetable for prayers.[145]

Religious Education and Schools

The instruction of the faithful in the beliefs and practices of religion is fundamental to Judaism, Christianity and Islam. As well as norms on preaching, Jewish, Christian and Muslim regulatory instruments make elaborate provision for the instruction of the faithful, particularly the young, and all have norms on religious schools: the Jewish *cheder*, Christian Sunday School and Muslim *madrassa*. Moreover, under civil law, state-maintained faith schools, foundation and voluntary schools may be designated by the Secretary of State as schools having a religious character if he is satisfied that the school was established by a religious body or for religious purposes; such an order must state the religion or religious denomination.[146] As to admissions, generally any parental preference will be respected; but there are exceptions, as to where 'compliance with the preference would prejudice the provision of efficient education or the efficient use of resources'.[147] Discrimination is forbidden with regard to school admissions.[148] However, schools designated as having a religious character enjoy an exception which may be relied on only if a school is over-subscribed – this allows the school to restrict admission on grounds of religion or belief;[149] the exception does not apply to other discrimination prohibitions by excluding pupils or by

---

[144] ELM: www.eastlondonmosque.org.uk/content/education-training.
[145] IFIS CUBE Network: Sample Constitution of an Islamic Society: 4.5: Facilities Manager.
[146] School Standards and Framework Act 1998, s. 69. The process is governed by secondary legislation: Designation of Schools having a Religious Character (England) Order 2013/ 2029.
[147] School Standards and Framework Act 1998, s. 86.
[148] Equality Act 2010, s. 85(1): this deals with admission and refusals to admit pupils.
[149] Equality Act 2010, Sch. 11, para. 5(a); School Admissions Code 2007, paras. 2.41–2.43; School Standards and Framework Act 1998: schools must comply with the Code.

subjecting them to any other detriment.[150] Moreover, attendance at or abstaining from attending a place of worship must not be required for admission to a maintained school.[151] In England, there is a large body of secondary legislation on faith school governance.[152] Whether all religious schools should be registered is much debated at present.[153]

Chedarim and Yeshivot

From the earliest Rabbinic times, the study of Torah (*Talmud Torah*) was considered as a supreme religious duty, and Jewish communities saw it as imperative to establish schools, including elementary schools (*chedarim*, singular *cheder*), and for more advanced study of Torah, *yeshivot* (singular *yeshivah*).[154] The tradition continues: a congregation must be 'committed to the study of Torah'.[155] The (Orthodox) United Synagogue is empowered 'to establish, maintain or otherwise run schools or other institutions, including schools or other institutions for further or higher education', and to employ staff for these purposes.[156] It makes provision

---

[150] Equality Act 2010, s. 82(2)(e)–(f).   [151] Education Act 1996, s. 398.

[152] E.g. School Governance (Constitution) (England) Regulations 2012; School Staffing (England) Regulations 2009 (amended 2012); for charging (which its governing body determines), see (under the Education Act 1996, s. 457) Education (School Sessions and Charges and Remissions Policies) (Information) (England) Regulations 1999; for behaviour (which the head teacher determines), see (for maintained schools) Education and Inspection Act 2006, s. 8, and (for academies and independent schools) Independent School Standards Regulations; for teacher appraisal (for governing body to determine), see e.g. the Education (School Teachers' Appraisal) (England) Regulations 2012; for admissions, see the School Admissions (Admission Arrangements and Co-ordination of Admission Arrangements (England) Regulations 2012; for complaints: as to maintained schools, Education Act 2002, s. 29, and for academies etc. Education (Independent Schools Standards) Regulations 2010, and for non-maintained special schools Education (Non-maintained Special Schools) Regulations 2011.

[153] Ofsted (Office for Standards in Education) estimates that there are 350 unregistered religious schools in Britain; for debate, see e.g. www.secularism.org.uk/unregistered-schools/.

[154] L. Jacobs, *Jewish Religion* (1999) 50–51, 240–241, 306–308. The root of *yeshivah* is *yashav*, 'to sit'.

[155] USCJ: Guide to Constitutions and Bylaws (2010) Art. II; see also *Affirmations* (2006) Arts. 12: it is committed to the study of Torah (*Talmud Torah*), 'the formal and informal education of children and adults in Jewish history and literature, thought and practice, and the Hebrew language, as the foundation of Jewish life and ... its perpetuation'; Art. 33: 'the equal status of boys and girls in religious education'; ELS: Con. Art. 4: the Council may provide 'religious education' and determine questions on the 'religious education of the children of members'; WCCMJ: By-Laws VII.

[156] US: Statutes 5.5.

for Jewish children to attend a Jewish school, which is to deliver 'a solid foundation in Jewish knowledge and practice, together with a love of Israel'; schools with the status in civil law of maintained schools teach the National Curriculum (with a tailor-made Jewish Studies curriculum) and are subject to inspection by the (civil) Office for Standards in Education (Ofsted). The United Synagogue: is the foundation body for ten Jewish schools; works on their behalf with government (central and local); offers training for their Foundation Governors and for Jewish day-school governors. In its voluntary aided schools, secular teaching is paid for by government. However, Jewish Studies (including Hebrew) are funded by parental voluntary contributions, such as some security costs. All United Synagogue primary schools co-operate in, for instance, sharing 'best practice' and developing courses on for instance multiculturalism in society today.[157] The United Synagogue Living and Learning Department also provides resources and 'best practice'.[158] The Chief Rabbi is 'the religious authority for dozens of Jewish schools' offering 'guidance' on 'inspiring and engaging educational programmes'.[159]

In 2009, the (civil) Supreme Court considered the policy of the Jewish Free School, requiring admission on the basis of a definition of Jewishness in accordance with the teaching of the Office of the Chief Rabbi; this was held to be discriminatory in so far as the Supreme Court held that it amounted to a test of ethnicity, which is unlawful under the Race Relations Act 1976 regardless of its religious content. Five justices considered that there was direct discrimination on the grounds of race; two considered that there was indirect discrimination; and two that there was no racial discrimination at all, but rather a lawful selection on the ground of religion in accord with doctrine.[160]

The Movement for Reform Judaism has detailed soft-law for its 'Jewish Schools' (*chedarim*) – admission is open to the children of synagogue members who are from four years six months old; a fee is payable.[161] Each synagogue should provide for a Chair of Education, Education Committee and teachers. First, the Chair of Education must: chair the Education Committee; through it, hire and provide for the welfare of the

---

[157] US: www.theus.org.uk/schools.
[158] US: www.theus.org.uk/article/about-living-and-learning-1.
[159] US: http://chiefrabbi.org/education/.
[160] *R (on the application of E) v. JFS Governing Body* [2009] UKSC 15.
[161] MRJ: Code of Practice, pp. 11–12: those seeking membership of a synagogue in order to have a child admitted are expected to remain members after the admission of their child to the school.

head teacher, teachers and Madrichim (assistants);[162] set the Curriculum with the Warden and Rabbi; liaise with the Head of Security; maintain the library; notify the Chair of House and Administrator of use of the building, class times and additional uses; notify the Administrator and Head of Security of the dates of terms; and oversee the Child Protection Co-ordinator and the production of the Cheder Handbook.[163]

Secondly, the Education Committee is responsible for the management of its Reform Synagogue Religion School and any other educational activities on behalf of the synagogue Council. Its Chair is elected each year at the Annual General Meeting.[164] The committee consists of a minimum of four: the Rabbi (if any), the Head Teacher (and/or one teacher), and the balance parents or other members of the synagogue. The Chair of the Council must receive notice of all committee meetings and may attend *ex officio*. Decisions are taken by majority vote (but the Chair has a casting vote) and minuted – all major changes of policy may need to be referred to the synagogue Council for approval.[165] The Chair of Education may attend all meetings of the teachers and Madrichim, after giving due notice, and the meetings of the Finance Committee, and must present an annual budget to the Finance Committee for approval by Council. The Education Committee may raise an annual levy for stationery or exceptional items subject to Council approval. All funds raised must be collected by a delegate of the Education Committee, deposited with the synagogue Treasurer and treated as a designated fund and only used for *cheder* or education requirements.[166]

Thirdly, the Head Teacher must monitor and manage the teachers and Madrichim. All *cheder* staff salaries are the responsibility of Council and must be included in the annual budgets of the Education Committee. Its Chair must recommend to Council, for all grades of staff, levels of salaries to be considered and acted upon by Council. The Madrichim are recruited from the children at the *cheder* provided one year has passed since their post-Bar/Bat Mitzvah. Priority is given to children with the best attendance record at Shabbat Services and *cheder* prior to Bar/Bat Mitzvah and who show continued involvement with the

---

[162] The singular is Madrih. The root of the word is *derech*, 'road, path or way'.

[163] MRJ: Code of Practice, p. 7.

[164] Nominees should have served at least 12 months on the Education Committee and must not be a member of the current teaching staff or a salaried member of the Synagogue.

[165] Any group may raise funds for the Cheder, but these funds must not be used for the salaries of the teaching staff unless agreed by Council.

[166] MRJ: Code of Practice, pp. 23–24.

community and/or furtherance of their Jewish studies post-Bar/Bat Mitzvah. The Head Teacher decides when a child is qualified or capable. Madrichim who have reached 16 may be given more responsibility if they have the ability. The work of assistance is arranged based on a rota determined by the Head Teacher who attempts to be fair when apportioning the number of weeks worked by each Madrih. All children who become Madrichim should be given various documents as to how they should work and behave on a Sunday. Once appointed, Madrichim are responsible to the Head Teacher directly for all aspects of their work and must not communicate to the Head Teacher through their parents or *vice versa*. If a parent has a problem with the process and is unable to resolve the matter with the Head Teacher, the matter may be drawn to the attention of and resolved by the Chair of the Education Committee. It is 'synagogue policy' that those advancing towards their Bar/Bat Mitzvah actively participate in the *cheder* (and synagogue life). It is 'customary' that when attending *cheder* all boys wear *kippot*; all girls may do so if they wish – it is not compulsory; Hebrew is taught according to ability not age. The synagogue Council, consulting the Committee, may suspend or alter these rules.[167]

In the United Synagogue of Conservative Judaism, the 'ideal Jew' should attend synagogue classes, read Jewish books, discuss Jewish issues with their family and friends, and study the prescribed Torah portion each week; but 'study is meaningful only if it leads to action' based on 'the teachings of Judaism'.[168] So, congregations should 'encourage, provide and/or sponsor age-appropriate formal and informal educational [programmes] for all members of the congregation and their families'. These should include a: nursery school; synagogue school; youth programs; Hebrew high school; family education; adult education; and travel to Israel for teens, college students, adults and families.[169] All education programmes (and prayer services) should be consistent with principles of 'dignity and moral conduct befitting a Jewish community', including: *hachnasot orchim* (hospitality), *derekh eretz* (respect), *kavod* (honour),

---

[167] MRJ: Code of Practice, pp. 24–26.

[168] USCJ: The 'Ideal' Conservative Jew: Eight Behavioural Expectations: Jewish Living.

[169] USCJ: Standards for Congregational Practice (2017): Standard VI: Schools should subscribe to the Statement of Aims of the Conservative Synagogue School as adopted by the Commission on Jewish Education. Congregations should support a Solomon Schechter day school in the local community, if feasible, and should refer to 'A Framework for Excellence in the Conservative Synagogue School'.

tzniyut (modesty), *anava* (humility), *tzedakah* (righteousness), *tikun olam* (repair of the world), and *hesed* (kindness).[170] Moreover, the United Synagogue of Conservative Judaism has an advisory Learning Team which offers guidance on, for example: the curriculum; school structure; teacher supervision and leadership; and school stakeholders, including parents, students, teachers and the education board.[171]

Instruction in the Faith and Sunday Schools

In keeping with its long history of formation for discipleship, and providing public education at church schools,[172] today historic churches share the principle of Christian law that a church has the right and duty to instruct the faithful.[173] Instruction by ministers and amongst the faithful in general (including children and young persons) may be by means of catechesis, Sunday school or other classes and the faithful should study Holy Scripture. In the Roman Catholic Church, catechesis, the ministry of the word directed to those who have responded to the faith, is the process by which 'through doctrinal formation . . . the faith of the people may be living, manifest and active'. The diocesan bishop, the Conference of Bishops, and pastors have special responsibilities to provide catechetical formation; the diocesan bishops must issue norms on the subject and foster and coordinate catechetical initiatives. Parish priests must ensure that: adequate catechesis is given for the celebration of the sacraments; children are properly prepared for confession and first holy communion; and, as far as conditions allow, formation is given to the mentally and physically disabled.[174] In Anglicanism too, priests and deacons must provide instruction in the faith for those entrusted to their charge,[175] especially children and young persons, who are to be instructed in the doctrine, sacraments and discipline of Christ, as the Lord has commanded and as found in Holy Scripture, and in the

---

[170] USCJ: Standards for Congregational Practice (2017): Standard VIII.
[171] USCJ: Congregational Education: https://uscj.org/leadership/congregational-education.
[172] See e.g. M. Hill *et al.*, *Religion and Law* (2014) 175.
[173] Christian Law Panel of Experts, *Principles of Christian Law* (2016) VI.2.2.
[174] CIC: c. 773: duty to catechise; c. 774: care for catechesis extends to all (especially parents); c. 775: diocesan bishop and Episcopal Conference; c. 776: parish priest; c. 777: recipients.
[175] PCLCCAC: Principle 48.2–4.

teaching and catechism.[176] In the Church of England, there are also substantial bodies of law on cathedral schools.[177]

The instruction of the faithful is likewise a key function in Protestant laws. Lutheran congregations must provide for the instruction of children and young people and may establish schools.[178] Methodists too should engage in their own private and collective reading of the Bible,[179] and, typically: 'Within the Societies of the Methodist Church provision shall be made for the Christian nurture of children and young people. The aim shall be to develop faith and commitment to Christ, as they share in worship and learning based on Holy Scripture.'[180] In the Methodist Church in Ireland, the main objective of Sunday Schools is 'to instruct and train the scholars in the doctrines, privileges, and duties of the Christian religion. The Holy Scriptures and, as far as possible, the Methodist Catechisms shall be used as the means of instruction and training. All the scholars shall be trained in the duty of regular attendance at public worship on the Lord's Day.' Sunday school is under the management of a Committee comprising the minister (President) and school officers – a Superintendent appointed by the Circuit Executive, a Secretary and, if necessary, a Treasurer, Librarian and a Missionary Secretary. The teachers must have good moral character, and in sympathy with the doctrine and discipline of Methodism. No one may continue as an officer or teacher who is at any time declared by the Committee, or by the Church Council or Circuit Executive, to be unfit as to general character or 'religious opinions' to take part in the religious education of the young. The Committee determine the programme of instruction in the school, arrange for examinations, inquire concerning absent scholars and deal with all those matters affecting the welfare of the school.[181]

---

[176] PCLCCAC: Principle 48.8. See e.g. Church of Ireland: Con. IX.27.

[177] See N. Doe, *The Legal Architecture of English Cathedrals* (London: Routledge, 2017) 175–180.

[178] LCGB: Rules and Regulations, Congregations, 2: it must 'as far as its resources and abilities make it possible', 'teach both adults and children through Bible studies, Confirmation and Baptism classes' and other means.

[179] MCI: Regulations, Discipline and Government, 3.01: 'The means of grace . . . include . . . Bible study [and] individual Bible study.'

[180] MCGB: Constitutional Practice and Discipline, Deed of Union 7; see also Standing Orders 050(2). See also MCI: Regulations, Discipline and Government, 11.02: the functions of class leaders.

[181] MCI: Regulations, Discipline and Government, 10.71–74

Likewise, Presbyterian ministers are under a duty to instruct children, young people and adults in the elements of Christian doctrine, and some churches impose this duty on parents and offer a right of church members to such instruction or catechism. There are also provisions about the establishment of a Sunday school in the local church. For example, in the Presbyterian Church in Ireland, the Kirk Session is to 'control the Sunday Schools of the congregation, and approve the teachers employed, the books used, and the regulations of the schools'. Above the local church, the Presbytery must 'foster Sunday School work within its bounds, requiring as far as possible that at least one school be maintained in connection with each congregation, having a programme which embraces study of Scripture, the Shorter Catechism, and the Missions and Agencies of the Church'.[182] Similar provisions are found in the United, Reformed, Congregational and Baptist traditions which also have Sunday schools.[183]

Madrassas

In Islamic tradition, a *madrassa* (school) was an educational institution of Islamic law, taught according to one or more of the schools of thought (Maliki, Hanafi, Hanbali, Shafi'i (Sunni) or Jafari (Shia)); also taught were Arabic grammar and literature, mathematics, logic and natural science. Islamic theology tuition was free, and food, lodging and medical care might also have been provided. Instruction consisted primarily of memorizing texts and the lectures of the instructor, who issued certificates to students allowing them to repeat his words.[184] In Britain today, madrassas are commonly classified as 'supplementary schools' for Muslims operating outside the mainstream (civil) education system, and offering instruction in Islamic subjects, including, but not limited

---

[182] PCI: Code, 37 and 77. See also PCW: Handbook of Rules, 3.2.2: the Presbytery supervises 'the work of the Sunday School, young people and children'; 3.4.2: General Assembly; J.L. Weatherhead, ed., *Constitution and Laws of the Church of Scotland* (1997) 132: 'Sunday School ... is under the supervision of the Kirk Session. The minister is head of the Sunday School.'

[183] UFCS: Manual of Practice and Procedure, I.III.17: the Session is to ensure that 'parents attend to the godly upbringing of their children, and to aid them by instituting a Sunday school' under 'the supervision of the Session'; BUGB: Model Trusts for Churches 2003, 5.1.4: a church is 'where children and adults are instructed in the Christian faith'.

[184] A. Black *et al.*, *Islamic Law* (2013) 50–51; M. Naqshbandi, *Islam and Muslims in Britain* (2012): Guide 4.13.

to, the Quran, *hadith* and jurisprudence; they are the subject of much public debate about transparency in their operation and potential impact on community cohesion, the educational development of children and child welfare.[185] They tend to be well-established, often connected to a mosque, often registered as a charity and considered by Muslims to be important in their strengthening of the cultural, religious and linguistic identity of their pupils.[186] They are also the subject of much soft-law regulation by various Muslim organisations.[187]

Modern regulatory instruments also deal with religious education, assigning either duties or rights to various authorities. For example, at Aberdeen Mosque and Islamic Centre, it is for the imam to provide for: 'the religious education for the children of members of the community', and a curriculum agreed with the Executive Committee; supervision of adult Islamic classes and Quranic studies; and pastoral care of students in learning institutions in Aberdeenshire, including making representations to the authorities if necessary.[188] Noor-Ul-Islam Mosque (Bury) itself must provide an educational centre for young Muslims, including a library and study facilities, for 'education in the principles of the Sunni Islamic faith'.[189] But at Central Jamia Masjid (Southall), the Board of Trustees may establish 'a library and a reading room'; arrange classes for children, youth and adults to teach the Holy Quran, Sunnah, and Arabic, English or Urdu; popularise Islam by lectures, meetings and educational, cultural and social functions 'consistent with the tenets and doctrines of Islam'; and: 'Three female Welfare and Education Officers shall be appointed ... to manage female Madrassah and welfare centre'; and madrassa fees are set out in the constitution.[190]

---

[185] M. Cherti and L. Bradley, *Inside Madrassas: Understanding and Engaging with British-Muslim Faith Supplementary Schools* (Institute for Public Policy Research, 2011) 3: there are around 2000 operating in the UK attended by around 250,000 Muslim children; they may also be styled 'mosque schools'. See also Department for Communities and Local Government, *The Training and Development of Muslim Faith Leaders: Current Practice and Future Possibilities* (2010): 3.7: most secondary-type Muslim institutions are known as *darul ulooms*; unlike Sunni schools, Shia schools do not train faith leaders – this occurs at the end of formal schooling: see above Chapter 3.

[186] M. Cherti and L. Bradley, *Inside Madrassas* (2011) 3, 17–18, 68–69.

[187] E.g. Guidance for Mosque Schools and other Islamic Studies Settings, and Faith Associates Guidance: www.sewsc.org.uk.

[188] AMIC: Con. Art. XIV.5.

[189] NUIM: Con. Art. 2. Model Constitution of an Islamic Organisation: Aims and Objectives 2: libraries.

[190] CJM: Con. Art. 3, 21 and 23. the fee is £5 10 per month.

By way of contrast, the Nasru-Lahi-Il-Fathi Society has an Education Committee to: make recommendations on educational matters to the Executive Committee; monitor 'the quality and relevance of lectures delivered by the preacher(s)'; liaise with the Mission Board so as to monitor the quality of lectures/seminars and to offer seminars for pilgrims to Mecca; monitor educational programmes for children; arrange for visiting Islamic Scholars to deliver prayers and lectures; and organise training, lectures and workshops to keep committee members abreast of the latest developments in the Islamic world and advise accordingly.[191] Muslims also work with secular authorities over education; for example, the Council for Mosques does so with Bradford Council Children's Services to support Muslim children and young people in State schools.[192]

With regard to particular madrassas, for instance, Birmingham Central Mosque runs an Evening Supplementary School (which also runs on Saturdays), under the umbrella of Birmingham Community Education and Training Services. It teaches Arabic, Islamic Studies and Qur'an Hifz (memorising the Quran). There are basic classes for younger children and intermediate classes for older children. Urdu is an optional subject for older pupils.[193] East London Mosque has a programme in Education and Training and has a Saturday Islamic School, a supervised evening madrassa to study Islam, a library, services for deaf children and recreational activities (e.g. Scouts).[194] And the London Central Mosque hosts the Al Qualam Weekend (Supplementary) School, providing 'basic Islamic instruction' for the children aged five to 16. The objectives of the school are *inter alia* to: (1) provide a clean Islamic environment; (2) teach Arabic and Islamic heritage; (3) strengthen pupils' faith, 'correct' their religious practice, and improve their behaviour; (4) train them to recite and understand the Quran correctly; (5) prepare them for GCSE examinations in Arabic and Islamic studies; (6) discipline the children about the need neither to exaggerate nor to abandon their religion, how to live in a multi-religious/cultural society, preserving their own identity and religion in order 'to integrate positively in the society and serve it'; (7) raise awareness about its goals; and (8) increase

---

[191] NASFAT: Con. Art. J. 7, N.2 and M. See also IFIS CUBE Network: Sample Constitution, 4.8.

[192] COM: www.councilformosques.org/community-centres/school-links/.

[193] BCM: https://centralmosque.org.uk/.

[194] ELM: www.eastlondonmosque.org.uk/content/education-training.

competence in its teaching team and administration in order to fulfil adequately the demand of the increasing number of pupils applying to join it.[195]

Islamic schools in receipt of State funding are inspected by the Office for Standards in Education.[196] For instance, an inspection of the Institute of Islamic Education (Jaamia Talimul Islam), an established *darul uloom* (Islamic seminary) at Dewsbury, West Yorkshire (founded in 1982), took place to advise the Secretary of State for Education and Skills about the school's suitability for continued registration as an independent school.[197] The Institute, connected to the Markazi mosque and overseen by a *shura* committee, provides full-time education for boys aged 12 to 16; in the morning, Islamic teaching occurs in the madrassa, and in the afternoon the school offers some (civil) National Curriculum subjects.[198] Its aim is to train *imams* and *ustaads* (Islamic studies teachers). Most students stay on for the *alim* (Islamic Studies) and *hifz* course (Quran memorisation), graduating after seven to nine years. The inspection found that: madrassa teaching was satisfactory and on occasions good; in the school, teaching was unsatisfactory in over half of the subjects; overall, pupils did not do well in public examinations; the spiritual, moral, social and cultural development of pupils was strong and their behaviour very good; and the Institute instilled 'a strong sense of duty'. It also found that, to comply with State regulations,[199] the school should, *inter alia*: produce and implement a written curriculum policy; give pupils experiences in aesthetic and creative learning; provide information about the teachers, and, on parental request, pupils' public examination results; and improve information on its complaints procedure.[200] The secular judiciary held recently that it is unlawful for an Islamic school to segregate pupils on the basis of gender; and: 'It is irrelevant ... that in adhering to its strict policy of segregation of sexes

[195] LCM: www.iccuk.org/page.php?section=education&page=school.

[196] That is, under section 163 of the Education Act 2002.

[197] Ofsted: Inspection Report (2005): https://reports.ofsted.gov.uk/provider/files/759347/urn/107791.

[198] Teaching in the mornings (Monday to Saturday) includes logic, history, theology, Islamic law and ethics, Quran recitation, memorisation and commentary, Arabic, Urdu; teaching in the afternoons (Monday to Friday) is e.g. English, mathematics, science, physical education, ICT and citizenship.

[199] That is, the Independent Schools Standards Regulations 2003.

[200] Ofsted: Inspection Report (2005): https://reports.ofsted.gov.uk/provider/files/759347/urn/107791.

the School is motivated by conscientious adherence to what it regards as the applicable tenets of Islam.'[201]

Various organisations have been established in recent decades to work in the field of Muslim education and schools, such as the Muslim Teachers Association, Association of Muslim Schools and Association for Muslim Supplementary Schools.[202] The aims of the Muslim Teachers' Association, founded 1979, are to: organise Muslim teachers working in state schools, Islamic schools and other educational settings in accordance with the guidance of the Quran and teachings of Mohammad; promote the professional development of Muslim teachers through training and support structures; offer advice and support to schools to promote equality of opportunity for all pupils, particularly Muslim pupils; enhance the education/welfare of Muslim teachers and pupils; provide advice and guidance for head teachers, government, local authorities and other organisations; represent Muslim teachers and pupils at all official levels in the United Kingdom; and promote greater knowledge/ understanding of the needs of Muslim teachers and pupils, who by virtue of their religious beliefs, are different from other teachers; supporting community cohesion; and facilitating good practice.[203]

The Association of Muslim Schools (founded 1992) coordinates the work of Muslim schools and shares best practice to advance the education of Muslim children. It is an umbrella body for registered Muslim schools (156 in 2013). A member Muslim school is one having Islam as its religious designation/character underpinning its values and ethos. The Association is recognised by the (civil) Department for Education to serve children/families from faith and non-faith backgrounds through direct education provision, charitable activities and joint initiatives with other service providers. The membership, across the independent, voluntary aided and free school spectrum, includes primary schools, secondary schools and residential schools, some which specialise in advanced Islamic study. The curriculum, across members,

---

[201] *Chief Inspector of Education, Children's Services and Skills* v. *Interim Executive Board of Al-Hijrah School* [2017] EWCA Civ. 1426: i.e. from Year 5.

[202] See also the British Association for Islamic Studies, managed by a Council; its elected Officers are e.g. the Chair, Secretary and Treasurer. Council meets once a year to support the Association through activities stipulated in a contract, e.g. having a website, membership database/mailing list and financial administration: Con. Art. 5 and 6: www.brais.ac.uk/about-brais/constitution.

[203] Muslim Teachers Association (UK): Con. (updated 2013) Art. 4; see also Art. 16: disciplinary action.

combines teachings of Islam alongside the (civil) National Curriculum within a faith-based context. Regulatory compliance and quality of education in schools are monitored and evaluated through inspections commissioned by the Department for Education, and carried out by either Ofsted or the Bridge Schools Inspectorate. The Executive Committee, elected by members, elects the officers, for example chairman and treasurer.[204]

The Association seeks to, *inter alia*: ensure the views and interests of Muslim schools are accurately and effectively presented to statutory bodies, educational organisations and the wider public; and promote education for children rooted in 'Islamic principles and values' and collaboration among member schools to raise educational standards, nurture creativity in the Islamic pedagogy, develop a new generation of role model educators and nurture excellence in the spiritual and moral character of their students. It also seeks to: provide a forum for those involved in Islamic education; and promote better understanding and positive relationships between different faiths in the United Kingdom for a harmonious and cohesive society that is based on principles of mutual respect, justice and sound acquisition and application of holistic education. The Association provides a variety of programmes,[205] and recommended policies.[206] The objectives of the Association for Muslim Supplementary Schools mirror these almost in order for madrassas to be centres of excellence in teaching and growth (*tarbiyyah*).[207]

Conclusion

Primary religious laws of Jews, Christians and Muslims require the profession of belief, the worship of God and study by and instruction of the followers in the faith. The secondary regulatory instruments of Jewish, Christian and Muslim organisations studied here implement the administration of these theocratic requirements, and share much in common in terms of their treatment of belief, worship and education. Whilst differences exist with regard to the authority competent to regulate these

---

[204] AMS: http://ams-uk.org/wp-content/uploads/2013/12/AMS-Brochure.pdf.
[205] There are programmes in e.g. School Improvement, Inspection Support and Effective Governance.
[206] AMS: Statutory School Policies: http://ams-uk.org/resources/policies/; for inspection reports, see: http://ams-uk.org/services/section-48-inspections/.
[207] Association for Muslim Supplementary Schools: www.amss.org.uk/.

matters, profound similarities between the legal systems reveal the following principles of religious law. Belief is rooted in the revelation of God as recorded and expounded in holy texts and pronouncements issued by those with authority to teach. The propagation of faith is a fundamental action and a divine imperative incumbent on all the faithful. The faithful should believe religious teaching and should not publicly manifest a position which is contrary to it – if they do so, disciplinary action may ensue. The worship of God is a fundamental action of all three religions and divinely instituted. Worship involves an intimate encounter between the faithful corporately and its individual members and the presence of God. Each religious organisation may use or develop texts or other forms of service for public worship. A religious organisation must provide for public worship. The faith leaders (Rabbi, minister and imam) are responsible for its conduct. The faithful must engage in regular attendance at worship, particularly on the days of religious significance. The administration of worship is subject to supervision by those authorities designated by law to provide this. The faith leaders are responsible for the religious instruction of the faithful. Each religion provides for religious schools (chedarim, Sunday schools and madrassas) to nurture the young, and may also provide for schools which are subject to regulation and inspection under State law and which receive state funding. Whilst duties to profess belief, worship God and study and instruct in the faith derive from primary religious law, and so have a theocratic basis, these are supplemented by legislation in Christianity and by both legislation and soft-law in Judaism and Islam.

The Rites of Passage

Judaism, Christianity and Islam have their own rites of passage which mark key stages in the spiritual lives of the faithful. Some of these rites are mandatory under primary religious law (and so suggest a theocratic dimension), some permissive and all are regulated by secondary systems of modern religious legislation and/or religious soft-law – some may also be administered in the context of worship at a religious ceremony, which may be performed at a synagogue, church or mosque. Historically, different theological understandings of the significance of some of these rituals have caused division within each of the three religions – and in part they continue to do so. This chapter compares the laws of Jewish, Christian and Muslim communities with regard to rites administered during childhood and adolescence, including rites of initiation. Next, follow the rites of spiritual development and commemoration. The chapter closes with a study of religious norms on funerals and the disposal of the human remains of the faithful. What follows examines these rites of passage in the classical religious law and the modern regulatory instruments of the religious groups studied, in terms of: their nature, purpose and effect; the prerequisites for admission to them, in the form of rights and duties; the preparation of candidates and others associated with their administration; the conditions required for their celebration; and the faith leaders responsible for their administration. The chapter exposes differences – the scope of legal diversity – and similarities from which it articulates principles of law of the Abrahamic faiths. The rite of marriage is studied separately in Chapter 8.

The Rites during Childhood and Adolescence

All three religions make provision for rites to be performed with regard to children and adolescents. Some rites are understood to be mandated by primary religious law. What follows studies norms on Jewish circumcision and the *bar/batmitzvah*, the Christian rite of baptism and/ or confirmation and the Islamic *aqiqah* and *khitan*.

Brit Milah and Bar/Bat Mitzvah

In Judaism, circumcision (the removal of the foreskin) is understood to manifest the 'sign of the flesh' of the covenant made by God with Abraham and is therefore known in Hebrew as *berit milah* (covenant of circumcision). This is first recorded in the book of Genesis where Abraham is instructed to circumcise all his male descendants (as he himself had been circumcised); and the moment of circumcision is stated to be when a boy is eight days old.[1] Jewish tradition understands that while the ideal is circumcision at this time, the rite may nevertheless be valid if carried out later or when the child is sufficiently able to undergo it.[2] An adult whose parents had not had him circumcised then must not remain uncircumcised but must undergo the rite as soon as possible. A male convert must be circumcised after becoming a member of the covenant but for one born a Jew the rite is an initiation not into Judaism but into the covenant, since Jewish status is established by birth.[3] In the early history of Reform Judaism, some advocated abolition of circumcision on the basis *inter alia* that it was cruel; but, today, Reform, Conservative and Orthodox Jews practise the rite.[4]

For example, within the Movement for Reform Judaism: 'Males have to undergo circumcision'; that is, baby boys who are under six months.[5] However, the *Beit Din* does not require the circumcision of a male child between the ages of six months and 16 years of age, but it may recommend a ritual circumciser (*mohel*) if this is requested.[6] In any event, the Brit Mila (Covenant of the Word) is 'a key life cycle observance for a Jewish family' to celebrate and remember God's covenant with Abraham

---

[1] Genesis 17:9–13: 'Thus shall my covenant be marked in your flesh as an everlasting pact'; as to age, see also Leviticus 12:1–3.

[2] See e.g. N.S. Hecht *et al.*, eds., *Jewish Law* (1996) 29, 60, 101.   [3] See above Chapter 2.

[4] For the Orthodox approach, see e.g. BAES: Bar and Bat Mitzvah Policy (2016); for the Conservative approach, see I. Klein, *Jewish Religious Practice* (1992) 419–432; see also USCJ: Guide to Constitutions (2010) Art. XV.3; for Liberal Judaism, see ULPS: *Affirmations* (2006) Art. 22: this affirms 'the importance of many of the traditional Jewish rites of passage, including ... ritual relating to birth, circumcision, baby-naming, [and] coming-of-age'; and MRJ: Areas of Responsibility and Codes of Practice Documents: pp. 7–8: new-born babies may be blessed.

[5] MRJ: Areas of Responsibility and Code of Practice Documents (Constitution): p. 10.

[6] MRJ: www.reformjudaism.org.uk/resources/life-cycle/.

and his people. A *mohel*, who must be authorised to act by the *Beit Din* (and all *mohalim* are fully trained and accredited doctors) must explain the significance of the rite. The baby is carried by his godmother (*kvaterin*) and handed to his godfather (*kvater*), while the opening prayers are said, and then passed to the *sandek* (the companion of the child) who holds the baby on his lap while circumcision is performed; *kiddush* wine is also to hand.[7] After the circumcision, further prayers are said, including a blessing over the wine and the naming of the baby. The choice of roles in the ceremony is that of the parents. Traditionally, the *sandek* is a Jewish male, often a grandfather or uncle of the baby (not the father). The *kvater* and the *kvaterin* are usually a Jewish couple who have not as yet had their own children. Traditionally, only men attend the ceremony. However, Reform communities encourage all to be present regardless of gender; but it is a matter of individual choice.[8] The *Beit Din* accepts physical and psychological reasons that may debar a male adult from circumcision; a letter is required, preferably from a *mohel*, or a Jewish doctor, explaining the reasons.[9] Liberal Judaism strongly recommends circumcision for male converts; however, if an exemption is sought, candidates must consult a doctor, normally a member of the Association of Liberal and Reform Mohalim. All converts are advised to perform the ritual of *tevilah* (ritual immersion in a *mikveh* (ritual bath)) as a valued way to confirm the change in status.[10]

A boy becomes *barmitzvah*, literally 'son of the commandment', on reaching his religious majority (13), at which point he is responsible for his actions and obliged to keep the Torah precepts. In the (Orthodox) United Synagogue, on the day of his thirteenth birthday (in the Hebrew calendar), the *barmitzvah* should go to *shul* (synagogue) in the morning, with his family, and wear his *tefillin* – that is, cube-shaped black leather boxes, containing four scriptural passages, attached to the head and arms and worn during morning prayers. If this is on a Monday or Thursday, or other time when the Torah is read, the boy receives a call-up (*aliyah*) to

---

[7] Usually, the *sandek* has a pillow on his lap, covered by a towel, and sits opposite the *mohel*. The circumcision usually takes two/three minutes, including application of a small dressing.

[8] In accordance with General Medical Council Guidelines, the *mohel* must obtain written consent from the parents informing them of the risks and appropriate anaesthetic and analgesic methods.

[9] MRJ: www.reformjudaism.org.uk/resources/life-cycle/.

[10] ULPJ: www.liberaljudaism.org/lifecycle/jewish-status-conversion/. See e.g. PLJC: Con. Art. 3.

the Torah, from which he may choose to read. After he completes his *aliyah*, his father recites a blessing of thanks for his son reaching adulthood. On the Shabbat after the ceremony, the boy receives an *aliyah* and may read a portion, if not all, of the *sedra* (Torah reading for that week from the Pentateuch), *maftir* (an extra portion) and *haftarah* (a reading from the Prophets linked to a theme in the *sedra*). Moreover: 'As befits this rite of passage, it is traditional to have a festive meal to celebrate a barmitzvah'; this may be a special *Kiddush* (see below), a meal at home or *shul* on Shabbat or some other event (provided by caterers licensed by the London Beth Din). Preparation for *barmitzvah* includes tuition by certified *barmitzvah* teachers. If a boy has special needs to the extent that he cannot celebrate the rite in the conventional way, this does not affect the Jewish status of the boy – 'neither does it violate any Jewish law'.[11]

In a member synagogue of the United Synagogue, permission must be granted to the son of a member to read a section of the Torah on becoming *barmitzvah* – if he has complied with requirements set by the United Synagogue and has satisfied the synagogue Rabbi of his competence to do so. To read the *maftir* and *haftarah*, he must comply with the same requirements and others of the United Synagogue and the Rabbi relating to attendance at religious study and attainment of religious knowledge. Not more than 36 months and not less than 18 months' notice must be given to the synagogue Administrator of the date of the Shabbat to celebrate his *barmitzvah* as well as an indication of the portions he will read and whether he will read *maftir* and *haftarah*.[12]

A girl, in the (Orthodox) United Synagogue, becomes *batmitzvah*, 'daughter of the commandment', on reaching her twelfth Hebrew birthday; and: 'In terms of Jewish law, girls become adults at this age in respect of being obligated to live a Jewish life and thereby accept an additional set of responsibilities'; a *batmitzvah* ceremony has become 'a normative part of communal life in recent years'. A girl may choose a *batmitzvah* in the synagogue, at home or elsewhere, or a ceremony of confirmation (*bat*

---

[11] US: www.theus.org.uk/article/bar-bat-mitzvah. Special provision is made for a boy who is profoundly deaf or who is unable to speak and so cannot fulfil the duty to hear/read the Torah portion.

[12] US: Bye-Laws, Sch. 4.1–5 (Regulations relating to Barmitzvahs); there are rules as to reserving the synagogue for the ceremony in accordance with precedence in membership (see above Chapter 6). See also e.g. the Orthodox NHAYS: Con. Art. 20: any member, subject to the agreement of the Rabbi and Wardens, wishing to celebrate the rite in the Synagogue, must be permitted to do so on giving adequate notice to the Secretary. Such agreement is not normally forthcoming for non-members.

chayil) with other girls. A *batmitzvah* ceremony is the most common and should be planned with the synagogue Rabbi. Girls prepare by way of study; and: 'It is customary for a girl to research and prepare a Devar Torah, a short speech in which she presents ideas about Jewish life and study.' The *batmitzvah* ceremony commonly occurs on Sunday structured around an afternoon service (*mincha*), though a growing number of communities also offer it on Shabbat. The girl recites prayers or readings, and may deliver her *dvar Torah* and make an item of Jewish art for the occasion.[13]

In the Movement for Reform Judaism, immediately prior to the *bar/batmitzvah*, the candidates must attend the Religion School (*cheder*) for at least two continuous years. During the 12 months prior to *bar/batmitzvah*, both the parent(s) and candidate must regularly attend Shabbat and Festival services – and the candidate must demonstrate knowledge and ability to participate competently and meaningfully in the ceremony. At the *bar/batmitzvah* ceremony, the candidate is expected to read a study passage, lead the *shema*, read the Ten Commandments or act as a Junior Warden – the child makes a solemn promise before the Ark to continue Jewish learning throughout life.[14] The synagogue Warden, consulting with the Religious Activities Committee, Rabbi and Education Chair: oversees compliance with the standards and the ceremony itself; liaises with parents as to, for instance, dates and Torah portions read; and works with the Rabbi and Chair of Education who decide on suitability of the child for the rite.[15] A *barmitzvah* should not be held on Sunday, as, for example, there is no Torah reading then.[16]

The United Synagogue of Conservative Judaism has soft-law on *bar* and *batmitzvah*, and events associated with them, which must be conducted 'in a dignified manner'; there are also norms on for example attire, music, and use of alcohol. Congregations should provide an

---

[13] US: www.theus.org.uk/article/bar-bat-mitzvah.

[14] MRJ: Code of Practice, p. 27; there are also detailed norms on the taking of photographs of children.

[15] MRJ: Code of Practice, p. 8. See also ULPS: *Affirmations* (2006) Art. 33: this affirms 'the equal status of boys and girls' and a *batmitzvah* complements *barmitzvah* at the age of 13; the Union also attaches great importance to the further ceremony, created by Liberal Judaism, of *Kabbalat Torah* (Acceptance of Torah or Confirmation) at the age of 15 or 16.

[16] S.B. Freehof, *Reform Responsa* (Cincinnati: Hebrew Union College Press, 1960) No. 4.

appropriate *Kiddush* after the ceremony; and: 'Hamotzi and Birkat HaMazon should be recited whenever required by Jewish law or local custom.'[17]

The Rites of Baptism and Confirmation

Christians over the ages have differed as to whether baptism and confirmation are distinct but related rites or whether they represent a single rite of initiation. However, all the historic churches studied here have rites of passage which mark the early stages in the spiritual life of the Christian. Certain churches call some rites sacraments and others call them ordinances.[18] First is the rite of baptism. It is a principle of Christian law that baptism is divinely instituted. A church may call baptism a sacrament or an ordinance. Baptism constitutes incorporation of a person into the Church of Christ. Baptism is validly administered with water in the name of the triune God. Baptism is administered ordinarily in public in church in the presence of the faithful by an ordained minister but extraordinarily in cases of necessity by a lay person. Baptism in a church may be of infants or adults to the extent prescribed by its law. A church may impose conditions for admission to baptism, but it must nurture the baptised person in the faith. Baptism should be susceptible to proof – but it cannot be repeated.[19]

For the Roman Catholic Church, baptism is the gate to the sacraments, necessary for salvation in fact or at least in intention, frees individuals from sin and constitutes their rebirth as children of God configured to Christ; by baptism, a person is incorporated into the Church – it cannot be repeated.[20] It is conferred by immersion or pouring.[21] In the case of infant baptism, parents and sponsors must be suitably instructed so that they 'understand the meaning of this sacrament and the obligations which attach to it'; those who have reached the age of reason (on completion of the seventh year) may also be baptised, as may adults.[22]

---

[17] USCJ: Standards for Congregational Practice (2017): Standard IV; *hamotzi* is a blessing before a meal and *birkat* a grace following a meal.

[18] See N. Doe, *Christian Law* (2013) 233–234.

[19] Christian Law Panel of Experts, *Principles of Christian Law* (2016) VII.1.1–10.

[20] CIC: cc. 204, 849; *Lumen Gentium*, Vatican II, Dogmatic Constitution (1965) 16; c. 205: 'The baptised are in full communion with the catholic Church.'

[21] CIC: c. 854; c. 853: outside the case of necessity, the water should be blessed.

[22] CIC: c. 851: preparation; c. 852: the age of reason; c. 11: the age of seven; c. 97: adulthood (18).

Parents must bring their children to be baptised, and parental consent is required for celebration to be licit.[23] Whilst there is a right to baptism, if the hope that the infant will be brought up in the Catholic religion is altogether lacking, baptism is to be put off; the parents must be informed of the reason.[24] Ordinarily, a minister baptises only those whose parents reside in his territorial cure of souls. An infant in danger of death is to be baptised without delay – and even if the parents of an infant in danger of death are comprised of both Catholic and a non-Catholic, that infant is validly and lawfully baptised 'even against the will of the parents'.[25] In the case of baptism of an adult in danger of death, the candidate must have 'some knowledge of the principal truths of the faith',[26] have manifested the will to receive baptism, and promise to observe 'the commandments of the Christian religion' in the event of survival.[27] A lay person may validly baptise in cases of necessity, but the normal place for baptism is on a Sunday in church.[28] Baptism should be administered in accordance with the order prescribed in the liturgical books, except in a case of urgent necessity when only what is required for its validity must be observed: 'washing with true water together with the required form of words'.[29] If there is doubt as to whether someone has been baptised, or its validity, and after serious enquiry the doubt persists, the person is baptised conditionally; confirmation may immediately follow baptism.[30] A baptism must be registered, and parents and/or sponsors must nurture the baptised person in the faith.[31]

The position is much the same in Anglicanism: the sacrament of baptism, instituted by Christ, is a sign of new birth by which those who receive it are incorporated into the Church of Christ.[32] Valid baptism is

---

[23] CIC: cc. 867–868: within 'the first few weeks' of birth, or in danger of death 'without delay'.

[24] CIC: cc. 867, 868.1 and 2.

[25] CIC: c. 867; c. 862: death; c. 868.2: lack of consent; cc. 870–871: a foundling is to be baptised unless proof of baptism is established; if aborted foetuses are alive, they are to be baptised if possible.

[26] CIC: c. 865.2.   [27] CIC: cc. 864–865: adults; c. 865.2: survival.

[28] CIC: cc. 861, 863: reservation to the bishop; c. 860: private houses/hospitals; cc. 856–857: Sundays.

[29] CIC: c. 850: prescribed order; c. 849: the formula.   [30] CIC: cc. 866, 869.

[31] CIC: cc. 875–878; c. 872: parents and sponsors; c. 873: one sponsor, male or female, is sufficient, but there may be two, one of each sex; c. 874: a sponsor must be 16 (unless exempted), a Catholic who has been confirmed and received the Eucharist, and not be the mother or father of the candidate.

[32] PCLCCAC: Principles 61.1 and 61.3; see also Articles of Religion (AR) (The Thirty-Nine Articles), Church of England, Arts. 25, 27: a dominical sacrament, baptism is 'a sign of Regeneration or new Birth, whereby . . . they that receive [it] are grafted into the Church';

administered with water, by pouring, sprinkling, immersion, submersion or other similar means, simultaneously with the words, 'I baptize you in the name of the Father and of the Son and of the Holy Spirit.'[33] Baptism by ordained ministers is the norm, but it may be administered by a lay person in an emergency, such as danger of death. Baptism should be administered publicly in the presence of the congregation but may be administered privately if permitted by law. Baptisms must be recorded. Valid baptism is indelible and cannot be repeated.[34] The number of godparents (or other sponsors) is customarily two – at least one should be of the same sex as the candidate, and both of an age prescribed by law. Parents or guardians may be sponsors. Subject to any permitted dispensations, sponsors must be baptised persons and should be communicants.[35] They are to help the baptised person grow in the knowledge and love of God and fellowship of the church. Parents and sponsors of infants must receive instruction prior to the baptism as to the sacrament itself and the Christian life entered by it, as are adults or others able to answer for themselves. No minister may without lawful cause refuse or unduly delay baptism of a child if the parents desire baptism. However, a minister may postpone it until the parents and sponsors are instructed and able to undertake their obligations. A minister should not baptise a child without parental consent. If a minister refuses or unduly delays to baptise a child, parents may apply to the bishop for directions. A minister refusing to baptise without lawful cause may be subject to discipline. When adults are baptised, they should be presented to the bishop for confirmation at the same time or as soon as possible.[36] If there is an uncertainty or reasonable doubt as to whether a candidate has been baptised previously, such person may be baptised conditionally.[37]

The Methodist Church of Great Britain permits infant and adult baptism. Except in an emergency, 'baptism shall be administered only

---

by it the promises of forgiveness of sin, and adoption as sons of God by the Holy Spirit, are signed and sealed, 'Faith is confirmed, and Grace increased by . . . prayer unto God'.

[33] PCLCCAC: Principle 61.2.

[34] PCLCCAC: Principle 61.5–10; 5. See e.g. Scottish Episcopal Church: Can. 27.3: public and private baptism.

[35] PCLCCAC: Principle 62.1–4. See e.g. Scottish Episcopal Church: Can. 27.2: in 'cases of necessity', one sponsor 'shall be deemed sufficient'; Church of England: Can. B23: this requires three godparents but also allows dispensation.

[36] PCLCCAC: Principles 62–63. See e.g. Church of England: Can. B22.4: 'No minister shall refuse or . . . delay to baptize any infant within his cure that is brought to the church to be baptized' (*Bland* v. *Archdeacon of Cheltenham* [1972] 1 All ER 1012).

[37] PCLCCAC: Principle 64.

after instruction has been given to the candidate or to the parents/ guardians of a candidate who is a young child'. Baptism is celebrated by a minister, but in an emergency may be administered 'by any person'. It is administered at public worship, but in exceptional circumstances (e.g. serious illness) at another time. If candidates are able to answer for themselves, the minister must be satisfied as to their repentance, faith and desire for baptism. It is administered by pouring water on the candidate or by dipping in water with the requisite words. However: 'It is contrary to the principles and usage of the Methodist Church to confer what purports to be baptism on any person known to have been already baptized at any time.' If it is uncertain whether a candidate has already been baptised, a conditional baptism may be administered. A baptism must be recorded in a register.[38]

By way of contrast, normally, Presbyterian law confines baptism to professing adults and children of professing members; there is no provision for sponsors or godparents. Baptism is 'a sign and seal that [which] declares . . . union with Christ . . . forgiveness of sins by washing . . . new life [and] adoption as His children . . . By this sacrament we are brought into Christ's Church.'[39] Elders must encourage parents to bring their children for baptism, which, ordinarily, is administered at a public service and extraordinarily in private or in an emergency by sprinkling of water or by immersion in the name of the Father, Son and Holy Spirit.[40] The parents or guardians must profess their own faith and promise to bring up the child in the faith and life of the church: if they do so, baptism must not be delayed; if they do not, baptism may be refused with the consent of Kirk Session. The congregation undertakes to support the child, but there are no godparents. Adult baptism is combined with confirmation. The minister must arrange for baptism, provide spiritual guidance of applicants, issues a certificate of baptism and records details in the baptismal register.[41] However, Believers' Baptism is the Baptist norm; for the Baptist Union: 'That Christian Baptism is the immersion in water into the Name of the Father, the Son and the Holy

---

[38] MCGB: Constitutional Practice and Discipline, Deed of Union 6; Standing Orders 010A, 054: it is reviewed periodically by the local Church Council.

[39] UFCS: Manual of Practice and Procedure, App. 6. See also PCW: Handbook of Rules, 9.1.

[40] J.L. Weatherhead, ed., Constitution and Laws of the Church of Scotland (1997) 32 and 109; Acts XVII, 1963 and IV, 1975; PCW: Handbook of Rules, 9.2.

[41] J.L. Weatherhead, ed., Constitution and Laws of the Church of Scotland (1997) 34, 108; PCI: Code, I.I.II.7(2); UFCS: Manual of Practice and Procedure, I.III.2. For similar norms, see URC: Manual A.1.1.

Ghost, of those who have professed repentance towards God and faith in our Lord Jesus Christ who "died for our sins according to the Scriptures"; was buried and rose again the third day."[42]

Secondly, according to the principles of Christian law: a church may make provision for a further rite accompanying/following baptism which may be styled confirmation or profession of faith. Candidates may undergo preparation and instruction prior to it.[43] By the rite of confirmation, which takes place broadly at puberty, the grace of the Holy Spirit is conveyed in a fuller manner to those who have already received it at baptism. There has been much theological discussion as to its precise significance and on the method of administration. Some consider it an integral stage in the process of Christian initiation (Catholics) whilst others do not practise it (Presbyterians); and in some, the rites of baptism and confirmation are separate (Anglicans).[44] In the Roman Catholic Church: 'the sacrament of confirmation impresses a character and by it the baptised, continuing on the path of Christian initiation, are enriched by the gift of the Holy Spirit'; it binds the person 'more perfectly to the church' and it obliges them more firmly 'to be witnesses of Christ by word and deed and to spread and defend the faith'.[45] The duty to ensure that confirmation is conferred on those who 'properly and reasonably request it' rests with the bishop; and parents and pastors are to see that the faithful are properly instructed to receive confirmation and that it is approached at the appropriate time, at 'about the age of discretion'. All baptised persons may receive confirmation; and, outside the danger of death, candidates must be suitably instructed, properly disposed and able to renew their baptismal promises.[46] It is administered by anointing the candidate with chrism on the forehead by the laying on of the hand and by the words prescribed in the liturgical books; it is desirable that it is celebrated in a church during the Mass.[47] The minister is a bishop but a priest may so act with a faculty to do so.[48] A candidate has a sponsor and confirmation must be registered.[49]

---

[42] BUGB: Con. 3.2; Model Trusts for Churches 2003, 2.8.2. For an identical formula, see BUS: Con. III.2.

[43] Christian Law Panel of Experts, *The Principles of Christian Law* (2016) VII.2.

[44] In the Orthodox Church, the baptism and confirmation are administered in a single rite.

[45] CIC: c. 879.

[46] CIC: cc. 885, 890 and 899; cc. 889–891: the Episcopal Conference may specify an age.

[47] CIC: c. 880; c. 881: it may be also celebrated apart from mass and in any fitting place.

[48] CIC: c. 882: a priest equivalent in law to a bishop, who has the mandate of the bishop or in danger of death any priest, has the faculty to confirm automatically by universal law.

[49] CIC: c. 892: the sponsor must fulfil c. 874; cc. 875–878: proof and registration.

Similar norms apply in Anglicanism: only a baptised person who has attained the age of discretion may be confirmed. Confirmation is a rite in which a person makes a profession of the faith and a mature reaffirmation of the commitment to Christ made at baptism. The minister of confirmation is the bishop who administers the rite with the laying on of hands and invocation of the Holy Spirit to strengthen the candidate in the Christian life. It should be administered at the Eucharist.[50] An ordained minister presents candidates to the bishop and the rite should be witnessed and recorded. All candidates must receive instruction in the Christian faith, including the Lord's Prayer, Creed, Ten Commandments and church catechism. When adults and children are able to answer for themselves, baptism and confirmation should be administered as a single rite; otherwise, confirmation should follow baptism as soon as is convenient.[51] Methodists too practise confirmation.[52]

By way of marked contrast, Presbyterians do not practise the rite of confirmation as such, but there is a rite for admission to full membership particularly for the purposes of receiving Holy Communion (see below). For example, in the Church of Scotland there is 'no "sacrament of confirmation"'; rather: 'The sacrament of baptism, being complete in itself, requires no subsequent confirmation'.[53] However, the church has an order of service for 'Confirmation and Admission to the Lord's Supper', namely 'a service of public profession of faith and admission to the Lord's Table'.[54] Similarly, for the United Reformed Church, the affirmation (or profession) of faith by which a person is publicly admitted to full membership is by the laying on of hands and giving and receiving the right hand of fellowship.[55] There is no confirmation in the Baptist tradition – rather, at a Believer's Baptism each candidate confirms their own faith.[56]

---

[50] PCLCCAC: Principle 65.1–8. See also AR, Art. 25: confirmation is 'not to be counted for [a sacrament] of the Gospel' – it is 'not . . . ordained of God'; Scottish Episcopal Church: Can. 30.1.

[51] PCLCCAC: Principle 65. See e.g. Church of Ireland: Con. IX.28.

[52] MCGB: Constitutional Practice and Discipline, Deed of Union 8(a)–(c); Standing Orders 054: confirmation registers.

[53] J.L. Weatherhead, ed., *Constitution and Laws of the Church of Scotland* (1997) 32–33.

[54] J.L. Weatherhead, ed., *Constitution and Laws of the Church of Scotland* (1997) 33 and 128. See also PCI: Code, para. 40(2): persons proposing to take communion for the first time shall be carefully instructed by the minister.

[55] URC: Manual A., Sch. A.   [56] See above for Believers' Baptism.

Aqiqah and Khitan

In Islam, since a child is born Muslim (see above Chapter 2),[57] rites applicable to birth are a matter of religious recommendation rather than obligation; according to custom, birth ritual (*aqiqah*) may involve shaving the child's head, distributing money to the poor, animal sacrifice (one for a girl, two for a boy) and naming the child (any name, provided it is not heathen).[58] Immediately after birth, the father recites the *adhan*, call to prayer, in the ear of the baby. This is the only ceremonial element of childbirth. At seven days old, after shaving the baby's hair, the hair is weighed and discarded. The amount of charity disbursed by the parents is equal to the weight of the baby's hair in silver. One or two sheep are also bought as sacrifices, with the meat being distributed to relatives, friends and the poor. Abortion is forbidden in Islamic law unless the life of the mother is in danger; non-destructive forms of contraception are permitted.[59]

Circumcision (*khitan*) is seen by some scholars as part of Muslim rites of purification (*taharah*) or else it may be traced back to the practice of Abraham. It has also been interpreted variously as a symbol of: self-discipline in the commandments of God; the inner development of reason; the submission of base passions to higher spiritual requisites; the physical recognition of the supremacy of God over the uncontrolled instincts; and the deeper religious commitment – the practice is not universal.[60] There is a custom that boys are circumcised before the age of 12,[61] preferably at seven days old. It is also normal for adult male converts to be advised to arrange their circumcision. Female circumcision is not a requirement of classical Islamic law.[62]

However, the modern regulatory instruments of the Muslim communities studied here are silent on circumcision. In point of fact, the opinions of Muslim scholars differ as to whether it is obligatory (*fard*)

---

[57] Muslims consider *all* children to be born in a state of sinlessness – implicitly, 'perfect Muslims'.

[58] J.L. Esposito, ed., *Oxford Dictionary of Islam* (2003) 24, 44.

[59] M. Naqshbandi, *Islam and Muslims in Britain* (2012): Guide 6.1.

[60] J.L. Esposito, ed., *Oxford Dictionary of Islam* (2003) 54.

[61] J. Hussain, *Islamic Law* (1999) 132; M. Rohe, *Islamic Law* (2014) 458.

[62] M. Naqshbandi, *Islam and Muslims in Britain* (2012): Guide 6.1.2: It is traditional among some African communities, Muslim and non-Muslim, especially around East Africa and the Horn of Africa, and some Arab communities, but very rare elsewhere in the Muslim community. The Messenger of Allah gave explicit advice to be sparing in the operation, advice that is normally interpreted as his accepting but not recommending the practice.

or the practice of Muhammad (*Sunnah*). While the Quran does not mention circumcision explicitly, for some, Muhammad was born without a foreskin or his grandfather Abd-al-Muttalib circumcised him when he was seven days old. Many early disciples were circumcised. Some *hadith* mention circumcision; Abu Hurayra, a Companion, is said to have held circumcision as *fitra* (the natural character of being human). Muhammad supposedly circumcised his grandsons Hasan and Husayn. Most Shia traditions regard the practice as obligatory. But some argue that it is forbidden (*haram*) on the basis that the Quran 4.119 forbids alteration of a body. There is no Muslim equivalent of a Jewish *mohel*; the circumciser is not required to be a Muslim; and circumcisions are usually performed in a hospital. The benefits of circumcision are also debated by Muslim scholars.[63] It has been held by the civil courts that if both parents do not agree to the circumcision of a boy, then a circumcision may not be performed, even if the Muslim father insists, without a court order. In any event, a court must consider what is in the best interests of the child, the religious environment of his home and the upbringing of the child will also be key.[64]

The Rites of Spiritual Development and Commemoration

All three religions have norms on the administration of rites which seek to enhance the spiritual development of the faithful or else to commemorate regularly events of religious significance. What follows examines ritual immersion, Kiddush, Pesach and ritual food preparation in Judaism; the celebration of Eucharist, Holy Communion or the Lord's Supper in Christianity; and the ritual preparation of food, Ramadan and pilgrimage in Islam. There are both differences and similarities between these rites.[65]

Mikveh, Kiddush and Kashrut

Judaism makes provision for many rites, designed around the concept of cleanliness, to assist the spiritual development of the faithful during their

---

[63] Mission Islam: www.missionislam.com/health/circumcisionislam.html.

[64] *Re J* (*Child's religious upbringing and circumcision*) [2000] 1 FLR 307 (CA).

[65] For civil law on the ritual killing of animals, see e.g. Slaughterhouses Act 1974 and Welfare of Animals (Slaughter or Killing) Regulations 1995: these protect Jewish and Muslim ritual methods.

lives.[66] Three are studied here: ritual immersion, the ritual preparation of food and the Passover meal. First, immersion in the ritual bath (*mikveh*, 'gathering of water') is understood to represent cleansing.[67] Today, in the Movement for Reform Judaism, for example, the *mikveh*, the pool of 'living water' (*mayyim hayyim*), is used 'as a Jewish ritual, generally to mark cycles and moments of transformation for both men and women', including weddings, menstrual cycles, celebrating festivals, Shabbat and conversion. The *mikveh* must contain water from a natural source. A person should enter it in a clean and naked state, and in as simple and humble a state as possible, taking time in 'a private sacred space to mark change and transformation'. The *mikveh* waters may be viewed as 'a kind of re-birth' at new life stages, adding layers to who they already are, or, where desired, metaphorically washing away experiences they wish to leave behind. The faithful are increasingly using the *mikveh* to mark a variety of life cycle events, from divorce to recovery from illness and dealing with infertility to marking special birthdays. The Bet Din may be consulted for a liturgy to use in the *mikveh*.[68]

Secondly, Kiddush is the sanctification of the Shabbat: on Friday night, when the Shabbat begins, the ceremony is carried out before sitting down to the Shabbat meal. A cup of wine is filled and held in the hand by the person presiding, usually but not necessarily the father, and the benediction over the wine recited, after which the Kiddush proper is recited; as a prelude to the ceremony, verses of the creation narrative which speak of the Shabbat (Genesis 2:1–3) are also recited. After the drinking of wine, the benediction over bread is recited and the family then partakes of the Shabbat meal.[69] The matter may be regulated by written norms. For instance, in the Movement for Reform Judaism, each synagogue should have a Kiddush Committee responsible for: liaising with families with regard to *B'Nei Mitzvot* Kiddush; preparation of any special Kiddush; purchasing wine and chola; preparing Friday night Kiddush; helping to organise the Seder for Passover; and organising the food for the Torah Breakfast.[70]

---

[66] The Talmudic Rabbis understood the verse 'Ye shall not make yourselves abominable' (Leviticus 11:43) as the basis for a host of religious practices which ensure cleanliness in body and spirit.

[67] Leviticus: 11.

[68] MRJ: www.reformjudaism.org.uk/resources/life-cycle/. See also, for a dispute as to a *mikveh*: *William Verry Limited* v. *North West London Communal Mikvah* [2004] EWHC 1300 (TCC).

[69] L. Jacobs, *Jewish Religion* (1999) 124–125.   [70] MRJ: Code of Practice, p. 15.

Thirdly, in virtue of their observance of dietary laws (*kashrut*),[71] Jews are required to eat only *kosher* ('right' or 'fit') food: 'laws governing production of Kosher food are complex'; they involve (but are not limited to) restrictions on what types of meat and fish may be eaten, which combinations of foods may be eaten together and how foods are prepared. Jews who observe the dietary laws may require all food to be prepared under supervision in order to be satisfied that no prohibited ingredients have been used.[72] Each Jewish tradition has its own regulatory system in this matter.[73] For instance, the Masorti Bet Din supervises preparation of *kosher* food under the Masorti Kosher label; caterers who are not usually *kosher* may apply for a one-day licence for a single event.[74] In the United Synagogue of Conservative Judaism: 'The observance of kashrut is a basic tenet of Conservative Judaism'; only kosher food is permitted in the synagogue or served at congregation-sponsored functions, regardless of location; and: 'Halakhic issues concerning the observance of kashrut should be resolved by the Rabbi in consultation with [the] lay leadership.'[75] And the Movement for Reform Judaism has a *kashrut* policy on the basis, in part, that 'sharing food is an important part of the Jewish religious experience'; all food brought into and prepared in the synagogue kitchen must be *kosher*;[76] for example, the synagogue and kitchen are dairy-only; no meat may be brought in or consumed there whether *kosher* or not; and foods, fish and dairy

---

[71] See Leviticus 11 and Deuteronomy 14: 3–21 for rules as to which animals, birds and fish are *kosher* and which *terefah* (literally 'torn' (from beasts)) and therefore forbidden; see also Esther 8:5 and Exodus 22:30.

[72] BDBJ: *The Employer's Guide to Judaism* (2004: updated 2015) Section 2: therefore, Jews may refuse foods labelled 'vegetarian' or wish to store and heat food separately from food that is not *kosher*.

[73] ULPS: *Affirmations* (2006) Art. 39. Also, *shechita* has been performed under the London Board for Shechita whose constituent members are the United Synagogue, Federation of Synagogues and Spanish and Portuguese Jews. Thus, Dayanim of the London Beth Din supervise *shechita* together with Dayanim from the Batei Din of those other bodies. Also, the Beth Din has a *kashrut* department to supervise and certify caterers, bakeries, restaurants and food manufacturers in the UK, and it supervises and certifies in the UK and many countries throughout the world, foods and items used in the manufacture of food: www.theus.org.uk/content/kashrut-researcher-kashrut-division-london-beth-din.

[74] AMS: www.masorti.org.uk/bet-din/bet-din.html.

[75] USCJ: Standards for Congregational Practice (2017): III: Congregations should refer to: 'Kashrut: Connecting the Physical to the Spiritual'; 'Jewish Dietary Laws'; 'Kosher: Sanctifying the Ordinary'; and 'Synagogue Policy on Bringing Foods Prepared in the Home into the Synagogue' (1988).

[76] MRJ. Code of Practice, 30.

products are regulated in detail. Any doubts or questions must be referred to the Rabbi or Religious Affairs Committee.[77] The renewal of *kashrut* licences, as a religious matter, is not subject to judicial review in the civil courts.[78]

The Passover (*Pesach*) may be offered as a brief case study of the interaction between cleanliness, Kiddush and *kosher*; it is the spring festival (held in the month of Adar after Purim) to commemorate the Exodus from Egypt and to celebrate the foundation of the Jewish nation/ people. For instance, the Movement for Reform Judaism has norms on 'Pesach Preparation and Communal Seder'. As to the preparation of the synagogue premises: the Cheder Kitchen and Shul Kitchen have to be prepared for Pesach and volunteers found to clean both; all unleavened food (*chumatz*) is removed (Exodus 12:15); and fridges are cleaned and cupboards taped up. All other items are stored behind the Ark. Pesach wine is purchased. Matzo has to be provided for Kiddush on the Friday and Saturday. There are special Pesach utensils behind the Ark. No *chumatz* is brought on to the premises (including into the kitchens) during Pesach.[79] With regard to the communal meal (*seder*), prior to Pesach, the faithful are notified about the event, bookings are made and collected by the Seder Organiser and money paid to the Treasurer. Once numbers are known, purchases are made of the main items from a *kosher* supplier and brought to the *shul*. A table plan is displayed on the door of the *shul*. A *haggadah* is the text recited at the *seder* on the first two nights of the Passover, and it includes the Exodus narrative; the *haggadot* have to be put out on the tables. The Organiser itemises the overall cost for payment by the Treasurer.[80]

The Eucharist, Holy Communion or Lord's Supper

The nature of the Eucharist, Holy Communion or Lord's Supper has been and is the subject of intense doctrinal disagreement in Christianity. However, for the historic churches, according to principles of Christian

---

[77] MRJ: Code of Practice, 30–31.

[78] See R v. *London Beth Din, ex parte Bloom* [1998] COD 131: a restaurateur sought review of a London Beth refusal to renew a *kashrut* licence; judicial review was declined on the basis that there was an insufficient public element in this essentially religious matter.

[79] MRJ: Code of Practice, 32.

[80] MRJ: Code of Practice, 31–32. For the Conservative tradition, see USCJ: Rabbinical Assembly, Pesach Guide (2016) which deals with e.g. utensils to be used, prohibited, and permitted foods.

law, the Eucharist, Holy Communion or Lord's Supper is instituted by Christ. The Eucharist and receiving Holy Communion are central to ecclesial life. The faithful should participate in the Eucharist and receive Holy Communion regularly. The Eucharist is presided over by such persons as are lawfully authorised and celebrated in an authorised place. A church should provide for reception of Holy Communion by the sick. Elements for the celebration of Holy Communion are bread and wine. A church may make provision for admission to it.[81] These principles derive from similarities between the norms of churches.[82]

Under Roman Catholic law: '[t]he most august sacrament is the blessed Eucharist, in which Christ the Lord himself is contained, offered and received, and by which the Church continually lives and grows'. Instituted by Christ, it is 'the memorial of the death and resurrection of the Lord, in which the sacrifice of the cross is forever perpetuated' and 'the summit and the source of all worship and Christian life'.[83] The faithful must hold the Eucharist in the highest honour, take an active part in its celebration, receive the sacrament frequently and reverence it with the greatest adoration.[84] In the Eucharist, Christ, 'through the ministry of the priest, offers himself, substantially present under the appearances of bread and wine, to God the Father, and gives himself as spiritual nourishment to the faithful'; therefore: 'The only minister, who, in the person of Christ, can bring into being the sacrament of the Eucharist, is a validly ordained priest.'[85] A priest may not celebrate the Eucharist without the participation of at least one of the faithful, unless there is a good and reasonable cause for doing so; deacons and lay persons may not perform actions which are reserved to the priest (e.g. the Eucharistic prayer) – but deacons, for example, prepare the altar, and laity may be permitted to distribute Holy Communion.[86] Any baptised person not forbidden by law is admitted to Holy Communion, as are children if they have sufficient knowledge and are carefully prepared so

---

[81] Christian Law Panel of Experts, *Principles of Christian Law* (2016) VII.3.

[82] For the exclusion of a person from Holy Communion, see above Chapter 2.

[83] CIC: c. 897; SC 47–48.

[84] CIC: c. 898: pastors must instruct the faithful about this duty.

[85] CIC: cc. 899–900; c. 904: daily celebration by priests; c. 905: a priest cannot celebrate more than once a day unless the bishop permits; c. 1378.2: lay people attempting to confect it are excommunicate.

[86] CIC: c. 906; SC 14; c. 907: prayers; c. 908: concelebration; c. 909: the priest must prepare himself by prayer; c. 910: ordinary minister; c. 911: bringing the sacrament to the sick (as viaticum).

that they understand and receive it with faith and devotion.[87] Excommunicates must not be admitted, nor anyone who is conscious of grave sin without having first been to confession.[88] The Eucharist must be offered in bread and in wine; but Holy Communion is to be given with bread alone or, under liturgical laws, with both or, in a case of necessity, with wine alone.[89] It may be celebrated on any day/hour in a sacred place (unless necessity requires otherwise), and norms exist for reservation and veneration of the Eucharist.[90] Roman Catholic canon law also makes provision for both pilgrimages and fasting.[91]

For Anglicans, the Holy Communion, Eucharist or Lord's Supper, is a sacrament instituted by Christ, the central act of worship, and an act of the whole church – and it must be maintained and duly administered by each church. Every confirmed person should receive it frequently and regularly. It should be administered in a church building, except for the communion of the sick or housebound, or in other cases with the consent of the bishop. The elements consecrated for Holy Communion are bread and wine and are to be received in both kinds. Presidency at the Holy Communion is reserved to a priest or bishop; a deacon or authorised lay minister may assist in distributing the elements.[92] The sacrament may be reserved for the sick and the housebound, those dying or in special need and for devotional services, if the bishop so permits.[93] To receive Holy Communion, normally, a person must be baptised and, where this is required by law, confirmed or ready and desirous of being confirmed.[94]

---

[87] CIC: c. 912: admission; c. 913: children in danger of death may receive if able to distinguish the Body of Christ from ordinary food; c. 914: children must be prepared for its reception.

[88] CIC: cc. 915–916.

[89] CIC: c. 924: a small quantity of water may be added to the wine; the bread must be wheaten, recently made and (c. 926) unleavened; the wine must be natural, made from grapes and not corrupt; c. 927: it is absolutely wrong to consecrate one element alone; cc. 928–930: language, vesture and posture.

[90] CIC: c. 931: time; c. 932: place; c. 933: for a good reason, with the bishop's consent, and if all scandal is eliminated, a priest may celebrate in the church of another tradition; cc. 934–944: reservation.

[91] CIC: c. 1230: pilgrimages to shrines; and c. 1249: fasting.

[92] PCLCCAC: Principle 66. AR, Arts. 25, 28. See e.g. Church of England: Can. B15.1: 'It is the duty of all who have been confirmed to receive the Holy Communion regularly and especially at . . . Christmas, Easter and Whitsun or Pentecost'; Can. B17.2: the bread may be leavened or unleavened but 'of the best and purest wheat flour', and the wine 'fermented juice of the grape and of good quality'.

[93] PCLCCAC: Principle 67. See e.g. Church of Ireland: Con. IX.14: administration to the sick in private homes.

[94] PCLCCAC: Principle 68. See e.g. Church of England: Can. B15A.

Whilst there remain profound doctrinal differences between Catholic and Protestant understandings of the sacrament (as to transubstantiation and consubstantiation), there are remarkable juridical similarities in terms of sacramental discipline. For example, Lutherans should participate in Holy Communion regularly,[95] and Methodists must receive bread and (non-alcoholic) wine.[96] The Methodist Church of Ireland has a duty to make 'due provision for the regular and ordered Service of Holy Communion'. Moreover: 'It is the duty and privilege of all its members to avail themselves of every opportunity to partake reverently and in faith of the Lord's Supper.'[97] Admission to the Lord's Supper is 'the privilege of members of the Church, and such members of the congregation, including children who wish to communicate, as the minister may judge to be eligible'; moreover, wine used in 'the ordinance shall be unfermented'.[98]

For Presbyterians: 'In the Sacrament of the Lord's Supper, the Church commemorates the Lord Jesus Christ and His sacrifice for us.' Christ's offering of himself to the faithful and their acceptance of this gift are 'represented' by the breaking of bread, the pouring of wine and the distributing of both by the minister: 'In the celebration the Church acts for Christ, and Christ acts through her'; its validity depends on its proper administration with a sincere aim, namely 'to show the Lord's death till He come'; and its 'efficacy depends on our acceptance of the gift of our Lord by faith'.[99] As to its administration, the Church of Scotland is typical. The Kirk Session decides when the Lord's Supper will be celebrated but only an ordained minister may administer it;[100] an elder may assist if authorised.[101] Members are entitled to (and should) receive communion and may do so by the 'common cup' in 'the ordinary elements of bread and wine', but an 'individual cup and unfermented wine are permitted'.[102] Baptised children may be admitted if their parents

---

[95] ELCIRE: Con. Art. 6: 'Members ... have the right to ... the use of the sacraments.'
[96] MCGB: Constitutional Practice and Discipline, Standing Orders 922(2): 'wine used shall be non-alcoholic'.
[97] MCI: Regulations, Discipline and Government, 1.01 and 2.06.
[98] MCI: Regulations, Discipline and Government, 3.05: there are exceptions to the admissions rule in paras. 4B.31 and 4G.16–21.
[99] PCW: Handbook of Rules, 9.3: the sacrament was instituted by Christ (Matt. 26.26–28).
[100] J.L. Weatherhead, ed., *Constitution and Laws of the Church of Scotland* (1997) 31. See also PCI: Code, I.II.II.37: public administration.
[101] UFCS: Manual of Practice and Procedure, I.III.7.
[102] J.L. Weatherhead, ed., *Constitution and Laws of the Church of Scotland* (1997) 109. See also PCW: Handbook of Rules, 2.2: a member must partake 'regularly' of the Lord's Supper.

request this.[103] The United Reformed Church has similar rules.[104] Baptists too regulate the Lord's Supper.[105]

Sawm, Hajj and Halal Food

It is an obligation on all Muslims to fast (*sawm*) in the month of Ramadan. The daily routine of fasting involves waking to have enough time for breakfast before first light, fasting without food or drink or ingested medication until immediately after sunset, and breaking the fast at that time. In mid-evening, there is a long period of extra prayer (*tarawih salah*), in which the entire Quran is recited over the 29/30 days of the month. It is highly recommended that Muslims read and recite as much of the Quran as they can individually during the month. Fasting does not apply to: anyone who is too sick to fast, or is on essential medication that is swallowed, injected or absorbed; women when menstruating, pregnant or suckling; or travellers (who may fast if it suits them). Those who are exempt must make up the missed fasts – unless they suffer from a long-term condition, who may instead feed a given number of the poor if they are able to afford it. There are certain other days in the year in which optional fasts are routinely made, and some people keep habitual fasts every Monday and Thursday. If any amount of food or drink is taken in genuine forgetfulness, fasting is not technically broken. The fast merely resumes from the point at which the error is remembered; there is no need to expel anything so taken. However, fasting is broken if anything, even something completely indigestible, is taken intentionally with the objective of mitigating hunger. Ramadan ends with the new moon of the following month and is followed by the feast day Eid-ul-Fitr, literally 'feast of fast-breaking'.[106] According to the Fatwa Committee UK, citing the verdict of the European Council for

---

[103] J.L. Weatherhead, ed., *Constitution and Laws of the Church of Scotland* (1997) 109; Act XV, 1992: children; Act III, 1985: the mentally disabled; PCW: Handbook of Rules, 9.3.

[104] URC: Man. A.15: 'When in obedience to the Lord's command his people show forth his sacrifice on the cross by the bread broken and the wine outpoured for them to eat and drink, he himself, risen and ascended, is present and gives himself to them for their spiritual nourishment and growth in grace.'

[105] See N. Doe, *Christian Law* (2013) 253–254.

[106] M. Naqshbandi, *Islam and Muslims in Britain* (2012): Guide 2.2.2. Birmingham Central Mosque has elaborate norms on Ramadan fasting set out in terms of what is compulsory (*fard*), recommended (*sunnah*), permissible (*nafl*), disliked (*makruh*) and forbidden (*haram*); also, e.g. women may choose to pray at home rather than in the mosque.

Fatwa and Research, a Muslim student may break their fast when their concentration during a period of examinations is affected by it and the student fears suffering severe exhaustion and hardship, is not able to delay the examination, and then makes up the missed fast – because: 'Allah wants ease for you, and He does not want hardship.'[107]

Secondly, a Muslim, who has the means to do so and is able to support his family for the duration, is under obligation to perform *hajj* once in a life-time.[108] *Hajj* requires a visit to Makkah (Mecca), Madinah (300 miles to the north), and Arafat nearby. It occurs during the second week of the month of *Dhul-Hijjah* (i.e. two months after Ramadan). Visits to Makkah and Madinah may be made at most other times too, but do not qualify as the *hajj* proper and are called *umrah*. Both include specific rituals: wearing *ihram* (for men two unstitched cloths); circumambulating the *Kaaba* (the black-shrouded *masjid* built by Abraham); making seven walks between the hillocks of Sa'fa and Marwah; and having the head shaved (for men) or a lock of hair cut (for women). The pilgrimage involves five continuous days of activity at Makkah, Madinah, then, on the Day of Hajj, on the plain of Arafat, and is followed with the feast day of Eid-ul-Adha (feast of sacrifice), where an animal is slaughtered for each adult in the family, and its meat distributed to relatives, friends and the poor. Stoning of three pillars occurs over the next three days at Madinah: the pillars represent three ancient idols that once stood there; the act symbolizes stoning the devil and rejection of idolatry. Before or after, pilgrims normally spend eight days at *Masjid an-Nabi*.[109] The modern regulatory instruments of the Muslim communities studied here rarely mention *hajj*.[110] However, the Muslim Council of Britain has guidance on it and a Travel Pharmacy Network which provides vaccinations, as well as advice on visas.[111]

Thirdly, there is dietary discipline. As the Quran prohibits fermented drinks due to their intoxicating potential, so Muslims are forbidden all association with intoxicating drinks (including buying, selling, delivering and consuming);[112] but alcohol may have valid surgical

---

[107] FCUK: Decision 1/1: citing ECFR Fatwa 6/25 (which cites Surat al-Baqarah: 185).

[108] See e.g. Al-Qadi al-Nu'man, *The Pillars of Islam* (2002) I.359–421; Quran 3:97. See also J. Hussain, *Islamic Law* (1999) 12, 14, 26, 61, 77, 187, 211.

[109] M. Naqshbandi, *Islam and Muslims in Britain* (2012): Guide 2.2.4: in all the pilgrimage takes about three weeks.

[110] See e.g. NASFAT: Con. Art. M.9: the Hajj and Umrah Committee.

[111] MCB: http://mcb.etraveltool.com/finder.

[112] J.L. Esposito, ed., *Oxford Dictionary of Islam* (2003) 140.

uses.[113] The Quran and *hadith* also forbid Muslims to consume carrion, spurting blood, pork and food consecrated to anything but God; and the Quran forbids consumption of any animal strangled, beaten or gored to death, or one that has died by falling. Ritual slaughter is required for domestic cattle, sheep, goats and fowl, which must be killed in the name of God by making a fatal incision across the throat of the animal.[114] Food that is lawful (*halal*) includes: fruit, vegetables and vegetable products except those mixed with alcohol; all fish and fish products (but those that are amphibious, such as crab, lobster, shrimp and prawns, are prohibited (*haram*)); meat or meat products from an animal slaughtered lawfully; dairy products (if they have no forbidden content); eggs (if cooked in a *halal* substance). Traditional Muslim eating practices are determined by elaborate Sunnah, such as sitting at a cloth spread on a clean, shoe-free floor or on a platform a few inches off the floor, washing hands before and after eating, and eating/drinking only with a washed right hand.[115]

However, modern regulatory instruments of Muslim communities provide for dietary discipline, and its administration by mosque committees and other bodies.[116] By way of illustration, the Council for Mosques (Bradford) has guidance on the subject: 'The provision and promotion of halal' by public sector providers in the district is 'an important consideration'. As such, the Council: should facilitate discussion with key organisations to agree a national framework to monitor and regulate halal, and it liaises with the Muslim Council of Britain to develop a national body for this; should work in partnership with the providers of school meals and schools in the Bradford district to ensure proper policies and procedures are in place regarding halal meals; oversee the work of its food inspector who monitors the *halal* system; and agree with Muslim retailers/suppliers a framework to regulate *halal* across the supply chain.[117]

The Funerary Rites

Each religion has elaborate norms applicable to funerals and the disposal of the human remains of the faithful. While the meaning of death and the

---

[113] M. Naqshbandi, *Islam and Muslims in Britain* (2012): Guide 8.1.

[114] J.L. Esposito, ed., *Oxford Dictionary of Islam* (2003) 68.

[115] M. Naqshbandi, *Islam and Muslims in Britain* (2012): Guide 8.1–4.

[116] See e.g. IFIS CUBE Network: Sample Constitution of an Islamic Society Art. 4.5: the Facilities Manager is responsible for meeting the catering team 'to organise Halaal food'.

[117] CFM: www.councilformosques.org/our-work/guidance/.

afterlife are matters of religious belief, norms applicable on death are a mixture of religious law and custom. What follows deals with norms on: the care and preparation of a body for a funeral; disposal of a body and conducting funerary rites; and Jewish and Muslim mourning.

K'vurah and Shivah

When a Jew dies, the funeral must take place as soon as possible following the death, sometimes on the day of the death (unless for instance an autopsy is required). After the funeral, the immediate family of the deceased (i.e. parents, children, siblings and spouses) mourn for seven days (the *shivah*, 'seven' in Hebrew). During the *shivah*, the immediate family stay at home, saying prayers and receiving condolences from well-wishers and often not working. Non-Jews may attend the funeral and *shivah*.[118] The movements within Judaism differ as to the acceptability of cremation over burial. The (Orthodox) United Synagogue, for example, may provide 'service and means for the burial of persons of the Jewish religion in accordance with the Form of Worship'.[119] The Jewish Joint Burial Society serves the United Synagogue, 27 Reform, 6 Masorti, 2 Liberal and 2 Independent communities in England – the Federation of Synagogues has its own Burial Society managed by Trustees.[120] At local level, the constitutions of synagogues also provides for rights to a Jewish burial or cremation; for example, at North London Reform Synagogue: 'Every member shall, subject to the terms of his admission into the Synagogue, be entitled to the right of burial for himself or any of his children under the age of 21 at a burial ground selected by the Council.' The Council must make suitable arrangements with the West London Synagogue of British Jews, or with some other body, in order to secure such 'burial rights'; the Council may also make regulations as to conditions to be observed 'in connection with graves, burials, cremations and funerals', in the absence of which 'the laws and practices of the West London Synagogue of British Jews shall, so far as

---

[118] BDBJ: *The Employer's Guide to Judaism* (2004: updated 2015) Section 2: it is recommended that men and women dress modestly (covering knees and elbows) – and men wear a skull-cap.

[119] US: Statutes 5.4. See also e.g. EHC: Con: Sch. of Regulations, 14: 'Register Books shall be kept . . . of all funerals performed under the auspices of the Congregation.'

[120] US: www.theus.org.uk/article/about-us-burial-society-0. The organisation also provides advice on burials and mourning and runs 13 cemeteries; and FOS: Law 32.

they are applicable, be observed.[121] At Elstree Liberal Synagogue too: 'Any child or person in the legal custody of a Full Member brought up in or of the Jewish faith, up to the age of 21 years and normally residing at the same address as their parent or guardian shall be included in [its] burial and funeral schemes.'[122] Again, Peterborough Liberal Jewish Community must provide 'burial and cremation services' for its members.[123]

The United Synagogue of Conservative Judaism may be offered as a detailed case study. 'Jewish law and tradition have endowed funeral and mourning practices with profound religious significance'; therefore: 'The laws, rules and customs of funerals and mourning are to be observed';[124] moreover: 'A Jewish funeral is a sacred rite and should be invested with both dignity and simplicity as taught by Jewish tradition'; even after death, the body, which once held a holy human life, retains its sanctity. To this end, Jewish funerals avoid ostentation; family and visitors reflect in dress and deportment the solemnity of the occasion; flowers and music are inappropriate; embalming and viewing are avoided, with interment as soon as possible after death.[125]

First, a Hevra Kadisha is a 'holy society' of volunteers which traditionally supervises funerals in Jewish communities; congregations are encouraged to establish a Hevra Kadisha to assist bereaved families; in some communities this is carried out by local cemetery societies or by funeral homes which observe Jewish customs and traditions, but the congregation Rabbi should be consulted on the acceptability of a funeral director. Moreover, preparation and burial of the body are highly valued commands (*mitzvot*), and an act of kindness (*chesed shel emet*) as the dead cannot repay this service. Families should consult the Rabbi as soon as possible after death and questions as to a funeral and periods of mourning should be referred to the Rabbi for guidance – and it is the duty of the community to assist the family of the deceased.[126]

Secondly: 'Jewish law requires that burial take place as soon as possible, preferably within 24 hours of death.' However, burial (*k'vurah*) may be delayed for legal reasons, such as: to transport the deceased; to enable

---

[121] NLRS: Laws, Art. 19.
[122] ELS: Con. Art. 5: Note. See also ULPS: *Affirmations* (2006) Art. 22: the importance of rites about death and mourning.
[123] PLJC: Con. Art. 3.
[124] USCJ: Standards for Congregational Practice (2017): Standard IV. See also Guide to Constitutions (2010) Art. XV: the Religious Committee may make rules as to funerals.
[125] USCJ: Guide to Jewish Funeral Practice (1992).
[126] USCJ: Guide to Jewish Funeral Practice: Introduction, 1 and 2.

close relatives to travel long distances to attend; or to avoid burial on Shabbat or another holy day.[127] Special cases such as death by accident or suicide, or of children under 30 days old, should be referred to the Rabbi for guidance. It is 'inappropriate' to make arrangements on Shabbat. Jewish tradition requires that the deceased not be left alone prior to burial. Hospitals should be requested to avoid disturbing the remains until the arrival of a guardian (*shomer*) to recite psalms (*tehellim*) there; and it is preferable that *shomrim* be members of the family, friends of the deceased or members of the congregation.[128]

Thirdly, Jewish law requires the deceased to be cleansed following a prescribed ritual (*taharah*), as a mark of respect, by a Hevra Kadisha prior to burial in plain white shrouds (*tachrichim*) to demonstrate the equality of all. A male is customarily buried wearing a *kipah* and his own *talit*. The casket (*aron*) must be made entirely of wood. The mourners for parents, spouses, children or siblings traditionally participate in the rite of *k'riah* (rending of garments) before the funeral – tearing of a visible portion of clothing (e.g. lapel, pocket or collar) which is then worn in the mourning period. In many communities, the mourner wears a black ribbon instead. The tearing for parents is on the left side over the heart and for other relatives on the right side. Between death and funeral, a bereaved person (*onen*), being an immediate member of the family of the deceased, is exempt from all affirmative religious obligations (e.g. reciting the three daily services) but is forbidden, for example, to drink wine, eat meat or indulge in luxuries (but there are exceptions).[129]

Fourthly, funerals may be held in the synagogue, funeral home or at the grave. The funeral service is usually brief and simple and normally includes the chanting of psalms (by the cantor), a traditional memorial prayer and a eulogy. Viewing the body publicly or privately is contrary to Jewish tradition. At a funeral, the casket may be covered with a specially prepared cloth or pall, and is borne from the funeral service to the grave by family or friends selected by the mourners. The pallbearers customarily stop seven times while carrying the casket to the grave. The mourners,

---

[127] Autopsies are contrary to Jewish law, being viewed as a desecration of the body. If an autopsy is recommended, the family may refuse, but if civil law requires one, it should be carried out under the supervision of a Rabbi. Organ donation may be seen as *K'vod Hamet* (respect for the dead); bringing healing to the living is permissible and may be considered a *mitzvah*. The Rabbi should be consulted. Embalming (unless required by civil law) and the use of cosmetics on the deceased are not permitted.

[128] USCJ: Guide to Jewish Funeral Practice, 3.

[129] USCJ: Guide to Jewish Funeral Practice, 4.

family and friends follow the casket as a mark of respect. In traditional practice, the casket is lowered into the earth and the grave filled, using a reversed shovel until a mound is formed over the casket. The Kaddish is recited at the grave after *k'vurah* is completed. There are different customs/variations and the Rabbi should be consulted. It is customary for the mourners to pass between two rows of people in attendance to receive traditional expressions of consolation, and, after the burial, to wash their hands on leaving the cemetery or before entering the house of mourning. As a rule, non-Jews may not be buried in a Jewish cemetery; the Rabbi should be consulted.[130]

Fifthly, cremation is against Jewish tradition and the family should be so advised by the Rabbi. If a family ignores the advice, the Rabbi may choose to officiate in the funeral parlour before cremation. Ashes should be interred in a Jewish cemetery in private without a Rabbi. An urn should have an opening so that the ashes come into contact with the earth.[131]

Sixthly, as to mourning, mourners are those whose parent, spouse, child or sibling has died. The seven days of *shivah* begin on the day of the burial. During the period, mourners are encouraged to absent themselves from work or school and remain at home. Public mourning observances are suspended on the Shabbat in view of the belief that the sanctity and serenity of this day supersedes personal grief. Mourners are permitted, and encouraged, to attend Shabbat services; but they are not called up to read the Torah (*aliyah*), may not conduct services and do not display the *k'riah* publicly. The major festivals terminate *shivah*. It is customary for: the name of the deceased to be recalled at the Shabbat service after the funeral; family and friends to arrange for a condolence meal (*seudat havra'a*); mirrors in the *shivah* home to be covered; a seven-day memorial candle to be kindled; the mourners to refrain from wearing leather shoes and males from shaving. Every day, the mourner recites Kaddish at the Shaharit, Minha and Ma'ariv service; a *minyan* is required (and if one cannot be assured, the mourner attends the synagogue service). During the first 30 days after burial, following observance of *shivah*, mourners continue to wear the *k'riah*, return to their work but refrain from public entertainment or social activities.

---

[130] USCJ: Guide to Jewish Funeral Practice 5.

[131] This position is the result of a *teshuva* adopted by the Rabbinical Assembly, Committee on Jewish Law and Standards in 1986. This is one of many *teshuvot* on death, burial and mourning.

Mourners for deceased parents must attend services daily to recite the Kaddish for 11 Hebrew months, and continue to refrain from public celebratory activities. The Kaddish is recited each year on the Hebrew calendar anniversary of the death when it is also customary to light a 24-hour candle, study a portion of Torah or Mishnah and donate *tzedakah*. Memorial prayers are recited on Yom Kippur, Sh'mini Atzeret, the eighth day of Pesach and second day of Shavuot. Some light a candle on each such occasion, others only on Yom Kippur.[132] An intermarried Jew may be buried in a Jewish cemetery; a Rabbi may not officiate at the funeral of a Jew who is intermarried and is to be buried in a cemetery of another faith group; a suicide considered to be the result of mental illness does not disqualify a Jew from burial in a Jewish cemetery.[133]

Whilst *halakhah* allows for the Jewish burial of an apostate even while forbidding mourning, Conservative Judaism would prohibit Jewish burial rites to the apostate.[134]

Christian Funeral Rites

Unlike Jews, generally, Christians have few funeral laws.[135] As such, the principles of Christian law on the matter are simply: the faithful who have died should be given a church funeral according to the norms of law; and disposal of human remains may be either by burial or by cremation accompanied by the administration of any service authorised for lawful use in a church.[136] For example, Roman Catholic canon law classifies a funeral as a 'sacramental',[137] and it provides for the anointing of the sick and dying.[138] The faithful are to be given a church funeral

---

[132] USCJ: Guide to Jewish Funeral Practice 6.

[133] USCJ: Guide to Jewish Funeral Practice 7.

[134] USCJ: Rabbinical Assembly, Committee on Jewish Law and Standards: Yoreh deah 340:5 (1994).

[135] Nor do most churches have the rite of confession. Yet, a church may practise private confession and absolution in the presence of an ordained minister if permitted by its law. The seal of the confessional is inviolable, save as may be provided by church law. A duty of confidentiality attaches to the exercise of ministry to the extent provided by law; Christian Law Panel of Experts, *Principles of Christian Law* (2016) VII.5.

[136] Christian Law Panel of Experts, *Principles of Christian Law* (2016) VII.6.

[137] CIC: c. 1166: 'Sacramentals are signs by which, somewhat after the fashion of the sacraments, effects, especially spiritual ones, are signified and are obtained through the intercession of the Church'; c. 1167: only the Apostolic See may establish them; c. 1168: the minister is a cleric but some sacramentals may be administered by qualified lay people; they also include blessings, vows and oaths.

[138] CIC. cc. 999-1007. this is a sacrament.

conducted according to the liturgical books; in its funeral rites 'the
Church prays for the spiritual support of the dead, honours their bodies,
and at the same time brings to the living the comfort of hope' – whereas
burial is recommended as a 'pious custom', cremation is not forbidden.[139] A funeral should normally be carried out in the parish church
of the deceased who should be buried in the parish cemetery if there is
one – if not, another is chosen.[140] A burial is registered.[141] For funerals,
catechumens are considered among the faithful, and children who die
before baptism but whose parents had intended their baptism may be
allowed a funeral by the bishop. However, unless they gave a sign of
repentance before death, funeral rites are denied to: notorious apostates,
heretics and schismatics; those who for anti-Christian motives chose
their bodies to be cremated; and other manifest sinners to whom a
funeral could not occur without public scandal – and in cases of doubt,
the bishop must be consulted and his judgment followed.[142]

In Anglican churches, to prepare a person for death a church may offer
anointing or imposition of hands. Disposal of a body may be either by
burial or by cremation. No minister may without lawful cause refuse or
delay disposal, in accordance with the funeral rites of a church, of the
remains of anyone brought to the designated place. Conducting funeral
rites for the non-baptised, suicides and excommunicates may be subject
to direction from the bishop. The minister is normally a bishop or priest
or, if neither is available, a deacon or an authorised lay person. The
choice of funeral rites, when alternatives are authorised, belongs to the
officiating minister consulting the family or friends of the deceased.
The remains of a Christian should be disposed of in a consecrated place
or, if not consecrated, in a place which has been blessed by a minister.[143]

---

[139] CIC: c. 1176: cremation is forbidden if 'chosen for reasons contrary to Christian teaching'.

[140] CIC: c. 1177: the faithful may choose another church with the consent of its minister; cc. 1178–1179: funerals of bishops and religious; c. 1180: 'All may, however, choose their cemetery . . . unless prohibited by law'; c. 1242: permission must be obtained to bury in a church unless it is e.g. a bishop.

[141] CIC: c. 1182; c. 1181: funeral offerings may be made; 'the poor are not deprived of a proper burial'.

[142] CIC: cc. 1183–1184.

[143] PCLCCAC: Principle 79. See e.g. Church of England: Can. B38.2: 'It shall be the duty of every minister to bury, according to the rites of the Church of England, the corpse or ashes of any person deceased within his cure of souls or of any parishioners or persons whose names are entered on the electoral roll' of the parish; B38.2: special rites may be permitted for suicides of unsound mind.

There is not a great deal of material on funerals in the Protestant juridical instruments studied here; however, in the (Presbyterian) Church of Scotland, burial or cremation is lawful, but a funeral service is not required – but this is the practice.[144]

Akhirah and Mayat

Islam understands that 'the entire purpose of life . . . is to earn reward in the next world [*akhirah*, afterlife] by worshipping Allah alone in the manner which He commanded and which was demonstrated by Muhammad'; the life of a person is measured on the Day of Judgment.[145] The Universal Islamic Declaration of Human Rights (1981) provides that: 'Just as in life, so also after death, the sanctity of a person's body shall be inviolable. It is the obligation of believers to see that a deceased person's body is handled with due solemnity.'[146] On the death of a Muslim, it is for the family of the deceased to prepare the body (*mayat*) for washing, perform the washing and lead funerary prayers. The body is washed three times (orifices being sealed with cotton), shrouded and perfumed. When death occurs during *hajj*, the shroud of a man must be seamless, and the face of a woman must be uncovered; if the person is martyred, the body is not washed and it is buried in the clothes in which they die.[147] Special prayers (*salat al-janazah*) are offered, often at the mosque. Throughout the washing, prayers and burial, the body is to face Mecca. The body must be buried as soon as possible, preferably before nightfall on the day of death. It is carried to the grave in an open bier, followed by a funeral party composed only of males, and buried without a coffin in a grave of sufficient depth to

---

[144] J.L. Weatherhead, ed., *Constitution and Laws of the Church of Scotland* (1997) 36: also, a dead body should be interred 'without any ceremony'.

[145] M. Naqshbandi, *Islam and Muslims in Britain* (2012): Guide 2.1.3: Submission to the *hudood*, the Islamic criminal code, ensures freedom from the punishment of sin in the afterlife. Children are born sinless and remain so until they reach puberty. The insane are also sinless, and they and children are guaranteed Paradise if they die in these states.

[146] UIDHR (1981): Art. 1.

[147] J.L. Esposito, ed., *Oxford Dictionary of Islam* (2003) 193: a martyr (*shahid*) is one who suffers or dies while performing a religious duty; death during pilgrimage or childbirth is a form of martyrdom; a martyr is freed from sin by that meritorious act and so entitled to immediate entry into paradise with a special status. For some Sunni scholars, ritual fasting, regular prayer, Quran reading, devotion to others and rectitude in giving are types of moral martyrdom; Shia Islam also values martyrdom (after that of Husayn in 680).

conceal odour and prevent abuse by animals. Close male relatives descend into the grave with the body to turn the face towards Mecca.[148] Cremation is prohibited as desecration of a body. One dying in a fire is a martyr.[149]

Muslim councils and mosques may offer funeral advice and services,[150] or else they list in their objects provision of a Muslim burial ground.[151] For instance, the objects of the Muslim Burial Council of Leicestershire are: the advancement of the Islamic faith by meeting the religious needs of the Muslim community by procedures and practices relating to burial; to advance the education of the general public in relation to Islamic burial; to relieve poverty and advance the education of Muslims through the provision of welfare advice on burial; and to assist in such associated charitable purposes as its Governing Body determines.[152] The Trustees may, for example: raise funds and invite and receive contributions; sell, lease or otherwise dispose of property comprised in the trust fund; appoint and constitute advisory committees; and employ its own staff.[153]

The Council has issued detailed guidance about funerals and burials, which must be carried out in 'a dignified manner and according to the rulings of the Islamic Shariah'; it also has guidance on organ donation and organ transplantation. As a general rule, in the whole process, a body should be handled with 'the utmost respect, gentleness and decency'. First, when a Muslim is near death, those around him/her are called on to

---

[148] J.L. Esposito, ed., *Oxford Dictionary of Islam* (2003) 88–89.

[149] M. Naqshbandi, *Islam and Muslims in Britain* (2012): Guide 6.4.

[150] The Council for Mosques (Bradford) provides burial services for Muslims at two designated sites, and works closely with the Bradford Council and Coroner for families to bury the dead 'in accordance with their religious requirements and practice': www.councilformosques.org/muslim-burial-services. At Birmingham Central Mosque, Yemeni and Somali 'sisters' prepare the bodies of women: www.centralmosque.org.uk. At East London Mosque and Islamic Centre: 'funeral rites for Muslims must be observed according to religious guidelines' and a funeral service is based at the mosque (e.g. to collect the body and to arrange prayers and the funeral): www.eastlondonmosque.org.uk.

[151] NUIM: Con. Art. 2: 'a Muslim burial ground'; CJM: Con. Art. 4.7: it is to 'assist in arrangements for the burial of deceased Muslims'; and Art. 22: 'The funeral service shall be provided to the Muslim community on a voluntary basis and free of costs, except the cost of the grave which is to be paid direct to the local authority' by the family of the deceased; AMIC: Art. 7.4: Funeral Assistance Committee.

[152] Muslim Burial Council of Leicestershire (MBCOL): Con. Art. 2.

[153] MBCOL: Con. Art. 3: Art. 4–7: eligibility, election and removal of Trustees; Art. 9: officers; Art. 10: membership is open to Muslim organisations and funeral arrangers; and Art. 11: Governing Body.

comfort and remind the person of God's mercy and forgiveness, and they are encouraged to recite Quranic verses. The person dying may also recite words of prayer, and it is recommended that a Muslim's last words should be the declaration of faith: 'I bear witness that there is no God but Allah' – but there should be no coercion to recite this. Offering water and physical comfort are also recommended. Secondly, upon death, those with the deceased are encouraged to pray for the departed and begin preparations for burial. Members of the same sex or of the immediate family should perform ritual washing (*ghusl*), removing any medical appliances, dressing incisions to prevent blood flow, closing the eyes of the deceased; they should also bind the lower jaw so that the mouth is held closed; fasten the ankles together; place the arms straight down the side of the body with straightened fingers; and wrap the body in a clean sheet. Muslims must strive to bury the deceased as soon as possible after death; therefore, it is not unusual for the deceased to be buried within 24 hours of death.[154]

Thirdly, to attend the *janazah* prayer at the mosque and the burial of a Muslim is *fard kifayah*, a religious duty, which, if performed by a few Muslims, absolves the rest of the community from this responsibility. If no one discharges the obligation, the entire Muslim community is con-sidered to be jointly accountable in the eyes of Allah.[155] The funeral prayer is a Muslim ritual which must be performed by Muslims, though observers are welcome. Muslim women commonly do not attend the funeral; but a non-Muslim woman may attend. The dress for men and (and non-Muslim women) should be modest; a headscarf is essential for women; shoes are removed before going into the prayer hall.[156] The congregation line up in rows behind the coffin to perform the funeral prayer for the deceased, then in two lines, they pass the coffin from shoulder to shoulder, taking it towards the gravesite. Visitors may follow the congregation as they move the coffin towards the grave. At the grave, the coffin is lowered usually by members of the family, and the grave filled. The Imam will then say final prayers at the graveside, and, following this, the congregation disperses while immediate family

---

[154] MBCOL: www.mbcol.org.uk/funeral-procedure.

[155] To avoid disputes about the body of a Muslim convert, when non-Muslim relatives may wish to dispose of it in a 'non-Islamic way', a convert should complete the MBCOL Statutory Declaration, for disposal to follow Islamic requirements, which should be lodged with a solicitor or local mosque.

[156] This means a shirt and trousers for men and an ankle length skirt, which should not be tight or transparent, together with a long-sleeved and high-necked top for the women.

members remain at the graveside for a short time in order to receive condolences.[157]

The Muslim Burial Council of Leicestershire also addresses organ transplantation or donation. It explains that for some Muslim scholars it is not permissible; but others permit it under certain conditions: 'To our knowledge no recognised Institution has given a general unconditional permission' for it; and 'it is impossible . . . to find express rulings concerning it in the classical works'. As such, the views of some scholars are based upon the 'general guidelines' of *shariah*. Some of the classical works suggest it is not permissible to derive benefit from a human body through transplants, since the body, dead or alive has great significance and is to be honoured – and the sanctity attached to it makes it unlawful to tamper with it. However, established principles (*qawa'id*) of Islamic jurisprudence, based on the teachings of the Quran and Sunnah, permit the use of unlawful things in cases of extreme necessity – for instance, when the life of a person is threatened, the rule against eating carrion or drinking wine is suspended. Organ transplantation may be permissible to save the life of another. The Council thus believes the issue needs further consideration in order 'to come to certainty' through 'honest debate and guidance from all of our learned Ulamaa'. As a result, the Council 'recommends' that 'individuals must clarify their personal position' on matters of organ transplantation 'with their local Mosque'.[158]

Conclusion

The rites of passage represent an important aspect of the journey through life of Jews, Christians and Muslims. All of the religious entities studied in this chapter provide in their laws for the administration of rites at the beginning of life and during adolescence. Male circumcision after birth in Judaism is normative, and, in Islam, some consider it to be permissive and others obligatory. It takes place after birth or at around the age of 12 – however, the Jewish religious office of circumciser has no obvious parallel in Islam.

Christian baptism echoes Jewish ritual washing in terms of action – but the effects differ – and in Christianity baptism incorporates a person

---

[157] MBCOL: www.mbcol.org.uk/funeral-procedure/attending-a-muslim-funeral-a-guide-for-non-muslims/.

[158] MBCOL: www.mbcol.org.uk/funeral-procedure/organ-transplantion/.   See   also M. Naqshbandi, *Islam and Muslims in Britain* (2012): Guide 6.4.1–10.

into the church universal, whereas Jewish immersion does not affect status. Muslims too have ritual washing, but later in life. Both Jews and Christians have a system of sponsors and instruction prior to these rites. The *bar/batmitzvah* in Judaism finds a conceptual parallel in Christian baptism (one effects admission to the covenant, the other to the church) as does confirmation (or mature profession of the faith) in adolescence or adulthood – and both religions cast their rules in terms of rights and duties. Muslim circumcision, performed in adolescence, may or may not be a conceptual equivalent to these – and the modern regulatory instruments of the Muslim communities studied here are silent on it.

With regard to rites in the spiritual development of the individual during adulthood, again there are juridical parallels in terms of action. Jewish ritual immersion and dietary discipline find no obvious parallel in Christianity, but the Christian celebration of the Eucharist, Holy Communion or Lord's Supper draws on the Jewish commemorative Passover. The rites of spiritual development in Islam are mandatory fasting, dietary discipline and pilgrimage. For all three religions, these are theocratic to the extent that they are understood as institutions of divine law and they are in turn regulated by detailed rules of primary religious law. However, while Jews and Christians have a large body of legislation, and sometimes religious soft-law, on these subjects, the principal vehicle used by the Muslim communities studied here is religious soft-law. With regard to funerary rites, Christians have few rules on the preparation of a body for disposal or funerals. By way of contrast, there is abundant Jewish and Islamic law on preparation of the body, the administration of funerals and the period of mourning after death. Elements of classical Jewish and Islamic law surface in the regulatory instruments of Jewish and Muslim organisations today, particularly with regard to bodies/societies responsible for burial. As to legal diversity, Christians permit cremation, Muslims do not and the Jewish traditions differ on the matter. Generally, however, across the subjects studied here, there is little diversity within and between the religions on all these matters – this area is, therefore, very fruitful for the articulation of common principles of religious law.

8

The Family, Marriage and Children

There has been considerable public debate in recent years about the civil recognition of religious law on marriage, particularly in the context of Islam.[1] The protection of children in family life and in religious contexts is also topical – including at Christian schools – as is that of radicalisation within the Muslim community.[2] Debates of this sort raise associated issues about how religious law deals with marriages conducted within the faith community (whether or not recognised by civil law), and the religious upbringing of children. These subjects also tell us much about the degree to which religious law impinges upon essentially private matters of family life and whether this is properly a matter of concern to religious organisations. The first two sections of the chapter explore the laws of Judaism, Christianity and Islam on religious marriages – their formation, dissolution and (where appropriate) annulment – and, briefly, their positions on civil partnerships and same-sex marriages. The third section examines religious law on children, including parental rights with respect to their religious upbringing, the religious autonomy of the child and norms on child protection (or safeguarding) in the life of the faith community itself. In the wider civil legal environment, the State must respect private and family life,[3] and men and women of marriageable age

---

[1] In 2008, the Archbishop of Canterbury saw it as 'unavoidable' that some *sharia* on e.g. marriage would be recognised by civil law: R. Williams, 'Civil and religious law in England: a religious perspective', 10 *Ecclesiastical Law Journal* (2008) 262. See also A. Shachar, 'Entangled: state and religion and the family', in R. Ahdar and N. Aroney, eds., *Shari'a in the West* (Oxford: Oxford University Press, 2010) Ch. 8.

[2] See e.g. *Raggett* v. *Society of Jesus Trust of 1929 for Roman Catholic Purposes & Anor* [2010] EWCA Civ. 1002 (27 August 2010): where school governors had accepted vicarious liability for the conduct of a Jesuit teacher alleged to have sexually abused a pupil and there was evidence of such abuse, it was a proper exercise for a judge to allow the action to proceed even though it was outside the limitation period and time-barred (under the Limitation Act 1980, s. 33); see also *Maga* v. *Trustees of the Birmingham Archdiocese of the Roman Catholic Church* [2010] EWCA Civ. 256 (16 March 2010).

[3] ECHR Art. 8.

have the right both to marry and to found a family, in accordance with the national laws governing the exercise of this right.[4] Moreover, the European Court of Human Rights has held that freedom of religion does not override national judicial proceedings instituted to protect a minor who has suffered as a result of entry to a marriage permitted under religious law.[5] The chapter also seeks to elucidate the extent of legal diversity/similarity within and across the faiths on these matters, and the degree to which norms are theocratic or the result of the use of practical reason.

Religious Marriage

The juridical instruments of Jewish, Christian and Muslim organisations studied here address the nature of marriage, formation of marriage (such as the rights and capacity of parties to marry), and its ritual solemnisation (including the role of faith leaders). The laws of some communities also address the conduct of the parties during the life of the marriage and the nurture of children born within marriage. In England and Wales, a marriage solemnised according to the rites of the established Church of England (which includes for this purpose the disestablished Church in Wales) is valid in civil law;[6] and a person having a qualifying connection with the parish has a right to be married in its church.[7] Civil law also recognises marriages conducted according to the usages of the Society of Friends (Quakers) and Jews (but only between two professing the Jewish religion);[8] civil and religious marriages are also recognised in Scotland.[9] According to State law, marriages may be solemnised in a

---

[4] ECHR Art. 12; see also Art. 14 on discrimination – this may also be relevant.

[5] *Khan* v. *UK*, Appl. No. 11579/85 (1986) 48 D&R 253: the abduction of and unlawful sexual intercourse with a 14 year old girl were not justified on the basis of a marriage under Islamic law; that an action etc. is 'permitted' by religion does not render it a lawful manifestation of religious freedom; see P. Taylor, *Freedom of Religion* (Cambridge: Cambridge University Press, 2005) 213.

[6] Marriage Act 1949, s. 26.

[7] Church of England Marriage Measure 2008; the special status of the church may be at odds with ECHR Art. 14: *R (Baiai, Trzcinska, Bigoku and Tilki)* v. *Secretary of State for the Home Department* [2006] EWHC 823, subsequently approved [2008] UKHL 53.

[8] Marriage Act 1949, s. 47 (Quakers), s. 26 (Jews).

[9] Scotland: marriages by habit and repute constitute valid marriages if begun before 2006: Family Law (Scotland) Act 2006; civil and religious marriages are governed by the Marriage (Scotland) Act 1977.

building which is certified as a place of worship and registered for the solemnisation of marriage.[10]

Erusin, Ketubah and Nissuin

Traditionally in Judaism, marriage is understood as a contract commanded by God by which a man and a woman unite to create a relationship in which God is directly involved (Deuteronomy 24:1). Whilst procreation is not its sole purpose, traditionally the spouses are expected to fulfil the commandment to have children (Genesis 1:28). Jewish law contains a list of forbidden marriages which, if attempted, are invalid.[11] Reform and Liberal Judaism recognize same-sex marriage and de-emphasize procreation – focusing on marriage as a bond between the parties – but Orthodox Judaism does not.[12] In Jewish law, marriage consists of two separate acts: betrothal (*erusin* or *kiddushin*, meaning sanctification), which effects a change in the status of the parties; and the marriage ceremony (*nissuin* or *chuppah*), which generates consequential rights and duties. At betrothal, the man gives the woman, in the presence of two unrelated male witnesses, an object of value (such as a ring), or a document declaratory of betrothal. The ceremony follows usually after one year.[13] The written marriage contract (*ketubah*) states the marital duties of the husband.[14] Under it, the man undertakes to protect, work for and sustain his wife, and to honour her rights; it also seeks to prevent the husband from divorcing the wife against her will. If divorce occurs, the man assumes the duty to provide a settlement (the amount also known as *ketubah*) for the woman or for any heir if the husband pre-deceases the wife. The duties of the wife are

---

[10] Pursuant to the Marriage Act 1949, ss. 41–42 and the Places of Worship Registration Act 1855.

[11] Leviticus 18:16–30; 20:9–22: e.g. one between a sister and brother or mother and son; but though a nephew may not marry his aunt, a niece may marry her uncle; the marriage of a male child born of an adulterous or incestuous union (*mamzer*) to a Jew is not permitted but a *mamzer* may marry a female equivalent (*mamzeret*); a *kohen* may not marry a divorcee; a man may marry his deceased wife's sister. See e.g. N.S. Hecht *et al.*, eds., *Jewish Law* (1996) 135–139 and I. Herzog, *Jewish Law* (1980) 23, 67, 151, 359. See also R. Warburg, 'Breach of a promise to marry', 17 *The Jewish Law Annual* (2008) 267–282.

[12] M. Elon, ed., *The Principles of Jewish Law* (Piscataway, NJ: Transaction Publishers, 2007) 353. Polygamy was proscribed in the eleventh century CE.

[13] Following betrothal, the contract could not be dissolved without a religious divorce.

[14] *Ketubah* is from the root *katav* – to write.

not traditionally set out in the contract; but such contracts in Reform Judaism may spell out the duties of both parties.[15] The traditional marriage ceremony is observed fully by Orthodox Jews and with minor variations by Reform and Conservative Judaism. First, after signing the *ketubah*, the parties are escorted by the parents under the wedding canopy (*chuppah*), where the ceremony is performed and which symbolizes the home of the groom; often Psalm 10 is recited, a blessing given, and the Rabbi (officiant) delivers a brief address. Secondly, the Rabbi takes a cup of wine and recites the prescribed benediction; the bride and groom sip the wine and the groom places a ring on the right-hand forefinger of the bride declaring: 'Behold, thou art consecrated unto me by this ring, according to the law of Moses and Israel' – the *ketubah* is then read publicly. Thirdly, after further blessings, the spouses sip the wine again and the groom customarily stamps on a glass, breaking it – this is to remind the parties of the destruction of the Temple.[16]

The modern Jewish regulatory instruments deploy aspects of these traditional norms in their treatment of marriage.[17] In the (Orthodox) United Synagogue, 'Marriage under a *chuppah* involves, amongst other things, the acceptance of all the conditions and requirements of Jewish law.'[18] At the time of the ceremony, the bridegroom or bride must be members of a local synagogue. A ceremony must not take place under its auspices without the written authorisation of the Chief Rabbi. The local Honorary Officers must appoint a Secretary for Marriages at the Synagogue; beforehand, the name of the appointee must be forwarded to the Board of Deputies of British Jews for certification by the civil Registrar General in accordance with the Marriage Act 1949. The Secretary for Marriages must be: an employee/member of the synagogue; present at every marriage under its auspices; and register all marriages (in books provided by the Registrar General). At least seven days before the ceremony, all documents required by the Marriage Act 1949, and the

---

[15] L. Jacobs, *Jewish Religion* (1999) 123–124; see e.g. Exodus 21:10. Married life is to be characterised by *shalom bayit* – literally 'peace of the home' – marital harmony.

[16] L. Jacobs, *Jewish Religion* (1999) 146–147.

[17] See also the Guidebook for Secretaries (for Marriages) of Synagogues: HM Passport Office, General Register Office (2017).

[18] 'Marriage ... involves the intertwining of two lives at many different levels. In order to succeed, it requires the unremitting efforts of both husband and wife to be attentive and sensitive to each other's needs. Included in this are their spiritual needs'; also: 'the marriage relationship is the ideal state for enhancing and harnessing the spirituality latent in every man and woman'.

Chief Rabbi's authorisation (see below), must be delivered to the synagogue Secretary for Marriages, and all marriage fees and charges paid in full to the Administrator of the synagogue. Prior to the ceremony, the *ketubah*, in a form approved by the Chief Rabbi, must be prepared by or on behalf of the Rabbi: a marriage must not take place unless the Rabbi (or appointee) is satisfied as to the accuracy of the contract. Immediately before the ceremony, the contract, and a copy for synagogue records must be signed in the presence of the bridegroom by two males approved by the Rabbi. Immediately after the ceremony, the *ketubah*, and the copy must be signed by the bride in her previous name and (except where a civil marriage has already taken place) the bridegroom and bride must sign the entry in the Register of Marriages and its copy and their signatories must be attested by two witnesses.[19]

Before the ceremony, the parties must also, at a meeting at the Marriage Authorisation Department at the Office of the Chief Rabbi, 'produce evidence to establish ... Jewish status and eligibility to marry in accordance with Jewish Law', as well as numerous prescribed documents.[20] Moreover, any party who has been married before should produce: their previous *ketubah* or the date and place of their previous marriage; the death certificate of a former spouse; or, if applicable, their Jewish divorce certificate and civil decree absolute (see below); the Registrar's certificate; and a letter from a close relative resident in the UK stating that they have not remarried since becoming widowed/divorced.[21] The United Synagogue 'assumes' that all couples will sign the *ketubah* (or Pre-Nuptial Agreement) and it encourages them strongly to do so.[22] Other synagogues in the Orthodox tradition may broadly mirror these legal rules.[23]

---

[19] US: Bye-Laws, Sch. 3.1–8 (Regulations).

[20] US: Marriage Authorisation Department of the Office of the Chief Rabbi: Notes to the Bride and Groom. Documents include: the ketubah of the parents (or, if not available, the date and place of their marriage); a birth certificate; the Registrar's certificates; a letter from a parent or other close relative living in the UK stating that the parties have never been married before; their Hebrew names, where known, and those of their fathers and whether their fathers are 'Cohen', 'Levi' or 'Israelite'.

[21] US: http://chiefrabbi.org/notes-to-the-bride-and-groom/. A charge is payable for administrative costs.

[22] US: The Office of the Chief Rabbi: http://chiefrabbi.org/background-pre-nuptial-agreement/.

[23] NHC: Con. 5.8–12: 'All Orthodox marriages shall take place in conformity with the directions of the Chief Rabbi of Great Britain complying with all legislation and statutes [on] marriage in England and Wales.' See also NHAYS: Con. Art. 19: compliance with

The Movement for Reform Judaism has similar norms. Each synagogue should have a Marriage Secretary who must: be conversant with Reform practices; confirm the couple's capacity to marry and, with the synagogue Administrator and Rabbi, their Jewish lineage; have custody of all relevant paperwork and certificates and ensure that the couple comply with the rules on registration; attend the ceremony; and carry out other duties such as writing certificates and organising witnesses.[24] The synagogue Administrator discharges a number of duties. First, the Administrator must discuss the marriage with the couple and check available dates with the Rabbi and Marriage Secretary prior to agreeing a date and time. Secondly, the Administrator must ensure the parties are aware of their duties to the synagogue, that they have been members of it for at least six months (i.e. in their own right not by right of their parents) and that they are aware of the costs and the services available (e.g. flowers, choir, organist). Thirdly, the Administrator acts as wedding organiser, and must *inter alia* ensure that: the Rabbi will be present and that there is wine, a glass and a *ketubah* available; a *chuppah* is erected, the synagogue is clean and ready, and a space is prepared for the veiling ceremony (*bedeken*). Next, he must: notify the singers, organise rehearsals, the organist and singer of the blessings; ensure that security is prepared; and notify the Honorary Secretary of the dates of the wedding and any *aufruf*.[25] In turn, at the local level, synagogues may have additional norms – for example, the Council of North London Reform Synagogue may make regulations in relation to 'the conditions to be observed and fees to be paid in connection with marriage in the Synagogue'.[26]

The Union of Liberal and Progressive Synagogues has norms on same-sex and mixed unions. It affirms 'the Jewish home as a "little sanctuary" (*mikdash m'at*), filled with the beauty of holiness, in which the values and traditions of Judaism can be exemplified, taught and transmitted from generation to generation'.[27] On the basis of 'the equal status of men and women in marriage law', the 'bride and bridegroom alike play an active role in the Jewish marriage service'; and because

---

'Civil Law' and members are 'entitled' to marry there – non-members may do so subject to approval by the Rabbi and Wardens.

[24] MRJ: Code of Practice, p. 15: the Synagogue Council appoints a Marriage Secretary and Assistant. See also P.S. Koebel, 'Reform Judaism and same-sex marriage: a halakhic inquiry', in W. Jacob and M. Zemer, *Gender Issues in Jewish Law* (2001) 169–183.

[25] MRJ: Code of Practice, p. 15: the *aufruf* is the *aliyah* for the groom (calling up to read the Torah).

[26] NLRS: Laws, Art. 19.   [27] ULPS. *Affirmations* (2006) Art 14

'there are loving, committed relationships other than marriage between a man and a woman, [it] recognises the right of Jewish same-sex couples, with and without children, to receive equal treatment in all areas of congregational life, including the right to celebrate their partnerships with a Service of Commitment conducted by a Rabbi'.[28] Moreover, congregations should provide the opportunity for mixed couples (a Jew and a non-Jew) to solemnise their partnerships with an Act of Prayer conducted by a Rabbi.[29] Member synagogues implement these norms.[30] For the United Synagogue of Conservative Judaism, marriage: 'marks [a] commitment to the Jewish people'; has 'an element of sanctity'; and involves a 'ceremony [which] evokes God's presence'.[31] However, interfaith marriages are prohibited by the Standards of Rabbinic Practice of the Rabbinical Assembly and so not permitted in the synagogue or any facility controlled by the congregation which thus may not engage anyone to conduct such marriages.[32]

Christian Marriage

Christians have a long juristic tradition as to the nature, formation, and solemnisation of marriage – complex bodies of church law on the subject were administered in the courts of the Church of England after the Reformation until 1857 and the enactment of parliamentary statute transferring jurisdiction to the civil courts.[33] Nonetheless, the historic churches retain norms on marriage. According to the principles of Christian law, the foundation of marriage is a lifelong union between one man and one woman. Marriage is instituted by God and for the well-being of the spouses. To be married validly in the eyes of the church, the parties must satisfy the conditions prescribed by church law and should be instructed in the nature and obligations of marriage. Marriage is

---

[28] ULPS: *Affirmations* (2006) Art. 34.
[29] ULPS: *Affirmations* (2006) Art. 36: such couples where possible should be buried in its cemeteries.
[30] See e.g. ELS: Con. Art. 4; PLJC: Con. Art. 3.
[31] USCJ: http://uscj.org/JewishLivingandLearning/Lifecycle/AKosherWedding.aspx.
[32] USCJ: Standards for Congregational Practice (2017): Standard IV: congregations should refer to 'A Return to the Mitzvah of Endogamy' (1992), 'May a Reception Following an Intermarriage be Held in a Conservative Synagogue?' (1987) and 'Congratulations to Mixed Marriage Families' (1989).
[33] See J.H. Baker, *An Introduction to English Legal History* (Oxford: Oxford University Press, 4th edn, 2007) 479–499: this provides an excellent overview up to the Matrimonial Causes Act 1857.

celebrated in the presence of an authorised person and should be regis-tered.[34] These principles derive from the similarities of the laws of the churches.

Under Roman Catholic canon law, Christian marriage is a divine institution: 'The marriage covenant, by which a man and a woman establish between themselves a partnership of their whole life, and which of its own very nature is ordered to the well-being of the spouses and to the procreation and upbringing of children, has, between the baptised, been raised by Christ the Lord to the dignity of a sacrament.' If two baptised persons' marriage is valid, their marriage is a sacrament – and the 'essential properties of marriage are unity and indissolubility'.[35] A marriage is brought into being by 'the lawfully manifested consent of persons who are legally capable'; consent is 'an act of will by which a man and a woman by an irrevocable covenant mutually give and accept one another for the purpose of establishing a marriage'.[36] Indeed, all those who are not prohibited by law have 'a right to marriage'; and baptism is required for sacramental marriage in church.[37] The 'diriment impedi-ments' prevent a person from validly contracting marriage: lack of age, physical impotence, prior marriage bond, consanguinity and affinity.[38] Persons incapable of contracting marriage include those who lack the sufficient use of reason, suffer from a grave lack of judgment concerning the essential matrimonial rights and duties and through causes of a psychological nature are unable to assume the essential obligations of marriage.[39] Other grounds vitiating consent include ignorance, error about the identity of the partner, fraud, simulation of consent, fear and force.[40] As a rule, only those marriages are valid which are contracted in the presence of a priest or deacon and two witnesses – the rite must be conducted in accordance with the liturgical books, and the essential element of the rite is the exchange of consents.[41] When there is doubt

---

[34] Christian Law Panel of Experts, *Principles of Christian Law* (2016) VII.4.

[35] CIC: c. 1055: 'a valid marriage contract cannot exist between baptised persons without its being by that very fact a sacrament'; c. 1056: essential properties.

[36] CIC: c. 1057: this consent cannot be supplied by any human power.

[37] CIC: c. 1058; c. 1059: the marriage of Catholics (even if only one party is Catholic) is governed by divine law and canon law, 'without prejudice to the competence of civil authority in respect of the merely civil effects of the marriage'.

[38] CIC: cc. 1083–1085: age, impotence and prior marriage; cc. 1091–1092: consanguinity and affinity.

[39] CIC: c. 1095.   [40] CIC: cc. 1096–1099, 1101–1103.

[41] CIC: c. 1108; cc. 1115–1116: place; cc. 1119–1120: Episcopal Conferences may approve local rites.

about the validity of a marriage there is a presumption it is valid until the contrary is proven; the annulment of marriages is the function of the tribunals of the church.[42] Pastors must provide assistance in the preparation of couples for marriage and the faithful must both support marriage and assist in the provision of pastoral care for spouses.[43]

The Anglican model is not dissimilar. Marriage, an honourable estate instituted by God, is an exclusive life-long union, signifying the mystical union that is between Christ and his Church. It is constituted on the free exchange of consents between one man and one woman joined together by God as husband and wife and lasting until the death of one spouse. Marriage is a creative relationship to share life together in the spirit of Christ for the: development of their personalities; procreation and nurture of children; right use of the natural instincts and affections; mutual society, help and comfort which the one ought to have for the other, in prosperity and adversity; and establishment of a home and family life.[44] Ministers must comply with civil law as to the formation of marriage and church law as to its solemnisation.[45] An ecclesiastical marriage is presumed valid if both parties: have a right under civil law to contract it; freely and knowingly consent to marry, without fraud, coercion, or mistake as to the identity or mental condition of the other party; do not fall within the prohibited degrees of relationship; have attained the required age, and, in the case of minors, have obtained the consent of their parents or guardians.[46] A church is free to impose for spiritual purposes such conditions for admission to ecclesiastical marriage as are prescribed by its law. While a Christian marriage is one between baptised persons, the law may provide for marriage where the normal requirement of baptism is not met. Generally, a minister may refuse to solemnise a marriage for such cause, which may include

---

[42] CIC: c. 1087: clerics 'invalidly attempt marriage'; c. 1088: chastity; c. 1086: disparity of cult.

[43] CIC: cc. 1063–1064; c. 1065: unconfirmed Catholics must receive confirmation before marriage; c. 1066: 'Before a marriage . . . it must be established that nothing stands in the way of its valid and lawful celebration'; c. 1067: the Episcopal Conference is to issue norms as to preliminaries (e.g. banns); c. 1069: the faithful must reveal to the parish priest or local ordinary impediments they know about.

[44] PCLCCAC: Principle 70; see also AR, Art. 25. See e.g. Church of England: Can. B30.1.

[45] PCLCCAC: Principle 71.1; 71.2: 'The parties to a marriage must satisfy the civil and ecclesiastical requirements for a valid marriage. Otherwise the minister should refuse solemnisation.'

[46] PCLCCAC: Principle 71.3. See e.g. Church of England: Can. B31–32.

conscientious objection, as is provided by the law.[47] A minister should instruct the parties in the nature, significance, purpose and responsibilities of marriage. Lawful notice of the date of the marriage must be given to the minister who must establish that no impediment obstructs its valid celebration under canon law and civil law; if any impediment is alleged, marriage should be deferred until the truth is established.[48] The ordinary minister is a priest or bishop, but the man and woman may also be understood as both recipients and ministers of marriage; deacons too may be authorised to solemnise marriage. The liturgical books must be used. A marriage is created by the free, competent and open consent of the parties in the presence of at least two witnesses. The marriage is recorded in registers maintained in the church for this purpose. A civil marriage may be followed by a blessing of it in the church.[49]

The Protestant churches also treat marriage as a divine institution and provide for its formation and solemnisation. By way of illustration, for the Methodist Church in Great Britain, marriage is 'a gift of God and . . . it is God's intention that a marriage should be a life-long union in body, mind and spirit of one man and one woman'. The solemnisation of marriage in church is open to those beyond its membership.[50] The marriage ceremony occurs after due counsel with the parties involved.[51] However, if a request is received 'to conduct prayers for a same-sex couple, the person approached should respond sensitively, pastorally and with due regard to established good practice' – 'no minister or layperson is required to act in any way contrary to his or her own conscience'; but: 'Methodist premises may not be used for the blessing

---

[47] PCLCCAC: Principle 71: a church may relax baptismal requirements for marriage by way of e.g. dispensation of a bishop; a person, being a member of, associated with, or resident in a parish of, a church, may be entitled to a church marriage. See e.g. Church of England Marriage Measure 2008: the common law right of parish residents extends to persons with a 'qualifying connection' to the parish.

[48] PCLCCAC: Principle 72.1–6; 72.4: it may be solemnised following e.g. publication of banns.

[49] PCLCCAC: Principle 73. For England, see e.g. M. Hill, *Ecclesiastical Law* (2007) paras. 5.31–5.50. The Scottish Episcopal Church permits same-sex marriages; the other Anglican churches do not.

[50] MCGB: Constitutional Practice and Discipline, Standing Orders 011A: 'The Methodist Church welcomes everyone, whether or not a member, who enquires about an intended marriage in any of its places of worship.'

[51] MCGB: Constitutional Practice and Discipline, Bk. VI, Pt. 2, s. 9: Christian Preparation for Marriage: Methodist Church Policy and Guidelines, s. 10, Guidelines for Inter-Faith Marriages, s. 14: the 'traditional teaching of the Church on human sexuality' is 'chastity for all outside marriage and fidelity within it'.

of same-sex relationships.'[52] Presbyterians have the same general approach. For the Presbyterian Churches of Wales, for instance, marriage is 'a holy estate instituted by God. It is based on natural tendencies and needs, and it is an expression of the Divine intention in our creation, to realise moral and spiritual ends.' It is 'the duty' of the church to 'explain the true nature of marriage to its members, to impress upon them the sacred responsibilities and obligations of married life, and to show how divine grace can help to maintain and enrich the marriage bond'; marriage 'essentially permanent in character should be upheld to the utmost'; there are also norms on the ceremony.[53] Very few rules about marriage are found in the instruments of Baptists.[54]

The Nikah, Mahr and Wali

In traditional Islam, marriage is understood as ordained by God as part of the divine guidance for all people; it is not obligatory but highly recommended. Marriage is a legal contract (*nikah*), not a religious rite but it has a religious or spiritual dimension. Engagement is not required but may be practised. Essential requirements (*rukun*) for marriage are that: the parties are a man and a woman of marriageable age (puberty) – a Muslim man may marry a 'woman of the book' (*kittabiyah*), including a Christian or Jew, but a Muslim woman may not marry a non-Muslim (unless he converts to Islam); the parties must not be prohibited by consanguinity or affinity; and the parties must consent to the marriage (and the consent of the bride's guardian (*wali*) may be required). Also, there must be an offer and acceptance (*ijab* and *qabul*) so as to form a contract; a dowry (*mahr*) must be paid by the groom to the bride; the parties should be equal in status (*kufw*) but not be engaged in *ihram* for *hajj* or *umrah*; and the bride must not be married (*iddah*) and the groom must not have more than three wives.[55] A husband and wife must display mutual care, respect and consideration to each other.[56]

---

[52] MCGB: Constitutional Practice and Discipline, Bk. VI, Pt. 2, s. 15: the Superintendent should be consulted in cases of doubt.

[53] PCW: Handbook of Rules, 9.4.   [54] See N. Doe, *Christian Law* (2013) 260.

[55] See e.g. J. Hussain, *Islamic Law* (1999) 60–75, 78; A. Black *et al.*, *Islamic Law* (2013) 111: 'And among His Signs is this, that He created for you mates from among yourselves, that you may dwell in tranquillity with them, and He has put love and mercy between your (hearts)': Quran: Sur Rum 30:21.

[56] See, however, for the traditional hegemony of husbands, F. Banda and L.F. Joffe, eds., *Women's Rights and Religious Law: Domestic and International Perspectives* (Abingdon: Routledge, 2016).

The Universal Islamic Declaration of Human Rights too treats marriage. It is a fundamental that 'the family shall be preserved, protected and honoured as the basis of all social life'. Every person is 'entitled to marry, to found a family and to bring up children in conformity with his religion, traditions and culture'. No one may be married against their will, or lose or suffer diminution of legal personality on account of marriage. Every spouse has 'such rights and privileges and carries such obligations as are stipulated by the Law' (i.e. *sharia*). Each partner is entitled 'to respect and consideration from the other' and a husband must maintain his wife and children according to his means. Motherhood is entitled to 'special respect, care and assistance on the part of the family and the public organs of the community (*Ummah*)'. And a married woman is entitled to: live in the house where her husband lives; receive the necessary means for maintaining a standard of living which is not inferior to that of her spouse; inherit from her husband, parents, children and other relatives; and enjoy strict confidentiality from her spouse as to disclosures detrimental to her interests.[57]

In England and Wales today, many Muslims choose not to enter a civil marriage for a wide range of reasons;[58] the problems which this may generate have resulted in a proposal that all Islamic marriages should be registered civilly,[59] not least to protect the women involved should there be a religious divorce (see below). In any event, the religious ceremony usually takes place in the mosque with the imam officiating; in the larger mosques registered civilly for marriages, the imam acts as registrar. However, there is no Islamic requirement for an imam or any other official to be present, merely for suitable witnesses. Marriage customs vary between communities, but the essential elements are the exchange of consents, the pledge or *nikah*, a dowry (*mahr*) from the husband to the wife, the presence of a *wali* (the guardian of the bride) and, after consummation, a feast (*walimah*) given by the husband for the

---

[57] UIDHR (1981): Arts. XIX and XX.

[58] *The Independent Review into the Application of Sharia Law in England and Wales* (February 2018), 13: reasons include: a lack of awareness that Islamic marriages need to be registered separately to be legal civilly; the belief that should the couple divorce, one partner may lose out financially in civil proceedings; appeasing the family; unreadiness to marry civilly; intending to register civilly after the *nikah* but not getting round to it; confusion that a *nikah* conducted overseas is valid, when a *nikah* conducted here would not be recognised; not wishing to marry civilly for cultural/religious reasons; and the rare practice of polygamy in some Muslim communities, which would be illegal in England and Wales.

[59] *The Independent Review into the Application of Sharia Law in England and Wales* (February 2018) 4–5.

community, to publicise the *nikah*. The imam delivers a traditional marriage sermon. If *masjid* officials are permitted under civil law to do so, the *nikah* may be combined with registration. Some Shias practise temporary marriage (*mutah*), in which a man declares fidelity to a woman for a prescribed period only; Sunni scholars reject this.[60] Moreover, arranged marriages may be common in some Muslim communities because of: restrictions on mixing between men and women; cultural traditions, especially matriarchal influence; and parental economic self-interest. In some very close communities, a *nikah* is performed between children as young as three or four.[61]

The regulatory instruments of mosques and Islamic centres often include provision of marriage among their objects.[62] First, a mosque may make no mention of civil law; for example, the East London Mosque and London Islamic Centre 'facilitates the solemnisation of an Islamic contract of marriage' and 'the couple is provided with an official Nikah certificate to show they have been married according to Islamic Law'.[63] Secondly, some provide for *nikah* following civil marriage. For instance, at London Central Mosque *nikah* is performed by an imam in Arabic or English; and 'a marriage contract according to Islamic (Shariah) Law' may be made. All who attend the ceremony are asked to observe 'the tradition of dressing in keeping with Islamic values' – admission to anyone who does not comply with this request may be refused. The following are required prior to the *nikah*: valid passports; the original Civil Marriage Certificate; proof of address; a Conversion Certificate, if applicable; two Muslim male witnesses, and *wali* (the bride's father or next of reliable male kin to the bride). Also required are a written declaration of the agreed Dowry (signed by both); if the bride has previously been married, an Islamic divorce or civil Decree Absolute; if the bride is not Muslim, a Statutory Declaration of consent. Payment of the prescribed fee is also required. The *nikah* ceremony itself takes place in the office of the imam. The *nikah* certificate may be issued in English/Arabic but not for any *nikah*, which is performed by imams from other mosques not linked with London Central Mosque.[64]

---

[60] M. Naqshbandi, *Islam and Muslims in Britain* (2012): Guide 6.2.2. In Muslim countries, it is unusual for the *nikah* to take place in the masjid.

[61] M. Naqshbandi, *Islam and Muslims in Britain* (2012): Guide 6.2.3; see also 3: 159 mosques in England and Wales are registered for marriage under the Marriage Act 1949.

[62] AMIC: Con. Art. I.1; XIV.5: performing the ceremony is a duty of the imam.

[63] East London Mosque Trust: www.eastlondonmosque.org.uk/.

[64] LCMICC: www.iccuk.org/page.php?section=social&page=matrimonials.

Thirdly, some mosques may celebrate a *nikah* and a civil marriage. Birmingham Central Mosque is authorised to do so,[65] and at the Islamic Sharia Council the *nikah* is conducted by an Imam and registered with the civil authorities.[66] Edinburgh Central Mosque too has a marriage service conducted in accordance with Scottish law. The parties must contact the imam and then notify the civil registrar. If the registrar is satisfied that there is no legal impediment, a Marriage Schedule is prepared and collected at the registration office. The parties must produce this to the Imam who will not solemnise a marriage without it being available at the time of the ceremony.[67]

Some Muslim organisations also have norms on forced marriages. For example, the Muslim Arbitration Tribunal seeks to stimulate awareness and discussion within the Muslim community about these, as well as support for victims. It may interview the potential victim and family, and, if satisfied that no coercion has been used, may issue a certificate for use as a supporting document for a spousal visa or as evidence before the civil court.[68] Indeed, State law enables a potential victim to seek from the family courts a Forced Marriage Protection Order.[69] Forcing marriage is a criminal offence.[70]

Religious Divorce

All three religions have rules which address the divorce and remarriage of the faithful. Under State law, uniquely, Anglican clergy in England and

---

[65] BCM: https://centralmosque.org.uk/services/marriage-bureau/.

[66] ISC: www.islamic-sharia.org/. The Council has dealt thus far with around 10,000 marriage cases, the majority concerning divorce. See above Chapter 5 for its work and composition.

[67] Edinburgh Central Mosque: www.edmosque.org/about-the-mosque/services/.

[68] MAT: www.matribunal.com/forced-marriages.php. The Tribunal offers its service because it considers that victims may be insufficiently confident to do so (due to e.g. the risk of recrimination by family members), and because the Muslim community itself is well placed to protect potential victims.

[69] Forced Marriage Act 2007: a forced marriage is one in which a person faces physical pressure to marry (e.g. threats, physical violence or sexual violence) or emotional and psychological pressure (e.g. made to feel they are bringing shame on their family). For Forced Marriage Protection Orders and the support of the Forced Marriage Unit (FMU), see: www.gov.uk/stop-forced-marriage.

[70] See also Anti-Social Behaviour, Crime and Policing Act 2014: it is a crime to force someone to marry, including: taking someone overseas to do so (whether or not the forced marriage takes place); marrying someone lacking mental capacity to consent to marriage (whether pressured to or not); and breaching a Forced Marriage Protection Order. The civil remedy of obtaining a Forced Marriage Protection Order continues alongside the criminal offence, so victims may choose how to be assisted

Wales have a statutory right to refuse, on grounds of conscience, to solemnise the marriage of divorced persons whose former marriages have been dissolved but whose former spouse is still living.[71] Civil law also recognises the existence (but not the civil binding effect) of Jewish divorce – the court may refuse to issue a civil decree absolute until a *get* has been granted by the Jewish husband to his wife.[72] Islamic divorce has, in recent years, been the subject of much debate around the rights of women and gender equality.[73]

The Get Procedure and Seder P'reidah

In classical Jewish law, a marriage is dissolved on the death of one of the spouses, or on divorce which is founded on the biblical text: 'When a man has taken a wife, and married her, and it comes to pass that she finds no favour in his eyes, because he has found some uncleanness in her, then let him write her a bill of divorcement, and give it into her hand, and send her out of his house: And when she is departed out of his house, she may go and be another man's wife.'[74] A bill of divorcement (*get*) is the document which effects the divorce and it must be issued by the husband voluntarily – traditionally, it is the woman who is married to the man, and not he to her, and so it is the husband who divorces his wife, not the wife who divorces her husband. If a husband refuses a *get*, the woman is an *agunah* (literally chained) and still bound in marriage – the marriage is dissolved only by the death of the husband or by a *get*. Even though the consent of the wife is not required for the divorce to be valid, the *ketubah* was designed to assist the wife in these circumstances (see above). While the Beth Din has no authority to sever the marriage bond – as this is achieved only by the parties voluntarily – the court does supervise the drafting and delivery of the *get* to ensure that halakhic procedures are satisfied, and the court may enforce the *ketubah*. Needless to say, there is no objection in Jewish law to divorce by mutual consent, though the Rabbinic courts seek to bring about reconciliation where this is possible.[75]

---

[71] Matrimonial Causes Act 1965, s. 8.

[72] See below the Divorce (Religious Marriages) Act 2002. See also M. Freeman, 'Is the Jewish get any business of the State?', in R. O'Dair and A. Lewis, eds., *Law and Religion* (Oxford: Oxford University Press, 2001) 365.

[73] See e.g. the studies in F. Banda and L.F. Joffe, eds., *Women's Rights and Religious Law: Domestic and International Perspectives* (London: Routledge, 2016).

[74] Deuteronomy 24:1–2.   [75] L. Jacobs, *Jewish Religion* (1999) 45–46.

The modern regulatory instruments of Jewish denominations deploy these elements of the classical law in various ways. First, the (Orthodox) United Synagogue assumes that all marrying couples will sign the *ketubah* (or Pre-Nuptial Agreement) and it encourages them to do so. In the *ketubah*, the couple undertakes that should their marriage run into serious difficulties, they would attend the Court of the Chief Rabbi (London Beth Din) to suggest a referral for counselling or mediation. However, if the relationship has deteriorated to the point where such support would be to no avail, the same meeting provides the Beth Din with an opportunity to discuss the possibility of *get* proceedings with the couple; on receiving a *get*, both parties are free to re-marry.[76]

A *get* is a document specially written at the instruction of the husband to be handed to his wife at the Beth Din. However, unlike a civil divorce, which may be instigated without the consent of both parties, a *get* may only be issued with the willing co-operation (or consent) of both husband and wife. If either party is obstructive, a 'stalemate' ensues in which neither is free to re-marry according to Jewish rites, even if they have been divorced in civil law. This deadlock, if prolonged unnecessarily, may, understandably, be enormously damaging for all concerned. A woman is particularly vulnerable: as she remains religiously married to her estranged husband, involvement with another man would be deemed adultery, with tragic consequences for children subsequently conceived. Neither party is required to establish grounds for divorce such as unreasonable behaviour, separation or adultery. All that has to be shown is that both the husband and the wife agree to the *get* taking place.[77]

As to process, on receipt of an application for a *get*, which is 'a religious ceremony', the London Beth Din invites both husband and wife to attend interviews at the Beth Din. At this, the first session, the Dayan (judge) will: check the relevant data relating to the writing of the *get* (e.g. details of their parties' English and Hebrew names); and ascertain if there are any issues which may cause delays at a later stage in the process. When a couple have separated, the normal expectation is that both parties will honour their responsibility to ensure that the *get* is completed within a few short months, regardless of whether all other issues in the divorce have been resolved. At a second session, the husband

[76] US: The Office of the Chief Rabbi: http://chiefrabbi.org/background-pre-nuptial-agreement/.
[77] US: www.theus.org.uk/article/divorce-0.

attends the Beth Din and instructs the Scribe to write the *get*; beforehand the husband will be asked to give proof of his identity and to confirm that he is giving the *get* of his own free will. The Scribe, with two witnesses (*eidim*) and the husband's representative (*shaliach*), where appropriate, adjourn to a writing room. The Scribe then writes the *get*. Once completed and checked by a Dayan, the *get* is ready to present to the wife. If the parties prefer not to meet, separate appointments may be arranged; the *get* is handed to the husband's representative and then to the wife on a separate occasion. The wife is asked if she is willing to receive it. If she is, her husband or (if not present his Shaliach), will recite a form of words at the request of the Dayanim, which indicates that on receipt of the *get* his wife will be free from the marriage. The *get* is then placed into the wife's hands: she must clasp it between them (there should be no rings on her fingers) and lift it above her head as a sign that she has acquired it for herself; put the *get* into her pocket or under one arm, turn and walk away several steps from her husband (or his Shaliach) as a sign that she has asserted her independence from him; and then hand the *get* back to the Dayan, so that it can be checked again by the witnesses. Once received, the *get* is the wife's property. However, it is standard practice to deposit the *get* with the Beth Din. Once the wife receives it, the Dayan reminds her of two restrictions on remarriage: a Cohen may not marry a divorcee; and 92 days should elapse before she may remarry. In due course, while the *get* is retained at the Beth Din, a *get* certificate is issued by it to both parties 'as evidence that they are properly divorced in accordance with Jewish law'.[78]

Moreover, if, in the written opinion of the London Beth Din, a member of the United Synagogue refuses to co-operate with the granting or receiving of a *get*, the privileges of membership must, as the Beth Din directs, be withheld for such period as the Beth Din advises.[79] Any member, who fails to give or receive a *get*, when directed by the Beth Din to do so, 'could forfeit the right to membership'. Such membership and all privileges and rights of membership may be terminated by the

---

[78] US: the Beth Din is assisted by volunteers who provide 'moral' support to either party if this is needed: www.theus.org.uk/article/divorce-0.

[79] The privileges include but are not limited to: being appointed Shaliach Tzibbur; Ba'al Tekiyah; Ba'al Koreh; Chatan Torah or Bereyshit; receiving an Aliyah when not a Chiyuv; entitlement to be an Honorary Officer, Local Honorary Officer or member of the Board of Management or represent the Synagogue on local and national organisations, the appointment to positions of responsibility e.g. taking Children's or Youth Services, as a teacher in the religion classes and/or Synagogue security.

Honorary Officers on the written authority of, and for such period as is determined by, the Beth Din itself.[80] The Beis Din of the (Orthodox) Federation of Synagogues operates a similar system.[81]

Secondly, within the Movement for Reform Judaism, whilst a *get* process is also available,[82] there is an alternative, namely an optional ceremony for divorce – *Seder P'reidah* – or Ritual of Release. This is intended to foster 'a spiritual setting for the termination of a marriage and provide a religious context for the expression of grief and loss'. However, the process is not intended 'to be a Reform version of a *get* and should not be construed as such'. Other rituals have also been designed for divorcing couples, for instance: meditations for use on leaving a home on divorce and moving to a new home; special recitations on starting another relationship; using the *havdalah* (traditionally a ceremony or prayer to mark the end of Shabbat) to signal a new phase of life; or an evening worship service, similar to the *minyan* for mourners after a death. However, none of these is meant to have halakhic validity; all have been prepared to provide comfort and consolation, and to reduce anger or bitterness that may attend a divorce. Many congregations also have 'caring community committees' to reach out to those divorced in much the same way they comfort families of the sick and the bereaved.[83]

Thirdly, the Conservative movement has also instituted *get* procedures designed to be sensitive to women's rights. Conservative Judaism has added what is known as the 'Lieberman Clause' to its *ketubah*, or 'marital licence' (so named after the late Jewish scholar Saul Lieberman), which is signed by both husband and wife and read during the wedding ceremony, and empowers the Conservative *Beit Din* to act on behalf of the woman and award her a *get*, even if the husband refuses. The Reconstructionist Movement, which includes women as members of the *beit din*, allows women the right to initiate a divorce proceeding.[84] The Conservative tradition also recognises civil marriage but not civil divorce.[85] However, the Union of Liberal and Progressive Synagogues, on the basis of 'the equal status of men and women in marriage law and ritual', objects 'to

---

81 FOS: www.federation.org.uk/wp-content/uploads/2017/08/federation_get-guide/.
82 MRJ: www.reformjudaism.org.uk/resources/life-cycle/. The Ritual of Release was introduced by the Central Conference of American Rabbis in 1983.
83 MRJ: https://reformjudaism.org/jewish-way-divorce.
84 MRJ: https://reformjudaism.org/jewish-way-divorce.
85 E.N. Dorff and A. Rosett, *A Living Tree: The Roots and Growth of Jewish Law* (Albany: New York State university 1900) 515ff.

the traditional *Get* (bill of divorce) by which the husband unilaterally "sends away" his wife and have created instead a reciprocal *Get*'.[86] The Assembly of Masorti Synagogues has a trained *mesader gittin* (a Rabbi qualified to write a *get*) to ensure all halakhic requirements are met in a supportive environment.[87]

Finally, civil law recognises that the refusal to issue a *get*, notwithstanding the fact that the wife had obtained a civil divorce. means that the woman is still seen as married in the eyes of the Jewish faith and therefore unable to re-marry under Jewish law, and the husband could withhold the *get* to seek advantage as to a financial settlement.[88] The Divorce (Religious Marriages) Act 2002 sought to overcome this by providing that if a marriage was solemnised in accordance with the usages of the Jews, the civil court may refuse to issue a decree absolute until a *get* has been granted to the wife.[89]

Divorce and Re-Marriage in Christianity

There are considerable traditional differences between churches as to the practice of marriage annulment, divorce amongst the faithful and the solemnisation of a church marriage following a civil dissolution.[90] However, for the historic churches, it is a principle of Christian law that marriage is a lifelong union which is terminated by the death of one of the spouses and may be dissolved when so determined by competent authority.[91] This principle derives from the similarities of the laws of the churches.

Within the Episcopal tradition, the Roman Catholic Church uses a system of marriage annulment and a restrictive approach to dissolution and second marriages: 'From a valid marriage there arises between the spouses a bond which of its own nature is permanent and exclusive';[92] and the 'essential properties of marriage are unity and indissolubility'.[93]

---

[86] ULPS: *Affirmations* (2006) Art. 34.

[87] AMS: www.masorti.org.uk/bet-din/bet-din.html.

[88] See e.g. Brett v. *Brett* [1969] 1 All ER 1007.

[89] Divorce (Religious Marriages) Act 2002 substituted a new section 10A into the Matrimonial Causes Act 1973; the Divorce (Scotland) Act 1976, s. 3A (inserted by s. 15 of the Family Law (Scotland) Act 2006) makes similar provision as to Scotland.

[90] See e.g. J. Witte, *From Sacrament to Contract: Marriage, Religion and Law in the Western Tradition* (Westminster: John Knox Press, 1997).

[91] Christian Law Panel of Experts, *Principles of Christian Law* (2016) VII.4.

[92] CIC: c. 1134.

[93] CIC: c. 1056: the essential properties; c. 1134: permanence and exclusivity.

When a marriage has been annulled by the church (because the criteria of validity have not been met), the parties are free to (re)marry.[94] However, if a union is terminated by a civil divorce, the canonical bond continues. Thus, a ratified and consummated marriage (between two baptised persons) cannot be dissolved by any human power or for any reason other than death, but the Pontiff may dissolve a non-consummated, ratified marriage for just cause at the request of both parties or one if the other is unwilling.[95] A marriage of two non-baptised persons is dissolved under the so-called Pauline Privilege, that is if one party becomes baptised as a convert and the other no longer wishes to cohabit, the convert is then free to marry another person.[96]

A somewhat different approach is used in Anglicanism.[97] The matrimonial bond is intended to be dissolved only by the death of one spouse. When this occurs, the surviving spouse is free to marry in church. However, when marital unity is imperilled, before recourse to civil law, the spouses are to approach the church which 'should labour that they may be reconciled'. If a harmonious or even tolerable relationship has in fact ceased to exist, a church may hold that while divorce is undesirable, it may be preferable to the continuance of a destructive relationship.[98] After the civil dissolution of a marriage, a church may permit a person whose former spouse is still alive to be married in church, and may stipulate conditions required for the solemnisation of such a marriage that it judges necessary to safeguard the holiness of marriage and the respect due to it. An ordained minister may refuse for reasons of conscience or other lawful cause to solemnise the marriage of a divorced person whose former spouse is still alive. A church may provide that the decision to solemnise such a marriage be made by a member of the clergy, as the case may be, either alone, or in consultation with the bishop, or with the consent of the bishop or such other competent authority prescribed by law. A person who has a civil divorce should

---

[94] CIC: cc. 1157, 1159: convalidation validates a marriage which was canonically valid *ab initio*.

[95] CIC: c. 1141; c. 1142.

[96] CIC: c. 1143; c. 1144: the non-baptised party is questioned on whether he/she wishes also to receive baptism and to cohabit; c. 1146: second marriage; cc. 1151–1155: separation while the bond remains.

[97] PCLCCAC: Principle 74: this deals with annulment; however, no provision is made for annulment within the church in the Church of England, Church in Wales or Scottish Episopal Church.

[98] PCLCCAC: Principle 75.1–4.

not by virtue of that fact alone be excluded from Holy Communion. Persons who re-marry during the lifetime of a former spouse and those married to them may receive Holy Communion subject to conditions operative under the law.[99]

There is little to distinguish between the Anglican model and those of Protestantism. For instance, in the Methodist Church of Great Britain, 'Divorce does not of itself prevent a person being married in any Methodist place of worship.' However: 'Under no circumstances does the Conference require any person authorised to conduct marriages who is subject to the discipline of the Church as a minister, deacon, probationer or member to officiate at the marriage of a particular couple should it be contrary to the dictates of his or her conscience to do so.' Therefore those authorised to conduct marriages 'but who for reasons of conscience will never officiate at the marriages of couples in particular circumstances shall refer such couples to an authorised colleague who is not so prevented'. Accordingly, if a couple seeks to be married in a Methodist place of worship, no objection to the performance by a particular minister, deacon, probationer or member of any duty in respect of their proposed marriage shall be entertained on such a ground.

This approach is also used in some Presbyterian churches: 'When a disagreement between husband and wife becomes apparent, an earnest endeavour should be made [by ministers and elders] to effect reconciliation ... in wisdom and gentleness' and to avoid resort to 'a court of law'. However: 'If and when all genuine efforts at reconciliation have failed and the husband and wife in all conscience have to accept the fact that the marriage bond has been irrevocably broken in spirit and in truth, then the Church, in accordance with the spirit of the New Testament teaching, cannot condemn persons for seeking a divorce.'[100] Nevertheless: 'The Church ... does not lay down rigid rules regarding the re-marriage in Church of divorced persons'; if the minister and elders consider that 'both the reasons for the previous divorce and for the re-marriage are genuine and sincere', it may take place but a minister may on grounds of conscience refuse to solemnise this and the Presbytery may

---

[99] PCLCCAC: Principle 75.5–9; 10: lack of parity of religion is not of itself a reason for seeking divorce. See e.g. Scotland: College of Bishops Guidelines (1981): no priest is 'required to officiate ... contrary to his conscience'; Church of Ireland: Con. IX.31.3–6: the cleric consults the bishop.

[100] PCW: Handbook of Rules, 9.4.

be approached to find another.[101] Divorced persons may also be admitted to the Holy Communion.[102]

Talaq, Khula and Faskh

In classical Islamic law, men seeking a divorce have the option of *talaq*, a form of unilateral divorce that they may issue themselves.[103] Women do not have this option, unless inserted as a term in the marriage contract. However, though there are some differences between the various schools of jurisprudence, today, for an Islamic divorce or dissolution of marriage, the woman may apply to a *sharia* council for a *khula* (which may be granted if the husband consents or is persuaded or even prevailed upon to consent) or *faskh* (which may be granted by a Muslim jurist to the wife against a husband unwilling to agree to a divorce).[104] Women may seek an Islamic divorce because, for example: the marriage has not been civilly registered and so civil divorce is not available; their own religious beliefs require them to be religiously divorced so as to move on in life; their family, in-laws or community may require a religious divorce before accepting the relationship is over; the concern that only religious divorce, rather than civil, will be recognised by Islamic jurisdictions overseas; the cost of a civil divorce may be prohibitive for some; Islamic divorce may be obtained more speedily; and misconceptions that Islamic divorce only is needed.[105]

---

[101] PCW: Handbook of Rules, 9.4: 'It is important to state that the Connexion does not lay on any minister the duty of officiating at the marriage of a divorced person if, in so doing, he would be acting against his own conscience and judgment, and that of the elders.' See also J.L. Weatherhead, ed., *Constitution and Laws of the Church of Scotland* (1997) 35; Act XXVI, 1959; URC: Manual M.

[102] PCW: Handbook of Rules, 9.4.

[103] M. Naqshbandi, *Islam and Muslims in Britain* (2012): Guide 6.2.5: The man repeats *talaq*, 'I cast you off', three times; and: 'A divorce is only permissible twice: after that the parties should either hold together on equitable terms, or separate with kindness' (Holy Qur'an, Surah Baqarah, v. 229).

[104] *The Independent Review into the Application of Sharia Law in England and Wales* (February 2018) 13.

[105] *The Independent Review into the Application of Sharia Law in England and Wales* (February 2018) 14: the evidence provided by the *sharia* councils indicated that when considering divorce applications, councils do not deal with issues such as arrangements for children and asset distribution. However, in some instances, during *khula* divorces, women were asked to make some financial concessions to the husband to secure the divorce including the return of the *mahr* (dower) and all other gifts received during the relationship. The review is aware of anecdotal evidence of councils issuing arrangements,

The Universal Islamic Declaration of Human Rights (1981) provides that every woman may seek and obtain dissolution of marriage (*khula*) in accordance with *sharia* before the courts, and, during the required period of waiting (*iddah*), to receive the means of maintenance commensurate with the resources of her husband, for herself as well as for the children she nurses or keeps, irrespective of her own financial status, earnings or any property that she may hold in her own right.[106] The Fatwa Committee UK has also found, following a decision of a *sharia* council which the husband rejected, that: 'the rulings issued by Islamic courts in Europe are binding, as long as their processes are diligent, and their works are recognized by the Muslim community'; however: 'we as a committee have no authority to judge if this Sharia body [in question] has done the annulment correctly'; since the wife wishes to resume the marriage, 'we advise for a new nikah to be performed. This will clear all doubts and both [parties] will be Islamically married and clear of any haram, since to have a relationship without Islamic approval is something that should not be taken lightly.'[107]

The Independent Review into the Application of Sharia Law in England and Wales, presented to Parliament by the Secretary of State for the Home Department (February 2018) found the vast majority using *sharia* councils are women, mostly (over 90 per cent) for an Islamic divorce.[108] As a significant number of Muslim couples fail to register civilly their religious marriages, some Muslim women do not have the option of obtaining a civil divorce. This demand will not end if the councils are banned and could lead to them going 'underground', making it harder to ensure good practice, and in women travelling overseas to obtain divorces, putting themselves at further risk. Therefore, as the review does not consider the closure of *sharia* councils a viable option, it proposes the registration of all Islamic marriages as well as awareness campaigns so

---

for children, that are claimed to be contrary to domestic law, but heard no direct evidence of this.

[106] UIDHR (1981): Art. XX.   [107] FCUK: Decision 8/3.

[108] *The Independent Review into the Application of Sharia Law in England and Wales* (Febraury 2018) 10: while *sharia* councils operate in Sunni communities, and are not prevalent in Shia communities, the review found that Shia couples consult a Grand Ayatollah (or an Ayatollah authorised by a Grand Ayatollah) for decisions on divorce. The review panel met two UK Shia organisations of which only one man had the authority, conferred from foreign Grand Ayatollahs, to pronounce an Islamic divorce.

that the demand for religious divorces from such councils will gradually reduce over time.[109]

In terms of practice, the Review found that all councils charge fees for processing divorces (but on occasion they waive fees for those who cannot afford them) to cover the administrative costs. Information-gathering is an inquisitorial process led by the council members to hear and test the quality of the evidence. All documentation was issued in English and whilst there was some evidence of deliberation in other languages, there was no evidence of individuals being disadvantaged by this. The evidence provided showed a range of practices, both good and bad. Examples of good practice include: reporting of family violence and child protection issues to the police; lowering or waiving fees for women unable to pay them; granting religious divorce as a formality on civil divorce; signposting to civil remedies e.g. as to arrangements for children; not asking women to reconcile relationships rather than obtaining divorce; declining to deal with any ancillary issues and referring users to civil courts; granting divorce in practically every case a woman sought it; including women as panel members; and (in some) having safeguarding policies for children.[110]

On the other hand, examples of bad practice include: inappropriate or unnecessary questioning about personal relationship matters; asking a forced marriage victim to attend with her family; insisting on mediation as a necessary preliminary; inviting women to make concessions to husbands to obtain a divorce – men are not asked (e.g. in *khula* agreements, husbands may demand excessive financial concessions from the wife); and inconsistency across councils in terms of decisions and processes. The review also found instances of: excessively lengthy process; no safeguarding policies or recognising the need for them; no clear signposting to the options available for civil divorce; considering all the evidence again for a religious divorce even after issue of a civil decree absolute; adopting civil legal terms inappropriately thereby confusing applicants over the legality of council decisions; the absence of women as panel members; panels including those who have only recently moved to Britain, and who do not have the required language skills and/or wider

---

[109] *The Independent Review into the Application of Sharia Law in England and Wales* (February 2018) 4–5.
[110] *The Independent Review into the Application of Sharia Law in England and Wales* (February 2018) 10–14.

understanding of British society; and varying/conflicting interpretations of Islamic law leading to inconsistencies.[111]

The review therefore makes three recommendations. First, the marriage law of the State should be amended to ensure that civil marriages are conducted and registered before or at the same time as the Islamic marriage ceremony (*nikah*), bringing Islamic marriage in line with civil law on Christian and Jewish marriage. Moreover, it should be a criminal offence for the celebrant of any marriage, including Islamic marriages, to fail to ensure that the religious marriage is also civilly registered; and civil law should recognise the existence (but not the civil binding effect) of an Islamic divorce (as it does the Jewish *get*) with the court empowered to refuse to issue a civil decree absolute until a *talaq* has been granted by the Muslim husband to his wife. Linking Islamic marriage to civil marriage would ensure that a greater number of women have the protection afforded to them in State family law and the right to a civil divorce, lessening the need to attend and simplifying the processes within *sharia* councils.[112]

Secondly, the review recommends awareness campaigns: cultural change is needed in Muslim communities for them to acknowledge women's rights in civil law, especially in areas of marriage and divorce. Educational programmes should be introduced to inform women of their rights and duties, including the legal protection civilly registered marriages provide. There is also a need to ensure that *sharia* councils operate within the law and comply with best practice, non-discriminatory processes and existing regulatory structures – a clear message must be sent that an arbitration that applies *sharia* in respect of financial remedies and/or child arrangements would not satisfy the Arbitration Act 1996 and its underlying protection.[113] Thirdly, on the basis that its first two recommendations aim to reduce gradually the use of *sharia* councils, the review recommends regulation – namely, that, in the medium term, the government should establish a body which would institute a code of practice for *sharia* councils to accept and implement on a self-regulatory

---

[111] *The Independent Review into the Application of Sharia Law in England and Wales* (February 2018) 14–16.

[112] That is, to amend the Marriage Act 1949 and Matrimonial Causes Act 1973, s. 10A: the *nikah* should be inserted by Statutory Instrument pursuant to s. 6.

[113] Awareness should also be raised in Muslim communities as to the availability of legal aid and the exceptions to the Legal Aid Sentencing and Punishment of Offenders Act 2012 (including the domestic violence and child protection exceptions), which mean that public funding is available to applicants.

basis. This body would include council panel members and specialist family law experts – in conducting the review, no *sharia* council was opposed to some form of regulation and some positively welcomed it.[114] The Muslim Arbitration Tribunal may be offered by way of illustration. A tribunal recognises that: 'A common problem faced by Muslim women is the request for an Islamic divorce from the husband. The wife may obtain a divorce in the civil courts; however, her husband may continue to deny her the Islamic divorce. As a result she may face stigma from the community, thus preventing her from re-marrying.' Therefore, the tribunal provides a service for women seeking 'to obtain an Islamic divorce by way of *khula* through the consent and co-operation of the husband'. The tribunal may issue a *khula* certificate within three or four months of an application. In the absence of the consent and/or co-operation of the husband, it may issue a declaration that the marriage is dissolved (*faskh*) provided its panel is satisfied that the necessary requirements have been met. It may also be able to provide advice regarding the Islamic divorce procedure if a civil divorce has been obtained. The tribunal also provides mediation for disputes as to dowry, children of the marriage and other family matters. It instructs two mediators from the panel to endeavour to reach a decision with which both sides are in agreement. However, the tribunal recognises that it is unable to deal with cases of domestic violence, which is a matter for the criminal law of the State – nevertheless, if secular criminal charges are brought that are associated with domestic violence, the parties may ask the tribunal to assist in reconciliation between them, which is observed and approved by the tribunal as an independent organisation. The tribunal may then pass the terms of the reconciliation to the Crown Prosecution Service through the local Police Domestic Violence Liaison Officers with a view to reconsidering the criminal charges. However, the tribunal acknowledges that the final decision whether to prosecute always remains with the Crown Prosecution Service.[115]

---

[114] This was the view of the majority on the review panel.
[115] MAT: www.matribunal.com/family-dispute-cases.php. See also ISC: www.islamic-sharia.org/: it conducts Islamic divorces only, in 'the light of Islamic family law', not 'the UK legal or judicial systems' – 'Civil marriages are dissolved by the British Courts and not by the Council'. For cultural perspectives about the relationship between religious marriages and civil marriages, see: www.lawandreligionuk.com/2018/03/21/integration-seeing-the-bigger-picture/.

The Protection of Children

Recent years have seen the development of far-reaching standards by civil authorities (including the Charity Commission) providing for the welfare of children, and its paramount importance has been recognised in both civic life and private organisations, including religious communities.[116] Moreover, in family life, with regard to adoption and custody, the religious upbringing of children and their autonomy, are the subject of civil law under which child welfare generally prevails over the exercise of religious freedom.[117] Under the Children Act 1989, the welfare of children is paramount, and this may include their religious well-being.[118] For example, a civil court must not deny a parent the care of a child simply because of that parent's religious beliefs – those beliefs need to be balanced against the welfare of the child, the rights of the other parent and the religious autonomy of the child.[119] Similarly, adoption agencies must give due consideration to the 'religious persuasion, racial origin and linguistic background' of a child; in one case, the court resisted an application that a Downs Syndrome child born to Orthodox Jews and fostered by non-practising Roman Catholics be returned to her natural parents – parents unable to care for a child cannot insist on the child being adopted or placed with carers who share the same religion.[120]

Children – Home and Synagogue

In Judaism, children are understood to be the greatest gift which may be bestowed by God on a marriage. Parents must care for their children who in turn must honour and pay respect to their parents.[121] Jewish law also enjoins that orphans and widows be cared for, and in the Talmudic

---

[116] See e.g. www.gov.uk/government/publications/working-together-to-safeguard-children-2; and www.gov.uk/government/organisations/disclosure-and-barring-service.

[117] See M. Hill et al., Religion and Law (2014) paras. 56, 313 and 458.

[118] Children Act 1996, s. 1(3)(d).

[119] Re J (Specific Issue Orders: Child's Religious Upbringing and Circumcision) [2000] 1 FLR 571.

[120] Adoption and Children Act 2002, s. 1(5); Re P (A Minor) (Residence Order: Child's Welfare) [1999] 2 FLR 573.

[121] See e.g. Exodus 20:12. The respect due from children to parents is in the Talmudic tradition conceived as the simple payment of a debt to those who brought the children into the world. See also B. Shmueli, 'Corporal punishment of children in Jewish law: a comparative study', 18 The Jewish Law Annual (2010) 137–212: this compares traditional and modern Jewish approaches to the subject.

tradition courts should appoint a guardian for orphans to administer faithfully any estate inherited.[122] While children inherit the estate of their father,[123] the Torah has elaborate rules on inheritance/succession.[124] According to Talmudic tradition, these only apply where the testator states that the disposition of the property is in the form of an inheritance; they do not apply if it is in the form of a gift.[125] As a result, most halakhic authorities agree that a will may be made in favour of anyone the testator wishes, provided it is in the form of a gift, not an inheritance – but property should be left to children. The order of priority of near relatives to inherit the estate of the deceased is: son, daughter, brothers, brothers of the father and kinsman (next nearest relatives on the side of the father); and a father takes precedence over all his children on the death of his son. A son born of an adulterous or incestuous union (a *mamzer*) inherits the estate of his natural father, thus 'the concept of an illegitimate child in this context is unknown in Jewish law'. A husband inherits the estate of his wife – but a wife does not inherit the estate of her husband yet she is entitled to claim her *ketubah*, which may provide that any daughters she bears to her husband will be maintained out of his estate when he dies. If a son dies before his father and leaves children, whether they are sons or daughters, they take precedence in inheriting the estate of their grandfather over his daughter (their aunt). A first-born son inherits a 'double portion' of the estate of his father – that is, not two-thirds of the whole estate but a portion that is double that received by his brothers.[126]

The modern regulatory practices of Jewish denominations may either incorporate or reject aspects of these elements of traditional Jewish law. For example, in the (Orthodox) United Synagogue, the London Beth Din oversees the process by which a non-Jewish child adopted by a Jewish couple may acquire Jewish status. Without certification of their Jewish status by the Beth Din, the child may not be admitted to an Orthodox Jewish school or allowed to marry in an Orthodox synagogue.[127] The Movement for Reform Judaism also regulates adoption, after the civil

---

[122] Deuteronomy 26:12; Exodus 22:21–23; Isaiah 1:17; Jeremiah 7:5–6; Job 29:12–13.

[123] L. Jacobs, *Jewish Religion* (1999) 294–295.

[124] Numbers 27:8–11; Deuteronomy 21:16–17.   [125] Mishnah, *Bava Batra* 8:5.

[126] L. Jacobs, *Jewish Religion* (1999) 243–244, 295; a girl is *mamzeret*. Deuteronomy 23:3: 'A mamzer shall not enter into the congregation of the Lord; even to his tenth generation'; so Isserles warns against disclosing *mamzer* status; in practice, today, generally, no investigation occurs to expose a *mamzer/mamzeret*.

[127] UB. www.theus.org.uk/article/adoption

legalities have been completed to settle the child's religious identity. Unless the parents know and have documentary proof that the adopted child was born of a Jewish mother, the child will not be considered legally part of 'the Jewish people' until the Jewish identity of the child is confirmed through the *Beit Din*.[128] Parents must consult the Rabbi who advises on the process, and complete the relevant form. The *Beit Din* does not require the circumcision of a male child between six months and 16 years of age, though, if requested, it will recommend a *mohel*. The parents are asked to attend the court with the child and sign a document promising to bring up the child as a Jew. If the child is old enough to attend *cheder* and children's services and activities, such attendance is expected and the court may discuss this in order to enable each child to appreciate the significance of the adoption process and to ensure that the Rabbis have considered the child's interests, and not just those of the parents. After the *Beit Din*, the parents must take the child into the *mikveh* for immersion in accordance with instructions given by the parents' Rabbi or the *Beit Din*. When formalities are concluded, their Rabbi may want to hold a welcoming ceremony for the child at the synagogue. As with the conversion of adults, the child's Jewish status is recognised by progressive synagogues worldwide, but not by Orthodox.[129] Some Reform responsa do not require immersion or circumcision in the case of the adoption of non-Jewish children; and they accept 'the validity of civil divorce and therefore must accept the decision of the civil courts as to custody of the children'.[130]

However, the Union of Liberal and Progressive Synagogues, because 'children are not to be held responsible for the actions of their parents', rejects the law of *mamzer*, which penalises offspring of unions 'prohibited by the biblical laws of consanguinity and affinity'.[131] Moreover, since genetically children inherit alike from both parents, but culturally the influence of either may prove the stronger, 'the traditional law of matrilineality cannot be justified'; so, on the basis of 'common sense',

---

[128] One reason for the process is that there have been many occasions when adopted children, brought up as part of a Jewish family involved in the community, think themselves Jewish, only to find out when they seek a *bar/batmitzvah* or to marry in a synagogue that they first have to convert to Judaism.

[129] MRJ: www.reformjudaism.org.uk/resources/life-cycle/. Also, if the child is male and no *brit milah* is carried out, the conversion may not be recognised by Masorti Judaism in the UK.

[130] S.B. Freehof, *Reform Responsa* (1960) Nos. 47 and 49.

[131] ULPS: *Affirmations* (2006) Art. 35: it cites Ezekiel 18.

children of 'mixed marriages' (of a Jew and a non-Jew) 'are to be treated alike, regardless of whether the mother or the father is the Jewish parent, and considered Jewish if so brought up'.[132] In turn, the child acquires rights: for example, at Wessex Liberal Jewish Community, until they marry or reach 21, the child of a member is entitled 'to all rights of membership', but not to vote nor to be appointed as a trustee;[133] and at Elstree Liberal Synagogue, a child/person in the legal custody of a full member, who has been brought up in, or is of, the Jewish faith, has not yet attained the age of 21 and normally resides at the same address as their parent or guardian, must be included in the burial/funeral schemes.[134]

The Jewish traditions today increasingly deal with the protection of children at the synagogue through soft-law. For example, the Movement for Reform Judaism has a Child Protection Policy Code of Practice. The Education Department of a synagogue has 'a moral and legal obligation' to ensure the Council, Chair of Education, Teachers and Madrichim treat children and young people with 'the highest possible standard of care' – the well-being of children is paramount. A synagogue itself must ensure that: (1) all adults who work with children/young people are aware of their responsibilities towards them and that training is available and reviewed regularly; (2) all who work with children/young people must respect their rights and their reasonable wishes and feelings; (3) all new staff and volunteers are recruited with due concern for their previous work and experience with children/young people, and that such experience is appropriate – disclosure and barring checks are to be undertaken on all those who are in regular supervisory contact with children/young people; (4) an induction process is undertaken to inform staff about the synagogue framework for safeguarding children and young people; (5) all safeguarding policy and codes of conduct are given to staff and volunteers, so they understand good practice and are not placed in situations where allegations could be made against them; (6) the Chair of Education with the *cheder* Head Teacher determine whether abuse occurs; (7) everyone at the synagogue refers concerns and disclosures to a higher authority; and (8) all suspicions and allegations of abuse will be taken seriously and responded to appropriately.[135] Each synagogue should also have a Child Protection Co-ordinator, appointed by the Council after the Annual General Meeting, who is to:

[132] ULPS: *Affirmations* (2006) Art. 36. [133] WLJC: Con. Art. 8.5.
[134] ELS; Con. Art. 5: Note. [135] MRJ. Code of Practice 38–39.

attend an approved course of training; be responsible to the Chair of Education; work with the Education Committee, Head Teacher and Chair of Education; receive reports on all matters of concern; provide training (using the resources of the National Society for the Prevention of Cruelty to Children); and co-ordinate training for adult teachers (not Madrichim) and Rabbi to recognise signs of abuse and know what to do if a pupil approaches them about it.[136]

At local level, a Reform synagogue may also have norms tailored to specific activities involving children, for example the Finchley Reform Synagogue has its Safeguarding Children and Child Protection Policy (2016). This deals with, *inter alia*: security; photographing children; working with statutory agencies; mandatory reporting; implementing the statutory Prevent duty to keep children safe from the dangers of radicalisation and extremism; confidentiality as to suspicions and investigations; family support; and the statutory framework of civil law upon which the standards in its soft law are based.[137]

Liberal Jewish communities too have a Safeguarding Policy,[138] as do Orthodox communities, such as at Stanmore and Canons Park Synagogue. Its policy is designed 'to safeguard the welfare of all young people attending the Synagogue and its activities by protecting them from physical, sexual and emotional abuse', and it applies to any person organising or supervising youth and children activities (leaders and assistants). Leaders must, for example: comply with the policy (such as in relation to suspicion, disclosure or allegation of child abuse); be satisfied that all those invited to act as assistants are 'fit and proper' persons; ensure their behaviour is appropriate; respect the trust placed in them; and ensure that activities are conducted in a safe manner without risk to the health of participants. The Youth Rabbi and Youth Committee must appoint a Child Protection Co-ordinator who is *inter alia* to record concerns, assist in implementing the policy, and advise on the suspension of leaders or assistants against whom complaints are made. The synagogue, subject to the requirements of civil law, has 'absolute discretion' to exclude from the synagogue premises and/or its activities, or to allow

---

[136] MRJ: Code of Practice 20.

[137] Finchley Reform Synagogue: Safeguarding Children and Child Protection Policy (2016): the guidance sets out the civil law framework including the Children Act 1989 and 2004, Protection of Children Act 1999, Data Protection Act 1998, Safeguarding Vulnerable Groups Act 2004 and Childcare Act 2006.

[138] WLJC: Policy: Safeguarding – Care (2013).

access subject to such conditions as it deems reasonable, a person who is a registered sex offender, convicted of, cautioned for, or found guilty by reason of insanity as to any offence relating to the physical, sexual or emotional abuse of young people, or who has been charged with such an offence.[139]

Some synagogues also make provision for the parental supervision of children; for instance, at Borehamwood and Elstree Synagogue, to provide for the well-being of children under 12 years of age whilst on synagogue premises, parents are 'strongly urged to ensure' that their children are under the care of the parents themselves or that of another responsible adult and remain within the designated activity. Moreover, any children congregating outside the building are a security risk and so will be asked to disperse with immediate effect. In the best interest of the entire community, members should assist with this policy by being aware of the movements and behaviour of their own children. The synagogue Honorary Officers, Board of Management, Employees and Voluntary Assistants, and United Synagogue do not accept liability/responsibility for any event, claim or contingency arising as a result of the conduct of parents, their children or anyone else disregarding any conditions set out in the synagogue policy.[140]

Churches, Children and Child Protection

Whilst Christian theology has a great deal to say about children,[141] and the church exercised extensive jurisdiction over inheritance, wills and probate,[142] the principles of Christian law of the historic churches are silent on children in family life, adoption, inheritance and child protection in church.[143] However, churches do sometimes deal with the religious upbringing of children. For the Roman Catholic Church, parents have the right and duty to educate their children, to choose freely schools for their Catholic education and to prepare them for reception of the sacraments – children adopted in accordance with civil law are

---

[139] Stanmore and Canons Park Synagogue (US): Child Protection and Anti-Bullying Policies (undated).

[140] BAES: Guidelines (November 2008) issued by the Honorary Officers.

[141] See e.g. J.F. Childress and J. Macquarrie, eds., A New Dictionary of Christian Ethics (London: SCM Press, 1986) 85.

[142] See e.g. R.H. Helmholz, The Canon Law and Ecclesiastical Jurisdiction from 597 to the 1640s (Oxford: Oxford University Press, 2004) 387–432.

[143] These subjects were not included in the work of the Christian Law Panel of Experts.

considered the children of those who have adopted them.[144] With respect
to marriages between a Catholic and a non-Catholic,[145] the local Ordinary may permit such a mixed marriage if there is a just and reasonable
cause and three conditions are met: the Catholic party must declare to be
prepared to remove dangers of defecting from the faith and make a
sincere promise to do all in their power to ensure that the children be
baptised and brought up in the Catholic Church; the other party is to
be informed in good time of these promises (so as to be aware of the
promise and duty of the Catholic party); and both parties are to be
instructed about the purposes and essential properties of marriage and
these are not excluded by either.[146] Canon law also regulates wills for
pious causes: testamentary freedom here is a matter of natural and canon
law, but formalities of civil law must be observed and heirs are bound to
fulfil the will of the testator; the Ordinary is the executor.[147] While they
have norms on mixed marriages, the religious upbringing of children and
wills are not generally addressed in laws of Anglicans, Methodists and
other churches in Britain.[148]

By way of contrast, child protection has been the subject of detailed
regulation within the churches across the traditions and of intense
scrutiny without.[149] Within the Roman Catholic Church,[150] the
Bishops' Conference of England and Wales has set up the National
Catholic Safeguarding Commission (NCSC), which directs the Catholic
Safeguarding Advisory Service (CSAS), the purpose of which is to
improve safeguarding practice in the church. Each diocese has a Safeguarding Commission, appointed by the bishop, to deal with reports of

---

[144] CIC: c. 226.2: education; c. 979: school; c. 914: sacraments; c. 110: adoption; c. 1140:
legitimacy.

[145] CIC: c. 1124; see also Pope Paul VI, *Matrimonia mixta* (1970).

[146] CIC: c. 1125; ED 150; the Episcopal Conference is to prescribe the way in which the
declarations and promises (which are always required) are to be made, and to determine
how they are to be established and how the non-Catholic party is to be informed of
them: CIC: c. 1126.

[147] CIC: cc. 1299–1301; see c. 1302 for trustees.

[148] N. Doe, 'Inter-church and inter-faith marriages in Anglican canon law', in N. Doe, ed.,
Marriage in Anglican and Roman Catholic Canon Law (Cardiff: Centre for Law and
Religion, 2009) 95; PCLCCAC does not deal with this. See also MCGB: Constitutional
Practice and Discipline, Book VI, Sect. 10: Guidance for Inter-Faith Marriages; and PCI:
Code, 85(5).

[149] It is currently the subject of investigation by the Independent Inquiry into Child
Sexual Abuse.

[150] For a critical study, see e.g. P. Gilligan, 'Clerical abuse and laicisation: rhetoric and reality
in the Catholic Church in England and Wales', 21 *Child Abuse Review* (2012) 427–443.

child abuse, to work with statutory agencies, to report annually to the NCSC and to appoint a Safeguarding Coordinator to disseminate best practice and national safeguarding policies in the diocese. Each parish and religious order has a Safeguarding Representative and a clerical adviser who reports to the Safeguarding Coordinator.[151] Ordination candidates are subject to psychological assessments, secular disclosure and barring service checks, referencing and interviews with the bishop and a selection advisory panel before being accepted for clerical formation.[152]

Anglican churches have also developed policies and norms to safeguard children. For example, the Church of England, in a wide range of policy statements and guidance documents, accepts, endorses and implements 'the principle' enshrined in the Children Act 1989 (and subsequent legislation and guidance) that the welfare of the child is paramount; as such it will: foster and encourage best practice by setting standards for working with children and young people and by supporting parents; work with statutory bodies, voluntary agencies and other faith communities to promote the safety and wellbeing of children and young people; act promptly if a concern is raised about a child or young person or about the behaviour of an adult; and work with appropriate statutory bodies if an investigation into child abuse is necessary. These documents have norms on such areas as: recruitment and risk assessment for those who may pose a risk to children and adults; the maintenance of safeguarding records; and responding to serious safeguarding concerns. In turn, each diocese has a safeguarding policy designed to implement the national policy.[153] Moreover, the Safeguarding and Clergy Discipline Measure 2016 seeks to provide a national statutory framework to ensure the church is a safer place for children/young adults by making the disciplinary processes under the Clergy Discipline Measure 2003 more effective as and when safeguarding issues arise – and to reduce the risk of abuse taking place. Canon law requires bishops to appoint diocesan safeguarding advisers, creates new powers to require clergy to undergo a risk assessment (conducted in accordance with regulations to be made by the House of Bishops and approved by General Synod) and imposes a

---

[151] CSAS: *Catholic Safeguarding Resource Area* (2017): www.csas.uk.net/resource-area/. In 2015, the NCSC approved the establishment of a Survivor Advisory Panel.

[152] Catholic Bishops' Conference of England and Wales: *A Charter for Priestly Formation for England and Wales* (2015).

[153] For the many documents, see: www.churchofengland.org/more/safeguarding.

duty on all clergy authorised to administer in a diocese to participate in training.[154]

Christian churches may also collaborate in norm-making for child protection. For instance, in Protestant traditions, in Wales, the Union of Welsh Independents, Baptist Union of Wales and Presbyterian Church of Wales have jointly produced a common Safeguarding Vulnerable Groups Handbook.[155] The document contains guidance on: the recruitment and selection process which all those working with vulnerable groups are required to undertake; working with children and young people; information on how to respond if there is a suspicion of, or allegations about, abuse; supporting those who are affected by abuse; and forms to be used to assist in operating the policy.[156]

Children at Home and at the Mosque

In Islam, children are considered a trust from Allah and not to be seen as possessions but blessings from God to be cherished. Children have a right to be loved, cared for and treated with kindness. Both parents share responsibility for caring for children, but, as a husband is required to maintain his wife, so he is responsible for the financial maintenance (nafaqah) of a son until he is grown up or a daughter until she is married. Children should be treated equally by their parents and they must respect and obey their parents – and reason and guidance are preferable means of discipline. The status of legitimate children is different from that of illegitimate children who have no claim upon their natural father. There is a presumption that on divorce a small child remains with the mother (hadhanah) – the age at which this ceases varies as between the Islamic schools and sex of the child, but the minimum age is two. A child who reaches the age of discretion may choose which parent to live with. A woman may lose the right to hadhanah if, for instance, she abjures Islam or ill-treats the child. A father retains guardianship over a child regardless of whether the mother has custody. Formal adoption is forbidden (Quran 33:4–5) and a child must carry its own name (as children

---

[154] Church of England: Canon C30.

[155] See: www.ebcpcw.cymru/en/training/safeguarding-children-and-vulnerable-adults/ policy-and-procedures.

[156] The handbook is driven in part by the secular Safeguarding Vulnerable Groups Act 2006 (Controlled Activity) (Wales) Regulations 2010, Disclosure and Barring Service (Core Functions) Order 2012, and Protection of Freedoms Act 2012.

need to know their origins); adopted children may not legally inherit, but informal adoption, 'embracing the child', exists enabling Muslims to confer financial benefits upon such children *inter vivos*.[157] Islamic inheritance law is complex and one of the most important areas in both theory and practice; its basic principles concern the classification of heirs and distribution/exclusion of property.[158]

According to the Universal Islamic Declaration of Human Rights (1981), alongside the duty on a husband to maintain their children according to his means: 'Every child has the right to be maintained and properly brought up by its parents, it being forbidden that children are made to work at an early age or that any burden is put on them which would arrest or harm their natural development.' Moreover: 'If parents are for some reason unable to discharge their obligations towards a child, it becomes the responsibility of the community to fulfil these obligations at public expense.'[159] The Fatwa Committee UK has also issued opinions as to the welfare of children.[160]

The recent independent review of the application of *sharia* law in England and Wales was critical of the safeguarding practices of some *sharia* councils (see above). However, soft-law instruments of mosques and Islamic centres increasingly contain norms on safeguarding;[161] and the Muslim Council of Britain and the National Council of Voluntary Youth Services agreed in 2015 a Memorandum of Understanding in order to formalise a partnership to support Muslim communities in safeguarding children and young people.[162] At local level, Darul Isra Muslim Community Centre (Cardiff), for example, 'will at all times endeavour to safeguard the welfare of all children in its care by protecting them from physical, sexual and emotional harm'. It recognises that 'abuse

[157] J. Hussain, *Islamic Law* (1999) 20, 79, 81–82, 126, 137, 196; J. Schacht, *Islamic Law* (1991) 166.

[158] A. Black et al., *Islamic Law* (2013) 200–204: the Quranic principles; Sunni law; and Shia law.

[159] UIDHR (1981): Art. XIX.

[160] See e.g. FCUK: Decision 11/3 (citing ECFR: Fatwa No. 68): 'Using medicine that is medically beneficial and protects children from diseases . . . is allowed; especially if there is no other alternative and not using the medicine will lead to greater harm and detriment.'

[161] See e.g. MINAB: http://minab.org.uk/news/47-events/past-/244-madrassah-manage mentteaching-a-safeguarding.html; Lancashire Council of Mosques: http://panlancashir escb.proceduresonline.com/pdfs/; and Faith Associates: http://www.faithassociates.co .uk/services/safeguarding-courses-for-mosques-and-madrassahs/.

[162] MCB: www.mcb.org.uk/mou-safeguarding-270315/.

of children can take many forms such as physical injury or neglect, sexual assault and emotional abuse' potentially carried out by those associated with the centre, for example parents, relatives, other trusted adults, other young people and strangers. The welfare of children is the 'highest priority' of staff. In the event of any suspicion, staff (who are overseen by the Child Protection Team) should note what is seen/heard in the incident book (time and place), sign it and consult immediately the relevant leader; it is the responsibility of the leader to initiate further action (e.g. referral to the Social Services, which should be contacted if a child requires urgent protection). It is for social services and police to decide whether a formal investigation is required.[163]

Finally, Muslim organisations may also be involved in matters of inheritance. For example, the Muslim Arbitration Tribunal deals with inheritance disputes, making 'a decision regarding the shares of the various parties concerned according to Islamic law'. If a party fails to comply with the decision, the other may seek to place it before the civil court as evidence of what the deceased intended, or before an Islamic court abroad. The tribunal also offers a service to those wishing to draft 'a will compliant with Islamic Law' on the basis of instructions provided by the testator. If any dispute about the will arises, the tribunal may provide a decision and resolve that dispute.[164]

Conclusion

All three religions have elaborate norms on marriage, divorce and children. All agree that marriage is contractual and a blessing from God and that it must be upheld by the faithful. The orthodox position is that marriage is a lifelong union between a man and a woman, instituted for the mutual affection and support of the parties, and may be ordered to procreation. To be married validly in the eyes of the faithful, the parties must satisfy the conditions prescribed by religious law – all three religions have theocratic rules on consanguinity and affinity. Judaism and Islam provide for the formation of a pre-nuptial agreement – Christianity does not. The elements of a marriage ceremony are largely customary, provided requirements for validity are met, including the consent of the parties. Jews and Muslims must ordinarily marry from within the faith, though exceptions may be permitted (such as for men in Islam) – and, as

---

[163] Darul Isra Muslim Community Centre (Cardiff): Policy (2010): Part B.
[164] MAT: www.matribunal.com/inheritance-disputes.php.

in for example Liberal Judaism, provision is made for mixed marriages by all Christian churches, though in some subject to conditions about the religious upbringing of the children. Marriage is normally celebrated at a service in a synagogue, church or mosque, in the presence of a faith leader and witnesses. A marriage must be registered in the books of the religious organisation in which it is celebrated. However, Liberal Judaism and some Christian churches today recognise same-sex marriages. The religious marriages performed in accordance with the usages of Jews and rites of many Christian churches may be recognised in civil law; an Islamic marriage is not *proprio vigore* recognised in civil law but may be celebrated, for example, following a civil marriage. There is a proposal before Parliament that all Muslim marriage ceremonies should be registered under civil law and so recognised, not least to protect the rights of women. According to religious law, a marriage is dissolved ordinarily by the death of one of the spouses and extraordinarily when recognised as such by competent religious authority. Orthodox, Reform and Conservative Judaism makes provision for the religious divorce before the Beth Din – through a *get* issued by a husband; and in Progressive Judaism by either the husband or wife. *Sharia* councils, prevalent among Sunni Muslims in Britain, may provide for divorce at the instance of both husband and wife, the husband alone, or the wife alone. Both parties are free to marry religiously after divorce. But religious divorces are not recognised in civil law. However, synagogues, churches and mosques may be licensed to perform religious marriages registrable under civil law. In Christianity, only the Roman Catholic Church has matrimonial tribunals which may declare a marriage invalid – dissolution is forbidden. However, in the other churches a minister may solemnise the marriage of a divorced person whose former spouse is alive to the extent that this is authorised by the law of a church and the conscience of the minister. The large bodies of classical religious law in Judaism and Islam on inheritance and wills do not find an echo in the laws of Christians today – churches follow the State on these. The protection of children in the activities of synagogues, churches and mosques is increasingly the subject of soft-law regulation by faith communities designed to meet the standards set by civic society and the numerous statutory frameworks applicable to the safeguarding of children under which the welfare of the child prevails over the collective religious freedom of faith communities and organisations.

9

The Property and Finance of the Faith Community

The juridical instruments of the Jewish, Christian and Muslim communities studied here contain elaborate rules which apply to their property and finances. The interplay between these and civil law is also very evident with regard to the administration of property and finance. Generally, as individual religious communities all need the capacity under civil law to acquire, administer and dispose of property, they utilise trusts and trustees and other secular entities with juridical personality under civil law. Ownership of property is vested in institutions at various levels: nationwide, regional and local. This chapter compares rules of religious organisations on the acquisition and disposal of property, the dissolution of organisations, places of worship (and their contents, particularly objects needed for the administration of worship), the control of finance, income in the form of offerings, taxes and investment, and expenditure in the form of the insurance of property, and the remuneration of faith leaders. The chapter elucidates the key differences between the laws of faith communities, as well as the similarities between them from which it is possible to induce common principles of religious law. Religious law also indicates that the faithful across our three religions are engaged in fundamentally the same actions with regard to property and finance.

The Ownership of Property

Whilst the legal objects of Jewish, Christian and Muslim religious organisations are essentially spiritual, even though these are played out in the public sphere of religious life, their engagement in the management of property reveals the temporal aspects of religious life. Key to these activities is the juridical concept of ownership. The laws of most faith communities deal with the right to acquire, own, administer and dispose of property; the need for juridical personality under civil law to enable these; the right of a community to frame norms on the acquisition, administration and disposal of property; adherence to these norms by religious units, particularly at local level; and the distribution of property on the dissolution of a religious organisation or its units.

Rekhush and Nekhasim – Karka and Mettaltelin

Classical Jewish law has a large body of complex rules on property (*rekhush*) and possessions or goods (*nekhasim*), tangible objects which are movable or immovable; a word for property less frequently used is *kinyan*, from *kanah*, to acquire or to own, which denotes both the object owned and the proprietary right to it.[1] There are three kinds of property: that which has an owner; ownerless property, when ownership has been abandoned or relinquished; and property belonging to the Temple (namely, in the Talmudic sources, *hekdesh*, or 'holy' property). In turn, property is divided into two categories: realty/land (*karka*) and movables or personal property (*mettaltelin*). To transfer property, a recognised act of acquisition must be performed as evidence of agreement – and many different forms of act are mentioned in the Talmudic sources, some Scriptural in origin, others introduced by the Rabbis. Realty may be acquired by money (*keseph*, silver), that is the payment of the purchase price; bond (*shetar*), the delivery of a deed of sale; and possession/occupation with the intention of acquisition (*hazakah*). Movables are acquired by, for example: *hagbahah* (literally 'lifting'), in which the object is raised at least three handbreadths from the ground, this being valid for all movables; *meshichah*, that is drawing the object towards oneself; and *mesirah*, a symbolic delivery of the object to be acquired. Movables cannot be acquired by *keseph* or *shetar*. In the view of some authorities, there is scriptural warrant for this.[2]

As seen in Chapter 1, modern legal instruments list the acquisition, maintenance and disposal of property among the objects of Jewish organisations. Property may be acquired at national, regional or local

---

[1] I. Herzog, *Jewish Law* (1965) I.65–68: property; 69–75: ownership; 77–81: movable and immovable property. For instance, the twelfth book of Maimonides' code covers e.g. sale and purchase (*mekhirah*), original acquisition and gifts (*zekhiyah u-muttanah*), and agency and partnership (*sheluhin ve-shuttafin*): see generally N.S. Hecht *et al.*, eds., *Jewish Law* (1996) 26, 48, 141, 278.

[2] L. Jacobs, 'Property in Jewish law', in Peter Elman, ed., *An introduction to Jewish Law* (London: Lincolns-Prager, 1958) 44–52; and G.J. Webber, 'The principles of the Jewish Law of property', 10 *Journal of Comparative Legislation and International Law* (1928) 82–93.

level. First, nationwide, for example, the (Orthodox) United Synagogue, a charity constituted under the United Synagogues Act 1870,[3] has power to: purchase, take on a lease or exchange, hire or otherwise acquire any property, rights and privileges necessary to promote its objects; make regulations for property, rights and privileges so acquired; and sell, let, mortgage or dispose of its property or assets, subject to such consents as may be required by civil law.[4] The title to any real or personal property held by the United Synagogue 'shall be vested in the United Synagogue Trusts Limited'. Moreover, in the execution of the trusts, 'the Trust Corporation ... shall, in all respects, conform to and comply with any lawful directions of the Honorary Officers'.[5] Property must be applied 'solely towards the promotion of its objects'; if the United Synagogue takes or holds any property subject to any trusts, it must only deal with the property as is allowed by law, having regard to such trusts; and, if it takes/holds property in England, Scotland, Wales or Northern Ireland subject to the jurisdiction of the Charity Commissioners for England and Wales, it must not sell, mortgage, charge or lease it without such authority, approval or consent as may be required by civil law – as regards any such acquired property, the Honorary Officers are accountable for their own acts and for the due administration of such property.[6] The Council may consider any decision of the Honorary Officers to sell/dispose of the site of any member synagogue or other of its properties and make representations to the Honorary Officers thereon.[7] The Federation of Synagogues has similar rules.[8]

Secondly, at regional level, the Wessex Liberal Jewish Community is typical. It is managed and administered by a Council composed of the Honorary Officers (elected by the Annual General Meeting) who serve as Charity Trustees under civil law.[9] These may buy, take on a lease or exchange, hire or otherwise acquire any property and maintain and equip it for use, and sell, lease or otherwise dispose of it (complying with the

[3] US: Statutes 1. See below for the Statutes and other regulatory instruments.
[4] US: Statutes 5.23–25.
[5] US: Statutes 52–53: i.e. other than sums of cash (see below). The Trust Corporation is appointed in accordance with Statutes 53.
[6] US: Statutes 45–46.
[7] US: Statutes 40. The Board of Trustees (i.e. Honorary Officers) is responsible for strategic and policy decisions in relation to US property. The Council may inter alia: elect and remove Trustees.
[8] FOS: Laws 15.3. See also USCJ: Bye-Laws 1.
[9] WLJC: Con. Art. 17: the trustees may also appoint trustees to act as officers.

civil charity legislation).[10] The property must be used solely to promote the objects of the community,[11] which, in turn, may only be dissolved at a special meeting, which must pass a resolution by no less than two-thirds of the members.[12]

Thirdly, the norms of synagogues are similar at local level across the denominations. For instance, the Movement for Reform Judaism has issued guidance to its member synagogues on a wide range of property matters (summarising that of the civil Charity Commission).[13] The title to synagogue property is vested in custodian trustees who are responsible for the safekeeping of documentary evidence as to title (e.g. deeds); however, custodian trustees have no power to manage the property and no role in the administration of the charity but must sign all documents relating to the purchase of property.[14] In turn, the managing trustees (Council Members) must: act together and not delegate control of the charity property to others; act strictly in accordance with the charity governing document; act in its interests only and without regard to their own private interests; manage its affairs prudently; not (without explicit authority) derive any personal benefit from the charity; and take proper professional advice on matters on which they are not competent.[15] These norms are repeated and may be embellished by member synagogues;[16] the Brighton and Hove Reform Synagogue, for example, is a Charitable Incorporated Organisation under civil law.[17] Member synagogues also deal with their own dissolution. North London Reform Synagogue is typical: it may be dissolved by a resolution passed by a two-third majority of those present and voting at a Special General Meeting convened for the purpose on 21 days' notice being given; the resolution may give instructions for the disposal of property held by it or in its name, but if any property remains after satisfying all debts and liabilities, such property must not be given to or distributed among the members of the

---

[10] WLJC: Con. Art. 18: moreover: 'No alteration of [the] constitution or any special resolution shall have retrospective effect to invalidate any prior act of the trustees.'

[11] WLJC: Con. Art. 4.1; see also Art. 5: benefits/payments to Charity Trustees and connected persons.

[12] WLJC: Con. Art. 6.

[13] MRJ: Code of Practice, p. 3; see also pp. 13–14 for maintenance of property and 'ritual artefacts'.

[14] MRJ: Code of Practice, p. 14.   [15] MRJ: Code of Practice, p. 3.

[16] ELS: Con. Art. 4. See also e.g. EHC: Con. Trust Deed 2–3.

[17] BHRS: Con. 1(h): i.e., under the Charitable Incorporated Organisations (General) Regulations 2001.

synagogue. Instead it must be given/transferred to such other charitable institution, having objects similar to some or all of the objects of the synagogue as the charity may determine, and if it cannot be so given, then to any such charitable purposes.[18]

The Principle of Christian Stewardship

As is the case historically,[19] the juridical instruments of the churches studied here all contain elaborate rules which apply to church property and finance, including the use and maintenance of church buildings and the offerings of the Christian faithful. The idea of Christian stewardship is fundamental. According to the principles of Christian law, a church has the right to acquire, administer and dispose of property, and to make rules on these matters. A church and/or institutions or bodies within it may seek legal personality under civil law to enable ownership of property. A church may also make provision for its own dissolution or that of institutions or bodies within it and for the distribution of property on dissolution. Property is held on trust for the benefit of the church and its work and such institutions are required to exercise proper stewardship of it.[20] These principles are induced from the laws of the historic churches studied.

The Roman Catholic Church claims for itself 'the inherent right, independently of any secular power, to acquire, retain, administer and alienate temporal goods, in pursuit of its proper objectives', namely: divine worship, providing support for clergy and other ministers, and works of the sacred apostolate and charity. The universal church, Apostolic See, particular churches and all other juridical persons are capable of acquiring, retaining, administering and alienating temporal goods in accordance with canon law. Under the supreme authority of the Roman Pontiff, ownership of temporal goods belongs to that juridical person which lawfully acquired them.[21] The church may acquire temporal goods in any way by which it is just for others to do so either by

---

[18] NLRS: Laws, Art. 22.

[19] See e.g. R.H. Helmholz, Ecclesiastical Jurisdiction (2004) 494–504.

[20] Christian Law Panel of Experts, Principles of Christian Law (2016) Principle IX.1: the ownership of property.

[21] CIC: c. 1254: the right to and objects of property; c. 1255: juridical persons; c. 1256: ownership; see also c. 1257: all temporal goods 'are regulated by the canons' and by the statutes of the juridical person in question; c. 1258: the 'church' for these purposes means the relevant juridical person.

natural or positive law – and the civil law of contract must be observed in this regard unless contrary to divine law or canon law; the permission of the competent authority is required for the valid alienation of goods which constitute the church's 'stable patrimony'.[22] The (national) Episcopal Conference sets the minimum and maximum values of property. Property over the maximum value is alienated only with the permission of the competent authority and if it is of special artistic or historical interest that of the Holy See. Property between the minimum and maximum values may be alienated with the permission of the bishop who must obtain the consent of the finance council and interested parties; if parish property is below the minimum, the competent authority is the pastor. Written evaluations must be obtained from experts to determine a suitable price and property must not be sold for less; the proceeds must be applied as the competent authority directs.[23] If permission has not been obtained, the disposal is canonically invalid.[24] Stable patrimony whose value falls below the minimum may be alienated by the owner without the permission of a higher authority.[25] Canon law forbids absolutely the disposal of certain sacred objects.[26] Ordinaries supervise the administration of temporal goods subject to the Pontiff who is 'the supreme administrator and steward of all ecclesiastical goods'.[27]

Anglican churches should satisfy the rules of civil law that apply to the acquisition, ownership, administration and alienation of church property, both real and personal; property is held by those authorities within a church which enjoy legal personality as trustees or other entities of a fiduciary nature under civil law and competence under church law.[28] Ecclesiastical authorities are the stewards of church property which they hold and administer to advance the mission of a church, and for the benefit and use of its members in accordance with church law.[29]

---

[22] CIC: c. 1259; c. 1290: civil contract law; c. 1291: permission of the competent authority.

[23] CIC: cc. 1292–1294.

[24] CIC: c. 1296: if the alienation is valid in civil law, the competent authority decides whether to vindicate the church's right; c. 1377: anyone alienating without required consents incurs a just penalty.

[25] CIC: c. 1285.   [26] CIC: c. 1190: 'It is absolutely forbidden to sell sacred relics.'

[27] CIC: cc. 1273–1289: administration of goods; c. 1276: the ordinary; c. 1284: duties of administrators.

[28] PCLCCAC: Principle 80.1–2. See e.g. Church in Wales: Con. II.56, III.2–5, 17, 20–21, 26: the Representative Body is incorporated by Royal Charter and holds property as trustees at provincial level.

[29] PCLCCAC: Principle 80.3–4.

As property is held in trust for a church, it should not be alienated or encumbered without such consents as may be prescribed by church law; church trustees may sell, purchase and exchange property as authorised by that law.[30] A central assembly of a church, or other designated body, may frame laws for the management and use of property.[31] Management and day-to-day administration of church property at local level is vested in parish assemblies or other entities, subject to such rights of the clergy as may be provided by law.[32] National, regional, provincial, diocesan, parish or other trustees function under the order and control of the appropriate assembly to which church law renders them accountable.[33]

Much the same arrangements are found in the Protestant churches. The property belonging to congregations of the Presbyterian Church of Scotland is held for them at national level by the general trustees or by local trustees (the office-holders of the local church such as the minister); the general trustees must approve the sale of most forms of church property and determine the use of the proceeds.[34] The Presbyterian Church of Ireland replicates this pattern with both general trustees and congregational trustees appointed 'to receive and hold the property of the congregation on trust for the congregation and subject to its directions' and those of the Congregational Committee.[35] In turn, the functions of the regional Presbytery include approval of the purchase, sale, exchange or lease of Presbytery property.[36] In the Methodist Church in Great Britain, the Conference may legislate on property matters and it manages all connexional property; and at local level: 'The Church Council shall transact all business required of it as managing trustees of the local

---

[30] PCLCCAC: Principle 80.5–6. See e.g. Church of Ireland: Con. XI.11: the Representative Body holds property subject to the control of General Synod; it may lease or sell property in a diocese with the consent of the Diocesan Council; X.11: movables used in services vest in it 'subject to any trusts affecting' them.

[31] PCLCCAC: Principle 80.7.

[32] PCLCCAC: Principle 80.9. See e.g. Church of England: M. Hill, *Ecclesiastical Law* (2007) 3.76: each bishop, archdeacon and incumbent is a corporation sole in civil law, and a parochial church council is a corporation aggregate; nationally, the Church Commissioners hold a wide range of properties.

[33] PCLCCAC: Principle 80.10.

[34] J.L. Weatherhead, ed., *Constitution and Laws of the Church of Scotland* (1997) 141; Church of Scotland (Property and Endowments) Act 1925; Acts XXVI, 1933 and VII, 1995 (as amended by Act XIII, 1996): these regulate the sale of buildings.

[35] PCI: Code, 53–57; 122: the general trustees are 'a body incorporated under Royal Charter in 1871', act under the Irish Presbyterian Church Acts 1871 and 1901 and are appointed by General Assembly.

[36] PCW: Handbook of Rules, 3.2.2. See also URC: Manual D Pt. I.2.

property';[37] the authority of the Conference applies to property held at national, district, circuit and local levels.[38]

The Baptist Union of Great Britain has a system of model trusts for its member local churches, with holding trustees at national level and managing trustees at local level.[39]

Mal, Milk and Amanah

In Islam, as God is the absolute and eternal owner of all things on earth, so human ownership (*milk*) of property (*mal*) is a form of trust (*amanah*) from God: its exercise must be for the benefit of humankind, sharia-compliant and ultimately accountable to God. Private property may be acquired through, for example, inheritance, gift or purchase – and the honest use of it may be considered a form of worship (*ibadat*). As such, in classical Islamic law, a *waqf* is 'the permanent dedication by a Muslim of any property for religious or charitable purposes, or for the benefit of the founder (*waqif*) and his descendants, in such a way that the owner's right is extinguished, and the property is considered to belong to God'. There are two types of *waqf*, and both must be established by the founder voluntarily: the family *waqf* (*waqf al ahli*), which is set up for the benefit of the founder and his relatives in order to provide for their needs and, after their death, to be used for charitable purposes; and the religious or charitable *waqf* (*waqf al-khayri*), established for religious objects (such as the foundation or maintenance of a mosque or cemetery) or charitable purposes (such as the welfare of the poor). The person appointed to administer the *waqf* is the *mutawali* (often initially the founder or one appointed by a judge) – a woman or non-Muslim may be appointed as *mutawali*. The conditions to establish a *waqf* (which may be established orally or in writing) are: the property must be owned by the founder; the founder must be an adult of sound mind; the *waqf* must be perpetual and commence before the death of the founder; a *waqf* must

---

[37] MCGB: Constitutional Practice and Discipline, Deed of Union 21; Standing Orders 901–903; Standing Orders 940.

[38] MCGB: Constitutional Practice and Discipline, Model Trusts 2–11: property is either local, circuit, district, connexional, conference or general; 13: trustees are authorised to apply property for e.g. charitable purposes, religious worship or services.

[39] BUGB: Model Trusts for Churches 2003 1–9: 'The Baptist Union Corporation Limited is the Holding Trustee for many churches' under the Baptist and Congregational Trusts Act 1951; '"Church property" means the land and buildings to which these Trusts relate . . . under the day to day management of the [local] church.'

be absolute (and for Shia Islam, unconditional); its object must be able to be identified with reasonable certainty; and if made when the founder is on his deathbed (*mard al-mawt*), it may not exceed one third of his estate without the consent of his heirs.[40] The legal instruments of some of the Muslim organisations studied here make reference to the *waqf* – but most do not.

For instance, according to the model constitution of an Islamic organisation issued by the Central Mosque, as to 'the status of Masjid and Waqf properties': 'The Masjid is and shall forever remain a Waqf (trust) property. As such, its ownership is vested solely with Allah. It cannot be owned by any individual, organization or community. It cannot be sold, exchanged, given away or demolished in anyway whatsoever. It shall at all times be subject to the Shari'ah law relating to Waqf and Masjids at all time'; and: 'All other Waqf (trust) properties held by the congregation shall be subject to the Shari'ah Law of Waqf at all times.'[41] Similarly, the Mosques and Imams National Advisory Board recommends that, where appropriate, member organisations should be registered as 'a charity, waqf or company' with a publicly displayed policy on matters of property (and finance), accessible policies on equality of opportunity, health and safety, hygiene, child protection (each policy having a clear system set out for monitoring implementation), and systematic risk assessment processes in place.[42]

By way of contrast, most of the Muslim entities studied here present their norms on property in the secular manner, without express reference to categories in classical Islamic law. First, with regard to rights to property, the Nasru-Lahi-Il-Fathi Society is typical: through its Board of Trustees, it may acquire, maintain and dispose of property in order to further the society objects.[43] Secondly, as to ownership, Markazi Jamia Masjid Riza and Islamic Centre (Huddersfield) is typical: the title to property which is and may be acquired for the purpose of the Masjid

---

[40] J. Hussain, *Islamic Law* (1999) 114–116, 160–162: there are parallels between a *waqf* and a trust in civil law. See also A. Black *et al.*, *Islamic Law* (2013) 194–200: property; and 204–212: 'Islamic trusts' (*awqaf*); and UIDHR (1981) Preamble: 'all economic resources shall be treated as Divine blessings bestowed upon mankind, to be enjoyed by all in accordance with the Law [and] the rules and the values set out in the Qur'an and the Sunnah'; see also XVI: the right to the protection of property.

[41] Model Constitution of an Islamic Organisation: General Meetings, Indemnities etc. See e.g. Lancaster Islamic Centre: Con. Shura Committee.

[42] MINAB: Standard 1 (2011): www.minab.org.uk/self-regulation/standards.html.

[43] NASFAT: Con. Art. C.

must be vested in the Trustees who must enter into a Deed of Trust setting out the purpose and conditions under which they hold the property in trust for the Masjid and Islamic Centre.[44] Some mosques distinguish between holding and custodian trustees. For example, the Executive Committee of Reading Muslim Council (a charity under civil law), which may acquire any property necessary to achieve its objects, and, subject to any consents required by civil law, dispose of that property,[45] must cause the title to all land held by or in trust for the charity to be vested either in a corporation entitled to act as a custodian trustee or in no fewer than three holding trustees who are appointed by it.[46]

Thirdly, the legal instruments provide for the dissolution of the organisation and for the disposal of its property as a result. Markazi Jamia Masjid Riza and Islamic Centre (Huddersfield) is, again, typical. If the members resolve to dissolve the charity, the trustees must remain in office as Charity Trustees and are responsible for winding up its affairs. The trustees must collect all assets and pay or make provision for all its liabilities, and apply any remaining property or money either directly for its objects, or transfer it to any charity/charities for purposes the same as or similar to its own objects, or dispose of it in such other manner as the Charity Commission for England and Wales may approve in writing in advance. Either before or at the same time that the members pass a resolution to dissolve the charity, they may also pass a resolution specifying the manner in which the trustees must apply the remaining property/assets and the trustees must comply with that resolution. In no circumstances may the assets be paid to or distributed among the members (unless a member is itself a charity). The trustees must notify the Charity Commission promptly that the charity has been dissolved, and, if obliged to do so for any accounting period, the final accounts.[47]

The Administration of Places of Worship

The principal forms of real and personal property used at the most local level include places of worship and their contents, associated buildings

---

[44] MJMRIC: Con. Arts. 7: Treasurer; 14: property; 15: finance; 18: dissolution.
[45] RMC: Con. Section C: it may also employ staff.
[46] RMC: Con. Section L: provided that property is not vested in the Official Custodian for Charities.
[47] MJMRIC: Con. Art. 18; see also e.g. RMC: Con. Section U.

(such as residences for faith leaders), and registers and records. The religious organisations studied here have detailed rules on these items in terms of their administration, care and maintenance.

The Synagogue

The synagogue is the building in which Jews worship and offer their prayers – 'synagogue' (from the Greek word meaning assembly) corresponds to the Hebrew *bet ha-keneset* – or 'house of assembly', namely, the place where Jews assemble. Strict decorum and reverence must be observed in the synagogue by worshippers who are to be aware that they are in the presence of God – and there is a section in the Shulhan Aruch on laws with regard to the sanctity of the synagogue. It is understood that when a synagogue can no longer be used it may be sold on the basis that its non-use means that its sanctity is lost; it may be sold for use as a church or mosque, but there is a common practice to sell the synagogue indirectly through a third party – it is also permissible to purchase a church or mosque for use as a synagogue provided the building does not contain any religious symbols present under its former use. The main function of the synagogue is for public worship; but it may be used for private prayer when not in use for public worship. There is a custom that the worshippers are to hurry to the synagogue for worship and prayer (based on Hosea 6:3) and to leave in an unhurried fashion – this indicates eagerness to be there and reluctance to leave.[48]

Modern regulatory instruments of Jewish entities across the traditions deal in detail with synagogue use. The (Orthodox) United Synagogue may found, build, maintain, conduct, promote and develop within the United Kingdom member synagogues which conform to the Form of Worship for persons of the Jewish religion.[49] The Honorary Officers may from time to time determine 'the maintenance and conduct' of a member synagogue, being one which conforms to the Polish or German ritual for

---

[48] L. Jacobs, *Jewish Religion* (1999) 251–253: little is known of the origins of the synagogue; with no explicit reference in the Bible, many have suggested that it originated in the period of the Babylonian exile after the destruction of the first Temple (586 BCE), as a small meeting-place for prayer (Ezekiel 11:16), and the Talmud (*Megillah* 29a) identifies the 'small sanctuary' with the synagogue. Moreover: 'There are no rules in Judaism regarding the architectural form of the synagogue building.'

[49] US: Statutes 4; and Health and Safety Policy and Procedures (2015) 1: policy statement (aims, employee duties, reviewing the policy); 2: health and safety structure; 3: responsibilities; 4: safety arrangements.

persons of the Jewish religion.[50] However, the Local Honorary Officers are, subject the directions of the Honorary Officers, responsible for 'the day-to-day administration and management of the Synagogue buildings and, consulting the United Synagogue, for keeping such buildings maintained to a proper standard'. The buildings are the property of the United Synagogue and the Local Honorary Officers must inform the Honorary Officers about any matters which come to their attention which materially affect their value, condition or status. The member synagogue must not arrange for 'structural alterations, significant improvements or repairs to the Synagogue buildings without the approval of the United Synagogue'; and the appointment of a professional advisor as to such works must be made only by the United Synagogue in consultation with the Local Honorary Officers. Yet: 'Minor repairs up to a limit of expenditure notified in writing by the Chief Executive, may be carried out at the discretion of the Local Honorary Officers.'[51] However, as seen in Chapter 3, the religious use of the synagogue is in the keeping its Rabbi (with a Cantor if appropriate) and Wardens (part of the team of Honorary Officers) 'under the overall guidance of the Chief Rabbi'.[52]

The Movement for Reform Judaism requires members to ensure that the synagogue is maintained in 'good condition' and to consider regularly whether it is being used to the best advantage of the charity; and the objects of member synagogues include 'the provision and maintenance of a place of worship'.[53] Similarly, in Liberal Judaism, at Elstree Liberal Synagogue, the Council may provide and maintain a place of worship for the conduct of religious services.[54] Indeed, some instruments specify the religious items required at a synagogue and provide for the vesting of title to them in trustees – for instance at Exeter Hebrew Congregation, where 'the Synagogue shall be available for all forms of Jewish worship',[55] the following must be vested in the trustees (unless the Committee of Management directs otherwise): 'six sifrei Torah, two pairs of rimmonim, two breastplates and four yadayim', as well as all furniture, fittings and other contents.[56] As the architectural features of a synagogue may be the

---

[50] US: Bye-Laws 2.   [51] US: Bye-Laws 22.3–4.
[52] US: www.theus.org.uk. See also FOS: Laws 2: it may 'establish and maintain Jewish places of worship'.
[53] MRJ: Code of Practice, p. 3; see also pp. 13–14 for maintenance of property and 'ritual artefacts'. See e.g. NLRS: Laws, Art. 1: 'provision and maintenance of a place of worship'; SSRS: Con. Art. 2.
[54] ELS: Con. Art. 4. See also WLJC: Con. Art. 3.
[55] EHC: Con. Schedule of Regulations, 12.   [56] EHC: Con. Trust Deed 2.

subject of responsa,[57] so too are its records regulated; for example: the Secretary of North Hendon Adath Yisroel Synagogue must 'maintain the records of the Synagogue and deposit them in a place of security and safety';[58] and in the Movement for Reform Judaism, the synagogue Honorary Secretary must maintain, for example, a stock of prayer books (for synagogue use and sale to members) and minutes of Council meetings.[59]

In similar vein, Orthodox synagogues may make express provision for seating and the separation of men and women through the use of the halakhic institution of a partition (mechitza);[60] for example, the consti-tution of Norwich Hebrew Congregation states: 'Each member is entitled to a seat in the Synagogue. Men and women are to be seated in separate areas of the Synagogue' – but the Committee may, at its discretion allocate and/or reallocate reserved seats to members or delegate that responsibility as it sees fit.[61] Likewise, North Hendon Adath Yisroel Synagogue constitution provides: 'Every full Member ... shall, subject to availability, be allocated a seat for himself or herself and, wherever possible, for each of his/her unmarried sons under the age of 21 and, in the Ladies Gallery, for his wife and his daughters under the age of 21.'[62] Stanmore and Canons Park Synagogue has soft-law on this: 'Male con-gregants are reminded that the Mehitza to separate men and women is in place at the back of the Shul' and 'are therefore respectfully asked not to occupy the seats behind the Mehitza as they are reserved for the use of women for all services except on Yomin Noraim'.[63] However, in Conser-vative Judaism: 'In almost all our Synagogues, men and women are seated together', on the basis of 'the equality of the sexes' and human dignity.[64]

---

[57] S.B. Freehof, Reform Responsa (1960) No. 11: a sukkah (traditionally a booth or hut roofed with branches, built against or near a house or synagogue and used during the Jewish festival of Sukkoth as a temporary dining or living area) built on the bimah of a synagogue (the raised platform on which the reading of the Torah takes place) is merely a decoration and cannot be regarded as a lawful sukkah.

[58] NHAYS: Con. Art. 16: records include the roll of members.

[59] MRJ: Code of Practice, p. 8.

[60] The rationale for such a partition is given in the Babylonian Talmud (Sukkah 51b, 52a).

[61] NHC: Laws and Con. 7; see 5.10 for services held there involving another Jewish tradition.

[62] NHAYS: Con. Art. 5.

[63] Stanmore and Canons Park Synagogue (US): www.sacps.org.uk/synagogue-etiquette .html.

[64] Statement of Principles of Conservative Judaism (1988) 38: both are created in the image of God.

As in the historical halakhic tradition, there are also norms on etiquette at synagogues. The Orthodox Borehamwood and Elstree Synagogue is a good example, and its guidelines seek to ensure time spent in
the synagogue is 'spiritually fulfilling'. First, as to dress: all boys and men
must wear a *kippah* (skullcap) while in the synagogue and its grounds; all
Jewish married ladies must wear a hat or other head covering while in the
synagogue; everyone 'is asked to dress modestly'. A person dressed
inappropriately may be asked to put on a coat or leave, in order 'to
maintain an appropriate level of respect for the holiness of the Synagogue'. Secondly, 'to maintain the dignity of the Religious Service', for
example: electronic devices are not to be used; applause is not appropriate at any time in a service; there are points in the service where talking is
absolutely forbidden – for example the reading of the Torah and when
the Ark (containing the Torah scrolls) is open – and it is 'disrespectful' to
talk during the sermon; worshippers should face the Ark when it is open
and are not to go behind the *bimah* (reading desk in the centre of the
synagogue) – those who persist in disturbing the service may be asked to
leave. There are also provisions on synagogue security.[65]
    Jewish Heritage UK plays a key role in the care/maintenance of
historic synagogues. It is a charity, with a Director and Board of
Trustees, and its objects are the preservation and conservation for the
benefit of the public of historic buildings and sites of Britain's Jewish
community and educating the public about them. Its primary concern
is to care for synagogues and maintain them in use for worship, as well
as ritual baths, communal buildings, schools, and hospitals. It also
monitors the condition of historic Jewish cemeteries (especially those
no longer in use).[66] Its 2015 quinquennial survey invited 45 historic
synagogues to participate; of 38 which did so, 92 per cent of buildings
were rated in a good or fair condition; 53 per cent showed significant
improvement; the remainder were a matter for concern or likely to
become so in the not too distant future. Some were active in hosting
school and civic groups, with impressive visitor numbers on Heritage
Open Days and similar events. Progress may be attributed to the
commitment and enthusiasm of individuals and the ability to access
funding. The survey stressed the importance of synagogues introducing

---

[65] BAES: Visiting Guidelines. For security, see also e.g. MRJ: Code of Practice, p. 16.
[66] Established in 2004, it became a Registered Charity in 2007: http://jewish-heritage-uk
.org/about.

a Maintenance Regime, and the need to train and mentor in good practice the custodians of historic synagogues.[67]

The Church Building and Sacred Objects

The historic churches share several principles of Christian law on sacred places and objects. A church may dedicate or otherwise set aside a building or other space, prescribed objects, and other forms of property, to worship and other sacred purposes. A place of worship, o other space, or sacred object, must be used in a manner which i consistent with its dedication. Responsibility for the use, care, and maintenance of these, vests in a designated person or body. Oversigh of the administration of church property vests in a competent ecclesi astical authority and a periodic appraisal of its condition may be the object of a lawful visitation.[68] These principles are induced from the similarities which exist between the legal systems of the churche. studied.

Under Roman Catholic canon law, sacred places are those assigned to divine worship or burial through their dedication or blessing by the diocesan bishop; and anything 'out of harmony with the holiness o the place is forbidden'. They are 'desecrated' by acts which in the judgment of the Ordinary are so serious and contrary to the sacred character of the place that worship may not be held there until the harm is repaired by the penitential rite prescribed in the liturgical books. No new church may be built without the bishop's consent if he is satisfied that this is for the good of souls and that the means to build it are available; before consenting, he must consult the Presbyteral Council and neighbouring rectors. The principles of liturgy and sacred art must be observed in erecting or restoring a church. Each church must be main- tained in a way which 'befits the house of God', and entry for sacred functions must be free of charge.[69] When a church cannot be used for worship and there is no possibility of restoration, the bishop may allow it

---

[67] *Synagogues at Risk: A Report on the Findings of the Second Quinquennial Survey of Historical Synagogues in Britain and Ireland* (Jewish Heritage UK, 2015) 3–4.

[68] Christian Law Panel of Experts, *Principles of Christian Law* (2016) IX.2: sacred places and objects.

[69] CIC, cc. 1210–1221: worship, preservation, entry; c. 553: vicars forane must ensure that 'the good appearance and condition of the churches and of sacred furnishings are carefully maintained'.

to be used for some secular but not unbecoming purpose. There are also norms on oratories, shrines, altars, cemeteries and records.[70] For Anglicans, likewise, buildings may be designated as places of public worship, which, with places for Christian burial, may be set aside for the purposes of God by consecration or dedication customarily performed by a bishop.[71] Such property may not be used for purposes inconsistent with the uses of God for which it is set aside; Wardens or other stewards must not allow churches to be profaned by any temporal use inconsistent with the sanctity of the place and sound doctrine.[72] The day-to-day control, direction and administration of places of worship vests in the parish council or other local assembly, which must ensure that proper care is taken of them and their contents, and endeavour to keep them decent, clean and in good repair.[73] Episcopal or other lawful consent, whether executive or judicial, must be obtained to alter, or add to, or remove property from places of worship to such extent and in such manner, and subject to such appeals, as may be prescribed by law.[74] An inventory should be kept of the contents of churches, and a church authority should inspect them and their contents at regular intervals as may be prescribed by law.[75] There are also norms on the maintenance of and access to records.[76] Moreover, provision is to be made for clergy to have appropriate accommodation which should be inspected periodically and whose occupation may be terminated or restricted only in accordance with law.[77]

As is the case in the Lutheran Church in Great Britain, in which it is the responsibility of the pastor to ensure that 'the facilities and buildings owned or used by the congregation are properly maintained and are

---

[70] CIC: cc. 1222–1234; cc. 1235–1239: the altar or table for the Eucharistic sacrifice should be fixed and dedicated; cc. 1240–1243: where possible the church (and parish) is to have its own cemeteries or at least an area in a public cemetery blessed and reserved for the deceased faithful; c. 535: parish records.

[71] PCLCCAC: Principle 81.1–3. See e.g. Church of Ireland: Con. IX.36: 'As often as churches are newly built or rebuilt, or churchyards are appointed for burial, they shall be dedicated and consecrated' by the bishop.

[72] PCLCCAC: Principle 81.5–6. See e.g. Church of Ireland: Con. IX.27.

[73] PCLCCAC: Principle 81.7. See e.g. Scottish Episcopal Church: Can. 35.3.

[74] PCLCCAC: Principle 81.8. See e.g. Church in Wales: Rules of the Diocesan Courts: the Diocesan Chancellor deals with such matters under the faculty jurisdiction.

[75] PCLCCAC: Principle 81. See e.g. Church of England: Can. F17: inventory.

[76] PCLCCAC: Principle 83. See e.g. Scottish Episcopal Church: Can. 42, Resolution 1: inspection of registers every 4 years.

[77] PCLCCAC: Principle 82; e.g. Church of Ireland: Con. IV.51.5: a vicar has a right to a 'free residence'

suitable for Christian worship',[78] so too in the Methodist Church of Ireland, the (local) Church Council is responsible for the 'maintenance letting and insurance of all the property entrusted to the Society, subject to such rights and obligations, if any, as may be vested in Local Trustees' The Council must appoint a Property Steward 'responsible to the Council for the proper maintenance of all property'. Also, a schedule of trust property in the circuit showing its state of repair must be submitted by the Circuit Trustees to the Circuit Executive annually and forwarded to the District Property Secretary; any structural alteration must be approved by the District Synod and Property Board; and the Circuit Superintendents must ensure that all renovations and repairs of trust property are considered by the trustees. Moreover, 'Trustees shall take care that Church property is restricted to Church uses only, in accordance with the provisions of the Trust Deed of the premises'; thus: 'the greatest possible care must be taken not to allow premises set apart for religious purposes to be used for entertainments which would bring offence to our people generally'; these include card playing, gambling, the sale, consumption or supply of alcohol, and preaching contrary to Methodist beliefs.[79] Methodists also have extensive provisions about the maintenance of records.[80]

Presbyterian laws require much the same action. For example, the local congregation in the Church of Scotland is responsible for the maintenance of its buildings. It must hold an annual inspection of its property and keep a Property Register to record inspections and any works carried out; the register is submitted annually to the Presbytery, which instructs full inspections of congregational property every five years. Again, if a congregation proposes to carry out work on a building, it must obtain the approval of the Presbytery – but the Presbytery may waive this requirement, provided the work costs no more than the financial limit fixed by the national General Assembly on the recommendation of the General Trustees; if the work costs more than this figure, and this is approved, the Presbytery must refer the matter to the Consultative Committee on Church Properties whose recommendation must be given due

---

[78] LCGB: Rules and Regulations, Responsibilities and Duties of Pastors, 1–24.
[79] MCI: Regulations, Discipline and Government, 10.06, 10.22, 10.63–69: political meetings are also prohibited.
[80] MCGB: Constitutional Practice and Discipline, Standing Orders 015; the one responsible for the archives for e.g. the circuit is the superintendent.

consideration by the Presbytery.[81] The use of a church building is also subject to regulation. Under Irish Presbyterian law: 'The minister shall be entitled to use the place of worship and other church buildings for the purposes of his office, subject to any direction of the Presbytery' but has 'no right to use the buildings or grant the use of them for any other purposes without the authority of the Kirk Session'.[82] Presbyterian laws also provide in some detail for the maintenance of Session, Presbytery and Assembly records and archives and manses.[83] Similar rules are to be found in the United Reformed Church and Baptist Union on church maintenance, records and manses.[84]

The Mosque Building

The only fundamental requirement for a *masjid* is that it is 'religiously' clean, that is free from contaminants whose presence require ritual purification, for example human or animal blood, urine, faecal matter, alcohol or matter not from *halal* animals. Therefore, it is a 'requirement to remove shoes when entering'. Normally, a *masjid* would have: facilities for ritual washing (*wudhu*), to prepare for prayers; a *mehrab* or alcove at the front of the praying area, to amplify the voice of the imam in *salah* and as a barrier (*sutra*) at the front of the *jamat*; a prayer mat (*musalah*) to mark out the imam's position; adjacent to this a pulpit (*mimbar*), for the Friday sermon; a wooden stave (*asaar*), which the imam customarily grasps when preaching; and copies of the Quran. Additional features like a dome or minaret (for a *muezzin* to issue the call to prayer) make the building distinctively Islamic, but have no essential religious significance.[85]

It is estimated that there are about 809 buildings registered (under the civil Places of Worship Registration Act 1855) as Muslim places of meeting for religious worship. The majority are Sunni (about 700–800 are Deoband and about 350 Bareilvi). Many Shias use Sunni mosques, although the reverse is rare.[86] In principle, all are open to anyone to perform Islamic duties at any time, and they welcome visitors. There are

[81] J.L. Weatherhead, ed., *Constitution and Laws of the Church of Scotland* (1997) 142; Act IX, 1979.
[82] PCI: Code, 82(1)–(2).   [83] PCI: Code, 41; PCW: Handbook of Rules, 4.10.
[84] See e.g. URC: Manual B.2: under the United Reformed Church Acts 1972, 1981 and 2000.
[85] M. Naqshbandi, *Islam and Muslims in Britain* (2012): Guide 4.1. For debate on building mosques, see A. Black *et al.*, *Islamic Law* (2013) 259–264.
[86] M. Naqshbandi, *Islam and Muslims in Britain* (2012). Guide 3.3.1.

various 'conventions' applicable to those who enter the mosque. First, the attire of men and women should be modest and as far as possible respec the Islamic dress code: men must be covered at least from the navel to the knee, and women entirely except for the face and hands. Secondly the separation of men and women: the five times daily congregationa prayer is enjoined on men, not on women (prayer by women is expectec to be discreet and private and therefore performed at home). Mos mosques make provision for women, and will allocate space wher requested. Larger mosques often have a gallery over the main room, part or all of which is for the use of women. During congregational prayer, it is usual for male visitors to wait at the back of the main room, but not sc for women. Thirdly, as there is an aversion among more strictly practis- ing Muslims to be photographed, consent must be obtained for this.[87]

The regulatory instruments of the Muslim entities studied here have norms on the maintenance of property. For example, under the model constitution issued by the Central Mosque, the Shura Committee of an Islamic organisation must maintain the masjid, madrassa, cemetery, lecture hall, meeting rooms and houses of residence for the Imam or Muadhins and it may equip these.[88] However: 'Only those persons who are adherents of the Islamic faith and referred to as Muslims shall have recourse to utilization of the facilities of the congregation', such as the right of entry to and use of the masjid and graveyard.[89] The Shura Committee must also maintain 'a detailed inventory of the assets of the congregation'.[90] At East London Mosque, a 'Radio Service provides access to the Adhan (Call to Prayer), Friday sermon, Tarawih (Ramadan evening prayers) and selected programmes for those who are at home'.[91] Under another model constitution, the mosque Facilities Manager is responsible for: cleaning the prayer space and mats (includ- ing for Friday prayers); ensuring the cleanliness of the ablution facilities (and reporting on this to the facilities committee); and keeping records of the society library and any other assets.[92]

Mosques may also have soft-law applicable to visitors. For example, at Birmingham Central Mosque: 'All adult visitors and children above the

---

[87] M. Naqshbandi, *Islam and Muslims in Britain* (2012): Guide 4.11–12.
[88] Model Constitution of an Islamic Organisation: Shura Committee 1–3.
[89] Model Constitution of an Islamic Organisation: www.central-mosque.com/fiqh/ ModelOfIslamicOrg.htm.
[90] Model Constitution of an Islamic Organisation: Shura Committee 11.
[91] ELMT: www.eastlondonmosque.org.uk/content/religious-spiritual.
[92] IFIS CUBE Network: Sample Con. of an Islamic Society Art. 4.5.

age of 12 are requested to observe modest dress when visiting the mosque' (for the latter a standard school uniform suffices). Female visitors may cover their heads if they wish, for example to enrich their own experience. There are also 'general rules' to enable visitors to 'respect the peace and prayer of worshippers inside the mosque'; visitors must: remove their shoes in certain specific areas around the mosque; keep food and drinks out of the mosque, except areas that have been designated as eating areas; not bring any animals into the mosque; keep the mosque building and courtyard clean by disposing of litter properly and safely; abide by the general rules of the mosque as displayed around the building; and not engage in smoking either inside the building or in the mosque courtyard.[93] Provision may also exist in the constitution of a mosque for its furniture/equipment,[94] and for the establishment and maintenance of a mosque library and reading room.[95]

The Control of Finance – Budgets, Accounts and Audit

Religious laws which regulate the control of finance generally mirror those on real and personal property. Rules address: those authorities charged to manage finances; the preparation and the approval of budgets; and accounts and their audit. As with the regulation of movable and immovable property, the foundation which underlies rules about finance is the principle of trusteeship, designed not least to honour those who donate to religion by systems of accountability; and, insofar as the entities studied are charities, many of these rules are shaped by standards set by civil law and the Charity Commission.[96] Classical religious law comes to the fore with respect to donating for pious causes. This section focuses in the main on the control of finance at local level.

Mammon and Maaser

Classical Jewish law has a large body of rules on money (*mammon* or *keseph*).[97] For example, tithes due from the faithful must be from corn,

---

[93] BCM: Advice (30 May 2015).   [94] See e.g. NUIM: Con. Art. 2.
[95] CJM: Con. Art. 4.1: library and reading room; Art. 4: acquisition and disposal of property.
[96] See the Charity Commission for England and Wales Statement of Recommended Practice (on budgets, accounting and reporting): www.gov.uk/government/publications/charities-sorp-2005.
[97] For an historical perspective, see e.g. N.S. Hecht *et al.*, eds., *Jewish Law* (1996) 326, 333, 335; for taxation, see 105, 169, 170, 283.

wine and oil (under biblical law), and from fruit and vegetables (under Rabbinic law). The farmer first separates from the yield a portion – a sixtieth, fiftieth or fortieth at the discretion of the farmer – as an offering or gift (*terumah*) to be made to a priest (*kohen*) and this is then treated as sacred food not to be eaten if the priest is in a state of ritual contamination or if the offering itself is contaminated – nor may it be eaten by a non-*kohen*. One tenth of the remaining produce (the first tithe or *maaser rishon*) is then separated and given to a Levite (i.e. a member of the tribe of Levi – the third son of Jacob – gatekeepers of the Temple), who, in turn, separates a tenth of his tithe and this (*terumat maaser*) is given to a *kohen* to be treated as the original *terumah*. The portion given to the Levite has no sanctity and may be eaten by an ordinary Israelite. The farmer separates a tenth of the remainder (the second tithe, or *maaser sheni*), which is taken to Jerusalem and consumed there in a spirit of sanctity. However, every third and sixth year of the cycle culminating in the Sabbatical year, the second tithe is given to the poor as 'the poor man's tithe' (*maaser ani*). After the destruction of the Temple, *maaser sheni* was redeemed for a small amount and this tithe could then be consumed by the farmer.[98] Today, it is understood that tithing laws apply only to Israel – farmers in the diaspora have no duty to give tithes – and, in so far as the purpose of tithes was the upkeep of the priests and Levites, the law has not survived destruction of the Temple. Rabbis also debate whether a tithe of money is voluntary or obligatory for Jews.[99]

In any event, modern regulatory instruments echo the broad idea of *maaser* with rules on subscriptions; and there are rules on accounts, budgets and investments.[100] The (Orthodox) United Synagogue may accept gifts and borrow or raise money for its objects on such terms and on such security as are thought fit.[101] First, its income must be applied 'solely towards the promotion of its objects'. No money may be paid or transferred by way of profit to its members, and no Honorary Officer or Council member may be appointed to any office paid by salary or fees, or receive other monetary benefit save for reasonable and proper expenses.[102] The United Synagogue may also employ and pay such

---

[98] I. Herzog, *Jewish Law* (1965) I.73, 216–217, 291; Numbers 18:21–32; Deuteronomy 14:22–27, 26:12.

[99] L. Jacobs, *Jewish Religion* (1999) 275–276. The practice in the State of Israel is a token.

[100] See e.g. FOS: Laws 15.3.   [101] US: Statutes 5.26.

[102] US: Statutes 45: Honorary Officers and Council members may be paid for professional services.

officers and staff as it thinks fit and make appropriate arrangements for the payment of the pensions, if any, of its employed officers/staff.[103]

Secondly, the United Synagogue may: procure contributions by personal or written appeals, public meetings or otherwise; invest its money and other property in such investments, securities or other property or on deposit or loan, in the United Kingdom or elsewhere as it thinks fit; appoint a person as an investment manager;[104] and delegate such person power to buy and sell investments in accordance with its investment policy (and revoke or vary this on reasonable and proper notice), giving directions to the investment manager as to the manner in which he is to report on all sales and purchases of investments made; and arrange as it thinks fit for any of its investments or income from those investments to be held by a corporate body as its nominee.[105]

Thirdly, the Treasurers must annually prepare and submit to the Council: at its June meeting each year, the annual accounts of the United Synagogue; and at its annual budget meeting (in November/December) a budget showing the estimated income and expenditure of the United Synagogue for the ensuing year. The Council may receive and consider any such budget and make representations on it to the Honorary Officers. If Council does not approve the budget as first presented to it, it may reject such budget and request the Honorary Officers to reconsider that budget and represent the budget to them, but the Council must not, if the budget is represented, reject it.[106]

At local level, each member synagogue of the United Synagogue must collect an annual membership subscription – the 'communal pay over' – from its members. A proportion of this is paid over to the United Synagogue to support it and for the services it provides. The remainder is retained and administered locally according to United Synagogue rules. The Local Honorary Officers are, subject to any direction of the Honorary Officers, to ensure the due and proper application of the synagogue's income/property. The Financial Representative must each year prepare and submit to the United Synagogue a budget, at the time and in the form directed by the Honorary Officers, setting out anticipated income and expenditure for the ensuing year.[107] The member synagogue must also contribute, at a rate set out in the budget of the United Synagogue in relation to that synagogue, a sum to cover the costs of the United

---

[103] US: Statutes 5.12.
[104] That is, within the meaning of the Financial Services Act, 1986.
[105] US: Statutes 5.28, 32.   [106] US: Statutes 39–40.   [107] US: Bye-Laws 22.1–2.

Synagogue, and such further contributions as the Local Honorary officers may from time to time decide.[108] The Local Honorary Officers must cause to be kept proper books or records of accounts (including member accounts) in a form determined by the national Honorary Officers. All books and account records kept by the synagogue 'should fully comply with ... relevant and other statutory requirements ... imposed by law'.[109]

Other Orthodox synagogues have analogous norms on, for example, budgets and accounting.[110]

For the Movement for Reform Judaism, a member synagogue is 'a well-run charity' if 'it is economically and effectively managed'.[111] First, each synagogue must have a Treasurer to: prepare forecasts and budgets, and with the Examiner the accounts; pay bills, salaries and expenses and bank all monies; with Council, advise on setting subscription rates; with the Administrator, collect dues, other fees and arrears, compile a fee schedule, and maintain a quarterly return to the Joint Jewish Burial Society; prepare the Monthly Finance report for Council; and compute and pay the tax and national insurance contributions to the Inland Revenue as to employees.[112] The synagogue Finance committee consists of the Council Chair, Honorary Treasurer, Assistant Honorary Treasurer and Administrator. The Council Chair may appoint a subscriptions officer to assist in collecting arrears, and invite any member who has financial skills to attend Finance Committee Meetings; the Treasurer must attend.[113]

Secondly, in its summary of the guidance of the Charity Commission for England and Wales, the member synagogue Trustees (Council Members) in managing the charity's finances must ensure, *inter alia*: bank accounts are operated by more than one person; all property is under the trustees' control; funds held for different purposes are kept in separate bank accounts; full and accurate accounting records are kept; and all money owed or due to the charity is collected in full. The trustees must spend income solely to achieve the objects of the charity (unless they have explicit authority to accumulate it) and with 'absolute fairness'

---

[108] US: Bye-Laws 23.   [109] US: Bye-Laws 24; see 25 for the annual report.
[110] See e.g. NHC: Laws and Con. 2, 4 and 6; and NHAYS: Con. Art. 5: membership fees.
[111] MRJ: Code of Practice, p. 4.
[112] MRJ: Code of Practice, pp. 6–7; see also p. 13: Finance Committee which deals with the state of the synagogue finance, preparation of budgets and fee increases.
[113] MRJ: Code of Practice, p. 37.

between persons qualified to benefit from the charity. When there are funds to invest, the trustees must: invest within the limits of the powers granted by the governing document or the civil Trustee Act 2000; monitor the performance of investments; avoid speculation and invest prudently to achieve both income and capital growth; and seek professional advice on what investments are most suitable.[114]

Thirdly, each synagogue should have an annual membership subscription.[115] The Finance Committee recommends rates and Council then decides. All members are rated according to their profile and the correct band. The Treasurer provides the Administrator with a monthly schedule of payments who then sends arrears letters, also monthly. Regular updates on the situation are sent to the Finance Committee; in all cases, confidentiality is observed. Should a member miss one payment, efforts are made to recover the sum. A member must not be removed for a minor infringement of the subscription rules. Small sums may be written off. If a series of subscriptions is unpaid, it must be determined whether the member has left the synagogue without informing it or whether there is hardship. If the member fails to respond, membership is suspended, but if the member pleads hardship, the Treasurer, Chair of Council and Administrator deal with the case quietly and with sympathy. A member seriously in arrears may be removed by the Administrator after notifying Council. If a member misses three payments without contacting the synagogue, termination of membership may be considered. Nobody is allowed to be more than one year in arrears; and: 'Common sense and compassion is ... used when dealing with subscription arrears.'[116]

Finally, when a synagogue raises funds by appealing to the public, it should: ensure the appeal is properly described, stating what the public's donations will be used for; not use methods which exert undue pressure on people to donate; approve in advance any fund-raising or advertising carried out on the charity's behalf; and require fund-raisers to hand over money raised by them before deducting their fees or expenses. Synagogue trustees risk personal liability if they: cause loss to the charity by acting unlawfully, imprudently or outside the terms of its governing document; or commit the charity to debts which amount to more than its assets. When a synagogue needs to employ staff it should give each employee a proper contract of employment and a written job description making

---

[114] MRJ: Code of Practice, p. 3.
[115] MRJ: Code of Practice, p. 11; see p. 13 for the Subscriptions Officer.
[116] MRJ: Code of Practice, pp. 37–38.

clear the extent of their authority to act on the charity's behalf.[117] These four sets of norms are repeated and/or embellished by member synagogues.[118]

The rules of Liberal communities are similar.[119] For example, the finances of Wessex Liberal Jewish Community are managed and administered by its Council (which includes the Treasurer).[120] Its Charity Trustees may: raise funds, but not undertake any permanent trading activity, in compliance with relevant civil law; borrow money and charge the property as security for repayment of money borrowed (complying with the Charity Act 2006); pay for goods or services necessary for the work of the charity; and open bank accounts and invest funds.[121] Income must be applied solely towards the objects of the community; a trustee may be reimbursed for 'reasonable expenses properly incurred' when acting on its behalf;[122] and the community may only be dissolved at a special meeting passing a resolution by no less than two-thirds of the members.[123] The trustees must comply with civil charity law as to keeping accounts for the preparation of annual statements of account, the transmission of these to the Charity Commission; and preparation of an annual report and return for transmission to the Commission. All cheques and payment instructions drawn on the charity bank or investment accounts must be signed or made jointly by two unrelated signatories authorised by Council.[124] The trustees must keep all the buildings of the charity in good repair and insure them to their full value against fire and other usual risks and they must have suitable insurance in respect of public liability and employer's liability.[125] The trustees set a scale for the subscriptions of members and may vary the subscription for the current year; addition or amendment of a levy requires approval of a

---

[117] MRJ: Code of Practice, p. 4; see also p. 13: fund-raising.
[118] See e.g. BHRS: Con. Art. 6: the application of income; Art. 7: payments to the Charity Trustees; Art. 12–20: Charity Trustees; Art. 22: Treasurer; Art. 31: accounts; and SSRS: Con. Art. 5: subscriptions; Art. 17: finance. See also NLRS: Law, Art. 12–13.
[119] ULPS: *Affirmations* (2006) are silent on financial matters.
[120] WLJC: Con. Art. 17: see above Chapter 4. See also e.g. PLJC: Con. Art. 5: subscriptions.
[121] WLJC: Con. Art. 18: moreover: 'No alteration of [the] constitution or any special resolution shall have retrospective effect to invalidate any prior act of the trustees.'
[122] WLJC: Con. Art. 4.1; see also Art. 5: benefits/payments to Charity Trustees and connected persons.
[123] WLJC: Con. Art. 6.
[124] WLJC: Con. Art. 27: accounts must be prepared in accordance with the Statement of Recommended Practice of the Charity Commission: see above n. 96.
[125] WLJC: Con. Art. 30.

resolution of the General Meeting; the trustees may reduce a subscription subject to a review on at least an annual basis; and subscriptions are payable in advance of the period covered.[126]

Likewise, the income and assets of the United Synagogue of Conservative Judaism are 'irrevocably dedicated for religious, educational, and other charitable purposes' and no part may be used to benefit any private person, except only for payment of reasonable compensation for services rendered and other payments so as to further its purposes.[127] Congregations should permit fund-raising under their auspices that is in keeping with 'Jewish law and custom'. Fund-raising likely to bring discredit to the congregation is not permitted, even if such activity is permitted under civil law.[128] The model constitution for *kehillot* also has norms on a range of financial matters.[129]

The Regulation of Finance in Christianity

There are several principles of Christian law common to the historic churches on the control of ecclesial finance, income and expenditure, some of which reflect ancient norms on the giving of tithes to the church.[130] As to the control of finance, a church has the right to make rules for the administration and control of its finances. Civil law applicable to financial accountability must be complied with. A church must ensure sound financial management, including the framing and approval by competent authority of an annual budget; should provide, with regard to each entity within it, for the keeping of accounts for approval by a competent authority; and must ensure that financial accounts are audited annually by qualified persons in order to promote proper stewardship in the church.[131] As to lawful income: a church has a right to receive funds. The faithful must contribute financially, according to their means, to the church's work. The officers of a church should encourage the faithful in the matter of offerings and collect and distribute these as prescribed. The

---

[126] WLJC: Con. Art. 8.12. See also ELS: Con. Art. 4, 6, 15–17; and EHC: Con. Trust Deed 2–4.

[127] USCJ: BL 1.3.

[128] USCJ: Standards for Congregational Practice (2017): Standard VII.

[129] USCJ: Guide to Constitutions (2010) Art. V: subscriptions; Art. VIII: Board of Trustees; Art. XV.3: Finance and Budget Committee.

[130] See e.g. R.H. Helmholz, *Ecclesiastical Jurisdiction* (2004) 40–43, 433–474.

[131] Christian Law Panel of Experts, *Principles of Christian Law* (2016) Principle IX.3: the control of finance.

local church and other entities may be required by competent authority to make a financial contribution to meet the wider institutional costs and needs of the church. A church which invests money should do so prudently and in ventures which are consistent with the ethical standards of the church.[132] As to expenditure, a church should: require the designated institutions or bodies within it to insure church property against loss; support and sustain those engaged in ministry according to their need and circumstance; and make suitable provision for ordained ministers who are in ill-health and for those who retire.[133] These principles derive from the laws of the churches.

First, as to the control of finance, in the Roman Catholic Church, while the Apostolic See regulates its own finances, each diocese has an institute to collect and manage funds through which the bishop is to satisfy those who serve the church and meet the needs of the diocese. The bishop is assisted by a finance council composed of at least three of the faithful skilled in financial affairs and in civil law and of outstanding integrity and appointed by the bishop for a five-year term. Administrators of temporal goods must present to the Ordinary an annual report, which in turn he is to present to the finance council for consideration. The council must prepare each year a budget of the income and expenditure foreseen, according to directions given by the bishop, for the governance of the diocese in the coming year. At the end of the year, it must examine a report of receipts and expenditure. The bishop must also appoint a finance officer to administer funds under the authority of the bishop in accordance with the budget determined by the finance council; the officer must report receipts and expenditure at the end of the year to the council. Moreover, each parish is to have a finance council acting in accordance with universal law and Episcopal directions.[134]

The principle of 'financial stewardship' is equally pivotal in Anglicanism. A church should be financially independent and self-supporting and each unit within it should be entrusted with a share in the responsibilities for, and control and direction of, the finances in that church. An ecclesiastical organisation must comply with such financial

---

[132] Christian Law Panel of Experts, *Principles of Christian Law* (2016) Principle IX.4: lawful income.

[133] Christian Law Panel of Experts, *Principles of Christian Law* (2016) Principle IX.5: ecclesiastical expenditure.

[134] CIC: cc. 1271–1277: diocesan funds; cc. 228, 492–494, 1276–1277, 1287: diocesan finance council; c. 537: parish finance council; c. 1280: every juridic person must have a finance council.

procedures and controls as are prescribed by church law, keep financial accounts and submit an annual report with the audited accounts to the appropriate church assembly in order for that assembly to review the financial management and affairs of that organisation.[135] Also, ministers must exercise propriety in financial matters.[136] Oversight of finance in an ecclesiastical unit in a church resides in its assembly, and day-to-day administration of funds by a lawfully constituted financial executive is under the general direction and control of the relevant assembly (such as a parish council). The bishop has no unilateral general control over diocesan finance. Funds must be used according to the terms of any gift by which they are acquired, and investigation of complaints of financial mismanagement should be carried out by an independent body with an appeal lying to an appropriate ecclesiastical authority.[137]

Protestants employ a similar pattern of budgets, accounting and audit at each level of the institutional church. For instance, the Conference of the Methodist Church in Great Britain may issue norms about finance. According to these, accounts must be kept of all moneys held at connexional, district, circuit or local church level. These must be audited annually in accordance with civil law. The Treasurer of any fund must oversee that fund, ensure that it is administered in accordance with the lawful instructions of the body to which the Treasurer is responsible, assist in the preparation of budgets, and monitor income and expenditure.[138] These rules apply to district, circuits and local funds. The Circuit Superintendent must ensure that auditors are appointed as to funds under the jurisdiction of the Circuit Meeting or Church Councils in the circuit. As to the latter, the local Church Council is 'to exercise responsible stewardship of its property and finance'.[139] The Treasurer must: receive 'all collections, gifts, donations, subscriptions and other moneys raised for the general church fund, the benevolence fund or the model trust fund and any money arising for such other accounts as the Church Council may direct'; meet all financial obligations on behalf of the Church Council; and present a statement of all such funds and

---

[135] PCLCCAC: Principle 84.

[136] PCLCCAC: Principle 85.1–5: a minister must ensure the highest standards, of honesty and care, in financial activities (e.g. keep church and personal finances separate).

[137] PCLCCAC: Principle 86. See e.g. Church in Wales: Con. VI.23: parish finance.

[138] MCGB: Constitutional Practice and Discipline, Standing Orders 012 and 012A.

[139] MCGB: Constitutional Practice and Discipline, Standing Orders 640; see also Standing Orders 621: the General Church Meeting (held annually) meets to discuss 'the condition of the Local Church, including its financial affairs'.

accounts to the Church Council and to such other committee or com
mittees as the Council may direct.[140] Moreover, the Council mus
appoint annually an auditor or independent examiner for all funds i
its jurisdiction.[141] As to the local church: 'The first charge on the genera
church fund shall be the sums required of the local church by th
assessment of the Circuit Meeting, which shall be paid into the circui
fund quarterly ... before the beginning of the quarter to which the
relate.'[142] Similarly, it is also a principle of Presbyterian law that budget
must be prepared, accounts kept and an annual audit of these made a
each level, Congregation, Presbytery and Assembly.[143] Similarly, i
Presbyterianism, a Presbytery exercises oversight of all funds received
or held on its own behalf, and appoints a Treasurer to prepare an annua
account and audit for approval by the Presbytery.[144] In turn, the Genera
Assembly is responsible for financial management and resourcing of th
life, worship and mission of the church; and budget and accounts ar
prepared for annual approval by General Assembly.[145] Similar arrange
ments operate at the various levels of the United Reformed Church a
well as in the Baptist Union of Great Britain.[146]

Secondly, as to income, the Roman Catholic Church asserts for itsel
'the inherent right to require from the faithful whatever is necessary fo
its proper objectives'. The faithful have the right to give freely to th
church, and the diocesan bishop must admonish them to assist so tha
the church has what is necessary for divine worship, apostolic works
works of charity and the sustenance of ministers. Thus, the faithful have a
duty 'to contribute to the support of the church by collections ..

---

[140] MCGB: Constitutional Practice and Discipline, Standing Orders 635; for the funds, se
Standing Orders 650–652, for the administration of accounts, Standing Orders 012.

[141] MCGB: Constitutional Practice and Discipline, Standing Orders 636; see also Standing
Orders 012.

[142] MCGB: Constitutional Practice and Discipline, Standing Orders 532, 635, 650.

[143] PCI: Code, 76: Presbytery must 'examine the ... accounts of each congregation ... ir
accordance with directions issued by the General Assembly'; 240: the Congregationa
Committee prepares p.a. accounts 'duly audited by auditors appointed by the congregation'; 286: Board of Finance of General Assembly.

[144] PCW: Handbook of Rules, 3.2: the Presbytery examines the income and expenditure of
its churches and prepares an annual report for the Association.

[145] PCW: Handbook of Rules, 3.3,4: Association funds; 3.4.2: financial matters, insurance
and property; PCI: Code, 122: 'The Auditors of Accounts of the General Assembly shall
annually audit the accounts of all the funds held by the [General] Trustees' and report to
the Assembly.

[146] URC: Manual B.2(1); BUGB: Con. 2: the Central Fund is administered by the
Trustee Board.

according to the norms laid down by the conference of bishops'. However, a minister may ask nothing to administer the sacraments beyond the offerings defined by competent authority. Offerings are determined by the provincial bishops but the local Ordinary may prescribe a special collection for specific parochial, diocesan, national or universal projects. The diocesan bishop may 'impose a moderate tax on public juridical persons subject to his authority'; *taxa* should be proportionate to income and imposed only after hearing the diocesan finance council and presbyteral council. The bishop may also impose an extraordinary (but moderate) tax on other physical and juridical persons 'only in cases of grave necessity' and with 'due regard for particular laws and customs'.[147] With the consent of the Ordinary, administrators of goods may invest money remaining after expenses are met; a report on investments is made to the Ordinary at the end of the year. Moneys assigned to a particular endowment must be invested cautiously and profitably, for the benefit of the relevant body, with the approval of the bishop who must consult interested parties and his finance council.[148]

Anglicanism is not dissimilar. Ordained ministers must instruct the faithful in their responsibilities towards missionary work, and give suitable opportunity for offerings to maintain that work. The faithful should make financial offerings according to their means. The duty to collect these at the time of public worship is vested in Wardens, and disposal of them is determined by a church assembly or other lawful authority. Fees payable for ministrations such as marriage and burials may be levied if authorised by church law.[149] A diocese should make a financial contribution to the national church to fund its activities, and a parish should contribute, through its assembly, a parish share or other such payment toward the finances of the diocese. A church may make legal provision as to the diocesan and parish share for: the duty to pay; the assessment of the sum due which should be fair and equitable; the timing of payment; appeals against the assessment; and sanctions for non-payment.[150]

---

[147] CIC: cc. 1260–1266; c. 1274: common fund; cc. 945–947: no commerce in the sacraments.

[148] CIC: cc. 1294, 1305; the parish finance council may not invest (c. 537); cc. 282 and 286: clerics.

[149] PCLCCAC: Principle 87. See e.g. Church of England: Parochial Church Councils (Powers) Measure 1956, s. 7: the council may with the minister 'determine the objects to which all moneys ... shall be allocated'.

[150] PCLCCAC: Principle 88. See e.g. Scottish Episcopal Church: Digest of Resolutions, 39: every congregation must contribute either directly or through such general fund or

Moreover, trustees may make such investments as are authorised by la▪ and these should be financially prudent and morally sound. Investment▪ are made subject to the direction of the appropriate assembly – bu church trustees are not liable personally for financial loss which ma result unless it is due to their own wilful default or culpable negligence.[15]

Similar arrangements are found in the Protestant Churches. Fo example, Methodists must engage in regular giving as 'a Christia▪ duty'.[152] The Circuit Superintendent ensures that all collections fo Connexional Funds are made at the proper times, and that these ar forwarded promptly to the relevant Treasurers.[153] Furthermore, the loca church must make a contribution to the Conference towards th expenses of the church by means of an apportionment determined b▪ it.[154] Also, trustees and prescribed bodies may invest funds in scheme▪ consistent with the prescribed ethical standards of the church.[155] How▪ ever, no local church may raise funds by means of any activity which i forbidden on Methodist property.[156] In similar vein, for the Church o Scotland, 'Christian liberality' is not simply 'a matter of providing for th▪ work of the Church, but primarily a grateful response to what God ha done for his people in Jesus Christ'.[157] Moreover, each congregation mu▪ make an annual contribution to central church funds on the basis of a▪ assessment made under the authority of General Assembly; if it fails t▪ meet the minimum required and a vacancy occurs in a congregation, th▪ Presbytery determines whether the shortfalls are justified. If they are not Presbytery must not allow the congregation to call a minister until, fo▪

Quota as the Diocesan Synod may require, to the diocese and to the general funds of th▪ General Synod'.

[151] PCLCCAC: Principle 89. See e.g. Church of Ireland: Con. X.10: the Representativ▪ Body's powers of investment are subject to the control of the General Synod.

[152] MCI: Regulations, Discipline and Government, 1.01 and 2.06: members are 'expected, a▪ far as they are able, to contribute to the funds of the Church' to support its missio▪ 'through regular giving, as far as can reasonably be expected'.

[153] MCI: Regulations, Discipline and Government, 4A.04.

[154] MCI: Regulations, Discipline and Government, 13.13ff: assessments on Circuits mad▪ under the authority of the Conference.

[155] MCI: Regulations, Discipline and Government, 10.70 and MCGB: Model Trusts 16.

[156] MCGB: Constitutional Practice and Discipline, Standing Orders 014: i.e. activity which not be permitted under Standing Orders 924,925 and 927.

[157] J.L. Weatherhead, ed., Constitution and Laws of the Church of Scotland (1997) 136 under the Weekly Freewill Offering, members undertake to give a regular weekly amount and this enables the financial board to place a realistic figure for income in it▪ annual budget.

example, the shortfalls have been met.[158] Presbyterian laws also provide for investments.[159] The Baptist Union also requires its member churches to make annual subscriptions.[160]

Thirdly, as to expenditure by way for instance of insurance, as in the Roman Catholic Church,[161] in Anglicanism, church assemblies, officers and other bodies should be aware of the risks associated with their activities. Church property, real and personal, and its occupation and usage, and individual church officers and activities, should be insured as appropriate against loss, damage and injury. A church should require appropriate bodies or persons within it to insure its property, use insurers of proven competence and specify the extent of the insurance required. Insurance policies should be regularly reviewed.[162] Protestant laws provide for much the same requirements. At local level, in the Irish Methodist Church, for example, the Church Council is responsible for the 'insurance of all the property entrusted to the Society, subject to such rights and obligations, if any, as may be vested in Local Trustees'.[163] Ministers too should take out insurance for their own property and liabilities, and the Circuit Superintendent must pay 'special attention to the insurance of churches, manses and other buildings against loss or damage by fire or any other cause'. Indeed, the Secretary of the Property Board must furnish annually the District Superintendent with a list of properties considered to be inadequately insured so that inquiry may be made at the District Synod.[164] Finally, the laws of churches provide for the financial maintenance of ordained ministers during their ministry and through pensions on retirement.[165]

---

[158] J.L. Weatherhead, ed., *Constitution and Laws of the Church of Scotland* (1997) 139; for shortfalls, see Act IX, 1996.

[159] PCW: Handbook of Rules, 3.2.3: the Resources and Properties Board is empowered to invest.

[160] BUGB: Con. 7.

[161] CIC: c. 1284.1: administrators of temporal goods must insure those goods.

[162] PCLCCAC: Principle 90. See e.g. Church in Wales: Church Fabric Regulations, 5: parish church councils must ensure 'all churches . . . and . . . contents are insured in accordance with the advice of the insurer'.

[163] MCI: Regulations, Discipline and Government, 10.06.

[164] MCI: Regulations, Discipline and Government, 29.16–19: personal, Sunday school insurance, and third party insurance.

[165] See e.g. CIC: cc. 281–282, 1272–1274; PCLCCAC: Principle 91–92; MCGB: Constitutional Practice and Discipline, Standing Orders 801, 805–807; J.L. Weatherhead, ed., *Constitution and Laws of the Church of Scotland* (1997) 136; URC: Manual B., 2(6).

The Finances of Muslims and Mosques

As Islamic law covers most aspects of Muslim life, so it has elaborate rules on financial matters, including commerce, so that through honest and fair business transactions Muslims may earn a living, support their families and give charity – and there must be no contract making during the Friday congregational prayer.[166] The Islamic law of contract (al-'aqd) deals with the formation of a contract, its binding effect, the option of withdrawal (khiyar), termination and remedies for breach of contract.[167] Those who engage in trade inter alia must have high moral values and behave equitably; they must not exploit others or obtain unfair profit, reduce competition in the marketplace or trade in haram goods. Unlawful gain (riba), often understood as 'interest', is prohibited, namely: 'an unlawful gain derived from the quantitative inequality of the counter-values in any transaction purporting to effect the exchange of two or more species (anwa') which belong to the same genus (jins) and are governed by the same efficient cause ('illa)'.[168] There is much debate among scholars on the propriety of Muslims lending and borrowing and prohibitions against charging interest on loans.[169] Most Islamic scholars today agree that the modern corporation is acceptable and that ethical investments may be made providing that the companies involved trade only in halal commodities. Islam also recognises the necessity for and dignity of labour and the entitlement of an employee to a fair wage and decent treatment by an employer.[170] As seen in Chapter 5, disputes as to such matters may be subject to Muslim arbitration.

Moreover, every Muslim who is the owner of more than a sharia-defined amount of property or savings, which is above their routine needs, is required to pay 2.5 per cent as zakat, literally for the 'purification' of their wealth. The money must be distributed to sharia-defined poor Muslims, for example those with insufficient means to be

---

[166] See e.g. Quran 62:9: no trading during Friday salat; 17:35: the exhortation to honesty in commercial transactions; 2:282: contracts as to future obligations should be written and witnessed.

[167] J. Schacht, Islamic Law (1991) 151; M. Rohe, Islamic Law (2014) 132–141, 495–499.

[168] N. Saleh, Unlawful Gain and Legitimate Profit in Islamic Law (1986) 13.

[169] J. Hussain, Islamic Law (1999) 162–164; reasons for the prohibition include: interest implies taking the property of another without giving anything in exchange; and dependence on interest discourages the person from working; the lender is likely to be wealthy and the borrower poor, and so taking interest is a form of exploitation. Some scholars argue that only excessive interest (usury) is forbidden.

[170] J. Hussain, Islamic Law (1999) 168–169; 176–194: Islamic banking.

assured of their next meal. Numerous charities and private initiatives exist to channel such funds for distribution to poor communities overseas. This distribution takes place in Ramadan as any obligatory religious act is deemed to be more virtuous in that month.[171] And, as the Council for Mosques (Bradford) explains: 'Giving charity (*zakah*) is the third pillar of Islam.'[172] Some mosques also require payment of members' subscriptions.[173]

What follows illustrates the rights to receive and raise funds and subscriptions, the control of finance, accounts and budgets and expenditure (including insurance) in three entities. First, the Muslim Council of Britain may be financed by affiliation fees, contributions, donations and funds from other legitimate sources. All monies raised by or on its behalf must be applied to further the objects of the Council and for no other purpose. Every member body must pay such annual affiliation fee as the General Assembly may determine, on the recommendation of the Finance and General Purpose Committee. It may also form or take over trust funds which, in the opinion of its National Council, may conveniently be administered by it. Legacies, gifts and funds (subject to any conditions imposed by the donor, testator or relevant trusts) must be vested in its trustees.[174] Its Finance and General Purpose Committee must: supervise fund-raising, the management of assets and disbursement of funds; be responsible for keeping proper accounts of all Council finances and for presenting annual audited accounts to the General Assembly; ensure compliance with any Financial Protocols agreed by the National Council; and set up a Secretariat with paid staff where necessary to carry out the day-to-day functions of the Council and ensure its efficient functioning. The Council Treasurer must: keep accounts of Council finances and be responsible for the management of its financial affairs; provide accounts for audit at least once a year by the auditors appointed by the annual meeting of the General Assembly; chair meetings of the Finance and General Purpose Committee; and determine the specific role and responsibility of the Assistant Treasurer in consultation with the Secretary General and keep the National Council

---

[171] Mehmood Naqshbandi, *Islam and Muslims in Britain* (2012): guide 2.2.3. See Quran 9:60.

[172] CFM: www.councilformosques.org/five-pillars-of-islam/.

[173] See e.g. LIS: Con. Membership: 1–3; RMC: Con. E.1: annual subscription; Model Constitution of an Islamic Organisation: Con. 1–8.

[174] MCB: Con. Art. 6

informed.[175] If the Council is dissolved (by special resolution of General Assembly), the office bearers must expeditiously realise all Council assets, pay its debts and liabilities and give surplus funds to a registered charity supporting Islamic causes.[176]

Secondly, at regional level, according to the model constitution issued by the Central Mosque, the Shura Committee of an Islamic organisation is authorised to: provide for the payment of salaries or remuneration of imams, *muadhins*, employees or other persons engaged in the work of the congregation; collect and canvass for and accept donations, bequests, endowments and other benefits for the congregation; and borrow for the purposes of the Board of Trustees without mortgaging any property of the Board or resorting to interest-based financing. The Committee is also to control and manage the assets and finances of the congregation in a responsible and transparent manner 'within the parameters of Islamic Law' and in compliance with standard civil accounting practice; and solicit for and use the funds of the congregation to further the objectives of the organisation and for any other cause deemed appropriate to enhance the cause of Islam and the Muslim community. Should funds be limited, the priority of order for expenditure must be the *masjid*, education, the cemetery and then other causes.[177] Members of the Committee must be indemnified and are not responsible for any loss or damage the congregation may sustain by reason of any *bona fide* act carried out in performing a function on behalf of the congregation. No one is personally liable for acts done on behalf of the congregation unless by dishonesty or wilful and manifest negligence. The mosque accounts are received and discussed at the ordinary general meeting.[178]

Thirdly, arrangements at local level mirror these norms. For example, at the Markazi Jamia Masjid Riza and Islamic Centre (Huddersfield), all monies raised by or on behalf of the *masjid* must be applied only to further the development and building of the organization. The Treasurer must keep proper accounts of the finances. The accounts must be audited at least once a year by a qualified accountant. The Management Committee must submit audited accounts for the last financial year to the

---

[175] MCB: Con. Art. 4.   [176] MCB: Con. Art. 10.
[177] Model Constitution of an Islamic Organisation: Shura Committee 1–3. See e.g. Lancaster Islamic Centre: Con. Aims 5.
[178] Model Constitution of an Islamic Organisation: www.central-mosque.com/fiqh/ModelOfIslamicOrg.htm. See also the MCW Model Declaration of Trust (2016) Art. 22: accounts.

Annual General Meeting, and appoint five of its voting members, including the Treasurer, to sign cheques and operate accounts in the name of the *masjid*.[179] The law of the State makes provision to accommodate aspects of Islamic financial practices.[180]

Conclusion

A comparative examination of the regulatory instruments of Jewish, Christian and Muslim entities on property and finance tells us much about the common actions in which the faithful are engaged across the religions studied here. They also tell us a great deal about the temporal aspects of religious law. Irrespective of the particular religion, the faithful, through their various institutional organisations: own, administer and dispose of real and personal property; set aside their places and objects of worship, forbidding activities with regard to them which are inconsistent with those sacred purposes; and give, receive and account for funds which must be used solely for the objectives of the organisation in question. There is very little legal diversity as within or as between the faiths on these matters. However, the laws of Christians collectively do not echo norms in classical Jewish and Islamic law about the making of contracts and other commercial transactions. Moreover, from the study of these regulatory instruments emerge principles of religious law common to all three faiths. A religious organisation has the right to acquire, administer and dispose of property, and should seek for its institutions legal personality under civil law to enable this. Property vests in prescribed institutions which act as its stewards holding it on trust for the benefit of the members and work of the institutions. Places and

---

179 MJMRIC: Con. Art. 7, 15 and 18. See also RMC: Con. Sections K-O and U; CJM: Con. Art. 5: application of income; 6: winding up; 7: funds; and Rules 31: accounts; 32: finance; 33: auditors; 34: indemnity; RMC: Con. I, L, and U; BCOM: Con. Art. 4: application of income; Art. 11: finance; NUIM: Con. Art. 7: accounts; Art. 8: the Treasurer; MCW: Imaan Islamic Society: Model Constitution (2007), Section E: finance; L: receipts and expenditure; N: accounts; O: annual report; P: returns; NASFAT: Con. Art. C and J; MJMRIC: Con. Arts. 7: Treasurer; 14: property; 15: finance; 18: dissolution; and AMIC: Con. Art. IV.8-9, V.11 and VII.

180 See M. Hill *et al.*, *Religion and Law* (2014) para. 345: e.g. the Finance Act 2005 provided for the direct-tax treatment of certain *sharia*-compliant financing vehicles e.g. cost-plus financing (*murabaha*) and participation or trust financing (*mudarabah*) would be treated for tax purposes in the same way as their traditional banking counterparts – the 'effective return' in a *murabaha* transaction and the 'profit share return' in a *mudarabah* transaction are now treated, for tax purposes, as payments of interest

objects of worship should be set aside, and any activities carried out should not be inconsistent with their spiritual purposes. Synagogues, churches and mosques commonly use religious soft-law, in the form of 'etiquette' or 'convention', with regard to correct conduct when people visit them. A religious organisation also has a right to receive, hold and invest income to further its objectives. Budgets should be prepared, and accounts kept and audited systematically. The faithful should regularly contribute according to their means to sustain the work of the organisation, and the institutions of government may acquire financial contributions by means of compulsory payments, particularly at the local level. Income should be spent only to further the objectives of the religious entity. In all of this, a religious organisation should comply with civil law applicable to its property and finances, not least to acquire/maintain charity status and meet Charity Commission standards.

10

The Religion, State and Society

We have already seen that one function of modern Jewish, Christian and Muslim regulatory instruments is to address the external relations of the religious organisation with individuals and bodies in the wider political, social and religious environment, such as: in relation to the availability to wider society of facilities to visit synagogues, churches and mosques; the public dimensions of profession of the faith and worship; and State law applicable to property and finance when the organisation seeks/acquires charitable status in civil law. We have also met many examples of religious law operating *praeter legem* (outside of or in the interstices of civil law, when the latter is silent on a matter), *secundum legem* (in accordance with civil law) and sometimes *contra legem* (against law), where such conflict is either civilly forbidden or else it is limited, excused, justified or otherwise permitted on the basis of religious liberty or a special exemption. This chapter explores further the rules of religious organisations in their external relations with the State and wider civil society, historically a matter on which all three faiths have differed in terms of the neutrality that they require or expect from the State in its legal posture towards religion. The chapter examines the stance of each faith towards the State, its nature and its functions and the working out of this stance in their modern regulatory instruments. The juridical approaches of the faith communities to human rights and religious freedom in wider society are dealt with in the second section. The third section deals with the approach of the religions to natural law – the existence of universal norms revealed to the whole of humankind.[1]

---

[1] Religious organisations under international law are much-debated today: see e.g. I. Clsmas, *Religious Actors and International Law* (Oxford: Oxford University Press, 2014).

The Relationship between the Religion and the State

As a general pattern, Jewish, Christian and Islamic laws all address: the nature and purpose of the State; the distinct identity and functions of the religion as opposed to those of the State; the need for co-operation between religious organisations and the State; the recognition and applicability of civil law to religious organisations; disobedience by the faithful to unjust laws; and the avoidance in disputes among the faithful of recourse to the courts of the State. Today, many government bodies may be charged with addressing religious issues/concerns; for example: the former Department for Communities and Local Government had a Race, Cohesion and Faiths Directorate which promoted interfaith activity and had a Cohesion and Faiths Unit (which advised on, for example, the Racial and Religious Hatred Act 2006 and Holocaust Memorial Day); the Department also had a Commission on Integration and Cohesion (to consider, *inter alia*, how local areas make the most of religious diversity);[2] the Equality and Human Rights Commission, a statutory body, whose responsibility is to protect, enforce and promote equality across the protected grounds, which includes religion;[3] and the Charity Commission, which deals with a significant number of faith-based charities.[4] The non-government Churches' Legislation Advisory Service also exists to: advance the charitable work (religious or otherwise) of churches and other religious entities by furthering their common interest in secular matters (other than education); advise such entities; conduct negotiations and liaise between them and government (such as parliament, central departments or local authorities); and monitor and alert members to developments in civil law and talk directly to government on religious issues.[5] Also, religious organisations generally have the status under civil law of unincorporated voluntary associations (unless e.g. incorporated under statute) and so their internal rules are classified as the terms of a contract entered into by the members of the organisation and such rules are enforceable to that extent (as to property or finance).[6]

---

[2] The Department published e.g. *Face to Face and Side by Side: A Framework for Inter Faith Dialogue and Social Action: Consultation* (London: Department for Communities and Local Government, December 2007). In 2018, the department became the Ministry of Housing, Communities and Local Government, with a Minister for Faith.

[3] It was set up under the Equality Act 2006.

[4] The Commission in 2005–2007 ran workshops for 800 such charities and has a Unit for this field.

[5] CLAS: www.churcheslegislation.org.uk/home.

[6] M. Hill *et al.*, *Religion and Law* (2014) 74–75.

Dina Demalkhuta Dina

The principle of *Dina Demalkhuta Dina* – the law of the land is the law – defines the relationship between Judaism and the (non-Jewish) State in Jewish law.[7] It has a long history, traceable to the work of the Babylonian jurist Mar Samuel (180–257 CE), and may be found in the Talmudic and later literature – and it means, broadly, that Jewish communities (including their courts) are 'bound by Jewish law itself to follow the law of the land' in such a way that some see this 'maxim' as a binding 'source' of Jewish law. The principle, which also represents a limitation on Rabbinic authority, is understood historically to be justified, variously, on the basis of: the divine right of kings; the king as 'the owner of the land'; the agreement of royal subjects to follow royal laws; and the recognition of secular authority in matters of money and property.[8]

However, the principle has its limits – and in these we see a high level of legal unity among the different Jewish traditions. For Orthodox Judaism: 'While it recognizes the right of a legitimate government to control land tenure and raise reasonable taxes', the State should leave Jewish authorities free to administer all "religious" matters including family law . . . internal commercial dealings and some aspects of criminal behaviour'; thus, the principle 'was not understood as a distinction between sacred (governed by *Torah*) and secular (governed by the ruling power)' – 'it was a claim that the *Torah* itself . . . regarded proprietary rights as a matter of human convention'.[9]

Limits on State competence were recognised by Reform Judaism in the nineteenth century. For example, the Braunschweig Conference 1844 held: 'Judaism will never yield up the right of independence, within its specific compass, and emphatically declines to tolerate all . . . interference

---

[7] Needless to say, the relationship between Jewish law and State law has been a subject of great importance and, especially after Emancipation in the late eighteenth and nineteenth centuries, in the history of the Jewish people in their diaspora communities living as minorities (large or small) across the world.

[8] I. Herzog, *Jewish Law* (1965) 24–32: the 'maxim' of the 'law of the (non-Jewish) state as a source of Jewish law'; Hecht *et al.*, eds., *Jewish Law* (1996) 90, 187; and S.L. Stone, 'Religion and state: models of separation from within Jewish law', 6 *International Journal of Constitutional Law* (2008) 631–661. For the rule against Jews using non-Jewish courts, see M. Elon, *Jewish Law* (1994) I.14. See also e.g. E. Quint, *A Restatement of Rabbinic Civil Law*, 2 Volumes (Northvale, NJ: Jason Aronson Inc., 1990).

[9] N. Solomon, 'Public law and traditional faith', in F. Cranmer, M. Hill, C. Kenny and R. Sandberg, eds., *The Confluence of Law and Religion* (Cambridge: Cambridge University Press, 2016) 161 at 165.

[by] the state in its inner development and its own religious affairs"
however: 'The Jew is obligated to regard as his native country the one to
which he belongs by birth and through civic conditions. He must defend
and obey all its laws'; and a Rabbi 'has only such rights as the State and
congregation invests in him'; for the Cleveland Conference 1855: Jewish
'Statutes and ordinances contrary to the laws of the land are invalid'; and
at Leipzig 1869: 'Judaism is in harmony with the principle of the unity of
the human race; of the equality of all before the law; of the equality of all
in duties and rights to the country and to the State; and with the full
liberty of the individual in his religious convictions' – but the 'autonomy
independence and self-government of Judaism in all religious matters
must be most sacredly preserved'.[10] Thus, for modern Reform scholars
'it is our religious duty to obey' the laws of 'a just government applying
equally to all citizens'; and those 'who violate these laws violate ... Jewish
law'.[11] Nevertheless, today: 'Most European Jews lack any sense of
living under a jurisdiction other than that of the country of which they
are citizens; they value living under governments which do not
discriminate ... on religious grounds, and [they] are content to regard
their religion as a private matter.'[12]

Similarly, for Conservative Judaism, as a matter of principle (applied
also to the State of Israel) the State should enable 'each religious community to handle its own ritual requirements'; and it is a *mitzvah* that Jewish
religious leaders 'denounce government policies which violate religious
and ethical norms'.[13] However, under its bye-laws: 'No substantial part of
the activities of the United Synagogue of Conservative Judaism may
involve carrying out propaganda or attempting to influence [secular]

[10] K. Kohler, 'The origin and function of ceremonies in Judaism', Central Conference of
American Rabbis, Yearbook, vol. I (Cincinnati: Bloch Publishing, 1891) 82, 83, 88, 124
101 and 108.

[11] S.B. Freehof, *Responsa for Our Time* (Cincinnati: The Hebrew Union College Press, 1977)
No. 54; see W. Jacob, 'The law of the land and Jewish law: opposition or concurrence', in
W. Jacob and M. Zemer, eds., *Re-Examining Progressive Halakhah* (2002) 71–90 at 84
75–78: Sephardic Jews embraced the principle more fully than Ashkenasic Jews.

[12] N. Solomon, 'Public law and traditional faith', in F. Cranmer, M. Hill, C. Kenny and
R. Sandberg, eds., *The Confluence of Law and Religion* (Cambridge: Cambridge University Press, 2016) 161 at 169–170: 'Their self-perception [is] more to do with historical
memory and social attachment than ... theology or law'.

[13] *Statement of Principles of Conservative Judaism* (1990) 29–30: 'the State of Israel must
encourage Jewish patterns of life in all [its] agencies'; 'Without being a theocracy, Israel
should reflect the highest religious and moral values of Judaism ... to maintain the Jewish
character and ambience of the State'; and: 'Religion as a moral influence is a blessing; as a
mere political power it is a menace.'

egislation, nor intervening in any political campaign involving a candidate for public office.'[14]

As seen already, modern regulatory instruments of Jewish organisations commonly provide for their own compliance with civil law,[15] and Rabbinic courts incorporate civil law in Jewish law for the purposes of adjudicating cases.[16] Jewish bodies may therefore utilise the State and its law for the purposes of their institutional lives. For example, the (Orthodox) United Synagogue was formed under the parliamentary United Synagogues Act 1870;[17] and on any question concerning the construction, application or alteration of its statutes, or about management, the Honorary Officers may apply to the Charity Commission whose opinion and advice is binding on the Honorary Officers.[18] The United Synagogue may also: (1) employ a Parliamentary Agent to review and advise on 'the passage of all intended or contemplated legislation within the United Kingdom or elsewhere including the European Union which may affect' it; (2) employ agents to liaise with local authorities in the United Kingdom and advise on any matter, whether legislation or otherwise, which may affect it; and (3) assemble in conference the representatives of voluntary organisations, government departments, statutory authorities and individuals in order to discuss such matters.[19]

A pivotal role in Jewish–State relations is played by the Board of Deputies of British Jews, known for statutory purposes as the London Committee of Deputies of the British Jews – the Board is 'the representative body of British Jewry'.[20] The Board is 'an independent organisation, free from outside control, and recognised as the body to make official representations on behalf of the Jewish Community of Great

---

[14] USCJ: Bylaws 1.3.
[15] See e.g. WLJC: Con. Art. 3: 'Nothing in this constitution shall authorise an application of the property of the charity for purposes which are not charitable in accordance with' civil charity law.
[16] See e.g. FOS: www.federation.org.uk/beis-din/din-torah-jewish-arbitration/; see Chapter 5.
[17] United Synagogues Act 1870; under the Charitable Trusts Act 1869, the Charity Commission's power to settle schemes was extended to registered places of worship; the 1870 Act had the first such scheme.
[18] US: Statutes 55.   [19] US: Statutes 5.13–15.
[20] BDBJ: Con. Art. 1. It traces its foundation to 1760 when seven deputies, appointed by the elders of the Spanish and Portuguese Congregations (Sephardic) formed a committee to pay homage to George III on his accession; at the same time, the Ashkenazi Community appointed its own committee and it was agreed at the end of 1760 that the two committees should hold joint meetings from time to time.

Britain to central and local government authorities, and other appropriate bodies'; in so doing it directs 'its policies to reflect the larges
practicable measure of common agreement'.[21] The Board must protect
support and defend the interests, religious rights and customs of Jew:
and the Jewish Community, and consider and, if necessary, make representations on all national and local government proposals, decisions
orders, regulations, public and private Acts and other measures, including those of the European Union, to government bodies and othe:
competent authorities. Next, it must defend and ensure the security
safety, well-being and standing of British Jews in co-operation with
statutory authorities and relevant parties; take such appropriate action
as lies within its power to advance the security, welfare and standing o:
Israel; and support and protect Jews and Jewish communities outside the
United Kingdom. It must also: initiate, undertake and co-ordinate
research into matters which affect the Jewish Community; promote a
better understanding of the Jewish Community within the United Kingdom and so develop relations with other ethnic and minority groups; and
co-ordinate, if appropriate and requested, Jewish communal activities
The Board may, for example, raise money for its activities. For all of these
purposes, the Board may associate with such other organisations as it
may consider appropriate.[22]

The Board has 300 or so Deputies elected by synagogue congregations,[23] synagogal organisations, representative councils or organisations,
and other bodies.[24] Elections occur every three years.[25] The Deputies
transact its business through Divisions, and work with the Honorary
Officers (President, Vice Presidents and Treasurer) and professional staff.
The Board meets eight times each year to debate matters and to consider
reports from its Divisions. There are four Divisional Boards: Community
Issues; Defence and Group Relations (for 'the political defence of the
Community and its relations with ethnic and other groups');

---

[21] BDBJ: Con. Art. 2.   [22] BDBJ: Con. Art. 3.

[23] Namely: 'ecclesiastical' authorities (Art. 37), i.e. in the case of Ashkenazim, the Ecclesiastical Authority of the United Hebrew Congregations of the Commonwealth, and in the
case of the Sephardim, that for the Spanish and Portuguese Jews' Congregation of
London.

[24] BDBJ: Con. Art. 4.

[25] BDBJ: Con. Art. 7: this also deals with the tenure of deputies (see also the Rules in
Appendix A); 5: the basis of representation; 6: eligibility of deputies; 8–10: representation
fees; 11: communal levy.

nternational Affairs; and Finance and Organisation. Each comprises
lected Deputies assisted by a professional Director.[26]

The Executive Committee of the Board, which includes the Honorary
)fficers with the President acting as chair, is 'responsible for and
ccountable to the Board for the management of the Board', as to, for
xample: recommending policy strategy and finance for approval by the
3oard; presenting for Board approval, and implementing and reporting
n, the triennial Board Plan; and monitoring income and expenditure.[27]
.he Executive Committee and Divisional Boards may appoint commit-
ees, and the Board may create Rules on for instance the election of
)eputies, Honorary Officers, Divisional Boards and their committees;
he Constitution Committee must 'rule on any question arising from the
nterpretation' of these Rules.[28] The President may act if an urgent matter
rises (with the concurrence of another Honorary Officer), and provision
s made in the event of the disability, death or resignation of the Presi-
lent, and for passing a Board motion of no confidence (with a two-third
najority) for any Honorary Officer and other procedural matters.[29] The
3oard also issues guidance.[30]

The Board must be guided in 'religious matters', including those
elating to marriages and 'the religious customs and usages of the Jews',
y the 'Ecclesiastical Authorities' to whom such matters must be referred.
However, this is without prejudice to the position of congregations,
groups of congregations and institutions not under the jurisdiction of
he Ecclesiastical Authorities which may be represented on the Board.
Moreover, nothing in this rule, or any decision given under it, can be
aken to represent the opinion of such congregation or group of congregations or institutions, nor to abridge the rights of action of, or affect in
ıny way, such congregations or groups of congregations or institutions.
Also, the Board must consult with those designated by such groups of

6 BDBJ: Con. Art. 12: Honorary Officers; 13: past presidents; 14: election of Honorary
   Officers at the first meeting of a triennium; 16: divisional structure; 17: election of
   divisional boards; 18: regions.
7 BDBJ: Con. Art. 15.
8 BDBJ: Con. Art. 19: committees; 20: Rules (see Appendices); 21: Constitution Committee.
9 BDBJ: Con. Art. 22: presidential action; 23: presidential disability etc.; 23A: motion of no
   confidence; 24: continuation in office; 25: quorum; 26: voting at meetings; 27: cessation or
   amalgamation of constituencies; 28: advocacy of views; 29: annual report; 30: dissolution
   of the Board.
0 E.g. BDBJ: The Employer's Guide to Judaism (2015): civil employment law and Jewish
   observance

congregations as their respective religious leaders determine for th
purpose on religious matters in any manner whatsoever concernin
them.[31] The Board may also make, alter or revoke Standing Orders i
order to regulate, manage and govern its meetings, affairs and busines
provided they are consistent with the constitution.[32] Amendments to th
constitution of the Board may be made only at a special meeting con
vened for this purpose with a two-third majority of Deputies present an
voting.[33]

Church–State Relations

The historic churches have diverse legal experiences in terms of thei
relationship to, or institutional separation from, the State. As to church-
state relations, therefore, a church should co-operate with the State i
matters of common concern, but each is independent in its own sphere
The faithful may participate in politics save to the extent prohibited b
church law. Co-operation between a church and the State may b
exercised on the basis of: the establishment of, or other formal relation
ship between, a church and the State; an agreement or civil legislation
negotiated freely with the State; the juridical personality which a church
or institutions within it may enjoy under civil law; the registration of
church under State law; and the fundamental institutional autonomy of
church in carrying out its lawful objectives and its freedom in these area
from intervention by the State.[34] These principles derive from the laws o
churches.

For the Roman Catholic Church: there is no authority except from
God; the 'political community and public authority are based on human
nature and therefore . . . belong to an order established by God'; politica
authority must be exercised within the limits of the moral order; and it is
'the role of the State to defend and promote the common good of civi
society', that is 'the sum total of social conditions which allow people . .

---

[31] BDBJ: Con. Art. 31; see above n. 23 for Ecclesiastical Authorities; see also Annexe (Cod
of Practice): the Board with the Ecclesiastical Authorities review developments in e.g
Parliament of concern to 'the religious well-being of the community' and 'conside
proposals to secure that purpose by legislative or other means'; on becoming aware of
matter, the Board must refer it to the Ecclesiastical Authorities and follow their guidance
see also 32: Secretary of Marriages; 33: gifts.

[32] BDBJ: Con. Art. 34.   [33] BDBJ: Con. Art. 35.

[34] Christian Law Panel of Experts, *Principles of Christian Law* (2016) X.1: church–state
relations.

o reach their fulfilment'. However, 'in their own domain, the political community and the church are independent from one another and autonomous' but should develop 'mutual co-operation' in favour of the welfare of all humans.[35] Indeed, the Latin Code recognises the qualified applicability of the law of the State to the church: 'When the law of the Church remits some issue to civil law, the latter is to be observed with the same effects in canon law, in so far as it is not contrary to divine law, and provided it is not otherwise stipulated in canon law.'[36] In other words, for the faithful, 'unjust laws … would not be binding in conscience'.[37] Moreover, canon law provides for the appointment of papal legates to States,[38] forbids clerics to hold public office if this means sharing in civil power,[39] asserts that church rights to appoint bishops are not conceded to civil authorities,[40] and enables church tribunals not to impose a penalty if the offender has been or is to be 'sufficiently punished by the civil authority'.[41]

This stance is shared broadly by Anglicans as to their view of the State,[42] co-operation with it, the applicability of civil law,[43] recourse to State courts in disputes between the faithful and deference to the State in its domain.[44] The Church of England is the established church in England – as a result, the Monarch is its titular head, takes an oath to uphold it and appoints its bishops (who may be Lords Spiritual in the House of Lords in Parliament); Measures of the General Synod must be approved by the Sovereign in Parliament, and Canons receive royal assent; but generally its institutions are legally separate and distinct from those of the State. Indeed, the Church of England in Wales was disestablished in 1920 and the Church in Wales today exists on the basis of a

---

[35] CCC: paras. 1918–1924, 1927; GS 26, 74, 76; Rom. 13.1: all authority is from God.

[36] CIC: c. 22; see e.g. c. 98.2: guardians; c. 110: adoption; c. 197: prescription; cc. 1059 and 1062: marriage; c. 1284.2: temporal goods; c. 1290: secular contract law.

[37] CCC: paras. 1897–1942; *Gaudium et Spes* (Vatican II, Pastoral Constitution, 1966) 29–31.

[38] CIC: cc. 362–367.

[39] CIC: c. 285.3; if 'it would serve a spiritual purpose' a bishop could dispense with this norm.

[40] CIC: c. 377.   [41] CIC: c. 1344.2.

[42] See AR, Art. 37: Of the Civil Magistrates: the monarch has 'the chief Government of all estates … Ecclesiastical or Civil' but does not administer God's Word or the Sacraments.

[43] PCLCCAC: Principle 46.2–3: processing data; 71–75: civil marriage; 77.5–7: civil law on disclosure of information in breach of the seal of the confessional; 80.1–2: trustees must comply with civil law.

[44] Church of Ireland: Con. VIII.26.4: the Court of General Synod hears no matter which 'in the opinion of the lay judges, is within the jurisdiction and more proper to be submitted to the … decision of a civil tribunal'.

statutory contract.[45] The Scottish Episcopal Church and the (Anglican Church of Ireland as it serves in Northern Ireland are institutionall separate from the State too.[46]

The Protestant Reformation in northern Europe saw the developmen of the principle that subjects should follow the religion of their rule: *cuius regio eius religio*;[47] the Lutheran doctrine of the 'two kingdoms' earthly and heavenly – is designed *inter alia* to guide the church in it relations with the world, especially government,[48] and Lutheran churc bodies today have juridical personality under civil law.[49] Whil Methodism generally advocates separation of church and State, th Methodist Church in Great Britain enjoys the protection of its trusts b State law devoted specially to it.[50] However: 'Managing trustees may nc sponsor meetings in support of political parties', but may permit occa sional use of Methodist property for political meetings by non-Methodi bodies and sponsor meetings to promote discussion of public issues i the context of Christian theology if this does not have a 'detrimenta effect on the peace and unity of the Church and its witness'.[51] Yet, in th Methodist Church in Ireland: 'No lawsuit relating to churches [or] Trus property shall be commenced without the consent of the General Com mittee through the Property Board, except by direction of the Confer ence'; otherwise the parties are responsible for costs incurred.[52]

Whilst the (Presbyterian) Church of Scotland is the national church and its autonomy is recognised and protected by the parliamentar Church of Scotland Act 1921, for the Presbyterian Church of Ireland Christ 'has appointed [in the church] a government distinct from civi authority', and 'its laws [are] founded on His authority' and 'directed t

---

[45] Welsh Church Act 1914 which disestablished the Church of England in Wales (a from 1920).

[46] See e.g. M. Hill *et al.*, *Religion and Law* (2014): 46, 47 and 53.

[47] J. Witte, *Law and Protestantism* (1990).

[48] Augsburg Confession 1530, Art. 16: 'all government and all established rule and law were instituted by God for the sake of good order, and ... Christians may without si occupy civil offices and engage in ... civil affairs'; also: 'the gospel does not overthrov civil authority, the state, and marriage but requires that all these be kept as true divin orders' (or 'orders of creation'), unless to do so would mean disobeying God (Acts 5:29)

[49] ELCIRE: Con. 1(1): under the (Irish) Taxes Consolidation Act 1997, s. 207.

[50] MCGB: Constitutional Practice and Discipline, Bk. I, Methodist Church Act 1976 (esp Sch. 2, Model Trusts), Methodist Church Act 1939, Methodist Church Funds Act 1960 see also MCI: Con. s. 7: the Methodist Church in Ireland Act (Northern Ireland 1928 and Methodist Church in Ireland Act (Saorstat Eireann) 1928.

[51] MCGB: Constitutional Practice and Discipline, Standing Orders 921.

[52] MCI: Regulations, Discipline and Government, 29.20.

the conscience'; 'their sanctions are spiritual'. However, 'although civil rulers are bound to render obedience to Christ in their own province, yet they ought not to attempt in any way to constrain anyone's religious beliefs, or invade the rights of conscience'.[53] Nevertheless, that church has State law devoted exclusively to it.[54] In the United Reformed Church too: 'Christ, the only ruler and head of the Church, has therein appointed a government distinct from civil government and in things spiritual not subordinate thereto', and 'civil authorities, being always subject to the rule of God, ought to respect the rights of conscience and of religious belief and to serve God's will of justice and peace for all humankind'.[55] Yet, again, the church has State law devoted exclusively to it.[56] Members of the United Free Church of Scotland should not approach the courts of the 'civil power' to resolve their disputes.[57] Similarly, whilst Baptists advocate the institutional separation of church and State, the Baptist Union of Great Britain is the subject of State law exclusively devoted to it.[58]

The Islamic Concept of State and the Non-Muslim State

In classical Islam, ideas of statehood are based on the principles of community, justice and leadership; the legitimacy of the ruler is derived from consultation (*shura*), the contract between the ruled and the ruler (*aqd*), and the oath of allegiance (*bayah*).[59] In Sunni thought, whilst theories of the state differ in terms of detail, generally, the state or political community is based on the sovereignty of God; the principal function of the ruler (*caliph*) must serve as the guardian of the community and of the faith and implement divine law as 'the Deputy of God' (*Khalifat Allah*) and is thus answerable to God; for most Sunni scholars, a *caliph* is elected by a council (*shura*), and does not hold a spiritual

---

[53] PCI: Code, I.III.13 and I.IV.15.   [54] PCI: Irish Presbyterian Church Act 1871.

[55] URC: Manual BU A, Sch. D, Version I, 8.

[56] URC: United Reformed Church Acts 1972, 1981 and 2000: on e.g. trusts for places of worship.

[57] UFCS: Con. V.II.8.   [58] BUGB: Baptist and Congregational Trusts Act 1961.

[59] J.L. Esposito, *Oxford Dictionary of Islam* (2003) 151; see also 49: caliphs are seen as successors to the Prophet, the political leader of Muslims. After the first four successors (see above Introduction), the caliphate became hereditary. The two main dynasties, Umayyads and Abbasids, dominated until 1258 CE. The Mamluk sultanate had Abbasids as titular caliphs in Cairo until the Ottoman conquest of Egypt in 1517. Ottoman sultans were widely recognised as caliphs until abolition of the caliphate in 1924.

office – though it has religious significance, especially with regard to the
unity of the Muslim 'nation' or *ummah* – but may be removed only in
exceptional circumstances; religious scholars provide religio-legal
advice.[60] According to Shia jurisprudence on the state (under the doctrine of *imamat*), however, authority vests in the leader (*imam*) who is
the Deputy of the Prophet (and appointed by him), and who rules on
behalf of God – the leader must therefore be a learned Islamic scholar
(*faqih*) and must possess prescribed personal characteristics, such as
justness and piety.[61]

The Universal Islamic Declaration of Human Rights, issued by the
Islamic Council of Europe in 1981,[62] acknowledges 'our obligation to
establish an Islamic order' in which: the 'rulers and the ruled alike are
subject to, and equal before, the Law' (i.e. *sharia*); 'obedience shall be
rendered only to those commands that are consonant with the Law'; and
'all worldly power shall be considered a sacred trust, to be exercised
within the limits prescribed by the Law'. Moreover, public affairs must be
conducted after mutual consultation (*shura*) between the believers qualified to decide; and every effort must be made to deliver humans from all
exploitation, injustice and oppression and ensure to everyone 'security,
dignity and liberty in terms set out in and by methods approved and
within the limits set by the Law'.[63] Importantly: 'It is the right and duty of
every Muslim to refuse to obey any command which is contrary to the
Law, no matter by whom it was issued';[64] everyone also has the right to
be protected from harassment by official agencies,[65] and to hold public
office; also: consultation (*shura*) is 'the basis of the administrative

---

[60] A. Black *et al.*, *Islamic Law* (2013) 12–14. See also e.g. H. Enayat, *Modern Islamic Political Thought* (London: Macmillan Press, 1982); and N. Feldman, *The Fall and Rise of the Islamic State* (Princeton, NJ: Princeton University Press, 2008).

[61] A. Sachedina, *The Justice Ruler in Shi'ite Islam: The Comprehensive Theory of the Jurist in Imamite Jurisprudence* (Oxford: Oxford University Press, 1988). E.g. Islamic Republic of Iran: Con. Art. 5: 'custody and leadership of Ummah devolve upon the just ['*adil*] and pious [*muttaqi*] scholar [*faquih*]'.

[62] Islamic Council of Europe 19 September 1981: see C.G. Weeramantry, *Islamic Jurisprudence* (1988) 176–183. See also: S. Azzam, 'Universal Islamic Declaration of Human Rights', 2 *The International Journal of Human Rights* (1998) 102–112. For a critical analysis, see A.E. Mayer, *Islam and Human Rights: Tradition and Politics* (Boulder, CO: Westview Press, 3rd edn, 2006) 76. See also the Cairo Declaration on Human Rights in Islam (1990).

[63] UIDHR (1981): Preamble.   [64] UIDHR (1981): Art. IV(e).

[65] UIDHR (1981): Art. VI; see also Art. VII: the right to protection against torture; Art. IX: asylum.

relationship between the government and the people', who, thus, are entitled to choose/remove their rulers.[66] However, some scholars today consider that 'State–religion–Muslim relations in non-Muslim countries are not succinctly defined in Islamic jurisprudence' because there is no precedent for Muslim minority communities formed by migration from Muslim lands 'to predominantly Christian countries'.[67] Moreover, for some, such Muslims should maintain a separate identity if in a minority.[68] Indeed, 'if the holy law is still maintained and enforced, even under infidel authority, that country may still be considered, for legal purposes, as part of the House of Islam', and so Islamic laws apply there.[69] Also, as Islam 'demands full allegiance from a person, once he has chosen freely to embrace it',[70] if *sharia* conflicts with the law of a non-Muslim State, 'it is divine law which must prevail' – and Muslims should 'contest, defend and protect themselves against "rational" and secular authority';[71] using *sharia* enables 'reassertion of Islamic identity', rather than submission to the laws of the country.[72]

Nevertheless, Muslim scholars have developed jurisprudence on 'citizenship' in non-Muslim states for Muslims belonging to the non-territorial category of the community of the faithful (*ummah*), as they seek to accommodate their faith in wider society.[73] For instance, using the classic Islamic division of the world into the territory of Islam or Muslim country (*dar al-Islam*), the territory of peace (*dar al-sulh*) and

---

[66] UIDHR (1981): Art. XI: public affairs; and Art. XIV: free association.

[67] I. Yilmaz, *Muslim Laws, Politics and Society in Modern Nation States: Dynamic Legal Pluralisms in England, Turkey and Pakistan* (Farnham: Ashgate, 2005) 45.

[68] K.A.E. Fadl, 'Islamic law and Muslim minorities', 1 *Islamic Law and Society* (1994) 141–187 at 179.

[69] B. Lewis, 'Legal and historical reflections on the position of Muslim populations under non-Muslim law', in B. Lewis and D. Schnapper, eds., *Muslims in Europe* (London: Pinter, 1994) 1–18 at 15.

[70] M.A. Kettani, 'Muslims in non-Muslim societies: challenges and opportunities', 11 *Journal of the Institute of Muslim Minority Affairs* (1990) 226–233 at 226.

[71] M. King, ed., *God's Law Versus State Law: The Construction of Islamic Identity in Western Europe* (London: Grey Seal, 1995) 4.

[72] J.S. Nielsen, *Muslims in Western Europe* (Edinburgh: Edinburgh University Press, 1987) 17.

[73] The status of a non-Muslim (*dhimmi*) resident in an Islamic state is beyond the scope of this study: see e.g. A. Black *et al.*, *Islamic Law* (2013) 71–72; and A.M. Emon, 'Shari'a and the rule of law: preserving the realm', in R. Griffith-Jones and M. Hill, eds., *Magna Carta, Religion and the Rule of Law* (Cambridge: Cambridge University Press, 2015) 196–214, especially 204–212.

the territory of war (*dar al-harb*), some scholars propose that a non Muslim political unit should be understood as *dar al-sulh*, namely: 'a neutral territory of peaceful coexistence between Muslims and non Muslims' where '[a]s protected persons under a pact of citizenship (through naturalisation), Muslim migrants become transformed into Muslim citizens'; in turn: 'By accepting citizenship . . . Muslim migrants accept and undertake to abide by laws, rules and regulations of their new homeland.' At the level of Islamic law, 'this approach is valid because *siyasa shar'iyya* [comprising measures bringing people to wellbeing] legitimated *qanun* or law-making by political authority in Muslim jurisdictions. This opens up *dar al-sulh* as a space for citizenship rights.'[74]

That Muslims in Britain are also citizens, and subject to civil law, is explored, for example, by Sheikh Kazi Luthfur Rahman, at the London Central Mosque and Islamic Cultural Centre.[75] On one hand: 'A true Muslim is bound to be content and satisfied with the decrees and decisions of Allah' to whom 'absolute and ultimate loyalty' is owed. On the other hand: a 'good Muslim Citizen in Britain' is *inter alia*: to fulfil contractual obligations, and 'citizenship is a form of covenant [to] be observed once it has been made';[76] to 'respect the law of the country and especially laws which are . . . for the health, safety and security of [the] public'; and to 'respect the tradition, custom and culture of other citizens while adhering to the Sunnah . . . as much as possible'.[77] For the Fatwa Committee UK, similarly: 'It is important for European Muslims to respect the law of the land . . . and not to break it, since they have entered into an agreement to obey and respect the laws of their country. Allah said: "O you who believe, uphold your agreement".'[78] It has also held: 'There is nothing wrong for Muslims to join the British army, since they are a part of the society and it is within their rights as resident of the country'; on joining, they may take the oath of allegiance to the Crown – if done 'by the Quran or by the name of Allah, there is nothing wrong with it'; and after joining, 'if they feel . . . their religious rights are not met, they should pursue the necessary [civil] legal channels' in the same

---

[74] See e.g. S.S. Ali, 'From Muslim migrants to Muslim citizens', in R. Griffith-Jones and M. Hill, eds., *Rule of Law* (2015) 157–175.

[75] 'Citizenship and Islam' (2016): www.iccuk.org/images/Citizenship_and_Islam1_Nov2016.pdf.

[76] He cites the Quran 5 (Al-Maidah: 1); and 17 (Al-Israa: 34).

[77] He cites Al-Adab Al-Mufrad 125 (of the jurist Al-Bukhari (d. 870 CE)).

[78] FCUK: Decision 2/3.

way as any other citizen.[79] It may be a crime under the law of the State to offend Islam through speech/literature.[80]

In principle, like the United Synagogue or Christian churches (see above), which have secured an Act of Parliament to provide for legal personality, protect institutional structures and regulate property and finance, so Muslim organisations may seek a parliamentary statute tailored to their needs. For example, statute recognises: the office of Dai al-Mutlaq, 'supreme head of Dawat-e-Hadiyah and its people professing Islam distinguished as the Shiah Fatimi Ismaili Tayyibi Dawoodi Bohras known as the Dawoodi Bohra Community'; its holder, 'duly appointed by an act of designation in accordance with the canons and principles of the mission known as Dawat-e-Hadiyah'; that 'the principles and tenets of Dawat-e-Hadiyah require that the Dai al-Mutlaq hold, control, administer and protect all properties and institutions of Dawat-e-Hadiyah and all such properties and institutions of the Dawoodi Bohra Community as are dedicated for the purposes of Dawat-e-Hadiyah and are recognised as such by the Dai al-Mutlaq'; and that the Act incorporates the Dai al-Mutlaq as a corporation sole capable of holding property in England and Wales and of suing and being sued.[81]

Engaging with civil law issues are also treated in the objects of Muslim organisations. For example, its constitution empowers the Muslim Council of Britain to be involved in: 'preparing the case for, and advocating, the responsibilities and rights of Muslims living in Britain'; establishing a position 'for the Muslim community within British society that is fair and based on due rights'; and working to eradicate 'disadvantages and forms of discrimination faced by Muslims'.[82] Similarly, the aims and objectives of British Muslims for Secular Democracy include raising awareness among British Muslims and the public about democracy, citizenship, and 'the separation of faith and state', so that 'faiths exert no undue influence on public policies'. It seeks to achieve this by, *inter alia*: facilitating discourse on 'secular democracy' and its benefits; raising awareness about 'religious influence on UK domestic and foreign policies', especially those having an 'undue effect on civil liberties'; addressing Islamophobia and prejudice against Muslims and Muslim

---

[79] FCUK: Decision 1/3.
[80] *Norwood* v. *DPP* [2003] EWHC Admin 1564: the Public Order Act 1986 was used to prosecute successfully the display of a poster showing events of 9/11 and the words 'Islam out of Britain'.
[81] Dawat e Hadiyah Act 1993.   [82] MCB: Con. Declaration of Intent and Art. 2.

communities and opposing radicalism and intolerant beliefs; and ensuring that practices of politicians/leaders are transparent.[83]

Religion and Human Rights

This section addresses the treatment of human rights in general and
religious freedom in particular in the legal and other instruments of
Jewish, Christian and Muslim organisations, who are themselves beneficiaries of civil human rights law. To varying degrees, these instruments
deal with the nature of human rights, the duty to promote them in civil
society, the establishment of institutions to work in the human rights
field, and the obligation of the faithful as individuals to respect human
rights. The State has recently developed a series of statutes which seek to
protect religious freedom, to regulate religious discrimination and to
forbid acts of religious hatred.[84]

Judaism, Human Rights and Wider Society

The Jewish approach to the secular category of human rights has been
the subject of considerable debate in recent years.[85] The Declaration on
Judaism and Human Rights (1974) affirms,[86] first, that: 'Human rights
are an integral part of the faith and tradition of Judaism. The beliefs that
man was created in the divine image, that the human family is one, and
that every person is obliged to deal justly with every other person are
basic sources of the Jewish commitment to human rights.'[87] Secondly, the
Universal Declaration of Human Rights 1948 remains 'a universally

---

[83] British Muslims for Secular Democracy: http://bmsd.org.uk/index.php/objectives/.

[84] For the Human Rights Act 1998 (incorporating religious freedom under ECHR Art. 9),
Equality Act 2010 (and regulations operative under it), and the Racial and Religious
Hatred Act 2006, see e.g. M. Hill et al., Religion and Law (2014) 43–48, 141–168.

[85] See e.g. M.R. Konvitz, ed., Judaism and Human Rights (New York: W.W. Norton, 1972)
13: 'There is no word ... for "human rights" in ... Scriptures or ... other ancient Jewish
text'; but this does not mean the ideals they stand for are not valued; and D. Novak, 'A
Jewish theory of human rights', in J. Witte and M.C. Green, eds., Religion and Human
Rights (Oxford: Oxford University Press, 2012) 27–41.

[86] McGill International Colloquium on Judaism and Human Rights, Declaration on Judaism and Human Rights (DJHR), adopted in Montreal 23 April 1974, by the Jacob
Blaustein Institute for the Advancement of Human Rights of the American Jewish
Committee, Canadian Jewish Congress, and Consultative Council of Jewish Organizations.

[87] DJHR: Art. I; and: 'The struggles of Jews for freedom from oppression and discrimination
in the modern era have helped advance the cause of human rights for all. Jews and Jewish

applicable standard for the human rights'; however, many nations vary in their values, needs and priorities. Civil and political rights are interdependent with, and indivisible from, economic, social and cultural rights. The continuing development of effective international law is essential to further just relationships between individuals and their governments, within a nation and among countries, and all nations should adopt bills of rights. Human rights laws should be interpreted in good faith to further the rights they promote, and applied impartially with a single standard for all, including in relation to religious intolerance and discrimination. All States should undertake or intensify action to safeguard the rights of all groups to their cultures.[88] The Declaration condemns depriving the rights of Jews. Moreover, Jewish communities must: preserve and sharpen the traditional sensitivity of 'the Jewish conscience' to the plight of the downtrodden, advocate for human rights and recognise that education is an important means to advancement. Recognising the commitment and contributions of other religions to human rights, there should be continued attempts for partnerships with them to bring the blessings of human rights, fundamental freedoms and dignity to all humankind.[89] The Board of Deputies of British Jews is also an advocate of human rights globally,[90] has an interest in promoting religious freedom and non-discrimination,[91] has called on both Jews and Muslims to stand together on issues including *halal* and *shechitah*, circumcision and marginalising extremists,[92] and it engages in interfaith dialogue.[93]

Beyond this, there are subtle differences between the traditions. Whilst not using the category of human rights explicitly, Orthodox Judaism recognises that: each human is made in the image of God with nonnegotiable dignity (Genesis 1:26); each is free, and moral life is a matter

organizations have significantly aided efforts to secure national and international protection of human rights.'

[88] DJHR: Art. II.   [89] DJHR: Art. III–IV.

[90] BDBJ: www.bod.org.uk/jonathan-arkush-irans-human-rights-record-is-dire-and-deteriorating/.

[91] BDBJ: www.bod.org.uk/political-party-manifestos-where-they-stand-on-issues-of-jewish-interest/.

[92] BDBJ: www.bod.org.uk/board-of-deputies-president-calls-for-muslims-and-jews-to-work-together-to-marginalise-extremists/.

[93] BDBJ: the Board promotes relations between different faith communities in the UK as to e.g. education, equality and extremism, and works with the Inter Faith Network, Council of Christians and Jews, and Three Faiths Forum: www.bod.org.uk/issues/interfaith-social-action/. See also e.g. the Shalom Declaration (2015) signed by Christians: http://shalom ihalui ulion.org/about.html

of choice (Deuteronomy 30:19); human life is sacred (Genesis 9:6); and marriage and the family (Hosea 2:19) represent the matrix of social life. Moreover, 'society is covenantal' – its members are responsible for one another's welfare; and a free society is 'on the biblical view a moral and not just a political achievement', its success dependent on its treatment of the most vulnerable. Therefore: 'all political authority is subject to the transcending authority of the divine', with 'moral limits to power' (Deuteronomy 16:18–20).[94] In turn, the United Synagogue commends the Equality and Human Rights Commission and its work.[95]

In similar vein, Reform Judaism is committed to bringing the Torah 'into the world when we strive to fulfil the highest ethical mandates in our relationships with others and with all God's creation'; and 'social action and social justice' represent 'a central prophetic focus of traditional Reform Jewish belief and practice'.[96] However, the Movement for Reform Judaism explicitly recognises the category human rights. It requires that the Council of a member synagogue must act 'with respect to the legal and human rights of the individual'.[97] Moreover, the Movement is also committed to 'campaigning against all violations of human rights' and 'to speak up for those who, through violence and inequality, are denied the ability to speak out about their suffering' – this in part on the basis of the Torah *mitzvah* to 'not stand idly by the blood of our neighbour' (Leviticus 19:16). Several of its Rabbis are involved in the work of Rabbis for Human Rights, a body which advocates human rights globally.[98]

The Union of Liberal and Progressive Synagogues too affirms 'the Jewish conception of humanity' created in the Divine Image, endowed with free will, capable of good and evil, mortal yet with a sense of eternity, able to have a direct relationship with God and 'divinely destined to lead to an age when all worship the One God ... and the reign of freedom, justice, love and peace will be permanently established

---

[94] Lord Sacks (Chief Rabbi, United Hebrew Congregations of the Commonwealth 1991–2013), 'The Great Covenant of Liberties', in R. Griffith-Jones and M. Hill, eds., *Rule of Law* (2015) 301–313.

[95] US: www.theus.org.uk/article/equality-and-human-rights-commission-call-evidence.

[96] Central Conference of American Rabbis: *A Statement of Principles for Reform Judaism* (CCA Yearbook, vol. 109, 2009) 110.

[97] MRJ: Code of Practice, p. 4. See also: www.reformjudaism.org.uk/human-rights-shabbat-10-december/.

[98] MRJ: www.reformjudaism.org.uk/shomrei-mishpat-protecting-human-rights/.

hroughout the world'.[99] It also affirms that God is 'Source of the Moral
Law', who demands that humans 'practise justice and mercy in their
dealings with one another',[100] and 'the establishment of just society'.[101]
The Union itself respects 'conscientious options' of its members,[102] as
well as other religions and supports dialogue with them, especially
Christianity and Islam, for 'mutual understanding, friendship and
enrichment'.[103] And on the basis of freedom and equality, for Conservative Judaism: 'justice and dignity for each human being can be achieved
within the framework of Halakhah'.[104]

Jewish religious freedom has been the subject of parliamentary
statute,[105] and activity in State courts as, for example, when a 'no
Saturdays off work' rule at a hairdressers was held to be indirect
discrimination in putting Jews in general, and the Jewish claimant in
particular, at a disadvantage on any given Saturday; although serving
clients on a Saturday was a legitimate aim, the employers should have
considered how, or if, they could re-arrange the claimant's duties and
customers for that Saturday.[106] Dress may also be an issue in the
context of employment. Some observant Jewish men and women
may have specific requirements regarding their dress. Some Jewish
men cover their heads at all times with a skull cap (*yarmulka, kappel*
or *kippah*). Some observant Jewish women wish to dress modestly,
which may include not wearing trousers, short skirts or short sleeves.
Some married Jewish women will also cover their hair, with a scarf,
hat or wig. Additionally, some observant Jews will not want to be in a
state of undress or have physical contact with members of the opposite
sex. For some strictly Orthodox individuals only, this may also extend
to shaking hands.[107]

---

[99] ULPS: *Affirmations* (2006) Arts. 3–4.   [100] ULPS: *Affirmations* (2006) Arts. 1–2.

[101] ULPS: *Affirmations* (2006) Art. 38.

[102] ULPS: *Affirmations* (2006) Art. 25; see also Art. 8: Israel.

[103] ULPS: *Affirmations* (2006) Art. 42.

[104] Statement of Principles of Conservative Judaism (1990): 29–30, 38. See also USCJ: The
'Ideal' Conservative Jew: Eight Behavioural Expectations: Jewish Living: social justice
programmes.

[105] E.g. Oaths Act 1978 s. 1(1): 'in the case of a Jew, the Old Testament' may be used.

[106] *Fugler* v. *MacMillan – London Hairstudios Limited* [2007] UKEAT 0009 07 30003 (30
March 2007).

[107] BDBJ: *The Employer's Guide to Judaism* (2015) Section 2.

Christianity, Human Rights and Religious Freedom

The provenance, nature and scope of human rights are much debated by Christian theologians and jurists, several of whom trace the concept to and often beyond the Reformation. According to the principles of Christian law of the historic churches: all humans, created in the image of God, share an equality of dignity and fundamental human rights; and a church should protect and defend human rights in society for all people.[108] Moreover, the faithful should promote social justice and charitable work as regulated by their church.[109] These principles derive from the laws of the churches.

The Roman Catholic Church teaches that the role of the State is 'to defend and protect the common good of civil society', which consists of 'respect for and promotion of the fundamental rights of the person, prosperity, or the development of the spiritual and temporal goods of society, and the peace and security of the community and its members'.[110] Moreover, the church claims for itself a right 'to true freedom to preach the faith, to proclaim its teaching about society, to carry out its task among people without hindrance, and to pass moral judgments even in matters relating to politics, whenever the fundamental rights of man or the salvation of souls requires it'.[111] The rights and duties of the faithful, set out in canon law, derive from the fundamental dignity of the individual as a human person and include inalienable and inviolable human rights.[112] However, the Church has been criticised in recent years in several cases, for instance on the applicability of human rights to the processes of its own tribunals (and fair trial standards),[113] and dismissal of an organist (separated from his wife) on grounds of adultery and bigamy (as to the right to family and private life).[114]

There is a large body of Anglican teaching and quasi-legislation on the promotion of human rights, much of it is found in resolutions of the

---

[108] Christian Law Panel of Experts, *Principles of Christian Law* (2016) X.2: human rights and religious freedom.

[109] Christian Law Panel of Experts, *Principles of Christian Law* (2016) X.3: social responsibility; and X.4: care in public institutions.

[110] CCC: paras. 1925–1927; GS 26, 84.   [111] GS 76; DH 14.

[112] CIC: c. 204: equality and dignity; c. 747: 'fundamental human rights'.

[113] *Pellegrini* v. *Italy*, App. No. 30882/96, 20 July 2001: applying ECHR Art. 9 to tribunal process.

[114] *Schüth* v. *Germany*, App. No. 1620/03, 23 September 2010: a church contract was not 'an unequivocal undertaking to live a life of abstinence in the event of separation or divorce', breaching ECHR Art. 8.

Lambeth Conference;[115] it is also a principle of law that: 'All persons are equal in dignity before God'; and that: 'All persons have inherent rights and duties inseparable from their dignity as human beings created in the image and likeness of God and called to salvation through Jesus Christ.'[116] Promotion of human rights and religious liberty is also pivotal in the doctrinal and juridical instruments of Protestants. For example, the Lutheran Church in Great Britain provides: 'This Church affirms the God-given human dignity of all people, rejoicing in the diversity of God's creation' and commits itself to 'struggle for justice, peace and the integrity of creation'.[117] With regard to the particular human right of religious freedom, the United Reformed Church in Great Britain declares that civil authorities, being always subject to the rule of God, ought to respect the rights of conscience and of religious belief and to serve God's will of justice and peace for all humankind'.[118] Presbyterians also hold to the view that: 'although civil rulers are bound to render obedience to Christ in their own province, yet they ought not to attempt in any way to constrain anyone's religious beliefs, or invade the rights of conscience'.[119] Very little distinguishes these approaches to human rights, and to religious freedom, from those which appear in the instruments of Baptist bodies.[120]

Islam and Human Rights

Human rights do not constitute a distinct category in traditional Islamic jurisprudence. Rather than that of a right (*haqq*), the focus of Islamic law is on duties (*taklif*) – duties towards God and duties towards others – and, therefore, for some scholars, to the extent that they exist, human rights are correlative to duties.[121] On the other hand, some today propose that 'Islamic law considers as obligatory and necessary those human rights that are due to each and every individual by virtue of his or her human nature'; human dignity is a divine gift (Quran 17:70).[122] Others

---

[115] See generally N. Doe, 'Canonical approaches to human rights in Anglican churches', in M. Hill, ed., *Religious Liberty and Human Rights* (Cardiff: University of Wales Press, 2002) 185.

[116] PCLCCAC: Principle 26.1 and 2.

[117] LCGB: Rules and Regulations, Statement of Faith, 9.

[118] URC: Man, BU A, Sch. D, Version I, 8.

[119] PCI: Code, I.III.13; this cites the Act of the Church of Scotland 1647.

[120] Baptist World Alliance: Const., Art. II.   [121] A. Black *et al.*, *Islamic Law* (2013) 20–22.

[122] A. Gomaa, 'Justice in Islamic legislation', in R. Griffith-Jones and M. Hill., eds., *Rule of Law* (2013) 177, 196 at 199.

seek to harmonize human rights under international law and elements of *sharia*, to the extent that Islamic law can serve to guarantee and enforce international human rights in and beyond the Muslim world.[123] However, some non-Muslims argue that *sharia* is incompatible with the system of human rights recognised in British law;[124] and the European Court of Human Rights has held: 'Shari'a which faithfully reflects the dogmas and divine rules of religion is stable and invariable'; it is difficult to reconcile it with the principles of democracy in the European Convention on Human Rights, and to declare respect for human rights while supporting *sharia* which 'clearly diverges' from Convention values, in, for example, its criminal law, its rules on women, and the way 'it intervenes in all spheres of private and public life in accordance with [its own] religious precepts'.[125]

Nevertheless, the Islamic Council of Europe issued the Universal Islamic Declaration of Human Rights in 1981, which was adopted by the Islamic Council in London in the same year.[126] It recognises that 'Allah has given mankind through His revelations in the Holy Qur'an and the Sunnah of His Blessed Prophet Muhammad an abiding legal and moral framework within which to establish and regulate human institutions and relationships'; 'human rights decreed by the Divine Law aim at conferring dignity and honour on mankind and are designed to eliminate oppression and injustice'; and 'by virtue of their Divine source they 'can neither be curtailed, abrogated nor disregarded by authorities ... or other institutions ... surrendered or alienated'.[127] It also recognises: 'all human beings shall be equal'; no one is to be subject to discrimination due to 'race, colour, sex, origin or language', and all

---

[123] See e.g. M.A. Baderin, *International Human Rights and Islamic Law* (Oxford: Oxford University Press, 2003) 47–168 (ICCPR).

[124] D. McGoldrick, 'The compatibility of an Islamic/shari'a law system or shari'a rules with the European Convention on Human Rights', in R. Griffith-Jones, ed., *Islam and English Law* (2013) 42.

[125] *Refah Partisi (Welfare Party) and Others* v. *Turkey* (no. 2) (2003) 37 EHRR 1 (GC) para. 72.

[126] It may be understood to apply to the *ummah*, world Islamic community, or to a Muslim state.

[127] Islamic Council of Europe 19 September 1981: see C.G. Weeramantry, *Islamic Jurisprudence* (1988) 176–183. See also: S. Azzam, 'Universal Islamic Declaration of Human Rights' (1998) 102–112. For a critical analysis (including translation from the original Arabic), see A.E. Mayer, *Islam and Human Rights* (2006) 76. See also the Cairo Declaration on Human Rights in Islam (1990).

ave rights to security, dignity and liberty in terms set out in and by
1eans approved and within the limits of the Law.[128]

The Declaration then presents the 'inviolable and inalienable human
ights that [the Council] consider[s] are enjoined by Islam'; however, in
1eir exercise, 'every person shall be subject only to such limitations as
re enjoined by the Law for the purpose of securing the due recognition
f, and respect for, the rights and the freedoms of others and of meeting
1e just requirements of morality, public order and the general welfare of
1e community (*ummah*)'.[129] The rights include: the right to life –
Human life is sacred and inviolable and every effort should be made to
1rotect it'; the right to freedom, on the basis that '[m]an is born free' and
1ere must be no restriction on this 'except under the authority and in
1ue process of the Law';[130] the right to equality – 'All persons are equal
1efore the Law' and so entitled to equal opportunities; the right to justice,
1ncluding 'the right to be treated in accordance with the Law', to protest
1gainst injustice (also a duty) and to remedies provided by the Law; and
1e right to a fair trial.[131] There are also rights to: the protection of
1onour and reputation, free association, dignity at work, family life,
1ducation, privacy and free movement.[132]

With regard to freedom of religion, and minority rights, the Declar-
1tion states: 'The Qur'anic principle "There is no compulsion in religion"
1hall govern religious rights of non-Muslim minorities. In a Muslim
1ountry, religious minorities shall have the choice to be governed in
1espect of their civil and personal matters by Islamic Law, or by their
1wn laws.'[133] As to freedom of speech, every person has the right 'to
1xpress his thoughts and beliefs so long as he remains within limits
1rescribed by the Law'. No one, however, is entitled 'to disseminate
1alsehood or to circulate reports which may outrage public decency, or
1o indulge in slander, innuendo or to cast defamatory aspersions on other
1ersons'; and: 'No one shall hold in contempt or ridicule the religious
1eliefs of others or incite public hostility against them; respect for the
1eligious feelings of others is obligatory on all Muslims.'[134] Everyone has

---

[28] UIDHR (1981): Preamble.
[29] UIDHR (1981): Explanatory Notes: each human right 'carries a corresponding duty'.
[30] UIDHR (1981): Art. 1.
[31] UIDHR (1981): Arts. II, III, IV and V. See also above Chapter 5.
[32] UIDHR (1981): Art. VIII: reputation; Art. XIV: association; Art. XVII: work; Art. XIX:
   family (see above Chapter 8); Art. XXI: education; Art. XXII: privacy; XXVIII: movement and residence.
[33] UIDHR (1981): Art. X.   [134] UIDHR (1981): Art. XII.

'the right to freedom of conscience and worship in accordance with hi religious beliefs'.[135]

By way of contrast, in Britain today, the regulatory instruments of th Muslim entities studied here do not expressly address human right Nevertheless, the organisations do pronounce on human rights. Fo example, the Muslim Council of Britain welcomed establishment of th civil Equality and Human Rights Commission to 'provide the require institutional support for a future Britain where all citizens, includin British Muslims, benefit from maximum equality of opportunity and ar able to fulfil their full potential'.[136] The Council also often expresses it opinion, or else urges secular government to act, on human rights issue and policy at home and overseas.[137] Further, Muslim bodies engage ii social justice initiatives and list these in their objects. For instance, th Council for Mosques (Bradford) lobbies on behalf of the Muslim com munity on local and national matters such as law and order, health education and interfaith relations.[138] Muslim bodies may also engage ii interfaith work. For example, Bolton Council of Mosques: sees dialogu with other religious communities as more important today than eve before; belongs to Bolton Interfaith Council; attends regular interfaith meetings with the Christian Churches and Hindu Forum; recognises a its 'duty' in the community to support other religious festivals; work with 'other religious groups to ensure the wider community is engaged and involved'; and provides training to promote interfaith an community cohesion.[139]

One area in which Muslim religious freedom is much-debated an often litigated is that in relation to dress, particularly in schools an employment.[140] However: 'For all the controversy that surrounds it . . there is no generally agreed single proper dress accepted by all Muslims' rather: 'individual Muslims claim a whole spectrum of requirements fo

---

[135] UIDHR (1981): Art. XIII.
[136] MCB: 19 November 2004: www.mcb.org.uk/mcb-welcomes-the-creation-of-a-new-com mission-for-equality-human-rights/.
[137] MCB: 20 May 2011: www.mcb.org.uk/our-government-must-not-look-the-other-way as-bahrain-commits-gross-violations-of-human-rights/.
[138] CFM: www.councilformosques.org/about-us/our-aims/.
[139] BCOM: www.thebcom.org/what-we-do.
[140] See e.g. R (on the application of Begum) v. Headteacher and Governors of Denbigh High School [2006] UKHL 15: banning a jilbab did not breach ECHR Art. 9.1; for criticism o this in Eweida and Others v. UK (2013) 57 EHRR 8, see M. Hill et al., Religion and Law (2014) paras. 77 and 80–82.

slamic dress according to their conscience and ... enthusiasm'.[141] First, he 'Islamic principles of dress' (with examples from the Sunnah) are that . man must cover himself 'from his navel to his knee at all times, and a voman must cover everything except her face and hands' but: 'How that ranslates into practice depends on interpretation of the Qur'an and junnah.'[142] Secondly, men may wear a sarong-like *izhar*, trouser-like *halwar*, and *kameez/qamees* (long shirt), headgear and beard. Thirdly, as vith men, the practice of women 'ranges from dress rooted in ethnicity, hrough token gestures of Islamic identity, to the full Sunnah' – but inlike for men, there are no 'specific examples from the Sunnah' describ-ng women's clothes, 'other than the general requirement of being loose, ind covering all except hands and face, or being fully covered under a veil [*niqaab*] and *burqa*-equivalent'; and some older generation vomen prefer to maintain their ethnic traditions, whether it is a sari and scarf (*shalwar-kameez* and *dupatta*), long skirt, blouse and scarf. But, for nen and women, any unwelcomed interference with dress would be considered an assault.[143]

Religion, Natural Law and Universal Duties

While the faithful of all three religions are bearers of human rights under civil law, and in different ways and to varying extents recognise fundamental rights flowing from the essential equality of humans who are made in the image of God, they differ considerably on the concept of natural law as the source of duties for all humankind. The term 'natural law' is used for a variety of doctrines which are often contested and differ in detail. At their core, they propose the existence of universal principles derived from nature, particularly human nature, which are normative, providing moral standards, or ethical constraints on human conduct, which determine what is right and wrong. These standards are applicable to all humans, discoverable through the use of reason, and should be used as a source of, and criterion to assess, the legitimacy of human action and human law. Natural law has played an important part historically in

---

[141] M. Naqshbandi, *Islam and Muslims in Britain* (2012): Guide 7.1.3.1: 'The least desirable outcome for all is where a particular Muslim organisation or an external non-Muslim body such as a court is asked to define Islamic dress – it cannot do so in undisputed terms', as its decision will 'inevitably include its own ethnic and factional prejudices'.

[142] M. Naqshbandi, *Islam and Muslims in Britain* (2012): Guide 7.1.3.2: 'Principles': this describes the dress of the Prophet Muhammad.

[143] M. Naqshbandi, *Islam and Muslims in Britain* (2012): Guide 7.1.3.3 1.

Christianity. By way of contrast, traditionally, it has played a small part in Judaism and Islam. However, today Jewish and Muslim scholars are beginning to develop their own natural law theory often drawing upon what many of them see as explicit or implicit natural law thinking in the classical sources of Jewish and Islamic law.[144]

Dat tiv'it

There are three basic approaches to natural law in Judaism. The traditional view is that natural law is not a category known to Jewish law, another is that natural law *doctrine* is present, but of marginal importance, in the historical Rabbinic tradition; and a minority of scholars propose that historical but marginal natural law thinking should have greater prominence in contemporary Judaism.[145] First, the traditional assertion is: 'In Judaism there is no natural law doctrine, and in principle there cannot be';[146] and so it is absent from standard contemporary texts on the sources of Jewish law.[147] The assertion is justified on various grounds. The idea of 'a natural order and natural laws is unknown in the [Hebrew] Bible'.[148] Only the Torah, the revealed law of God, is acceptable to *halakha*; there is no room in this monist system for a parallel authority – the Torah is the fullest expression of the revealed law of God available to humans and sufficient for every question arising in life. Some Torah commands may in any event be 'rationally justified' or have a 'non-evident rationality', and 'fulfilling [them] puts us in a position . . . to understand their justifications'.[149] As there is no distinction between law and morals, no moral code independent of divine law, so there is no universal law discoverable by reason without appeal to God; rather *halakha* already contains 'moral rights and duties'.[150] In short, the concept of natural law jars with the legal monism of Judaism: the source

[144] N. Doe, 'Natural law in an interfaith context: the Abrahamic religions', in N. Doe, ed *Christianity and Natural Law* (Cambridge: Cambridge University Press, 2017) 184–204

[145] J. Macy, 'Natural law', in A.A. Cohen and P. Mends-Flohr, eds., *20th Century Jewish Religious Thought* (Philadelphia, PA: The Jewish Publication Society, 2009) 663–672.

[146] M. Fox, 'Maimonides and Aquinas and natural law', *Dinei* 3 (1971): 5. See also B.S Jackson, 'The Jewish view of natural law', *Journal of Jewish Studies* (2001): 136–145.

[147] See, typically, N.S. Hecht et al., eds., *Jewish Law* (1996).

[148] L. Jacobs, *Jewish Religion* (1999) 167.

[149] J.A. Jacob, 'The reasons of the commandments: rational tradition without natural law' in J.A. Jacob, ed., *Reason, Religion and Natural Law* (Oxford: Oxford University Press 2012) 106ff.

[150] I. Herzog, *Jewish Law* (1980) Vol. 1, 381: 'Moral Rights and Duties in Jewish Law'.

of halakhic norms is the written and oral law, not natural law – no valid norms exist outside the revealed law of God.

Secondly, however, some scholars suggest that the pre-revelation Noahide laws imply that 'all human beings know either instinctively or by tradition what constitutes ... the basic rules which all humans are expected to follow', that is 'the Torah for the Gentile world' which a 'son of Noah' (*ben Noah*), Gentile, must keep to belong among 'the righteous of the nations'.[151] Of the seven commands Noah reiterated after the Flood, one deals with courts and the others forbid blasphemy, idolatry, adultery and incest, homicide, robbery and eating the flesh of a living animal. Several medieval scholars also recognized universal duties in 'the reasons for the commandments' of the Torah which may not appear in the Torah and not be totally dependent on divine command. For example, for Saadia Gaon (d. 942): 'As human beings require a prophet, besides their own reason, to explain to them the revealed commandments, so they require other commands, besides the revealed ones. The goodness of these other commandments is rooted in human reason and understood through it'; and for Judah Halevi (d. 1141): 'There are the rational laws, being the basis and the preamble of the divine law, preceding it in character and time, [and] ordinances especially given to Israel as a corollary to rational laws.'[152] While the use by Maimonides (d. 1204) of natural law theory is much-debated,[153] the first Jewish thinker to use the term 'natural law' (*dat tiv'it*) was Yosef Albo (d. 1444) for whom there are three kinds of law: 'positive law' made by humans; divine law 'ordered by God' through a messenger (like Moses); and natural law, which is 'the same among all peoples, at all times, and in all places'.[154] Therefore: 'a fully-fledged natural law theory in the modern sense is absent in the medieval Jewish tradition' but it has 'natural law sentiments'; medieval thinkers were 'moving toward a natural law theory, according to which moral truths are universally binding, reflective of our human nature, and accessible to human reasoning'.[155] The trend continued in later centuries; for instance, according to the Talmudic scholar

---

[151] L. Jacobs, *Jewish Religion* (1999) 169.

[152] A. Sagi, 'Natural law and *halakha*' (2000) 167–171, and 181.

[153] O. Leaman, 'Maimonides and natural law', *Jewish Law Annual* 6 (1987) 78–93.

[154] J. David, 'Maimonides, nature and natural law', 5 *Journal of Law, Philosophy and Culture* (2010) 67–82, at 78–90.

[155] T. Rudavsky, 'Natural law in Judaism: a reconsideration', in J.A. Jacobs, ed., *Reason, Religion and Natural Law: From Plato to Spinoza* (Oxford: Oxford University Press, 2012) 83 at 105.

Samuel Glasner (d. 1924): 'As for things that human beings find revolting and loathsome, even had the Torah not forbidden them, all ... who would [do them] are even more abominable than one violating an explicit biblical prohibition.'[156]

Thirdly, there are modern scholars who use natural law thinking. For example, the contemporary Jewish scholar David Novak advocates adoption of natural law theory in Judaism today. He bases his position on a multitude of texts cited from scripture and the classical Rabbinic tradition. First, natural law originates in God: it is created by God, exists as a God-given commandment (*mitzvah*) and represents what God has willed for all humans. Secondly, natural law is discoverable 'when practical or moral reason is properly exercised'. Thirdly, natural law is different from the laws of nature: sub-rational impulses only become the concern of natural law as 'moral law' when they involve interpersonal human relationships – and some moral norms may be known by instinct before being revealed in the Torah. Fourthly, therefore, natural law governs all inter-human relations, unlike the revealed law of God which is addressed 'to a particular human society'; and: 'When the reason of the commands is universal and thus immediately evident to all *a priori*, the command can be considered a natural law precept'; when the reason is neither universal nor evident to all, it may be known through revelation *a posteriori*. Fifthly, revelation is 'the maximal manifestation of God's law', and natural law 'the minimal manifestation of God's law', which allows 'the normative claim of revealed law to be intelligible' and used to test human law.[157]

Jus Naturale

Natural law has enjoyed a prominent place in Christianity. Many see Paul's Letter to the Romans as containing a germ of the idea: 'When Gentiles who have not the law do by nature what the law requires, they are a law to themselves, even though they do not have the law. They show that what the law requires is written in their hearts' (Romans 2.14–15).[158] The doctrine was developed by the early Church Fathers, and in the medieval period Aquinas (d. 1274) argued (along Aristotelian lines):

---

[156] A. Sagi, 'Natural law and *halakha*' (2000) 172–174.

[157] D. Novak, 'Natural law and Judaism', in A. M. Emon, M. Levering and D. Novak, *Natural Law: A Jewish, Christian and Islamic Trialogue* (Oxford: Oxford University Press, 2014) Ch. 1.

[158] See e.g. F.J. Contreras, ed., *The Threads of Natural Law: Unravelling a Philosophical Tradition* (New York: Springer, 2013).

humans are rational creatures, with the capacity to reason; by using reason to reflect on human nature, we may discover the specific ends toward which we naturally tend (e.g. to live) and general end for which God created us (salvation in eternal communion with God). On discovering these ends, we can determine the means to achieve them. This understanding of God's plan for humans, implanted in us by His act of creation, is natural law – a participation in the eternal law of God – and from natural law, we deduce moral duties. Elements of the theory were retained at the Reformation in the sixteenth century; for instance, John Calvin (d. 1564) proposes that humans have a 'sense of divinity', or a 'sense of God', or 'the seed of religion', corrupted but not obliterated by sin; but for certain knowledge of God humans need the Word of God.[159]

However, partly because of the doctrine of original sin, later Reformation theology generally rejected the competence of fallen human reason to engage in 'natural theology', a view asserted by Karl Barth (1886–1968): when gentiles 'show that what the law requires is written on their hearts' (Romans 2.15), 'they show precisely that they no longer cling to any human resources, including "natural law"'.[160] Generally, therefore, natural law theory is rejected for a variety of reasons. It is flawed because it moves from observable facts to moral principles; it attempts to base ethics (ought) on a non-moral account of what human beings are like (is) – but what humans are like does not tell us what they ought to be like morally. The picture of human nature is likely to be as controversial as the moral conclusions at which it arrives – that picture is itself the product of a moral outlook rather than an independently established basis by which a moral outlook can be supported. That human reason alone (and fallen human reason at that), reflecting on human nature, can understand God's will for us, undermines the need for God's grace, devalues the revelation in Christ – if humans can know what is good in God's eyes, this unacceptably exalts human reason. Also, natural law theory plays down or denies specifically Christian ethics – whereas Christianity actually requires a radically new set of imperatives instituted by Christ.[161]

---

[159] N. Doe, *Fundamental Authority in Late Medieval English Law* (Cambridge: Cambridge University Press, 1990) 62–64 (Aquinas); and P. Helm, *John Calvin's Ideas* (Oxford: Oxford University Press, 2006) 370–374.

[160] K. Barth, *The Epistle of Paul to the Romans* (Oxford: Oxford University Press, 1933) 68.

[161] G.J. Hughes, 'Natural law', in J.F. Childress and J. Macquarrie, eds., *A New Dictionary of Christian Ethics* (London: SCM Press, 1986) 412–414.

Nevertheless, there are today Catholic, Orthodox, Lutheran, Reformed and other scholars, who propose natural law theory, rooted in the idea that God imprints upon all a capacity to discern the ordering which God has instituted for us, whether the discoverability of universal ethical principles is affected by sin, or not.[162] For example, the Anglican theologian Nigel Biggar proposes that to 'affirm natural law' means: there is a form of flourishing given in and with the nature of human beings; reflection on human nature can achieve an understanding of that flourishing and its basic goods; and reflection on our experience can produce a grasp of kinds of disposition and action that respect and promote those goods. Moreover, all humans are, despite their sinfulness, 'somewhat' capable of an accurate grasp of basic goods and their practical requirements; and so there are areas of ethical agreement between Christians and others. However, none of this 'makes the Christian theological salvation narrative ethically irrelevant. It does not say that sinful humans have the motivation to do sufficiently what they know to be right, apart from penitence, faith, gratitude, and hope that the story of God's salvific initiative inspires' – nor does it mean they have the power, unaided by biblical tradition, to know completely what is good, virtuous or right.[163] At the same time, however, with the exception of Roman Catholic canon law, and in ecumenical dialogue, natural law is not expressly used in the modern juridical texts of churches, though they do invoke concepts of divine law, the revealed law of God, as well as large moral ideas rooted in ethical standards which may be conceived as universal.[164]

Natural Law in Islamic Jurisprudence

In Islam, *sharia* is created by God and must be obeyed. Reason alone cannot oblige obedience – at most, it corroborates what is established by texts endowed with divine authority.[165] Therefore, there is no natural law

---

[162] See N. Doe, ed., *Christianity and Natural Law* (Cambridge: Cambridge University Press, 2017).

[163] N. Biggar, *Behaving in Public: How to Do Christian Ethics* (Grand Rapids, MI: William B. Eerdmans, 2011) 41–42.

[164] See N. Doe, ed., *Natural Law* (2017) 28–35 (Roman Catholic canon law); 167–171 (ecumenism); see other studies in this volume for the approach of the historic churches to natural law thinking. For concepts of moral law and conscience, see N. Doe, *Christian Law* (2013).

[165] A.M. Emon, *Islamic Natural Law Theories* (Oxford: Oxford University Press, 2010).

tradition in Islam.[166] Rather, the dominant thesis is that of 'scriptural positivism' – namely, the supremacy of the Quran, which rejects a role for reason in law, theology and philosophy. Moreover, traditionally, for legal theory (*usul al-fiqh*), if there is no scripture on a specific issue, there is a state of legal suspension (*tawaqquf*) and no coherent way to determine divine law on the matter. In such a case, it is not possible to attribute to God a ruling with normative force – all determinations of the divine law must find expression, either directly or indirectly, from scripture.[167]

However, some scholars consider that human beings may speak authoritatively on the basis of reason without recourse to the revealed divine law.[168] Moreover, whilst the Quran is the revealed word of God and the foundation of *sharia*, 'claiming that God is the sole legislator and that human-made law has no legitimacy cannot be sustained'; humans have no direct access to God's will following the revelation, which ceased at the death of the Prophet, but, as humans 'do not have perfect access to the will of God, they are not able to be the executor of the Divine Will without involving their subjectivity in the process'.[169] Thus, as seen in Chapter 1, other sources of law imply the use of human reason and experience: the consensus of jurists; reasoning by analogy; jurisprudence; and custom. As a *mujtahid* is one who exercises independent reasoning (*ijtihad*) in the interpretation of law, so *aql* is intelligence or natural human knowledge (in Ismaili thought, intellect as divine emanation) a source for *sharia*.[170]

Scholars propose that pre-modern Sunni jurists recognised the authority of reason – whether and how reason alone may require good and prohibit bad, and so justify norms under *sharia*. For these jurists, nature links the divine will and human reason. God created nature for the benefit of humanity. Since nature reflects His goodness, it fuses both fact

[166] G. Makdisi, *Ibn 'Aqil: Religion and Culture in Classical Islam* (Edinburgh: Edinburgh University Press, 1997) 130; P. Crone, *God's Rule – Government and Islam: Six Centuries of Medieval Islamic Political Thought* (New York: Columbia University Press, 2004) 263–264.

[167] A.M. Emon, 'Natural law and natural rights in Islamic law', 20 *Journal of Law and Religion* (2004–2005) 351–395 at 351.

[168] F. Griffel, 'The harmony of natural law and Shari'a in Islamist theology', in A. Amanat and F. Griffel, eds., *Islamic Law in the Contemporary Context* (Palo Alto, CA: Stanford University Press, 2007) 38–61.

[169] A. Black et al., *Islamic Law* (2014) 9.

[170] J.L. Esposito, ed., *Oxford Dictionary of Islam* (2003) 22, 214.

(what is) and value (what ought to be). Consequently, as a divinely created good, nature can be investigated to reach empirical and normative conclusions about right and wrong. Within these broad categories however, scholars adopt different positions on human nature.[171] Their starting point is the Quran 30:30: 'So [prophet] as a man of pure faith [hanif], stand firm and true in your devotion to religion. This is a natural disposition [fitra] God instilled in mankind – there is no altering God's creation – and this is the right religion, though most people do not know it.'[172] So, fitra is the original state in which humans were created by God and being a hanif is to follow this disposition towards God: 'Every child is born according to the fitra'; it is parents who make their child Jewish or Christian; but due to the temptations of evil, revelation is used by God to return humans to the right path.[173]

Three pre-modern schools of thought are relevant here: the Mutazilites proposed that human reason may discover the will of God independently of revelation; the Asharites rejected this idea – the revealed law of God is the sole moral criterion for humans; and the later Asharites accepted a limited scope for reason under divine law and sharia. The Mutazilites are those (notably Wasil Ibn Ata (d. 748)) who withdrew (i'tazala is 'to withdraw') from the school of Hasan of Basra (Hasan al-Basri). They considered the created order (of nature) (fitra) to contain the same norms as revealed in the Quran (which was created not eternal); there is harmony between reason and revelation and God's command is not the sole criterion to determine the correctness of an act – the command by itself is insufficient as an agent for action. Therefore, that which is not prohibited either by scripture or a rational universal obligation (wajib) is permitted.[174]

However, Asharites considered that rational deduction from the empirical observation of nature devalues revelation, undermines the omnipotence of God and erroneously suggests that the created order is sufficient to disclose the will of God.[175] This Sunni school, founded by Abu al-Hasan al-Ashari (d. 935), and associated with Hanbali, Shafi'ite

---

[171] See generally A.M. Emon, *Islamic Natural Law Theories* (2010).

[172] Translated by M.A.S. Abdel Haleem, *The Qur'an* (Oxford: Oxford University Press, 2004).

[173] U. Rubin, 'Hanif', in J.D. McAuliffe, ed., *Encyclopaedia of the Qur'an* (Leiden: Brill, 2001–6).

[174] A. Emon, 'Natural law' (2004–2005) at 355; he labels this the 'hard natural law' theory.

[175] R.M. Frank, 'Moral obligations in classical Muslim theology', 11 *Journal of Religious Ethics* (1983) 205–223, at 207–210.

and Maliki jurisprudence, offered a voluntarist critique of the Mutazilites, and was later understood to express Islamic orthodoxy. That God cannot do evil and must reward/punish humans because of their reasoned determinations, undermines God's omnipotence: morality is willed by God; it does not exist objectively; nor is it discoverable independently by unaided human reason. The view that humans have the capacity to judge right and wrong assumes that God can or cannot prescribe for them, and so implies limits on His power. Moreover, conclusions from reason alone are arbitrary, shaped by circumstance, subjectivity, desire and intuition, and should not be confused with a ruling of God; to hold otherwise means that revelation would be irrelevant. Rather, the role of reason is to prove the truth of revelation, interpret that truth and perhaps extend it to uncovered areas according to approved methods.[176]

The Asharite Al-Ghazali (d. 1111) adopts a more nuanced position: 'Every human is originally created with the belief in the one God', a belief rooted in the soul, though some people turn away from God. However, God is a legitimate subject of human understanding. Thus, independent of revelation, norms may be deduced from self-evident principles and observations of nature. Therefore, revelation and conclusions of reason may be identical but this does not apply to normative judgments on human conduct and *sharia*. Laws to determine which actions are good or bad cannot be drawn from nature or the human mind, but must be based on the revealed texts.[177] Later Asharite scholars, therefore, developed the idea that reason may be used, as a matter of God's grace (*fadl; tafaddul*), when definitive revelatory scripture is silent.[178]

Thirdly, this later Asharite approach surfaces in the work of some modern scholars. For example, Muhammad Abduh (1849–1905) proposes that judgments on human conduct need not be based solely upon revelation – universals may be known through reason. Yet, the faculty of reason (*quwwat al-aql*) is not exercisable by everyone – only those 'trained in the use of reason' (*uqala*) who know right from wrong through their rational capacity are able to lay down 'rules of justice'.

---

[176] A. Emon, *Islamic Natural Law Theories* (2010) Chapter 3: he labels this the voluntarist school.

[177] F. Griffel, 'Natural law' (2007) n. 42: he cites M. Kerr, *Islamic Reform: The Political and Legal Theories of Muhammad Abduh and Rashid Rida* (Berkeley, CA: University of California Press, 1966) 58–66.

[178] Scholars include: Fakhr al-Din al-Razi (d. 1209); Najm al-Din al-Tufi (d. 1316); and Abu Ishaq al-Shatibi (d. 1388); A. Emon, *Islamic Natural Law* (2010) Ch. 4: he labels this 'soft natural law'.

But, as experience shows that people do not listen to those trained in the use of reason or obey their deductions from it, society is prepared to submit to a higher authority than reason: prophecy. Consequently, only revealed law adequately prescribes actions in this life and rewards/punishments in the next – and thus gives a clearer incentive to do right than is given by reason: 'the unequal distribution of the faculty of reason among humans required human societies to accept divine law rather than natural law'.[179]

Finally, according to Abu al-Ala Mawdudi (1904–1979), moral values are absolute and set out in *sharia* as allowed actions (*marufat*) and disallowed actions (*munkarat*): *marufat* 'have always been accepted as "good" by human conscience', and *munkarat* 'have always been condemned by human nature as "evil"'; and so, *marufat* are in harmony with nature and *munkarat* against it. *Sharia*, in defining precisely *marufat* and *munkarat*, clearly indicates the standards to which individuals and society should aspire. However: 'The Quran leaves no room for the impression that the divine law may mean merely the law of nature and nothing more.' Rather: 'humankind should order the affairs of its ethical and social life in accordance with the law that is Sharia, that God has communicated through His Prophets ... It denies in the clearest terms the right of humans to exercise any discretion in such matters as have been decided by God and His Prophet.' Furthermore: 'Even if this world and its natural laws (*qawanin tabi'iyya*) are sufficient and adequate for what is within the human essence of mineral, organic and animal elements, they cease to be sufficient for his creational element' which 'needs a different order for the universe, an order in which the only governing law is the creational law and in which the natural law is only auxiliary to it.'[180]

Conclusion

Primary religious law and secondary religious law studied here tell us something about how Jews, Christians and Muslims co-operate with the State, comply with its laws, and value human rights. Classic *halakhah* requires Jews to obey the law of the land; the United Synagogue uses

[179] F. Griffel, 'Natural law' (2007) at n. 47, 53–55.

[180] A.A. Mawdudi, *Islam ka nizam i hayat: The Islamic Way of Life*, K. Ahmad and K. Murad, ed. and trans. (Leicester: Islamic Foundation, 1986) 17–21; and: *The Islamic Law and Constitution* (Lahore: Islamic Publications, 2nd edn, 1960) 75.

parliamentary statute as the basis for its constitution; and the Board of Deputies of British Jews has its parliamentary agents to liaise with the State. Christian churches consider that the political community is instituted by God – but church and State are institutionally distinct and discharge separate functions, though they should co-operate with each other in matters of common concern, and each church and its faithful must comply with State law in so far as obedience is just and conscionable. Christian churches may also operate under parliamentary statutes exclusively devoted to them. By way of contrast, in the absence of precise classical jurisprudence on the place of Muslims in non-Muslim States, today the concept of citizenship is being developed by Muslim scholars to explain their duty to obey State law – and the regulatory instruments of Muslim entities often expressly invoke civil law standards in their norms. Only one example has been found, however, of a Muslim group using parliamentary statute for its constitution as a corporate entity. Generally, as with Jewish and Christian bodies, Muslim organisations are classified in civil law as voluntary associations, though their internal rules may be enforceable as such in, for example, property and finance matters, and on the basis of their charitable status. The faithful of all three religions are the beneficiaries of civil human rights law, which they value, and there are both Jewish and Islamic Declarations of Human Rights. However, the modern regulatory instruments of Jewish and Muslim organisations are generally silent on human rights – though, unlike Christians, Jews and Muslims in Britain have their own conceptual equivalents. In turn, there are several radical similarities and differences in the approaches of Judaism, Christianity and Islam to natural law doctrine, not only as between these faiths, but also within each faith. Whereas natural law doctrine has historically played a prominent part in most Christian traditions, though some contest its potential to devalue revelation in Christ, in Judaism and Islam it is a minority position: the revealed law is sufficient of itself and human reason is not a freestanding normative category independent of revelation – though reason has a place for example as an aid to interpret revelation; but some scholars argue that it should play a greater part in Judaism and Islam today. However, debate about a shared concept of divine law, communicated at creation to all humans as a universal law of duties, but whose imperfect human apprehension is perfected by a knowledge of the revealed law (to which reason is a servant) is clearly worthwhile as a means of identifying common ground in dialogue between the Abrahamic faiths.

~

Conclusion

This study has used a generous understanding of religious law to includ
historical, classical or traditional (primary) laws of Judaism, Christianit
and Islam (*halakhah, ius canonicum* and *sharia*) as well as the (second
ary) modern laws of Jewish, Christian and Muslim religious organisa
tions in the United Kingdom found in their formal regulatory
instruments (typically in constitutions of the faith communities) and
informal instruments or soft-law (guidance, codes of practice or policy)
The findings, which bring into question assumptions, in public debate
on the pervasiveness, character and scope of religious law in society, ar
as follows.

First, religious law exists as legal fact in society today – in both guises
classical and modern. Religious law is used by Jews, Christians and
Muslims in a very wide range of areas in the lives of the faithful. In thi
sense, the scope or reach of religious law is extensive. Therefore, th
position is rather more nuanced than the contemporary understanding o
the civil courts, typified in the judgment of Sir James Munby 2012
namely: 'for the devout Christian ... there is likely to be some degre
of distinction between the secular and the divine ... matters quotidiar
and matters religious', but for Haredi Jews 'the distinction is, at root
meaningless', as 'every aspect of their lives ... is governed by ... purel
religious law', as is the case for 'the devout Muslim', for whom 'ever
aspect of ... existence is governed by the Quran and Sharia' – religiou
law constitutes the 'rules for living'.[1] Religious law is indeed 'rules fo
living'. In point of fact, all Jews, Christians and Muslims who belong to ;
particular religious organisation use religious law to regulate much o
most if not the whole of their lives. In terms of subject matter of religiou
law, they all have rules on, for example: the daily life of the faithfu
outside the synagogue, church or mosque; the appointment anc

---

[1] *Re G* [2012] EWCA Civ. 1233: on the education of Haredi/Chareidi children.

unctions of their faith leaders; the institutional structure and governance
of their religious organisations; the informal resolution of complaints and
conflicts; the formal processing of prescribed matters by judicial fora; the
definition of beliefs, administration of worship, and education/instruc-
ion of the faithful in religious schools; the rites of passage marking stages
in life; marriage and divorce; and the property and finances of their
religious organisations. But, unlike Jews and Muslims, Christians have
few explicit laws on, for example, inheritance, family life, and commercial
activities – but Christians in following the State on these matters are
governed in the exercise of their civil legal rights by the fundamental
principles of Christian law. Nevertheless, on the other hand, unlike
Christians, Jews and Muslims have few detailed laws on, for example,
the ordination or other admission of faith leaders, disciplinary processes
applicable to faith leaders or the structure and authority of organisations
at regional level; and, unlike Jews and Christians, Muslims have few
explicit, detailed or developed laws on the binding effect on the faithful
of civil law.

Secondly, nonetheless, all three faiths have a *general* jurisprudence on
the submission of the faithful to the law of the State. Beyond obedience to
civil law on the basis of appreciation of its civic worth or the threat of
civil sanction in the event of disobedience, in Judaism this is achieved by
the principle that the law of the land must be followed (*dina demalkhuta
dina*), in Christianity through the principle that the faithful must defer to
civil law in matters within the competence of the State (in the Protestant
tradition this is based on the doctrine of the two kingdoms) and in Islam
through the (much-debated) principle about the territory of peace (*dar
al-sulh*) in which obedience to the law of a non-Muslim State may be
rooted in a pact or covenant of citizenship freely entered by Muslims.
Also, Jewish, Christian and Muslim organisations all incorporate, or
defer expressly to elements of civil law in their regulatory instruments,
most typically in the fields of charity law with respect to the property and
finances of their organisations. It may be presumed that Jews, Christians
and Muslims would not make any regulatory instruments for themselves
that are not halakhah–gospel–sharia compliant. Yet, all three religions
ultimately reserve for the faithful the religious right to disobey civil law
contrary to divine law – and for them to deal with the civil consequences.

Thirdly, elements of religious law (both ancient and modern), and/or
decisions of religious authorities which are based on it, are recognised
either expressly or tacitly by the civil law of the State and its institutions.
The constitution of the State, through its law, recognises the constitutions

of the three Abrahamic religions. For example, all Jewish, Christian and Muslim organisations enjoy:

(1) The status or position under civil law of voluntary religious associations, and their internal rules are classified as the terms of a contract entered into by the members of the religious organisation (the civil doctrine of consensual compact).

(2) The collective right under the Human Rights Act 1998 (and the European Convention on Human Rights), as their members enjoy the individual right, to religious freedom – unless State interference in its exercise is prescribed by civil law, for a legitimate aim, or necessary for democracy.

(3) The enforcement in State courts of their internal religious rules or the administration of property and finance or to vindicate some civil right.

(4) The protection of their autonomy in terms of freedom from State intervention in the administration of religious law as to disciplinary processes against their faith leaders (when such process does not have a public/governmental element and is therefore not susceptible to judicial review).

(5) The protection of State employment law for their faith leaders when there is legal evidence of a relationship of employment.

(6) The administration of justice in their arbitral tribunals on the basis of religious law (under the Arbitration Act 1996).

(7) The freedom to educate or instruct the faithful in supplementary religious schools (which if registered are subject to inspection by the State).

(8) The advantages of charitable status (for the advancement of religion, provided there is a public benefit, and the civil standards of accountability are satisfied in their financial activities (which themselves may be regulated by religious law, such as the religious duty of the faithful to give financially) – again many religious organisations are registered charities under civil law and their constitutions (which contain religious law and often explicitly refer to sources of the primary religious law) are recognised by the civil Charity Commission.

(9) Freedom to administer religious law on divorce or, with Jews and Muslims, on the ritual slaughter of animals, if standards set out in civil law are satisfied.

(10) The facility to negotiate with government the enactment of parliamentary statute to facilitate and protect the institutional

structures of their religious organisations (e.g. the United Synagogues Act 1870, the Methodist Church Act 1976, and the Dawat-
e-Hadiyah Act 1993). However, no Jewish or Muslim religious
organisation enjoys precisely the same legal position as that of the
Church of England (by law established), the national Church of
Scotland (under statute autonomous) or the Church in Wales (by
law disestablished from the State) with its vestiges of the former
legal establishment in relation to for example marriage, prisons and
burial.

In short, there is an abundance of evidence from the law of the State
and the decisions of the civil courts that religious law may operate freely,
provided the political stakes are not too high, on the basis of either the
express or the tacit approval of the State and its institutions. To this
extent, the law of the State already provides, to some considerable extent,
accommodation of religious law elucidated in 2008 by the then
Archbishop of Canterbury, Dr Rowan Williams. Equally, the legal evidence seems to refute the understanding that religious law has no
jurisdiction under civil law, an understanding which was enunciated in
Parliament in 2008 by Bridget Prentice MP, Under Secretary in the
Ministry of Justice, in relation to 'Shari'a law',[2] or that of the current
Archbishop of Canterbury, Justin Welby, in 2017 who did not think that
we should have elements of sharia law in the English jurisprudence
system' and that 'English courts always have to prevail, under all circum-
tances, always'.[3] The position is more nuanced: the State does accommodate religious law with civil law. The religious legal instruments are
vehicles for mutual accommodation between State and religion – again,
the State would not recognise them unless they were consistent with civil
law; and the faith organisations would not make them if they were
inconsistent with religious law.

Fourthly, much religious law is theocratic, in origin, conception and
form. All three faiths use the category of divine law, the law of God
revealed to humankind and recorded in a sacred text which has a high
normative authority and content applicable to the faithful. All Jewish
religious organisations recognise and to a greater or lesser extent defer to

---

For the lecture, and the Written Parliamentary Answer by Bridget Prentice MP, and other
reactions to the lecture and the issues raised in it, see R. Griffith-Jones, ed., *Islam and
English Law* (2013) 20–33 and 35 and the other studies therein.
Church Times (9 February 2018) 6.

the Torah and its halakhic interpretation. All Christian churches emplo
the category of the Word of God and recognise it, either alone c
alongside tradition, as the ultimate norm in matters of faith and orde
All Muslim religious organisations recognise the supremacy of the Qura
and (its interpretation in the) Sunnah as divine law – the moder
regulatory instruments of many Muslim organisations also explicitl
make reference to these as forming the foundation of *sharia*. The theo
cratic element of religious law indicates that, as one commentator puts i
'religious law has a religious character in that it has distinct source
purposes and subject matters' which differ from other forms of lav
'owing to the way in which its ultimate foundation comes from
supernatural cause; a reality external to the individual'.[4] The supernatura
character of religious law is also found in its purposes: all three faith
recognise that the purpose of the revealed divine law is to guide th
faithful, in their relations with God and each other, as they walk throug|
life along the path to the hereafter. Religious law is 'religious' in virtue c
the subjects with which it deals; such as: the life of the faithful; th
spiritual qualities required for faith leaders; the profession of religiou
belief; the administration of worship and sacred rites; and the discover
of universal principles implanted in humans at creation.[5] Needless to say
the religiosity of the modern regulatory instruments studied in thi
volume is also provided by the very character of their makers: they ar
made by and for Jews, Christians and Muslims. What also comes to th
fore in key areas is the inherent adaptability of classic religious law.

Fifthly, on the other hand, there are features of religious law which ar
more temporal, secular or functional than has been presumed. Alongsid
its supernatural elements, religious law has a legal character – it is th
product of a legal order and displays axiomatic characteristics of law ii
that it seeks to stabilize human conduct; indeed: 'the religious and lega

---

[4] R. Sandberg, 'The Reformation of religious law', *Quaderni di Diritto e Politica Ecclesiastic*
(2017) 97–110.

[5] See however A. Huxley, 'Introduction', in A. Huxley, ed., *Religion, Law and Tradition*
(2002) 1: talk of religious laws often invokes an understanding that such phenomena ar
largely historical relics. Huxley prefers to refer to religious law as 'Old World Law texts' o
'Obsolescent Written Law'. He argues that emphasis is to be given to the 'O' word in both
of these formulations since 'what critically differentiates these ... systems from the norma
Comparative Law fodder is oldness, obsolescence or, if you prefer, history'. This approach
however, underplays the dynamic nature of religious law: the way in which religious law
are created, interpreted and applied in the day-to-day life of faith communities. These
insights, though valuable, do not necessitate rejection of religious law as a category.

dimensions of religious law overlap' so much so that the 'dual religious and legal character of religious law is its key definitional attribute' – and its functional aspects may be shared by secular law.[6] For instance, the modern religious regulatory instruments studied here are recognisable as law' in so far as they bind the faithful, are administered or implemented by designated religious officers, and are enforceable within the respective religious organisations through prescribed internal processes and by designated religious authorities. Like their secular counterparts, they consist of rules which require (precepts), forbid (prohibitions) or enable permissions). They are interpreted primarily within the religious community through the use of juristic techniques of interpretation shared with most secular legal systems (text and context, intent and effect). Religious law may be relaxed in a particular case on the basis of necessity and circumstance or for the attainment of a higher goal. And the regulatory instruments deal with temporal matters such as the changeable institutional structures of the organisation, maintenance of records of meetings and rites, and the proper administration of budgets and accounts. Many of the norms studied here are more than social conventions.[7] Moreover, once more, religious regulatory instruments (secondary religious law) may be properly conceived as religious law in so far as we must assume that Jews, Christians and Muslims would not make rules for themselves that are not *halakhah*–gospel–*sharia* compliant.

Sixthly, much religious law is driven by civil law and standards of wider society – this may be styled the internal secularisation of religious law. There is evidence that Jewish, Christian and Muslim religious organisations accept and incorporate in their regulatory instruments secular standards such as: consultation, for example in making appointments of faith leaders; giving reasons for decisions (e.g. for a refusal to admit a candidate to organisational membership); the professionalisation of management (e.g. training staff and volunteers with regard to the safeguarding of children at synagogues, churches and mosques); the

---

[5] R. Sandberg, 'The Reformation of religious law' (2017): he cites e.g. the work of N. Luhmann, *Law as a Social System* (Oxford: Oxford University Press, 2004); *A Systems Theory of Religion* (Stanford, CA: Stanford University Press, 2013); and *A Sociological Theory of Law* (London: Routledge, 2nd edn, 2014).

[7] See e.g. M. Malik, *Minority Legal Orders in the UK* (London: British Academy, 2012) 23: the author distinguishes legal norms 'where an individual or group can point to distinct norms that regulate normative social order' and legal orders 'that indicate that there are mechanisms for institutionalised norm enforcement'.

application of equality standards in the religious activities; and the use of secular budget and accounting standards. Further (empirical) research needed as to the precise extent to which such norms are driven by wider society. We have also met many examples of religious law operating *praeter legem* (outside of or in the interstices of civil law, when the latter is silent on a matter), *secundum legem* (in accordance with civil law), and occasionally *contra legem* (against civil law), where such conflict is either civilly forbidden or else it is limited, excused, justified or otherwise permitted on the basis of religious liberty or a special exemption. Nevertheless, there are also the contested areas, such as whether: Muslim religious marriages should be registered civilly; whether human rights should apply directly within religious communities; and whether and religious schools, Jewish, Christian and Muslim, should be registered civilly. Indeed, further work is needed as to how if at all the primary and secondary religious law of Jewish, Christian and Muslim communities in Britain today contribute to what is perceived by some as the isolation or vulnerability which adherents may experience in wider society.[8]

Seventhly, while modern regulatory instruments in the form of the legislation of the religious organisations (such as their constitutions) are formally binding on the faithful, there is a shared experience among Jews, Christians and Muslims in their extensive use of religious soft-law. A notable innovation in the regulatory life of these religious organisations in recent years has been the dramatic increase in the volume of nationwide or local quasi-legislation, or soft-law, in the form of guidelines, policy documents or codes of practice. This exists today in relation to a wide range of issues. Nationwide, a great deal of quasi-legislation has been issued, for instance, on better protection for the safeguarding of children and vulnerable adults; on nationwide standards of governance in those religious communities which employ a local or congregational system of polity; and on etiquette to be followed by those outside the faith when visiting, and health and safety regimes at, synagogues, churches and mosques. Jews and Muslims also produce a host of policy and guidance documents on religious matters, such as the ritual preparation of a body for burial or the preparation of a synagogue or

---

[8] See e.g. *The Independent Review into the Application of Sharia Law in England and Wales* (February 2018), Foreword: 'The observance of *sharia* ... has also been regarded by some as keeping many Muslims isolated, entrenched and with little social and psychological stake in wider British citizenship and civic life', particularly women.

mosque for particular religious festivals. Sometimes soft-laws are declaratory of primary religious law, or of formal regulatory instruments, or they add to or else supplement these. Unlike formal regulatory instruments, religious soft-law often gives reasons for its norms.

Eighthly, religion and religious belief are juridified through their deployment in the modern regulatory instruments of Jews, Christians and Muslims, and the translation of elements of classical Jewish, Christian and Islamic law into norms of conduct as interpreted and applied by the faithful to their secondary religious law. This practice means that, conceptually, the modern regulatory instruments of these religious organisations law may be understood as 'religion in action', or 'applied religious belief': the translation of religious belief into norms of conduct. In this sense, religious belief becomes the primary stimulus for law: it proposes values – the primary source of religious law – it contemplates action – the primary focus of religious law – and it animates these values in norms of conduct – the primary character of law. In turn, religion is governed by rational laws: these are deduced rationally from faith – God reveals the divine law; the faithful reflect on revelation through the use of reason; deductions based on faith are translated into norms of conduct; and the reasons for these are found in the faith. In this sense, much secondary religious law is the product of the use of practical reason. For example, the religious belief in Liberal Judaism that men and women are equal in so far as they are both made in the image of God is translated into the rule that the ordination of women Rabbis is allowed; the Roman Catholic belief that Jesus commissioned Peter as Pope is translated into the rule that no one may judge the Pope; and the Muslim belief that Allah wants what is best for the faithful is translated by the Fatwa Committee UK into the ruling that a Muslim student sitting examinations may be relieved from fasting in Ramadan.

Ninthly, religious law is pluralistic. There are profound differences between the laws of Jews, Christians and Muslims, as there is a high level of juristic pluralism, in the form of the multiplication of micro-legal systems, within and across the three religions. As to the substantive differences, for example: a person has Jewish status if their mother is Jewish; a person acquires Christian status through incorporation into the church universal at baptism; a person has Muslim status if the father is Muslim (but provision is made for conversion in all three faiths). There is also juridical diversity/difference in the topics addressed, the breadth or coverage of these topics, or the depth at which they are regulated – that is, in the details of the rules. As to legal pluralism within the

religions, for example: Orthodox Jews consider *halakhah* to bind
Reformed Judaism does not, and Conservatives consider it binding
but susceptible to evolution with changes in circumstance; Roman
Catholics forbid the ordination of women as priests, the Anglican
Churches in Britain permit this, and the Baptists do not understand
their ministers to be priests with a sacerdotal function; Sunni Islam
does not require circumcision, most Shia traditions regard the practice
of circumcision as obligatory but many Sunni jurists argue that it
is forbidden on the basis that the Quran prohibits the alteration of a
body. These examples may be multiplied greatly on the evidence
studied here.

Tenthly, the profound similarities between the laws of Jews, Christians
and Muslims enable the articulation of principles of religious law
common to these three Abrahamic faiths. Such articulation could be
the focus of debate in response to the call of the Woolf Commission in
2015 for a 'national conversation [to] be launched ... by leaders of faith
communities and opinion leaders in other ethical traditions to create a
shared understanding of the fundamental values underlying public life'
with a view, 'within the tradition of Magna Carta and other such declarations of rights over the centuries', to the formulation of 'a statement of
principles to guide the development and evaluation of policies relating to
the common good'.[9] What emerges from this study is that: (1) there are
principles of religious law common to Judaism, Christianity and Islam –
their existence can be factually established by empirical observation,
comparison and induction; (2) the religious organisations of each religion contribute through their own regulatory instruments to this store of
principles; (3) the principles have a strong sacred content and are
fundamental to the self-understanding of the faithful; (4) they have a
living force and contain within themselves the possibility of further
development and articulation; and (5) these principles demonstrate a
degree of unity between the religions, stimulate common actions, and
should be fed into interfaith dialogue for greater mutual understanding.

In short, the juristic traditions of all three faiths coalesce productively
when articulated as common principles of religious law, which, through
the translation of divergent religious beliefs into convergent norms of
conduct, stimulate shared actions among the faithful regardless of their

---

[9] Woolf Commission, *Living with Difference* (2015) 3.14.

religious affiliation. This fact must count for something in the quest for fuller interfaith dialogue. A statement of them appears in the Appendix which follows – this contains for debate a proposed Charter of Abrahamic Law with principles of law common to all three Jewish, Christian and Islamic faiths – one of the fruits of comparative religious law.

Appendix

Toward a Charter of Abrahamic Law

A STATEMENT OF PRINCIPLES OF RELIGIOUS LAW

Common to Judaism, Christianity and Islam

A principle of religious law common to the Jewish, Christian and Islamic organisations studied here is a foundational proposition or maxim of general applicability which is induced from the similarities of their regulatory systems; derives from their religious beliefs, juristic traditions or religious practices; expresses a basic sacred truth or ethical value; and is implicit in, or underlies, their classical laws and juridical systems. Their articulation here is based on the proposition that: (1) there are principles of religious law common to these religions and their existence can be factually established by empirical observation and comparison; (2) the religious organisations contribute through their own regulatory instruments to this store of principles; (3) the principles have a strong theocratic content and are fundamental to the self-understanding of each religion; (4) these principles have a living force and contain within them the possibility of further development and articulation; and (5) these principles demonstrate a degree of unity between the Abrahamic faiths, stimulate common religious actions and should be fed into the interfaith enterprise to enhance mutual understanding.

Section I Religious Organisations and Their Systems of Law

1. The Religious Organisation

1. A religious organisation as an institution may define itself by its autonomy, polity and objects.
2. A religious organisation is a community which may be nationwide, regional, or local.

3. A religious organisation has a distinct membership, or other body of persons associated with it, which may be organised in territorial or non-territorial units, such as congregations.
4. A religious organisation is autonomous in its system of governance or polity.
5. A religious organisation has among its objects the advancement of belief, the administration of rites and service to the wider community.

2.   Religious Regulation

1. The laws of religious organisations are found in a variety of formal sources, including constitutions, codes of canon law, statutes and bye-laws.
2. Customs may have juridical force to the extent permitted by religious law.
3. Religious soft-law, which includes guidelines, codes of practice and policy documents, is designed to complement formal written law and consists of rules that are nevertheless prescriptive in form and generate the expectation of compliance.

3.   The Servant Law

1. Religious law exists to serve a religious organisation in promoting its objects.
2. Laws contribute to constituting a religious organisation and facilitate and order its activities.
3. Religious beliefs may shape law and law may realise certain religious propositions in norms of conduct and behaviour.
4. Religious law is sourced ultimately in the revealed law of God as expressed in sacred texts.

4.   The Structure, Effect and Relaxation of Norms

1. Religious law principally deals with the lives of the faithful, faith leaders, institutional government, belief, worship, rites and property.
2. Religious law consists of various juridical formulae, such as precepts, prohibitions and permissions, and may be cast as principles and rules, rights and duties, functions and powers and may be binding or exhortatory.
3. All members of a religious organisation are subject to its laws, as are its component institutions, to the extent that the law provides.
4. Laws are prospective and should not be retrospective in effect unless this is clearly provided for in the laws themselves, and should be clear, stable and coherent, and later laws may abrogate earlier laws.
5. A religious organisation may have in place a mechanism for the enforcement and vindication of the rights and duties of the faithful, but a law may

be relaxed by competent religious authority for the spiritual good of the individual and the common good of the religious community.

Section II   The Faithful

1.   Membership of a Religious Organisation

1. All the faithful should be equal in dignity.
2. A religious community is made up of those incorporated into it in accordance with its proper laws and customs.
3. A religious organisation should serve, in appropriate ways, all who seek its assistance regardless of membership.
4. The names of persons belonging to a religious organisation may be entered on one or more rolls or other registers of membership subject to such conditions as may be prescribed by law.
5. Names may be removed from such rolls and registers in accordance with the law.

2.   The Functions of the Faithful

1. The law of a religious organisation should generally set out the basic rights and duties of all its members.
2. The faithful should promote the objects of the religious organisation and bear witness to the faith through their lives in the world.
3. The faithful should engage in the collective religious life, in professing the faith, participating in worship and enjoying its rites.
4. The faithful should maintain such religious standards in their private lives as are prescribed by law.
5. The faithful should practise daily devotion, private prayer, reading sacred texts and self-discipline; uphold religious values; and be of service to the wider community.
6. Children at synagogues, churches and mosques must be safeguarded in accordance with the highest standards that ensure their welfare and protection.

Section III   Faith Leaders

1.   Admission as a Faith Leader

1. Religious organisations may set apart persons, by way of ordination or other means, for leadership, including teaching and leading in worship.
2. A religious organisation may distinguish between different types of faith leader.

3. Candidates must be called by the religious community to serve as faith leaders, and their suitability tested through selection, examination and training by competent authority.

2. Religious Offices

1. A religious office is a position constituted by law or custom.
2. A religious office exists independently of the person who occupies it.
3. A religious office enables the discharge of functions of the particular role attaching to it.
4. A religious office may be held by a person or persons with such qualifications as are prescribed by law or custom.
5. A religious office is filled by a variety of means, often by appointment or election.
6. The authority which attaches to a religious office is determined by or under the law.
7. The authority to exercise religious office ceases upon lawful dissolution of the office, expiration of the stated term of office, attainment of the prescribed age limit, or the death, resignation, transfer, retirement or removal of the office holder.

3. The Functions of Faith Leaders

1. Faith leaders must be duly authorised by their religious organisation in order to function.
2. Faith leaders are to preach, teach the faith, administer rites and provide pastoral care.
3. Faith leaders must lead their private lives in a manner which befits their function.
4. Faith leaders may engage in such other occupations, including offices held beyond the religious organisation, as are not forbidden by law or competent authority.
5. Faith leaders are accountable to the competent authority in the manner prescribed by law.

Section IV   Religious Governance

1. Systems of Religious Polity

1. A system of government used by a religious organisation may reflect its conception of divine law.
2. A religious organisation should have institutions to legislate, administer and adjudicate for its own governance.
3. A religious institution has such power, authority or jurisdiction as is assigned to it by law.

4. A religious institution must comply with the law and may be subject in the exercise of its functions to such substantive and procedural limitations as may be prescribed by law.
5. Religious institutions may be organised at national, regional and/or local level.

2.   Nationwide Religious Organisations

1. A religious tradition may have a nationwide organisation.
2. A religious community organised with a nationwide reach may have such institutional structure as is prescribed by the regulatory instruments applicable to it.
3. The autonomy and functions of a nationwide religious entity, and its governing body, may include the authority to legislate, administer and adjudicate on matters within its competence.
4. A nationwide religious governing body is composed of such members of the faithful as are elected or otherwise appointed to it in accordance with law.

3.   Regional Religious Organisations

1. Nationwide religious entities may have regional structures.
2. Regional religious organisations may have such institutions as are prescribed by the law applicable to it.
3. A regional religious institution exercises such authority and functions as are conferred on it by the religious community to which it belongs or the constituent entities associated with it.
4. A regional religious institution is composed of such members of the faithful as are elected or otherwise appointed to it by those competent to do so under the law.

4.   Local Religious Organisations

1. Regional religious units may be divided into or constituted by local religious organisations or congregations existing at the most localised level of institutional religious life.
2. A local religious organisation, its assembly and other institutions, such as a council, meeting or other body, has such authority and functions as are lawfully inherent to it or conferred upon it by the institutions of the wider religious entity to which it may belong.
3. The governing body of a local religious organisation is composed of those members of the faithful who are lawfully elected or otherwise appointed to it.

Section V   *The Resolution of Religious Disputes*

1.   The Interpretation of Law

. Laws should be interpreted by reference to their text, context and precedent.

. A religious organisation has authority to interpret its own law.

. For the interpretation of law, recourse may be had to the purposes of the law, the mind of the legislator, and religious faith and practice.

2.   Informal Dispute Resolution

. Religious disputes may be settled by a variety of informal means, including a complaints process or other administrative process.

.. The competent authority may settle the matter in a process short of formal process in the manner and to the extent provided by law.

.. Anyone with a sufficient interest in the matter may challenge a decision by recourse to the relevant and competent authority.

3.   Religious Courts and Tribunals

. A religious community may have a system of courts, tribunals or other such bodies to provide for the judicial or formal arbitral or other resolution of religious disputes.

.. Religious courts, tribunals or other such bodies may have a nationwide, regional and/or local competence to the extent permitted by the relevant law.

.. The establishment, composition and jurisdiction of judicial bodies are determined by the law applicable to them.

.. Religious courts, tribunals and other such bodies are established by competent authority, administered by qualified personnel and may be tiered in terms of any original and appellate jurisdiction.

.. Religious courts, tribunals and other bodies exercise such authority over the faithful as is conferred upon them by law.

4.   Due Process

.. Every effort must be made by the faithful to settle their disputes amicably, lawfully, justly and equitably, without recourse in the first instance to religious courts and tribunals.

.. Formal process is mandatory if religious law or civil law require it.

.. Judicial or arbitral process may be composed of informal resolution, investigation, a hearing and/or such other elements as may be prescribed by law including an appeal.

4. The faithful must be judged according to law and procedures must secur‹ fair, impartial and due process.
5. The parties have the right to notice, to be heard, to question evidence, to a‹ unbiased hearing and where appropriate to an appeal.

5. Religious Offences and Sanctions

1. A religious organisation may institute a system of religious offences.
2. Religious offences and defences to them are to be clearly defined in writin, and a court, tribunal or other body acting in a judicial capacity must giv‹ reasons for its finding.
3. A religious organisation has a right to impose spiritual and other lawfu censures, penalties and sanctions upon the faithful, provided a breach o‹ religious law has been established.
4. Sanctions should be lawful and just.
5. A religion may enable the removal of sanctions.

Section VI   Belief, Worship and Education

1.   The Definition of Belief

1. Religious beliefs may have elements which themselves may generate norm of conduct.
2. Religious beliefs may be interpreted to the extent and in the manne prescribed by law.

2.   Profession of Faith

1. The profession of faith is a fundamental religious action and a divine imperative incumbent on all the faithful.
2. A religious organisation has the right and the duty to instruct the faithful in the context of a religious school, and to proclaim the faith.
3. Preaching is inherent to faith leadership.
4. Authorised persons may deliver sermons or other forms of preaching.
5. Sacred texts must be treated respectfully and coherently, building or tradition and scholarship in order to illuminate, challenge and transform thinking and doing.

3.   Discipline in Matters of Belief

1. A religious organisation has a right to enforce its own standards of belief.
2. The faithful should respect, honour and uphold the religious beliefs of their community.
3. A religious organisation has the right to determine the limits of permissible religious opinion, and to interpret its own beliefs.

4.   The Nature and Forms of Worship

. The worship of God is a fundamental obligation of religion.

.. Each religious organisation and those bodies within it which are competent to do so may develop texts or other forms of service for public worship, provided these are consistent with divine law.

.. Forms of worship may be found in a book of rites or liturgy, a book of prayer, a directory of worship or other instrument.

5.   The Administration of Public Worship

.. A religious organisation must provide for public worship.

.. Faith leaders are particularly responsible for the conduct of public worship.

.. Regular attendance at worship, particularly on holy days, is an expectation on the faithful.

.. The administration of worship in a local religious congregation is subject to supervision by those authorities designated by law to provide this.

Section VII   The Rites of Passage

1.   Rituals in the Early Years of Life

. A religious organisation may practise the customary rituals after the birth of a child.

.. A religious organisation may impose conditions for the administration of such rituals.

.. Rituals performed after the birth of a child cannot be repeated.

.. A religious organisation may make provision for a further rite in adolescence, following the rituals performed after birth to confirm the religious status of the individual involved.

.. Candidates may undergo preparation and instruction prior to the administration of this further rite, which should be administered in accordance with religious practice.

2.   Rites of Spiritual Development or Commemoration

. Rituals performed during adulthood may include ritual immersion, dietary discipline, commemorative meals and pilgrimages.

.. Such rites may be understood to be required by divine law.

. The faithful must participate in such rituals to the extent required or permitted by law.

3. Marriage

1. The foundation of marriage is a union between one man and one woma*
   for their mutual well-being.
2. There is no marriage unless the parties freely consent to marry.
3. Parties to a marriage may enter a pre-nuptial agreement to the exten*
   provided by law.
4. To be married in the eyes of religion, the parties must satisfy the condition
   prescribed by law and should be instructed in the nature and the obliga*
   tions of marriage.
5. Marriage is celebrated in the presence of an authorised faith leader an*
   witnesses.
6. Religious marriages may be registered civilly.
7. A marriage is ended by the death of one of the spouses and may b*
   dissolved when so determined by competent religious authority.

4. Funerals

1. The body of a deceased person is owed the greatest of respect.
2. The faithful who have died should be given a funeral according t*
   religious rites.
3. Disposal of human remains may be either by burial or by cremation, to th*
   extent permitted by law, accompanied by the administration of any rite*
   authorised for lawful use, and followed by such period of mourning as i*
   customary.

Section VIII   Property and Finances of a Religious Organisation

1. The Ownership of Property

1. A religious organisation has the right to acquire, administer and dispose o*
   property.
2. A religious organisation and/or institutions or bodies within it may see*
   legal personality under civil law to enable ownership of property.
3. A religious organisation may have rules about the acquisition, ownership*
   administration, sale or other form of disposal of its property.
4. A religious organisation may have in place provision for its own dissolutior*
   or that of institutions or bodies within it and for the distribution o*
   property on dissolution.
5. Property which vests in institutions is held on trust for the benefit of th*
   organisation and its work, and such institutions are required to exercis*
   proper stewardship of that property.

2. Places and Objects of Worship

A religious organisation may dedicate or otherwise set aside a building or other space, prescribed objects, and other forms of property, for worship and for other religious purposes.

A place of worship, or other space or object, must be used in a manner which is consistent with its religious purposes.

Responsibility for the use, care and maintenance of places of worship and objects in them, vests in a designated person or body.

Oversight of the administration of property vests in competent authority and a periodic appraisal of its condition may be the object of a lawful visitation or inspection.

3. The Control of Finance

A religious organisation has the right to make rules for the administration and control of its finances.

The civil law applicable to financial accountability must be complied with.

A religious organisation must ensure sound financial management, including the framing and approval by competent authority of an annual budget.

A religious organisation should provide, with regard to each entity within it, for the keeping of accounts for approval by a competent authority.

A religious organisation must ensure that financial accounts are audited annually by qualified persons.

4. Lawful Income

A religious organisation has a right to receive funds.

The faithful must contribute financially, according to their means, to the work of the religious organisation and other pious causes.

The officers of a religious organisation should encourage the faithful in the matter of offerings and collect and distribute these as prescribed.

A religious organisation and other entities may be required by competent authority to make a financial contribution to meet the wider institutional costs and needs of the religion.

A religious organisation may invest money to the extent permitted by its law, and if permitted should do so prudently and in ventures which are consistent with its religious and ethical standards.

5. Ecclesiastical Expenditure

A religious organisation should require the designated institutions or bodies within it to insure its property against loss.

A religious organisation should support and sustain those engaged in faith leadership according to their need and circumstance.

3. A religious organisation should make suitable provision for faith leaders who are in ill-health and for those who retire.

Section IX   Religion and State Relations

1.   Religion–State Relations

1. A religious organisation should co-operate with the State in matters of common concern, but each is independent in its own sphere.
2. The faithful may participate in politics save to the extent prohibited by religious law.
3. The faithful should obey the law of the State on the basis of their citizenship.
4. Co-operation between a religious organisation and the State may be exercised on the basis of:
   (1) the establishment of, or other formal relationship between, it and the State;
   (2) an agreement or civil legislation negotiated freely with the State;
   (3) the juridical personality, which it or institutions within it may enjoy under civil law;
   (4) its registration in accordance with the provisions of any applicable State law;
   (5) the fundamental institutional autonomy of the religious organisation in carrying out its lawful objects and its freedom in these areas from intervention by the State.

2.   Human Rights and Religious Freedom

1. All humans, having been created in the image of God, share an equality of dignity and fundamental or human rights.
2. A religious organisation should protect and defend human rights in society for all people.

3.   Universal Duties

1. Divine law is the source of universal duties owed by one human to another.
2. Universal duties are communicated to all humankind at creation.
3. The imperfect human apprehension of such universal duties is perfected by knowledge of the revealed law of God.

BIBLIOGRAPHY

Primary Sources

1. Jewish materials

Adas Yeshurun Synagogue (USA): *Constitution*: http://adasyeshurun.net/wp-con
tent/uploads/2016/09/ConstitutionandBylaws.pdf.

Assembly of Masorti Synagogues: www.masorti.org.uk/bet-din/bet-din.html; www
.masorti.org.uk/bet-din/bet-din.html.

Association of United Synagogue Women: *Constitution* (2009).

Borehamwood and Elstree Synagogue (US): *Guidelines: Complaints Procedure*
(undated); *Guidelines: Zero Tolerance* (undated); *Bar and Bat Mitzvah Policy*
(2016); *Guidelines* (November 2008); *Visiting Guidelines* (undated):
www.borehamwoodshul.org/.

Board of Deputies of British Jews: *Constitution* (2008): www.bod.org.uk/wp-con
tent/uploads/2014/10/Constitution2008-09-21.pdf; *The Employer's Guide
to Judaism* (2004: updated 2015): www.bod.org.uk/; on human rights,
see: www.bod.org.uk/jonathan-arkush-irans-human-rights-record-is-dire-
and-deteriorating/; www.bod.org.uk/political-party-manifestos-where-they-
stand-on-issues-of-jewish-interest/; www.bod.org.uk/board-of-deputies-
president-calls-for-muslims-and-jews-to-work-together-to-marginalise-exre
mists/; www.bod.org.uk/issues/interfaith-social-action/.

Brighton and Hove Reform Synagogue: *Constitution* (2013): www.bh-rs.org/
constitution.

Cambridge Traditional Jewish Congregation: *Declaration of Trust* (1981, with
amendments to 2016).

Exeter Hebrew Congregation: *Constitution, Schedule of Regulations and Trust Deed*
(4 May 1994).

Federation of Synagogues (Orthodox): *Laws* (adopted in 1948 and amended 2014):
www.federation.org.uk/; www.federation.org.uk/arbitration/; www.feder
ation.org.uk/beis-din/din-torah-jewish-arbitration/; www.federation.org.uk/
small-claims-beis-din/; www.federation.org.uk/wp-content/uploads/2017/
08/federation_get-guide_a4_aug17.pdf; https://reformjudaism.org/jewish-
way-divorce.

Finchley Reform Synagogue: *Safeguarding Children and Child Protection Poli*
(2016): https://frsonline.org/.

Jewish Heritage: http://jewish-heritage-uk.org/about; and *Synagogues at Ris*
A Report on the Findings of the Second Quinquennial Survey of Historic
Synagogues in Britain and Ireland (Jewish Heritage UK, 2015).

Jewish Joint Burial Society: www.jjbs.org.uk/.

Jewish Leadership Council: www.thejlc.org/.

Leo Baeck College (London): www.lbc.ac.uk.

Liberal Synagogue Elstree: *Constitution* (2015): www.tlse.org.uk/tlse_constitution
2005.pdf.

London Beth Din: www.theus.org.uk/article/about-london-beth-din.

Declaration on Judaism and Human Rights, adopted in Montreal on 23 April 197
by the Jacob Blaustein Institute for the Advancement of Human Rights *(*
the American Jewish Committee, Canadian Jewish Congress, and Consult*(*
tive Council of Jewish Organizations, at the McGill International Coll*(*
quium on Judaism and Human Rights.

Movement for Reform Judaism: *Code of Practice*: www.reformjudaism.org.uk
www.reformjudaism.org.uk/resources/life-cycle/;   www.reformjudaism.o*(*
.uk/publications/;   https://reformjudaism.org/jewish-way-divorce;   ww*(*
.reformjudaism.org.uk/human-rights-shabbat-10-december/; www.reform*j*
daism.org.uk/shomrei-mishpat-protecting-human-rights/.

North Hendon Adath Yisroel Synagogue (Orthodox): *Constitution* (2013).

Norwich Hebrew Congregation: *Laws and Constitution* (adopted 1951 an
amended 1958, 1978, 2012 and 2016).

North London Reform Synagogue: *Laws of Sha'arei Tsedek* (Amendments t
1999).

Office of the Chief Rabbi: http://chiefrabbi.org/dvar-torah/; Marriage Authorisa
tion Department of the Office of the Chief Rabbi: Notes to the Bride an
Groom: http://chiefrabbi.org/notes-to-the-bride-and-groom/; http://chie
rabbi.org/background-pre-nuptial-agreement/;   http://chiefrabbi.org/chief
rabbi-ephraim-mirvis-must-fight-slavery/.

Peterborough Liberal Jewish Community: *Constitution* (2014): www.pljc.org.uk.

Rabbinical Assembly (USCJ): *Pesach Guide* (2016): www.rabbinicalassembly.org
www.rabbinicalassembly.org/jewish-law/committee-jewish-law-and-standards.

Shalom Declaration (2015): http://shalomdeclaration.org/about.html.

Stanmore and Canons Park Synagogue (US): *Child Protection and Anti-Bullyin*
Policies (undated): www.sacps.org.uk/synagogue-etiquette.html.

Sukkat   Shalom   Reform   Synagogue   (Wanstead):   *Constitution*   (2014*)*
www.sukkatshalom.org.uk.

Union of Liberal and Progressive Synagogues: *Affirmations of Liberal Judaism*
(London: Revised Edition, 2006); www.liberaljudaism.org/what-we-do/all

ance-for-progressive-judaism/; www.liberaljudaism.org/what-we-do/music/; www.liberaljudaism.org/lifecycle/jewish-status-conversion/; www.liberalju daism.org/2016/10/join-the-human-rights-shabbat-programme/.

United Synagogue (Orthodox): *Constitution, Statutes* (Revised 2016), *Bye-laws* (2010); *Health and Safety Policy and Procedures* (2015): www.theus.org.uk/; www.theus.org.uk/article/conversion-2; www.theus.org.uk/article/litigation; www.theus.org.uk/article/about-london-beth-din; http://chiefrabbi.org/ dvar-torah/; www.theus.org.uk/article/rcus; www.theus.org.uk/schools; www.theus.org.uk/article/about-living-and-learning-1; http://chiefrabbi.org/ education/; www.theus.org.uk/article/bar-bat-mitzvah; www.theus.org.uk/ article/about-us-burial-society-0; http://chiefrabbi.org/background-pre-nup tial-agreement/; www.theus.org.uk/article/divorce-0; www.theus.org.uk/art icle/adoption; www.theus.org.uk/article/equality-and-human-rights-commis sion-call-evidence.

United Synagogue of Conservative Judaism: *Bye-laws* (adopted 2011 and 2012, amended 2013–2016); *Standards for Congregational Practice* (1957, as amended 2017); *Statement of Principles of Conservative Judaism* (1988); *A Guide to Writing and Revising Congregational Constitutions and Bylaws* (2010); *The 'Ideal' Conservative Jew: Eight Behavioural Expectations; Jewish Living* (1957, as amended 2017): with explanations by the Committee on Congregational Standards; *Crafting a Contract Between the Synagogue and the Professional: Protecting the Partnership While Providing for Separation; Model Rabbinic Engagement Agreement – Synagogue with Rabbi; Putting the Partnership Under the Microscope: The Process of Review and Assessment of a Congregation's Professionals and Leadership; Model Guidelines for Congre gational Policy Against Harassment*; Committee on Jewish Law and Stand ards, and Kehilla Affiliations and Standards Committee: *Standards* (2010); *Shabbat Observance; Yad LaTorah – Laws and Customs of the Torah Service: A Guide for Gabba'im and Torah Readers; Kashrut: Connecting the Physical to the Spiritual; Jewish Dietary Laws, Kosher: Sanctifying the Ordinary; Synagogue Policy on Bringing Foods Prepared in the Home into the Syna gogue* (1988); *Guide to Jewish Funeral Practice: A Return to the Mitzvah of Endogamy* (1992); *May a Reception Following an Intermarriage be Held in a Conservative Synagogue* (1987) *and Congratulations to Mixed Marriage Families* (1989): http://uscj.org/LeadingKehilla/Resources/MediationArbitra tion/CommitteeonCongregationalStandards.aspx; http://uscj.org/HumanRe sources/LegalUpdates/GuidelinesforPolicyAgainstHarassment.aspx; http:// uscj.org/HumanResources/LegalUpdates/GuidelinesforPolicyAgainstHarass ment.aspx. www.uscj.org/; www.uscj.org/Aboutus/OurStructure/Mission Statement.aspx; www.rabbinicalassembly.org/sites/default/files/assets/public/ halakhah/teshuvot/19912000/bergman_unconverted.pdf; http://uscj.org/

JewishLivingandLearning/Lifecycle/JewishFuneralPractice/GuidetoJewis
FuneralPractice.aspx.

World Council of Conservative-Masorti Judaism (Masorti Olami) (o
World Council of Conservative Synagogues): *By-Laws* (2010): www
.masorti.org.uk/bet-din/bet-din.html; www.mbd.org.uk/site/page/beth-din.

Wessex Liberal Jewish Community: *Constitution* (2011); *Policy: Safeguarding*
Care (2013).

2. Christian materials

Anglican Communion Legal Advisers Network: *The Principles of Canon Law*
Common to the Churches of the Anglican Communion (Anglican Commu
nion Office, London, 2008).

Baptist Union of Great Britain: *Constitution* (undated); Baptist Union Corporation
Guidelines, *Baptist Model Trusts for Churches* (2003); *Baptists in Ecumenica*
Partnerships (2008); *Orders and Prayers for Church Worship: A Manual fo*
Ministers, compiled by E.A. Payne and S.F. Winward (Baptist Union o
Great Britain and Ireland, London, 1960, reprinted 1972).

Baptist Union of Scotland: *Constitution* and *Standing Orders of the Council and*
Assembly (undated).

Baptist World Alliance: *Constitution, and Bylaws of the General Council* (2004).

Christian Law Panel of Experts: *A Statement of Principles of Christian Law* (Rome
2016).

Church in Wales (Anglican): *The Constitution of the Church in Wales* (2006); *The*
Book of Common Prayer (1984).

Church of England (Anglican): *Canons of the Church of England* (1964–2017)
Book of Common Prayer (1662); legislation: Parochial Church Councils
(Powers) Measure 1956; Church of England (Worship and Doctrine) Meas-
ure 1974; Church of England Marriage Measure 2008; Safeguarding and
Clergy Discipline Measure 2016; and: www.churchofengland.org/more/
safeguarding.

Church of Ireland (Anglican): *The Constitution of the Church of Ireland* (2003).

Church of Scotland: *The Constitution and Laws of the Church of Scotland*, edited
by J.L. Weatherhead (Church of Scotland, Board of Practice and Procedure,
Edinburgh, 1997).

Evangelical Lutheran Church in Ireland: *Evangelical Lutheran Church in Ireland:*
Constitution (2011).

Lutheran Church in Great Britain: *Rules and Regulations* (2011).

Lutheran World Federation: *Constitution* and *Bylaws* (2010); *The Lutheran World*
Federation as a Communion of Churches (LWF, Geneva, 2003).

Methodist Church in Great Britain: *The Constitutional Practice and Discipline of*
the Methodist Church (2009); *Guidelines for Churches dealing with Extremist*

Political Parties (2003); *Rules and Regulations for Faith and Worship: The Local Preachers' Training Course* (2006); *Handbook for Probation: Formation in Ministry* (2007); *Guidance on the Stationing of Ministers and Deacons.*

Methodist Church in Ireland: *Code of Pastoral Practice*; *Constitution* (2010); *Regulations, Discipline and Government* (2010).

Presbyterian Church in Ireland: *The Code: Book of the Constitution and Government* (2010).

Presbyterian Church of Wales (*Eglwys Bresbyteraidd Cymru*): *Constitution* (2009); *Handbook of Order and Rules* (2010); *Constitution for a Local Church* (2009); *Employee Handbook* (undated); *Safeguarding Children: Handbook*: www.ebcpcw.cymru/en/training/safeguarding-children-and-vulnerable-adul ts/policy-and-procedures.

Roman Catholic Church: G. Chapman, *Catechism of the Catholic Church* (London: Continuum International Publishing, 1994); *Codex Iuris Canonici*, Code of Canon Law (1983), promulgated by *Sacrae disciplinae leges* (1983); *Dignitatis Humanae* (Vatican II, Decree, 1965); *Gaudium et Spes* (Vatican II, Pastoral Constitution, 1966); *Lumen Gentium* (Vatican II, Dogmatic Constitution, 1965); Apostolic Constitution *Fidei Depositum*, on the publication of the Catechism of the Catholic Church, prepared following the Second Vatican Council, Pope John Paul II (1994); *Catholic Safeguarding Resource Area* (2017): www.csas.uk.net/resource-area/; Catholic Bishops' Conference of England and Wales: *A Charter for Priestly Formation for England and Wales* (2015); *Pastor Bonus* (1988).

Scottish Episcopal Church (Anglican): *Code of Canons* (2006).

United Free Church of Scotland: *Manual of Practice and Procedure* (2011).

United Reformed Church: *Manual* (2008); *Model Constitution for Local Churches* (2010).

World Alliance of Reformed Churches: *Constitution* (2003).

World Communion of Reformed Churches: *Constitution* and *Bylaws* (2010).

3. Islamic materials

Al-Ikhlas Centre (Cardiff): *Policy* (undated)

Al-Khoei Foundation: http://religiouseducationcouncil.org.uk/members/rec-members/al-khoei-foundation

Aberdeen Mosque and Islamic Centre: *Constitution* (2000): www.aberdeenmosque .org/.

Association for Muslim Supplementary Schools: www.amss.org.uk/.

Association of Muslim Schools: *Statutory School Policies*: http://ams-uk.org/ resources/policies/; for inspection reports, see: http://ams-uk.org/services/ section-48-inspections/.

Birmingham Central Mosque: *Seven Articles of Muslim Faith*; *Advice* (30 Ma 2015): https://centralmosque.org.uk/.

Bolton Council of Mosques: *Constitution* (undated); *Five Pillars of Islam* www.thebcom.org/.

British Association for Islamic Studies: *Constitution* (undated): www.brais.ac.uk about-brais/constitution.

British Muslims for Secular Democracy: http://bmsd.org.uk/index.php/objectives.

Cairo Declaration on Human Rights in Islam (1990).

Central Jamia Masjid (Southall): *Constitution* (2016).

Central Mosque: *Model Constitution of an Islamic Organisation* (2004): https:/ centralmosque.org.uk/; www.central-mosque.com/fiqh/ModelOfIslamicOrg .htm; www.central-mosque.com/fiqh/WhoShouldBeImaam.htm; https://ce tralmosque.org.uk/services/marriage-bureau/.

Council for Mosques (Bradford): *Constitution*; Guidance; Burial Service; Fiv Pillars of Islam: www.councilformosques.org/about-us/constitution-and membership/; www.councilformosques.org/our-work/guidance/; www.cou cilformosques.org/muslim-burial-services/;   www.councilformosques.org five-pillars-of-islam/; www.councilformosques.org/about-us/our-aims/.

Cube Network: *Sample Constitution of an Islamic Society*: http://cubenetwork.org/

Darul Isra Muslim Community Centre (Cardiff): *Policy* (2010).

East London Mosque and London Muslim Centre (and East London Mosqu Trust): www.eastlondonmosque.org.uk/; www.eastlondonmosque.org.uk content/religious-spiritual;   www.eastlondonmosque.org.uk/content/educ tion-training; www.eastlondonmosque.org.uk/content/education-training.

Edinburgh Central Mosque: www.edmosque.org/about-the-mosque/services/.

European Council for Fatwa and Research: Final Statement: 25th Ordinary Session (Istanbul, 6–10 October 2015): Fatwa 2/25.

Faith Associates: *Muslim Women's Guide to Mosque Governance, Managemen and Service Delivery* (2016) www.faithassociates.co.uk/training-faith leaders/; www.faithassociates.co.uk/beacon-mosque/; www.faithassociate .co.uk/category/case-study/communications-strategy/; www.faithassociate .co.uk/training-faith-leaders/.

Fatwa Committee (UK): http://cubenetwork.org/.

Guidance for Mosque Schools and other Islamic Studies Settings (Newport Gwent): www.sewsc.org.uk.

Hijaz College Islamic University (Nuneaton): www.hijazcollege.com/.

Inter Firm Islamic Societies: https://westernmuslimuk.com/tag/inter-firm-islamic societies/.

Islamic College (London): www.islamic-college.ac.uk.

Islamic Council of Europe: *Universal Islamic Declaration of Human Rights* (1981)

Islamic Sharia Council: www.islamic-sharia.org/.

Kingston Muslim Association: *Constitution* (2006): http://kingstonmosque.net/.

Lancaster Islamic Society: *Constitution* (1994): www.lancasterislamicsociety.co.uk/.

London Central Mosque Trust and Islamic Cultural Centre: www.iccuk.org/.

Madrassa.co.uk: *Madrassah Standards: Frameworks*: www.madrassah.co.uk/stand ards/.

Markazi Jamia Masjid Riza and Islamic Centre (Huddersfield): *Constitution* (undated): http://masjidriza.com/1/about-us/masjid-constitution.

Mission Islam: www.missionislam.com/health/circumcisionislam.html.

Mosques and Imams National Advisory Board: *Standards* (2011): www.minab.org.uk/self-regulation/standards.html.

Muslim Arbitration Tribunal: *Procedural Rules*: www.matribunal.com/.

Muslim Burial Council of Leicestershire: *Constitution* (2004); *Funeral Procedure* (undated): www.mbcol.org.uk/funeral-procedure.

Muslim College (London): www.muslimcollege.ac.uk.

Muslim Council of Britain: *Constitution* (2012); *Community Guidelines to Imams and British Muslim Organisations* (2004): www.mcb.org.uk/mcb-commu nity-guidelines-to-imams-and-british-muslim-organisations/; www.mcb .org.uk/mcb-welcomes-the-creation-of-a-new-commission-for-equality-hu man-rights/; www.mcb.org.uk/our-government-must-not-look-the-other-way-as-bahrain-commits-gross-violations-of-human-rights/.

Muslim Council of Wales: *Imaan Islamic Society: Model Constitution* (2007); *Model Declaration of Trust* (2016).

Muslim Teachers Association (UK): *Constitution* (1979, updated 2013): www.mta-uk.org/.

Naqshbandi, Mehmood, *Islam and Muslims in Britain: A Guide for Non-Muslims* (London, 2012).

Nasru-Lahi-Il-Fathi Society of Nigeria, United Kingdom and Ireland: *Constitution* (2006).

Noor-Ul-Islam Mosque (Bury): *Constitution* (undated): www.noorulislam.org/.

Palmers Green Mosque, Muslim Community and Education Centre for Islamic Studies: *Complaints Policy* (undated): www.mcec.org.uk/.

Reading Muslim Council: *Constitution* (undated): www.readingmuslim council.org.uk/our-constitution/.

The Qur'an, translated by M.A.S. Abdel Haleem (Oxford: Oxford University Press, 2004).

4. The Law of the State

Parliamentary Statutes

Adoption and Children Act 2002.

Anti-Social Behaviour, Crime and Policing Act 2014.

Arbitration Act 1996.

Baptist and Congregational Trusts Act 1951.
Baptist and Congregational Trusts Act 1961.
Charitable Trusts Act 1869.
Charities Act 1993 and 2011.
Childcare Act 2006.
Children Act 1989.
Children Act 1996.
Children Act 2004.
Church of Scotland Act 1921.
Church of Scotland (Property and Endowments) Act 1925.
Data Protection Act 1998.
Dawat-e-Hadiyah Act 1993.
Divorce (Religious Marriages) Act 2002.
Divorce (Scotland) Act 1976.
Education Act 1996.
Education Act 2002.
Education and Inspection Act 2006.
Equality Act 2010.
Family Law (Scotland) Act 2006.
Financial Services Act 1986.
Forced Marriage Act 2007.
Human Rights Act 1998.
Irish Church Act 1869.
Irish Presbyterian Church Act 1871.
Legal Aid Sentencing and Punishment of Offenders Act 2012.
Limitation Act 1980.
Marriage Act 1949.
Marriage (Scotland) Act 1977.
Matrimonial Causes Act 1965.
Matrimonial Causes Act 1973.
Methodist Church Acts 1939, 1976, 1979.
Methodist Church Funds Act 1960.
Methodist Church in Ireland Act (Northern Ireland) 1928.
Methodist Church in Ireland Act (Saorstat Eireann) 1928.
Oaths Act 1978.
Places of Worship Registration Act 1855.
Protection of Children Act 1999.
Protection of Freedoms Act 2012.
Public Order Act 1986.
Safeguarding Vulnerable Groups Act 2004.
Racial and Religious Hatred Act 2006.
School Standards and Framework Act 1998.

Slaughterhouses Act 1974.
Trustee Act 2000.
United Reformed Church Acts 1972, 1981 and 2000.
United Synagogues Act 1870.
Welsh Church Act 1914.

Secondary Legislation

Admissions (Admission Arrangements and Co-ordination of Admission Arrangements) (England) Regulations 2012.
Charitable Incorporated Organisations (General) Regulations 2012.
Civil Registration Act 2004 (Republic of Ireland) and Marriage (Northern Ireland) Order 2003 (UK).
Designation of Schools having a Religious Character (England) Order 2013.
Disclosure and Barring Service (Core Functions) Order 2012.
Education (Independent Schools Standards) Regulations 2010.
Education (Non-maintained Special Schools) Regulations 2011.
Education (School Sessions and Charges and Remissions Policies) (Information) (England) Regulations 1999.
Education (School Teachers' Appraisal) (England) Regulations 2012.
Independent School Standards Regulations.
Safeguarding Vulnerable Groups Act 2006 (Controlled Activity) (Wales) Regulations 2010.
School Admissions Code for 2007.
School Governance (Constitution) (England) Regulations 2007 and 2012.
School Staffing (England) Regulations 2009.
Welfare of Animals (Slaughter or Killing) Regulations 1995.

Judicial Decisions

Ahmad v. Inner London Education Authority [1978] QB 36.
AI v. MT [2013] EWHC 100 (Fam).
Brett v. Brett [1969] 1 All ER 1007.
Chief Inspector of Education, Children's Services and Skills v. Interim Executive Board of Al-Hijrah School [2017] EWCA Civ. 1426.
Cohen v. Baram [1994] 2 Lloyd's Rep. 138.
Eweida and Others v. United Kingdom (2013) 57 EHRR 8.
Fugler v. MacMillan – London Hairstudios Limited [2007] UKEAT 0009 07 30003 (30 March 2007).
Hasan v. Redcoat Community Centre (2013) East London Employment Tribunal (unreported).
Hoffmann v. Austria (1993) 17 EHRR 293.
Khan v. UK, Appl. No. 11579/85 (1986) 48 D&R 253.
Khon v. Wagschal and Ors [2007] EWCA Civ 1022.

Maga v. *Trustees of the Birmingham Archdiocese of the Roman Catholic Church* [2010] EWCA Civ 256.

McFarlane v. *Relate Avon Ltd* [2010] EWCA Civ 771.

Middleton v. *Crofts* (1736) 2 Atkins 650.

Norwood v. *DPP* [2003] EWHC Admin 1564.

Pellegrini v. *Italy*, Appl. No. 30882/96, 20 July 2001.

President of the Methodist Conference v. *Preston* [2013] UKSC 29.

R (Baiai, Trzcinska, Bigoku and Tilki) v. *Secretary of State for the Home Department* [2006] EWHC 823, subsequently approved [2008] UKHL 53.

R v. *Chief Rabbi, ex parte Wachmann* [1992] 1 WLR 1036.

R v. *Imam of Bury Park, ex parte Sulaiman Ali* [1994] COD 142.

R v. *London Beth Din ex parte Bloom* [1998] COD 131.

R (on the application of Begum) v. *Headteacher and Governors of Denbigh High School* [2006] UKHL 15.

R (on the application of E) v. *JFS Governing Body* [2009] UKSC 15.

Raggett v. *Society of Jesus Trust of 1929 for Roman Catholic Purposes & Anor* [2010] EWCA Civ 1002.

Refah Partisi (Welfare Party) and Others v. *Turkey* (no 2) (2003) 37 EHRR 1 (GC).

Re J (Specific Issue Orders: Child's Religious Upbringing and Circumcision) [2000] 1 FLR 571.

Re G [2012] EWCA Civ 1233.

Re J (Child's religious upbringing and circumcision) [2000] 1 FLR 307 (CA).

Re P (A Minor) (Residence Order: Child's Welfare) [1999] 2 FLR 573.

Schüth v. *Germany*, App. No. 1620/03, 23 Sept. 2010.

Soleimany v. *Soleimany* [1999] QB 785.

Ur-Rehman v. *Doncaster Jahia Mosque* [2012] UKEAT 0117-12-1008.

William Verry Limited v. *North West London Communal Mikvah* [2004] EWHC 1300 (TCC).

Secondary Sources

Abrahams, I., *Judaism* (London: Constable, 1917).

Abu-Rabi, I.M., *Intellectual Origins of Islamic Resurgence in the Modern Arab World* (Albany, NY: State University of New York Press, 1996).

Ahdar, R. and I. Leigh, *Religious Freedom in the Liberal State* (Oxford: Oxford University Press, 2nd edn, 2013).

Alexy, R., *The Argument from Injustice: A Reply to Legal Positivism* (Oxford: Oxford University Press, 2002).

Ali, S.S., 'From Muslim migrants to Muslim citizens' in R. Griffith-Jones and M. Hill, eds., *Magna Carta, Religion and the Rule of Law* (Cambridge: Cambridge University Press, 2015) 157–175.

l-qadi al-Nu'man, *The Pillars of Islam*, translated by A.A.A. Fyzee and revised by I.K.H. Poonawala (Oxford: Oxford University Press, 2002).

rkes, H., *Constitutional Illusions and Anchoring Truths: The Touchstone of the Natural Law* (Cambridge: Cambridge University Press, 2010).

rsheim, H. and P. Slotte, *The Juridification of Religion?* (Leiden: Brill, 2017).

zzam, S., 'Universal Islamic Declaration of Human Rights', 2 *The International Journal of Human Rights* (1998) 102–112.

aderin, M.A., *International Human Rights and Islamic Law* (Oxford: Oxford University Press, 2003) 47–168.

anda, F. and L.F. Joffe, eds., *Women's Rights and Religious Law: Domestic and International Perspectives* (London: Routledge, 2016).

arrett, D., 'Tackling radicalisation: the limitations of the anti-radicalisation prevent duty', *European Human Rights Law Review* (2016) 531.

arth, K., *The Epistle of Paul to the Romans* (Oxford: Oxford University Press, 1933).

assiouni, M.C., *The Shari'a and Islamic Criminal Justice in Time of War and Peace* (Cambridge: Cambridge University Press, 2014).

eckford, J.A. and J.T. Richardson, 'Religion and regulation', in J.A. Beckford and N.J. Demerath, eds., *The Sage Handbook of the Sociology of Religion* (London: Sage, 2007) 396.

en-Menahem, H., 'The judicial process and the nature of Jewish law', in N. Hecht, B.S. Jackson, D. Piattelli, S.M. Passamaneck and A.M. Rabello, eds., *An Introduction to the History and Sources of Jewish Law* (Oxford: Clarendon Press, 1996) 421–437.

ertea, S., 'Legal argumentation theory and the concept of law', in F.H. van Eemeren *et al.*, eds., *Anyone Who Has a View: Theoretical Contributions to the Study of Argumentation* (Netherlands: Kluwer, 2003) 213.

iggar, N., *Behaving in Public: How to Do Christian Ethics* (Grand Rapids, MI: William B. Eerdmans, 2011).

lack, A., H. Esmaeili and N. Hosen, *Modern Perspectives on Islamic Law* (Cheltenham: Edward Elgar, 2013).

leich, J.D., 'Judaism and natural law', *Jewish Law Annual* 7 (1988) 5.

ottoni, R., R. Cristofori and S. Ferrari, eds., *Religious Rules, State Law, and Normative Pluralism – A Comparative Overview* (Springer, 2016).

owen, J.R., *On British Islam: Religion, Law and Everyday Practice in Shari'a Councils* (Princeton, NJ: Princeton University Press, 2016).

radney, A., *Law and Faith in a Sceptical Age* (Abingdon: Routledge, 2008).

rand, C.O. and R.S. Norman, eds., *Perspectives on Church Government: Five Views of Church Polity* (Nashville, TN: Boardman & Holman, 2004).

rems, E., *The Experiences of Face Veil Wearers in Europe and the Law* (Cambridge: Cambridge University Press, 2014).

Broyde, M.J., *Sharia Tribunals, Rabbinical Courts and Christian Panels* (Oxford Oxford University Press, 2017).

Brundage, J.A., *Medieval Canon Law* (London: Longman, 1995).

Budziszewski, J., *The Line Through the Heart: Natural Law as Fact, Theory, an Sign of Contradiction* (Wilmington, DE: ISI Books, 2009).

Burnside, J., *God, Justice and Society: Aspects of Law and Legality in the Bibl* (Oxford: Oxford University Press, 2010).

Cameron, E., *The European Reformation* (Oxford: Oxford University Press, 1991

Cane, P., C. Evans and Z. Robinson, eds., *Law and Religion in Theoretical an Historical Context* (Cambridge: Cambridge University Press, 2008).

Chadwick, H., *East and West: The Making of a Rift in the Church* (Oxford: Oxfor University Press, 2003).

Chapman, G., ed., *Catechism of the Catholic Church* (London: Continuum Inter national Publishing, 1994).

Charity Commission, *Guidance: Changing Your Charity's Governing* (Documen CC36) (5 August 2011), www.gov.uk/government/publications/changing your-charitys-governing-document-cc36/changing-your-charitys-governing document-cc36.

Cherti, M. and L. Bradley, *Inside Madrassas: Understanding and Engaging wit British–Muslim Faith Supplementary Schools* (Institute for Public Polic Research, 2011).

Childress, J.F. and J. Macquarrie, eds., *A New Dictionary of Christian Ethic* (London: SCM Press, 1986).

Churches Legislation Advisory Service: www.churcheslegislation.org.uk/home.

Cismas, I., *Religious Actors and International Law* (Oxford: Oxford Universit Press, 2014).

Coertzen, P., *Church and Order: A Reformed Perspective* (Leuven: Peeters, 1998).

Cohen, J., 'Halakhah and the modern temper', in W. Jacob, ed., *Beyond th Letter of the Law: Essays on Diversity in the Halakhah*, in the series Studie in Progressive Halakhah (Pittsburgh, PA: Rodef Shalom Press, 2004 92–155.

Contreras, F.J., ed., *The Threads of Natural Law: Unravelling a Philosophica Tradition* (New York: Springer, 2013).

Coulson, N., *A History of Islamic Law* (Edinburgh: Edinburgh University Press 1964).

Cranmer, F., M. Hill, C. Kenny and R. Sandberg, eds., *The Confluence of Law an Religion: Interdisciplinary Reflections of the Work of Norman Doe* (Cam bridge: Cambridge University Press, 2016).

Crone, P., *God's Rule – Government and Islam: Six Centuries of Medieval Islami Political Thought* (New York: Columbia University Press, 2004).

Cross, F.L. and E.A. Livingstone, eds., *Oxford Dictionary of the Christian Churc* (Oxford: Oxford University Press, 2005).

Danby, H., *The Mishnah: Translated from the Hebrew with Introduction and Brief Explanatory Notes* (Oxford: Oxford University Press, 1933).

Daube, D., *Studies in Biblical Law* (Cambridge: Cambridge University Press, 2008).

David, J., 'Maimonides, nature and natural law', *Journal of Law, Philosophy and Culture*, 5 (2010) 67–82.

Davis, D.R., *The Spirit of Hindu Law* (Cambridge: Cambridge University Press, 2010).

Department for Communities and Local Government, *The Training and Development of Muslim Faith Leaders: Current Practice and Future Possibilities* (London: Department for Communities and Local Government 2010).

Face to Face and Side by Side: A Framework for Inter Faith Dialogue and Social Action: Consultation (London: Department for Communities and Local Government, December 2007).

Deweese, C.W., *Baptist Church Covenants* (Nashville, TN: Boardman Press, 1990).

Doe, N., *The Legal Architecture of English Cathedrals* (London: Routledge, 2017).

'Natural law in an interfaith context: the Abrahamic religions', in N. Doe, ed., *Christianity and Natural Law* (Cambridge: Cambridge University Press, 2017) 184–204.

Christian Law: Contemporary Principles (Cambridge: Cambridge University Press, 2013).

Law and Religion in Europe: A Comparative Introduction (Oxford: Oxford University Press, 2011).

'Canon law and communion', 6 *Ecclesiastical Law Journal* (2002) 241.

'Canonical approaches to human rights in Anglican churches', in M. Hill, ed., *Religious Liberty and Human Rights* (Cardiff: University of Wales Press, 2002) 185.

The Law of the Church in Wales (Cardiff: University of Wales Press, 2002).

Canon Law in the Anglican Communion: A Worldwide Perspective (Oxford: Clarendon Press, 1998).

The Legal Framework of the Church of England: A Critical Study in a Comparative Context (Oxford: Clarendon Press, 1996).

'Canonical doctrines of judicial precedent: a comparative study', 54 *The Jurist* (1994) 205.

Fundamental Authority in Late Medieval English Law (Cambridge: Cambridge University Press, 1990).

Doe, N., ed., *Christianity and Natural Law* (Cambridge: Cambridge University Press, 2017).

Doi, A.R.I., *Shari'ah: The Islamic Law* (London: Ta Ha Publishers, 1984).

Dorff, E.N. and A. Rosett, *A Living Tree: The Roots and Growth of Jewish Law* (Albany: New York State University, 1988).

Douglas, G., N. Doe, S. Gilliat-Ray, R. Sandberg and A. Khan, *Social Cohesion and Civil Law: Marriage, Divorce and Religious Courts* (Cardiff: Cardiff University, 2011).

Edge, P., *Religion and Law* (Aldershot: Ashgate, 2006).

Elon, M., *Jewish Law: History, Sources, Principles* (Philadelphia and Jerusalem Jewish Publication Society, 1994).

Elon, M, ed., *The Principles of Jewish Law* (Piscataway, NJ: Transaction Publishers 2007).

Emon, A.M., 'Shari'a and the rule of law: preserving the realm', in R. Griffith-Jone and M. Hill, eds., *Magna Carta, Religion and the Rule of Law* (Cambridge Cambridge University Press, 2015) 196–214.

Islamic Natural Law Theories (Oxford: Oxford University Press, 2010).

'Natural law and natural rights in Islamic law', *Journal of Law and Religion* 2 (2004–2005) 351–395.

Emon, A.M., M. Levering and D. Novak, *Natural Law: A Jewish, Christian an Islamic Trialogue* (Oxford: Oxford University Press, 2014).

Enayat, H., *Modern Islamic Politic Thought* (London: Macmillan Press, 1982).

Esposito, J.L., ed., *The Oxford Dictionary of Islam* (Oxford: Oxford Universit Press, 2003).

Ettinger, S., 'The prohibition against consulting two authorities and the nature o halakhic truth', 18 *The Jewish Law Annual* (2010) 1–19.

Fadl, K.A.E., 'Islamic law and Muslim minorities', 1 *Islamic Law and Society* (1994 141–187.

Feldman, N., *The Fall and Rise of the Islamic State* (Princeton, NJ: Princeton University Press, 2008).

Ferrari, S., *Lo spirito dei diritti religiosi: Ebraismo, cristianismo e islam a confront* (Milan: Il Mulino, 2002).

Fox, M., 'Maimonides and Aquinas and natural law', *Dinei* 3 (1971) 5.

Frank, R.M., 'Moral obligations in classical Muslim theology', *Journal of Religiou Ethics* 11 (1983) 205–223.

Frankel, Z., *On Changes in Judaism* (1845).

Freehof, S.B., *Responsa for Our Time* (Cincinnati, OH: The Hebrew Union Colleg Press, 1977).

Reform Jewish Practice and Its Rabbinic Background (New York: Union o American Hebrew Organisations, 1963).

Reform Judaism and the Legal Tradition: The Tintner Memorial Lecture (New York: Association of Reform Rabbis, 1961).

Reform Responsa (Cincinnati, OH: Hebrew Union College Press, 1960).

Freeman, M., 'Is the Jewish get any business of the State?', in R. O'Dair and A Lewis, eds., *Law and Religion* (Oxford: Oxford University Press, 2001) 365

French, R.R. and M.A. Nathan, eds., *Buddhism and Law: An Introductior* (Cambridge: Cambridge University Press, 2014).

Friedman, J.S., 'A critique of Solomon B. Freehof's concept of minhag and Reforn Jewish Practice', in W. Jacob and M. Zemer, eds., *Re-Examining Progressiv Halakhah* (New York/Oxford: Berghahn Books, 2002) 111.

aon, S., *The Book of Beliefs and Opinions*, translated by S. Rosenblatt (New Haven, CT: Yale University Press, 1989).

illigan, P., 'Clerical abuse and laicisation: rhetoric and reality in the Catholic Church in England and Wales', 21 *Child Abuse Review* (2012) 427–443.

inzberg, L., *Students, Scholars and Saints* (Philadelphia: Jewish Publication Society, 1928) 112.

olinkin, D., 'The responsa of Rabbi Solomon B. Freehof: a reappraisal', in W. Jacob, ed., *Beyond the Letter of the Law: Essays on Diversity in the Halakhah, Studies in Progressive Halakhah* (Pittsburgh, PA: Rodef Shalom Press, 2004).

omaa, A., 'Justice in Islamic legislation', in R. Griffith-Jones and M. Hill., eds., *Magna Carta, Religion and the Rule of Law* (Cambridge: Cambridge University Press, 2015) 177–195.

oodliff, P., 'Baptist church polity and practice', 168 *Law and Justice* (2012) 3.

ordis, R., *The Dynamics of Judaism* (Bloomington, IN: Indiana University Press, 1990).

reenberg, S., ed., *The Ordination of Women as Rabbis: Studies and Responsa* (New York: The Jewish Theological Seminary of America, 1988).

riffel, F., 'The Harmony of Natural Law and Shari'a in Islamist Theology', in A. Amanat and F. Griffel, eds., *Islamic Law in the Contemporary Context* (Palo Alto, CA: Stanford University Press, 2007) 38–61.

riffith-Jones, R., ed., *Islam and English Law: Rights, Responsibilities and the Place of Shari'a* (Cambridge: Cambridge University Press, 2013).

uidebook for Secretaries (for Marriages) of Synagogues: HM Passport Office, General Register Office (2017).

aas, P., 'German Romanticism and the Jews: the intellectual basis for halakhic reform', in W. Jacob, ed., *Beyond the Letter of the Law: Essays on Diversity in the Halakhah*, in the series Studies in Progressive Halakhah (Pittsburgh, PA: Rodef Shalom Press, 2004) 4.

alivini, D.W., *Mishnah, Midrash and Gemara* (Cambridge, MA: Harvard University Press, 1986).

allaq, W., *Sharia: Theory, Practice, Transformation* (Cambridge: Cambridge University Press, 2009).

amilton, C., *Family, Law and Religion* (London: Sweet & Maxwell, 1995).

echt, N.S., B.S. Jackson, S.M. Passamaneck, D. Piatelli and A.M. Rabello, eds., *An Introduction to the History and Sources of Jewish Law* (Oxford: Oxford University Press, 1996).

elm, P., *John Calvin's Ideas* (Oxford: Oxford University Press, 2006).

elmholz, R.H., *The Canon Law and Ecclesiastical Jurisdiction from 597 to the 1640s* (Oxford: Oxford University Press, 2004).

The Spirit of Classical Canon Law (Athens, GA & London: University of Georgia Press, 1996).

Herzog, I., *The Main Institutions of Jewish Law*, 2 volumes (London and Ne York: The Soncino Press Limited, 1939, Paperback edn, 1980).

Hill, M., *Ecclesiastical Law* (Oxford: Oxford University Press, 4th edn, 2018).

Hill, M. and N. Doe, 'Principles of Christian law', 19 *Ecclesiastical Law Journ* (2017) 138–155.

Hill, M., R. Sandberg and N. Doe, *Religion and Law in the United Kingdo* (Netherlands: Wolters Kluwer, 2nd edn, 2014).

Hourani, G.F., *Reason and Tradition in Islamic Ethics* (Cambridge: Cambridg University Press, 1985).

Hughes, G.J., 'Natural law', in J.F. Childress and J. Macquarrie, eds., *A Ne Dictionary of Christian Ethics* (London: SCM Press, 1986), 412–414.

Hussain, A., 'Legal pluralism, religious conservatism', in R. Sandberg, ed., *Religio and Legal Pluralism* (Aldershot: Ashgate, 2015) 151.

Hussain, J., *Islamic Law and Society* (Leichhardt, New South Wales: The Fede ation Press, 1999).

Huxley, A., ed., *Religion, Law and Tradition* (Abingdon: Routledge, 2002).

Jackson, B.S., 'Judaism as a religious legal system', in A. Huxley, ed., *Religion, La and Tradition: Comparative Studies in Religious Law* (Abingdon: Routledg 2002) 34.

'The Jewish view of natural law', 52 *Journal of Jewish Studies* (200 136–145.

Jacob, J.A., 'The reasons of the commandments: rational tradition without natur law', in J.A. Jacob, ed., *Reason, Religion and Natural Law* (Oxford: Oxfor University Press, 2012) 106.

Jacob, W., 'Writing responsa: a personal journey', in W. Jacob, ed., *Beyond th Letter of the Law: Essays on Diversity in the Halakhah*, Studies in Progressiv Halakhah (Pittsburgh, PA: Rodef Shalom Press, 2004) 103.

'The law of the land and Jewish law: opposition or concurrence', in W. Jaco and M. Zemer, eds., *Re-Examining Progressive Halakhah* (New York Oxford: Berghahn Books, 2002) 71–90.

Jacob, W., ed., *Beyond the Letter of the Law: Essays on Diversity in the Halakha* Studies in Progressive Halakhah (Pittsburgh, PA: Rodef Shalom Pres 2004).

Jacob, W. and M. Zemer, *Conversion to Judaism* (Pittsburgh, PA: Rodef Shalom Press, 1994).

Jacob, W. and M. Zemer, ed., *Gender Issues in Jewish Law: Essays and Respons* (New York: Berghahn Books, 2001).

Jacobs, L., *Jewish Preaching: Homilies and Sermons* (Vallentine Mitchell, 2004).

'Property in Jewish law', in Peter Elman, ed., *An introduction to Jewish La* (London: Lincolns-Prager, 1958) 44–52.

Jacobs, L., ed., *Concise Companion to the Jewish Religion* (Oxford: Oxford Univer sity Press, 1999).

arrar, R. and L. Collard, *A model for collaboration in designing and delivering Islamic Studies modules between a HE institution and a Muslim community college* (University of Westminster, 2012).

ewish Policy Research Report (for the Board of Deputies of British Jews): *Synagogue Membership in the United Kingdom in 2016* (2017), compiled by D.C. Mashiah and J. Boyd (2017).

Kamali, M.H., *Shariah Law: An Introduction* (Oxford: One World, 2008).

Kerr, M., *Islamic Reform: The Political and Legal Theories of Muhammad Abduh and Rashid Rida* (Berkeley, CA: University of California Press, 1966).

Kettani, M.A., 'Muslims in non-Muslim societies: challenges and opportunities', 11 *Journal of the Institute of Muslim Minority Affairs* (1990) 226–233.

Khadduri, M. (translator), *Islamic Jurisprudence: Shafi'i's Risala* (Baltimore: Johns Hopkins University Press, 1961).

King, M., ed., *God's Law Versus State Law: The Construction of Islamic Identity in Western Europe* (London: Grey Seal, 1995).

Klein, I., *A Guide to Jewish Religious Practice* (New York and Jerusalem: The Jewish Theological Seminary of America, 1979, 1992).

Koebel, P.S., 'Reform Judaism and same-sex marriage: a halakhic inquiry', in W. Jacob and M. Zemer, eds., *Gender Issues in Jewish Law* (Oxford: Bergahn Books, 2001) 169–183.

Kohler, K., 'The origin and function of ceremonies in Judaism', 17 *CCAR Yearbook* (1907) 208.

Konvitz, M.R., ed., *Judaism and Human Rights* (New York: W.W. Norton, 1972).

Kwak, A-J., ed., *Holy Writ: Interpretation in Law and Religion* (Aldershot: Ashgate, 2009).

Leaman, O., 'Maimonides and natural law', *Jewish Law Annual* 6 (1987) 78–93.

Levering, M., 'Natural Law and Christianity', in A.M. Emon, M. Levering and D. Novak, *Natural Law: A Jewish, Christian and Islamic Trialogue* (Oxford: Oxford University Press, 2014) Ch. 2.

Jewish-Christian Dialogue in the Life of Wisdom: Engagement with the Theology of David Novak (London: Continuum, 2010), Chs. 3 and 4.

Lewis, B., 'Legal and historical reflections on the position of Muslim populations under non-Muslim law', in B. Lewis and D. Schnapper, eds., *Muslims in Europe* (London: Pinter, 1994) 1–18.

Lichtenstein, A., 'Does Jewish tradition recognize an ethic independent of halakha?', in M. Fox, ed., *Modern Jewish Ethics: Theory and Practice* (Columbus, OH: Ohio State University Press, 1975) 62.

Lord Philips of Worth Matravers, 'Equality before the law' (2008) 161 *Law and Justice* 75.

Luhmann, N., *A Sociological Theory of Law* (Abingdon: Routledge, 2nd edn, 2014).

A Systems Theory of Religion (Stanford, CA: Stanford University Press, 2013).

Law as a Social System (Oxford: Oxford University Press, 2004).

Macy, M., 'Natural law', in A.A. Cohen and P. Mends-Flohr, eds., *20th Centu* *Jewish Religious Thought* (Philadelphia, PA: The Jewish Publication Societ 2009) 663–672.

Makdisi, G., *Ibn 'Aqil: Religion and Culture in Classical Islam* (Edinburgh: Edi burgh University Press, 1997).

Malik, M., *Minority Legal Orders in the UK* (London: British Academy, 2012).

Mayer, A.E., *Islam and Human Rights: Tradition and Politics* (Boulder, CO: Wes view Press, 3rd edn, 2006).

McGoldrick, D., 'The compatibility of an Islamic/shari'a law system or shari'a rul with the European Convention on Human Rights', in R. Griffith-Jones, ec *Islam and English Law* (Cambridge: Cambridge University Press, 201: 42–71.

Menski, W.F., *Hindu Law* (Oxford: Oxford University Press, 2003).

Morrisey, F., 'Papal and curial pronouncements: their canonical significance in th light of the 1983 code of canon law', 50 *The Jurist* (1990) 102.

Mukadam, M. and A. Scott-Baumann, *The Training and Development of Musli Faith Leaders: Current Practice and Future Possibilities* (London: Depar ment for Communities and Local Government, 2010).

Naqshbandi, M., *Islam and Muslims in Britain: A Guide for Non-Muslin* (London: City of London Police, 2012).

Ner-David, H., *Life on the Fringes: A Feminist Journey Toward Traditional Ra binic Ordination* (Needham, MA: JFL Books, 2000).

Neusner, J. and T. Sonn, *Comparing Religions through Law: Judaism and Isla* (Abingdon: Routledge, 1999).

Newman, L.E., *Past Imperatives – Studies in the History and Theory of Jewish Ethi* (Albany, NY: State University of New York Press, 1998).

Nielsen, J.S., *Muslims in Western Europe* (Edinburgh: Edinburgh University Pres 1987).

Novak, D., 'A Jewish theory of human rights', in J. Witte and M.C. Green, ed *Religion and Human Rights* (Oxford: Oxford University Press, 2012) 27–4

Ofsted: Inspection Report (2005): https://reports.ofsted.gov.uk/provider/file 759347/urn/107791.

Ombres, R., 'The removal of parish priests', 1 *Priests & People* (1987) 9–12.

Örsy, L., *Theology and Canon Law: New Horizons for Legislation and Interpre ation* (Collegeville, MN: The Liturgical Press, 1992).

Othman, A., '"And amicable settlement is best": *sulh* and dispute resolution i Islamic law', 21 *Arab Law Quarterly* (2007) 64–77.

Patsavos, L., *Manual on Orthodox Canon Law* (New York, Hellenic College, Hol Cross Orthodox School of Theology, 1975).

Picken, G., ed., *Islamic Law*, 4 volumes (Abingdon: Routledge, 2010).

Quint, E., *A Restatement of Rabbinic Civil Law*, 2 Volumes (Northvale, NJ: Jaso Aronson Inc., 1990).

Rayner, J., 'Ethics versus ritual', in W. Jacob, ed., *Beyond the Letter of the Law: Essays on Diversity in the Halakhah*, Studies in Progressive Halakhah (Pittsburgh, PA: Rodef Shalom Press, 2004) 119.

Reinhart, A.K., *Before Revelation: The Boundaries of Muslim Moral Thought* (Albany, NY: State University of New York Press, 1995).

Rheins, R.S., '*Asu Seyag LaTorah*: make a fence to protect the Torah', in W. Jacob and M. Zemer, eds., *Re-Examining Progressive Halakhah* (New York: Berghahn Books, 2002) 91.

Rivers, J., *The Law of Organized Religions* (Oxford: Oxford University Press, 2011).

Rodopoulos, P., *An Overview of Orthodox Canon Law* (Rollinsford, NH: Orthodox Research Institute, 2007).

Rohe, M., *Islamic Law in Past and Present*, trans. G. Goldbloom (Leiden: Brill, 2014).

Rosen, L., *The Justice of Islam* (Oxford: Oxford University Press, 2000).

Ruane, N.J., *Sacrifice and Gender in Biblical Law* (Cambridge: Cambridge University Press, 2013).

Rubin, U., 'Hanif', in J.D. McAuliffe, ed., *Encyclopaedia of the Qur'an* (Leiden: Brill, 2001–2006).

Rudavsky, T., 'Natural Law in Judaism: a reconsideration', in J.A. Jacobs, ed., *Reason, Religion and Natural Law: From Plato to Spinoza* (Oxford: Oxford University Press, 2012) 83.

Sachedina, A., *The Justice Ruler in Shi'ite Islam: The Comprehensive Theory of the Jurist in Imamite Jurisprudence* (Oxford: Oxford University Press, 1988).

Sacks, Lord Jonathan (Chief Rabbi of the United Hebrew Congregations of the Commonwealth 1991–2013), 'The Great Covenant of Liberties', in R. Griffith-Jones and M. Hill, eds., *Magna Carta, Religion and the Rule of Law* (Cambridge: Cambridge University Press, 2015) 301–313.

Sagi, A., 'Natural law and *Halakha*: a critical analysis', *Jewish Law Annual* 13 (2000) 149–196.

Saleh, N., *Unlawful Gain and Legitimate Profit in Islamic Law* (Cambridge: Cambridge University Press, 1986).

Sandberg, R., 'The reformation of religious law', *Quaderni di Diritto e Politica Ecclesiastica* (2017) 97–110.

Religion, Law and Society (Cambridge: Cambridge University Press, 2014).

Law and Religion (Cambridge: Cambridge University Press, 2011).

Sandberg, R., ed., *Religion and Legal Pluralism* (Aldershot: Ashgate, 2015).

Saperstein, M., *Jewish Preaching 1200–1800* (New Haven, CT: Yale University Press, 1992).

Schacht, J., *An Introduction to Islamic Law* (Oxford: The Clarendon Press, 1982).

Schechter, S., *Studies in Judaism* (Philadelphia: Jewish Publication Society, 1945).

Sezgin, Y., *Human Rights under State-Enforced Religious Family Laws in Israel, Egypt and India* (Cambridge: Cambridge University Press, 2013).

Shachar, A., *Multicultural Jurisdictions: Cultural Differences and Women's Right* (Cambridge: Cambridge University Press, 2013).

'Entangled: state and religion and the family', in R. Ahdar and N. Aroney, eds *Shari'a in the West* (Oxford: Oxford University Press, 2010) Ch. 8.

Sheehy, G., *et al*, *The Canon Law: Letter and Spirit* (Dublin: Veritas, 1995).

Sheikh Kazi Luthfur Rahman, 'Citizenship and Islam': www.iccuk.org/images Citizenship_and_Islam1_Nov2016.pdf.

Shmueli, B., 'Corporal punishment of children in Jewish law: a comparative study' 18 *The Jewish Law Annual* (2010) 137–212.

Silberg, M., *Talmudic Law and the Modern State*, translated by B.Z. Bokser (New York: Burning Bush Press, 1973).

Solomon, N., 'Public law and traditional faith', in F. Cranmer, M. Hill, C. Kenny and R. Sandberg (eds.), *The Confluence of Law and Religion* (Cambridge: Cambridge University Press, 2016) 161.

Sparkes, D.C., *The Constitutions of the Baptist Union of Great Britain* (London: Baptist Union of Great Britain, 1996).

Stone, S.L., 'Religion and state: models of separation from within Jewish law', 6 *International Journal of Constitutional Law* (2008) 631–661.

Strack, H.L. and G. Stemberger, *Introduction to the Talmud and Midrash*, translated and edited by M. Bockmuehl (Minneapolis, MN: Fortress Press, 2nd edn, 1996).

Taylor, P.M., *Freedom of Religion* (Cambridge: Cambridge University Press, 2005).

The Independent Review into the Application of Sharia Law in England and Wales presented to Parliament by the Secretary of State for the Home Department by Command of Her Majesty (February 2018) Cm 9560.

The Official Report of the Lambeth Conference 1998 (Harrisburg, PA: Morehouse Publishing, 1999).

Thompson, S., *Prenuptial Agreements and the Presumption of Free Choice: Issues of Power in Theory and Practice* (Oxford: Hart, 2015).

Vyver, J.D. van der and J. Witte, eds., *Religious Human Rights in Global Perspective: Legal Perspectives* (The Hague: Martinus Nijhoff, 1995).

Warburg, R., 'Breach of a promise to marry', 17 *The Jewish Law Annual* (2008) 267–282.

Washofsky, M., 'Against method: liberal halakhah between theory and practice', in W. Jacob, ed., *Beyond the Letter of the Law: Essays on Diversity in the Halakhah*, Studies in Progressive Halakhah (Pittsburgh, PA: Rodef Shalom Press, 2004) 17.

'Taking precedent seriously: on halakhah as a rhetorical practice', in W. Jacob and M. Zemer, eds., *Re-Examining Progressive Halakhah* (New York/Oxford: Berghahn Books, 2002) 1.

Weatherhead, J.L., ed., *The Constitution and Laws of the Church of Scotland* (Edinburgh: Board of Practice and Procedure, 1997).

Webber, G.J., 'The principles of the Jewish Law of property', 10 *Journal of Comparative Legislation and International Law* (1928) 82–93.

Weeramantry, C.G., *Islamic Jurisprudence: An International Perspective* (London: Macmillan, 1988).

Weiss, B., *The Spirit of Islamic Law* (Athens, GA: University of Georgia Press, 1998).

Williams, R, 'Civil and religious law in England' (7 February 2008) in R. Griffith-Jones, ed., *Islam and English Law: Rights, Responsibilities and the Place of Shari'a* (Cambridge: Cambridge University Press, 2013) 20–33; and *Ecclesiastical Law Journal* (2008) 262.

Witte, J., *Law and Protestantism: The Legal Teachings of the Protestant Reformation* (Cambridge: Cambridge University Press, 2002).

From Sacrament to Contract: Marriage, Religion and Law in the Western Tradition (Westminster: John Knox Press, 1997).

Witte, J. and F.S. Alexander, eds., *Christianity and Law* (Cambridge: Cambridge University Press, 2008).

Woolf Commission, *Living with Difference*, Report of the Commission on Religion and Belief in British Public Life (2015).

Yilmaz, I., *Muslim Laws, Politics and Society in Modern Nation States: Dynamic Legal Pluralisms in England, Turkey and Pakistan* (Farnham: Ashgate, 2005).

Zemer, M., *Evolving Halakhah* (Woodstock, VT: Jewish Lights Publishing, 1998); the book was first published in Hebrew as *The Sane Halakhah* (Tel Aviv: Dvir, 1993).

Zucca, L., *Law, State and Religion in the New Europe* (Cambridge: Cambridge University Press, 2012).

INDEX

434 INDEX